T0305314

Developing and Enhancing Teamwork in Organizations

The Professional Practice Series

The Professional Practice Series is sponsored by The Society for Industrial and Organizational Psychology, Inc. (SIOP). The series was launched in 1988 to provide industrial and organizational psychologists, organizational scientists and practitioners, human resources professionals, managers, executives, and those interested in organizational behavior and performance with volumes that are insightful, current, informative, and relevant to *organizational practice*. The volumes in the Professional Practice Series are guided by five tenets designed to enhance future organizational practice:

1. Focus on practice, but grounded in science
2. Translate organizational science into practice by generating guidelines, principles, and lessons learned that can shape and guide practice
3. Showcase the application of industrial and organizational psychology to solve problems
4. Document and demonstrate best industrial and organizational-based practices
5. Stimulate research needed to guide future organizational practice

The volumes seek to inform those interested in practice with guidance, insights, and advice on how to apply the concepts, findings, methods, and tools derived from industrial and organizational psychology to solve human-related organizational problems.

Previous Professional Practice Series volumes include:

Published by Jossey-Bass

Advancing Executive Coaching: Setting the Course for Successful Leadership Coaching
Gina Hernez-Broom, Lisa A. Boyce, Editors

Technology-Enhanced Assessment of Talent
Nancy T. Tippins, Seymour Adler, Editors

Going Global: Practical Applications and Recommendations for HR and OD Professionals in the Global Workplace
Kyle Lundby with Jeffrey Jolton

Strategy-Driven Talent Management: A Leadership Imperative
Rob Silzer, Ben E. Dowell, Editors

Performance Management: Putting Research into Practice
James W. Smither, Manuel London, Editors

Alternative Validation Strategies: Developing New and Leveraging Existing Validity Evidence
S. Morton McPhail

Getting Action from Organizational Surveys: New Concepts, Technologies, and Applications
Allen I. Kraut

Customer Service Delivery
Lawrence Fogli, Editor

Employment Discrimination Litigation
Frank J. Landy, Editor

The Brave New World of eHR
Hal G. Gueutal, Dianna L. Stone, Editors

Improving Learning Transfer in Organizations
Elwood F. Holton III, Timothy T. Baldwin, Editors

Resizing the Organization
Kenneth P. De Meuse, Mitchell Lee Marks, Editors

Implementing Organizational Interventions
Jerry W. Hedge, Elaine D. Pulakos, Editors

Organization Development
Janine Waclawski, Allan H. Church, Editors

Creating, Implementing, and Managing Effective Training and Development
Kurt Kraiger, Editor

The 21st Century Executive: Innovative Practices for Building Leadership at the Top
Rob Silzer, Editor

Managing Selection in Changing Organizations
Jerard F. Kehoe, Editor

Evolving Practices in Human Resource Management
Allen I. Kraut, Abraham K. Korman, Editors

Individual Psychological Assessment: Predicting Behavior in Organizational Settings
Richard Jeanneret, Rob Silzer, Editors

Performance Appraisal
James W. Smither, Editor

Organizational Surveys
Allen I. Kraut, Editor

Employees, Careers, and Job Creating
Manuel London, Editor

Managing Human Resources for Environmental Sustainability
Susan E. Jackson, Deniz S. Ones, Stephan Dilchert, Editors

Published by Guilford Press

Diagnosis for Organizational Change
Ann Howard and Associates

Human Dilemmas in Work Organizations
Abraham K. Korman and Associates

Diversity in the Workplace
Susan E. Jackson and Associates

Working with Organizations and Their People
Douglas W. Bray and Associates

The Professional Practice Series

This volume is dedicated to the life and work of Richard Hackman (1940–2013), who's theories, thinking, research and approach to understanding team effectiveness inspired, guided and motivated all of us . . .

Developing and Enhancing Teamwork in Organizations

Evidence-Based Best Practices and Guidelines

Eduardo Salas

Scott I. Tannenbaum

Debra J. Cohen

Gary Latham

Editors

Cohen photo courtesy of Society of Human Resource Management
Cover design: Wiley

Published by Jossey-Bass

A Wiley Brand

One Montgomery Street, Suite 1200, San Francisco, CA 94104-4594

www.josseybass.com

For additional copies/bulk purchases of this book in the U.S. please contact 800-274-4434.

Jossey-Bass books and products are available through most bookstores. To contact Jossey-Bass directly call our Customer Care Department within the U.S. at 800-274-4434, outside the U.S. at 317-572-3985, fax 317-572-4002, or visit www.josseybass.com.

Jossey-Bass publishes in a variety of print and electronic formats and by print-on-demand. Some material included with standard print versions of this book may not be included in e-books or in print-on-demand. If this book refers to media such as a CD or DVD that is not included in the version you purchased, you may download this material at http://booksupport.wiley.com. For more information about Wiley products, visit www.wiley.com.

Library of Congress Cataloging-in-Publication Data

Developing and enhancing teamwork in organizations: evidence-based best practices and guidelines / Eduardo Salas, Scott I. Tannenbaum, Debra Cohen, Gary Latham, editors.
pages cm. – (The professional practice series)
Includes index.
ISBN 978-1-118-14589-0 (cloth); ISBN 978-1-118-62716-7 (ebk.);
ISBN 978-1-118-42095-9 (ebk.); ISBN 978-1-118-41922-9 (ebk.)
1. Teams in the workplace. I. Salas, Eduardo.
HD66.D4727 2013
658.4'022–dc23

2013008456

Printed in the United States of America

HB Printing 10 9 8 7 6 5 4 3 2 1

Contents

	Foreword	xiii
	The Editors	xv
	The Contributors	xvii
Part 1: Why Teamwork Matters in Organizations		**1**
1	**Teamwork in Financial Institutions—Does It Really Matter?** Michael J. Castellana, CEO, SEFCU	**3**
2	**Do Teams' Leaders Really Matter?** COL Casey Haskins, U.S. Military Academy, West Point	**6**
3	**Teamwork Matters** Peter J. Pronovost, Johns Hopkins University	**11**
4	**Making a Difference with Health Care Teams** Victor V. Buzachero, Scripps Health	**13**
5	**Developing Leaders on Any Team** George O'Leary, Head Football Coach, University of Central Florida	**17**
6	**Teamwork and Spaceflight—An Evolving Relationship** Daniel W. Tani, Astronaut, NASA	**22**
Part 2: The Organization and Its Influence		**25**
1	**Silent Killers of Team Performance: How Honest, Collective, and Public Conversations Can Overcome Them** Michael Beer, Harvard Business School and TruePoint	**27**

2 **How Organizational Process Maturity Improved Software Team Performance** 48
Bill Curtis, CAST Software
3 **Leading a Team to a Major Technological Development** 85
Kazem Rassouli, University of Toronto, Rotman School of Management

Part 3: The Team Leaders 119

4 **Building Great Leadership Teams for Complex Problems** 121
Ruth Wageman, Harvard University
5 **Developing High-Impact Teams to Lead Strategic Change** 154
Kate Beatty and Roland B. Smith, Center for Creative Leadership
6 **Leading Executive Teams: The Good, the Bad, and the Ugly** 182
Susan R. Meisinger, Society for Human Resource Management
7 **Leading from the Helm: Lessons from America's Cup Sailing Teams** 208
Mark A. Clark, American University

Part 4: The Organizational Context 237

8 **Virtual Teams: The How To's of Making "Being Virtually There" Successful** 239
Debra J. Cohen and Alexander Alonso, Society for Human Resource Management
9 **Trust and Conflict at a Distance: How Can I Improve Relational Outcomes in Distributed Work Groups?** 268
Jeanne Wilson, The College of William and Mary

10 **Teamwork Improvement in Health Care: A Decade of Lessons Learned Every Organization Should Know** 298
Sandra A. Almeida, MD, LLC, Healthcare Consulting, Heidi King, TRICARE Management Activity, and Mary L. Salisbury, The Cedar Institute, Inc.

11 **Why Teamwork Matters: Enabling Health Care Team Effectiveness for the Delivery of High-Quality Patient Care** 331
Joanne Lyubovnikova, Aston University, and Michael A. West, Lancaster University

12 **Rethinking Team Diversity Management: Evidence-Based Strategies for Coping with Diversity Threats** 373
Mirko Antino, Universidad Complutense de Madrid, Ramón Rico, Universidad AutonOma de Madrid, Miriam Sánchez-Manzanares, Universidad Carlos III de Madrid, and Dora C. Lau, Chinese University of Hong Kong

13 **High Performance in Temporally Separated Team Work** 406
J. Alberto Espinosa, Kogod School of Business, American University

Part 5: The Assessments, Applications, and Interventions for Teams 439

14 **Designing, Delivering, and Evaluating Team Training in Organizations: Principles That Work** 441
Megan E. Gregory, Jennifer Feitosa, Tripp Driskell, and Eduardo Salas, Department of Psychology, Institute for Simulation and Training, University of Central Florida, and William Brandon Vessey, EASI/Wyle, NASA Johnson Space Center

15 Conducting Team Debriefings That Work: Lessons from Research and Practice 488
Scott I. Tannenbaum, Rebecca L. Beard, and Christopher P. Cerasoli, Group for Organizational Effectiveness, Inc.

16 Achieving Optimal Team Composition for Success 520
John E. Mathieu, University of Connecticut, Scott I. Tannenbaum, Jamie S. Donsbach, and George M. Alliger, Group for Organizational Effectiveness, Inc.

17 How, When, and Why You Should Measure Team Performance 552
Kimberly A. Smith-Jentsch, Mary Jane Sierra, and Christopher William Wiese, University of Central Florida

18 Team Time Management: Psychological Insights for Timely Project Performance 581
Josette M.P. Gevers and Christel G. Rutte, Einhoven University of Technology, Netherlands

19 Five Simple Processes That Improve High-Risk Team Effectiveness 609
Michaela Kolbe, ETH Zurich, Switzerland

Part 6: Summary 645

20 Enhancing the Practice of Teamwork in Organizations: Emerging Themes 647
Stephanie Zajac and Eduardo Salas, University of Central Florida

Name Index 661
Subject Index 680

Foreword

This latest volume in the SIOP Professional Practice Series was sparked and inspired by a Leading Edge Conference sponsored by the Society for Industrial and Organizational Psychology held in the fall of 2010. That conference was designed to bring together leading-edge practitioners and academics to exchange views and knowledge about effective teams and help lead to better practice in that area.

Gary Latham chaired that Leading Edge Conference, in his final role as president of SIOP. The conference theme he chose was work teams. The co-chairs of the conference were Scott Tannenbaum, who brought together leading scientists on work teams, and Debra Cohen, who brought together leading practitioners. Eduardo Salas, who was SIOP president-elect, represents both aspects, as he is a scientist-practitioner on work teams and hence was selected as the primary editor of this book.

Using the best results from the conference, Eduardo Salas and his colleagues, who were all involved in key roles for that conference, employed the presentations and concepts as a framework to bring the contents of this volume to us. After reflecting on the conference's presentations and experience, all of the content in this book was updated and new material was added beyond that covered in the conference itself.

As one can see in the table of contents, the settings and outcomes of team performance described in this book cover a wide range of activities and industries. We learn about teamwork in the NASA organization supporting astronauts, superior performance in football, and also in the military and industry. We are also treated to some fascinating chapters concerning health care organizations and their delivery of vital services.

The range of contributors to this volume includes about one-quarter from outside of the United States, reflecting the global importance of this topic and the wealth of experience available around the world. The editors are to be commended for honoring and sharing this broad set of viewpoints.

The wide range of contributors' work settings and experiences also adds to the value of this book. The contributors include internal and external consultants, highly regarded academics and professors, as well as the full-time staff of many of these organizations.

It is fascinating to read about the range of challenges that face teams in today's organizations. Many are made up of a diverse set of team members, varying in experience, education and training, and other personal characteristics. Many teams include people who are not in the same room together, are geographically dispersed, and often connected only by electronic media. Welcome to the new world of work!

The problems and settings in which we see teams playing a vital part include several high-risk enterprises, such as military and high-technology units. Others require complex problem-solving skills in environments of great uncertainty and political sensitivity. In such situations, no single person can accomplish the work required. Only teams will be able to do what needs to be done, but only effective teams will suffice. Fortunately, this book helps us understand what must be done to make such teams effective.

It is particularly refreshing to see this volume focus on what we know will work to develop and enhance team performance in organizations. The contributors are dedicated and consistent in offering evidence-based practices. In other words, they use research to support the many specifics offered here for good team performance and ways to enhance teamwork. The presentations in this volume are extremely helpful to the serious researcher or practitioner attempting to improve team performance.

Our field owes thanks to the editors of this book for bringing it all together. Debra Cohen, Gary Latham, Eduardo Salas, and Scott Tannenbaum are well-respected and esteemed scholars and practitioners on the topic of effective teams. This volume demonstrates why they are so highly regarded. Their efforts and those of the chapter contributors certainly enrich our understanding of effective work teams.

Rye, New York ALLEN I. KRAUT, Series Editor
January 1, 2013

The Editors

Eduardo Salas, Ph.D., is the Pegasus Professor of Psychology and university Trustee Chair at the University of Central Florida, where he also holds an appointment as program director for the Human Systems Integration Research Department at the Institute for Simulation and Training. Dr. Salas has co-authored more than 450 journal articles and book chapters and has co-edited twenty-five books. He received his Ph.D. in industrial and organizational psychology from Old Dominion University in 1984.

Scott I. Tannenbaum, Ph.D., is president of the Group for Organizational Effectiveness (gOE), an Albany, New York–based consulting and research firm he co-founded in 1987. Under his leadership, gOE has provided advice, tools, and training to more than four hundred organizations, including more than thirty Fortune 100 companies. He has worked with and supported a wide array of teams, including medical, drilling, aviation, sales, banking, combat, and leadership teams. Dr. Tannenbaum has written more than sixty publications and given over one hundred professional presentations. He has authored books on knowledge management and human resource technologies, reviewed for twenty professional journals, and served as the Principal Investigator on numerous research contracts and grants.

Debra J. Cohen, Ph.D., SPHR, is senior vice president, Knowledge Development, for the Society for Human Resource Management (SHRM) and is responsible for the Society's Knowledge Development Division, which includes the SHRM Knowledge Center (including the Society Library), the Research Department, Academic Initiatives, HR Standards, and Thought Leadership. Dr. Cohen joined SHRM in May of 2000 as the director of Research. Prior to joining SHRM, Dr. Cohen spent fifteen years as an academician teaching HRM at George Washington University and George Mason University. Dr. Cohen has published more than forty articles and book chapters and has been published in a variety of journals, including *Journal of Management, Academy of Management Journal, Personnel Psychology, Human Resource Management,* and many others. Dr. Cohen received her Ph.D. in management and human resources in 1987 and her master's degree in labor and human resources in 1982, both from The Ohio State University. She received her bachelor of science in communications from Ohio University. She is a frequent presenter at national, international, and regional conferences and has spoken to a wide variety of audiences. Prior to her academic career, she was a practicing human resources manager in training and development.

Gary Latham, Ph.D., is the Secretary of State Professor of Organizational Effectiveness in the Rotman School of Management. He is a past president of the Canadian Psychological Association and the Society for Industrial-Organizational Psychology, and President Elect of the Work and Organizational Psychological Division I of the International Association of Applied Psychological. In addition, he has been awarded the status of Fellow in the Academy of Management, American Psychological Association, Association for Psychological Science, Canadian Psychological Association, International Association of Applied Psychology, Society for Industrial-Organizational Psychology, and the Royal Society of Canada. Dr. Latham has served on the board of governors for the Center for Creative Leadership and currently serves on the board of directors for the Society for Human Resource Management.

The Contributors

Essay 1

Michael J. Castellana, CPA, president and CEO of SEFCU, leads the largest credit union in the Capital Region and the seventh largest in the State of New York. Castellana joined SEFCU more than twenty-three years ago as a member of the executive management team and during his tenure has seen the credit union grow both geographically and in overall size. Castellana directs all functional areas of the credit union and is responsible for its business planning and asset management. In addition, he serves as chairman of the SEFCU Foundation, a nonprofit affiliation Castellana formed to pool the time, talent, and financial resources of SEFCU staff in support of children's causes.

Outside of SEFCU, Castellana is also an active leader in the community. He is chairman of the board of directors of the Capitalize Albany Corporation and serves on the boards of the American Cancer Society's HopeClub, the University at Albany Foundation and Tech Valley Connect. He also sits on the advisory boards of Big Brothers/Big Sisters, Little Sisters of the Poor, St. Anne Institute, the University at Albany MBA Advisory Council, the Dean's Council of the Lally School of Management of RPI, the President's Advisory Council of Hudson Valley Community College, and the Federal Reserve Bank of New York's Community Depository Institutions Advisory Council of which he was recently named chair. Castellana is also a member of the AICPA and the NYSCPA.

Essay 2

Casey Haskins served twenty-nine years as an Army officer, retiring in 2011 as a colonel. In his Army career, he commanded units from platoon through brigade and served in a variety of staff positions, in the United States and overseas. He earned a reputation as one of the Army's most innovative trainers, as well as for a distinctly new approach to planning and leading organizations, which has since been adopted by a number of organizations around the world and continues to influence the Army as a whole. At the time of his 2010 presentation to the SIOP Leading Edge Consortium, he was the director of military instruction at West Point. Since retiring from the Army, Casey has worked as an independent consultant and trainer and has started his own business, Deep Insights LLC.

Essay 3

Peter J. Pronovost, MD, Ph.D., FCCM, is a practicing anesthesiologist and critical care physician and a professor in the departments of Anesthesiology and Critical Care Medicine, Surgery, and Health Policy and Management who is dedicated to finding ways to make hospitals and health care safer for patients. He is senior vice president for patient safety and quality and Director of the Armstrong Institute for Patient Safety and Quality, Johns Hopkins Medicine.

Dr. Pronovost developed a scientifically proven method for reducing the deadly infections associated with central line catheters. His simple but effective checklist protocol virtually eliminated these infections, saving 1,500 lives and $100 million annually across the State of Michigan. This infection prevention program is being implemented across the United States and in several countries around the globe.

Dr. Pronovost regularly addresses Congress on the importance of patient safety, prompting a report by the U.S. House of Representatives' Committee on Oversight and Government Reform strongly endorsing the ICU infection prevention program. He has chronicled his work helping improve patient safety in his new book, *Safe Patients, Smart Hospitals: How One Doctor's Checklist Can Help Us Change Health Care from the Inside Out.* He has also published more than four hundred articles related to patient outcomes, safety, and the measurement and evaluation of safety efforts. He serves in an advisory capacity to the World Health Organizations' World Alliance for Patient Safety.

He has won many awards, including the coveted MacArthur Fellowship in 2008, and was named by *Time* magazine as one of the world's one hundred "most influential people."

Essay 4

Victor V. Buzachero is corporate senior vice president for innovation, human resources and performance management, Scripps Health. He joined Scripps Health in September 2001 and has since led Scripps Health to national recognition as a top employer by AARP the past seven years, *Working Mother* magazine for the past five years, and *Fortune* magazine's Top 100 Employers in 2008, 2009, 2010, and 2011. He has led several new and successful initiatives, including a comprehensive employee wellness program, implementing an annual management cycle that integrates strategic planning, capital planning, operations planning, performance management, and talent management, as well as decertifying the California Nurses Association to maintain the only non-union health system in California. Buzachero's leadership has helped grow Scripps Health to a $2.4 billion integrated delivery health system. Prior to coming to Scripps Health, he held top executive level positions at organizations such as Providence Health System, Banner Health System, Presbyterian Health System (Texas Health Resources), and Baptist Health System. During his tenure at these organizations, Buzachero developed and successfully implemented programs on leadership development, service excellence, reduction in employee turnover, improved employee satisfaction, as well as an e-health strategy. Additionally, he served as vice president of marketing (hospital acquisitions) for Quorum Health and was co-owner and principal of a national labor relations and executive compensation consultancy. In 1999 Franklin Covey honored Buzachero with the "Organization of Excellence" award for his prominent efforts in organization development and effectiveness and in 2011 he was honored by *HR Executive* magazine as a top HR executive for the year. He is frequently sought out to speak at the national level on ROI in health care and work force initiatives and labor relations among many other topics. He is the current chairman of the American Hospital Association Solutions Board, in addition to serving on other boards.

Essay 5

George O'Leary has been the head football coach at the University of Central Florida since 2004. Under O'Leary, UCF has made three appearances in conference championship games and won conference titles in 2007 and 2010. UCF has also gone to four bowl games with O'Leary at the helm. O'Leary has been voted conference coach of the year three times, and was *SportsIllustrated.*com's national coach of the year in 2005.

O'Leary is also known for his success while the head coach of Georgia Tech from 1994 to 2001. Georgia Tech went to five straight bowl games, beat their arch-rival Georgia three years in a row, and won the conference title in 1998. While the head coach at Georgia Tech, O'Leary was named conference coach of the year twice and Bobby Dodd national coach of the year in 2000.

O'Leary began his career in 1968 with a very successful high school career then stints as defensive line coach at Syracuse, defensive coordinator at Georgia Tech, defensive line coach for the San Diego Chargers, defensive line coach for the Minnesota Vikings, and defensive coordinator for the Vikings. O'Leary attended the University of New Hampshire and earned his degree in physical education.

Essay 6

Astronaut Daniel W. Tani was selected as an astronaut candidate by NASA in April 1996 and reported to the Johnson Space Center in August 1996. Having completed two years of training and evaluation, he qualified for flight assignment as a mission specialist in 1998. He held technical duties in the Astronaut Office Computer Support Branch and EVA Branch and has served as a crew support astronaut (CSA) for Expedition 4. Tani flew on STS-108 in 2001 and has logged more than eleven days in space, including over four EVA hours in one space walk. In 2002, he was a crewmember on the Aquarius undersea research habitat for nine days as part of the NEEMO-2 mission (NASA Extreme Environment Mission Operations). Tani then trained and qualified as the backup flight engineer for Expedition 11, which launched aboard the Soyuz TMA-6 in April 2005. A veteran of two spaceflights, Tani has logged more than 131 days in space and thirty-nine hours and eleven minutes in six EVAs.

After Tani received his bachelor's degree from MIT, he worked at Hughes Aircraft Corporation in El Segundo, California, as a design engineer in the Space and Communications group. In 1986, he returned to MIT and received his master's degree in mechanical engineering in 1988, specializing in human factors and group decision making. After graduation, Tani worked for Bolt Beranek and Newman in Cambridge, Massachusetts, in the experimental psychology department. In 1988, Tani joined Orbital Sciences Corporation (OSC) in Dulles, Virginia, initially as a senior structures engineer and then as the mission operations manager for the Transfer Orbit Stage (TOS). In that role, he served as the TOS flight operations lead, working with NASA/JSC mission control in support of the deployment of the ACTS/TOS payload during the STS-51 mission in September 1993. Tani then moved to the Pegasus program at OSC as the launch operations manager. In that capacity, he served as lead for the development of procedures and constraints for the launching of the air-launched Pegasus unmanned rocket. Tani also was responsible for defining, training, and leading the team of engineers who worked in the launch and control room.

Chapter 1

Michael Beer is Cahners-Rabb Professor of Business Administration, Emeritus, at the Harvard Business School and co-founder and chairman of TruePoint, a management consultancy whose mission is to help senior teams transform their organizations into high-commitment, high-performance enterprises. He is a well-known authority in the areas of organization effectiveness, organization change, and human resource management. Beer is the author of eleven books, including *High Commitment, High Performance* (2009) and *Higher Ambition* (2011). He is the recipient of numerous professional and academic honors, among them the

Academy of Management's Scholar-Practitioner Award and the Society of Human Resource Management's Michael C. Losey Research Award.

Chapter 2

Bill Curtis, Ph.D., received his M.A. in psychology from the University of Texas and his Ph.D. in organizational psychology and statistics from Texas Christian University in 1975. He taught behavioral statistics at the University of Washington, where he participated in research on leadership, sports psychology, and programmer selection. During 1977 he was a staff psychologist at Weyerhaeuser, where he worked on organizational effectiveness programs and co-developed training for a performance appraisal system. In 1978 he joined GE's Space Division, where he led experimental research on software development methods and validated the predictive value of software metrics. Later at the ITT Programming Technology Center he developed a global software productivity and quality measurement system. He joined MCC, the American fifth-generation computer research consortium, in 1983 and led research on advanced user interface technologies and the software design process. He joined the Software Engineering Institute at Carnegie Mellon University in 1991 as director of the Software Process Program and led the project that produced the "capability maturity model" (CMM), which has become the global standard for evaluating the capability of software development organizations. He later developed the People CMM and business process maturity model. He co-founded TeraQuest, which became the global leader in CMM-based consulting services and was acquired by Borland in 2005. He is currently a senior vice president and chief scientist of CAST Software, which has developed a technology for measuring the structural quality of software systems. He is also the director of the Consortium for IT Software Quality, which is developing global standards for measuring software size and structural quality. He has published four books and more than 150 articles. In 2007 he was elected a Fellow of the Institute of Electrical and Electronics Engineers (IEEE) for his contributions to software process improvement, software measurement, and the psychology of programming.

Chapter 3

Kazem Rassouli, Ph.D., earned his master's and Ph.D. degrees in chemical engineering from the University of London. He began his career as a process engineer and soon rose to the rank of management at Iran-Japan Petrochemical Complex. In 1986, Dr. Rassouli became the director of Esfahan Nuclear Technology Center, about which he has written in this book. In 1998, International Atomic Energy Agency (IAEA-Vienna) invited him to share his latter experience in a project management guide-book and also evaluate the effectiveness of IAEA in planning and execution of $70M projects worldwide. Dr. Rassouli has held several management positions for the R&D programs and engineering divisions of Ontario Power Generation. He has also taught (and now teaches) MIS at the Rotman School of Management, University of Toronto.

Chapter 4

Ruth Wageman, Ph.D., received her doctorate from Harvard in 1993 and returned there in 2006 as an associate in the Department of Psychology, after serving as a professor at the Columbia University Graduate School of Business and the Tuck School of Dartmouth College. She presently leads the ReThink Health Stewardship initiative of the Rippel Foundation, which focuses on developing multi-stakeholder leadership teams to transform health care. Her research and teaching interests focus on the design and leadership of effective leadership teams, especially ones with civic and social change purposes.

Chapter 5

Kate Beatty, Ph.D., is director of global portfolio management at the Center for Creative Leadership and is responsible for the quality and relevancy of CCL's portfolio worldwide. She conducts research, writes, and speaks to a wide variety of audiences in her areas of expertise: strategic leadership and teams. Dr. Beatty is co-author of *Becoming a Strategic Leader: Your Role in Your Organization's Enduring Success,* as well as numerous articles and book chapters. She has a B.S. in electrical engineering from the University of Illinois and an M.S. and Ph.D. in organizational psychology from Saint Louis University. She can be reached at beattyk@ccl.org.

Roland B. Smith, Ph.D., is a senior faculty member and lead researcher at the Center for Creative Leadership. His work includes facilitating the Leadership at the Peak program for senior executives and leading other custom engagements. He is currently a member of the Organizational Leadership practice group and leads CCL's Legal Sector practice. Dr. Smith serves as the lead researcher for both the senior executive research initiative (SERI) and the Global Institute for Talent Sustainability (GIFTS). In addition, he currently serves as the Skeens Watson visiting professor of leadership at Elon School of Law. Dr. Smith can be reached at smithro@ccl.org.

Chapter 6

Susan R. Meisinger, SPHR, JD, is a widely read columnist on HR leadership for *HRExecutive Online.* She speaks and consults on human resource management issues and is the former president and CEO of the Society for Human Resource Management (SHRM), the world's largest professional association devoted to human resource management. Prior to joining SHRM, Meisinger was appointed by President Ronald Reagan as a deputy under secretary in the U.S. Department of Labor, responsible for more than four thousand employees and enforcement of more than ninety U.S. employment laws. Meisinger is a former board member for the World Federation of Personnel Management Associations, SHRM, the HR Certification Institute, and has corporate board experience. She is a Fellow of the National Academy of Human Resources and the Human Resource Policy Institute. She currently sits on the board of the Certified Financial Planners Board of Standards, the Kronos Workforce Institute Advisory Board, and the National Academy of Human Resources board of directors. Meisinger also co-authored and edited *The Future of Human Resource Management,* published in 2005 by John Wiley & Sons.

Chapter 7

Mark A. Clark (Ph.D., Arizona State University) is an associate professor of management, Kogod School of Business, American University in Washington, D.C. He has more than twenty years of experience in team training, workforce analysis, program development, and action consulting. His research centers on team performance contexts, investigating the effects of culture, diversity, knowledge, and strategic human capital practices. He has published more than two dozen scholarly journal articles and book chapters in academic outlets, including *Group Dynamics, Human Resource Management, Academy of Management Journal,* and *Journal of Applied Psychology,* and has presented more than forty research papers at international, national, and regional conferences.

Chapter 8

Debra J. Cohen, Ph.D., SPHR, is senior vice president, knowledge development, for the Society for Human Resource Management (SHRM) and is responsible for the society's Knowledge Development Division, which includes the SHRM Knowledge Center (including the Society Library), the Research Department, Academic Initiatives, HR Standards, and Thought Leadership. Dr. Cohen joined SHRM in May of 2000 as the director of research. Prior to joining SHRM, Dr. Cohen spent fifteen years as an academician teaching HRM at George Washington University and George Mason University. Dr. Cohen has published more than forty articles and book chapters and has been published in a variety of journals, including *Journal of Management, Academy of Management Journal, Personnel Psychology, Human Resource Management,* and many others. Dr. Cohen received her Ph.D. in management and human resources in 1987 and her master's degree in labor and human resources in 1982, both from The Ohio State University. She received her bachelor of science in communications from Ohio University. She is a frequent presenter at national, international, and regional conferences and has spoken to a wide variety of audiences. Prior to her academic career, she was a practicing human resources manager in training and development.

Alexander Alonso, Ph.D., in his role as vice president for research at the Society for Human Resource Management, is responsible for all SHRM research activities, including the development of SHRM's Competency Self-Assessment and HR Professionals Competency Model. He also oversees the teams responsible for research products such as People Insight engagement tools, SHRM Benchmarking Services, and the Workplace and Employment Trends Center. Prior to joining SHRM in 2011, Dr. Alonso worked with numerous subject-matter experts worldwide with the aim of identifying performance standards, developing competency models, designing organizational assessments, and conducting job analyses. Among other assignments, he led a project for SHRM to study the state of HR education and supported the development of assessments for university accreditation. Dr. Alonso was part of the team recognized by the Society for Industrial and Organizational Psychology with the 2007 M. Scott Myers Award for Applied Research in the Workplace for the development of the federal standard for medical team training, TeamSTEPPS. He was also honored by the American Psychological Association with the 2009 Presidential Citation for Innovative Practice for supporting the development of a competency model for team triage in emergency medicine. He has published works in peer-reviewed journals such as *Journal of Applied Psychology, Personality and Individual Differences, Quality and Safety in Health Care,* and *Human Resources Management Review.* He has also served as the chairperson for the SIOP International Affairs Committee and as the vice president for programs of the Personnel Testing Council of Metropolitan Washington. Dr. Alonso received his doctorate in industrial-organizational psychology from Florida International University in 2003.

Chapter 9

Jeanne Wilson, Ph.D., is an associate professor at the Mason School of Business, The College of William & Mary. She received her Ph.D. in organizational behavior and theory from Carnegie Mellon University. Dr. Wilson's research focuses on new organizational forms, particularly distributed work groups and the role of distance in work relationships. She has studied the development of trust over time in distributed groups, knowledge transfer in teams that cross organizational boundaries, and attributions about performance in international project teams. Her current projects include examining the effects of distance on construal levels and developing a scale to measure perceptions of proximity.

Chapter 10

Sandra A. Almeida, MD, MPH, is the founder and president of Sandra A. Almeida, MD, LLC Healthcare Consulting, and a Captain in the U.S. Navy Reserves (retired). She is a board-certified preventive medicine and public health physician with more than twenty-five years of experience in diverse professional positions, including academic faculty appointments, clinical and research positions, military assignments, and health care consulting. Dr. Almeida has more than twenty years of experience in health care–related organizational safety and team performance improvement. From 1985 to 1993 she served as an active duty U.S. Naval flight surgeon and aeromedical safety officer supporting both U.S. Navy and Marine Corps commands. During that time she helped pioneer the Department of Defense aircrew team performance improvement effort as one of the Marine Corp's first Aircrew Coordination Training instructors. From 1993 to 1995, Dr. Almeida completed her medical training at the University of California San Diego–San Diego State University Preventive Medicine Residency Program and in 1996 took a faculty position at the residency as Director of Research and Thesis Affairs. She has been consulting since 1993 for both government and private-sector organizations, with a focus on the application of epidemiological methods to advance the quality, safety, and therapeutic capacity of modern health care. For the past eight years Dr. Almeida has worked extensively as a principal medical and scientific consultant for the Department of Defense Patient Safety Program. She has assisted in various aspects of program and curricula development, instruction, implementation, and evaluation. She is one of the original authors of TeamSTEPPS®. She currently leads the Patient Safety Program's Evaluation Workgroup, holding principal responsibility for the development and implementation of the TeamSTEPPS evaluation program. Dr. Almeida received her medical degree with honors at Dartmouth Medical School in 1984.

Heidi King, MS, FACHE, BCC, CPPS, is the acting director for the Department of Defense (DoD) Patient Safety Program and director for the Patient Safety Solutions Center in the Office of the Chief Medical Officer at TRICARE Management Activity, which serves 9.6 million DoD beneficiaries. She delivers innovative solutions to engage, educate, and equip patient-care teams to institutionalize evidence-based safe practices. King promotes the integration of teamwork principles into practice through education, training, research, and outreach. She is a servant leader transforming health care through the spread, impact, and sustainment of high-performing teams in DoD and beyond. King is the lead architect of award-winning TeamSTEPPS®, an evidence-based medical teamwork system aimed at improving communication to optimize patient outcomes and promote a culture of team-driven care. She co-directs the National Implementation of TeamSTEPPS project through an interagency partnership with the Agency for Healthcare Research and Quality, now adopted by military and civilian organizations internationally, with translations in several different languages. King is leading a key Military Health System strategic initiative, Implementing Evidence-Based Practices to Improve Quality and Safety, aimed at decreasing preventable patient harm and readmissions, as DoD is a federal partner in the Partnership for Patients national campaign. King is a recognized speaker, author, collaborator, and certified coach. She is an active steering council member of the Improvement Science Research Network and serves on several boards and expert panels. She received the distinguished Office of the Secretary of Defense Medal for Exceptional Civilian Service in 2007, the National Patient Safety Foundation Chairman's Medal in 2009 for inspiring and leading change through improvement strategies while creating a culture of respect, openness, learning, and team dynamics, and was a 2012 finalist for the Service to America Medal.

Mary L. Salisbury, MSN, RN, is president of The Cedar Institute, Inc., and a subcontractor of the DoD Patient Safety Program. She is a Northeastern University master's-prepared nurse commanding forty-two years of continuous service with a clinical focus in operative, critical care, and emergency medicine and a current focus on safety in health care. As founder and president of The Cedar Institute, Inc., Salisbury provides services to both military and civilian health care organizations. A member of the original team working to translate the principles of crew resource management into health care, Salisbury remains a participating author and designer of the TeamSTEPPS® learning and evaluation methodologies and engagement lead for the DoD Patient Safety Solution Center. In these roles, Salisbury encourages bold commitment to the questions: "What would it take to ensure excellence in the patient and caregiver experience? To ensure all can engage in safe systems of health care excellence? To ensure all care is given by safe hands?"

Chapter 11

Joanne Lyubovnikova, Ph.D., is a lecturer in work and organizational psychology at Aston University. She graduated with a BSc (Hons) in social psychology from Loughborough University (2005) and an MSc in work and organizational psychology from Aston University (2006), before receiving her Ph.D. in 2010, also from Aston University. Her doctoral research focused on the prevalence and measurement of real teams in organizations. Furthermore, Dr. Lyubovnikova has been involved in a number of large scale research projects examining teamworking in the English National Health Service. Her research interests focus on the antecedents of team effectiveness, particularly in relation to engagement, diversity, and virtual team working.

Michael A. West, Ph.D., is professor of work and organizational psychology at Lancaster University Management School, senior research fellow at The Work Foundation, and an emeritus professor at Aston University. He graduated from the University of Wales in 1973 and received his Ph.D. in 1977. He has published more than two hundred articles for scientific and practitioner publications, as well as multiple books and book chapters. His areas of research interest are team and organizational innovation and effectiveness, particularly in relation to the organization of health services. He lectures widely both nationally and internationally about the results of his research and his solutions for developing effective and innovative organizations.

Chapter 12

Mirko Antino, Ph.D., is an assistant professor of research methods at Complutense University of Madrid, faculty of psychology. He received his Ph.D. in the Department of Social Psychology in the same university. He also received a master's in methodology of health and behavioural sciences. His actual research interests include team diversity, team structure, team performance measurement, and social networks (he is member of the INSNA). His research has appeared in the *Journal of Applied Psychology, Psicothema, Revista de Psicologia, Revue economique et sociale,* and *Journal of Business Strategy,* among others. He can be reached at m.antino@psi.ucm.es.

Ramón Rico, Ph.D., is an associate professor of organizational behavior in the Department of Social Psychology and Methodology at the Autonomous University of Madrid. He received his Ph.D. from the same university and is currently a visiting professor at the Institute for Simulation and Training at the University of Central Florida. His work has been published in the *Academy of Management Review, Journal of Management, Journal of Business and Psychology, European Journal of Work and Organizational Psychology, International Journal of Psychology, Social Science Information, Spanish Journal of Psychology, Psicothema,* and *Journal of Managerial Psychology.* His current research interests include shared cognition, team diversity, virtuality, task design characteristics, multi-team systems, and team process and effectiveness. He can be reached at ramon.rico@uam.es.

Dora C. Lau, Ph.D., University of British Columbia, is an associate professor at the Chinese University of Hong Kong. Her research interests include demographic diversity and faultlines, relational trust, team dynamics, upper-echelon composition and organizational impact, family business challenges and management, and Chinese management. She has published extensively in top-tiered journals such as *Academy of Management Review, Academy of Management Journal,* and *Journal of Applied Psychology.* Dr. Lau has served as the associate editor of the *Journal of Trust Research* and also guest-edited a special issue for the *Asia Pacific Journal of Management* on leadership in Asia.

Miriam Sánchez-Manzanares, Ph.D., is an assistant professor of organizational behavior at the Department of Business Administration at Carlos III University of Madrid. She received her Ph.D. from the joint doctoral program in organizational behavior at Complutense University of Madrid. Her current research interests include the impact of diversity faultlines on teamwork behavior; shared cognition, adaptation, and performance in teams; and virtual teams. Her papers have appeared in the *Academy of Management Review, Journal of Applied Psychology,* and *Journal of Management,* among others. She can be reached at msmanzan@emp.uc3m.es.

Chapter 13

J. Alberto Espinosa, Ph.D., is a professor and chair of the Information Technology Department at the Kogod School of Business at American University. He holds doctoral and master's degrees in information systems from the Tepper School of Business at Carnegie Mellon University. He also earned an MBA and is a mechanical engineer. His research focuses on coordination and performance across global boundaries, particularly distance and time zones. His work has been published in leading scholarly journals, including *Management Science; Organization Science; Information Systems Research;* the *Journal of Management Information Systems; IEEE Transactions on Engineering Management; Communications of the ACM; Information, Technology and People;* and *Software Process: Improvement and Practice.* He also has almost twenty years of global work experience.

Chapter 14

Megan E. Gregory is a doctoral student in industrial/organizational psychology at the University of Central Florida and a graduate research associate at the Institute for Simulation and Training. Her research interests include teams, training, decision making, and stress, especially within the medical and health care fields. She is particularly interested in research that has the potential to improve both patient safety and the work experiences of health care providers.

Jennifer Feitosa is a doctoral student in the industrial/organizational psychology program at the University of Central Florida, where she earned a B.S. in psychology in 2010 with honors. As a graduate research associate at the Institute for Simulation and Training, her research interests include team composition, social identity, and statistical methods, with an emphasis on the impact of culture. She is currently involved in projects investigating aspects of team dynamics, funded by the Army Research Institute, an MURI grant, and National Aeronautics and Space Administration.

Tripp Driskell is a doctoral student in the applied experimental and human factors program at the University of Central Florida. He received his master's in human factors from Embry-Riddle Aeronautical University.

William Brandon Vessey, Ph.D., is currently the senior scientist managing team risk within the NASA Behavioral Health and Performance Research Element at the Johnson Space Center. He received his MS and Ph.D. in industrial and organizational psychology from the University of Oklahoma in 2012 with a minor in quantitative psychology. His primary research interests fall into the broad categories of teams, leadership, and creativity, with a specific focus on team leadership and collective leadership. His work has appeared in several books and journals, including *The Leadership Quarterly, Creativity Research Journal,* and *Creativity and Innovation Management.*

Chapter 15

Scott I. Tannenbaum, Ph.D., is president of the Group for Organizational Effectiveness (gOE), an Albany, New York–based consulting and research firm he co-founded in 1987. Under his leadership, gOE has provided advice, tools, and training to more than four hundred organizations, including more than thirty Fortune 100 companies. He has worked with and supported a wide array of teams, including medical, drilling, aviation, sales, banking, combat, and leadership teams. Dr. Tannenbaum has written more than sixty publications and given over one hundred professional presentations. He has authored books on knowledge management and human resource technologies, reviewed for twenty professional journals, and served as the Principal Investigator on numerous research contracts and grants.

Rebecca L. Beard is a co-founder and executive vice president of the Group for Organizational Effectiveness, Inc. (gOE) with more than twenty-five years of consulting experience in the areas of employee, management, and organization development. Her work includes diagnostic, research, and implementation efforts; evaluating organizational, managerial, team, and individual effectiveness; training needs analysis; supporting change efforts; creating innovative training interventions; developing competency programs, certification programs, and performance management tools; and enhancing internal HR and OD effectiveness. She received her MS in psychology from Old Dominion University and was part of the team that won SIOP's 2007 M. Scott Meyers Award for applied research.

Christopher P. Cerasoli is a research associate with the Group for Organizational Effectiveness, Inc. (gOE), an Albany, New York–based research and consulting firm. He received his master's from the State University of New York at Albany, where he is currently a Ph.D. candidate in industrial/organizational psychology.

Chapter 16

John E. Mathieu, Ph.D., is a professor of management at the University of Connecticut and holds the Cizik Chair in Management at UConn. His primary areas of interest include models of team and multi-team effectiveness, leadership, training effectiveness, and cross-level models of organizational behavior. He has more than one hundred publications, two hundred presentations at national and international conferences, and has been a PI or co-PI on more than $6.5M in grants and contracts. He is a Fellow of the APA, SIOP, and the Academy of Management. He serves on numerous prestigious editorial boards and holds a Ph.D. in industrial/organizational psychology from Old Dominion University.

Jamie S. Donsbach, Ph.D., is a senior consultant with the Group for Organizational Effectiveness (gOE), a consulting and research firm. Since joining gOE in 2003, Dr. Donsbach has supported corporate and public-sector customers with a variety of organizational needs, such as enhancing team effectiveness, training, identifying competency gaps, managing performance, and developing/validating assessment tools. Throughout her career she has enjoyed advising and supporting teams at all stages of the team life cycle. Her research interests include team development, leadership, and organizational support. Dr. Donsbach received her doctorate in industrial/organizational psychology from the University at Albany, State University of New York.

George M. Alliger, Ph.D., is vice president of solutions for the Group for Organizational Effectiveness. He holds a Ph.D. in industrial/organizational psychology from the University of Akron and a master's in clinical psychology from Xavier University. Dr. Alliger has conducted research and published extensively in the area of training, including methods and analysis. His roles in meta-analytic research of criteria for training evaluation, and in developing the architecture and methods for the Mission Essential Competencies for the USAF, have led to awards from ASTD and SIOP. He also has managed numerous job analyses, training evaluation, test development, and performance certification projects.

Chapter 17

Kimberly A. Smith-Jentsch, Ph.D., is an associate professor in the department of psychology at the University of Central Florida and director of their doctoral program in industrial and organizational psychology. She received her Ph.D. in psychology from the University of South Florida in 1994. Dr. Smith-Jentsch is a Fellow of APA Division 14 (Society for Industrial and Organizational Psychology) and a member of the editorial board for the *Journal of Applied Psychology*. Her publications in the areas of team performance measurement and training have been cited more than one thousand times.

Mary Jane Sierra is a doctoral candidate in the industrial/organizational psychology program at the University of Central Florida. She earned her B.A. in psychology from Stony Brook University and her M.A. in forensic psychology from John Jay College of Criminal Justice. Sierra has experience working in numerous research and applied settings spanning the private, public, and non-profit sectors. Her research and applied work have focused on selection, training, teams, leadership, stress, deviance, organizational culture, and multilevel theory. She is particularly dedicated to examining issues concerning personnel in high-risk occupations, such as military, law enforcement, and public safety officials.

Christopher William Wiese is a doctoral candidate in the industrial/organizational psychology program at the University of Central Florida. In 2008, he graduated from the University of Central Florida with a bachelor of science degree in psychology. His research and applied work have focused on teams, virtual teams, assessment centers, team mental models, shared leadership, culture, communication, and technology. Furthermore, he has used this knowledge in his consulting and volunteer work with the entities in both the public and private sectors. He is particularly interested in team cognition, assessment center validity, and leadership in culturally diverse virtual teams.

Chapter 18

Josette M.P. Gevers, Ph.D., is an assistant professor of work and organizational psychology at the Department of Industrial Engineering and Innovation Sciences at Eindhoven University of Technology. She received her Ph.D. from the same university in 2004.

Her research interests include team process and performance, team cognition, and the effects of time in organizational behavior.

Christel G. Rutte, Ph.D., received her MSc and Ph.D. degrees in psychology at the University of Groningen, The Netherlands. In 1999 she was appointed as full professor of organizational psychology at Eindhoven University of Technology, The Netherlands. In 2007 she was appointed as full professor of work and organizational psychology at Tilburg University, The Netherlands. Her main research interests are team processes, management of individual and team performance, and individual and team time management.

Chapter 19

Michaela Kolbe, Ph.D., is a senior researcher and lecturer at the ETH Zurich, Switzerland. Using micro-level behavior observation in the clinical as well as simulated setting, she has been studying the relationship between interaction patterns and performance in teams, mainly in acute care teams. In her current research, she focuses on the promotion of "speaking up" and on advancing debriefing techniques for simulated-based team trainings. Dr. Kolbe is also working as a systemic family therapist and holds a Ph.D. in psychology.

Chapter 20

Stephanie Zajac is a second-year student in the Industrial/Organizational Psychology Master's program at the University of Central Florida. She is currently a graduate research assistant working under the direction of Dr. Eduardo Salas for the Institute of Simulation and Training, where she is involved with a diverse range of both basic and applied research. Her main areas of interest include the cognitive variables and affective states that facilitate effective team processes, as well as team training development and leadership. She has been involved with the development of a number of training programs for agencies, including Veteran's Health Administration and the Coalition for Psychology in Schools and Education.

Part One

Why Teamwork Matters in Organizations

ESSAY ONE

Teamwork in Financial Institutions—Does It Really Matter?

Michael J. Castellana
CEO, SEFCU

Not only do effective team-based behaviors "matter" in financial institutions but a case can be made that they have, and will continue to, predict success and failure. It is well documented that the functioning of a team has a direct and significant correlation to achieving its stated goals. For any particular team, the case for a positive correlation is short and indisputable. But what happens when an organization is an ecosystem of independent and often competing teams? Such is the case for most financial institutions—both those that remain today as well as those that have become casualties of industry evolution and business cycle disruption. In such an environment, teamwork may be the difference between thriving and ceasing to exist.

Most financial institutions are balance-sheet driven, with organizational structures dictated by line of business that further align with financial statement category. For example, there will likely be a lending division with component reporting units for commercial, retail, and residential products. The aggregation of the individual obligations of these products will appear on the company's balance sheet as commercial loans outstanding, auto loans, credit card loans, and so on. Often the balance sheet and income statement become the de facto report cards of the institution.

Supporting these "balance sheet–oriented" divisions will be teams from areas like human resources, facilities, information technology, customer service, debt recovery, and more. A financial services organization could easily have twenty-five or more balance sheet divisions below the corporate level and a like number of support divisions. As you visualize the organizational chart, each of these divisions will be made up of multiple teams with more granular objectives in support of their respective business units.

Unfortunately, the organizational chart will resemble the classic row of silos with a corporate ring at the top. Most business units, regardless of size, are managed through measurable and clearly defined metrics. These metrics within one silo should cascade down from the divisional lead and help define success for each individual team. While seemingly simple within the divisional silo, the metrics of one silo often come at the expense of another silo or of those support teams referenced above. For example, the real estate lending team has a metric on loans originated, and clearly more is better. However, the loss mitigation team has a metric related to delinquent loans where one bad mortgage boosts the metric in the wrong direction by hundreds of thousands of dollars. The typical conflicts in success metrics for silo component teams in financial institutions could fill this book. Wall Street and Main Street are littered with the names of once proud financial brands that could not coordinate the tension among individual, team, and divisional success metrics in such a way that it created a win vertically (divisional), a win horizontally (across multiple divisions), and a win corporately (mission-based attainment).

It may be illustrative to look at my own institution and our methods in dealing with silo conflict. SEFCU is a $2.4 billion credit union serving many of the population centers in upstate New York. We were chartered and have operated in an uninterrupted manner since 1934. We have more than forty branches, 750 employees, and two wholly owned subsidiaries (a mortgage bank and an insurance agency). While we have many of the structural characteristics detailed above, we attack silo conflict through a shared sense of purpose and a focus on corporate culture. The combination of these elements and a "just do the right thing" approach to empowerment provide the decision-making guidance necessary to overcome silo conflict.

We have adopted a "banking with a purpose" (BWP) business model. This overarching approach has four pillars, starting with our *employees*, followed by our *members* (customers), then our *community*, and finally our *business partners*. We elevate our employees to the top of the priority list—if they are not ready, engaged, and working together, the rest of the model fails. We then address the needs of both our current and future customers. We also contribute a minimum of 20 percent of our net income to our community in a variety of forms of philanthropy. This approach gives the prior two pillars (employees and customers) something to take pride in and an opportunity to be part of something much bigger than themselves or their divisions. Finally, we have a programmatic approach to working with our business partners to ensure they benefit from their association with the SEFCU ecosystem. For each of these four pillars, we have success metrics that define both organizational and team success.

We have fostered a six-point corporate culture, including member service, teamwork, continuous improvement, change management, fun, and wellness. While non-numeric, this "way of doing business" is reiterated in both word and action at all levels. These elements define how we will operate on the inside of SEFCU's four walls.

BWP + Corporate Culture, SEFCU-Style, become the lens through which we can identify, measure, and react to team success metrics horizontally, vertically, and at the corporate level. Our not-for-profit approach mutes an overemphasis on balance sheet success metrics, and our relatively small size provides for a more narrow structural height and depth—again giving us a better chance to overcome silo-based team metric conflict.

In sum, we recognize that if we do not properly promote teamwork throughout our ecosystem, we lose. At our financial institution, we use our mission, business model, metrics, training, incentives, structure, culture, decision making, and even physical space arrangements to promote collaboration and a sense of shared purpose. When it comes to financial institutions, teamwork matters.

ESSAY TWO

Do Teams' Leaders Really Matter?

COL Casey Haskins
U.S. Military Academy, West Point

Sooner or later, every discussion about teams leads to the topic of leaders. People believe that leaders matter a great deal and that leadership is the main factor in determining a team's performance, for good or bad. Part of this belief appears to be inborn; across cultures, people defer more and give more weight to authority figures than to others. But much of our belief in leadership is acquired as well, soaked up from our culture, especially the stories we tell. In our stories, leaders often play a dominant role. They are the heroes, and the notion that they are the most important members of the team is drummed into us as children. Very often, the people telling the stories are leaders, too, whether parents or teachers or preachers. Leaders tell stories of other leaders, and we absorb the lesson that leaders matter. It's no surprise that the "great man" theory of history still dominates in most people's thinking. While it has been criticized for millennia, its central idea has never been dismissed.

We typically assign the credit (or blame) for important events to leaders, even when we know intellectually that those events were largely beyond their power, and in spite of knowing the critical roles others played—even when it's clear that the contributions of the rest of the team were probably at least as important as the leader's. In our minds, for example, it's still Abraham Lincoln who won the Civil War. Never mind the contributions—

up to and including death—of literally millions of others on the Union side. Never mind that Lincoln himself wrote, "I claim not to have controlled events, but confess plainly that events controlled me." Logically, we realize he was correct, but still it was his sheer persistence and determination that won the war. This just feels right. It's how the world works—how we think it does, anyway.

Recently, though, a number of researchers have started to question this received wisdom. They've asked how much leaders really do contribute and whether teams would be better off with more shared leadership—or even with no leaders at all. The debate they've sparked now comes up regularly during discussions about teams and discussions about leadership. And the truth is the revisionists have compiled a lot of evidence to support their view that leaders matter less than we think. Most leaders—the evidence is quite clear on this—are pretty average. Replace one and an organization will soon resume its previous course. While the team's satisfaction may go up or down, its overall performance will change very little. In fact, some studies show that the difference between highly rated CEOs and poorly rated ones is, at most, a few percentage points in the company's performance. Why all the fuss then?

Here are two reasons leaders really do matter—just not always in the ways we think.

The first reason is that looking at averages is not the right approach. We do it almost automatically, assuming that leaders will be normally distributed: that is, that leader talent—and therefore leaders' results—will look like a bell curve. Identifying the curve's center and how far it's spread (its variance) will therefore tell us a lot. However, this is a mistake. Talent is indeed (at least approximately) bell-shaped, but results are not. Rather, they are distributed according to a "power law." While we are correct to expect a bell curve of leader talent, that's really irrelevant when judging the impact they have. We should look for an exponential curve instead—a very different proposition—and we should pay much more attention to the extremes than to the middle.

This dichotomy between a population (normally distributed) and the results of that population's interactions (distributed exponentially) is typical of complex systems. Results of complex interactions always follow a power law, even when the things that produce them don't. In a now-familiar example, although measures of general talent in the population approximate a bell curve, income and wealth are exponential—a fact that provoked Occupiers' protests against the privileged "1 percent."

In a power-law distribution like this, we should expect that most leaders won't make all that much difference, a few will make some difference, a handful will make a really big difference, and—only occasionally—one or two will have an impact profound enough to shatter the status quo.

And, at least in the Army, that does indeed describe what we see.

The Army is an interesting place to study leadership. In many ways it's the closest thing to a controlled experiment we can find: lots of identical organizations doing nearly identical things in very similar circumstances. Usually, the biggest difference between those organizations is the leaders who are put in charge. But despite all their similarities, some teams achieve markedly different results. Part of that difference can no doubt be ascribed to circumstances and luck—but not all of it. Too much is consistent and predictable to be random chance.

When we look deeper, we find, as expected, that most leaders do matter a little, yet their time in command doesn't have much of an impact one way or another on the team's performance; it's more a question of style than dramatically different results. Yet there are a few leaders who consistently make a big difference in every unit they're assigned to. Some of them improve team performance significantly. Sometimes a bad leader slips through the cracks and has an equally dramatic effect, but for the worse. Taken altogether, the size of effects leaders have on their teams is not bell-shaped but exponential—and it's usually the ones near the end of the curve who make it into the history books.

Arguing, as the revisionists do, that leaders don't matter because the average leader doesn't make much difference to the team's performance, is like arguing that the stock market doesn't matter because most days it doesn't move much, or earthquakes don't matter because they're typically too small to be felt. Both arguments are true, but both miss the point.

This brings us to a second reason why leaders matter more than other members of the team. Success and failure are not symmetric. To a leader, they are not just two sides of the same coin. That's because leaders cannot succeed by themselves. Success requires the whole team. A leader can work hard and do all the right things: build a good plan, develop the members of the team, inspire them, put in place the right incentives, and find a good balance between empowerment and control. Still, at the end of the day, success comes down to execution on the part of lots of individual team members—and to luck.

Dwight Eisenhower prepared two press statements for D-Day. The brief statement he actually released credited the hard work and heroism of the Allied soldiers, sailors, and airmen who did the difficult fighting and dying at Normandy. Since then, in fact, historians have identified about fifty individuals in that day's fight who made a critical difference. Absent any single one of their contributions, the battle might have swung the other way. And after all, the Supreme Allied Commander who had launched them was still in England. But they did what they did, and the invasion succeeded.

Eisenhower's other press release, never issued, heaped upon himself the blame for D-Day's failure. This may sound like nothing more than a gimmick (distribute the credit, accept the blame), but there was something deeper at work. Ike knew that failure differs from success in a key way: It takes the whole team to win a battle, but a commander can lose it all by himself. Misread a situation, or make one bad decision, and the whole enterprise can tip into disaster. George Armstrong Custer, always a brave commander if not always a prudent one, condemned his men to death with a single fateful misjudgment at Little Big Horn. That is why Ike had to have a second statement ready—he could not know beforehand whether he had gotten things right.

And this is another reason that studies of leaders and their contributions often veer off track: They equate failure with a lack of success—but failure and success are not really mirror images.

It is true: Most leaders really don't make that much difference in the end. At the same time, it's undeniable that a few men and women have an outsized influence on their organizations, that the whole team achieves very different results with them in charge than when someone else is there. Some leaders manage to pull this off consistently, achieving superior results in a variety of circumstances—often despite considerable shortcomings in their teams. Looking at averages conceals these dramatic differences near the curve's end. It's the outliers who matter most. And while even the best leaders must rely on the whole team to win, the most mediocre have it in their power to cause disaster all by themselves.

So in the end, the common belief that leaders do matter is right. The studies that conclude they don't are wrong.

ESSAY THREE

Teamwork Matters

Peter J. Pronovost, MD, Ph.D.
Johns Hopkins University

Effective teamwork is essential in all aspects of life, but especially so in health care. Over decades-long investigations, teamwork failure has repeatedly surfaced as a major cause of preventable deaths and adverse events. Poor communication and teamwork are major causes of all types of sentinel events, from retained foreign objects to perinatal events and medication errors. Wherever we look, teamwork lapses harm patients.

Along with a dismal recount of how clinicians interact, we are seeing hopeful signs that teamwork can be improved. Rather than an abstract concept, effective teamwork involves a concrete set of skills and behaviors that clinicians can learn and, when they do learn, they save lives. The Veterans Health Administration (VHA), for instance, implemented a national team training program in hospitals with surgical services and experienced a significant decrease in surgical mortality. The program was based on aviation's theory of crew resource management and included tools and strategies that taught clinicians the skills needed to work as an effective team.

The skills taught by the VHA may seem innate, yet too few clinicians have or use these skills in the workplace. Medical schools and nursing schools spend insufficient time teaching these skills and often lack the experts to teach them. As a result, clinicians often do not see how teamwork and communication contribute to excellent patient care, often focusing on the individual "hero" in caring for patients. We need to ensure that medical students and nursing students graduate with expertise in teamwork, a skill they will use every day. Students spend a substantial amount of time memorizing facts and staring into microscopes. While the basic sciences are important for their training, most students will not use this knowledge when they step into the hospital or outpatient setting.

Gone are the days when one physician is solely responsible for a patient's outcome. Health care is complex, with specialized physicians, nurses, laboratory technicians, managers, and others all doing their jobs to move patient care forward. What pulls their skills together and makes health care work is effective teamwork. To be effective, teams need to focus on common goals and ensure that everyone is bringing his or her best to realize those goals.

A number of actions can help improve patient outcomes by improving teamwork and applying the skills in this book. First, training programs need experts qualified to provide teamwork training. Second, health professional schools and residency programs need to foster effective teamwork and communication skills and ensure their graduates have the skills necessary to be part of a high-performing team, a team that includes patients and their families. Health care organizations need to provide mechanisms to monitor and improve teamwork skills. For example, a member of the care team, with appropriate training, can be assigned the role of observing teamwork and providing feedback on performance. Finally, medical specialty boards could include teamwork as a core competency for board certification.

We have made major advances in medicine to treat patients, but limited advances in teamwork to help patients. This book provides the tools teachers and learners need, tools that will ultimately save lives. We must ensure that these tools are practiced.

ESSAY FOUR

Making a Difference with Health Care Teams

Victor V. Buzachero

Scripps Health

Health care is an industry that is considered one of the most complex in the world. In fact, Peter Drucker said, "The hospital is, altogether, the most complex human organization ever devised." The industry is comprised of payers and consumers who seek care from independent physicians who use services at independent hospitals. These health care organizations are comprised of a vast number of product and service operations that work together to serve doctors and patients. Integrated delivery systems or networks weave together the services of payers, physicians, and hospitals in an effort to do all things for the patient.

Teams in health care are utmost in criticality. The team brings together vastly unique constituents and stakeholders to provide a unified experience of care for patients to achieve the best outcomes. Without the use of teams in health care, the patient care experience would involve a series of events delivered in silo fashion that would have to be knit together by the patient. These teams are high-performing in nature, focused on the patient first, creating the highest quality outcome, and avoiding the blind man scenario of describing the elephant by touch approach to care for the patient.

The health care industry uniquely consists of tax-exempt organizations that exist to serve the communities in which they operate. Given the complexity and various independent components that make up the industry, organizations, or communities served, people work together to provide health care to patients through multiple team models, each serving unique purposes. There are five basic teams in health care today:

- *Team of Equals*—Boards of directors or trustees, committees of physicians, or teams of executives that serve to govern the organization and represent constituents.
- *Command-and-Control Teams*—Teams that operate in emergency or crises situations during times of disaster, emergency care, or intense, highly technical, life-threatening situations.
- *Expert Leader–Dominated Teams*—Teams comprised of care providers under the direction of a physician or expert in functional areas to deliver care.
- *Multi-Disciplinary Teams*—Groups representing many functions or areas of expertise that work to develop processes, procedures, and operating policies between and among disparate groups so they are effective together.
- *Co-Management Teams*—A newer team concept that blends clinical and administrative leadership together to jointly manage processes, systems, or ventures to achieve mutually beneficial outcomes.

Health Care Teams Explored

Team of Equals

These teams exist with a mission to serve, for example, a community, and therefore represent some sort of constituency. In this role, typically there is a primus, or leader, selected by the team to facilitate rather than lead. The facilitator is to guide the team of equals in fulfillment of their responsibility. This includes generative discussions that craft vision to determine direction, oversee areas entrusted to them, and define how they relate to the environment. In this capacity, all members are to contribute and the outcomes are expected to be greater than the sum of the parts.

Command-and-Control Teams

These teams are comprised of a hierarchal structure that is needed when a group of people must come together in situations of high risk and uncertain, changing environments to deliver outcomes that are not always known. In a crisis or an emergency situation such as an earthquake, terrorist attack, or major accident such as an airline crash, the team must assemble and execute rapidly in highly intense, life-threatening situations. The team enlists a military type structure with a pre-established command center (hospital incident command center) and prescribed roles for members working under the direct control of the command center leader. Planning, reporting, and execution are directed explicitly by the incident commander. The team shifts, post-action, to complete an after-action review to ascertain how the team performed, and what variables surfaced. The team then co-creates revised processes and roles for the next crisis.

Expert Leader–Dominated Teams

Led by a leader that is considered a subject matter or functional expert, these teams are generally led by an MD who directs the assessment of information and prescribes action to a clinical team that implements the plan. The clinical team will be guided by a manager/leader who will coordinate, oversee, and provide much of the care directed by the MD. Consensus decision making is limited because the subject-matter expert is deemed to have superior know-how. These teams function much like command-and-control teams; however, the intensity is less and the duration of the work is much longer. One remarkable difference is that, in many settings, the subject-matter expert is not employed by the organization but is governed by a "team of equals" (committee of medical staff). These types of teams can also be functional in imaging, nursing, laboratory, and pharmacy areas.

Multi-Disciplinary Teams

These are teams that represent something different in the health care setting. Functioning much like a project team, they take on issues and decisions that cannot be completed solely by a functional/expert team because they address items that cross areas of expertise and serve all functional teams or may even require the teams to work collectively to achieve an outcome. These teams may take on process improvement roles, develop policy and procedures, or define how activity will flow from one area to another to assure seamless transition and effective relationships. The teams may function on a time-limited schedule or may have ongoing roles for the organization, like a patient safety team. These teams can also undertake compliance and licensing requirements to demonstrate the quality of the institution. Of course, these teams function best when there is mutual interdependency pertaining to the issue. They function by means of a consensus approach and are political in nature.

Co-Management Teams

Teams to co-manage areas arise when mutually interdependent, but independent, groups come together to achieve outcomes. These co-management teams are useful in leading and managing service or product lines that include co-management by administration and clinical (physician) leaders to operate the service or product lines. The team will have co-leaders, each of whom has a unique role. Leads are in the administrative and clinical areas and counsel each other. The team is comprised of additional administrative and clinical members, but likely dominated by those in clinical areas. Both share accountability for outcomes, including risk, reward, or penalty. The group functions in consensus decision making with the two dominant leaders maintaining veto power. Additionally, special ad hoc groups will serve the team to educate, study, and research various issues to guide the decision making.

These five unique team models allow for the optimal approach based on emerging situations. Circumstances in health care environments are constant in one thing: change. Changing circumstances should employ the appropriate model for the new circumstance. The seasoned leader will deploy all five team models throughout the enterprise simultaneously to achieve peak performance.

ESSAY FIVE

Developing Leaders on Any Team

George O'Leary
Head Football Coach, University of Central Florida

"This organization has no leadership."

"I need more leaders on this team."

How many times have you heard those statements, and agreed with them because you know what they're going through?

You shouldn't have! Every group has leaders in it, and you don't need more leaders; you just need the right leaders in the group to step up and take charge. An organization with the right leadership, even if it's only one individual, will run like a well-oiled machine. The trick is to make sure the right leaders step up.

An example I like to use while on the speaking circuit is this: At every table of ten people, one will be a winner, one will be a loser, and the other eight are trying to figure out which one to follow. For some laughs, I usually then ask whether they know which people at their tables are the losers. I've had people nod their heads yes, and some have actually pointed the person out!

After being in the coaching ranks for more than forty years at the high school, college, and pro level, I have seen thousands of young men from every walk of life bond together and select who the leaders of their team will be. Usually, this is done before any official captains voting is done. It takes place day in, day out, in the locker room and on the field. Winning teams picked the winner at the table as their leader; losing teams decided to follow the loser. It's that simple.

So how can you influence the group to gravitate toward the winner and see the loser for who he is? You first need to identify the different types of people in your organization. You then need to help the person or people you identified as winners to see themselves the way you see them. Finally, you need to make sure the support is in place for those individuals to be successful.

You can generally categorize everyone on your team into three groups: winners, losers, and followers. Your leaders are going to come from the winners and losers. It's imperative that the winners end up as the true leaders of your team! Here are some quick ways to identify which category each person falls into:

1. *Winners:* The main characteristic I always look for is that he or she has to be willing to be respected rather than liked. It takes a certain maturity to understand what that means and to put it into action while among peers; that's what separates the true leaders from the rest of the group. This quality is why a leader is going to stand up for what's right and put guys in their place who aren't doing it right. This is the quality that allows you to trust a leader when you aren't around to make sure the team is doing what needs to be done. It allows him or her to give 100 percent and push everyone around to be their best, despite the loser in the group telling people that they should sit back and take it easy. Finally, their teammates will trust a leader to do what's right. That part, though, is based on teamwork, and I'll show how that fits into leadership a little later.
2. *Followers:* Most people would rather have a group of friends who like them and have no clue whether those people respect them or not; those aren't your leaders. They are the eight looking for direction. This group should be pretty easy to identify. Your main duty here is to make sure they look up to the individuals you identified as winners.
3. *Losers:* I wish there was a better term for it, but it's what they are. Without much effort, they will find every way possible to lose and will take down everyone around them in the process. The loser is the most harmful person on your team because he sees himself as a leader and is competing against the true winners on your team for which direction the team will go. A strong caution I'll give is that in most groups the loudest

person, the one who talks the most, isn't necessarily the best leader of the group. In fact, a lot of the time that person is the opposite of what you want. He's the loser at the table, and he has to be loud because his voice is his only way of capturing people's attention; he has no other redeeming qualities to attract followers. I guess in a way he is a leader, as some will inevitably end up following him, but as soon as the going gets tough, the loser will fold and leave everyone else to fend for themselves. A winner, in contrast, will have your team bond even closer together when facing adversity. A loser will convince others to protect themselves rather than sacrifice for the person standing next to him. He's the cancer on the team that you have to isolate and eventually cut out.

Once you've identified the winners in the group, if they are natural-born leaders, it should be a quick and easy transition for them to take over the team and be very successful. Make no mistake about it, though: A natural-born leader is extremely tough to come across. A good way to think of it is that a natural leader is not just noticed, but remembered. For your other leaders, though, it takes more work. They are the reluctant leaders. They give 100 percent and look down at guys who take shortcuts. They just haven't found their way of inspiring those around them. Sometimes, it's their self-confidence lagging a bit. Other times, it might be they aren't quite ready to make the jump from being liked to being respected; they understand the difference, but need an extra push to separate from the pack. Unfortunately, there isn't any sure-fire way to help every one of these individuals to step up. Each person is unique, so it's important you get to know them as well as you can and develop a plan you think will work for whatever is holding that person back from being his or her best. Keep in mind that you aren't trying to create something from nothing. You know they have it in them, and you are just trying to get it out of them with that little push.

While some require a more individual plan of action, in general you can build up team leadership by first meeting with your leaders individually in your office and let them know you see them as the true winners on the team. You won't believe what kind of confidence that instills in a person! Then tell them what the expectations are of leaders in your organization. Finally, let them know that it's their team and you have their back. After all, these are the individuals you identified to trust with the team's future success! The next step is to make the public aware of who the leaders are. I usually do this during team meetings, but there are two sides to it. I will commend the leaders in front of their peers for a job well done, but will also get after them if they aren't pulling their weight. Say, for instance, you have a "no hat" policy, where individuals are supposed to take off their hats upon entering the building. As time goes by, you see more and more people not taking their hats off. That is something I would bring up in a team meeting by first letting the leaders know they need to have everyone following the rules and then let the group know that the leaders will be enforcing those rules.

That last statement is important because it helps build in the support structure you want for the leaders. It lets the entire organization know who is in charge. It helps the reluctant leaders step up, since they can fall back on your authority when asking others to fall in line. If someone wants to challenge a leader on a decision, there is no question of whose side you are going to take. That builds up the trust the leaders have in you and builds the confidence they have in themselves when making decisions. Remember, you can do all of this because you properly identified these individuals as the best leaders of your team; they are the winners, and they will have the followers believing that they are winners as well! Before long, your entire organization will believe they are winners, and that is a tough thing for any opponent to overcome.

Up to this point, I have covered leadership from a coach's point of view, but what really matters is how the other players view the leaders. The whole reason you are putting in all of this work is so the team buys in to what you're selling. This is where teamwork becomes vital! That trust you want the team to have in the leaders starts off as little things. While you keep track of the big picture, the team only cares about the immediate future; what happens from one play to the next. Let's say you are grooming your quarterback to be a leader on the team. Will the quarterback throw the ball at the right point during the receiver's route? He has to if he wants to be a leader and build teamwork! He has to do it repeatedly for the receivers to trust him to throw at the right time. Once that trust is built, the receivers might not like it when the quarterback throws to someone else, but they will trust that the quarterback made the right decision and will respect that decision. That's just one small example of how leadership and teamwork are both built at the same time.

Once they get the little things right, like throwing the ball on time, don't be afraid to test them. Force the players to rely on each other to do the job. Get them out of their comfort zones during practice. A great way I have found to accomplish this is through competition. Break the team into groups and watch how the groups instantly work together to beat the other groups. These events are also a perfect time to give the leaders of the team some experience by being the "captains" of each group. Trust me, the players might figure out what you're up to, but it still won't stop them from working together and pushing each other. Teamwork-building exercises don't just have to be during practice, either. You can do different things throughout the year, whether it's in the weight room, conditioning, or meetings. Building teamwork, just like building leadership, will lead to great team chemistry. When an entire team gets to that point of trust and respect among all others, great things will happen.

The next time you are at a conference or banquet sitting at a table full of people, look around the table. Can you identify the loser? Who's the winner? Most importantly, can you get the rest to follow the right person? If you can do that, you will be successful at any level!

ESSAY SIX

Teamwork and Spaceflight—An Evolving Relationship

Daniel W. Tani
Astronaut, NASA

Currently, the concepts of teamwork are tightly tied into astronaut selection, training, and qualifications. But it has not always been that way.

In the early days of America's human space flight program, the original astronauts were selected from among the military's finest test pilots. The criteria for selection were clearly technical excellence, operational skills, and probably charm and other public skills. The concepts of teamwork and crew resource management (CRM)—a team training strategy—had not yet infused the military pilot environment, and these space pioneers were essentially asked to test fly spacecraft the same way they did their aircraft—with reliance on their own skills and expertise.

As more astronauts were selected for the lunar program, there was still no conscious effort to teach or develop teamwork skills. Any positive team dynamics were a result of random personality mix—certainly not a result of explicit training. As crews became larger (two in the Gemini program and three in the Apollo), they must have faced interpersonal issues, but there were no public fallouts due to lacking team skills . . . until. . . .

Skylab was America's first orbiting space station—three different three-person crews were sent to live on Skylab, with the longest mission lasting eighty-four days. The dynamics between the on-orbit crew and the ground team quickly became strained with these longer missions (classic "us versus them" team dynamics). Famously, one crew "mutinied" and refused to work or even talk to the ground for more than one day. This event brought the issue of teamwork front and center at NASA.

With the transitions through the Space Shuttle, MIR Space Station, and now International Space Station (ISS) programs, the mission has become increasingly complex, the required skill set of the crews has become very broad, and the diversity of astronauts has become much greater. As a result, explicit teamwork skill training has become mandatory—a must for mission success. On the ISS, a crew consists of three or six astronauts, from at least two different countries—usually more. Because these astronauts live and work together in a small space for months at a time, the success of each crew depends on strong teamwork skills, and the ultimate success of each mission (defined as both technical outcome and happy returning crew members) is tightly tied to the teamwork that they exhibited.

Not only do mission requirements require keen teamwork skills but so does the training program for the ISS, which can last for several years. Astronauts-in-training are exposed to many cultures and languages (Russian, Japanese, French, German) and organizations with whom they must work. All of these interactions require highly developed teamwork skills to bridge the cultural, language, and organizational boundaries.

In the astronaut office, the term most often used is "expeditionary behavior," which encompasses leadership and followership skills, self-reliance and self-care, understanding of roles and responsibilities, communication, and conflict resolution—all aspects of successful teamwork in a long duration, high-stress, hazardous environment. Not only are crew members explicitly taught these concepts and skills in a classroom environment, but they are run through many training events to stress and expand their skill sets. Today, every astronaut who is chosen to live on the ISS for a six-month expedition has gone through wilderness training (via the National Outdoor Leadership School, a leadership building experience), a deep-sea expedition (in the Aquarius underwater research lab), winter and sea survival events held in

Russia, and other events designed to challenge their intra- and interpersonal relationships.

So far, the inclusion of teamwork training into general astronaut and ISS crew training has been a great success. Crews return home better friends than they were when they launched; mission goals have been accomplished with great success; and rarely are there conflicts within a crew or between the crews and the ground—and never has it been displayed Skylab-style. NASA has realized the importance of great teamwork—and that these skills are rarely inherent in the astronauts. They must be taught, developed, and reinforced.

Part Two

The Organization and Its Influence

CHAPTER ONE

Silent Killers of Team Performance

How Honest, Collective, and Public Conversations Can Overcome Them

Michael Beer
Harvard Business School and TruePoint

A central problem organizations face is that of coordination. Organizations are formed to enable their members to accomplish a result none could accomplish alone (Beer & Walton, 1990a). Substantial evidence exists, however, that differentiated functional departments, businesses and/or country/regions with different capabilities, time horizons, interpersonal orientations and cultures, present a major challenge (Lawrence & Lorsch, 1967a). This challenge has been shown to be greatest in uncertain and dynamic environments where high levels of responsiveness to change are essential (Lawrence & Lorsch, 1967a).

Research has shown that organizations that successfully integrate diverse value creating activities employ well-designed high-performance teams that cut across organizational boundaries. Such teams are led by individuals who have a general management orientation and good leadership skills, and through superior capacity to confront and resolve conflict are able to avoid political battles and solve problems (Lawrence & Lorsch, 1967a). Unfortunately, too many organizations have been unable to design and foster high-performance teams (Hackman, 2002).

Consider the Santa Rosa Systems Division (SRSD) of Hewlett-Packard, a division in HP's Test and Measurement Sector (Beer & Rogers, 1997). Historically, its single-purpose frequency measuring devices were sold to engineers to enable them to measure accurately frequencies emitted by the products they were designing. The emerging and growing telecommunication market in the 1990s created a demand for rugged multi-purpose frequency measurement devices (systems) in manufacturing cell phones, for example. Hewlett-Packard created a new division to enter this market. The division was given fourteen product lines that had been developed in other divisions. Its general manager was charged with responsibility to manage these legacy products for revenue and profits while at the same time identifying and developing new technology platforms. SRSD's senior leaders created three cross-functional business teams led by section managers in R&D. Each team was charged with managing the legacy products for revenue and profits and overseeing the development of strategically important new products.

Two years later, SRSD had not met its revenue and profit goals by a wide margin. Moreover, there was considerable conflict on the three business teams. On the Receiver Products and Stimulus Response business team, Custom Systems (CS) representatives who were charged with using legacy products to develop a customized systems solution complained that virtually all the time in business team meetings was spent on R&D projects to develop new technology, and none on CS's efforts to sell legacy systems. For example, in the Receiver Products business, CS had developed a growing business in satellite test equipment by using their applications engineering skills to integrate legacy products into a system that solved measurement problems associated with satellites. Little discussion and focus were given to this accomplishment and its potential. R&D engineers, on the other hand, resented the time and engineering resources CS put on customized systems. Similar problems existed in the Systems Products business team, where a natural tension existed between the time given to R&D projects needed to sustain a declining product line and time given to selling custom systems that met immediate customer demands. A "cold war" broke out between Custom Systems and R&D over engineering resources and, to a lesser extent, with the marketing department, whose limited resources made it impossible to serve both R&D and CS.

In this chapter I discuss six silent barriers—barriers that are undiscussable publicly—that twenty years of action research using the "strategic fitness process" (SFP) have been found to undermine the development and implementation of high-performance teams. These barriers represent an unhealthy organizational and management context for teams. I argue that process interventions, such as effective coaching and team development, training, and even changes in team leadership, will not succeed unless they are accompanied by changes in these six silent barriers. And I will explain how honest, collective, and public conversations enabled by SFP, which revealed the six silent barriers, are a powerful means for improving team effectiveness and performance. The distinctive contribution of the research findings in this chapter is that they show the connection between multiple barriers, how they interact to cause ineffective cross-boundary teams, and how the system of organizing and managing that undermines teams can be changed rapidly and sustainably.

Silent Barriers to Team Performance

The "strategic fitness process" (Beer & Eisenstat, 2004), an action science and intervention method described later in this chapter, has been employed in the last twenty years in dozens of organizations at the operating, business, and corporate levels to enable lower-level employees to speak the truth to senior managers about the state of effectiveness of their organization. Senior management teams are required to develop a compelling two-page strategic direction for the organization and then select and commission a task force of approximately eight of their best people to interview approximately one hundred key employees across the organization about strengths and barriers to implementation of the strategic direction. Upper management then receives feedback from the task force about the findings. A content analysis of findings from two studies, each involving twelve organizations, consistently revealed six silent barriers to organizational effectiveness. Effectiveness is defined as the organization's alignment (structure, systems, people, rewards, leadership, and organizational behavior) with its espoused strategy, and therefore the organization's capacity to implement that strategy (Beer & Eisenstat, 2000; Beer, 2011). The most prominent of the barriers is poor coordination across silos caused by non-existent or ineffective teams. That organizational silence, the inability to confront difficult organizational and strategic issues, undermines the development of an effective organization has been well documented in multiple studies (Argyris, 1985; Morrison & Milliken, 2000).

Task forces also uniformly reported that their organization's strength was its people. We concluded that the six silent barriers undermined the capacity of capable and motivated people to implement the organization's strategy, particularly their ability to coordinate and effectively function as teams.

To summarize their findings for senior teams, task forces conducted a rigorous analysis of their data with the help of a scholar-consultant. Acting as researchers, we then conducted a content analysis of task force findings in two-dozen organizations. That analysis yielded the following six barriers:

1. Unclear strategy, values, and/or conflicting priorities;
2. An ineffective senior team;
3. A top-down or a laissez faire leader;
4. Poor coordination and communication across functions, businesses, or geographic entities;
5. Inadequate leadership development and leadership resources below the top; and
6. Poor vertical communication down, and particularly up.

The central barrier to strategy execution is *poor coordination* (Barrier 4). In virtually all cases, coordination was undermined by the lack of properly designed cross-boundary teams and, in a few cases, the complete lack of such teams. If teams existed, membership in them was not always well-defined. Members continued to report exclusively to their function, business, or geographic region. The team leader had little or no authority to make final decisions if consensus could not be achieved, and/or the leader and team were not given or held responsible for a final business or project outcome. The inability of SRSD to achieve its strategic goals of *exploiting* legacy systems for short-term performance, while at the same time successfully *exploring* and developing new product lines, was a direct consequence of these mistakes in the design of cross-functional business teams.

Consider the recollection of SRSD's general manager about how he conceived the functioning of business teams:

> [I] made clear [my] expectations for . . . business team members by articulating the areas for which they had individual functional responsibility and the areas in which they were to work together. R&D was responsible for developing new systems platforms. Custom Systems (CS) was responsible for generating sales of customized systems put together from legacy general-purpose instruments. Marketing was responsible for generating orders and customers support. The area in which functional representatives on the team were expected to work together was new product definition and long-term business strategies that would result in a profitable business. (Beer & Rogers, 1997, p. 6)

Section managers from R&D who ran the R&D effort aligned with that business were given responsibility for leading the team. They and the team were not, however, held accountable for the overall performance (revenue and profit) of the business they were managing, nor were they given any authority with regard to business decisions or given career authority over team members (for example, performance evaluation, coaching, and recommendations about future positions).

In this description, all the design problems discussed earlier are apparent. SRSD's business teams were not real teams (Hackman, 2002; Wegeman, 1995). Each team member was responsible for his/her functional task and accountable to his or her functional boss, with no accountability to the team leader, who had no authority to make decisions or hold members accountable for effective membership in the team. And teams were not accountable for team performance. Team leaders from R&D continued to be only accountable for developing new technical platforms or systems. So it is not a surprise that members from CS became frustrated when discussions in meetings did not include a review of CS successes in generating revenue and profits or their urgent need for engineers from R&D to support them in building an application engineering business from legacy products. Without that support, CS engineers could not exploit the opportunities for revenue and profits they were finding. In effect, business teams were unable to make crucial tradeoff decisions between allocating engineering resources to exploit legacy products for short-term revenue and profits, and engineering resources needed to explore new technical systems solutions needed for long-term success.

Across almost all of the organizations studied, team ineffectiveness was a function of insufficient down-the-line leaders, with a general management perspective brought about by inadequate efforts to develop such leaders (Barrier 5). As the SRSD case illustrates, section managers, who were assigned to lead business teams, had spent their whole careers in engineering positions and had no cross-functional experiences outside R&D. They therefore lacked the general management perspective needed to see the businesses they were leading as more than developing new technology platforms. They failed to grasp the strategic interdependence of managing for the short and long term. Their tendency to see problems from an R&D perspective made it impossible for them to develop trust and confidence from team members in other functions. In effect, these team leaders were not integrators who possessed a balanced perspective (Lawrence & Lorsch, 1967b). Confronted with this finding, SRSD's senior team admitted that there were no credible candidates within the division. They had not been developed.

In most instances, the reason for the paucity of leaders with a general management perspective was the ineffectiveness of senior teams (Barrier 2). Why? Senior teams had not spent enough time reviewing their key people and high potentials and did not provide them with cross-functional experiences that would stretch them. This behavior was often a function of an ineffective leadership team whose members were selfishly holding onto good people they needed to meet their unit's goals.

Just as important, senior team ineffectiveness also undermined the strategic management of the business. Senior teams in all the businesses we studied did not spend enough time as a team (1) developing and agreeing on a strategy and values that would guide organizational behavior such as collaboration so essential to effective teams, (2) reviewing team progress, (3) reordering the relative priority of the initiatives assigned to each team, based on what they learned from these reviews, and (4) reallocating resources accordingly. These findings suggest a simple but uncomfortable rule of thumb for assessing and developing lower-level cross-boundary teams: The effectiveness and performance teams cannot be higher than the effectiveness and performance of the senior management team.

SRSD is again a good example. The task force reported, "Members of the top team operate within their own functional silos. They are like a group of fiefdoms that refuse to cooperate effectively for fear that they will lose power" (Beer & Rogers, 1997, p. 1). In fact, the senior team met sporadically. When they did, they discussed administrative matters, as opposed to strategic issues that they and the general manager feared would lead to unmanageable conflict. So no regular reviews of each business team's progress in developing a profitable business occurred. Engineering managers who ran the teams therefore did not receive the advice or coaching they desperately needed to make up for their lack of general management experience. Indeed, this problem became so acute that one member of the senior team took it upon himself to organize meetings with team leaders and a few other senior team members to review business team activities and coach team leaders. SRSD's team problems and this makeshift solution were, of course, the consequence of the general manager's false assumptions about the design of cross-functional teams, namely that team members were individually responsible for achieving their functional goals and that the only task for the business team as a group was to define new products and develop a long-term strategy.

Lacking a strategic management process, it is not surprising that task forces in the organizations we studied reported to their senior teams that people in the organization perceived that strategy and values were unclear and that there were conflicting priorities (Barrier 1). Because senior management teams did not meet as a group to develop strategy (this was typically done by the general manager in conjunction with the chief strategy officer or chief marketing officer), senior team members sent different messages to their respective functions, businesses, or geographic regions. And they prioritized their initiatives without sufficient concern for and understanding of the interdependence of their activity with that of others. And because ineffective senior management teams did not agree on values, such as collaboration and accountability, to which they expected team members to adhere, this further weakened team effectiveness and performance, although poor team design was the more important cause.

This was very much the case at SRSD. The task force reported to the senior management team: "We have two competing strategies that are battling each other for the same resources. The resultant factions around these two strategies are tearing this organization apart. SRSD is still not sure what kind of business it wants to be" (Beer & Rogers, 1997, p. 1). The battle at SRSD was between R&D and CS for scarce engineering resources and the limited resources of marketing that each department felt it needed to achieve its goals. Not surprisingly, the task force reported, "There is a cold war going on between R&D and the Custom Systems department" (Beer & Rogers, 1997, p. 1).

Task forces in all the organizations we studied reported, typically with a good deal of anxiety, that interviewees saw leadership by the head of the organization, business unit head, CEO, or operating unit head, as a barrier (Barrier 3). This feedback was understandably less direct, rarely couched in personal terms, than their report about other barriers. From an analysis of the leaders' practices people saw as problematic, we concluded that leaders were either too top down or too laissez faire. They either became involved in problems that were best handled at lower levels or were in some other way too directive, or they were too hands-off, not identifying and forcing fact-based constructive conflict that resolved problems about which there were different opinions.

We concluded that top-down or hands-off laissez faire leadership was a function of conflict aversion by the organization's head. In effect, leaders avoided debate by being directive or by not engaging others in strategically important discussions about which there are typically different perspectives. Conflict aversion prevented leaders and their senior teams from rapid learning about lower-level and senior team ineffectiveness and, of course, slowed remedial action. SRSD's general manager fit the profile. He was a laissez faire leader who managed his team in a "star" pattern, meeting individually with each senior team member. This created distrust among senior team members and prevented the senior team from engaging in discussions of strategic and organizational problems that the general manager feared might lead to conflict. Others we studied avoided debate by forcing their views on others.

We came to call the barriers the "silent killers" (Beer & Eisenstat, 2000). Like cholesterol and hypertension that silently undermine human health, the silent killers silently undermined the health of the organization. They were perceived by those interviewed by the task force to be the root cause of organizational ineffectiveness. But they were typically discussed only in private conversations between trusted colleagues. Poor or closed vertical communication (Barrier 6) made the barriers undiscussible publicly. That is, all parties to the problem of underperforming teams could not find a way to hold a collective, honest, fact-based conversation that would enable systemic change—change in all six silent barriers simultaneously—thus leading to change in both "hard" facets such as organization and team design and "soft" facets such as leadership and organizational behavior, skills, and attitudes, both senior team behavior and behavior within lower level teams. Thus, everyone knew about the barriers, but the leadership team was either not motivated to and/or did not know how to create a safe, honest, and collective conversation that would reveal them.

Such feedback would have allowed senior teams we studied to validate what they already suspected (Our interviews with senior teams revealed that they knew about the barriers.) By "validate," I mean coming to see threatening feedback about difficult problems as objective, not constructed by a few biased or politically motivated individuals or subgroups. Unable to discuss the barriers publicly (within the senior team and with lower levels), senior management teams could not come to agreement among themselves about what was blocking effectiveness, nor could they engage lower levels in honest conversation about problems and solutions that would enable the redesign of teams, change in senior team effectiveness, and changes in team leaders if necessary.

All this made the barriers self-sealing. In all the organizations we studied, the barriers had been in place for some time. At SRSD, ineffective coordination and dysfunctional business teams had been in place for two years. Indeed, in informal conversations at breaks and over coffee, I learned about these problems six months before SFP was implemented when I conducted a workshop for the top forty managers in SRSD using a case about another organization that had similar coordination problems. When asked whether they had shared their perceptions with SRSD's general manager, the answer was no. It was not until the senior team employed the strategic fitness process that the barriers became discussible and were ultimately overcome. In some cases, SRSD being one, changes in organizational and team design were made during the three-day fitness meeting (see below). In other cases, it required more engagement over a period of weeks or months to arrive at a new design.

We concluded that the six silent killers together are a syndrome. All six barriers were typically reported together and were interdependent in the manner described above. They are stress points in organizations. That is, they are hard to get right due to the human problems created by differentiation and hierarchy (Beer, 2009, p. 111). And these stress points can become major fault lines when organizations are faced with new market realities that require rethinking strategy, organization, and team design, as well as organizational behavior, the situation in which SRSD found itself.

Figure 1.1 shows this interdependence. The first three barriers, ineffective senior team, ineffective leader, and unclear strategy and conflicting priorities, are interdependent. They make it impossible to develop an effective team that can create a high-quality direction for the organization, a direction to which all members of the senior team are committed. The fourth and fifth barriers, poor coordination due to ineffective or nonexistent cross-boundary teams and insufficient down-the-line leaders with the general management capability to lead teams, preclude effective high-quality execution of the strategy. That is, poorly designed, led, and managed teams don't succeed in creating the coordination required to execute the strategy. The sixth barrier, poor vertical communication, had two components. The first, downward communication, was poor because senior leaders did not spend enough time communicating about strategic direction. The second, inability of lower-level team members to "speak truth

Figure 1.1. The Silent Killer Syndrome: Barriers to Team Performance

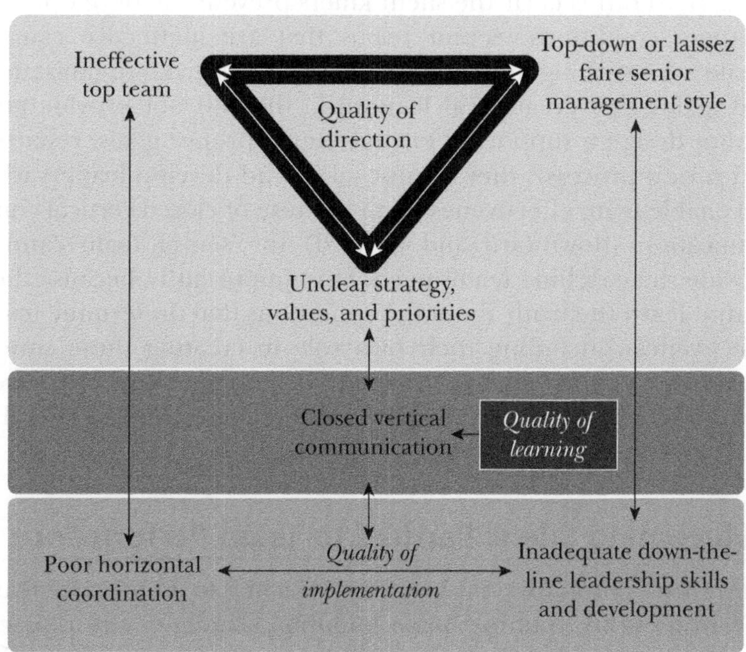

to power," made it impossible for a senior management team to learn about the barriers and take corrective action—improve their own effectiveness, redesign the organization and team structure (clarifying or changing roles and responsibilities), and make changes in leadership behavior through development or replacement. In effect, organizations with silent barriers are unable to learn about what is working and not working and redesign themselves.

The argument that six silent killers undermine team effectiveness and performance maps very closely the findings of Richard Hackman (2002), who has studied teams for almost two decades. He concluded that five conditions have to be present for teams to be effective. "The team (1) is a real team not a team in name only, (2) has a compelling direction for its work, (3) has an enabling structure that facilitates rather than impedes teamwork,

(4) operates within a supportive organizational context, and (5) has available ample expert coaching in teamwork" (Hackman, 2002, p. 31). It is clear the silent killers prevent the development of these conditions. Senior teams that are ineffective cannot create a compelling direction, they cannot design an organization and teams that create real teamwork, they do not provide and cannot design a supportive environment (proper goals, rewards, and review process), they cannot select and develop leaders who will enable team effectiveness, and because of closed vertical communication (downward and upward) the senior team cannot provide the coaching teams need. Most importantly, because they cannot learn the truth about the conditions that undermine team effectiveness, including their own role in creating these conditions, they cannot change them. How senior teams and lower levels might learn the truth so they can change conditions is the subject of the next section.

Overcoming Silent Barriers to Team Performance

The most frequently employed approaches to improving team effectiveness are training, team building, coaching, and replacement of team leaders. Indeed, SRSD began with this training—the workshop I conducted. These interventions by themselves have been shown to be largely ineffectual, as Hackman (2002) found in his research and experience. This is our finding as well (Beer, Eisenstat, & Spector, 1990). No one who has been called on to consult and coach an ineffective team could come away from this experience without realizing that the cause of a team's ineffectiveness is largely outside the team's control. The silent killers had been in existence since the founding of SRSD. The workshop I conducted in SRSD six months before they employed SFP clarified the problems but did not enable key managers to confront them collectively and change the situation, an example of the futility of training as an intervention.

What was lacking in many other organizations we have worked with and studied, SRSD included, was a means for creating what we have come to call an *honest, collective, and public conversation.* By *honest* I mean that the whole truth about silent barriers is revealed. Embarrassing and potentially threatening issues are not left unreported. By *collective* I mean that the conversation involves the senior team and a cross-section of people in the organization who serve on teams or are affected by their efficacy. By *public* I mean that everyone in the organization connected to the coordination and team problems hears the results of the task force findings and what the senior team will do about them, and they are given an opportunity to challenge the change plan. As Hackman notes, the solution to team effectiveness problems is not coaching, the replacement of poor leaders with great leaders, or better communication as singular interventions (Hackman, 2002). Honest, collective, and public conversations motivated by an intervention such as SFP help senior management teams learn the "unvarnished truth" about the syndrome of multiple barriers, the unhealthy context in which underperforming cross-boundary teams are embedded, and motivate them to transform barriers into strengths that will support team performance.

In too many organizations, this does not happen. Coordination due to the lack of teams or poorly designed teams is not subject to open discussion. Decades of research finds (Argyris, 1990; Beer & Eisenstat, 2000) that open discussions threaten senior management's assumptions and self-esteem ("We must not be good leaders"), thus triggering defensive routines. Recent research suggests that organizational silence is caused by individuals' implicit theories about the negative consequences of speaking up and that these theories cannot easily be altered by the most open of leaders (Detert & Edmondson, 2011). Even if leaders were to learn about the intensity of concerns regarding coordination in their organization, our research suggests that they do not act on them because feedback from one or two people is simply not substantively and emotionally compelling enough to confront uncomfortable truths. Leaders can easily rationalize that the feedback is not valid, biased, or does not represent what is really going on. The threat inherent in owning up to effectiveness problems causes many senior managers, and their senior teams, to distance themselves emotionally from problems, thus reducing their sense of urgency to deal with them, our research shows.

The strategic fitness process (SFP) developed by Russ Eisenstat and me enables the organization and its leaders to gain the benefits of open feedback, while eliminating the negative

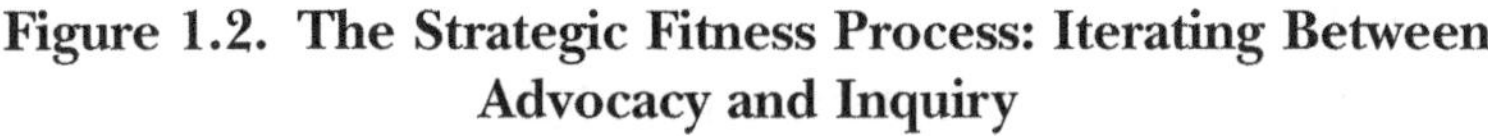

Figure 1.2. The Strategic Fitness Process: Iterating Between Advocacy and Inquiry

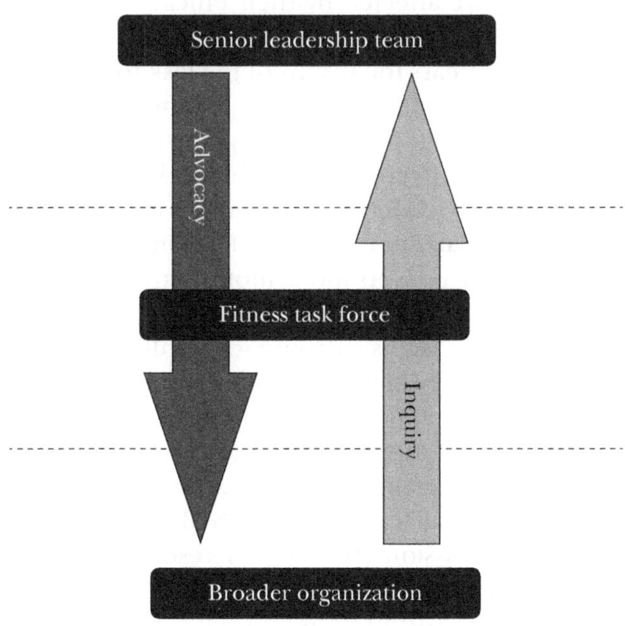

consequences of speaking up for lower-level people. It has proven to be a useful research method that revealed the silent killers and also a powerful intervention method capable of overcoming them and turning them into strengths, our research shows (Beer, 2011; Beer & Eisenstat, 2000, 2004). The method iterates between advocacy and inquiry. As Figure 1.2 shows, the senior team (1) advocates a compelling strategic direction and (2) commissions a task force to inquire into strengths and barriers to strategy execution as perceived by people in the organization (usually one hundred key people). The senior team then decides on and advocates changes and moves into an inquiry phase about quality of their change plan by asking the task force to critique that plan. The iteration of advocacy and inquiry is designed to reduce potential defensive behavior by senior teams and make it possible for task forces to tell senior teams the truth.

Figure 1.3 shows a carefully designed process that is typically facilitated by consultants. They are also a substantive resource to

Figure 1.3. Steps in the Strategic Fitness Process

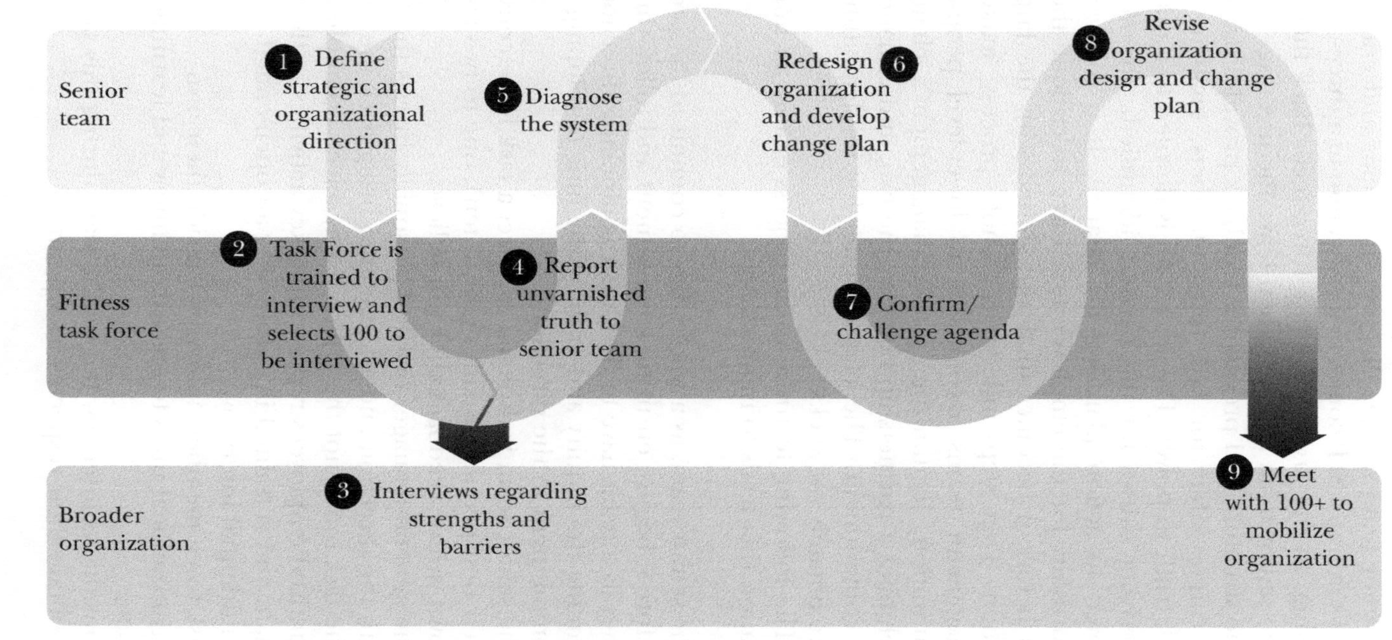

the senior team as they diagnose problems and craft organizational solutions. SFP comes to a crescendo in a three-day "fitness" meeting. In the *first day* the task force feeds back their findings to the senior team and they then leave the meeting. The design of the structure and process for feedback provides psychological and career safety for task force members, enabling them to speak truth to power. The *second day* is devoted to a diagnosis of underlying causes for the barriers identified. The *third day* is devoted to action planning for change. It is followed by an opportunity for the employee task force to critique the change plan before it becomes final and shared with the larger organization. That step, indeed the whole process, makes senior management teams accountable to lower-level people in the organization, legitimizing senior management's change plan, developing a partnership between the two, and enhancing trust and commitment. The elapsed time for implementing SFP is approximately six weeks.

The following features in the process enable an honest conversation that leads to rapid change:

- The senior team, as a whole, has to commit to the process before it begins, ensuring commitment and follow-through.
- They as a team have to develop a compelling direction, framing the inquiry and at the same time developing their commitment to the direction.
- The senior team is directed to select a task force consisting of their best people (usually eight to ten), one to two levels down, whose feedback they will believe.
- The general manager or CEO personally invests the task force with the direction and asks them to bring back the truth.
- The task force, not the senior team, selects a sample of one hundred employees representing key activities in the value chain and is trained in conducting an open-ended confidential interview.
- Task force members interview outside their own organizational units to ensure openness and learning for them.
- Consultants interview the senior team during this same period to obtain their respective viewpoints.

- When the interviews have been completed (usually a three-week period), the task force is guided through a rigorous analysis that identifies key barriers and strengths to be fed back to senior management.
- A three-day "fitness" meeting is the forum for data feedback, diagnosis, and planning of change. The following features of this meeting are key to the success of the process:
  - Consultants present ground rules for non-defensive dialogue.
  - A "fishbowl" method for feedback—the task force sits in a circle discussing their feedback, theme by theme, uninterrupted while senior team members sit in an outer "U" listening—enables task force members to deliver the "unvarnished" truth without fearing that what they say will affect their careers. It also makes it harder for the senior team to be defensive and thus enables them to learn.
  - The "fishbowl" enables the task force to paint a rich and emotionally compelling picture of how the organization is functioning. Once they have received the feedback, senior teams understand that if they do not act they undermine their credibility and legitimacy as leaders.
  - Because the task force leaves after their feedback, the senior team can discuss sensitive problems—for example, their own effectiveness—honestly among themselves.
  - Facilitators frame problems and provide analytic frameworks as needed to enable senior teams to conduct a systemic diagnosis of the organization and craft new organizational architecture and management process. Neither they nor the task force recommend specific solutions.
- The senior team is required to share their change plan with the task force. The task force meets alone to critique the plan. Because they deliver their critique of the plan as a group, they are able to confront the senior team with deficiencies in the plan with minimum fear of retribution.
- Change is launched when the senior team reports what they heard, along with their diagnosis and action plan, in a meeting that includes the one hundred people interviewed, the task force, and other key members of the organization. This step mobilizes the organization to action.

The power of the SFP to create conditions for effective coordination and teamwork comes from the systemic nature of the process. It brings all hard and soft facets of the problem together for a simultaneous solution. It emotionally connects senior teams to unpleasant truths. It makes them accountable to the people in the organization—particularly those on teams—to take action. Consider the following quote from a member of SRSD's senior team after feedback from the task force had been delivered:

> I was taking a lot of notes, but all I could think of the whole time was how did it get this bad? The discussion between the top team and how we worked together was even more painful. The whole thing was easily the worst day of my HP career. In my room that night I was considering writing a resignation letter, until I realized that Scott [the general manager] probably wouldn't accept it. It hit me that we were in it up to our necks and now there was no turning back. (Beer & Rogers, 1997)

Our research has shown that in 80 percent of the cases studied SFP turned the six silent killers into strengths, thus creating the conditions for greater organizational and team effectiveness (Beer, 2011). Consider the outcome at SRSD, the most transformed of the twelve units in the study:

- Clarified the strategy and priorities;
- Redesigned the SRSD from a functional to a matrix organization, thus redefining the role of business teams and the authority of business heads, making team members responsible to the business team leader as well as their functional bosses;
- Recognizing that engineering managers did not have the experience or general management perspective required to lead business teams, the senior team assigned four of its members that responsibility in addition to their functional role;
- Began a successful process of senior team development that:
  - Increased interpersonal trust;
  - Redefined how decisions were to be made and conflict managed;

- Redefined the senior team's role in conducting a quarterly strategic review of business teams and reallocation of resources as priorities changed.

The structural and procedural changes described above were implemented in approximately three months, much faster than the months of piecemeal change typically associated with these types of changes, although the supporting organizational behavior and attitudes were developed in action over time. Revenues and profits improved dramatically in five years that followed SFP, and five years later the head of the Test and Measurement Sector praised SRSD's accomplishments, seeing them among the top business units in the sector.

Comparing the most- and least-successful applications of SFP enabled us to identify several interdependent conditions associated with successful applications of SFP. They were (1) a perceived gap between performance aspiration and actual performance, often brought about by frame-breaking changes in the environment, (2) the general manager or CEO possessed non-hierarchical values aligned with honest, collective, and public conversations, and (3) the head of the organization was open to learning. The latter was often associated with a new general manager or CEO, new to the job of general management and/or just recently appointed to lead the organization. Because they had recently taken charge of the organization, silent barriers surfaced by the task force were attributed to the former leader and therefore did not threaten the leader, although there are a number of instances in which leaders who had been in place for some time, SRSD's general manager included, successfully employed SFP. The personality, characteristics, and leadership style of the general manager or CEO played no role.

SFP is not a magic bullet, nor is it a universal solution to ineffective organizations and underperforming teams because not all leaders are ready to undertake such a counter-conventional process. Nevertheless, our action research shows how the syndrome of silent killers undermines organizational and cross-boundary team performance, and it demonstrates that honest, collective, and public conversations about these barriers can improve both senior-team and lower-level team performance rapidly and with commitment for all parties. Given the rapid pace of change, open organization-wide conversations promise to enable organizations and their leaders to adapt faster to changing circumstances. A wider acceptance of non-hierarchical values among leaders will, however, be required to enable wider use of honest, collective conversations as a means for improving team performance.

References

Argyris, C. (1985). *Strategic change and defensive routines.* Boston: Pitman.

Argyris, C. (1990). *Overcoming organizational defenses.* Needham, MA: Allyn & Bacon.

Beer, M. (2009). *High commitment, high performance: How to build a resilient organization for sustained advantage.* San Francisco: Jossey-Bass.

Beer, M. (2011). Developing an effective organization: Intervention method, empirical evidence and theory. In A.B. Shani, R.W. Woodman, & W.A. Pasmore (Eds.), *Research in organizational change and development, Vol. 19.* Bingley, UK, Emerald Group Publishing.

Beer, M., & Eisenstat, R. (2000). The silent killers of strategy implementation and learning. *Sloan Management Review, 4*(4), 29–40.

Beer, M., & Eisenstat, R. (2004). How to have an honest conversation about your strategy. *Harvard Business Review, 82*(2), 82–89.

Beer, M, Eisenstat, R., & Spector, B. (1990, December). Why change programs do not produce change. *Harvard Business Review,* pp. 158–166.

Beer, M., & Rogers, G.C. (1997). Hewlett-Packard's Santa Rosa Systems Division: The trials and tribulations of a legacy, Case No. 9-498-011. Boston: Harvard Business School Press.

Beer, M., & Walton, E. (1990, February). Developing the competitive organization: Interventions and strategies. *American Psychologist, 45*(2).

Detert, J.R., & Edmondson, A.C. (2011). Implicit voice theories: Taken for granted rules of self-censorship at work. *Academy of Management Journal, 54*(3), 461–488.

Hackman, J. R. (2002). *Leading teams.* Boston: Harvard Business School Press.

Lawrence, P.R., & Lorsch, J.W. (1967a). *Organization and environment: Managing differentiation and integration.* Boston: Harvard Business School Press.

Lawrence, P.R., & Lorsch, J.W. (1967b, November/December). New management job: The role of the integrator. *Harvard Business Review,* pp. 142–151.

Morrison, E.W., & Milliken, F.J. (2000). Organizational silence: A barrier to change and development in a pluralistic world. *Academy of Management Review, 25*(4), 706–725.

Wegeman, R. (1995). Interdependence and group effectiveness. *Administrative Science Quarterly, 40,* 145–180.

CHAPTER TWO

How Organizational Process Maturity Improved Software Team Performance

Bill Curtis

CAST Software

Overview

The short history of software development is a litany of missed schedules, overrun budgets, defective products, and failed projects frequently described as the "software crisis." The past four decades have seen a progression of methods designed to improve team performance in software development. Software is a knowledge-intense industry in which external factors can have greater control over team performance and behavior than variables internal to the team. The most effective method has been the Process Maturity Framework, a unique approach to organization development that successfully transformed both team and organizational performance across large segments of the software development industry. The primary objective of this chapter is to explain how managing factors external to the team, such as the maturity of an organization's engineering processes, enabled dramatic improvements in software team performance. Along the way I will provide "Points for Practitioners" to guide those managing and improving the performance of teams working on knowledge-intense tasks like software development.

The Impact of Individual Differences

Software teams are often unjustly derided as loose federations of undisciplined mavericks who hide behind a myth of artistic mastery. Many software developers still discuss their work as artistry or craft rather than as an engineering discipline. However, the plague of defects in most software products argues that artistic mastery does not equate to engineering soundness. Software engineering, a term coined in 1968, is a young discipline. The analytic equations that dominate more established fields of engineering are rare in software development. Consequently, individual capability plays an extraordinarily large role in the performance of software teams. Unfortunately, excessive focus on individual capability has obscured a deeper understanding of the situational conditions that have undermined the capability and performance of software teams for decades.

Curtis (1981) confirmed that the range of performance differences among competent software development professionals in tasks such as finding defects could be over 20 to 1, and even among top performers, differences of greater than 3 to 1 are common. Using repeated measures designs, Curtis, Sheppard, Kruesi-Bailey, and Boehm-Davis (1989) demonstrated that up to half the variation in software development tasks such as understanding, coding, and debugging software was accounted for by individual differences among developers. In behavioral research on software development through the early 1980s, the individual differences variation in experiments kept overwhelming the hypothesized main effects for software engineering techniques such as programming methods, tools, and specification formats. Consequently, in the mid-1980s I switched my research methods from controlled experiments to techniques more characteristic of cognitive science such as thinking-aloud protocols, in order to better understand the sources of such large variations in individual and team software development performance.

These large individual differences were measured in controlled environments that were unaffected by the impact of situational factors external to a team. In studying the productivity of large projects, Boehm, Abts, Brown, Chulani, Clark,

Horowitz, Madachy, Reifer, and Steece (2000) replicated Boehm's (1981) results from two decades earlier by finding that differences between high-performing teams (roughly 90th percentile) and low-performing teams (roughly 10th percentile) differed by almost 4 to 1 and dramatically outweighed the impact of any other factor affecting software development productivity. For instance, the technical complexity of the project accounted for performance differences of only 2 to 1. Much to the chagrin of the computer science community, Boehm concluded that managing team and individual capabilities offered the greatest opportunity for improving software development productivity.

In a field study of the design process for large, software-intensive systems, Curtis, Krasner, and Iscoe (1988) identified the three most significant challenges facing project teams as being the thin spread of application domain knowledge among team members, breakdowns in communication and coordination, and volatile requirements. The thin spread of application domain knowledge—such as knowledge of banking, telecommunications, avionics, or retail sales—is an important source of individual differences among developers that is separate from knowledge of computing techniques. Wide variation in domain knowledge, combined with the amount of technical knowledge required to design complex systems, creates large individual performance differences that distinguish a small number of exceptional designers from a much larger contingent of merely competent designers who lack sufficient domain knowledge to synthesize successful solutions for large, complex systems.

The other two challenges to team performance often had roots that were external to the team. Breakdowns in communication and coordination frequently represent team process issues that were often caused by managers or customers external to the team. Finally, volatile requirements are external factors that are among the most frequently cited factors causing project overruns and failures. The challenge for teams is to develop processes and techniques for managing coordination problems and changing requirements, since these problems are pervasive in software development.

Points for Practitioners

1. The more knowledge-intense the work, the larger the role individual and team capability will play in productivity. Even simple measures of knowledge, skills, abilities, and other characteristics (KSAOs) from related experience should be highly weighted in estimating project costs and schedules.
2. In commercial environments, external factors can strongly affect performance unless a team has processes for managing them.

Dissecting a Software Design Team

In taking a more macro-cognitive approach (Lyons, Lum, Fiore, Salas, Warner, & Letsky, 2012) to studying teams working on complex problems, Walz and her colleagues (Walz, Elam, Krasner, & Curtis, 1987; Walz, Elam, & Curtis, 1993) coded videotaped interactions from eighteen meetings of a software design team in an industrial research center designing an innovative database technology. Figure 2.1 displays the percentage of interactions that represented agreement among team members at each team meeting. Contrary to expectations, agreement did not monotonically increase across the course of the project. Rather, it increased sufficient to produce scheduled work products. However, unresolved issues were back in play after the interim work product had been released. These results were resonant with findings by Levesque, Wilson, and Wholey (2001) that mental models in software design teams did not necessarily converge over time. Interestingly, the greatest convergence of team agreement occurred near the point in the design process that would be predicted by Gersick's (1988) punctuated model of team equilibrium. The change in this team was the acceptance of one member's proposal for a novel model for object-oriented databases that then became the focus of the team's remaining design activity.

As we started our research on the software design process at MCC in the mid-1980s, we had proposed a model of how coalitions

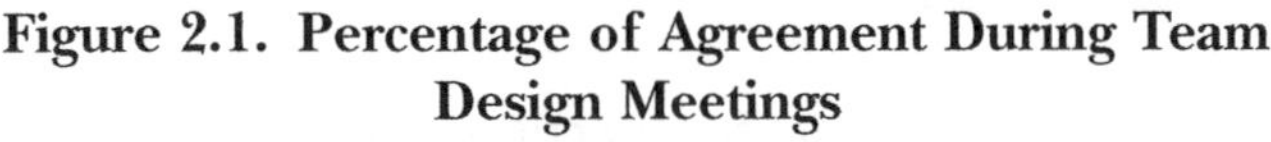

Figure 2.1. Percentage of Agreement During Team Design Meetings

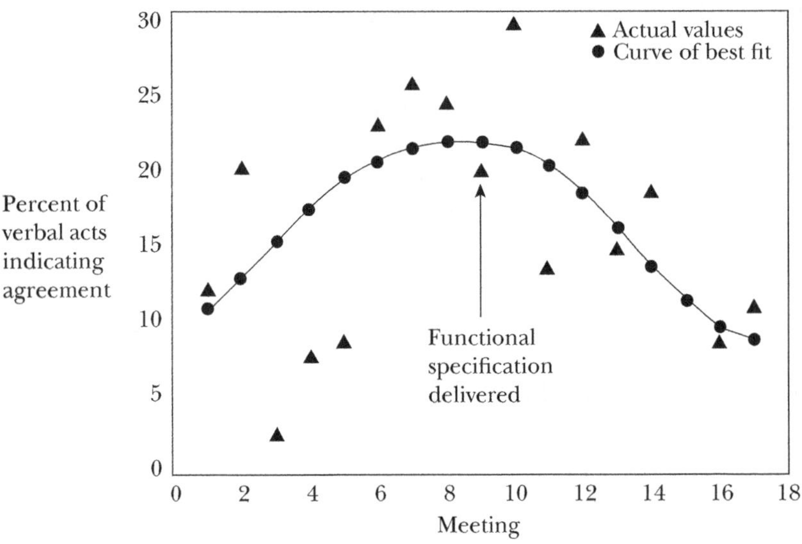

of team members would initially form around different preliminary models of the solution. Then through a dialectic team process they would ultimately reach a unified solution (a team mental model) from the merger of the various preliminary models. This is far from what we observed. Although many design alternatives were proposed by different team members, in complex problem spaces we rarely observed teams producing a unified solution model through the merging of these preliminary alternatives.

Just as Curtis, Krasner, and Iscoe (1988) had identified in their field study of the design of large systems, exceptional designers dominated design teams because few members of the team had sufficient technical and domain knowledge to synthesize a workable solution. Rather, after the team had struggled with design options, exceptional designers would be able to synthesize enough concepts to propose a solution, much of which they may have carried forward from previous experience. The remainder of the team activity was typically spent in debating and refining this proposed design. If the design solution was emergent, much of the emergence occurred in one or, at most, a very limited number of heads.

In essence, it appeared easier to integrate solution knowledge in a single head than to integrate it across heads. Thus the solution process in complex designs often required initial debate to produce enough information for a superior designer to synthesize a workable initial solution, which then became the team's de facto working solution (Figure 2.2). This solution was then refined through the team's dialectic process, even if individual mental models of the solution never fully converged. We did not propose that this method of developing a team's solution was common to all teams, but rather that we had observed it in an extremely knowledge-intense team task at a time when the software engineering community believed that a more egalitarian process was typical and even desirable. Thus, reaching enough of a team solution to make progress did not necessarily require the converging of individual mental models, but rather the acceptance of one as the team's working model, even if team members' individual cognitive representations of it were flawed or incomplete.

Points for Practitioners

1. Participative, egalitarian models of team solution-making are very popular, but not necessarily descriptive of solution development in knowledge-intense work where knowledge of at least one of the critical domains is thinly spread across the team.
2. Accept that a few knowledgeable members may dominate the team process, especially if the team begins converging on their solution.
3. Do not require that team members achieve complete agreement with the proposed solution, since this is unlikely, but rather they achieve enough consensus so that progress can be made.

Measuring Software Team Performance

A significant challenge in studying software development teams has been the definition of performance measures. The most common measures of performance have been productivity, quality, and much less often, team attitudes. Productivity and quality

Figure 2.2. A Model of Factors Affecting Software Team Performance

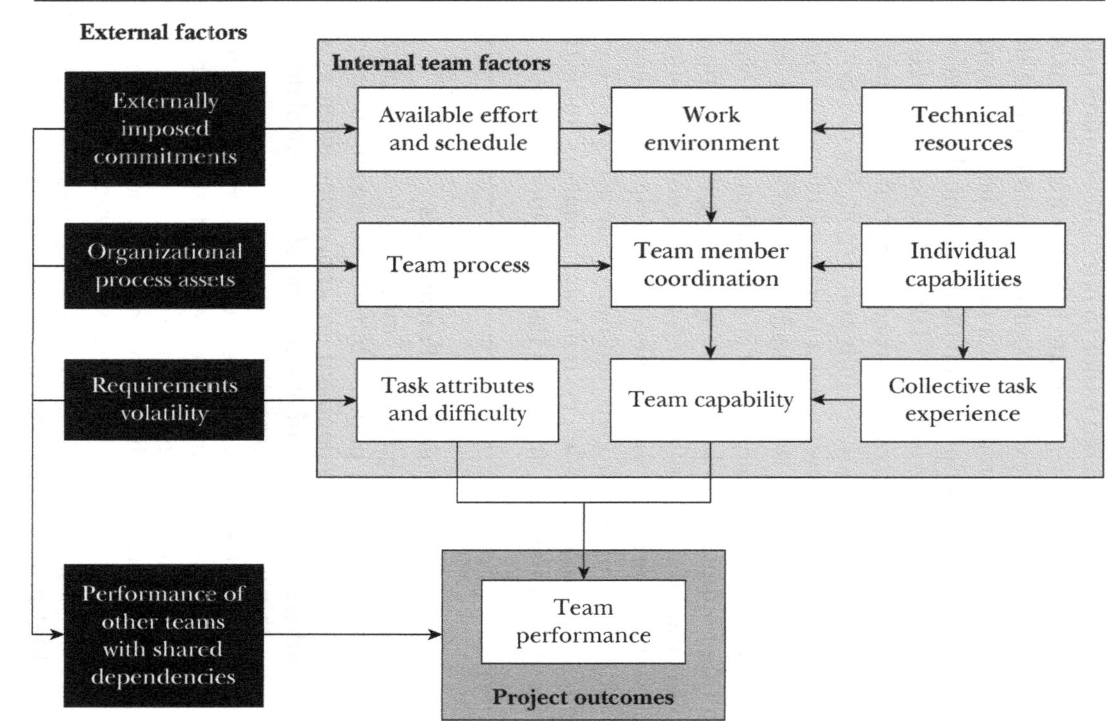

measures are controversial and no widely accepted standard for their definition has been established.

For instance, productivity is frequently measured by the number of lines of code (or computer instructions) that are produced in a period of time. However, the number of lines of code in a computer program can vary by a factor of 10, depending on the definition used for what constitutes a single line (Jones, 1997). Other measures such as the number of functional elements in a program also suffer from ambiguities in their definition that lead to significant variance in their counting. Worse still, there are many ways that lines of code per unit of time can be gamed, and most developers are skilled in manipulating them.

Quality has also been difficult to quantify because of inconsistencies in measuring defects. If the test cases written to assess the defects in a system are prepared by someone with a weak understanding of the system, its requirements, or its operational environment, then the test cases will be insufficient to detect all the defects in a program. Consequently, defining dependent variables in research on teams that produce knowledge artifacts such as software presents a challenging, but not insurmountable hurdle.

Fortunately, recent developments in measurement technology have made it easier to capture measures of size and quality automatically (Sappidi, Curtis, & Szynkarski, 2011). The measurement tools enforce consistent counting with the measurement specifications programmed into the system, reducing the subjectivity that had been a consistent problem with manually counted measures. The quality of performance measures has been getting better, but the adoption of measurement tools into software development organizations can move no faster than the maturity of the organization.

Point for Practitioners

1. Measuring knowledge-intense artifacts such as software is in its infancy. Consequently, measures of team productivity and quality must be interpreted with care, as they are susceptible to strong contextual influences within software systems as well as manipulation by developers.

Early Team Methods to Improve Productivity and Quality

Since the 1970s, the organization and structure of software teams has been manipulated to improve productivity and quality. In early software development projects, teams were often constructed by collecting a group of engineers who had learned a computer language and placing them under the responsibility of a team lead, who usually had no training in management or team leadership. Since the heritage of software development grew from individuals writing their own programs, and since large programs could be divided into collections of small programs called modules, early teams frequently resembled loose collections of individuals working in close proximity on independent tasks. However, by the mid-1970s it became clear that these loosely federated teams were producing inconsistent results and defective systems.

In the early days of software engineering, Harlan Mills (1971) designed the "chief programmer team" to organize the roles required to support the work of talented developers. Mills, himself an extraordinary developer, recognized the broad range of skill differences among developers and designed a team structure to accommodate it. Thus, most of the software was expected to be produced by the chief programmer and several talented assistants. Other team roles were defined to perform support functions such as testing or documenting the emerging software. The failure of chief programmer teams to gain widespread adoption resulted from the simple fact that there were not enough exceptionally talented developers to fill all the chief programmer roles needed on large projects. In fact, in studying the design and development of large systems, Curtis, Krasner, and Iscoe (1988) rarely found evidence of more than one exceptional software designer for every three projects, and their sample typically consisted of the more successful projects in the companies they studied.

In contrast to chief programmer teams, Gerald Weinberg (1979), a software developer who earned a Ph.D. in psychology, pioneered a participative team structure called "egoless teams." Egoless teams were designed around the principle that, although developer skills differed widely, different developers could take a leadership role for the tasks in which they were well-skilled. In this more participative approach, team leadership could shift among individuals at different stages of a project on which the evolving tasks highlighted the need for different skills. Although not widely adopted, Weinberg's egoless teams set a precedent for the development of "agile methods" (Larman, 2004), a more recent collection of techniques for organizing software teams.

Most computer scientists believed that the best way to improve software productivity and quality was to improve the languages and tools used by software developers. During the 1970s their focus was on better languages and rules for writing readable and correct programs. Although the benefits of "structured programming" were demonstrated in classical human factors-style experiments (Sheppard, Curtis, Milliman, & Love, 1979), the size of computer programs was growing exponentially by the end of the 1970s, and better languages and coding techniques were no longer adequate to ensure productivity and quality in large systems. Consequently, in the 1980s the computer science community turned its focus to better methods and tools for designing large complex systems. "Computer aided software engineering" (CASE) tools were sold with promises of order-of-magnitude improvements in productivity and quality. Unfortunately, by the middle of the 1980s the emerging productivity data showed only 10 percent gains when development teams were augmented with these tools. This gain was embarrassing, since Boehm (1987) reported that year-on-year gains from experience without new tools appeared to average 7 percent.

There were two responses to this dilemma in the computer science community. The first, and it included the largest segment, was the development of even more advanced computer languages and tools. A much smaller group that emerged from the user interface research community focused on developing technology for "computer supported cooperative work" (CSCW), or "groupware" for short. This community saw the importance of coordinating interactions among team members, especially as systems were growing more complex. Experimental tests of groupware tools demonstrated mixed results (Jarvenpaa, Rao, & Huber, 1988) because these tools did not address the critical factors affecting software team performance such as previous knowledge of the application domain. However, there loomed a much larger external threat to software team performance that had to be addressed first.

The Process Maturity Framework

By the mid-1980s it became clear that better computer languages, design methods, and software development tools were producing only slight productivity and quality gains in practice. Clearly, the problem lay outside of the factors that were affected by the tools of the trade. By the late 1980s, Watts Humphrey (1988) began arguing that the problem was not with languages and tools, and that most development teams were capable of doing quality work. Rather, he believed that the fundamental problem lay with the absence of management and process discipline. In essence, software organizations were abrogating their responsibility to establish effective management control over development, subjecting software development teams to death-march projects (Yourdon, 1997) caused when management made unachievable commitments. Development teams too often met the challenge by sacrificing successful development practices in the rush to meet irrational schedules.

Humphrey's approach was radical because it focused on the process rather than the technology. Humphrey had visited Phil Crosby's Quality College and learned about his Quality Maturity Grid (Crosby, 1979). Crosby believed that best practices had to be adopted in stages. These stages extended from initial exploration to full adoption and ultimately to professional mastery. He argued that the maturity of any business practice could be rated on this scale. Thus, an organization could adopt a collection of best practices and periodically assess how mature each practice was in its adoption cycle.

Humphrey embraced the maturity concept, but realized that adopting and maturing practices individually was ineffective. In fact, software development teams had been adopting new practices and technologies for two decades with little improvement to show for the effort. Humphrey believed that the biggest problem facing most software teams was unachievable commitments and, if not brought under management control, they could undermine the benefits of any practice.

Humphrey argued that, before adopting new languages, programming practices, or tools, an organization first needed to stabilize the environment in which software teams worked. Stabilizing the team environment required that commitments be balanced with resources so that software teams were not thrown into firefighting chaos by demanding they achieve more than was possible within their allotted schedules. The only way to avoid the death-march projects (Yourdon, 1997) that were continually thrust on software teams was to enforce a discipline of team and project planning on which rational schedules and commitments could be based. Planning was coupled with a discipline of tracking the actual rate of progress in order to take corrective action when estimates were wrong and to provide the data needed to make future schedules and commitments more realistic. Thus, the improvement journey began with management protecting software teams from unrealistic and destabilizing commitments.

Humphrey wanted to apply the practices of statistical quality management and continual improvement (Deming, 1982) to software teams, but he realized this could never work unless they worked in a disciplined, stable environment. He transformed Crosby's model into the "process maturity framework" (Humphrey, 1989). In the context of Humphrey's model, maturity does not represent a natural evolutionary process that organizations or teams undergo across time as described in the team maturation process developed by Morgan, Salas, and Glickman (1993). To the contrary, the process maturity framework treats maturity as the result of a guided change process whereby each evolutionary stage places requirements on how organizations and teams conduct their work.

Most of the software development world considered the process maturity framework to be a model of software best practices with a precedence order for their implementation. However, as will be revealed over the next several sections, this framework was an innovative model of organization development that transformed the capability of many software development organizations and the performance of their teams. Humphrey had only passing familiarity with the organization development literature, and he was not trying to advance theory and practice in this area. He arrived at the process maturity framework by proposing an order in which impediments had to be removed to enable an organization to adopt and continually improve an integrated system of effective software development practices.

Humphrey believed that software development organizations already had competent programming staffs and that their capability could be improved through better selection and training methods. However, he did not believe rising competency would be sufficient to solve the software crisis. The crisis was one of management and team discipline, which had to be addressed first. Thus, in the late 1980s after an executive career at IBM, Humphrey joined the Software Engineering Institute (SEI) at Carnegie Mellon University and launched the software process movement that transformed a large segment of the software development industry.

Points for Practitioners

1. In an industry dependent on teams to produce knowledge-intense products, the largest threat to team performance may be the lack of management control over commitments.
2. Improving individual and team competency may not be sufficient to overcome problems when root causes are external to the team.

The Capability Maturity Model

Originally the process maturity framework consisted of a discussion of software development practices by maturity level in Humphrey's (1989) book, a loosely defined assessment method, and a self-assessment questionnaire about development practices (Humphrey, 1988). In 1991 Humphrey asked me to succeed him as director of the Software Process Program at the SEI when he stepped toward retirement. The U.S. Department of Defense was beginning to use Humphrey's assessment method to qualify and rate bidders on large software-intensive system contracts. I realized quickly that we had to have a well-defined model with clearly delineated practices at each maturity level if the assessments were to be credible when used as one of the evaluation criteria on multi-million-dollar contracts. I organized a team at the SEI to produce a version of the process maturity framework for software development with clearly defined practices and criteria for advancing through the maturity levels. In August 1991 we released the first version of the "capability maturity model for software" or CMM (Paulk, Weber, Curtis, & Chrissis, 1995), which was adopted as a de facto global for software development organizations by the mid-1990s.

Over the past two decades many different CMMs have been developed to apply the process maturity framework to other types of business processes. Consequently, improvement programs guided by CMMs in business environments such as banking, medical services, and hardware manufacturing have demonstrated that the improvement guidelines in the process maturity framework are relevant to many work environments (Weber & Curtis, 2004).

A CMM is a prescriptive roadmap for guiding the evolutionary transformation of an organization through five stages of continual process improvement. Each of these five evolutionary stages, called "maturity levels," is a well-defined organizational plateau in the continual improvement of an organization's business processes. The ordering of the maturity levels is based on a precedence order for eliminating the primary barriers to sustainable improvement. At each maturity level an organization implements sets of integrated practices, called "process areas," that build new capabilities for improving performance on top of the foundations established at previous maturity levels.

Table 2.1 presents the staging of the maturity levels with a brief description of the behavioral characteristics of an organization at each level and the types of problems they must solve in getting to the next level. The names of the maturity levels differ from those of the original CMM to make them more descriptive, since titles for the levels have differed across subsequent maturity models. We will provide more elaborate descriptions of the guidance and practices at each maturity level over the next five sections, followed by a section with the empirical evidence from case studies that validated the CMM's effectiveness in successful improvement programs.

Table 2.1. Maturity Levels of the Process Maturity Framework

Maturity Level	*Behavioral Characteristics*	*Problems to Solve*
Level 5 Innovating	The organization takes responsibility for making proactive improvements that close gaps between existing performance and business objectives. Teams expect to adopt frequent innovations.	Innovations must be standardized and optimized across teams. New problems will most often come from external challenges which the organization can now address through its innovation infrastructure.
Level 4 Optimized	Work processes and outcomes are managed statistically to understand and reduce causes of variation. Measures at each process step are used to predict final outcomes and take corrective action early. Continual incremental improvements to work processes optimize their performance. Plans are based on statistical characterizations of the end-to-end process and its constituent parts.	Optimizations to the existing work processes may not be sufficient to meet competitive challenges, customer expectations, or future mission objectives. Existing work processes can be made obsolete by advances in technology, methods, or training. Teams may stagnate in existing processes and become less competitive or efficient over time.
Level 3 Standardized	Standard end-to-end business processes are defined including each team's work methods and interfaces to other teams. Experiences and measures are shared across teams. Teams plan and manage their work by adapting standard processes to local conditions. Repositories are used to capture and share process assets such as plans, measures, tailoring guidelines, lessons learned, successful solutions, etc.	Measures have not been analyzed to develop statistical characterizations of the performance of standard processes. Consequently, quality and costs are not managed predicatively across teams in the end-to-end business process. Causes of variation in team performance are not well understood. Work processes have not been optimized to the local conditions affecting each team.

Level 2 Stabilized	Managers ensure that commitments are based on planning that balances resources with workloads. Work products are controlled to ensure acceptable quality. Progress is tracked to take corrective action. Lessons are captured to improve future planning. Team performance is reviewed and coaching on how to perform good practices is available.	Different teams use different practices based on their past experience. Measures are defined differently across teams. Teams struggle to learn from other teams since different practices and measures are hard to compare. Little economy of scale or organizational learning.
Level 1 Inconsistent	Commitments are made without planning. Team work processes are undefined and ad hoc. Work is managed through personal relationships. Managers rely on individual motivation and heroic effort to meet unrealistic schedules. Products are released without adequate quality checks.	Poor management of workload and resources. Lack of commitment to disciplined work procedures. Best practices sacrificed to schedule pressure. Constant task-switching and firefighting as priorities shift. Inconsistent quality and rampant rework. Low respect for management.

Level 1—Inconsistent

Level 1 environments are characterized primarily by their inconsistency, and especially by large variations in their results. Some teams and managers have established stable, effective work environments, but this is often the exception. Teams in low maturity environments rely heavily on exceptional individuals (heroes), personal interactions rather than defined procedures, and tacit knowledge. These attributes do not provide a foundation for organizational competitiveness or sustainable improvement. If asked whether their organization adds value to their work, most teams in Level 1 environments would answer, "No!"

Change management and improvement programs in Level 1 environments that focused on extending common practices across the entire organization have had a consistent history of failure in software organizations. Quite simply, project managers and team leaders who were firefighting overcommitted projects had little time to worry about new practices and little experience in sustaining them under stress. Developers on low maturity teams had no time to learn new practices and often sacrificed disciplined practices in the chaotic rush of trying to meet unachievable commitments. In essence, there was little infrastructure of disciplined practices within teams on which organization-wide practices could be overlaid. Until a software team's work environment could be stabilized, it rarely improved its performance or learned from the experience of other teams. Humphrey realized that he had to address team issues before he addressed organizational issues.

Points for Practitioners

1. In immature environments performing knowledge-intense work, reliance on heroes is a symptom rather than a solution. Identify the causes of instability in team performance.
2. Managers who manage primarily through interactions rather than establishing disciplined procedures will have difficulty improving the performance of their teams.

Level 2—Stabilized

The objective in advancing to Level 2 (often called the Managed Level) is to stabilize the work environment so that teams are not forced to sacrifice effective processes and work procedures in order to achieve unreasonable commitments. Thus, the focus is on management—typically project managers or team leaders, although management responsibilities may be shared among team members. To stabilize the team environment, CMMs introduce practices in several process areas to plan and manage commitments, control the versions and quality of team work products, and ensure adherence to stabilizing practices.

Management must uphold the planning and commitment process if teams are to avoid devolving back to the inconsistent adhocracy of Level 1. The focus at Level 2 is on enabling teams to meet their commitments with practices they have been able to perform successfully in the past, rather than forcing teams to adopt common, organization-wide practices. Once teams are able to repeat successful work practices in a stable environment, the organization can evaluate which practices are most effective for wider deployment across teams. Organizations that achieve Level 2 have reported reducing their rework by half, since teams make fewer mistakes and find them earlier when not placed under unrealistic schedule pressures (Dion, 1993).

Points for Practitioners

In order to stabilize the team work environment:

1. The requirements and expectations for a team's work should be documented and changes to them managed in order to establish a basis for planning team activities and commitments.
2. Team work must be planned so that commitments are balanced with resources and schedules, enabling teams to repeat and sustain disciplined practices that have been successful in the past.
3. Work progress must be measured and tracked so that corrective action can be taken when progress falls

Continued

behind expectations, commitments can be renegotiated if assumptions or estimates were wrong, and lessons should be captured.

4. Only the minimally necessary end-to-end team work process should be implemented initially, and a team should draw on its experience for practices it has been able to perform successfully.
5. Mechanisms should be established within each team to control the versions and quality of work products, especially those passed to other teams.
6. Periodic review and coaching should be available to managers, team leaders, and team members to ensure they are able to sustain practices that stabilize their work environment.

Level 3—Standardized

Once teams are successful in meeting their commitments with disciplined, repeatable practices, the organization can compare work across teams to see which practices work best. These practices can then be integrated into standard work processes to achieve an economy of scale when deployed organization-wide. Organizations progressing to Level 3 typically establish a centralized improvement group that can synthesize best practices from team experience and deploy these best practices through training, consulting, and change management programs across the organization. To standardize the work of similar teams across an organizational environment, CMMs introduce practices in several process areas that define standard processes and measures and the means to support their adoption.

Learning can be deployed more rapidly across teams in Level 3 organizations since common work processes make the experience and work assets of each team relevant to other teams. For instance, lessons about how to adapt processes to different situations and challenges can be captured and rapidly deployed through organizational repositories and other communication mechanisms such as social media. Thus, Level 3 establishes a strong foundation for organizational learning and common training that was not present when teams could use different, locally defined work procedures.

At Level 3 the organization's infrastructure begins exercising a strong, positive influence on team performance. Teams can initiate projects using proven process descriptions with defined roles and work procedures that they can tailor to their specific conditions, rather than struggle to invent a team process. Thus, the effort spent in the storming and norming phases of Tuckman's (1995) developmental stages or the storming, norming, performing, and reforming stages of Morgan, Salas, and Glickman's (1993) more recent TEAM model is substantially reduced because the team does not have to invent a work process from scratch. Rather, a team can adapt an existing, well-defined process using tailoring guidelines from the organization's experience. Standard organizational processes and lessons learned regarding them are strong external factors that can enhance team performance in Level 3 organizations.

Points for Practitioners

In order to standardize the work of teams in an organization:

1. The best work practices drawn from teams should be integrated into standard end-to-end work processes with tailoring guidelines for adapting them to use in different situations.
2. Standard measures should be defined at the practice or process level and collected regularly for analysis.
3. Organizational repositories of experience, work artifacts, intermediate performance results, and final outcomes from using standard processes should be established for use by teams in planning, managing, and evaluating their work.
4. An organizational improvement or change management group should be established to plan and manage the definition, deployment, and sustained use of standard processes, measures, repositories, training, and other organizational assets that aid teams.

Level 4—Optimized

The implementation of common process-level and task measures at Level 3 provides a foundation for managing work processes quantitatively. Although the original CMM and its successors used "optimized" as the title of Level 5, it is more appropriate at Level 4. Level 4 focuses on optimizing existing work processes through a combination of techniques such as statistical process control, root cause analysis, incremental improvement (Kaizen), lean, and related techniques (Siviy, Penn, & Stoddard, 2008). Thus, by collecting and analyzing process performance data across teams, an organization can establish the performance capability of its processes statistically and identify factors that cause variation in their results. This knowledge enables teams to quantitatively manage their performance by understanding, controlling, and minimizing sources of variation in their work. These statistical process management techniques were pioneered by William Shewhart (1931) and provide the foundation for the popular Six Sigma approach to process improvement. To improve the work of teams at Level 4, CMMs introduce practices in process areas that continually optimize their performance.

Level 4 practices enable software teams to accurately predict final outcomes at many points during their development process. This predictability is enabled because statistically stable work processes produce intermediate results that are good predictors of cost, quality, and other outcomes. For instance, the teams developing the Space Shuttle's primary avionics software system used statistical techniques to predict the number of defects they expected to make in developing each new version of their software as well as the rate at which they expected to find these defects through their various inspection and testing methods (Paulk, Weber, Curtis, & Chrissis, 1995). While software cannot be proven to be defect-free, the software produced by these teams did not experience an operational problem due to their programming in over ten years of flight.

Points for Practitioners

In order to optimize the work of teams in an organization:

1. Train teams in the use of statistical process management, root cause analysis, and related techniques for continually optimizing the performance of their work and the precision of their results.
2. Continually analyze measures at the organizational level to understand how standard practices perform under different conditions and to establish performance baselines that are useful to teams.
3. Continually analyze measures at the team level to identify causes of variation in performance or results that can be minimized or eliminated.
4. Develop predictive models of team performance that can be used throughout the team's work to predict team and/or organizational results, and use these predictions to take early corrective actions.

Level 5—Innovating

Although teams continually optimize the performance and results of their current work processes at Level 4, these processes may not be capable of achieving the outcomes demanded by customers or a competitive market. In this case the only solution is to innovate, to make a disruptive change in practices or technologies that produces a dramatic leap in performance. Unfortunately, software teams rarely have the resources or time to experiment with innovations. Consequently, at Level 5 organizational management establishes proactive improvement activities such as advanced automation, process re-engineering, innovative workforce practices, R&D projects, and other actions to close the gaps between the current capability of its standard work processes and the capability needed to achieve challenging business objectives. To improve the work of teams at Level 5, CMMs introduce practices in process areas to produce and deploy innovations.

Achieving a Level 5 capability sets an organization on the path of continual innovation. Continual innovation is necessary because many of an organization's standard processes become obsolete or uncompetitive in as little as two years. Consequently, organizations that believe implementing a standard process is sufficient may eventually find their teams performing below competitive levels. However, continual innovation will not lead to consistent competitive gains unless teams already have the capability for using and optimizing standard practices and processes.

Points for Practitioners

In order to provide teams with innovations to improve their performance:

1. Establish an organization-level capability to focus on identifying and deploying innovations.
2. Experiment with candidate innovations to ensure their effectiveness and learn lessons about how to best deploy them.
3. Deploy innovations selected through Level 5 practices as standardized Level 3 processes that can be optimized using Level 4 techniques to achieve their maximal effectiveness, and use this approach as the continuous Plan-Do-Check-Act improvement cycle recommended by Deming (1982).

Validating the CMM

Most of the quantitative evidence validating the effectiveness of the capability maturity model has been provided through case studies since the level of analysis is the organization. Generally, the data in these studies are aggregated over teams and projects to establish an organizational baseline characterizing typical project performance. Thus, these validation studies reside at what Ployhart (2012) describes as the "meso" level—a level that sits between the micro level of individuals and teams characteristic of most psychologically based research and the macro level of business outcomes pursued by management theorists.

In summarizing results from fourteen case studies, Herbsleb, Zubrow, Goldenson, Hayes, and Paulk (1997) found evidence for consistent gains from Level 1 to Level 3 in software quality, productivity, schedule and budget adherence, customer satisfaction, and staff morale. They reported the median annual productivity gain to be 35 percent, while the median annual reduction in defects adjusted for the size of the product was 39 percent. It typically took an organization approximately eighteen months to improve from one maturity level to the next, as this requires an organization-wide change. These results were corroborated by detailed case studies from Schlumberger (Wohlwend & Rosenbaum, 1994), the U.S. Air Force (Lawlis, Flowe, & Thordahl, 1995), Motorola (Diaz & Sligo, 1997), Telcordia Technologies (Pitterman, 2000), Tata Consultancy Services (Keeni, 2000), Computer Sciences Corporation (McGarry & Decker, 2002), and an IT services firm (Harter, Krishnan, & Slaughter, 2000). Clark (2000) and Galin and Avrahami (2006) have analyzed data from many projects collected from numerous companies to further validate the effectiveness of the CMM.

In conducting a successful CMM-based improvement program at Raytheon, Dion (1993) identified one of the largest sources of beneficial results to be reductions in rework. Based on analyzing time card data where rework activity was separately recorded during the improvement program, Dion found that improved development processes in teams and projects reduced rework from 41 percent of total effort at Level 1, to 21 percent at Level 2, and 11 percent at Level 3. Thus, at least through Level 3 the improvements in productivity, schedule and budget adherence, and delivery time are very much affected by practices that help teams avoid making mistakes, as well as helping teams detect their mistakes earlier in their work process. Reducing rework in addition to other efficiency factors implemented through Level 3 improved productivity by a factor of 2.3 compared to results at Level 1.

Adopting the CMM to Workforce Development

During the early 1990s most organizations applying the CMM thought of it as a model of best practices in software development. However, after realizing the organization development potential of the process maturity framework, I launched the development of a new CMM that replaced the software development practices in the original CMM with workforce development practices such as selection, performance management, communication, competency development, compensation, and team building. Rather than implement isolated personnel management techniques, the people CMM (Curtis, Hefley, & Miller, 2002) integrated them into a system of workforce practices that were implemented in stages. Each maturity level established a new, more sophisticated level of capability for improving the effectiveness and value of an organization's workforce.

Just as with the CMM for software, the initial focus for improvement was at the team and work unit level because organization-wide workforce practices could not be effective if managers and team leaders lacked the ability to manage the performance and skill needs of their teams and work units. In another example of this evolutionary approach, team-based practices progressed from developing basic coordination and communications skills within teams at Level 2, to deploying standard domain-based team processes at Level 3, which when mastered provided the foundation for team empowerment and quantitative performance management at Level 4.

The people CMM was adopted most heavily in organizations that were already familiar with the CMM for software, such as defense contractors, Indian outsourcers, and IT departments in large organizations. Benefits of people CMM–based improvement programs were reported in areas, such as reductions in voluntary attrition, as well as increases in productivity, quality, and staff morale (Curtis, Hefley, & Miller, 2003). Once the general change management and organization development potential of the process maturity framework had been understood and validated, it was extended to numerous other disciplines such as services and business processes (Weber & Curtis, 2004).

Points for Practitioners

1. Workforce development and human capital management practices should be implemented as a system of integrated workforce processes that can be continually improved using guidelines from the process maturity framework.
2. The first step in workforce development is to ensure that managers and team leaders can perform the tasks required to manage the skill needs and performance of their teams and work units.
3. In a mature organization a system of integrated workforce development processes should be focused on growing and sustaining the critical competencies (knowledge, skills, abilities, and other characteristics; KSAOs) required to drive the business strategy.
4. Continual improvement techniques such as plan-do-check-act cycles, statistical process management, and root cause analysis can be applied effectively to workforce development activities.

The Team Software Process

After developing the process maturity framework, Humphrey (1995) turned his attention to developing a disciplined method that software developers could use in improving the maturity of their own personal development processes. In essence he was giving individuals the disciplines they would need to work in high maturity (CMM Levels 4 and 5) development organizations. His philosophy was that developers had to study their own personal habits in developing software and measure their effectiveness in terms of work efficiency, pace, and mistakes.

Individual developers differ both in their style of performing common software development tasks and in the results they achieve. Humphrey's personal software process (1997) taught developers to identify and measure each of the steps in their personal processes of designing, coding, inspecting, and testing the software components they were assigned to build. Humphrey adapted the techniques of continual process improvement for use with knowledge-intense tasks, and he frequently likened it to how world-class athletes studied their performance to shorten their times. As developers established a quantitative understanding of their own development behaviors and capabilities, they were able to accurately estimate the time it would take to build a software component. In addition, as they performed root cause analyses of their mistakes, they dramatically reduced the number of defects in their work products (Seshagiri, 2012).

Humphrey (1999) next aggregated the personal processes of individual software team members into a team software process. Once developers had mastered the basics of their own personal work styles, they were better prepared to undertake a team process that integrated disciplined software engineering practices with team planning, coordination, and management. Although the team software process was designed before the "big five" were published, it appears to incorporate practices covering each of the big five team processes (Salas, Sims, & Burke, 2005).

Team members were trained first in the personal software process and then introduced to how these practices should be integrated into the team software process. Software projects were initiated in team launch workshops where team members jointly planned their projects and made achievable commitments. Team estimates for effort became more accurate because they were built from estimates by individuals who understood their own capability quantitatively. The hallmark of the team software process was the constant availability of data on performance and the quality of work products at the individual and team levels throughout the project cycle. Teams used predictive models of expected progress toward quality targets to manage team performance and address software quality issues early in the development process (Webb, 2010). The quality of software products developed by teams using the team software process has been proven to be better in organizations such as Microsoft IT, Intuit, and NAVAIR (Davis & Mullaney, 2003).

NAVAIR trained their software development teams in the team software process and dramatically improved their results for on-time deliveries, productivity, and the density of defects in delivered products (Carleton, Kellogg, & Schwalb, 2010). NAVAIR extended the method for use on both systems engineering and integrated engineering teams. In large weapons systems development, software development teams are embedded within an integrated systems environment working alongside systems and hardware engineering teams in a multi-team system (Mathieu, Marks, & Zaccaro, 2001). Improvements at the software team level do not automatically translate into improvements for the whole system unless teams in other engineering areas also adopt disciplined processes. In particular, a lack of discipline at the systems engineering level can undermine improved results from hardware and software teams because system engineers are the central team integrating the work of other engineering disciplines.

At NAVAIR the team software process was extended into a method called "team process integration" that was trained to all engineering teams. Teams in other engineering disciplines experienced the same improved results achieved by software teams, suggesting that the team-based practices underlying the team software process were generalizable to other engineering disciplines, at a minimum, and quite likely to teams in other business areas working on complex problems that require expertise in multiple domains. Research on the personal and team software process methods continues at the Software Engineering Institute, and they have been adopted in a national program for training software engineers in Mexico.

Points for Practitioners

1. Knowledge-intense and creative work processes such as those performed by software developers can be measured and continually improved at the individual and team levels.
2. Team estimates and performance can be dramatically improved when team members can characterize their ability to perform work tasks quantitatively and share their data with the team.
3. Launch workshops at the beginning of team projects are effective planning mechanisms to help ensure

Continued

understanding and buy-in to the team's commitments and work procedures.

4. Individuals and teams can improve the quality of their work products by analyzing and eliminating the root causes of their mistakes and product defects.
5. High-maturity organizational capabilities are most easily developed when individuals and teams undergo the same transformation in their own personal or team work processes simultaneously.

Teams in the Context of Software Organizations

For half a century the "software crisis" has demonstrated the overwhelming effect that external conditions can have on the performance and outcomes of competent software teams. Fortunately, the case study data available over the last two decades on improvement programs guided by the CMM demonstrate that well-designed interventions focusing on a combination of organizational and team processes can produce dramatic improvements in performance. Even more powerful has been a combination of CMM-based organization-wide improvements coupled with the disciplined team software process to accelerate growth in the maturity and performance of an organization's business processes.

A critical issue calling for research regards whether improvements in the maturity of team processes can drive organizational process maturity in the absence of an organizational improvement program, or whether improvements in team processes must be orchestrated as part of an organizational improvement program in order to be sustained. Humphrey believed that engineers could force an organization to mature by adopting disciplined processes on their own volition. However, there have been case studies of organizations that were not successful in adopting and sustaining the personal or team software processes, even though they experienced some of the performance benefits (Morisio, 2000). What is no longer in question is that organizational improvement programs driven by a staged model of improvement that focuses on stabilizing software teams first can produce dramatic improvements in performance, outcomes, and morale (Herbsleb, Zubrow, Goldenson, Hayes, & Paulk, 1997).

The process maturity framework is an organizationally based intervention that assumes team stability is a required foundation for organizational improvement. Having stabilized the team environment, an organization can marshal its resources to provide strong improvement assets to teams in the form of standard processes with tailoring guidelines, quantitative performance baselines, predictive performance models, organization-wide workforce development activities, and centralized support for organizing and transferring knowledge among teams. Consequently, in software organizations, and probably in most complex organizations (Salas, Goodwin, & Burke, 2008), team performance cannot be predicted without assessing the maturity of the organization's business processes, since an organization's behavior and infrastructure can substantially degrade or enhance the performance of its teams. Figure 2.2 presents a model of software team performance that summarizes much of the research and practical experience discussed in this chapter.

This model depicts a software team within a multi-team environment. If it does not share dependencies on other teams, then the effect for other teams can be removed. The factors within the internal team milieu are not substantially different from those in other team performance models. However, the critical features of this model are the significant impacts from three external factors:

1. *Externally imposed commitments and constraints*—The most significant factor inflicting crisis on software teams has been the willingness of management to make commitments without adequate planning, with the usual result being unachievable schedules. Until this factor is controlled, it will undermine team performance, and beneficial factors internal to the team will rarely be able to demonstrate their full impact. In an immature organization, the effect of this factor is negative, but in a mature organization its effect is neutral since it is under the control of planning that balances resources with commitments and readjusts when progress differs from plans.

2. *Organizational process assets*—The effectiveness of a team is multiplied when it can reuse project plans and histories, defined processes, performance baselines, predictive models, and lessons learned from the experience of other teams. In low-maturity organizations with few assets, the contribution of this factor is near zero, but in high-maturity organizations the benefits in terms of reduced start-up time, avoidance of problem conditions, and productivity from reusing previous solutions can at least double team productivity (Dion, 1993).
3. *Requirements volatility*—The complexity of the original requirements assigned at project initiation is part of the task attributes that are internal team factors. However, the frequency with which requirements are added or changed by customers without the team being able to adjust effort, scope, or schedule is an external factor that can inject chaos into team performance. In an immature organization the effect of this factor is negative, but in a mature organization its effect is neutralized by actions that adjust schedule, scope, or effort to avoid harmful effects on team performance.

As the process maturity of an organization improves, it exerts a strong positive influence on software team performance by providing assets from past experience that relieves the team from having to develop them through expensive trial and error. Teams can outperform the maturity and capability of their organization's processes if they are lucky enough to have an exceptional designer. Conversely, they can underperform the capability and maturity of the organization's processes if the relevant knowledge and experience of team members are low. Nevertheless, over time and across projects, the maturity of the organization's business and engineering processes has been shown in case studies to be a strong determinant of software team performance by controlling the effect of external factors depicted in Figure 2.2.

In a multi-team environment, dependencies on other teams can constrain or accelerate performance, depending on the discipline and performance of other teams. In a mature organization the performance of all teams is enhanced by the same organizational assets, processes, and disciplines, and therefore the joint performance of dependent teams should be enhanced. However, in an immature organization, these external factors will limit how much any team's performance can beneficially affect the performance of other teams. Consequently, the maturity of an organization's business processes will be a primary determinant of whether a team's contribution will translate into project success or will be lost in the inefficiency of an undisciplined organization.

Points for Practitioners

1. In organizations with low process maturity, team performance will be difficult to improve until external factors that negatively affect it are controlled. Organizational development programs must address these factors to be successful.
2. In multi-team situations, process maturity will be critical in translating team performance into organizational performance through its influence on inter-team coordination.

Conclusion

This chapter reviewed the evolution of software teams from the early years of software engineering through the recent transformation of large segments of the software industry by the process maturity framework. Lessons learned with software teams may be relevant to teams in many areas of knowledge-intense work. One of the most critical lessons to emerge from the historical review of software team performance regards the exceptional impact external factors can have on team performance. Factors such as the control of requirements and commitments and the maturity of an organization's work processes have been addressed successfully in organizational change programs guided by the process maturity framework.

The process maturity framework is an innovative model of organization development that incorporates teams as a central focus of the change process. This framework addresses the long-term improvement of an organization's work processes, including those performed by teams, through a series of prescriptive stages that are not a natural evolutionary path. Rather, these stages constitute a model of planned organization development using the organization's work processes as the primary agent of change. This framework is important to team-based organizations because it systematically eliminates barriers to the continual improvement of team performance. The effectiveness of this approach has been validated in case studies of software development, workforce development, and business process improvement, and it is an excellent guide for those conducting change management programs for knowledge-intense work teams.

References

Boehm, B.W. (1981). *Software engineering economics.* Upper Saddle River, NJ: Prentice Hall.

Boehm, B.W. (1987). Improving software productivity. *IEEE computer, 20*(9), 43–57.

Boehm, B.W., Abts, C., Brown, A.W., Chulani, S., Clark, B.K., Horowitz, E., Madachy, R., Reifer, D., & Steece, B. (2000). *Software cost estimation with COCOMO II.* Upper Saddle River, NJ: Prentice Hall.

Carleton, A., Kellogg, D., & Schwalb, J. (2010). Extending the TSP to systems engineering: Early results from team process integration. *Crosstalk: The Journal of Defense Software Engineering, 22,* 23–27.

Clark, B.K. (2000). Quantifying the effects of process improvement on effort. *IEEE Software, 17*(6), 65–70.

Crosby, P. (1979). *Quality is free: The art of making quality certain.* New York: McGraw-Hill.

Curtis, B. (1981). Substantiating programmer variability. *Proceedings of the IEEE, 69,* 846.

Curtis, B., Hefley, W.E., & Miller, S.A. (2002). *People capability maturity model: Guidelines for improving the workforce.* Reading, MA: Addison-Wesley.

Curtis, B., Hefley, W.E., & Miller, S.A. (2003). Experiences applying the people capability maturity model. *Crosstalk: The Journal of Defense Software Engineering, 16*(4), 9–13.

Curtis, B., Krasner, H., & Iscoe, N. (1988). A field study of the software design process for large systems. *Communications of the ACM, 31,* 1268–1287.

Curtis, B., Sheppard, S.B., Kruesi-Bailey, V., Bailey, J., & Boehm-Davis, D. (1989). Experimental evaluation of software specification formats. *Journal of Systems and Software, 9*(2), 167–207.

Davis, N., & Mullaney, J. (2003). *The team software process (TSP) in practice: A summary of recent results (Technical Report CMU/SEI-2003-TR-014).* Pittsburgh: Software Engineering Institute, Carnegie Mellon University.

Deming, W.E. (1982). *Out of the crisis.* Cambridge, MA: Massachusetts Institute of Technology, Center for Advanced Engineering Study.

Diaz, M., & Sligo, J. (1997). How software process improvement helped Motorola. *IEEE Software, 14*(5), 75–81.

Dion, R. (1993). Process improvement and the corporate balance sheet. *IEEE Software, 10*(4), 28–35.

Galin, D., & Avrahami, M. (2006). Are CMM program investments beneficial: Analyzing past studies? *IEEE Software, 23*(6), 81–86.

Gersick, C.J.G. (1988). Time and transition in work teams: Toward a new model of team development. *Academy of Management Journal, 31,* 9–41.

Harter, D.E., Krishnan, M.S., & Slaughter, S.A. (2000). Effects of process maturity on quality, cycle time, and effort in software product development. *Management Science, 46,* 451–466.

Herbsleb, J., Zubrow, D., Goldenson, D., Hayes, W., & Paulk, M. (1997). Software quality and the capability maturity model. *Communications of the ACM, 40,* 30–40.

Humphrey, W.S. (1988). Characterizing the software process: A maturity framework. *IEEE Software, 15*(2), 73–79.

Humphrey, W.S. (1989). *Managing the software process.* Reading, MA: Addison-Wesley.

Humphrey, W.S. (1995). *A discipline for software engineering.* Reading, MA: Addison-Wesley.

Humphrey, W.S. (1997). *Introduction to the personal software process.* Reading, MA: Addison-Wesley.

Humphrey, W.S. (1999). *Introduction to the team software process.* Reading, MA: Addison-Wesley.

Jarvenpaa, S.L., Rao, V.S., & Huber, G.P. (1988). Computer support for meetings of groups working on unstructured problems: A field experiment. *MIS Quarterly, 12,* 645–666.

Jones, C. (1997). *Applied software measurement.* New York: McGraw-Hill.

Keeni, G. (2000). The evolution of quality processes at Tata Consultancy Services. *IEEE Software, 17*(4), 79–88.

Larman, C. (2004). *Agile and iterative development.* Reading, MA: Addison-Wesley.

Lawlis, P.K., Flowe, R.M., & Thordahl, J.B. (1995). A correlational study of the CMM and software development performance. *Crosstalk: The Journal of Defense Software Engineering, 8,* 21–25.

Levesque, L.L., Wilson, J.M., & Wholey, D.R. (2001). Cognitive divergence and shared mental models in software development project teams. *Journal of Organizational Behavior, 22,* 135–144.

Lyons, R., Lum, H., Fiore, S.M., Salas, E., Warner, N., & Letsky, M.P. (2012). Considering the influence of task complexity on macrocognitive team processes. In E. Salas, S.M. Fiore, & M.P. Letsky (Eds.), *Theories of team cognition: Cross-disciplinary perspectives.* New York: Taylor & Francis.

Mathieu, J.E., Marks, M.A., & Zaccaro, S.J. (2001). Multi-team systems. In N. Anderson, D. Ones, H.K. Sinangil, & C. Viswesvaran (Eds.), *International handbook of work and organizational psychology* (pp. 289–313). London: Sage.

McGarry, F., & Decker, B. (2002). Attaining Level 5 in CMM process maturity. *IEEE Software, 17*(6), 87–96.

Mills, H. (1971). *Chief programmer teams, principles, and procedures (IBM FSD Report FSC71–510).* Gaithersburg, MD: IBM Federal Systems Division.

Mohrman, S.A., Cohen, S.G., & Mohrman, A.M. (1995). *Designing team-based organizations.* San Francisco: Jossey-Bass.

Morgan, B.B., Jr., Salas, E., & Glickman, A.S. (1993). An analysis of team evolution and maturation. *Journal of General Psychology, 120,* 277–291.

Morisio, M. (2000). Applying the PSP in industry. *IEEE Software, 17*(6), 90–95.

Paulk, M.C., Weber, C.V., Curtis, B., & Chrissis, M.B. (1995). *The capability maturity model: Guidelines for improving the software process.* Reading, MA: Addison-Wesley.

Pitterman, B. (2000). Telcordia Technologies: The journey to high maturity. *IEEE Software, 17*(4), 89–96.

Ployhart, R.E. (2012). The psychology of competitive advantage: An adjacent possibility. *Industrial and Organizational Psychology: Perspectives in Science and Practice, 5,* 62–81.

Salas, E., Goodwin, G.F., & Burke, C.S. (2008). *Team effectiveness in complex organizations: Cross-disciplinary perspectives and approaches.* New York: Taylor & Francis.

Salas, E., Sims, D.E., & Burke, C.S. (2005). Is there "big five" in teamwork? *Small Group Research, 36,* 555–599.

Sappidi, J., Curtis, B., & Szynkarski, A. (2011). *CRASH: CAST report on application software health 2011/2012.* New York: CAST Software.

Seshagiri, G. (2012). High maturity pays off. *Crosstalk: The Journal of Defense Software Engineering, 24,* 9–14.

Sheppard, S.B., Curtis, B., Milliman, P., & Love, T. (1979). Modern coding practices and programmer performance. *IEEE Computer, 12*(12), 41–49.

Shewhart, W.A. (1931). *Economic control of quality of manufactured product.* New York: Van Nostrand.

Siviy, J.M., Penn, M.L., & Stoddard, R.W. (2008). *CMMI and Six Sigma: Partners in process improvement.* Reading, MA: Addison-Wesley.

Tuckman, B.W. (1965). Developmental sequence in small groups. *Psychological Bulletin, 63,* 384–399.

Walz, D.B., Elam, J.J., & Curtis, B. (1993). Inside a software design team: Knowledge acquisition, sharing, and integration. *Communications of the ACM, 36*(10), 63–77.

Walz, D.B., Elam, J.J., Krasner, H., & Curtis, B. (1987). A methodology for studying software design teams: An investigation of conflict behaviors in the requirements definition phase. In G.M. Olson, S.B. Sheppard, & E. Soloway (Eds.), *Empirical studies of programmers: Second workshop* (pp. 83–99). New York: Academic Press.

Weinberg, G. (1979). *The psychology of computer programming.* New York: Van Nostrand Reinhold.

Webb, D.R. (2010). Updating the TSP quality plan using Monte Carlo simulation. *Crosstalk: The Journal of Defense Software Engineering, 22,* 14–21.

Weber, C.V., & Curtis, B. (2004). *Business process maturity model.* Needham, MA: Object Management Group.

Wohlwend, H., & Rosenbaum, S. (1994). Schlumberger's software improvement program. *IEEE Transactions of Software Engineering, 20,* 833–839.

Yourdon, E. (1997). *Death march: The complete software developer's guide to surviving "mission impossible" projects.* Upper Saddle River, NJ: Prentice Hall.

CHAPTER THREE

Leading a Team to a Major Technological Development

Kazem Rassouli
University of Toronto, Rotman School of Management

Overview

This chapter analyzes the steps taken to lead a team that turned around a troubled organization by bringing about major organizational changes and technological development over a period of ten years. It introduces a framework of integrating the actions and deliverables of the proposed steps to ensure a structured and top-down approach of: *defining the problem; developing the solutions, vision, goals and change plan; instituting governance; managing resources and stakeholders; implementing and measuring success.* In each of these steps, the design, practices, and the interplay between the critical elements of building and leading the team are analyzed with references to published research. The mechanisms and the intensity of the interactions between the external and internal factors affecting the success of this technology development team are discussed and the adopted change strategies are outlined. This chapter finally reviews the joint efforts of management and staff of this organization to define the problem and solutions; develop change strategies, vision, and goals; plan for resources and activities; establish the internal infrastructure and the external agreements with the stakeholders and suppliers; implement the change plan to achieve the goals and vision; measure successes; and adjust the plan during implementation.

Leading a Team to a Major Technological Development

This chapter reviews the circumstances that led to a major technological development by a team of mostly fresh engineers in a region of the world that is less expected to embrace the management tools that have long been proven successful elsewhere. It introduces ten major steps of leading (inspiring and enabling) the team to develop and implement major organizational and behavioral changes for success. They include *review of the background* of the prevailing situation; *definition of the problem* and the underlying causes; *development of a conceptual solution; establishing change policies and strategies; crafting vision, goals, and associated change plan; stakeholder engagement and management; instituting governance; staffing and training; implementation and measurement of success;* and finally, *keeping staff inspired and motivated* to stay the course of instigated changes for success. Table 3.1 summarizes the objectives and the activities of these steps, including key limitations and advice on their applications.

In each of these steps, the design and the interplay between the critical elements of building and leading the team are analyzed. As will be seen, the acquisition of a technological capability was the overall objective of this team. The planned technological facilities were the specific objectives, the development and execution of which was the vehicle for developing the team's capabilities over the life of the associated projects. This created an interesting synergy between acquiring the intended technological capability and the application of its products where the creators were also the end-users of the technological facilities they had developed themselves.

Although the external and internal factors affecting the success of a technology development team are somewhat common to all geographical regions, the mechanisms and the intensity of their interactions depended on the socio-political setting, the techno-economic infrastructure, and the regulatory environment of the location in which this team aspired to grow and succeed. The interactions within and between the external and internal forces were continually changing, thus requiring the implementation of new strategies to position the team for success.

Table 3.1. Objectives (Deliverables) and Actions of the Ten Steps in Leading a Team to a Major Change

Step	*Objectives (Deliverables)*	*Comments and Limitations*
Review the Background	Customer expectation, organization's mandate and strategic goals. Regulatory, socio-economic and political environment (for/against). Infrastructure (staff, facilities, governance) strengths and weaknesses. Business plan, achievements, successes, failures, underlying causes.	Use review of history and interviews with staff and stakeholders. Limitations: time-consuming, diversified, and possible biased views. Use proposed review framework.
Define the Problem(s)	Validity and viability of organization's goals in the current environment. Gaps between business plan and achievements, shortfalls, barriers, causes. Infrastructure weaknesses and environmental constraints, causes.	Use interviews, specialized meetings, and brainstorming workshops. Limitations: like Step 1 plus inadequacy of information.
Develop a Conceptual Solution	New organization's vision, goals, and strategies for viable operations. Business gap closure strategies, plan and assurance of success. Changes to the infrastructure to implement strategies and meet the goals.	Use consultants, specialized meetings, and brainstorming workshops. Limitations: like Step 2 plus prediction of future.

Continued

Table 3.1. Continued

Step	*Objectives (Deliverables)*	*Comments and Limitations*
Develop Change Strategies	Define the change scope, content, timing, stakeholders' impacts. Identify the positive and negative reactions and opportunities for change. Develop change strategies using inputs of Steps 1 through 3 and stakeholders.	Use interview, meetings, and brainstorming workshop with stakeholders. Limitations: like Step 3 plus strong resistance to change.
Craft Vision, Goals, and Change Plan	Develop a mission for existence and a vision for magnificence. Develop overall and specific goals that fulfill mission and realize vision. Specify deliverables, resources, and action plan to achieve the goals.	Use consultants, specialized meetings, and workshop with stakeholders. Limitations: like Step 4 plus stakeholders' commitment.
Involve and Manage Stakeholders	Obtain their inputs, issues, buy-in for the needs and specifics of change. Set expectations, contributions, and relative roles and responsibilities. Agree on the change plan, inputs, deliverables, interfaces, and reporting.	Use interviews and specialized meetings. Limitations: like Step 5 plus maintaining stakeholders' engagement and motivation.
Establish Governance	Develop organization, functions, and programs to meet mandate and goals. Develop procedures, guides, data sheets, templates, and forms.	Use consultants and expert staffs. Limitations: high costs and bureaucracy.

Table 3.1. Continued

Step	*Objectives (Deliverables)*	*Comments and Limitations*
Staff, train, and develop staffs	Job analysis, staffing/training requirements, selection criteria/processes. Interview, hiring, training, assignments, development, coaching plans. Performance monitoring, compensation, reward, productive environment.	Use consultants and expert staffs. Limitations: resistance to new hires, cultural segregation, external influences.
Measure and Monitor Success	Establish performance metrics (adequacy, quality, timeliness) for provision of resources and actions to achieve planned deliverables and goals. Identify inadequate performances and issues to improve plan/infrastructure.	Use consultants and expert staffs. Limitations: reward system for "individual vs. team behaviors."
Keep Staff Motivated	Monitor organizational environment and changes to planning assumptions. Revise change strategies and action plan to address the risks to success.	Use consultants and expert staffs. Limitations: external influences.

This chapter begins with an examination of the background to the Esfahan Nuclear Technology Center (ENTC or Center) in Iran as the start of the infrastructural changes that led to the successful development and implementation of several projects over a period of fifteen years. It then examines the two-year joint efforts of ENTC management and staff (as the first step in building a team for success) to: (a) define the problem and required long-term solutions; (b) develop and agree upon the vision and goals; and finally (c) plan for resources and activities that ensured the attainment of the planned goals and vision. Development of the internal infrastructure (organization, governance, staff, and facilities) and the external agreements with the stakeholders and suppliers are then analyzed. This chapter concludes with a brief review of major successes and the lessons learned during the implementation of the projects over a fifteen-year time span.

Background

The Esfahan Nuclear Technology Centre (ENTC) was established in 1975 to provide technical support to the several nuclear power plants (NPPs) planned to be built in pre-revolution Iran. By the time of the Iranian revolution in 1979, only a conceptual design and some temporary offices were completed for the ENTC on a very large piece of land, 15 km southeast of the city of Esfahan. Of the several planned NPPs, only two were under construction in Bushehr (a southern city of Iran), one at roughly 30 percent and the other around 60 percent progress. Following the Iranian revolution, the foreign contractors of ENTC and BNPP (Technique Atom of France and KWU of Germany) abandoned both projects.

With the dawn of the Iraq-Iran war and shift of national priorities in the early 1980s, the grand pre-revolution nuclear program of Iran shrank drastically. Having no customer, no goal, no funding, and only 250 staff members (about 20 percent technical), the ENTC experienced nearly seven years of indecision, decline, and frequent management changes (five in seven years). The central and local governments were pushing for its closure. Most of its land had been confiscated by the City of Esfahan. Local residents also disliked the Center due to their concern over nuclear safety and its impact on their land value.

Lack of clear goals and well-established strategies by the ENTC sponsor organization (Atomic Energy Organization of Iran [AEOI]) wasn't helping either. Furthermore, the Iranian government could not support the need and priority for an expensive nuclear technology investment in this war-stricken country. The frequent management changes had resulted in a series of failed initiatives. The Center's staff had thus lost faith, and so had little respect for the senior management directions. Employee morale and performance were low. Lines of communication between management and staff had been largely broken, and unofficial organizations and centers of power had emerged. Management of the Center, while admitting lack of purpose, long-term plan, achievements, governance, and staff morale, were nevertheless quick to blame others or circumstances. In short, the entire Center and its sponsor organization (AEOI) appeared to have learned helplessness, as characterized by Latham (2009).

Definition of the Problem and a Conceptual Solution

It's customarily said in Iran that "a *good definition of a problem is half the solution.*" This is because most solutions often lie on the flip side of the problem. The identification and definition of the ENTC problems involved a long and painstaking exercise over a six-month period. This was achieved through: (a) review of relevant ENTC documented history; (b) interviews with several knowledgeable staff; (c) brainstorming sessions and workshops with the ENTC departments; (d) and meetings with government officials and other stakeholders, who had a vested interest in the Center.

This background review focused on ENTC design documents, plans, reports, and correspondence. This was done to identify: (a) the overall and specific objectives of ENTC; (b) its projects and facilities; (c) organization and governance; (d) departments and job functions; (e) resources and funding; (f) staffing and training; (g) progress reports and results achieved; (h) problems and barriers; and (i) operating environment and key players. This review provided a fact-based understanding of the Center's background. It also provided a long list of information gaps, open-ended questions, and the names of several individuals for interviews (employees and stakeholders). The interviews further helped with: (a) substantiating the background information; (b) filling in the information gaps; (c) defining the problems; (d) finding the underlying causes; and (e) identifying potential solutions.

The interviews were very much welcomed by the interviewees and the entire ENTC staff. They acted as a morale booster for the staff, who thought they had been forgotten altogether in the past several years. They wanted to be heard, after years of being ordered around aimlessly; thus, I made sure I was a good listener and a careful note-taker. The interviews also filled my knowledge gap in understanding the past and potential solutions for the future.

The two months of one-on-one interviews and discussions with the staff and the stakeholders revolved around: the reasons why and how the Center was established; who it was planned to serve; what their expectations were; what the objectives of the proposed design were; whether they were still valid under the prevailing socioeconomic and political environment (especially with the absence of foreign contractors); and what the barriers and causes of the failures in achieving the designed objectives were.

It has been shown that encouraging dissent, with a moderate amount of collective self-efficacy, can prevent faulty *groupthink* decisions; that is, employees agreeing with that which they know is wrong so as to be seen as team players (Latham, 2009; Tasa & Whyte, 2005). As much as answers to the above questions were important, equally valuable was encouraging dissent and stimulating the employees' sense of urgency for the gravity of the situation at hand. Their critical thinking and participation in defining the problem in order to propose genuine solutions and required changes were truly needed.

This approach proved to be highly motivating and created a strong sense of commitment among many of the respondents, whose inputs were used to develop the change plan and some of whom acted as champions of change during the implementation phase. Commitment is shown to have a powerful source of motivation in that it leads to perseverance in the course of action even in the face of obstacles. People who are committed to their organization continue to set and commit to high goals (Meyer, Becker, & Vandenberghe, 2004; Meyer & Herscovitch, 2001).

The common theme in the interviewees' complaints, whether internal or external, was that ENTC had no clear mission to exist, no clear goals to pursue, no clear customer to serve, no serious work to do, no governance to comply, no performance to measure, no career to develop, no achievement to celebrate, and no satisfaction to thrive. ENTC had, in fact, morphed into "Esfahan No-Clear Technology Center." Figuratively speaking, ENTC appeared to need changing to "Esfahan New-Clear Technology Center"—by developing and implementing "new-clear mission to exist, new-clear goals to pursue, new-clear customer to serve, new-clear objectives to achieve and so on." Such "transition statements" from negative to positive (Latham, 2009) or from problem to solution were, in fact, at the core of my follow-up discussions with the ENTC departments, which inspired the staffs to develop and implement new vision and strategies on the ruins of the past. The inspired team then transformed ENTC to what has now captured the attention of the world for its indigenous nuclear technology capability.

Within a month, from the background reviews and many pages of interview notes, a framework for communicating the past and developing a pathway to the future was developed. The internal elements of this framework were as follows:

1. Potential vision and goals that portrayed the future state of ENTC;
2. The specific deliverables that would facilitate the achievements of the goals and vision;
3. The required knowledge and resources that the team either had, or otherwise needed to have, in order to transform their actions into the specified deliverables;
4. Tools and facilities required to execute the plan efficiently and effectively; and
5. Opportunities and constraints in acquiring needed knowledge and resources as well as in taking necessary actions to achieve the specified deliverables.

As for the external elements of this framework, the following questions were posed:

1. How could the central sponsor organizations (AEOI and Department of Planning and Budget of Iran) include ENTC's goals in the national energy plan (i.e., how could ENTC exist)?
2. What were the potential oppositions or support from local governments and the Members of Parliament?
3. What were the local/national regulatory jurisdictions that govern the ENTC activities?
4. What were the interests of the international organizations (for example, IAEA) and firms (for example, suppliers) in ENTC goals and objectives?

5. What were the current and future opportunities and constraints that could either support or limit ENTC in pursuit of its goals?

This 10-point framework of Q/A was a very useful tool for compiling the information obtained from the background reviews and interviews. It was also a very effective communication tool with the staff and stakeholders in the post-interview meetings in order to present the background and the future in a structured way. The meetings with each technology development department were organized in a workshop format for a week, in order to introduce the results of the initial assessment, seek their input on the overall direction of the Center, and discuss their role and contribution to build the Center's future. This joint development of the vision, goals, and implementation strategies, as supported by research (Latham, Mitchell, & Dossett, 1978), created a shared sense of ownership for the plan and a shared commitment to implement it.

Development and Communication of Policies and Strategies

Regular communication and engagement of ENTC employees were of vital importance to the successful development and implementation of the change plan. Giving people a voice is seen by employees as a sign of fairness (Greenberg, 1987; Greenberg, 2006) as well as genuineness and commitment of the management for an effective change (Latham, 2009). Communication of the review framework and development of the ENTC vision and strategies were conducted through weeks of presentations and brainstorming sessions with each technology development department. Even though the proposed changes were going to shake the Center to its core, sincere and up-front communication created the awareness, engagement, and sense of urgency for the required changes.

The first order of each departmental meeting was to understand and agree on the change framework. On the one hand, it was used to review and understand the past; on the other hand, to help define the future in a structured way. A summary of key policies and strategies that were developed and agreed on in these brainstorming sessions is as follows:

1. There was a need for relevant and motivating vision and goals that appealed to the entire ENTC; one that inspired employees to take action. Research has shown that goal setting is among the most effective ways to motivate people on the job (Mitchell & Daniels, 2003).
2. The vision and the associated goals should spur the employees to form specialized teams and empower them to achieve their deliverables.
3. Considering ENTC's past failed initiatives, for the vision to be motivating, the staff should first believe it is achievable and important to them. Then they would trust and commit to it materially and emotionally. With the highly educated staff, this was achieved by engaging them in all steps of developing strategies to attain the vision and goals.
4. ENTC's vision and goals were not tied to the fate of the BNPP. However, it was sufficiently inclusive to serve the BNPP, if and when it was completed. This was because viability of ENTC's vision over the long term depended on a powerful customer for nuclear technology.
5. ENTC's vision and goals were aligned with the global trends of technological development, and the policies of the International Atomic Energy Agency (IAEA). This alignment facilitated international contracts and IAEA's technical assistance, while avoiding the usual negative publicities and political nuisances around ENTC activities.
6. The vision and goals maximized the use of domestic resources, while capitalizing on the international expertise to develop indigenous capabilities (staffs and facilities) in nuclear technology. This provided unique professional developmental opportunities for the technical employees and motivated them to acquire expertise in highly complex technological fields. Experiments have revealed that employees who are given specific high goals, attainable within a realistic time, show superior performance (Latham, Mitchell, & Dossett, 1978).

7. A long-term development plan was needed to facilitate gradual acquisition of capability in the design and construction of research reactors and nuclear materials production facilities.
8. Various projects with increasing complexity over time were planned to be executed, enabling the acquisition of challenging expertise while achieving the complex technological goals in the long term. This facilitated the gradual acquisition of expertise in the design and construction of nuclear facilities, while establishing the required engineering and production facilities as the ENTC's technological infrastructure.
9. IAEA technical supports as well as external experts and contractors were required for the transfer of technology in nuclear reactor design and nuclear material production.
10. Technology development departments functioned as developers of conceptual and basic design for the facilities and projects in the long-term plan.
11. A multi-disciplinary engineering team would process the basic design through detail design, procurement, and supervision of construction and installation activities.
12. AEOI and government approval of the program were required to fund and support the change plan over the course of its development and implementation.
13. Staffing and training were the cornerstone to the development and implementation of the plan, since expertise for the implementation of the strategies resided in knowledgeable employees. Research has shown that training followed by motivation proportionately improved staff performance (Maier, 1955, as cited in Latham, 2009).
14. A set of well-defined and transparent administrative and technical governance was required to promote discipline, clarity in requirements, consistency in decisions, efficiency in processes, effectiveness in delivery, and most importantly, effective teamwork. This built confidence, credibility, trust, and integrity between management and staff, which in turn facilitated reliable, consistent, fair, and satisfying operations. Most importantly, it minimized the confusion, mistakes, blame, and rumors that had demoralized everyone in the past.

15. A well-defined monitoring and control infrastructure was required to measure the adequacy, timeliness, and quality performance of the staff and projects, particularly their deliverables against the established goals. A well-known axiom in business and management is that "what gets measured gets done" (Locke & Latham, 1990, as cited in Latham, 2009). Performance is found to increase significantly when managers conduct regular assessment of their staffs' performance (Walker & Smither, 1999). This performance monitoring system was not designed to be a penalizing tool for deficiencies or mistakes, but to reward good performance and identify sub-target performances for improvement opportunities. It's been said that "*The person who does not make mistakes is unlikely to make anything.*" Empowering staff into action, with adequate training and constructive criticism, enables them to achieve high goals and learn from their mistakes (Ford & Heaton, 2000, as cited in Latham, 2009).
16. A performance-based compensation system was required that rewarded the staff and their teams for implementing and achieving ENTC strategies and goals. This, as shown by research (Latham, 2009), created job satisfaction and motivated them to become and remain higher performers. Praise, feedback, participation in decision making, and monetary incentives are shown to increase performance when they lead to the setting of and commitment to a specific, high goal (Latham & Locke, 2006).
17. Respectful and professional interactions with the central and local governments, local community, and other domestic and international stakeholders were required to secure their buy-in and support, while avoiding their potential hostility and political sabotage, which could hinder the achievement of the Center's objectives.

These policies and strategies were used as the basis for the development of the ENTC vision, goals, plans, staffing, training, organization, governance, performance assurance, stakeholder management, and so forth. The departmental discussions, with emphasis on due process, created a strong sense of trust, enthusiasm, ownership, and commitment to the vision and goals among the staff. Because the Center was about to have: a meaningful vision; adequately resourced goals (achievable); a prestigious multidisciplinary team to perform challenging tasks; training and professional development; opportunities for developing unique skills; clear roles and responsibilities; technical and administrative governance systems; performance-based compensation; and a state-of-the-art IT infrastructure, a great job is said to "consist of task variety, feedback, recognition, responsibility, opportunities for acquiring new skills, advancement, and most of all, autonomy" (Hackman & Oldham, 1975; Hackman & Oldham, 1976).

By this time, I had already selected and hired nearly fifty engineers to establish the immediately needed engineering department and project management office. In addition, an experienced engineering firm was hired to help with the development of engineering governance for a multidisciplinary detail design, procurement, and project management department, while training its newly hired engineers.

With the end of the Iraq-Iran war in sight, Iran was showing an appetite for new development programs to advance its five-year plan. Several meetings with the Department of Energy (DOE) at the Ministry of Budget and Planning (MBP) resulted in a preliminary agreement for a program of infrastructure development in nuclear technology. The idea of a nuclear technology infrastructure, which supports future developments in nuclear energy applications, as well as the Bushehr NPPs, was appealing to the AEOI, the governor of Esfahan, and the local Members of Parliament (MPs). What was soon needed by the DOE was a long-term development plan that outlined the details of "what was to be done; to achieve what, by when; at what cost; to what benefits."

Under the direction of a steering committee, several working groups in various technological fields were formed at the ENTC, including both the old and new staffs. The teams were tasked to develop the vision, goals, projects, staffing, facilities, schedule, and budget, taking into account the policies and strategies developed in the departmental meetings. The vision of the ENTC was defined to be "The technological and engineering capability (staff and facilities) in design and construction of nuclear reactors and nuclear material production facilities."

Within a few weeks, a proposal for a ten-year development plan was drafted for the ENTC. This plan contained several hundred pages of detailed plans for nearly forty projects. The program proposal started with the overall objectives of the Center within the context of future technological needs of the country for nuclear research and nuclear power generation. It then outlined the policies and strategies, the mandate and objectives of the Center, the projects and facilities that ensured achievement of those objectives, required activities and resources, project schedules and milestones, budget and annual cash flow, together with staffing and training plans.

The program was a huge success with the AOEI, the DOE, and the parliamentary committee for the national energy program. The follow-up deliberations at the DOE and the Parliament for the final approval of the program (within the first ten-year development plan of post-war Iran) went smoothly. Within a year and a half since its dismal state, the ENTC had a long-term program for nuclear technology development and a well-funded position within Iran's long-term development plan. The battle of ENTC was half won! With the approval of its budget, the ENTC was back on its feet. Within a few years, the ENTC was listed among the top ten priority projects of the country. And within a decade, the ENTC was on the world map for its indigenous nuclear technology capability.

Vision Statement

The interviews and departmental discussions initially focused on the determination of ENTC's mandate. Among the questions asked were: Who would miss us if we ceased to exist? Who would need our expertise as a service provider? What would be their expectations of the ENTC? Having often heard similar questions in the past, the staff's first priority was to create an ENTC mandate with which they could identify and a vision statement that would inspire them.

Considering the policies and strategies developed during the departmental discussions, the mandate of the Center was defined as "to provide design and engineering services for construction of nuclear reactors and nuclear material production facilities."

The overall goal of the ENTC was hence "to acquire required technological and engineering capability (staff and facilities)," and its associated vision was "the capability to fulfill the mandate, i.e., the capability to provide design and engineering services for construction of future nuclear facilities."

Commitment to this vision of high-tech capability required that staff first believe it was achievable and, second, that it was worth their effort to do so. Staff capability could be achieved through initial training and then actual design and engineering of facilities that help enhance their capability in the process. Consequently, several projects in each technological field were planned that increased in complexity over time. This strategy, as noted by Latham (2009), allowed the staff to understand and trust the relationships among the expected capability, their required actions, and the desired outcome.

The stretched challenge of gaining unique expertise in highly complex and prestigious fields served as a great motivator for the technical employees. This was very much needed, following years of disappointments and dismay. Research has shown that challenging and specific goals are effective motivators and lead to higher staff performance (Locke, 2000; Locke & Latham, 2002). Moreover, the facilities installed through execution of these projects established the nuclear infrastructure (facilities and governance) needed to complement the staff's capability in achieving the ENTC's vision; namely: "the capability in design and engineering services for construction of future nuclear facilities."

It has been noted that a vision must appeal to the emotion of people (Latham, 2009). Having seen the nuclear technological advances in the training centers abroad, this vision served as a great source of inspiration that energized the technical staff to put in their best to realize a dream high-tech capability that they had long aspired for. And that was what the ENTC vision had in it for them. This vision also appealed to the central and local governments, who were pursuing indigenous capability in the post-revolution of Iranian industries, which were generally sanctioned by the West. More specifically, the proposed nuclear technology capability could help in pursuing the huge investments in the BNPP and ENTC, which were abandoned by the foreign contractors.

Goals and Change Plan

The ENTC vision was designed to be achieved through specific goals in order to provide the required staff training and establish the nuclear technology infrastructure, so that nuclear technology capability (vision) is realized. Having defined the infrastructure as the ways (know-how, engineering, and administrative governance) and means (facilities) of providing design and engineering services (the capability): (a) several infrastructure facilities were planned to be installed at the ENTC; (b) design and construction of the infrastructure facilities were planned to be performed by the staff as a training exercise; and (c) engineering and administrative governance was developed (again as a training and performance enhancing/assurance tool) to help staff develop and implement the facilities and provide required support services.

A series of consultations with the ENTC staff (who were trained abroad), IAEA experts, and the French preliminary design documents produced a partial list of nuclear support facilities that are common to all nuclear technology centers. Next additions to the list of infrastructure facilities were projects that fulfilled the new mandate of the ENTC (that is, design and construction of research and engineering reactors, together with nuclear material production facilities). And finally, the list was completed with the training and technical support facilities, common services, utilities, and offices found in most industrial establishments.

Professional staff often questioned the technical feasibility of the complex technological challenges in the ten-year plan. Short-term objectives and deliverables were set in order to facilitate short but sure steps and also provide opportunities for adjustment or improvements to the plan, based on the lessons learned. Hence, planning for short-term projects or sub-projects increased employee confidence and commitment to long-term goals, whereas a distant goal seemed too far off to motivate the staff to attain it. It has been shown that staff set with sub-goals perform better than those who only have a long-term goal (Latham & Seijts, 1999). High and challenging goals, set with specific deliverables (in quantity, quality, and time) and attainable within a realistic time, allow evaluation of staff performance;

make necessary adjustments when potential deviations are predicted; and create perseverance until the goals are attained (Latham & Locke, 2006; Latham & Locke, 2007; Locke & Latham, 2002).

Increasing staff capability was planned to be achieved through initial training, followed by participation in the design and construction of the nuclear facilities, under the supervision of the owner of technology or experienced engineering firms. These facilities were planned to increase in complexity, over the ten-year cycle of the ENTC development plan, as ENTC progressed toward establishing its planned nuclear technology infrastructure. In other words, staff's design and engineering capabilities developed with increasing complexity of the applied technologies.

The capability development strategy involved the technology development staff and the engineering departments in all stages of project development, from conceptual and basic design to the detail and procurement engineering. This was followed by the construction, installation, and commissioning of the facilities. A detailed engineering governance system was also developed as an important training tool to help the team with qualified steps of design and documentation of engineering activities. This governance system included standards, procedures, design guides, checklists, look-up tables, data sheets, and templates. This resulted in products that were acceptable to the supervising and verifying contractors (owners of technologies, licensors, and experienced firms). At this level of competency, the staff and governance elements of the nuclear technology infrastructure could be claimed to have been successfully established.

The defined scope, resources, costs, and specifics of the deliverables allowed the projects office to develop performance metrics to measure the progress of activities and projects toward achieving the ENTC goals. Such project performance metrics created focus and accountability toward attaining ENTC goals. They produced a clear definition of what defined accomplishment and drastically improved staff and departmental performance toward desirable targets.

Development of the vision, specific goals, and action plans, with full participation of staff, achieved many of the established principles and planning strategies. It provided a professionally relevant and realizable plan on how achieving the vision of a rare capability would make the staff and the stakeholders proud to identify with. They later acted as champions of change during the implementation phase. The move from a conceptual vision statement to concrete implementation steps (showing the interplay among vision, goals, projects, resources, and plan) created a strong sense of belief and certainty about the future of ENTC, compared to the several years' worth of empty rhetoric. This integrated plan, with defined contribution and interactions among disciplines, united the previously adrift and fragmented staff around a common vision, with a shared commitment to work together and score success as a team.

The performance metrics provided a clear definition of what was important and what defined accomplishment. They were the basis for rewarding good performance and the identification of inadequate performances for improvement opportunities. The gap between the "needs" and "haves" of the ENTC development plan served as the basis for negotiations with domestic and international agencies and firms for staff training and supervision; know-how and technological contracts; engineering and construction services; engineering tools and IT infrastructure; as well as supply and fabrication of equipment.

Stakeholder Involvement and Management

Stakeholders had very central roles is the fall and rise of the ENTC. The key stakeholders at the time of ENTC planning included AEOI, the provincial governor of Esfahan, the MPs of the local ridings, the mayor of Esfahan, the residents of villages surrounding ENTC, the DOE (MBP), and the Parliament that approved the country's annual plan and budget.

Review of the ENTC background soon indicated that the local governments strongly questioned the added value of and the future need for ENTC. The City of Esfahan, with the support of the Esfahan governor, had already confiscated a majority of the ENTC lands and was pushing for its total closure so that its un-utilized lands and assets could be used for the immediate needs of the municipal development plan. Moreover, the central government didn't want to be seen supporting an expensive investment in the cash-strapped, war-torn Iran. Local farmers and their elected MPs were also against continuation of ENTC operation due to their concerns with the unutilized ENTC resources, nuclear safety, and its impact on their land value.

Of all the stakeholders, the director of DOE (MBP) was the least at odds with ENTC. He indicated that he would lobby on behalf of the ENTC (with the minister, the cabinet, and Parliament) if we submitted a justifiable long-term plan that outlined what we wanted to do, when, to what benefit, and at what cost. All the while, for the reasons given above, AEOI was keeping a low profile and so was content with keeping the ENTC's status quo until the opportunity for investment and ENTC development arose.

Several agenda items were prepared to be discussed with the stakeholders, including such questions as: What are your issues and concerns with current and future operations of ENTC? How do you propose to address the impacts of closing ENTC (loss of jobs and associated social issues, loss of opportunity in nuclear technology development and applications)? How do you view the proposed ENTC change plan, which could also benefit your goals (job opportunities, unique nuclear training facilities, unique capability in nuclear material testing and research, unique nuclear technology capability that creates opportunities for the future nuclear applications in the country)? What are the strengths and weaknesses of the ENTC plan, in your view, and how do you wish to contribute to improve it? What regulatory frameworks do you want the activities of ENTC to be governed by? What current or future opportunities and constraints do you see in the activities of ENTC? How could you help?

The meetings with the opposing stakeholders (AEOI was the only supporter, but silent) indicated that, while each had his own specific reasons to oppose ENTC's continued operation, their issues had a few common themes. They were not told what ENTC was doing. They didn't know how ENTC operations could negatively or positively affect them. Their interfaces and respective roles and responsibilities with ENTC were not clear to them. There was no clear understanding, no clear benefit, no clear expectations, no clear relationship, no clear communication, no clear roles and responsibilities with respect to the stakeholders.

While all these concerns justified long-overdue answers, the stakeholders' craving for recognition was most apparent in these meetings. Lack of acknowledgment and respect for their existence, authority, expectations, and their having a say had gradually moved them to the "enemy line." Once again, a straightforward solution to these concerns was to "transition" the stakeholders' complaints into statements of needs and expectations (Latham, 2009).

Better still was engaging the stakeholders in a dialogue to give them a voice, and a chance to influence the ENTC planning and decision-making process (Latham, 2009). In the subsequent meetings, a summary of ENTC's background; the volume of investment in staff training, facilities, and preliminary design; ENTC's draft vision, mandates, goals, projects; and how implementation of ENTC's change plan could benefit or impact them were explained. This engagement was not merely a communication tool to tell the stakeholders what ENTC had already decided. On the contrary, it was a genuine, engaged dialogue to help both sides understand the objectives, the issues and opportunities, the logic and process behind the ENTC plan, how they could contribute to improve it, how it could impact them, and how they could help and gain benefit from it.

The dialogue with the stakeholders was also intended to understand their needs, concerns, jurisdictional authority, interfaces, and respective roles and responsibilities. The concluding solutions and strategies included stakeholders' share of views and needs in the planning process, which facilitated their buy-in to the ENTC change plan.

Stakeholders' discussions also helped with establishing a communication plan of who submits and receives what, when, how, and to what level of detail during the development and implementation of the ENTC change plan. This was critical to keeping the stakeholders engaged during the planning and execution stages, when their continued support and interface were required. This also gave them the assurance that this engagement at the planning stage would continue during the implementation of the change plan.

Finally, engaging the stakeholders was intended to seek opportunities (legally, materially, and morally) for their support for the implementation of the change plan. Surprisingly, these presumed adversaries were quite forthcoming in suggesting ideas to support the plan, or to remove constraints within their jurisdictions, to help the implementation. One interesting observation was the sharp and ironic change in the position of the Esfahan mayor from an adversary to an advocate. The same mayor, who had been busy confiscating ENTC land for municipal use, offered several pieces of land in the prime locations of Esfahan for the housing of ENTC staff. He later organized several meetings to discuss the confiscated land and install fences, at the City's cost, on the agreed boundaries to ensure the security of ENTC facilities.

Governance

Arguably the most challenging part of developing the ENTC change plan was to convince staff of the need for a detailed engineering and administrative governance. They viewed governance as a bureaucratic burden, which could inhibit innovation, creativity, and efficiency. Ironically, they didn't appreciate the fact that confusion and inconsistency, lack of clarity and transparency, frequent changes and ad-hoc decisions, frequent blame and chaos, unfair treatments and favoritism, and lack of controls and accountability (that they had previously complained about) were mostly due to lack of a well-thought-out, comprehensive, and integrated governance system. Once the departmental discussions drilled down to the root causes of their complaints, it became abundantly clear that lack of established requirements, processes, controls, and accountability had in most cases resulted in the very situations they were complaining about. Therefore it was agreed that a detailed engineering and administrative governance system could help staff with the requirements of what they needed to deliver, to whom, with what inputs and activities, from whom and how, following which rules and standards.

Staff later appreciated that a comprehensive, structured, and integrated set of governance would help promote clarity, discipline, efficiency, and productivity. This is because every member of the team worked to the same set of standards, expectations, requirements, and processes; while their respective roles and responsibilities were clear to all. The teamwork efficiency and productivity gains hence resulted from timely exchange of respective deliverables—in specified quantity and quality. Compliance with the governance system also led to consistent and credible behavior, which in turn resulted in an effective team.

The team later realized that ENTC governance was, in fact, a very useful and effective training and guiding tool to facilitate efficient execution of their duties. It was helping them with the processes (the "how") of "what" they had to do and "what" to deliver: effectively; expeditiously; and most importantly, successfully, per qualifying requirements of the governance. For example, the inputs to a design activity were previously formatted in a data sheet for adequacy, quality reviews, and validation (QA), before being processed according to established design guidelines and standards, so that a qualified design product was produced.

Quantity and quality gates (requirements, resources, processes, and deliverables) for all steps of engineering and administrative governance also helped with the development of work management (activity and resource planning) tools and control metrics, so that the adequacy, the quality, and the progress of the planned work were routinely monitored and reported. This system of work-monitoring metrics was also used to measure and reward good performance or to identify opportunities for improvements in the organization, governance, tools, resources, and training.

At the time when ENTC decided to install a networked information system (PC-based network of hardware and software that was emerging in the market to improve the efficiency and effectiveness of business operations and management), the established governance was a great asset to automate and link many of the already established engineering and administrative requirements, processes, resources, and their interfaces. Establishing information systems (IS) based on the governance's standards, procedures, and guides (IS processes and decision logics), supported by checklists, look-up tables, data sheets, templates, and forms (IS input/output screens), also helped in establishing paperless operations and decisions. This engineering management system was integrated with resource and project management systems (human resource, material, tools, budget, costs, standard activities, deliverables, schedule, etc.) to produce various monitoring and control reports on staff/project performance; all based on the foundation of the ENTC governance.

From an organizational and administrative perspective, ENTC governance provided well-defined, transparent, and auditable operations, since all steps of an assignment or transaction followed approved procedures or guidelines. It helped with the orientation and ease of addition of new staff on the team, who could use its defined requirements and steps to execute their duties, with little or no supervision. Similarly, it allowed staff rotations and substitutions when training, promotions, or organizational changes were required. The motto among the ENTC team was that the governance system and practices should operate so seamlessly, reliably, and consistently that no one would become indispensable in ENTC, including its director.

Staffing, Training, and Professional Development

The departmental meeting participants soon agreed that successful achievement of the challenging vision and strategic goals critically relied on the knowledge, training, skills, and expertise of ENTC staff. Staff had already proven their instrumental role in the definition and planning of the ENTC change plan. They would soon play a central role in the development of the know-how, design, engineering, implementation, and utilization of the projects. For this, ENTC needed the know-how in the fields of reactor technology and nuclear material production. Absence of an engineering team was a critical impediment to translating the technological know-how to engineering documents required to procure and install the technological facilities in the field.

An engineering department, supported by a project management office, was therefore established. An experienced engineering firm was contracted to help develop engineering governance and train the newly hired engineers in the required disciplines. Several foreign companies were also contracted to provide the required know-how and oversee the design, engineering, procurement, construction, and commissioning of the nuclear facilities.

Formulating and implementing recruitment, performance appraisal, and compensation plans that were aligned with the defined strategies and goals was the next critical step. This was to ensure that the staff had the competencies and behaviors required to achieve the ENTC goals. This required attracting, retaining, and engaging the diverse talents needed for the execution of the plan; developing their expertise; creating a productive work environment; and continually coaching and monitoring their performance.

Extensive job analysis with documented job descriptions (as part of ENTC governance), together with long-term hiring and training plans, were the first order of business to ensure that ENTC was staffed with the most talented and effective employees possible. Requisite hiring, as the first step of this strategic plan, was easily facilitated by the proximity of the ENTC to the prestigious Esfahan University of Engineering and Technology, as well as the extensive talent pool that existed in Esfahan, as it is the most industrial city in Iran. A comprehensive set of recruiting requirements, selection criteria, procedures, and forms was developed. This was done to ensure that the "right" and "best" possible talents were hired (Latham, 2009). Other administrative governing documents were also developed for training and professional development, performance-based compensation, and team performance management.

Based on the established governance, several hundred staff member were hired during the course of executing the projects. This was the first test of the adequacy and organizational integrity of the ENTC governance for fair screening, tests, interviews, and selection of candidates. Staff training and development were the next critical step in setting up (enabling) the teams for success at the onset of the execution of ENTC's development plan.

Following the initial orientation and familiarization with the ENTC governance, projects, departmental functions, and job descriptions, staff training was further advanced to the level of on-the-job training. Technology development departments, with the help of the engineering department, translated the technological know-how received from technology owners into procurement and construction documents to help national contractors build the projected facility. The owner of the technology oversaw all steps and deliverables of the basic and detail engineering, through construction and commissioning, so that the specified technological development was achieved before signing off on the project closure with the contracted technologist. These activities proved to be highly motivating for the new hires, and for the experienced staff.

While staff hiring and training were critical requirements to start implementation of ENTC's change plan, motivation became the cornerstone to retaining and keeping them inspired to drive their expertise into results. The implementation stage revealed that, while the former was simple but relatively expensive to attain, the latter was very complex and inexpensive to achieve. The former step dealt with defining the job functions, staffing needs, training, and professional development of individual staff members. However, the latter dealt with group dynamics. On a daily basis, the team received a large volume of information on cultural, political, and socioeconomic aspects of their lives from their team members and the society at large. Because the source, the content, and the volume of this "muted group training" were largely unknown, we were dealing with much more complex issues when adding the nature of group dynamics.

Starting with hiring, the majority of the employees welcomed the fresh blood in support of the execution of the plan. However, some staff perceived the new hires as a threat to their job security. To make matters worse, implementation of the staffing plan relied on the training and mentoring of the new hires by the latter group. Moreover, while the addition of the highly talented and enthusiastic graduates helped dilute the remnants of resistance to change, their differences in attitude, culture, and work ethic created some friction.

The next set of challenges to creating effective teams that would deliver as planned was the implementation of a performance-based reward system for "individual versus team behaviors." There were employees who were individually high performers, but poor team players. Organizational and payoff decisions based on such behavioral differences were at times questioned on the grounds of unfair or biased assessment.

Moreover, some staff were either indifferent or opposed to the ENTC change plan due to their own ideological or political reasons. Some were doubtful about the feasibility of the very ambitious plan, and others questioned its priority for a country at war. The engaged process of developing goals and projects from the proposed vision was helpful to a great extent to address the former issue. However, the latter concern remained a socio-political issue for some time, despite them knowing that approval of the ENTC development plan by the government and Parliament was consistent with the country's priorities.

Although such dissents once erupted to a vocal opposition to the validity and the value of the change plan, it gradually faded with the emerging developments. With the end of the war and early successes of the ENTC development plan, those who questioned the priority or the feasibility of the ambitious plan appeared to back off considerably. Regular departmental meetings were held to review progress and issues pertinent to the projects, departments, staff, and the overall performance of the Center. I also allocated one afternoon of each month for one-on-one meetings with the staff, upon their request, in order to discuss their issues and concerns in all aspects of their work and lives. I encouraged my management team to also hold the same meetings with their staffs to hear their views and complaints about ENTC. Staff doesn't have to agree with management decisions and actions, but they do need to understand the basis of their assessment (Folger, Konovsky, & Cropanzano, 1992; Greenberg, 1987) in order to stay motivated and engaged.

Implementation and Measurement of Success

Within a few years, ENTC was a very different organization. The team had an approved long-term plan and several technology development projects were under way. Based on the approved plan, ENTC started implementing its staffing and training plan, establishing its governance and IT infrastructure, engaging IAEA technical cooperation in its activities, contracting national and international firms, and executing its projects with the help and supervision of the external contractors and IAEA. It grew from nearly 250 staff members (with fewer than fifty technical personnel) to nearly one thousand, 50 percent of whom were technologists and engineers.

Extensive pre-engineering governing documents and a QA system, based on IAEA's and international standards and best practices, were established. This included the entire cycle of project design, engineering, procurement, construction, installation, and commissioning activities, comprising policies, organization, roles and responsibilities, standards, procedures, forms, design guides, and specifications.

An integrated network of IT and IS infrastructure was established across ENTC to run various engineering, management, and administrative software, based on the requirements and processes of the established governance. Within three to four years, ENTC grew from a single PC to hundreds of workstations, in a large local area network of mainframes and servers; executing advanced modeling, engineering, management, and administrative application software.

IAEA Technical Corporation (IAEA-TC) was engaged to support the development and execution of a number of ENTC projects. Frequent visits by IAEA-TC and IAEA safeguard staff, including top IAEA officials such as the director-general (DG) and deputy DGs of TC and safeguard, were arranged. These provided the needed technical and training supports as well as the international transparency required to fend off potential negative publicity about ENTC activities. ENTC was praised in the DG report to the IAEA Board of Governors for its well-established and orchestrated program of nuclear technology development in support of nuclear power generation in Iran.

Several international contracts for training, technology transfer, and supervision of engineering, procurement, and construction of the projects were secured. The requirements and the processes of acquiring expertise through joint design and engineering together with construction and operation oversight were stipulated in these contracts. Hence, the contracted nuclear facilities initially became the vehicle for training in basic and detailed design, as well as construction of nuclear facilities. They were later used as the experimental facility for further technological development.

Several national contracts were also secured for civil construction, procurement, fabrication, installation, and commissioning of the facilities under the supervision of the engineering team and the oversight of the international contractors. Many technology development projects were going through various stages of basic or detailed engineering, procurement, or construction. The

Center, which once was under serious threat of closure, had become one of the top-ten priority projects of the country. An extensive plan of building new houses and improving the living conditions of the staff in the nearby housing complex was executed. This was one of the key morale-boosting strategies that was included and approved in the ENTC development plan.

Staff performance was found to increase significantly when managers appraised their performance (Walker & Smither, 1999). A set of performance metrics was established that measured the departmental and staff performance (adequacy, quality, and timeliness of provision of planned needs) to check the projects against specified deliverables. These metrics were effective communication tools at the regular departmental meetings and the New Year celebrations to provide ongoing feedback to the staff. These meetings provided summary reports about the performance of the departments, the projects, and ENTC as a whole. They were intended to celebrate successes and identify issues to correct the adverse conditions or recover from substandard performance. These progress metrics were also reported to the stakeholders, to seek their advice and support and to maintain their engagement through sharing of information. Frequent visits of high-ranking Iranian officials were encouraged to maintain their commitment and support for the implementation of the ENTC development plan.

Compensation and incentive pay, based on a combination of individual, departmental, and project performance, ensured that staff and management efforts were rewarded for their effectiveness in delivering on ENTC goals. Projects and departmental performance were assessed against allocated resources, while an individual's performance was measured against assigned work. Each department was treated like a business unit that was rewarded for the value of the work it delivered as a team against the resources it received.

Keeping Staff Inspired and Motivated

Two years into the implementation phase, the ENTC started celebrating the completion of one or two projects each year. With the start of the larger and more complex projects, the engineering activities inside and outside the country grew in volume. Reams of engineering drawings and specifications were expected to be produced. Thousands of acres of land had to be developed, and hundred-thousand tons of equipment were planned to be procured, installed, and commissioned. Top national companies were about to start the construction and installation of the facilities. Interacting with the more highly paid staff of the contractors could bring up feelings of injustice among ENTC staff. Maintaining the motivation and commitment of the trained staff hence became a challenge, with a potential risk of staff turnover.

To address this issue, it was decided to spin off some operations into three staff-owned-and-operated private companies: one for engineering, one for construction, and one for support services. The engineering company was formed and nearly three hundred ENTC employees were transferred to it. The Center rented its offices and leased all the necessary computers, tools, and equipment to the newly formed company. All engineering activities of the Center, with some guarantee for future work, were contracted out to the company. While executing the ENTC contracts, the engineering company soon started contracting many projects outside the ENTC. Sense of ownership had greatly enhanced their efficiency and productivity.

A year later, a staff-cooperative company for construction and technical support services was established. Nearly two hundred ENTC staff were transferred to it and similar rules of engagement with the engineering company were applied. Most of the less-complex construction and installation activities and technical support services were contracted to this construction company. An environment of ownership and rewards similar to that in the engineering company was established. Within a year, this company was contracting many more projects external to the ENTC.

Less than a year later, the third private company was established to provide logistics support and general services to ENTC. Nearly 150 of the remaining staff of the Center were transferred to this staff-owned cooperative company. All supply-chain activities, transportation, office services, restaurants, housing, and other common services were contracted to this company.

With the formation of the three private companies, the Center shrank from one thousand staff members to fewer than three hundred within two years. Contracted engineering and construction projects and associated support services performed much better under the new entities, while staff earned much more than before; a win-for-all situation. These transitions were orchestrated through a well-defined and documented governance and transition plan, led by a group of cheerleaders.

Performance-based compensation and incentive pay systems were established in all companies according to their project earnings. Formation of the private companies inspired great incentives for higher organizational and personal efficiencies and improved productivity, since they were now working for themselves. It created a sense of ownership, responsibility, and accountability that fuelled great dynamics, never experienced at ENTC before. ENTC control gates were drastically reduced from numerous behavioral and task-based metrics and controls to a few project-based deliverables specified in the binding contracts. The new sense of ownership drove many of the desired behaviors and performance that ENTC planned to achieve through its complex performance management and control system. It bred a new sense of responsibility for what they now owned and accountability for what they now delivered.

To close, I would like to reflect on an informal exchange at a dinner table with a group of high-ranking experts from a foreign nuclear technology center. They had been visiting the Center to negotiate potential joint projects with our technologists. On their last day they visited the historic sites of Esfahan, ending with a dinner banquet, with the participation of ENTC's negotiating team. After the dinner and a few formal exchanges about the week's achievements, the head of this delegation asked me: "Why do the Esfahanies say Esfahan is half of the world?"

This proverb is often used by Esfahan's tour guides when they introduce the historic sites of Esfahan to sightseers. I was taken off-guard by this question in front of my staff, most of whom were residents of Esfahan. I also realized that, for the visiting delegation, the Esfahan's historic sites were no comparison to their own tourist and historical sites, let alone being equal to half of the world's. So they were all seriously puzzled by the suggestion that Esfahan's historic sites were equivalent to half of what existed elsewhere in the world. So I had no choice but to be truthful in my answer and say: "Because the Esfahanies haven't seen the other half."

I believe that the prime cause of the dismal circumstances of ENTC before planning and implementing the drastic changes was the failure of its players (managers, stakeholders, and staff) to see the other half. What I believe contributed to the success of the proposed ENTC change plan was the intense engagement and negotiations of all halves to create a whole, which facilitated the success of ENTC.

References

Folger, R., Konovsky, M., & Cropanzano, R. (1992). A due process metaphor for performance appraisal. *Research in Organizational Behavior, 14*, 129–177.

Greenberg, J. (1987). A taxonomy of organizational justice theories. *Academy of Management Review, 12*, 9–22.

Greenberg, J. (2006). Losing sleep over organizational injustice: Attenuating insomniac reactions to underpayment inequity with supervisory training in interactional justice. *Journal of Applied Psychology, 91*, 58–69.

Hackman, J.R., & Oldham, G.R. (1975). Development of the job diagnostic survey. *Journal of Applied Psychology, 60*, 159–170.

Hackman, J.R., & Oldham, G.R. (1976). Motivation through the design of work: Test of a theory. *Organizational Behavior and Human Performance, 16*, 250–279.

Latham, G.P. (2009). *Becoming the evidence-based manager.* Mountain View, CA: Davies-Black.

Latham, G.P., & Locke, E.A. (2006). Enhancing the benefits and overcoming the pitfalls of goal setting. *Organization Dynamics, 35*, 332–340.

Latham, G.P., & Locke, E.A. (2007). New developments in and directions for goal setting. *European Psychologist, 12*, 290–300.

Latham, G.P., Mitchell, T.R., & Dossett, D.L. (1978). The importance of participative goal setting and anticipated rewards on goal difficulty and job performance. *Journal of Applied Psychology, 63,* 163–171.

Latham, G.P., & Seijts, G.H. (1999). The effects of proximal and distal goals on performance on a moderately complex task. *Journal of Organizational Behavior, 20,* 421–429.

Locke, E.A. (2000). Motivation, cognition, and action: An analysis of studies of task goals and knowledge. *Applied Psychology: An International Review, 49,* 408–429.

Locke, E.A., & Latham, G.P. (2002). Building a practically useful theory of goal setting and task motivation: A 35-year odyssey. *American Psychologist, 57,* 705–717.

Meyer, J.P., Becker, T.E., & Vandenberghe, C. (2004). Employee commitment and motivation: A conceptual analysis and interpretative model. *Journal of Applied Psychology, 89,* 991–1007.

Meyer, J.P., & Herscovitch, L. (2001). Commitment in the workplace: Toward a general model. *Human Resource Management Review, 11,* 299–326.

Mitchell, T.R., & Daniels, D. (2003). Motivation. In W.C. Borman, D.R. Ilgen, & R.J. Klimoski (Eds.), *Handbook of psychology, 12: Industrial organizational psychology* (pp. 225–254). Hoboken, NJ: John Wiley & Sons.

Tasa, K., & Whyte, K. (2005). Collective efficacy and vigilant problem solving in group decision making: A non-linear model. *Organizational Behavior and Human Decision Making Processes, 96,* 119–129.

Walker, A.G., & Smither, J.W. (1999). A five-year study of upward feedback: What managers do with their results matters. *Personnel Psychology, 52,* 393–423.

Part Three

The Team Leaders

CHAPTER FOUR

Building Great Leadership Teams for Complex Problems

Ruth Wageman
Harvard University

Leadership functions increasingly are fulfilled not by a heroic individual but rather by leadership *teams* (Ancona & Nadler, 1989; Hambrick, 1997; Wageman, Nunes, Burruss, & Hackman, 2008). Leadership teams appear to be common in contemporary life and, for many complex enterprises, a necessity.

At the top of organizations, for example, the rapid changes and increasing complexity and interdependence of organizations' environments may have made the top leadership role too large for any one person to accomplish, no matter how talented (Bennis, 1997). At the same time, *cross-organizational* leadership teams are increasing in prevalence in public life. Multi-stakeholder leadership teams are frequently formed, for example, when community and societal needs require the resources and capabilities of multiple, independent institutions to solve them. Many observers have noted that these kinds of societal problems are increasing in frequency in the world (Sayles & Chandler, 2009). In the public sector and in civic life, for instance, we are seeing an increase in climate-related crises like flooded cities, droughts, severe wildfires, oil spills, and epidemics, which are creating the requirements for cross-entity and cross-sector collaborations, bringing together leaders from municipalities, non-governmental organizations (NGOs), and local businesses. All these entities hold critical leadership roles in bringing about a sustainable solution. These multi-stakeholder collaborations benefit from shared authority and broad resources held by members appointed from relevant stakeholder groups (Mendonca, Beroggi, & Wallace, 2001; Leonard & Howitt, 2006; Sayles & Chandler, 2009). Leadership teams of many kinds thus have considerable potential compared to individuals fulfilling leadership functions independently. They have more resources, more diverse perspectives, broader networks of key constituencies, and the potential to develop context-specific strategies to solve unique local problems.

While the great strengths and potential of leadership teams are compelling, it is also the case that such teams struggle with significant challenges to their effectiveness. The purposes of this chapter are first to draw upon everything that is known about leadership teams to identify the key challenges teams face whose core purpose is to provide leadership, collectively, to complex systems. I summarize these as a set of "tripwires" that cause leadership teams to stumble (Hackman, 1994). Throughout, I provide illustrations of why these potential tripwires are so common for leadership teams, especially those that operate across organizations. Second, for each tripwire, there is a parallel positive condition that can be put in place to increase the chances that leadership teams will avoid the pitfalls and develop into fully effective teams that provide all the leadership that is needed by the complex undertakings they govern. These conditions can be put in place from the beginning of the life of a leadership team to establish a positive trajectory for their work, but, as will be seen, also need considerable monitoring and adjustment throughout the unfolding of a complex undertaking (see Table 4.1 for a summary of tripwires and conditions).

Leadership Teams

A leadership team is a group of individuals, each of whom has personal responsibility for leading some part of a system but who is also interdependent for the purpose of providing overall leadership to a larger enterprise. The most commonly written about kind of leadership team is the one at the top of an organization—

Table 4.1. Tripwires and Conditions for Great Leadership Teams

Tripwires	*Conditions*
1. Unclear purposes	**1. Compelling direction**
Differences in individual interests	Use narrative to find shared values
Conceptual challenge	Identify interdependencies
Teams are poorer than individuals at defining purposes	Authorize an individual
2. The wrong people are convening	**2. Convene the right people**
Representing institutions	Look for systems thinkers
Too senior	Recompose over time
No teamwork skills	Assess empathy and integrity
3. Meetings are a waste of time	**3. Create enabling structure**
Avoiding conflict	Create interdependent tasks
Different cultures	Establish ground rules
Assume "we're all grownups"	Do midcourse reviews and revise norms

the senior management team. Typically composed of the CEO and his or her direct reports, each member of a top management team has a separate, individual leadership responsibility. In a global for-profit company, for example, that responsibility might be for a geographical region, for a set of major customers, or for a particular function. But members of such teams also have *collective* responsibility for aligning the various parts of the organization into a coherent whole and fostering its overall effectiveness.

Less frequently studied and less well understood are leadership teams that bring together the resources of multiple enterprises for purposes of solving difficult problems or for leading major change in complex systems. Yet these kinds of leadership teams are both increasingly critical and especially difficult to design, launch, and lead well. And the consequences of their successes and failures have lasting impact on the communities in which they operate . . . for better or for worse.

A pair of examples from two different U.S. communities serves to illustrate. Note that in each case, key aspects of the composition, origin, and challenges they faced were quite similar in many respects. Yet the results of their convening were radically different.

Team 1

In a town in the Pacific Northwest, a group of leaders convened to address the health care needs of citizens in four surrounding counties who lacked adequate health insurance. These patients were often unable or reluctant to seek care when they needed it and lacked the resources to engage the kind of primary and preventive care that promotes good health over time. As a consequence, their care was usually urgent and typically sought in emergency rooms, creating burdens on the hospitals, the community, and the patients themselves.

Convened by a senior leader from one major hospital in the region, a leadership group formed to include two senior leaders from major local employers, senior leaders from both hospitals, from two primary care practices, and from one major health insurer.

In the course of their work, this team of leaders from a range of institutions mobilized volunteer health care workers to support this underserved population and eventually created a new community health center to meet the needs of the underinsured.

Since that time and over the subsequent twenty years, different configurations of leaders from these institutions have undertaken additional problem-solving collaborations. For example, they created a single sleep lab jointly owned by both hospitals, thereby preventing the overinvestment of funds in redundant and competing resources; they have conducted a community-wide health needs assessment with over one hundred institutional partners; and they have identified a set of health priorities for their region. The pattern of configuring and reconfiguring different groups of leaders from these institutions to address health and health care challenges in the area continues, and this community has, unusually, a governance body composed of members from many institutions, including the citizenry, that collectively tackle problems and set future priorities for health.

Team 2

In a small city in the Northeast, eight leaders came together to address how to provide care to the underinsured in their community. Convened by respected leaders from the public health department, the leadership group that formed ultimately included three hospital CEOs, one senior leader from a mental health provider, one from a children's health center, and one from a major private health care insurer in the region. This leadership group met monthly over two years, but were unable to agree on an approach to solving the problem for which they had initially convened. Significant conflicts arose among members about just what their purposes and approach should be and how to take action together. While they produced a high-quality assessment of local health care needs in the region, at this writing they have enacted no significant changes in access to care for the uninsured. Their sense of efficacy as a group to tackle the problems of their community is very low. The group members still meet, but some individuals report that they largely attend so that no decisions are made behind their backs.

These two teams convened functionally similar groups to respond to similar local pressures. Yet they differed widely in effectiveness. Let me begin our analysis by establishing what we mean by an effective leadership team. Effective leadership teams (1) meet the needs of the *constituencies* they serve, (2) grow in *capacity* to solve increasingly challenging problems over time, and (3) on balance, contribute to the *development of individual leaders* (Hackman, 2002; Wageman & Hackman, 2009) rather than undermine their commitment and effectiveness. Team 1 above showed markedly positive signs on all three criteria of effectiveness, spawning increasing success and offering many leaders opportunities to tackle significant societal problems. Team 2, by contrast, not only failed to address critical community problems but have burned out collaborative capacity in the process. Without significant turnover among the leaders in this latter community, it may never build the kind of collaborative leadership capacity needed to address the challenges faced in the region. The continuing ineffectiveness of the leadership group is in no way trivial for this community.

What are the conditions that increase the chances of outcomes like that of Team 1 and help to avoid the pitfalls that undermined Team 2? The focus of this chapter is to draw upon research about leadership teams, as well as field observations of multi-stakeholder leadership teams in practice, to identify what most gets in the way of leadership team effectiveness and, more practically, what leaders operating in such teams can do about it. To do so, I draw upon an array of field studies of leadership teams, my own and others (Ancona & Nadler, 1989; Berg, 2005; Ganz & Wageman, 2008; Gerencser, Kelly, Napolitano, & Van Lee, 2008; Hambrick & D'Aveni, 1996; Li & Hambrick, 2005; Wageman & Hackman, 2009; Wageman, Nunes, Burruss, & Hackman, 2008), to make sense of these challenges and pose potential solutions.

Tripwire 1: What Is the Purpose of This Leadership Team?

Every team needs a compelling purpose. For team purposes to engage members' motivation and to orient them in a common direction, those purposes must be *consequential, challenging,* and *clear* (Hackman, 2002; Wageman, Nunes, Burruss, & Hackman, 2008). These three ideas are straightforward in concept, but must be brought to life in unique ways for every team.

For example, team purpose must be challenging enough to engage members' capabilities, but not so impossible as to be demoralizing. To achieve the right degree of challenge, someone must identify what a particular team of leaders is ready for at a given point in its life. Early on, when leaders are undertaking their first collaborative initiatives, the level of challenge they can handle may be much lower than when they have matured significantly as a collaboration. We have seen, for example, that multi-stakeholder leadership teams who undertake a clear task, such as collectively building a shared model of the causes of their local problems or designing a forum for interchange with a broader set of leaders, are able to build the collaborative "muscle" they need to later undertake the greater challenges involved in addressing problems that raise significant conflicts among the interests of the institutions—such as deciding that the community served by two competing hospitals needs only one cancer center, not two.

A team purpose must also be consequential: crucial enough to be treated as a significant priority of the individuals on the leadership team, even when their institutional responsibilities demand a lot of them. And, finally, a leadership team purpose must be clear. Members must be able to imagine what will be accomplished as a consequence of their work and, above all, what the role is that only this team of leaders, of all people in this community or organization, can play in bringing that about.

Teams of other kinds—front-line production teams, quality teams, or task forces—often suffer from a lack of consequentiality in their purposes. Considerable research has demonstrated that, for such teams, the work they do often is inadequately connected to larger, more meaningful objectives, to the lives and work of others, or to the effectiveness of the organization as a whole. Not so with leadership teams. They tend to experience their purposes as highly consequential for the well-being of others or of the shared enterprise. And they typically do experience their shared leadership work as a significant challenge to their capabilities, a meaningful stretch. It is *clarity* of purpose that is the most difficult feature of compelling team purposes to establish for leadership teams.

Leadership teams are no less in need of clarity than any other kind of team. Indeed, they may be *more* in need of explicit attention to defining clear purposes than other teams. As Edmondson, Roberto, and Watkins (2001) point out, leadership teams tend to face highly unstructured task streams: continuously changing flows of overlapping problem-solving and decision-making situations. Moreover, teams of leaders have a greater need to deal with unpredictable events in the external environment than do many kinds of teams (Ancona & Nadler, 1989; Berg, 2005). The very amorphousness of their work makes the team purposes difficult to specify.

Data from a study of leadership teams across nations and sectors illustrate this (Wageman, Nunes, Burruss, & Hackman, 2008). These data show the average scores for consequentiality,

Figure 4.1. Leadership Team Purposes Lack Clarity

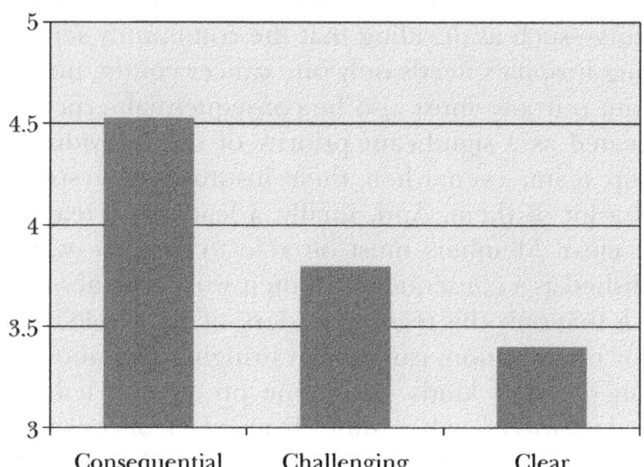

challenge, and clarity across more than a hundred leadership teams of many kinds, on a scale from 1 = very poor to 5 = excellent (see Figure 4.1). As one leadership team member described his team's purpose: "So, our team purpose is really important, and it's going to be very tough to pull off . . . if only we knew what it was."

Obstacles to Clarity of Purpose

There are three main reasons why the purposes of leadership teams can be especially unclear: (1) differences among the interests and priorities of the individuals prevent alignment of purpose at the team level; (2) articulating purpose for a leadership team can be an extraordinary conceptual challenge; and (3) in teams of peers, defining purpose is a joint task—and teams are notoriously poor at articulating purposes collaboratively. I elaborate on each of these obstacles, below, and then turn to the question of what leadership teams can do to address them, drawing on examples and illustrations of real teams facing these challenges successfully.

Differences in Interests

A significant challenge to clarity of purpose for leadership teams is that when a group of leaders convenes, the tacit assumption that all are "signed on" to a shared enterprise, or that members view themselves as a leadership group, may be excessively optimistic. In leadership teams at the top of an organization, for example, members often construe themselves as representing their own units there in the team to gain what they can and protect what they can for their own constituents, even at cost to other leaders at the table. In multi-stakeholder leadership teams, that stance is even more likely. Members of such teams do not operate within the boundary of a single enterprise with a clear organizational purpose. Rather, they gather, typically because they have been convened by someone from outside their own organization who perceives a problem that is beyond the scope of any one institution to solve. Often, members have responded to an invitation to such a leadership team because their institutions, too, have an interest in seeing that problem solved. For example, Gerencser, Kelly, Napolitano, and Van Lee (2008) describe an inspiring example of how one senior leader from Hewlett-Packard, out of great personal sorrow and determination, eventually convened a group that drew in members of UNESCO, engineering educators, the World Bank, and the Nigerian Society of Engineers, among others, to radically transform the quality and availability of science and engineering education in Africa. This shared perception of a problem is, as will be seen, a vital resource for establishing clear purpose for the leadership team. Nonetheless, the primary construal of individuals' roles in the group is generally that they are there to represent the well-being of their own institutions or organizational units in the joint work.

Finding a clear, shared purpose that is largely congruent with the interests of the individual institutions is important for a novice multi-stakeholder leadership group to have any chance of accomplishing something together (Berg, 2005; Gerencser, Kelly, Napolitano, & Van Lee, 2008; Hemmati, Dodds, Enayati, & McHarry, 2002). But because decisions about purpose always involve choosing *not* to do some things as well as what the team *will* do, articulating a direction for the leadership group may require members to forgo goals that some deem personally valuable (Hackman, 2002). That necessity poses significant emotional challenges to a newly formed group, whose impulse may be to include all individual motives in the interests of initial harmony—resulting in very little focus for the team. The expression "a camel is a horse designed by a committee" is about this very issue: the tendency of peer groups to sand down the sharpest edges of a single vision or values in the interest of including all their personal goals. The challenge, then, is to find purposes that both reflect the values that are common across the individuals and institutions and at the same time not to overemphasize the satisfaction of individual motives relative to the shared ones. That is a tough balancing act for any group of leaders to navigate gracefully.

Conceptual Challenge

Defining a compelling team purpose for leadership teams is also an extraordinary conceptual challenge (Wageman, Nunes, Burruss, & Hackman, 2008). Specifying just what a team composed of leaders shares responsibility for, and doing so in a way that is clear, tangible, and motivating, poses special problems compared to other kinds of teams. Because leadership tasks can be amorphous—just what tasks does a team of leaders do together?—the transition from imagining the outcomes of their work to specifying the unique role of the leadership team in bringing that about takes considerable abstract conceptualization skill (Wageman & Hackman, 2009; Wageman, Nunes, Burruss, & Hackman, 2008). Although individuals' leadership responsibilities within their organizations generally are very clear indeed, just how a collection of leaders together can provide something more than the sum of individuals' responsibilities is difficult for many leaders to articulate. For example, many leadership teams have loosely defined purposes, such as "providing the leadership to improve the well being of our community" or "leading the development of a solution to our problems." This lack of specificity about what the team does together—what leadership functions they fulfill to bring about the desired change, whether that is setting collective priorities, seeking resources, or launching and guiding an innovation—impairs their ability to orient themselves and to engage with each other on key issues. When members have little clarity about why they convene as a leadership team and what they expect to accomplish together that no other team can do, they may sporadically meet and discuss a variety of issues—some important, others less so—but gain little traction and experience no progress. This pattern, which characterized Team 2 described earlier, meant that the only thing coming from the team was frustration and increasing pessimism about their ability to accomplish anything meaningful.

Teams Are Poor at Articulating Purposes Together

Leadership teams can struggle to arrive at a sharp enough direction statement to guide collective action. Defining and clarifying a purpose drawing on multiple perspectives and different interests is often a particularly difficult challenge for very diverse groups like the multi-stakeholder leadership teams described above. Articulating purpose is not a function that is well-executed by groups, but is rather done more effectively by individuals with excellent conceptual skill and dexterity with language (Hackman, 2002, pp. 224–225). Hackman describes, for example, a small cooperative newspaper, in which members of the cooperative were personally committed to the values of democracy and wanted to enact those values by involving all members in setting aspirations. In spite of considerable time and energy invested in the debate, they were never able to reach agreement on a sharp collective purpose concrete enough to guide behavior.

Similarly, in a study of activist teams (Ganz & Wageman, 2008), clarity of team purpose was significantly lower for self-governing leadership teams than for any other kinds of front-line task performing teams we studied or for senior leadership teams, all of which typically have purposes established by an *individual* with authority to call others to a specific set of actions.

Much has been written about how leaders can go about creating clarity of purpose for teams that report to them, and the crucial role of authority in creating clarity (Hackman, 2002; Podolny, Khurana, & Besharov, 2010; West, Borilla, Dawson,

Brodbeck, Shapiro, & Haward, 2003). But multi-stakeholder leadership groups are typically composed of peers under the aegis of no one institution, and members hold no authority over one another. As a consequence, there is no natural designate to articulate purposes for the team. Such leadership teams may be convened by an individual who has some vision for what the team may accomplish and yet hold no particular legitimacy for calling others to that purpose except their own personal qualities. Multi-stakeholder leadership teams thus have to navigate yet another tricky balancing act between engaging the members in defining purposes that are meaningful to them and their institutions and avoiding the sanding-down process and messy compromises that tend to characterize purposes articulated by groups.

Condition 1: Create a Compelling and Clear Purpose for the Team

Clarity of purpose is possible even for multi-stakeholder leadership teams. The set of actions involved in establishing compelling purposes is a short list, and we will address each in turn: (1) identify key interdependencies among team members' institutions; (2) use personal narrative to locate deeply held and shared values; and (3) authorize an individual to articulate the purpose on behalf of the group.

Identify Interdependencies

The work of leadership for members of any leadership team involves making collective decisions on behalf of a larger whole, while simultaneously acting on behalf of their individual constituents. Multi-stakeholder leadership teams convene because of a specific problem to solve that is not under the control of any one of their institutions and will benefit from a combining of resources across these entities. They may also convene, as in the example of Team 1, believing that some long-term cross-institutional entity will be needed to address future problems and make community-wide decisions.

Therefore, articulating shared purpose begins with explicitly engaging both these questions: (1) What *resources* do each of us bring that can make us more able to solve the immediate challenge we face? and (2) What *capacity* do we need for the future? The answers generated in a discussion of these questions can point to specific leadership activities that this group can undertake as a team. Those specific activities begin pointing the way to a larger definition of team purpose.

For example, one multi-stakeholder leadership team perceived that with a hospital CEO, a senior officer from a major local employer, and the regional private medical insurer at the table, they had the resources together to undertake an experiment. They construed their purpose as creating, testing, and learning from an innovative way of providing health care and benefits to a significant local population. They undertook to engage together in a local action experiment, the lessons of which might be applied and expanded throughout the broader community. Other members of this group served, for this experiment, as a kind of advisory council. Over time, different configurations of leaders engaged in other innovations, and the group built additional collaborative capacity in their own leadership team and throughout their community by engaging in consultative work to each other around key institutional challenges.

The example above illustrates three of the four kinds of leadership teams we have observed in our research. These different ways of operating as a team—collective decision making, coordinating a single initiative together, consulting to one another—are all legitimate uses of a leadership team. The greater the interdependence, the greater the impact of the team (Wageman, Nunes, Burruss, & Hackman, 2008). The four types are as follows: (1) least interdependent is the information sharing or alignment team. These teams do not make, decide, or perform anything together; rather, their purpose is to exchange information in ways that enable the individual leaders to do their independent leadership activities more effectively. Many coalitions are such teams, engaging in information sharing in the hopes that informing each other of their own activities may create alignment across related undertakings; (2) more interdependent still is a leadership group in which members actively consult to one another, enabling the individual leaders to act more effectively based on advice and counsel from other members; (3) third, and more interdependent still, is the coordinating team—a team that collectively manages the timing, sequencing, and interdependencies in implementing some change or innovation; and (4) finally, most interdependent of all, is the decision-making group, which establishes strategic priorities and allocates resources together by some joint decision-making process.

The team described above discovered for itself a range of ways of operating as a leadership team that involved most of these activities at one time or another. But it was their insight about combining resources and undertaking the coordination of an experiment together that developed their capacity to operate with a high degree of interdependence, taught them critical lessons about how to work together, and launched the other forms of activity that supported those purposes. They went beyond the mere information-sharing that is the simpler and less impactful purposes of most coalitions (as compared with decision-making teams), creating a platform for accomplishing not just their initial undertaking but building the capacity for further action.

Use Narrative to Identify Shared Values

In our work with self-governing activist teams (Ganz & Wageman, 2008), we found that engaging individual leaders in developing their public narratives enabled groups of leaders to articulate to themselves, and to others who called them personally, to take on leadership of the particular challenge before them. Drawing on choice points in their personal histories, participants illustrate for others the values that underlie their motives to lead.

The function that engaging individuals in public narratives can serve for leadership *groups* is twofold. First, developing one's narrative enables individuals to clarify for themselves as persons, not just as representatives of their institutions, why this team's purposes may be consequential for them and deeply connected to their own values. Second, it enables the leaders as a group to identify the *shared* themes in their values and experience a deep and genuine connection of purpose with each other, even in a highly diverse group. Those shared values can begin building a platform of trust among members that will serve them well when the challenge of dealing with different interests among their institutions inevitably arises.

Authorize an Individual to Articulate Purpose

Having an individual in the team given the authority to set direction helps with clarity. For senior leadership teams at the top of an organization, the chief executive can identify key decisions that the team makes together and study the themes in those decisions to establish an overarching purpose. Doing so requires first conceptualizing what a leadership team can do *as a team* to provide essential leadership to the larger entity. That kind of cognitive work requires creative conceptualization, something that comes best from an individual rather than from a team (Hackman, 2002).

For teams of peers, no such authority exists naturally. But teams that have articulated shared values through public narrative and who have identified the key activities and interdependencies at least for their initial undertakings have excellent raw material from which to generate their overarching purpose in ways that make it possible to imagine just what it would look like for them to accomplish it—and to see their unique role in bringing that about. We have seen that one particularly effective way of going from raw material to clear purpose is by iterating between individual purpose statements and group reflection. Once a group has generated its shared values and its interdependencies, for example, they can authorize one member of the team who is particularly articulate and has high levels of conceptual ability to shape a purpose on behalf of the team. That individual can then bring the creative work she or he has done back to the team for their reactions. A designated individual may then do some additional modifications based on the group's responses. The trick is not to become caught up in group editing or, worse, group writing, something that easily captures an opinionated team of leaders (Ganz & Wageman, 2008).

This iterative process—the group generates shared values and activities, an individual uses his or her creativity to sharpen those into a shared purpose, the team responds and ratifies—uses the best of what both teams and individuals are uniquely suited to do well on behalf of a leadership team.

Tripwire 2: The Wrong People Are Convening

Leadership teams often suffer from the consequences of poorly considered choices about just who is at the table. There are three main errors most frequently made about the composition of leadership teams. First is convening people who will represent the key stakeholder groups in the community or organization. When people are invited as representatives, they act as representatives—of their particular interests, and not of the whole. Second is convening very senior people under the assumption that the most senior people will have the authority to make decisions on behalf of their institutions. The logic of that choice is not in itself faulty, but the consequences are more often that these individuals are impossible to convene or chronically designating replacements at meetings, killing the momentum of the leadership group. Third is convening a group without any assessment of the individuals' collaborative abilities, resulting in minimal competence to work together, or even including dangerous "derailers" on the team.

Convening People to Represent Their Constituencies or Organizations

The logic of choosing individuals who collectively represent the constituent parts of the system and who can bring the resources of those parts to the table is sound. Solving complex problems in communities and organizations and bringing about a new state of the system requires broad perspectives, significant authority, and considerable resources. The cost of issuing invitations solely on the basis of who can represent a key group or entity, however, is convening a group that, ironically, suffers from an inability to act on behalf of the whole system when they convene. When the individuals are invited as representatives, they will construe themselves as being on the team for the purpose of representing their own institutions' interests. Ironically, the very breadth of composition can result in myopia that prevents them from seeing the whole.

Moreover, leaders' legitimate roles as representatives of their particular organizations or constituents can cause them to make negative assumptions about other team members' motives (Berg, 2005). Members interpret the meaning of each others' statements as primarily being about serving the interests of the groups they represent. Thus, leadership team dynamics tend to embody and express the intergroup relationships—positive and negative—that pervade the larger community, especially when those relationships are inherently competitive (e.g., for investments, for clients, for recognition or credit). Finally, the most compelling personal motives of leadership team members often are historically more about being individual leaders than about being team members. Most senior leaders do not construe themselves as team members, but rather prefer to operate independently and to exercise considerable authority over others. Together, personal motives, role definitions, and the incentives in the system create a natural tendency for the dynamics of leadership teams to shift from trying to make the best collective decision possible for the whole to trying to win decision contests with other team members (Lewicki, Saunders, & Minton, 1999).

Choosing the Most Senior People

As noted above, the logic of convening senior leaders—because they have considerable authority to act on behalf of their institutions and bring to bear their resources—has merit. The problems arise when two aspects of the leadership team's work intersect with this compositional choice. First, senior leaders typically have jobs that already require more of their time than many can manage, resulting in leaders who are generally unavailable. And when they come from different institutions, the rhythms of their personal calendars are almost certainly different. It becomes a significant challenge even to convene such a group at all. Keeping any kind of momentum going or coping with the need to revisit and refresh memories of prior work becomes a constant struggle.

Second, when teams continue to struggle to define clear purposes or engage significant leadership tasks, the motivation for senior leaders to attend meetings declines. Up against demanding and consequential leadership responsibilities in their own institutions, the work of a multi-stakeholder leadership team has a significant hill to climb. It must be compelling enough to claim the attention of persons who have little to spare—and often the work of these teams fails to achieve that degree of significance, as will be seen. What often results as a consequence is that the members of such groups make unilateral decisions not to attend any given meeting, a matter we will return to with the next tripwire.

Paying No Attention to Demonstrable Teamwork Skills

I do not mean to insult senior leaders, but it has been my observation that people do not become CEOs, or mayors, or chief ministers because of their ability to work well with peers. The typical leadership habits and routines of senior leaders may, in fact, militate against effective teamwork. Among the characteristics frequently admired and reinforced in senior leaders are decisiveness (the ability to choose a course of action and stick with it), personal vision (the tendency to have strong views about how things ought to be), and dominance (the inclination to impose one's point of view) (Glynn & DeJordy, 2010; Zaccaro, Rittman, & Marks 2001).

None of these characteristics in large quantities is helpful in the work of a leadership team, especially one composed of peers. The challenge for such teams is to co-create vision, to sift through complex options and make choices that move toward a shared goal, to minimize harm to the individuals' institutions, and to experiment with new ways of proceeding, learn with others, and take actions in concert with others. Those collective leadership functions require quite a different set of leadership characteristics, among them systems perspective, empathy, and integrity. We will return to these particular capacities shortly in addressing the process of composing a multi-stakeholder leadership team effectively.

Keeping Known Derailers in the Team

Many team members can, with determination and appropriate coaching, expand their self-images beyond that of individual leaders and develop the kinds of teamwork competencies needed for work with peers. But there is another type of characteristic that poses a serious risk to the success of any team, which we term team "derailers." These are characteristics that undermine the effectiveness of any team.

According to our research (Wageman, Nunes, Burruss, & Hackman, 2008), derailers often display at least one of two characteristics that are relatively rare among top leaders. The first manifests as a victim mentality. When they are asked about their career histories, one hears a story dominated with occasions when the individual felt unfairly treated, his or her work unfairly assessed and contributions unrecognized. Years later, the bitterness is still fresh, and one hears no recognition that the individual had in any way contributed to the problem. And there is no sign that he or she has taken any constructive lessons from those past challenges.

The second observable characteristic of derailers is their negative perceptions of other people. Their descriptions of others are filled with sweeping judgmental statements: "He's a bad leader." "She's a fool." They apply disparaging adjectives to other people, efforts, or strategies. While there is no simple test that will identify every derailer, there are some symptoms one can readily observe. These include individuals who:

- Frequently complain about others, including publicly;
- Bring out the worst in other team members;
- Attack people instead of critiquing ideas;
- Raise disagreements outside the team, but decline to say them in the room;
- Contravene group agreements when acting independently; and
- Claim to understand the impact of such behavior, but show no change.

In my ten and more years of studying leadership teams, I have observed that the single matter that most keeps senior leaders awake at night about their teams is the challenge of removing a destructive individual, especially if that individual is in control of critical resources or is a powerful individual in other respects. While some courageous leaders do take the risks of removing these individuals from the team, many seek alternatives that enable them to have a functional leadership team without risk of losing this individual's support altogether. For multi-stakeholder leadership teams, the risk is political. Disinviting from the team a senior leader from another institution, a significant figure in the community, will likely mean that person becoming an implacable opponent to anything the group undertakes thereafter. The most constructive instances I have seen of dealing with this challenge effectively have involved groups that shaped their activities to reduce interdependence with that individual, engaging them in the team only consultatively and around specific questions. Doing so meant altering the meeting and work pattern of the group, a considerable coordination cost at the very least.

Condition 2: Convene the Right People

Convening the right people to a leadership team is not just selecting people by position or title or membership in a key institution. It also requires establishing that these individuals bring the capabilities to work as a team and think about the system in which they operate as a whole, not just their own institutions. Ideally, a convener should consider three key teamwork capacities.

Look for Behavioral Signs of Empathy and Integrity

Leadership teams must be able to engage in robust discussions that explore divergent ways to address a systemic problem or seize an opportunity. Two competencies that consistently enable teams to engage in real and robust discussions of strategic issues that result in shared understanding and a collective decision are *integrity* and *empathy*. There are ways to observe signs of these competencies in potential team members.

Empathy

This competency shows itself in the way an individual deals with the spoken words of other leadership team members, especially when they raise concerns about the direction of a team's movement with respect to the impact it will have on his or her area of responsibility. In our research, empathy manifested itself in three ways in individuals' behavior: (1) reflecting back understanding of the *content* of a concern another person has just raised; (2) expressing understanding of the *significance* that concern holds for the *speaker*, and (3) the ability to respond to the *feelings* the speaker has attached to that concern.

Leaders who are high in empathy can paraphrase their colleagues, they identify the underlying institutional concern that others raise, and they address such a concern directly in their responses, rather than turning the discussion in another direction. Without empathy, teams cannot build trust, reach meaningful consensus, or make tough decisions. When members do not feel that others have understood their concerns, they are unable to assume that a team decision will deal adequately with the ways in which they feel quite understandably protective and responsible for their own institutions and constituencies. Without the belief that their concerns are understood *and taken into account in the decision process*, they will raise and re-raise objections, leading to a team that has consistent trouble arriving at solutions.

Integrity

The team competency "integrity" does not just refer to its popular definition of being generally honest. Integrity in a leadership team involves owning one's opinions and speaking out during the interactions of the team, articulating honest objections and concerns in ways that the team can address together. And it involves undertaking the actions agreed in the presence of others once out of sight of one's fellow leaders. Integrity in our research manifested in four ways:

- Putting on the table for discussion by the group any issues that affect multiple people around the table—even when the implications of that issue are largest for one's own institution or area of responsibility;
- Keeping discussions that take place among the leaders confidential;
- Implementing the decisions as agreed by the team; and
- Holding the team accountable to make decisions that are consistent with the values and precedents the team already has set.

A team composed of people high in both integrity and empathy is protected against a common destructive pattern among leadership teams, especially multi-stakeholder groups. That pattern is a continuing routine of agreements that do not hold, leaders taking unilateral actions that materially affect the work of the team and its constituents, and continual revisiting of matters that members thought had already been settled.

Look for Systems Thinking

Another competency that plays a role in making leadership teams successful is conceptual thinking, or the ability to perceive patterns and synthesize complex information. At its basic form, it is the ability to identify patterns from divergent sources of data. At its most sophisticated, it is the ability to understand the interrelations among the different institutions, processes, and groups in a community and how they dynamically influence one another to produce current results. The presence of systems thinking in one or two members of the team can raise the level of systems thinking in the group as a whole. In convening a leadership team, look for individuals who naturally think beyond their institutions' internal dynamics and reflect on its interrelations with other groups and organizations. When you ask individuals to think about the whole community, persons who are good systems thinkers quickly move beyond their institutional roles and think about consequences for a larger community. It requires a relaxed, reflective time to test for this competency: systems thinking emerges when a leader has the latitude to reflect and not in the heat of fighting fires on one's home turf.

Composing—and Recomposing—a Leadership Team

If a leadership team is to be effective, the convener must ensure that the members collectively understand and can represent the entire community. That heuristic does not translate into every institution or group having a seat at the table. As needed, senior leaders and specialists can be invited to contribute to the core team's work when it could benefit from their particular expertise or knowledge.

One hypothesis is that to compose a leadership team well that has the full array of capacities—time and authority to do significant work, teamwork competencies, systems perspective—involves iterating the membership. We have seen conveners of multistakeholder teams conduct relationship-building conversations with many potential team members before inviting an initial set to the table. That process allows for exploring leadership practices and styles, personal values, and potential for commitment to the team's ongoing work.

Moreover, some research has shown that the right group of leaders to envision collaborative work across institutions to alter a community or solve large problems may not be the best group of people to carry that work forward (Gerencser, Kelly, Napolitano, & Van Lee, 2008; Hemmati, Dodds, Enayati, & McHarry, 2002). One possible process for iterating leadership team formation over time is to convene an initial set of very senior leaders from diverse institutions, attending to their values and their vision for change, and engaging them in co-visioning for the future. Those leaders can then ultimately be asked to identify the "right people" for an ongoing collaboration, taking into account the competencies needed to do that work together, and providing the resources and time needed for *this* group to lead the work.

Tripwire 3: Meetings Are a Waste of Time

It is ironic that senior leaders who already are overloaded tend to waste significant amounts of time when they convene. Leadership teams often focus on surprisingly trivial matters. They do make decisions together—but often about issues that are not consequential for the team's core leadership work. When I examined the survey scores for the leadership teams I studied, I found that the average meaningfulness of the leadership teams' tasks was M = 3.83, well below the ideal of 5.

There are three main forces that push leadership teams in the direction of ineffective and wheel-spinning meetings: (1) conflicts among individual interests and an inability to manage that conflict effectively; (2) variation among members' implicit expectations of how the group should operate; and (3) the tacit assumption that because members are all competent leaders there is no need to be explicit about what effective team processes they wish to employ.

Conflict Between Individual and Collective Interests

Leadership teams may avoid the critical questions because, when they do address important matters, they risk becoming caught up in seemingly irresolvable conflicts. Conflicts in leadership teams often stem from members' views that their main responsibilities are to maximize the effectiveness of the unit or institution they lead (Ancona & Nadler, 1989; Berg, 2005). There is a real risk that making decisions together that maximize *overall* effectiveness will result in outcomes that are inconvenient, costly, or threatening to the institutions headed by certain team members. That kind of discussion requires considerable skill at sustaining and managing tensions without personalizing conflict or resolving it in premature or suboptimal ways. But it also requires the willingness to engage in the real issues in the first place—and many leadership teams are reluctant to raise the most consequential matters precisely because dealing with them collectively will require a kind of social dexterity that is rare.

Variations in Institutional Cultures and Norms

Leaders who come from different institutions also bring with them institutional cultures and norms that vary—and these differences are seldom overtly noted or addressed. One significant cultural norm that varies across institutions is how to act when there is a conflict between the demands of one's individual job and the work of the team. As noted earlier, senior leaders who find the work of the leadership team less compelling than their own individual responsibilities can often decide independently of one another not to appear at a given team meeting because of demanding responsibilities in their home institutions. In some organizations, that is a normal institutional practice, and sending a lower-level leader as a delegate in one's stead is commonplace. When the work of the leadership team is mere information sharing, that may be a reasonable practice. But when the work of the team is decision making—as it should be—lower-level leaders cannot make decisions with the same degree of authority and therefore create a barrier to progress on the shared work of the team. This pattern can result in lengthy delays, lost momentum in the work, and most difficult to deal with, under-bounded teams who continually revisit prior work.

We found that the boundaries of leadership teams are unusually porous and blurred. Indeed, members of such teams often do not even know that they do not know who is on the team. According to our findings (Wageman & Hackman, 2009), leadership team members have great confidence in their knowledge of team membership, responding to items such as "Team membership is quite clear—everybody knows exactly who is and is not on this team" in the upper regions of the 5-point boundedness scale (M = 4.51). But when individual members report the *number of members* in the team, the data tell a different story. Of the more than 150 leadership teams I have studied, only twenty-one (14 percent) were in agreement about the number of team members. And their estimates of team size often were in the double digits—far too large to accomplish anything meaningful together. Poor boundaries are a significant problem for any team. How can "we" do anything meaningful or learn to work together effectively if we don't know who "we" are?

Assuming That "We Are All Grownups"

I have used a lighthearted turn of phrase to convey the underlying assumption that prevents leadership teams from articulating ground rules for their interactions that might enable them to be more effective. Members of such teams do invariably have substantial experience leading and working with others, and they likely have learned many lessons over time about how to lead effectively—and yet those effective practices seldom are what emerges naturally when a new group convenes. Rather, whatever behavior the team tolerates becomes part of the rules of engagement. In the absence of formal team norms, members each assume their own code of conduct, which typically begins a descent into what I call lowest-common-denominator behavior. If one member is late to a meeting and is not confronted—a likely scenario in a team of peers—then the new norm is that being late once is acceptable. Inevitably, another member tests the boundaries and is late to two meetings and also is not confronted. And now the norm is that being late to *two* meetings is acceptable. How long before lateness is itself the norm?

The example above is relatively overt and addressable. More common and less tractable is a tacit norm in which members keep to themselves whatever reservations they have about the direction of group decisions—and conserve, unspoken, their right to act against the agreements of the group.

Yet for all the difficulty poor emergent norms cause leadership teams, members often are hesitant to create formal rules and hold each other accountable to them. It may feel uncomfortable or may be experienced as a violation of autonomy for the individuals involved.

Condition 3: Create an Enabling Structure for the Team

As seen in Figure 4.2, outstanding leadership teams—those that accomplish their purposes and grow in capacity over time—work

Figure 4.2. Outstanding Leadership Teams Have Enabling Structures

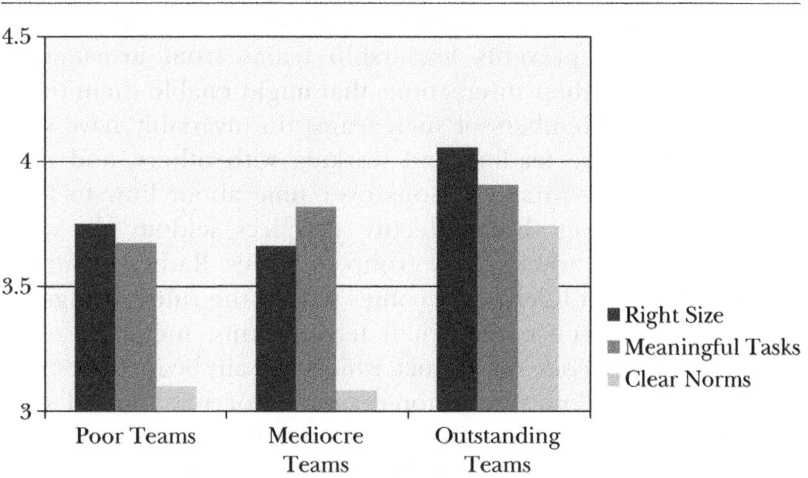

on meaningful tasks, are small and well-bounded, and, above all, have clearly specified norms of conduct. Poor teams—those that meet none of their constituencies needs and develop no capacity over time—suffer from trivial tasks, are overlarge and underbounded, and, above all, have no explicit ground rules about how they work together.

What is involved in creating enabling structures for leadership teams whose members come from different institutions? We find two key activities to be especially useful to creating an enabling structure for such teams: (1) paying careful attention to how agendas are crafted for the team's work and (2) designing a facilitated and iterative process of establishing explicit ground rules for the team's collaborative work.

Crafting Agendas Focused on Meaningful, Interdependent Activities

Leading a team of leaders requires that someone pay careful attention to the tasks members do in their work together, to prevent an unintended downward slide to mere information sharing or diversions into long discussions about trivial matters. Edmondson, Roberto, and Watkins (2001) point out that there is no single or fixed task list for leadership teams, given the shifting nature of work they perform. What is required, these authors emphasize, is continuous attention to task demands and team process needs as they evolve over time. Special attention is warranted when a team is choosing an initial collaborative task, as it has strong influence on trust that is built, the team's sense of efficacy that it can handle the challenges and conflicts that arise, and the way the processes of the group will evolve over time (Gerencser, Kelly, Napolitano, & Van Lee, 2008; Hemmati, Dodds, Enayati, & McHarry, 2002).

Our observations of leadership teams suggest that having a single individual hold responsibility for the agenda, although that role can rotate over time, helps create genuine interdependence and meaningful collaborative work when the group convenes. Absent explicit attention by one person, a team as a whole typically generates a long list of small items, each of which is relevant mainly for only one or two leaders at the table—which results in predictable negative consequences for member attention and effort. By contrast, having one individual thinking about the strategic work of the group and creating a short list of key decisions or activities that require robust discussion and coherent action enhances the level of commitment exhibited by team members and their willingness to seek solutions that integrate multiple interests. Keeping the work both meaningful and interdependent requires selecting team tasks carefully each time the team convenes. It is a function fulfilled repeatedly rather than once in the team's lifetime.

Put Constructive Norms in Place from the Beginning, and Revisit Them over Time

We have observed that establishing effective team norms is an iterative process. Often, a leadership team needs to begin with extremely basic rules in order to get anywhere at all as a team: do not interrupt others, elicit others' views in the discussion, put cell phones away, show up on time. But the norms necessary to enable a leadership group to address complex challenges for their constituencies are often considerably more nuanced. All the outstanding teams we have studied arrived at a set of norms tailored to the unique challenges the team faced, and what they learned was most needed to enable their particular work. Excellent norms tended to be clear, few in number, and behaviorally specific.

There are, nonetheless, a handful of widely shared norms that we have seen across many effective leadership teams. These include making individual leaders' institutional concerns *discussable* in the team. A norm that advocates speaking and acting as if one is *only* considering the collective outcome can have perverse effects. In the absence of explicit discussion of institutional interests, other team members are likely to assume that a position taken by one individual is really intended to promote the interests of that leader's own constituency. They expend considerable energy trying to figure out just what the hidden agendas are. By inviting members to make their institutional concerns explicit, those concerns become part of what the team can deal with in its choices and actions.

Other norms we have seen commonly emerge to support the work of leadership teams include reliable attendance at meetings (no sending delegates to fuzz the team boundaries); if a decision or event affects more than one entity represented around the table, put it on the table for the team to deal with; if you disagree, say so at the time; consensus is the ideal decision rule, or at the very least agreement among members to test out a course of action and revisit it together; and what members say and agree when in private as a team is what members will say and do outside the team.

Putting effective norms in place for a team is, as noted, an iterative process. The more sophisticated ground rules described above come about not by natural emergence over time, nor by explicit statements at the beginning of a team's life. Rather, they come about because the team has (usually via the intervention of a skilled facilitator) engaged in active reflection during a natural pause in their efforts, about what is getting in the way of their being more effective together. Active and deliberate reflection on their own experiences as a team is the primary source of insight and motivation for leaders to develop norms of conduct that are meaningful to them, constructive for their work, and likely to be taken up and enforced by the team as a whole.

Conclusion

We have seen that the natural setup of leadership teams, as well as their emergent processes, can undermine their ability to meet the needs of their constituencies and grow in capacity over time. I have argued that leadership team effectiveness requires identifying the systemic conditions that create obstacles to leadership team effectiveness and then creating design features that elicit and reinforce effective collaboration over time. Consistent with this kind of systems perspective, I want to conclude by underscoring two overarching lessons about creating conditions for the effectiveness of leadership teams, especially multi-stakeholder leadership teams. These two lessons are (1) pay attention to beginnings and (2) treat natural breakpoints in the work as opportunities for relaunch.

Beginnings

When in the life of a team do leaders' choices have the most possible impact on the quality of the team's accomplishments? The three conditions underscored in this chapter—compelling purpose, the right people, enabling structures—all are best put in place right from the beginning of the life of a group. Groups, like all complex systems, get on powerfully over-determined trajectories, for better or for worse. It is considerably easier to establish a leadership team onto a positive trajectory than to attempt in real time to correct a downward course. Indeed, Hackman (2011) estimates that about 60 percent of the variance in team effectiveness is influenced by the quality of *prework* (identifying the right people, thinking through purposes) done before the team even exists, and another 30 percent is influenced by the quality of the team's *launch.* If that estimate is right, then paying exquisite attention to the up-front processes of considering different potential team members, engaging the team in well-designed processes for articulating their own aspirations, and putting structures in place to get a leadership team off to a well-executed start are well worth the time and energy required.

Relaunch

Nevertheless, leadership teams face chronic patterns of team membership change, team dissolution, shifts in the major tasks they undertake, all creating moments when the original team, however well-launched, must be revisited. In the case of multi-stakeholder leadership teams, team membership can change with the cycle of elections, with turnover in institutional leadership teams, with the changing relevance of particular institutions to the collaborative work being undertaken by the team. Moreover, as community challenges shift, the people and resources best suited to tackle those problems may call for a reconfiguration of the key leaders engaged in addressing them.

Each time that happens, a leadership team can usefully be restructured and relaunched all over again. Because of the impact of beginnings, these moments of change can be real opportunities to enhance the effectiveness of collaborative leadership teams, providing the moment for a powerful reshaping of the team onto an increasingly positive trajectory over time.

References and Further Reading

Ancona, D., & Nadler, D.A. (1989, Fall). Top hats and executive tales: Designing the senior team. *Sloan Management Review*, pp. 19–29.

Bennis, W. (1997, Winter). The secret of great groups. *Leader to leader.*

Berg, D.N. (2005). Senior executive teams: Not what you think. *Consulting Psychology Journal, 57*, 107–117.

Edmondson, A., Roberto, M., & Watkins, M. (2001). Negotiating asymmetry: A model of top management team effectiveness. Working paper, Harvard Business School.

Ganz, M., & Wageman, R. (2008). Leadership development in a civic organization: Multi-level influences on effectiveness. Working Paper, Harvard Kennedy School of Government.

Gerencser, M., Kelly, C., Napolitano, F., & Van Lee, R. (2008). *Megacommunities.* New York: Palgrave MacMillan.

Glynn, M.A., & Dejordy, R. (2010). Leadership through an organization behavior lens: A look at the last half-century of research. In N. Nohria & R. Khurana (Eds.), *Handbook of leadership theory and practice* (pp. 119–157). Boston: Harvard Business School Press.

Hackman, J.R. (1994). Trip wires in designing and leading work groups. *The Occupational Psychologist, 2*, 3–8.

Hackman, J.R. (2002). *Leading teams: Setting the stage for great performances.* Boston: Harvard Business School Press.

Hackman, J.R. (2011). *Collaborative intelligence: Using teams to solve hard problems.* San Francisco: Berrett-Koehler.

Hambrick, D.C. (1997). Corporate coherence and the top management team. In D.C. Hambrick, D.A. Nadler, & M.L. Tushman (Eds.), *Navigating change: How CEOs, top teams, and boards steer transformation.* Boston: Harvard Business School Press.

Hambrick, D.C. (2000). Fragmentation and other problems CEOs have with their top management teams. *California Management Review, 37*, 110–131.

Hambrick, D.C. (2007). Upper echelons theory: An update. *Academy of Management Review, 32*, 334–343.

Hambrick, D.C., & D'Aveni, R.A. (1996). Top team deterioration as part of the downward spiral of large corporate bankruptcies. *Management Science, 38*, 1445–1466.

Hemmati, M., Dodds, F., Enayati, J., & McHarry, J. (2002). *Multi-stakeholder processes for governance and sustainability: Beyond deadlock and conflict.* London: Earthscan.

Katzenbach, J.R. (1997). *Teams at the top: Unleashing the potential of both teams and individual leaders.* Boston: Harvard Business School Press.

Leonard, H.B., & Howitt, A.M. (2006). Katrina as prelude: Preparing for and responding to Katrina-class disturbances in the United States. *Journal of Homeland Security and Emergency Management*, pp. 1–20.

Lewicki, R.J., Saunders, D.M., & Minton, J.W. (1999). *Negotiation.* New York: McGraw-Hill.

Li, J.T., & Hambrick, D.C. (2005). Factional groups: A new vantage on demographic faultlines, conflict and disintegration in work teams. *Academy of Management Journal, 48*, 794–813.

Mendonca, D., Beroggi, G.E.G., & Wallace, W. (2001). Decision support for improvisation during emergency response operations. *International Journal of Emergency Management, 1*(1), 30–38.

Podolny, J.M., Khurana, R., & Besharov, M.L. (2010). Revisiting the meaning of leadership. In N. Nohria & R. Khurana (Eds.), *The handbook of leadership theory and practice.* Boston: Harvard Business School Press.

Sayles, L.R., & Chandler, M.K. (2009). *Managing large systems: Organizations for the future.* New York: Harper & Row.

Smith, K.G., Smith, K.A., Olian, J.D., & Sims, H.P., Jr. (1994). Top management team demography and process: The role of social integration and communication. *Administrative Science Quarterly, 39*, 412–438.

Wageman, R., Gardner, H., & Mortensen, M. (2012). The changing ecology of teams: New directions for teams research. *Journal of Organizational Behavior, 10*, 1–15.

Wageman, R., & Hackman, J.R. (2009). What makes teams of leaders leadable? In N. Nohria & R. Khurana (Eds.), *Advancing leadership.* Boston: Harvard Business School Press.

Wageman, R., Hackman, J.R., & Lehman, E.V. (2005). The team diagnostic survey: Development of an instrument. *Journal of Applied Behavioral Science, 41,* 373–398.

Wageman, R., Nunes, D.A., Burruss, J.A., & Hackman, J.R. (2008). *Senior leadership teams: What it takes to make them great.* Boston: Harvard Business School Press.

West, M.A., Borilla, C.S., Dawson, J.F., Brodbeck, F., Shapiro, D.A., & Haward, B. (2003). Leadership clarity and team innovation in health care. *The Leadership Quarterly, 14,* 393–410.

Zaccaro, S.J., & Banks, D. (2001). Leadership, vision, and organizational effectiveness. In S.J. Zaccaro & R.J. Klimoski (Eds.), *The nature of organizational leadership.* San Francisco: Jossey-Bass.

Zaccaro, S.J., Rittman, A.L., & Marks, M.A. (2001). Team leadership. *The Leadership Quarterly, 12*(4), 451–483.

CHAPTER FIVE

Developing High-Impact Teams to Lead Strategic Change

Kate Beatty
and Roland B. Smith
Center for Creative Leadership

How are strategic objectives best achieved? How do organizations navigate challenges in a way that meets short-term objectives, while also building future capabilities? How do leaders enhance individual and collective capabilities to execute on their strategy?

True, high-impact teams can be the lever organizations need to deliver on these challenges. In this chapter, we will define what is meant by high-impact teams, the types of strategic changes they are suited to address, and how effective leadership can be developed to help them reach their potential.

Much of the information in this chapter is based on the work of the Center for Creative Leadership (CCL), a top-ranked, global provider of executive education that accelerates strategy and business results by leveraging the leadership potential of individuals and organizations. The mission of the Center is to advance the understanding, practice, and development of leadership for the benefit of society worldwide. Founded in 1970 as a nonprofit educational institution focused exclusively on leadership education and research, CCL annually serves more than twenty thousand individuals from more than two thousand organizations globally—including more than eighty of the Fortune 100 and key organizations in the public, nonprofit, and education sectors. CCL conducts research on an ongoing basis and shares it broadly through papers, conferences, and publications. CCL also uses research to build its portfolio of courses, products, services, and publications. Elements of this chapter are based on research and content related to two of CCL's open enrollment programs (Leading Teams for Impact and Leading High-Performance Teams), as well as on our customized work with functional and cross-functional teams.

Leadership of High-Impact Teams

As we look at high-impact teams, we are specifically interested in group performance and collaborative decision making. We also are interested in team leaders, collective team leadership, and the role both play in generating process gains and process losses. We have worked with a variety of teams formed to achieve some identified outcome, ranging from completion of a specific task through leading large-scale, strategic change. These strategic leadership teams, in particular, quickly realize that the success of their efforts is impacted by dynamics within and across teams, as well as variables inside and outside the enterprise.

In all of these cases, our definition of a high-impact team includes three key elements (Ginnett, 1996; Morgenson, DuRue, & Karam, 2010):

- High-impact teams produce results that go above and beyond what is required by their stakeholders.
- Team members are satisfied with the experience and feel committed to the team and fellow members, such that they are interested in working again with each other.
- Team members learn over time; that is, their efficiency and performance on a *future* task is better than their performance on a *current* task as they learn to adapt to changing conditions.

In today's world, where technology creates unprecedented access to vast volumes of information and global interconnectedness is the norm, teams have new challenges if they are to reach the level of high-impact performance. They are dealing with very complex business issues, so success is not guaranteed. They are often dispersed across the globe and must deal with time zone and cultural differences, as well as with the inherent challenges in working virtually versus face to face. Finally, while advances in technology provide for ready access to information, technology itself does not make sense of the information. That task, of course, is the work of the team.

As the world becomes more complex, so does the role of leadership to help the team succeed. No longer can one leader have all the answers, nor does one leader typically have all the skills and strengths the team needs to be successful. More and more, the work of creating direction, alignment, and commitment requires leadership to be shared by members of the collective (Van Velsor, McCauley, & Ruderman, 2010). The concept of collective leadership is not new to the world of team leadership. In fact, research on the related topic of shared leadership dates back to the 1960s (Bowers, Seashore, & Marrow, 1967). Yet in our experience, teams rarely leverage the power of collective leadership to its fullest.

Most research has traditionally focused on team roles, internal processes, and the individual functions of team leaders. A recent review of literature (Morgenson, DeRue, & Karam, 2010) provides evidence of this historical focus. (See Table 5.1, Team Leadership Functions.)

Going forward, we advocate for a new definition of team leadership that is supported by research and practice. This definition must focus more broadly on the collective capacity of the team to produce impact by creating direction, alignment, and commitment across an organization. (See Figure 5.1.) In this collective capacity, team members lock arms together and share the responsibility for leadership. Similarly, the team is proactive about its place within the system of the organization, mindful of its connections to other teams, critical work groups, and functions, and key influencers within the enterprise. The role of the individual team leader does not go away. In fact, due to the power inherent in his or her role, the leader must intentionally create the conditions for the team to develop and enact this collective capacity.

Table 5.1 Team Leadership Functions

Leadership Function
Transition phase
Compose team
Define mission
Establish expectations and goals
Structure and plan
Train and develop team
Sensemaking
Provide feedback
Action phase
Monitor team
Manage team boundaries
Challenge team
Perform team task
Solve problems
Provide resources
Encourage team self-management
Support social climate

Source: Morgenson, DeRue, and Karam, 2010, p. 10.

The Nature of Strategic Change

Organizations experience change almost constantly, and those changes take on a variety of forms. For example, an organization might change suppliers, bring in a new leader, or need to adapt to new regulations. Several researchers and practitioners (such as Kirton, 1989; Musselwhite & Jones, 2004) have attempted to codify different types of change and help us understand how to lead and manage ourselves and others through these experiences. While many different ways of describing change exist, for purposes of this chapter we will focus on change that is *strategic* in nature. We define *strategy* as the deliberate pattern of choices an organization makes for long-term success that is reflected in activities and investments throughout the organization. Different strategies will be reflected by different patterns. *Strategic change, therefore, is a shift in the connected and interdependent patterns of activities and investments an organization makes to achieve success.*

Office Depot provides a helpful example of strategic change (Peters, 2011). Kevin Peters assumed the role of president for

Figure 5.1. Views of Teams and Team Leadership

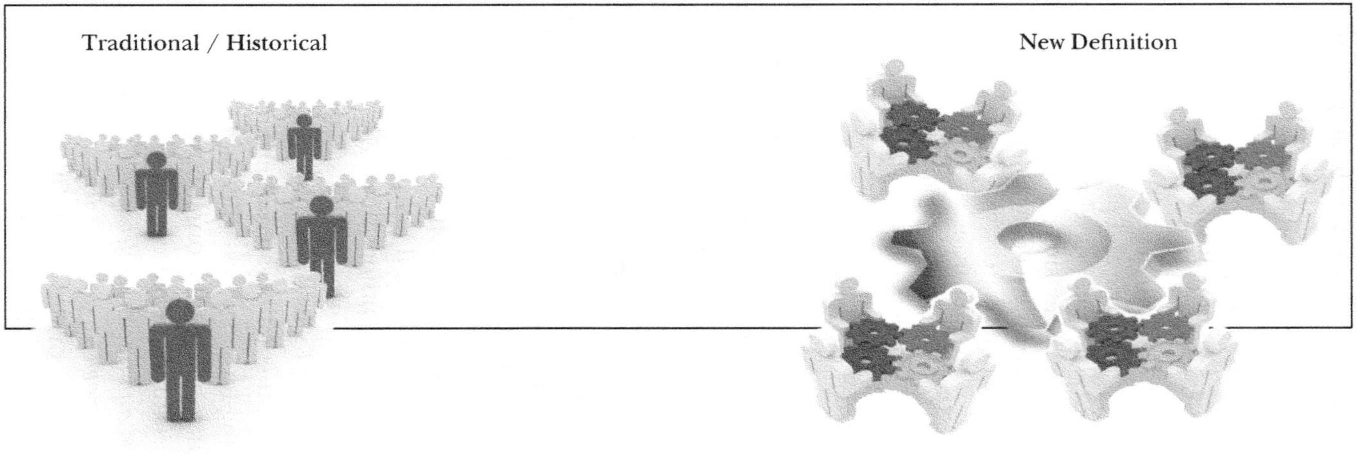

Traditional / Historical

New Definition

North America in 2010 during a significant economic downturn. Sales were falling, and the decline was greater for Office Depot than for its competitors. Peters sought to understand why. He found patterns in the organization emphasizing things that did not play a significant role in driving customer purchases, for example, keeping the shelves stocked and the stores clean. What was missing was a clear focus on the customer experience. So he sought to shift patterns and make Office Depot more customer-centric.

There are several characteristics of strategic change, whether it happens at Office Depot or another organization.

Strategic Change Is Broad in Scope

Strategic change has impact and connections that cross organizational units and boundaries. This is part of why "pattern" is so important to strategy and strategic change. Organizations create sustainable competitive advantage by instilling an interconnected web of activities that touches different parts of the business. This kind of complexity is difficult for competitors to replicate.

At Office Depot, for example, the new pattern of customer experience has tentacles into multiple parts of the business. It started with store planning. Stores were very large and presented obstacles for shopping. The company has reduced store size and designed a more convenient layout focused on the most popular products. Associates are being retrained to focus on customer service (for example, learning to ask more open-ended questions in conversations with customers) and on creating efficiencies in other activities that are necessary but not fundamental drivers for sales (such as restocking). The company is beginning to offer additional services desired by customers, such as copying, shipping, and computer repair. The thread tying these initiatives together is a focus on creating a convenient customer experience.

Strategic Change Takes Time

Strategic change does not happen overnight. Most organizational patterns have existed for some time and have become well-honed. Shifting to new activities, beliefs, and practices is no small order. Kevin Peters says of his Office Depot experience: "You can't drive changes like this overnight. Our business has been around since 1986, and that's a long time for employees and customers to establish expectations and behaviors. These changes won't be completed in the next month or the next quarter—maybe not even in the next year" (p. 50).

With a time horizon on the order of years, versus months or quarters, some team members may struggle with strategic change. They are accustomed to seeing the results of their efforts in a fairly short period of time. In particular, those individuals focused on operations and efficiency may struggle with this aspect of leading strategic change (Hughes & Beatty, 2005).

Strategic Change Requires Management of Multiple Dimensions

Team members often aspire to know all that will happen and will need to take place to achieve strategic change. But with the level of complexity and breadth associated with this type of change, learning is required along the way. It can only happen if team members are paying attention to and managing activities and events in multiple dimensions:

- *Task level:* Are the specific steps we are undertaking being completed as intended? Are they having the intended impact?
- *Tactical level:* Are clusters of related tasks or events in sync with each other? Is coordination among team members happening as expected?
- *Transformational level:* Are the team's activities connected with the activities of other teams as needed in order to align various elements of the strategy across the business?

Team members must be able to move flexibly and with agility across these dimensions to ensure strategic change takes place. It would be nice to stay at the transformational level. But if the strategic intent is not well understood, then alignment across tactics and tasks cannot happen. Strategic team members need to connect data and lessons in one dimension to what is happening in other dimensions. The interplay among the dimensions is fertile ground for critical learning.

Strategic Change Requires Systematic and Contextual Understanding of the Challenges

No strategic challenge sits in isolation. In fact, we have found that strategic challenges usually consist of several integrated and linked challenges. When CCL asked senior leaders attending its Leadership at the Peak program to describe their challenges (Smith & Campbell, 2010), four challenges topped the list: the ability to lead and influence across multiple groups and constituencies; strategic issues; talent management; and business operations and organizational performance. Most, though, described these challenges as multifaceted. In other words, you would not be able to address a particular challenge effectively without addressing other links in the challenge chain.

For example, the challenge described by one senior executive is shown in Figure 5.2. This particular challenge is made up of several smaller challenges: *convincing* other leaders to develop and own strategies, *instilling* customer orientation, *instilling* positive public perceptions, and *generating* measurable outcomes. While there are several different components, they all need to be addressed together to achieve success.

Given the complexity of strategic challenges and the need to lead and influence effectively across multiple boundaries, it becomes even clearer that teams are a necessary leadership vehicle. The difficulty is that teams often are given just one part of the challenge chain. To produce high impact, they must use

Figure 5.2. Example of a Challenge Chain

Strategic Issues
"Convincing [other leaders to develop and own strategies] that [instill customer orientation and positive public perceptions] through [measurable outcomes.]"
Business Operations and Performance
Leading Across Multiple Groups

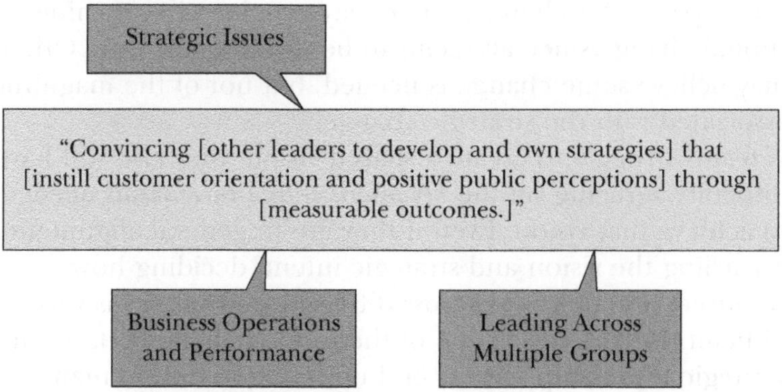

contextual mapping and boundary-spanning strategies to understand and address the underlying complexity. Leaders must master connecting and bridging strategies in order to guide their team through vertical, horizontal, stakeholder, demographic, and geographic boundaries (Ernst & Chrobot-Mason, 2011).

Challenges Teams Experience in Leading Strategic Change

No doubt, it is difficult to lead strategic change. In fact, studies show 66 to 75 percent of major change efforts fail to reach their intended outcomes (Beer, 2001; Cameron & Quinn, 1999). We believe strategic leadership teams play a critical role in leading change efforts that succeed. Teams bring a diversity of perspectives that is critical to assessing the complex factors involved in the change; deciding how to move forward; and aligning implementation efforts within the network of the organization.

Unfortunately, few teams are effective at exerting strategic leadership. In our work with teams, we are intrigued by how often there is a lack of shared vision of the future, and even more surprised by how often team members fail to realize different opinions exist. They seldom take time to dig beneath the surface of vision statements and understand whether everyone thinks similarly about the implications for the organization. As a result, team members face a number of challenges that keep them from enacting their leadership role effectively:

- They may not agree on the *importance or urgency* associated with a particular change. Some may wonder why anything should change since all seems to be working just fine. Others may believe some change is needed, but not of the magnitude associated with the strategic change.
- If teams struggle to create a shared vision, they also will have difficulty agreeing on the *key priorities and investments* needed to achieve that vision. Even if they are in general alignment regarding the vision and strategic intent, deciding how resources are allocated across different possibilities is very difficult. In fact, this is one of the most challenging tasks of strategic leadership. Teams end up trying to do too many

things because they cannot arrive at the difficult decisions needed to focus their investments. Data collected by CCL from more than twelve thousand strategic leadership team members over the past twelve years tells the story. In a ranking of team strengths, the ability to be discriminating about what the team *will and will not do* is consistently at the bottom of the list.

- In some cases, individuals on the team may experience a *threat to their own position, resources, or other personal interests.* Perhaps the change involves a shift in power or investment away from an individual's functional area. Or the change is initiated by another team member who is receiving a lot of attention and represents competition for the next promotion or bonus. It becomes very difficult to subjugate personal needs to the needs of the organization.
- Finally, many teams find it difficult to complement a short-term focus on results with a *longer-term focus on building capabilities* both for themselves and the organization. They have an established pattern of working to accomplish what needs to be done today. Large changes, such as a shift to a more collective form of team leadership, are easily ignored, especially when they cannot be broken down into manageable and knowable steps. In CCL's survey of team strengths, striking an appropriate balance between near-term and long-term needs was ranked third from the bottom.

The lowest-rated item from CCL's survey of the strategic leadership capabilities of teams is the ability to focus energy only on productive activities so that time is not wasted. It is ironic that many teams resist the shift to a more collective form of leadership because they appreciate what appears to be focus and productivity coming from a single leadership voice—yet they consistently report a lack of productivity and focus.

Enhancing the Team's Ability to Lead Strategic Change: Tools for Leaders and Practitioners

To enhance the ability to create direction, alignment, and commitment in the midst of strategic change, team members must realize they are part of a network of patterns embedded in the organization—and that they themselves are impacted by these patterns. So they need to change themselves as they change the rest of the organization. Unfortunately, this is not an automatic realization. Senior leadership teams in particular may think everyone *else* needs to do something differently. They have done the work to set the strategic direction; now others should fall in line and implement it.

As others acknowledge, react to, and begin to experiment with the changes, they may find areas where the planning needs to take shape (Musselwhite & Jones, 2004). If senior leaders want ownership and buy-in, they must flex with these changes. But even more fundamentally, when the culture of the organization is at odds with the requirements of the change (as it often is), beliefs and practices must change. This requires the senior team itself to make significant changes in how it creates direction, alignment, and commitment (McGuire & Rhodes, 2009).

Teams must make three critical shifts to lead strategic change effectively. Team members and leaders will need to share leadership so that it is a collective process, versus a role held by an individual on the team, and then leverage the collective leadership to create direction, alignment, and commitment throughout the organization. The proverbial ball is in the team leader's court first. Specifically, the team leader must begin to share power and leadership (Navigator), encourage the team to see its place in the system and influence accordingly (Interconnected Influencer and Contextual Cartographer), and build the team's ability to span boundaries (Engineer). Each is described in greater detail below.

Shift 1: Collective as Leader (Navigator and Crew)

Vance Tang, former president and CEO of Kone Americas, tells the story of the transformation of his organization (Tang & Moore, 2009). Kone is an industrial engineering company of around 34,000 employees, with sales of about five billion Euros worldwide. It specializes in people-moving systems—elevators and escalators—and has a presence in fifty countries. The North American organization represents about one-quarter of the company.

When Tang took over, the company was doing fine, but there were several opportunities to achieve more. For example, there were many silos limiting cross-group interactions and collaboration. A hub-and-spoke leadership model maximized efficiency and operational excellence, but did not foster new ideas or a customer focus. The company also was not attracting a diverse base of top-notch talent.

Tang and Chuck Moore, his senior VP of human resources, began conversations with each other and with CCL regarding how they could enhance and develop leadership to create energy, excitement, collaboration, and customer focus. At first, they thought sending people to leadership programs would do the trick. But as the discussions ensued, they came to realize much more was needed. In an interview, Moore commented, "I realized at that point in time that we're not talking about an HR program. We're not talking about HR owning the program. We're talking about shared leadership. And for this to be successful, leadership—at the senior level—has to own it and has to participate as we go forward, to design and to develop and to deliver this experience and development opportunity with our people" (Tang & Moore, 2009).

Similarly, Tang said, "I think it was not just a mindset change, but it was a transformational moment for us to recognize that this was a much harder problem. . . . This is a really more complicated journey that required Chuck and me to be very collaborative and very interdependent without even knowing those words. And as we gained from each other's perspectives, we began to share that same experience across our team. And it really started the journey—the culture journey, the leader journey we had under way."

Teams form habits, just as people do. These habits impact many different areas, including the ways teams create or discourage direction, alignment, and commitment. For example, a team may have habits around decision making that look like this: the leader presents the situation, people share their perspectives while the leader listens, and the leader makes the decision. Perhaps, though, the decision is frequently consistent with one team member's point of view—someone who has worked closely with the leader for a long time. So while others are willing to share their perspectives, they don't do so in a committed way. They believe the leader will just go along with this other individual. They also believe the two talk outside of meetings and align before discussing issues with the group. So once a decision is made, people don't feel a commitment to it or embrace it with enthusiasm. Habits are connected to the beliefs they hold regarding how decisions are made. The logic is this: the way teams enact leadership cannot change until habits change. And habits won't change until beliefs and practices change (McGuire & Rhodes, 2009).

One important area where beliefs, practices, and habits must change has to do with where the responsibility for leadership lies. This shift is particularly challenging, because it involves how the team approaches every situation. Consciously or not, members ask themselves:

- Am I "on point" or is someone else taking responsibility at this meeting?
- Who is the decision-maker here?
- Should I step in now and try to help, or will that undercut someone else's authority?

Ultimately, the team leader and team members have to view themselves as responsible for leadership, even when someone else is designated as the formal leader. This is one of the many ways in which teams must shift their "inside out" practices to complement the "outside in" shift initiated during times of change.

How do teams go about making this shift to a collective leadership mindset? CCL's research shows two things differentiate teams that make an effective transition from those that don't (McGuire & Rhodes, 2009): shifting roles/identity and displaying risk and vulnerability in a way that invites others into the change. Each is described below, along with tools for practitioners and leaders who seek to make this shift.

Role/Identity Shift

Role shift in the context of collective leadership means far more than a change on an organization chart. One's *role experience* is likely influenced by upbringing, by traditions about how authority is granted via organization hierarchies, and by geographic culture, organizational culture, personal values, and so forth. Role experience includes all implicit and explicit expectations about roles and responsibilities. These expectations must be held out for examination, with questions asked about how assumptions and beliefs are driving behavior and whether they are holding the team back from collective leadership.

It is one thing for a team member to see the opportunity missed by not "stepping up" to own more responsibility for the work of the team. It is another for a team leader to feel comfortable letting go of the reins. This individual likely wakes up thinking about how to move work along and keep team members aligned and committed. Plus, the team leader is the individual the rest of the organization looks to and holds accountable for team performance. The leader will feel a greater sense of responsibility and will undoubtedly pressure the team to succeed in a markedly different way than other team members.

We have seen team leaders be very effective in shifting their identity from "leader," or *the* person responsible for the outcome of the team, to *guide,* or the person who educates and models the way for the team as they explore unchartered territory (McGuire & Rhodes, 2009). Guides are naturally curious about what comes next, reflective as they pass through new terrain to capture lessons of experience, and ready to use those lessons to prepare their team for what is to come. Similarly, the term "guide" conveys the sense that the person is here *for* others, helping them to explore and learn as they go. While "leader" can convey that sense, it also carries meaning that others are here *for* the leader, to carry out his or her wishes.

In working with teams and their leaders, we will often ask, "If your leader is to be your guide, what should your leader continue to do, stop doing, and start doing?" Similarly, we ask, "What should you do more of, less of, or stop doing?" These types of questions result in a discussion that can begin to shift the dynamic regarding an individual's identity within the team.

Teams that successfully make the shift in role and identity do so through honest and open dialogue. A tool that can help to get that conversation started is shown in Exhibit 5.1.

Exhibit 5.1. Team Leadership Responsibility Tool

Instructions: The purpose of the tool is to help team members diagnose, discuss, and develop their identity regarding where the responsibility lies for leadership of the team. The team works together to complete the tool. Give all team members copies of the tool and ask them to decide where on the continuum of responsibility the team is functioning now. Each person should mark this with an "X." This describes the team members' current beliefs, practices, and identity regarding the leadership role. Next, ask each member to decide where on the continuum the team will be required to be in order to lead strategic change. Have each person mark this with a "Y." Each member should then share their assessment, and their rationale. Finally, discuss the differing options, the gaps between current and future, and how the team can move forward.

Members who rate team functioning toward the *left* generally view all direction and decisions as being made by the team leader, with minimal to no group input. Individual and group objectives, as well as how to achieve those objectives and how to coordinate among members, are all determined by the leader. Compliance of team members, rather than commitment, is the goal. Work flow is designed by the team leader, and team meetings typically are for information distribution purposes only. While observing the team, it would be clear who the team leader is, as he or she would direct all communication flow and would be the sole person making decisions.

Members who rate team functioning toward the *right* generally view vision and strategic direction setting as a full team responsibility. Decisions around implementation are also shared, with commitment (versus compliance) to those decisions as the goal. They are dedicated to a team identity that is more than the separate independent efforts of each individual's area. The team is also committed to and intentional about learning; therefore feedback and honest dialogue are free-flowing. While observing the team, it would be difficult to know who the team leader is, as each member is fully participating and contributing to progress and decisions.

Most teams fall somewhere between these two ends of the continuum: where is your team now (X), and where does the team need to be to lead the strategic change in front of you (Y)?

Responsibility of Leader **Everyone's Responsibility**

Risk and Vulnerability as Invitation

Those who value a hierarchical form of leadership, achievement, and competence are likely to feel they must present themselves as "knowing" and competent. But in times of strategic change, no one has the right answers all the time. Team leaders and members must be open to taking risks and experiencing vulnerability.

Vance Tang of Kone described his feelings beautifully (Tang & Moore, 2009): "Every time that we got together, I still had that anxiety because I didn't have a clear path that I could share back with my colleagues and my peers of how we were going to achieve this. And we all had to learn, whether it was me or the senior leadership team, how to deal with that ambiguity. And that was a huge step for us because we were very operationally focused. We know how to get things done. This was different. We had to discover, collectively, together, interdependently. That was a challenge. That was a real challenge."

A sense of ambiguity leaves people feeling at risk and vulnerable. What happens then is critical. Do team members quickly push back into the areas where they feel comfortable—where someone has the answer and can move forward? If so, and if it is allowed, they quickly learn that people aren't serious about moving to collective leadership. It is good talk, but there is no real commitment to making it happen. Alternatively, in these moments when teams and their members are on the edge of vulnerability, they can choose to build trust with each other, learn together, inquire, pull new perspectives out on the table, build on each other's ideas and thoughts, and treat mistakes as learning opportunities versus failures. The leader or guide can play a critical role during these times by acknowledging uncomfortable feelings and urging everyone to stay with it.

When a team leader demonstrates risk and vulnerability, it can have a tremendous, sea-changing effect. There is an opportunity to invite others into the process and share the responsibilities of leadership. People enjoy being invited into problem solving, and they are appreciative of the opportunity to bring their strengths to the work at hand. This type of public learning can break through the power dynamics that tend to keep things in the organization as they are—whether or not change is desired. It signals to the rest of the organization that change is necessary,

Exhibit 5.2. Storytelling as Invitation

Leaders can send powerful messages through the stories that they tell. Stories engage different parts of our brains, including the areas associated with images and emotion. In this way, they can convey information that typical conversational language does not convey and enhance understanding of the speaker's message. Additionally, people remember stories much better than they remember statements. When leaders are attempting to shift the power dynamics in teams, they need to gain the attention of team members and let them know they are serious about this invitation. Stories can facilitate this process.

Develop a story to share with your team, using the following prompts:

Think of a time when you did not know the best course of action or how to proceed in a situation:

- What was the situation, and what challenge or challenges did you need to overcome?
- What was new or different about this situation for you?
- How did you come to realize you needed the help of others?
- What did you do to enlist their help?
- What did they do that was helpful to you?
- What was the result?
- How is the situation in your story similar to the situation you are facing with your team?
- What possibilities excite you if team members step up to assume more responsibility and engage in new and different ways?

help is needed, and everyone is in the development process together.

Storytelling can be a powerful tool in such situations (see Exhibit 5.2). The leader can describe what it was like to not know something and ask for help, and what happened next. It sets the stage for the team to know that it is okay to be vulnerable and that their contributions are needed to fill the gap where vulnerability is felt.

Shift 2: Interconnected Influence Agent (Influencer) and Contextual Cartographer

A team that shares the same vision and direction is aligned and committed to success and can accomplish amazing things for the organization. Football player and coach Knute Rockne once stated that a team in an ordinary frame of mind will do only ordinary things. In the proper emotional state, though, a team will do extraordinary things. Emotional state, or "group affect," includes mutual support, trust, and cooperation within the team, qualities determined by the members' influence behaviors.

Team leaders should encourage the team to reflect on these questions:

- Which influence tactics does your team use most frequently with each other? Which work?
- Which influence tactics does your team most frequently use with key populations across the extended organization? Which work?
- Which tactics does the team need to change in order to influence more effectively?

A team leader's ability to influence and align team members behind a shared vision and common goals is fundamental to group success. However, strengthening the team's ability to influence the larger organization is even more critical in strategic change—and more complex. It includes other relevant forms of influence besides proactive tactics, such as political and impression management tactics and how information is communicated and filtered to indirectly influence decisions made by others (Yukl, 2011). High-impact team leaders need to embrace their role as interconnected agents of influence and become competent with tools that allow their teams to study and map these areas. In this way, the team can learn where it fits within the broader network of the enterprise and how to plug into the organizational power grid—the web of relationships, information flow, communication patterns, and influence that *"gets things done"* within an organization (Cross, Parker, & Cross, 2004). This should not be the singular responsibility of the designated team leader, but a collective responsibility. The team must learn to map the energy reserves within the enterprise that can fuel strategic change.

The Role of Network Mapping

Strategic change is about altering the patterns of choices and information flow across the system to create new connections in the system and to enhance existing connections. Mapping is a helpful tool, providing a baseline metric to assess team influence and to highlight critical hubs of knowledge, influence, communication, and relationships. Maps help the team stay aligned, create a strategy to navigate complex and ambiguous environments, and ultimately achieve its objective. Through a network lens, teams manage at inflection points across the organization to align information flow and decisions with their strategic goals. In Figure 5.3, Cross, Ehrlich, Dawson, and Helferich (2008) share an example of two account teams—one underperforming and one high-performing. The high-performing team has enhanced information flow necessary to tackle strategic challenges.

Mapping can provide a practical approach for increasing team effectiveness impact. For example, CCL was asked to help an organization create high-impact client teams to drive more effective business development. The diagram at the top in Figure 5.4 is an initial mapping of one of the existing client teams. The four squares represent individual team members, while the arrows reflect who is sought out by whom for important information and expertise. As shown, one member of the team is disconnected—neither sought out for information and expertise nor seeking it from others.

To increase impact and effectiveness, the team looked beyond its internal mapping to examine how it is situated within the larger enterprise. By mapping the constellation of individual connections in the "expanded" network, the team leader, team, and enterprise have a baseline for success and a clear path forward. (See bottom half of Figure 5.4.) Key pockets of knowledge, as well as critical relationships and communication hubs, can now be leveraged effectively.

Finally, as shown in Table 5.2, Cross, Ehrlich, Dawson, and Helferich (2008) have identified six key network mapping questions that can contribute to team success. Teams answering these questions can quickly build their collective capability to accelerate

Figure 5.3. High-Performing and Low-Performing Team Information Flow

Underperforming Team

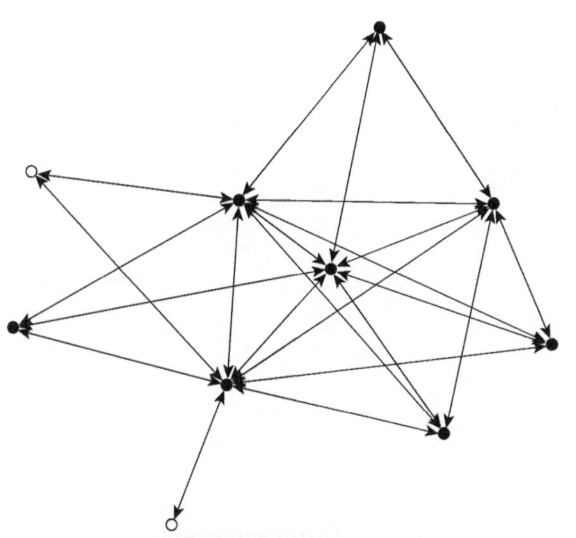

High-Performing Team

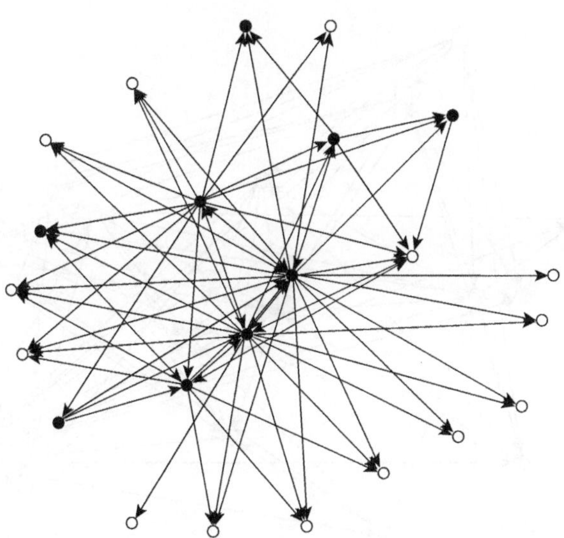

Source: Cross, Ehrlich, Dawson, and Helferich, 2008.

Figure 5.4. Creating a High-Impact Team for Business Development

Current Team Network

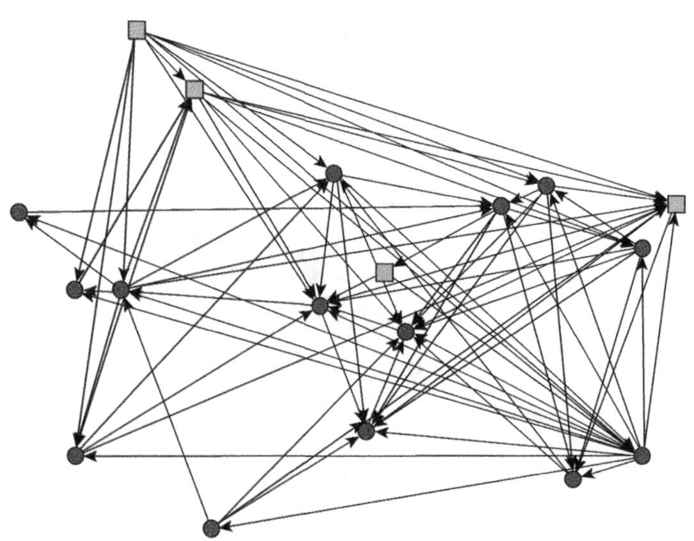

Table 5.2 The Changing Face of Teams

Team Levers	*Traditional View*	*Network View*
Are the right voices influencing team trajectory?	Leader as ultimate decision-maker and direction-setter. Process and content roles in team provide structure.	Decision making and direction setting influence shifts based on expertise. Leader and followers set climate for shifts in responsibility.
Is the team "appropriately" connected for the task at hand?	Information and decision-making networks either over-connected or hierarchical.	Information and decision-making networks are focused on an archetype for success based on point in process.
Has the team cultivated important external relationships?	Not heavily emphasized either to others within an organization or to experts outside an organization.	Heavily emphasized and targeted both within and outside organization to bring the best expertise to bear.
Are value-added collaborations occurring in the team network?	Principally just information and decision-making interactions.	A focus on value added interactions in terms of both performance and team members' engagement.
Do underlying relationship qualities yield effective collaboration?	Communication focus on joint commitment to goals, benevolence-based trust, and group process and harmony.	Information focus on awareness of expertise, timely accessibility, competence-based trust, and execution of commitments made to teammates.
What organizational factors are key to effective collaboration?	Matrix reporting structures, 360-degree performance feedback, team-based collaborative technologies, and flexible organizational affiliation.	Positive organizational network momentum, supported by consistent meaningful exposure to others' expertise, organization-wide collaborative technologies, and flexible workflow.

Source: Cross, Ehrlich, Dawson, and Helferich, 2008.

effectiveness and expand impact. By being more purposeful about mapping the network, they can navigate, create critical connections, and strengthen relationships.

A tool that can easily be utilized to expose teams to network mapping is shown in Exhibit 5.3. It represents a surface look the comprehensive process needed to capture the context in which the team operates—one that typically involves comprehensive surveys to define and map key stakeholders, senior executives, and vital knowledge centers.

Exhibit 5.3. Team Network Analysis

Instructions: List all key stakeholders of your team's project or accomplishments (those that are impacted by it; those who you need to rely on for successful implementation).

Complete the worksheet below. Assess each stakeholder or stakeholder group according to:

- Its power to accelerate or block your team's successful implementation
- Its alignment or commitment to your team's goals
- The extent of closeness in the relationship and trust between your team and the stakeholder

Map your stakeholders on a sheet of flip-chart paper.

1. Place stakeholders in relative distance from the team (greater distances indicate less alignment with the team's goals).
2. Draw the stakeholders' circle size based on your assessment of their power.
3. Attach stakeholders to your team's own circle with 1, 2, or 3 lines (indicates trust in relationship).
4. Attach stakeholders to each other with lines (indicates their relationships to each other).

Examine the map.

- What insights can you gain about stakeholder support for your team's goals?
- Where is key support missing?
- What strategies do you need to consider that will build stakeholder commitment?
- How will you accomplish this?

Team Social Network

Stakeholder	Assessed Power to Affect Your Project			Extent of Alignment of Your Goals vs. Their Goals			Strength of Your Relationship (Trust)		
	∘	○	◯	Close	Medium	Far	I	II	III
1. Example: SPONSOR		○			Medium			**II**	
2.									
3.									
4.									
5.									
6.									

Based on Cross, Parker, and Cross, 2004.

Shift 3: Boundary Spanning, Bridge Building (the Engineer)

High-impact teams are boundary spanners, connecting disparate parts of the enterprise to create direction, alignment, and commitment in service of strategic change. High-impact team leaders are engineers who create the infrastructure to encourage boundary spanning skills in all team members. Ernst and Chrobot-Mason (2011) discuss five types of boundaries teams need to address:

- *Vertical boundaries* across levels, rank, seniority, authority, power;
- *Horizontal boundaries* across functions, units, peers, expertise;
- *Stakeholder boundaries* between an organization and its interchange with external partners (alliances, value chains, customers/clients, shareholders, governments, communities, etc.);
- *Demographic boundaries* between diverse groups, including the full range of human diversity (from gender to race, from education to ideology); and
- *Geographic boundaries* across distance, locations, cultures, regions, markets.

Interestingly, the first step in collaborating more effectively is to clearly understand and manage boundaries (Figure 5.5). Two practices are creating safety (buffering) and fostering respect (reflecting). Once boundaries are managed, then teams can focus on forging common ground. This phase is critical in that it focuses on building trust (connecting) and developing community (mobilizing). The final phase is discovering new frontiers. This phase is important for driving sustainable strategic change and is where high-impact teams need to spend the majority of their time. They need to strengthen interdependence both inside and outside the team (weaving) and enable reinvention (transforming).

Teams and team leaders have successfully leveraged boundary spanning to achieve strategic change in many private, public, and nonprofit organizations (see Ernst and Chrobot-Mason, 2011). As teams apply the sequence of practices in Figure 5.5, they realize moving from Managing Boundaries to Discovering New Frontiers requires a shift from the leader to the collective as responsible for

Figure 5.5. Boundary-Spanning Strategies and Practices for High-Impact Teams

Strategy	Practices	Definition (with outcomes in italics)
1. Managing Boundaries *Taps into the power of differentiation and the need for distinctiveness, divergence, and uniqueness within groups.*	Buffering	Monitor and protect the flow of information and resources across groups to *define boundaries and create safety.*
	Reflecting	Represent distinct perspectives and facilitate knowledge-exchange across groups to *understand boundaries and foster respect.*
2. Forging Common Ground *Taps into the power of integration and the need for unity, convergence, and belonging across groups.*	Connecting	Link people and bridge divided groups to *suspend boundaries and build trust.*
	Mobilizing	Craft common purpose and shared identity across groups to *reframe boundaries and develop community.*
3. Discovering New Frontiers *Taps into the power of simultaneous differentiation and the power of adaptation and transformation.*	Weaving	Draw out and integrate group differences within a larger whole to *interlace boundaries and advance interdependence.*
	Transforming	Bring multiple groups together in emergent, new directions to *cross-cut boundaries and enable reinvention.*

Source: Ernst and Chrobot-Mason, 2011.

leadership; a collective that expands through the worldview of interconnected influence agent; and bridge-building that facilitates emergence of new frontiers required to successfully institutionalize strategic change.

Conclusion

High-impact teams can be key levers for sustainable strategic change. However, teams today are generally not functioning in a high-impact way to effectively lead strategic change. To improve, they must make fundamental shifts in their beliefs, practices, and collective behavior and develop a new set of abilities. There is still a role for an individual team leader, but the *collective* leadership capability of the entire team becomes an important strategic resource. Together, team members understand internal relationships, roles, and communication flow across the breadth of an enterprise. They are able to establish new connections, span gaps, and create direction, alignment, and commitment around important strategic goals. Ultimately, they drive transformative results for the organizations they serve.

References

Bowers, J.B., Seashore, D.G., & Marrow, S.E. (1967). *Management by participation: Creating a climate for personal and organizational development.* New York: Harper & Row.

Beer, M. (2001). How to develop an organization capable of sustained high performance: Embrace the drive for results-capability development paradox. *Organization Dynamics, 29* (4), 233–247.

Cameron, K.S., & Quinn, R.E. (1999). *Diagnosing and changing organizational culture.* Reading, MA: Addison-Wesley.

Cross, R., Ehrlich, K., Dawson, R., & Helferich, J. (2008). Managing collaboration: Improving team effectiveness with a network perspective. *California Management Review, 50*(4), 78–99.

Cross R.L., Parker, A., & Cross, R. (2004). *The hidden power of social networks: Understanding how work really gets done in organizations.* Boston: Harvard Business School Press.

Ernst, C., & Chrobot-Mason, D. (2011). *Boundary spanning leadership: Six practices for solving problems, driving innovation, and transforming organizations.* New York: McGraw-Hill.

Ginnett, R.C. 1996. Team effectiveness leadership model: Identifying leverage points for change. *Proceedings of the 1996 Psychology in the Department of Defense Symposium.* Colorado Springs, Colorado.

Hughes, R.L., & Beatty, K.C. (2005). *Becoming a strategic leader: Your role in your organization's enduring success.* San Francisco: Jossey-Bass.

Kirton, M.J. (1989). *Adaptors & Innovators: Styles of Creativity and Problem Solving.* London: Routledge Publishing.

McGuire, J.B., & Rhodes, G.B. (2009). *Transforming your leadership culture.* San Francisco: Jossey-Bass.

Morgenson, F.P., DeRue, D.S., & Karam, E.P. (2010). Leadership in teams: A functional approach to understanding leadership structures and processes. *Journal of Management, 36*(1), 5–39.

Musselwhite, C., & Jones, R. (2004). *Dangerous opportunity: Making change work.* Greensboro, NC: Chris Musselwhite.

Peters, K. (2011). Office Depot's president on how "mystery shopping" helped spark a turnaround. *Harvard Business Review, 89*(11), 47–50.

Smith, R.B., & Campbell, M. (2010). C-suite challenges and the economic meltdown: What's next for senior leaders? *HR People & Strategy, 33*(4).

Tang, V., & Moore, C. (2009, October 1). Transforming your organization: The Kone story. Webinar available to the public through the Center for Creative Leadership's webinar series.

Van Velsor, E., McCauley, C.D., & Ruderman, M.N. (Eds.). (2010). *Handbook of leadership development.* San Francisco: Jossey-Bass.

Yukl, G. (2011). Personal communication to Roland Smith, December 13, 2011.

CHAPTER SIX

Leading Executive Teams

The Good, the Bad, and the Ugly

Susan R. Meisinger, SPHR, JD

Former President, Society for Human Resource Management

I'm willing to bet that virtually every leader who has ever been responsible for leading and relying on a team of executives has, at some point, found him- or herself muttering, "Geez; that was ugly. I feel like I'm dealing with children." And well-paid children, at that!

It's usually muttered in the context of a disagreement among and between executive team members, one or both of whom have brought it to the leader for a decision. While much of a leader's job involves making difficult decisions that no one else can make, leaders rarely embrace the extra time and effort required to make decisions on issues that could have been handled by executives on their team without the leader's involvement.

Leaders Must Recognize That Executive Teams Are Different

Frequently, the attributes that enabled a team member to reach the executive suite are the very attributes that can create friction and problems among the executive team members. Top executives who are smart, driven, competitive, and committed to their jobs have usually been very successful at each stage of their careers. They aren't accustomed to failure, and at the executive suite level, a failure can be a significant blow to a career.

While the dynamics of an executive team are fundamentally subject to the same dynamics of most work teams, discussed at length in this book, for executive teams, the stakes are often more significant for the individual members and to the organization as a whole. This creates some additional dynamics.

Members of the executive team who have been successful in large part due to their real or perceived superior intellect must now work with others of equal or greater intellect. This may be a new experience for some, akin to when a star in the high school basketball team plays in his or her first college game. The bar has been raised, and he may require coaching to help him learn when to recognize that his peers may have greater strengths in some areas and that it's appropriate to trust them.

Furthermore, when operating on an executive team, individual success is much more linked—not just in outcomes but often in compensation—to the overall success of the business, not just the executive's area of responsibility. This makes executives much more dependent on their peers' performance than in previous roles and may cause heightened anxiety and tension between team members when business challenges arise.

Time also becomes a much dearer commodity as an executive moves up within an organization. At the same time these people are adding areas of responsibility and gaining a broader span of control, they are also facing important demands to dedicate scarce time resources to collaborate with other executive team members in decisions critical to the business. Failure to pause and act as a team to fully debate and deliberate about business issues because of the press of time can lead to abrupt and expedient decision making that fails to consider long-term implications.

Finally, the operation of an executive team is different because employees watch the executive team closely, trying to discern the direction of the firm, particularly during tough economic periods. If employees see a high-performing group of executives, they are reassured and much less likely to be distracted from their tasks.

The operation of the executive team is also likely to be modeled elsewhere in the organization. If employees see that members of the executive team are not working collaboratively, it's likely to have a ripple impact throughout the organization. After all, if my department head doesn't get along with your department head, why should I have to get along with you? Alternatively, if I know that my department head talks regularly to your department head in a collegial and effective style, I'm much more likely to help you out.

Executive Teams Need Care and Feeding

So is there such a thing as an executive team that operates smoothly, like a well-oiled machine, in perfect harmony, with a shared vision and consistently outstanding results? Perhaps; but they're as rare as ducks' teeth. And while an executive team may operate smoothly for a period of time, it rarely lasts, because the world doesn't stand still. Business conditions change; team members come and go; restructurings, mergers, and acquisitions happen.

This constant, almost organic, change within organizations and therefore the executive teams is in constant need of care and feeding by their leader. In a business environment that feels as though it rests on shifting sands, with rapid changes in a global economy, where business models that thrived last year may die next year, leaders must pay greater attention to the dynamics of their executive teams. Failure to do so may put the enterprise in real jeopardy.

For if members of the executive team, who are collectively responsible for all aspects of the business, are unable to function together effectively, then the seeds of failure for the business will be planted. Dysfunctional teams will lead to failures of communication on key business issues. There will be distrust and disagreement over critical resource allocations. Decisions will be delayed because of failure to work together on an answer, placing entire departments or business units in limbo while they await clear direction from the executive team.

Leaders Must Do Their Work Through Executive Teams

Successful CEOs understand that they are responsible for the entire enterprise. That's the job; they're the ones who answer to the board. But smart CEOs also understand that, while they're responsible for everything, they can't do everything. They must get things done through and with an executive team—one hopes one that is made up of extraordinary leaders in their own right. CEOs know that these are the people who will push the corporate strategy and expectations down throughout an organization while creating the culture and ensuring execution of the strategy.

Leaders must understand and leverage what the research has taught us: that "teamwork at the top promotes better decision making and increases the involvement and commitment of key executives." However, there's also considerable research that suggests that senior teams find teamwork difficult (Edmondson & Smith, 2006, p. 6).

Leaders must lead a team of executives in such a way that open sharing and debate on competing viewpoints are encouraged, but without behaviors or actions that disturb the trust among team members and fail to address the true issues. This means overcoming some of the "group think" behaviors first identified in the 1970s by research psychologist Irving Janis, who described it as "a mode of thinking that people engage in when deeply involved in a cohesive in-group, when the members' strivings for unanimity override their motivation to realistically appraise alternative courses of action" (Janis, 1972).

This also means that leaders have to accept and overcome what research has also shown—that groups tend to "suppress dissent, focus discussion on things that they already agree about rather than what they disagree about, have more extreme attitudes and judgments on a wide array of issues and decisions than the individuals they comprise, have greater confidence in the correctness of their decisions and attitudes than individuals, and lead individuals to publicly endorse decisions and attitudes that they view as normal for the group, even when they privately hold reservations" (Ben-Hur, Jonsen, & Kinley, 2010).

It's no small challenge.

Leaders Must Know Themselves First

Perhaps the most important consideration in predicting how well an executive team will operate is the leader of the team.

Frequently, a CEO is the individual who will have a major impact on how team members operate. There's no single style required to be effective as a CEO—consider the diversity of corporate CEOs around the globe, with broad variations in values, personalities, attitudes, strengths, and weaknesses. Drucker asserted that effective leaders ask themselves, "What needs to be done?" and then ask, "Of those things that would make a difference, which are right for me?" (Karlgaard, 2004).

If, for example, the leader does find him- or herself muttering "it's like dealing with children," he or she must also ask whether he or she might be acting like an over-controlling or perhaps absent parent. This requires an honest understanding and assessment of one's style, strengths, and weaknesses. Assessment processes and resultant feedback can help leaders gain clarity about their own style, but then, to paraphrase Gandhi, leaders must "be the change they want to see."

Leaders of executive teams have to know when to remain silent. Frequently, top executives are where they are because they have a clear vision of what needs to be done and have the drive and intellect to know how best to get there. When leading an executive team, clarity of vision is still important, but there will be greater dependence on the contributions made by the members of the team than in previous roles. Simply stated, leaders who once could drive change within their own units or departments will now need help to drive it throughout an entire organization. To do that, they'll need to listen; they can't be so forceful and compelling that they suck the air out the room so others don't even speak. Or "They can start by using the four most important words in leadership—What do you think?—as the first step in empowering others to share in the leadership of their collective destiny" (Pearce, 2004, p. 52).

There are benefits to the organization when a leader remains silent and first listens to executive team members. It increases the likelihood that everyone's ideas will be voiced; since team members may not know what the leader's views are, they are less fearful of publicly differing from or disagreeing with their leader. Furthermore, the leader has the benefit of additional input that may shape, change, and ultimately improve his or her original thinking or opinion.

This also means knowing when to force members of an executive team to resolve issues by working together, rather than elevating the issue to the leader's desk. Among the many lessons I learned while leading executive teams was that allowing executive team members, who often saw things differently, to bring their disagreements to me for resolution wasn't the best way to lead the team. I learned that, by requiring the executives to jointly prepare a decision memo for me that set out both sides of an issue, I forced them to discuss the subject objectively as they prepared the memo. The result: during the discussion they gained a better understanding of one another's perspectives and were able to resolve issues without my involvement.

Leaders of executive teams should also diagnose their own tolerance to conflict, understanding that their aversion to it may dampen open debate or lead to some subjects being deemed as "forbidden" for discussion. For some leaders, conflict causes discomfort and evokes a flight response. For others, conflict is energizing, evoking a fight response. Leaders need to know which response is more likely for them and moderate their responses accordingly.

Part of "know thyself" requires the realization that the leader's own assessment of the executive team is very possibly flawed. While most top executives believe they're able to accurately assess their teams, research suggests this may not be the case. They may have a higher opinion of how the executive team is performing than the team itself has.

In a survey of 124 CEOs and 579 senior executives at large and mid-size firms from around the world in a range of industries, 52 percent of the non-CEOs said that their teams were doing poorly in critical areas. However, just 28 percent of the chief executives reported problems. The areas surveyed included thinking innovatively, cross-marketing, leading change, overseeing talent development, and building a company culture. Rating their teams' overall effectiveness on a 7-point scale (7 being the best), the CEOs gave an average score of 5.39 out of 7 on their teams' overall effectiveness, while the other executives gave an average score of only 4.02. The research also included a survey of sixty top HR executives from Fortune 500 companies, and only 6 percent of those reported that "the executives in our C-suite are a well-integrated team" (Rosen & Adair, 2007).

In summary, the leaders of executive teams must recognize the importance of their own roles in maximizing meaningful contributions from the team by understanding their own styles and limitations, modeling behavior that they want from executive team members, and recognizing that they may overestimate the success of these efforts.

Leaders and Executive Teams Must Develop a Shared Understanding About the Culture

Every organization has a culture that evolves, sometimes intentionally, sometimes unintentionally. The business press is full of examples of corporate cultures that are considered part and parcel of the organization's successes, such as Google, Facebook, and Zappos.

The leader must work with the executive team to provide clarity on what kind of culture should be sought and maintained to ensure business success. This means having agreement on the core values that guide the organization's internal conduct as well as its relationship with the external world. Similarly, members of the executive team must have a shared and clear understanding of the vision for the organization, so that if an employee asks any member of the team about the vision, the answer will be the same. For example, the core values for Zappos are as follows:

> "As we grow as a company, it has become more and more important to explicitly define the core values from which we develop our culture, our brand, and our business strategies. These are the ten core values that we live by: (1) Deliver WOW Through Service; (2) Embrace and Drive Change; (3) Create Fun and a Little Weirdness; (4) Be Adventurous, Creative, and Open-Minded; (5) Pursue Growth and Learning; (6) Build Open and Honest Relationships with Communication; (7) Build a Positive Team and Family Spirit; (8) Do More with Less; (9) Be Passionate and Determined; (10) Be Humble." (Zappos, n.d.)

Another example of core values comes from Google:

> "As we keep looking toward the future, these core principles guide our actions. (1) Focus on the user and all else will follow. (2) It's best to do one thing really, really well. (3) Fast is better

than slow. (4) Democracy on the web works. (5) You don't need to be at your desk to need an answer. (6) You can make money without doing evil. (7) There's always more information out there. (8) The need for information crosses all borders. (9) You can be serious without a suit. (10) Great just isn't good enough." (Google, n.d.)

Leaders Must Be Clear on Who Is on the Executive Team

Executive teams have to be "bounded"; that is to say, leaders must provide clarity on who is a member of the team. When data were collected and analyzed on more than 120 top teams by researchers, they found that the executive teams thought that they had unambiguous boundaries. But when executive members were asked to describe their team, fewer than 10 percent agreed about who was on it (Hackman, Wageman, Nunes, & Burruss, 2008).

Executive leaders are often the culprit in allowing this ambiguity to exist, either through erroneous concerns about being viewed as too exclusive or sheer inertia. This in turn increases the chances of dysfunctional team behavior, since executives aren't clear on who is responsible for what or who is appropriate to be involved in critical strategy discussions and decisions. As noted by researcher Hackman (2008), "in truth, putting together a team involves some ruthless decisions about membership; not everyone who wants to be on the team should be included, and some individuals should be forced off" (Coutu, 2009).

Just as clarity on the membership of the executive team is important, research also suggests that big is not always better. Bigger teams require more attention and time for managing the links and relationships between and among the team members. According to Hackman, having a "huge senior leadership team—say, one that includes all the CEO's direct reports—may be worse than having no team at all" (Coutu, 2009).

Define the Role of the Executive Team

It's unlikely that an executive team will be successful if members of the team don't understand what the team should or should not be doing. Leaders need to make sure that executive team members know what the leader expects from the team, as key decision-makers for the organization. Leaders must also make it clear to executive team members that they have responsibilities to support each other. The leader must gather the team together and be direct about what are considered bad political behaviors and be willing to back threats with actions.

Members of the executive team must understand that the executive team is their "first team." The people who report to them—whether a department, division, or subsidiary—are their "second team." The role of the executive team is to work together on the "first team" to make decisions that apply to the organization as a whole. Their role is not to represent the interests of the people and organization that report to them. Ready (2004, p. 88) describes this role as that of an "enterprise leader" or "anyone accountable for the economic and social welfare of the total enterprise, across divisions, businesses, functions and locations. An enterprise leader might run a business unit or oversee a major function, but will make decisions with the entire corporations in mind." When Sam Palmisano became chairman and CEO of IBM, he changed the name of IBM's Enterprise Leadership Group to the Enterprise Leadership Team. This symbolic—and ultimately effective—technique helped drive home the expectation that IBM's leaders were on a "first team"; they were not simply a group of leaders for the company.

For those joining an executive team for the first time, this can be a challenge. In the past, key relationships in the organization were vertical: up to his or her manager and down to his or her direct reports. Upon joining the executive team, those key relationships shift from the vertical to the horizontal, to the "first team" and not his or her functional group.

Why is this important?

When executive team members understand that their priority is to work collaboratively with each other, as key leaders of the business, they are more likely to focus on what's in the best interests of the overall business, rather than the demands of their particular area of responsibility. It provides clarity to team members when faced with a difficult decision that forces them to weigh what's best for the organization as a whole against what the impact might be on their own divisions or units. In all cases, they must place priority on what's best for the "first team"—the overall organization.

For many, this is a difficult transition. Many successful executives have thrived in a culture in which departmental or division success is recognized and rewarded. Others have been successful because of their unique expertise in a narrow area that is critical to the business, which hasn't required a focus on leadership competencies or, even more importantly, leadership team competencies.

Spending time discussing the topic of the leadership role of the executive team allows team members to share any assumptions they may have about their responsibilities as leaders and to recognize biases they may have acquired in other roles. It is hoped that open and frank conversations about past leadership experiences can also serve to build greater trust and understanding among and between members of the team.

Equally important to working as a first team is the need to ensure that executive team members have agreement and understand what they should spend their time on. This isn't always readily apparent, and when executive teams don't have clarity and agreement on how they'll spend their time, time will be wasted on topics that are not important or don't require executive team input. Worse, individual members may promote their own personal interests. Without a shared understanding, conflicts will occur.

A survey of six hundred executives conducted by McKinsey revealed that only "38 percent said their teams focused on work that truly benefited from a top-team perspective. Only 35 percent said their top teams allocated the right amount of time among the various topics they considered important, such as strategy and people" (Kruyt, Malan, & Tuffield, 2001).

Frequently, CEOs and executive teams fail to take time to discuss and agree on the priorities that only the executive team can address. Topics that demand collective action are treated as interchangeable with topics that require brief information-sharing. As a result, the executive team falls into familiar patterns of discussion, reviewing agenda items that have been reviewed in past meetings, which are de facto departmental or divisional reports that do not really need discussion and decisions by the group. Some executive team members try to use meetings for show and tell, particularly if they don't feel they've had enough time with the leader. Team members listen politely, monitoring the presentations to ensure that no one has taken actions or made decisions that impact "their" areas of responsibility. Meetings are boring and endless. More importantly, they siphon time away from discussions of real issues that have enterprise-wide implications.

In a rapidly changing, networked world, this model simply won't work. Whereas once business silos might have been able to operate side-by-side, today's customers are much more likely to demand an integrated solution. Technology is allowing for crossover in functions that historically have been separated, requiring executive teams to grapple with new issues of resource allocation, complex processes, and business priorities. Consider, for example, the explosion of the Internet and e-commerce, which requires organizations to work collaboratively to maximize the value of the technology. Decisions must be made on who controls the design and allocation of a website's "real estate"; who is responsible for writing the content on the site; who ensures the proper vetting and posting of the content; and who ensures the e-commerce integrates properly with the financial system and that the sales are properly integrated with inventory control and logistics. Similarly, rapid changes and growth in social media are taking executive teams into previously unchartered territory as they try to balance the benefits of extending their marketing reach, while potentially diluting the brand with multiple parties using the new media.

One way to sharpen the discussion about what the team will spend its time on is to have clarity on issues that are not subject to team consensus and who is accountable for what. If each team member understands what decisions he or she has responsibility for and authority to make, and knows who must be included in the decision-making process, less time will be spent on how, when, and by whom a decision may be made.

This assignment of accountability is never finished. Executive team leaders must continually revisit issues of responsibility, accountability, and decision authority. Businesses are always changing, and where once a decision could be made and one executive held accountable, a merger, acquisition, or new line of business could require reassessment on what parties should be involved in what decisions. Sometimes, executive teams fail to recognize this and individuals continue to make decisions they have always been accountable for in the past, causing conflicts to arise.

When executive team members have clarity on accountabilities and team priorities and recognize that their group is their first team, they can focus on debating strategic topics, making clear decisions, and establishing company priorities.

Operational Responsibilities of the Executive Team Must Be Clear

Just as the executive team will be responsible for debating and setting strategic direction and priorities, it will also be responsible for holding itself and the organization accountable for delivering results. Therefore, regular sessions of the team, during which progress is measured against the strategy and plans, are critical. Regular business reviews, where executive team members assess business performance against quarterly financial and operation goals, will allow mid-course corrections and the early identification of problems and opportunities. At the same time, an assessment can be made against annual and/or multiple-year goals and whether the organization continues to remain focused on the priorities that have been set by the executive team.

Even when they have clarity on what they will do as an executive team and what their individual and collective accountabilities are, leaders must ensure their team will work well together. How will they handle the inevitable conflicts that arise over competing strategic directions, priorities, and resource demands?

Leaders Must Focus on Developing Trust Among Executive Team Members

Research on teams has helped us to understand that open communication and the development of honest, candid conversations are keys to their effectiveness (Douglas, Martin, & Krapels, 2006; Goodbody, 2005, 1994; Hirst & Mann, 2004; Katzenbach &

Smith, 1993; Ng & Liang, 2005; Patrashkova-Volzdoska, McComb, Green, & Compton, 2003; Peters & Fletchers, 2004; Scholtes, Joiner, & Streibel, 1996), and this is especially true for executive teams.

But ensuring that open, honest, and candid conversations take place is easy to expect, and often hard to achieve. Leaders must spell out their expectations that, even when team members disagree, they have a responsibility and are expected to speak out.

In his leadership fable, *The Five Dysfunctions of a Team*, Lencioni identified the absence of trust as the first dysfunction, noting that, without trust, "teamwork is all but impossible." He defined trust as "the confidence among team members that their peers' intentions are good, and that there is no reason to be protective or careful around the group. In essence, teammates must get comfortable with one another" (Lencioni, 2002, pp. 195–196). This type of trust requires team members, who have fought so hard to get on the executive team by demonstrating their superior knowledge and expertise, to now allow their colleagues to see that they have weaknesses and may need help from them from time to time.

Trust is not something that is established overnight, although Lencioni suggested some exercises to help speed up the development of trust within a team, such as team members sharing personal histories, 360-degree assessment tools, or sharing their individual perspective on each other's strengths and opportunities for improvement on the team (p. 199).

Lencioni also suggested the use of personality and behavioral preference profiles as a tool to help individual team members better understand and empathize with each other (p. 199). Tools such as the Myers-Briggs Type Indicator (MBTI) are useful in helping executives recognize that individuals have different preferences in how they perceive the world and make decisions and that no one way is better than another—they are just different. By understanding differences and being given a common vocabulary to discuss them, colleagues are better equipped to understand why an executive team member approached an issue as he or she did. This can prevent team members from assuming that someone on the team behaved as he or she did out of spite or simply to be disruptive.

Greater understanding of individual styles enables greater development of trust. This is important because research suggests that within-group trust is a moderating factor that helps executive teams gain the benefits of task- or issue-focused conflict without suffering the costs of personal or relationship conflict (Simons & Peterson, 2007).

Leaders Must Expect Executive Team Conflict, But All Conflict Is Not Equal

But what happens when there's the potential for or a history of conflict that hampers continuing trust, meaningful communication, and candid exchanges? Do meetings even allow for lively conflict? After all, avoiding disagreement may result in short meetings, but it may also mean that the team is actually avoiding tough discussions. A calm and quiet meeting may mean conformity rather than consensus or just reflect a fear of "making waves."

Understanding the types of conflict that are likely to arise in teams helps. Often referred to as "task conflict," these are disagreements about the task at hand. Task conflict frequently arises when team members have differences in viewpoints, ideas, and opinions. Examples include conflicts about distribution of resources, procedures and policies, judgments and interpretation of facts (DeDreu & Weingart, 2003, p. 741). Said another way, task conflicts are those that can be resolved by recourse to logic and facts (Edmondson & Smith, 2006, p. 6). While such disagreements can be helpful in preventing group think, and encourage creativity and understanding because diverse perspectives are voiced, task conflicts can, if not managed well and acknowledged appropriately, create discord within a team. Managing task conflict requires the leader to communicate clear expectations that the executives will listen to each other respectfully and consider diverse approaches and opinions as they are voiced.

Discord can often evolve from task conflict to "relationship conflict," which may preclude any fruitful debate in the first place. Relationship conflict arises where the real conflict is between individuals rather than about a task. If opposing values or interests are deeply held, relationship conflicts are likely. Examples of relationship conflict are conflicts about personal taste, political preferences, grudges, and interpersonal style (DeDreu & Weingart, 2003, p. 741).

One type of conflict isn't better than another; research has shown strong negative correlations between relationship conflict, team performance, and team member satisfaction, as well as strong negative correlations between task conflict, team performance, and team member satisfaction (DeDreu & Weingart, 2003). As a practical matter, as issues are discussed and debated, the nature of the conflict can sometimes shift from task to relationship and back. People and their actions are, after all, not easily compartmentalized.

Researchers Edmondson and Smith suggested three practices that may help with successfully resolving conflict on executive teams (Edmondson & Smith, 2006).

First, by educating members of the executive team about basic principles of the nature of conflict and our reactions to it, they can learn to manage themselves, learn to reflect on their reactions to conflict, and reframe the situation. The goal is to help team members recognize the nature of their reactions to conflict, then step back so they are able to consider alternative interpretations. Executives are "well served by asking the question, 'How am I interpreting the situation such that I'm reacting this way?'" (Edmondson & Smith, 2006, p. 14).

Second, executive team members should manage conversations, channeling their reactions into productive discussion. Rather than react to a relationship conflict by hardening their positions or ducking the topic completely, leaders must help team members confront the issue and understand why they reacted as they did. This helps the team cool down and focus on whether deeper issues need to be discussed.

Third, team members must acknowledge that they have responsibility for managing relationships with their peers. This means getting to know each other's goals and concerns and focusing on building trust (Edmondson & Smith, 2006).

All of this is not easy and often requires a rejection of corporate cultures that frown on acknowledging emotions or resist open conversations about why things aren't working. It is more likely that executive teams will simply place responsibility for conflict on certain individuals, rather than delve into the why of it all.

For that reason, a facilitator may be useful to help them understand how they make decisions and the politics and biases involved. A disinterested third party is often able to observe the process, provide feedback, and challenge individuals' thought processes, helping the team overcome obstacles to success.

Executive Teams Must Be Provided Proper Rewards and Recognition

As noted earlier, many come to the executive team after having been very successful in leading a unit or division and being recognized and rewarded for that success. After all, a simple truism is that people do what they're paid to do.

To help ensure that team members recognize that they are now responsible for the results of the entire enterprise, it is critical that the performance management, rewards, and recognition systems be designed to drive the behaviors required. This provides an effective tool to ensure that members act in the best interests of the entire team, rather than a single unit.

While there is no shortage of performance management approaches that can drive first team behaviors and outcomes (and there are many consultants willing to use them), there are two critical features for their design. First, the program must both reward and/or hold accountable the entire team for over-arching business outcomes. The measures that are used should be linked to the overall corporate strategy (revenue growth, profit, earnings before income and tax, share value—whatever fits the company's strategy) and clearly telegraph that a portion of their reward is linked to how well the overall team performs, as demonstrated in business results.

Second, the program must reward and/or hold team members accountable for their behavior when working with each other. In other words, if an executive team member is able to meet financial or other goals, but does so by leaving a path of disruption and destruction, he or she must be held accountable for this behavior, rather than rewarded for it.

Leaders Must Deal with Good, Bad, and Ugly Executive Team Members

Or bring in and keep the good, try a makeover on the ugly, and get rid of the bad!

Jim Collins is well-known for his encouragement to leaders to ensure that they have "the right people on the bus" before deciding where the bus should go (Collins, 2001). Similarly, building and maintaining a cohesive leadership team is the first discipline in Lencioni's The Four Obsessions of an Extraordinary Executive.

Leaders won't always have the luxury of building an executive team from scratch; frequently, they become first among what used to be equals when promoted over peers. Sometimes they inherit a team, and sometimes they take on leadership of a team that's a hybrid of some sort, the result of a merger or acquisition. Regardless, the team is likely to change over time as people come and go and the organization grows or changes.

The Ugly

What happens when a leader has an "ugly" team member—someone who is not performing? What should the leader do when a member of the executive team is not delivering the business results expected, nor demonstrating the expected behaviors of a leader in the organization? When a leader considers the questions "Would I hire this person again?" or "Would I care if he was quitting?" and realizes the answer to either question is "no," it's probably an ugly team member.

If so, the leader has to recognize that this person will act as a cancer on the team if not dealt with. Left unaddressed, the person's continued role on the team will be seen as inequitable and can be used as an excuse for any other failings of the team. Failure to hold the team member accountable also has implications for the broader organization, because other managers and leaders in the organization will feel comfortable modeling that failure. After all, if a member of the executive team isn't held accountable, why should someone undertake the difficult and uncomfortable task of holding his or her own team members accountable? Unfortunately, because taking adverse action against senior executives can sometimes be complicated, expensive, and time-consuming, it's frequently avoided.

Delaying action will be expensive to the organization in the long term, so leaders must act quickly to move a dysfunctional executive team member out. While this seems simple, a surprising number of CEOs, when asked to reflect on mistakes they'd made when first assuming their role as CEO, replied that they wished they had moved more quickly to replace poor performers on the executive team.

The Bad

What if the executive team member is valuable in most instances, but sometimes just acts badly? Coaching, direct feedback on expectations, 360-degree assessments, and other human resource developmental options are available to address the rough edges of a team member acting badly. However, leaders must hold the person accountable for demonstrating improvement if he or she hopes to stay.

The Good

Bringing the "good" onto the team is one of a leader's greatest responsibilities. Succession planning is a critical part of ensuring the sustainability of an organization. It allows team members to gain some familiarity with employees who may be future colleagues on the executive team. It involves a robust discussion about potential future leaders for the organization and forces the executive team to recognize what skills and abilities are necessary for the executive team to work successfully on behalf of the organization.

It is surprising how often organizations, even those with robust succession planning programs, discriminate against the internal candidates they worked so hard to identify, candidates they probably know the best. Internal candidates are known for all aspects of performance, not just past successes and demonstrated capabilities, but any mistakes made along the way. An internal candidate is sometimes overlooked because of past mistakes or missteps. The internal candidate's ability to rapidly contribute to the organization because of his or her knowledge of the business, the market, the workforce, the formal and informal networks within the organization, or its systems and processes is overlooked or undervalued.

Rather than risk selection of an internal candidate with known weaknesses, an external candidate is selected—after only a few hours of interviewing and reference checking. Since there are few perfect candidates, it's just as likely external candidates will have weaknesses that will be unknown until they become apparent over time.

Leaders have to ask themselves which will best serve the current and future business needs of the organization: a known quantity with weaknesses that can be addressed or a new quantity whose weaknesses will be discovered in the future?

However a position is to be filled, members of the executive team should be involved in the selection process. This doesn't mean that the leader should delegate the decision to others. It also doesn't mean that the successful candidate should be chosen by consensus. It is the leader's role to make the selection decision. Well-organized and orchestrated panel interviews of finalists identified by the leader are extremely helpful in selecting new executive team members for a number of reasons.

First, such interviews tend to be more focused. With multiple individuals asking questions, it is less likely that time will be spent on general conversations with little meaningful information shared. The interview should contain behavioral or situational questions that reveal how the candidate has behaved or would behave in different circumstances (see Adler, 2007, and Overman, 2007, for more on panel interviews; see Latham, 2009, for more on selecting applicants).

Whereas a single interviewer can become distracted, multiple interviewers provide time to reflect on what's been said. Follow-up questions are more likely, which enables the candidate to respond with greater depth and interviewers to learn more. Time is saved, as this method eliminates the need for a series of interviews, and there is a shared experience for members of the team because all have heard the same information. Thus, their assessment of the candidate is likely to be more accurate. Panel interviews also provide the leader an opportunity to observe the interaction of the candidate with members of the team and to draw his or her own conclusions on how successful the person is likely to be in working with the team.

And finally, such interviews allow the candidate to meet and judge for him- or herself whether this is an executive team he or she would like to join, and if not, it will allow the person to drop out of the process.

Much has been written on leadership competencies required to be successful in executive positions. When I was CEO of the Society for Human Resource Management, publishers regularly sent me newly published books on all aspects of leadership to check out. Similarly, leaders who are charged with selecting their executive teams have to sort through the various models and determine for themselves what they should look for in executives to carry the organization forward. Some of the competencies that I have found strengthened the leadership teams I have worked with are:

- *Emotional intelligence* or the ability to be self-aware and perceive the effect one may be having on others, understand the emotional makeup of others, and moderate the effect as appropriate (see Goleman, Boyatzis, & McKee, 2002, for a discussion on emotional intelligence). Emotional intelligence enables executive team members to be better equipped to deal with the task and relationship conflict that is certain to arise within an executive team. Being able to understand one's own emotions and the effect you have on others is critical to enable changes in behavior that will help to resolve conflicts and enable progress to be made.
- *Functional intelligence or a proven track record.* One of the best predictors of future performance is past performance. This means looking for candidates who have demonstrated competencies in various functional areas, having produced high-quality work in diverse situations over extended periods of time.
- *Intellect.* Leaders should have the self-esteem required to bring in people that are smarter than they are. As Will Rogers said, "A man only learns in two ways, one by reading, and the

other by association with smarter people." Said another way, general mental ability is correlated with better job performance (Schmidt & Hunter, 1998). Smarter is better.

- *Political savvy.* While closely related to emotional intelligence, savvy refers to the ability to identify the internal and external politics that have an impact on the work of the organization. Individuals with political savvy recognize that there are always political implications—large or small—with all decisions.
- *Curiosity.* In my experience, executive candidates who demonstrate the desire to seek information and knowledge, are broadly read, and have interests outside of their careers bring real value to an organization. People who are curious are often interested in exploring and learning about new ways of doing business and are frequently able to spot important trends or changes in the business environment that may impact the company.
- *Global competence.* Even if the organization is purely domestic, candidates with experience working, traveling, or living abroad often have learned to adapt to change and to operate in unfamiliar surroundings. This experience can prove to be very useful as they help lead an organization through change.

Leaders Must Recognize That Location, Location, Location Matters with Executive Teams

The executive team is assembled, the good have been retained, the bad and ugly dealt with, and the leader is positioned to work with the executives to help drive the organization to new heights. But there's one last topic that should be considered.

While not generally the subject of open discussion and debate, office real estate—and more importantly its location—can have an impact on executive team effectiveness and dynamics (Steele, 2009). While placement of offices may lead to petty resentments that can be ignored, it makes sense to acknowledge the fact that office placement matters and that it can impact how the executive team functions.

Day-to-day contacts between executives are affected by office placement, which in turn is likely to impact the flow of information. Who hasn't suddenly remembered to share information with someone when running into the person in the hallway or at the coffee machine?

It's for this reason that some leaders prefer to have executive teams co-located where they can rapidly touch base to resolve issues. While being clustered may result in greater communication, it also runs the risk of reducing the visibility of the executive team within the organization unless team members make a conscious effort to be visible to employees.

Some leaders decide that dispersed offices are a better option because, for whatever reason, the nature of the business is better served by having executives closer to the people who report to them, because of the need for greater information flow within the units. While this option may result in executive team members being more visible throughout the organization, it may mean less contact among executive team members. In this case, team members have to consider ways to allow for the informal interactions that can facilitate the free flow of information.

Certainly, there is no one right or wrong way to address the issue of physical location of executive team members. What is important is that the executive team members acknowledge that, whether they are co-located or scattered, they must be mindful of the impact on team dynamics and the culture of the organization.

In considering additional ways to use office real estate to help the executive team function, Steele suggested establishing a shared common space for the team, reasoning that "accidental contacts allow for much quicker sharing of opinions, ideas, or questions as they arise rather than discussing them at some later time" (Steele, 2009, p. 23). This in turn may increase the likelihood that team members may be able to rapidly recognize and seize an opportunity.

Conclusion

Leading an executive team is full of challenges and requires thoughtful consideration of a plethora of issues. But when done successfully, the rewards are many: an opportunity to work with people you respect, admire, and learn from, while leading an organization to successfully achieving its vision.

Five Suggestions for Leading Executive Teams

1. Recognize that an executive team is different from other management teams because this team is collectively responsible for the performance of the overall enterprise. Behavioral biases toward operating in silos must be overcome, with executive team members understanding that their "first" team is the executive team.
2. Leaders must be vigilant in monitoring their own behavior and understand that how an executive team operates is driven in large part by modeling the leader's behavior and because the leader tolerates, permits, or encourages those behaviors.
3. The most effective executive teams are those on which team members have clarity on roles and responsibilities; leaders are responsible for ensuring that such clarity exists.
4. Leaders and executive teams must dedicate time and attention to the team's dynamics and recognize that those dynamics will change with the addition or loss of any member. It's the leader's role to ensure that new dynamics that improve the team are embraced and those that harm the team's performance are rejected.
5. Leaders must allow executive teams to have productive conflict, with meaningful communication and candid exchanges, but refuse to accept conflict if it is personal and hampers continuing trust.

References

Adler, L. (2007). Using the panel interview to save time and increase accuracy. The Adler Group. Retrieved from www.adlerconcepts.com/resources/column/newsletter/using_the panel_interview_to_s.php.

Ben-Hur, S., Jonsen, K., & Kinley, N. (2010). Why the best executive teams sometimes make the worst decisions: Beware of groupthink. Retrieved from www.imd.org/research/challenges/TC073-10.cfm.

Collins, J. (2001). Good to great. *Fast Company*. Retrieved from www.jimcollins.com/article_topics/articles/good-to-great.html.

Coutu, D. (2009). Why teams don't work: An interview with J. Richard Hackman. *Harvard Business Review*. Retrieved from http://hbr.org/2009/05/why-teams-dont-work/ar/1.

DeDreu, C.K.W., & Weingart, L.R. (2003). Task versus relationship conflict, team performance, and team satisfaction: A meta-analysis. *Journal of Applied Psychology, 88*(4), 741–749.

Douglas, C., Martin, J.S., & Krapels, R.H. (2006).Communication in the transition to self-directed work teams. *Journal of Business Communication, 43*(4), 295–321.

Edmondson, A.C., & Smith, D.M. (2006). Too hot to handle? How to manage relationship conflict. *California Management Review, 49*(1), 6–31.

Goleman, D., Boyatzis, R.E., & McKee, A. (2002). *Primal leadership: Learning to lead with emotional intelligence.* Boston, MA: Harvard Business School Press.

Goodbody, J. (2005). Critical success factors for global virtual teams. *Strategic Communication Management, 9*(2), 18–21.

Google. (n.d.). Ten things we know to be true. Retrieved July 26, 2012, from www.google.com/about/company/philosophy/

Hackman, J.R., Wageman, R., Nunes, D., & Burruss, J. (2008). *Senior leadership teams: What it takes to make them great.* Boston: Harvard Business School Press.

Hirst, G., & Mann, L. (2004). A model of R&D leadership and team communication: The relationship with project performance. *R&D Management, 34*(2), 147–160.

Janis, I.L. (1972). *Victims of groupthink.* Boston: Houghton-Mifflin.

Karlgaard, R. (2004). Peter Drucker on leadership. *Forbes.* Retrieved from www.forbes.com/2004/11/19/cz_rk_1119drucker.html.

Katzenbach, J.R., & Smith, D.K. (1993). *The wisdom of teams: Creating the high-performance organization.* Boston: Harvard Business School Press.

Kruyt, M., Malan, J., & Tuffield, R. (2001). Three steps to building a better top team. McKinsey Quarterly. Retrieved from www.mckinseyquarterly.com/Three_steps_to_building_a_better_top team_2743.

Latham, G. (2009). *Becoming the evidence-based manager: Making the science of management work for you.* Mountain View, CA: Davies-Black/Society for Human Resource Management.

Lencioni, P. (2002). *The five dysfunctions of a team: A leadership fable.* San Francisco: Jossey-Bass.

Ng, P.T., & Liang, T.Y. (2005). Speaking the unspeakable: The paper dialogue approach. *International Journal of Human Resources Development and Management, 5*(2) 190–203.

Overman, S. (2007, January 1). Staffing management: Multiple choice. *Staffing Management Magazine, 3*(1). Retrieved from www.shrm.org/Publications/StaffingManagement Magazine/EditorialContent/Pages/0701_overman.aspx.

Patrashkova-Volzdoska, R.R., McComb, S.A., Green, S.G., & Compton, W.D. (2003). Examining a curvilinear relationship between communication frequency and team performance in cross-functional project teams. *IEEE Transactions on Engineering Management, 50*(3), 262–269.

Pearce, C.L. (2004). The future of leadership: Combining vertical and shared leadership to transform knowledge work. *Academy of Management Executive, 18*(2), 47–57.

Peters, L.D., & Fletcher, K.P. (2004). A market-based approach to understanding communication and teamworking. *Academy of Marketing Science.* www.amsreview.org/articles/peters02-2004.pdf.

Ready, D.A. (2004). Leading at the enterprise level. *MIT Sloan Management Review.* Retrieved from http://hbr.org/product/leading-at-the-enterprise-level/an/SMR141-PDF-ENG.

Rosen, R.M., & Adair, F. (2007). CEOs misperceive top teams' performance. *Harvard Business Review.* Retrieved from http://hbr.org/2007/09/ceos_misperceive-top-teams-performance/ar/1.

Schmidt, F.L., & Hunter, J.E. (1998). The validity and utility of selection methods in personnel psychology: Practical and theoretical implications of 85 years of research findings. *Psychological Bulletin, 124*(2), 262–274.

Scholtes, P., Joiner, B.L., & Streibel, B.J. (1996). *The team handbook* (2nd ed.). Madison, WI: Joiner Associates.

Simons, T., & Peterson, R. (2007). Why trust matters in top management teams: Keeping conflict constructive. *Cornell Hospitality Reports,* 7(14). Retrieved from www.hotelschool.cornell.edu/research/chr/pubs/reports/abstract-14582.html.

Steele, F. (2009). The ecology of the new executive team. *Leader to Leader,* pp. 20–26.

Zappos. (n.d.). Retrieved July 26, 2012, from http://about.zappos.com/our-unique-culture/zappos-core-values.

CHAPTER SEVEN

Leading from the Helm

Lessons from America's Cup Sailing Teams

Mark A. Clark

Kogod School of Business, American University

Overview

Running a high-performing professional team involves challenges that may be met through a variety of leadership approaches. Because each team has idiosyncratic resources and goals, the style most effective for one team may not be appropriate for another. Further, those who aspire to team leadership have varying capabilities. This chapter depicts the challenges of four leaders of America's Cup sailing teams, illustrating the confluence of personal style, team structure, and idiosyncratic team goals. The leaders choose strategies to meet their team challenges with varying success, imparting team leadership lessons to (1) identify team goals and resources; (2) examine personal leadership styles, beliefs, and fit; (3) create a structure and process to leverage team strengths; (4) coach for peak performance at the right time; and (5) build in feedback, acknowledge wins, and plan for the future.

The author would like to express gratitude to Elizabeth (Hall) Gaston, world-class in both sailing and as a graduate assistant, for gaining access to our first teams and biking the Port of Valencia with me in pursuit of the next interview.

> "The leader can never close the gap between himself and the group. If he does, he is no longer what he must be. He must walk a tightrope between the consent he must win and the control he must exert."
>
> —Vince Lombardi, NFL Green Bay Packers

As the words of the great Coach Lombardi imply, leading a team is both a difficult and ongoing challenge. A good leader must account for the specific context—team goals, culture, personalities, connections, and resources—in deciding how to most effectively influence his or her team. This means that a leader must know him- or herself, including beliefs, behavioral styles, and skills, as well as potential other sources of leadership and influence within the team. Leaders must also understand the norms, practices, and typical processes that enable their particular teams to operate. Each team's idiosyncratic resources, goals, and processes will vary in its fit with the capabilities of those who aspire to leadership, implying that the approach most effective for one team may not be appropriate for another. This effect may be magnified in teams at the peak of their profession, where mere high performance is a minimal standard.

This chapter depicts the challenges of leaders of such teams in the America's Cup sailing races, illustrating the confluence of personal style with teams of idiosyncratic goals, resources, structure, and cultures. The leaders chose strategies from autocratic direction to empowering members, with varying success in meeting their team challenges. Together, they offer lessons in team leadership that can be applied to settings as widely varied as ocean swells viewed from a sailboat's helm:

1. Identify team goals and resources;
2. Examine personal leadership styles, beliefs, and fit with the team members;
3. Create a structure and process that leverages the team's strengths;
4. Coach for peak performance at the right time; and
5. Build in feedback, acknowledge wins, and plan for the future.

Following a brief review of core team leadership theories, I will elaborate on each of these areas, then look in on leaders of various America's Cup teams whose actions provoke thought on the application of such lessons.

Defining Team Leadership

At its most basic level, team leadership may be defined as a set of characteristics and actions associated with moving teams toward their goals by influencing member attention, efforts, development, and coordination. This definition blends classic views of individual leadership as both characteristics of individuals (a *property*) and the *processes* which he or she instigates (Bass, 1990) with modern views of team effectiveness. Team leadership properties may include characteristics such as integrity and extroversion as well as competencies such as listening skills. Process leadership may include organizing practices, communication tactics, decision-making modes, empathetic appeals, and other means of directing and coordinating action. Team leader effectiveness may be deemed a combination of the design of a team and the functional behaviors of the leader in relation to members' developmental needs at the time best suited for a team's maturity (cf. Hackman & Wageman, 2005; Kozlowski, Gully, Salas, & Cannon-Bowers, 1996; Zaccaro, Rittman, & Marks, 2001).

Team leaders must first be attuned to the task or goal of the collective, while also balancing attention to the unique needs of each individual and the interaction among them from both social and task perspectives (Hackman, 1987). Members work best when they are actively engaged—when they feel accepted into the team's social system and are guided incrementally toward the team's goals. This often means that the leader(s) must find success through motivating others to be involved, fomenting relationships, and structuring the goal system to give clear feedback. The leader might have to take a backseat in order for these systems and relationships to function properly. Thus, while leaders may be necessary for teamwork, their presence can threaten team dynamics and subsequent performance. This dilemma is known as the *paradox of team leadership* (Manz & Sims, 1995).

Traditional and relatively more modern leadership theories—such as universal, contingency, transformational, servant leadership—can each provide lessons helpful to those wishing to lead teams (Bass, 1990). *Universal* approaches explain leadership through the property elements discussed above: a set of unique qualities, ideal type, or style inherent in a particular leader. From this, those who lead teams can identify those traits and skills that best fit their teams and work to enhance them. *Contingency* approaches examine the style and traits of leaders in context, designating appropriate actions for a given situation. Team leaders mindful of contingencies will watch for the interaction of factors within or outside the team which influence collective performance, including situational context, behaviors, member composition, goal-setting, and stakeholder acceptance.

Transformational leadership has gained much attention in recent years as a more personal means of influencing others. Leaders transform their workplaces through providing vision and empowering members and teams to plan and enact their values. Once these values are implanted into team members' minds and hearts through the charismatic efforts of the leader, members become allies in monitoring progress—their own and those of their teammates—toward collective goals. This *super leadership* allows members to run teams on their own, while appointed leaders might fill other roles, such as developing coaching skills and managing the boundary between the team and its organizational context (Manz & Sims, 1991). Finally, *servant leadership* (Greenleaf, 1970) aims to turn the traditional ego model of leadership on its head, changing the focus to empowering and developing others through humble service, courage, vision, and inspiration. By defining team leadership in terms of influence, mutual support, and service, this implies that leadership can emerge from multiple places within the team, outside formal lines of authority, through expertise, charisma, networks, or political skill.

Team leaders may act as developmental guides, motivators, and liaisons connecting the mission or purpose to the members of the team. To be effective, it has been proposed that they should focus on performing functions that would otherwise impede member progress (cf. Hackman & Wageman, 2005; Zaccaro, Rittman, & Marks, 2001). This view demands that leaders both provide feedback to team members on their developmental goals as well as listen to the members' own assessments of individual and collective progress. Importantly, leaders must time their efforts to be in sequence with the rhythms of the team and the demands set upon them (Kozlowski, Gully, Salas, & Cannon-Bowers, 1996). This means observing the team and its members to gain a sense of their needs, formulating a plan, then choosing the best opportunity to help the team focus on its development and direction. Combined with the contingency approach to leadership described above, this view demands that team leaders assess the situation, including relevant personal and organizational factors, potential barriers, and temporal orientation, before choosing the most appropriate approach.

Team Leadership in Context: Sailing Teams

It's no coincidence that many great team insights come from the world of sports. Sporting events provide teams with relatively clear goals, timelines, finite resources, and competition from other entrants. At the same time, sports teams parallel other work teams in the dynamic changes which may occur within the team and the competitive environment. Long seasons and multiple playoff rounds act as a crucible, testing member limits while shaping team processes and leader behavior. Winning an America's Cup, or even getting a team to the point where it can compete, is a prodigious task. Those charged with a Cup team must be aware of the effects of the influence that personal and organizational practices have on members, considering both immediate consequences and long-term outcomes. Much can be learned from the triumphs, failures, and the many forms of success in the America's Cup teams.

Two trained interviewers spoke with members of professional sailing teams participating in the America's Cup, an international sailing competition. The teams were primarily based in a Mediterranean port, with interviews conducted onsite or in the Eastern United States, although the members' home countries spanned the globe. Each team is a major enterprise, with major corporate sponsors and budgets ranging from approximately

$30 million to over $200 million. All interviewees were solicited through a mix of personal contacts, cold calls, and the snowball technique (whereby one interviewee nominates others). The interviewers proceeded through structured qualitative inquiry, modeled after Strauss and Corbin (1998), where interviewees were encouraged to tell their stories in their own voices. The interviewers followed an interview protocol, speaking with team leaders and members over a period of several months. Interviews were professionally transcribed, using qualitative content analysis to ascertain the presence and scope of construct relationships, themes, and findings.

Setting: Leadership in the America's Cup

> "There would be three or four teams pretty much on the same level, [but] what makes a difference is in the management of the personalities and all the pressures."
>
> —Niccolo Porzio di Camporotondo

As expressed in his quote above, the head of Regatta Operations for the 32nd America's Cup understood that success in the competition depends on the way in which team leaders set the course and navigate the challenges associated with their disparate resources. The course was the specialized goal structure and resource pool of each team, which included their targeted placement in the sailing race as well as considerations such as national pride, individual prestige, and promoting the team sponsors. Each team, after all, was really a multi-unit syndicate, with some degree of independence among subteams in areas including design, shore, management, and sailors. The challenges came from within the team—high-quality personnel and equipment, both requiring careful treatment—as well as from the actions of the competitors and eyes of spectators worldwide.

Navigating the challenges varied according to the style of each team's leader, with no particular style assuring success across all teams. To be sure, putting together a winning Cup run—or enhancing the sponsor's brand, or any other planned goal—is not an easy task. A winning run has not only the elements of a business enterprise, but in fact exemplifies what the business world wants to become—highly responsive teams of experts, using cutting-edge technology in a highly competitive industry to leave challengers in their wake.

History. The America's Cup has been the most renowned prize in sailing, dating from the 1851 British challenge taken on by the yacht *America*, which brought the trophy to the United States. After defending its possession for more than one hundred years, since 1983 the United States found itself just one among many viable contenders to win the Cup. (See Exhibit 7.1 for a history of the race.) In the modern, more professional event, teams from Australia, New Zealand, and Europe competed on a scale well beyond the ken of the race originators. Gone were the amateur sailors and millionaires who supported teams of decades past. The best teams now trained year-round with billionaire funding and corporate sponsorship. Teams had to recruit the top in the marine industry to design and build their boats just to stay on par. Managing a team is a year-round job, equivalent to a major sports franchise in the United States. Although as a challenge cup the particulars can change for any cycle, typically the America's Cup is a multiyear series, in which boats and crews are developed early then raced in Acts and tournaments for two or three years for the right to face the Cup Defender in the final one-on-one racing series.

In 2007 for the first time, an independent group, America's Cup Management (ACM) (see Exhibit 7.2), was given charge of the event. While Camporotondo and his colleagues directed the races and generally promoted the sport, the individual teams managed themselves. Each challenger put forth a six-figure entry fee and invested tens of millions in individual syndicates. None of them, however, believed he could buy performance with dollars. Good funding could bring the required elements to the shore, but the race was as much a contest of leadership as of boat design.

Looking over the field of America's Cup entrants, it was apparent that each team had its challenges. The port buzzed with the skirmishes between BMW Oracle's majority owner and his charismatic skipper. Meanwhile, defending team Alinghi, who at one time struggled to replace the heart of their team, seemed to have

Exhibit 7.1. A Short History of the America's Cup

The America's Cup, one of the oldest sporting trophies in the world, began its history with an 1851 race around the Isle of Wight hosted by the British Yacht Club. The event was famously witnessed by the United Kingdom's Queen Victoria, who asked her attendant which boat was in second while watching the New York Yacht Club's schooner, America, salute her as it sailed past in the leading position. His reply came to epitomize the America's Cup pursuit: "Your Majesty, there is no second."

The Cup was subsequently named for the winning schooner, rather than for its patron country, as is sometimes assumed, and was carried triumphantly home to the young United States of America. The Commodore arranged for its disposition as a Deed of Gift to the New York Yacht Club, to be held as "a perpetual challenge cup for friendly competition between nations." Since then, thirty-three times a challenge has been accepted by the Cup Defender, with each race subject to changes in the location, boat type, and other details outlined in the challenge.

The United States held the Cup (and the sporting world's longest winning streak) until 1983, when the series was interrupted by a win from an upstart Australian team. Dennis Connor won it back for the United States in 1987 and in 1988, famously bending the rules in his Defender run with a faster catamaran against single-hulled challengers caught unaware of the loophole in the challenge rules. Connor moved the Cup competition to San Diego, California (from the previous U.S. base in Newport, Rhode Island), thus beginning the modern Cup era abound with further changes. Teams that had traditionally drawn their members from a single home country became increasingly of mixed international membership. New design rules and advances in technology such as carbon fiber construction pushed each team's yacht design further to the cutting edge, increasing the need for sophisticated modeling and heavy financial investment.

The Cup remained in the United States until 1995 when another parvenu nation, this time New Zealand, took the Cup to the other side of the world for the second time. New Zealand then became the first country other than the United States to successfully defend the Cup in 2000. However, in 2003, Team Alinghi grabbed the Cup with a team of international sailors,

Continued

with many taken from Team New Zealand's 2000 crew. With an official yacht club based in Geneva, Switzerland, and no waters large enough to hold an event of this kind, Alinghi chose to enhance the Port of Valencia on the Mediterranean coast of Spain to hold the next challenge.

Twelve teams competed in the multi-year event, which culminated in the 2007 finals of the 32nd America's Cup: Alinghi (Defender), BMW Oracle (US-Britain), Shosholoza (South Africa), China Team, Areva (France), Desafio Espanol, Emirates (New Zealand), Victory Challenge (Sweden), Team United Germany, with three from Italy: Luna Rossa, +39, and Mascalzone Latino. As can be seen, most teams represented a country, although the majority employ an international mix of staff and sailors. Two countries' teams, China Team and Shosholoza, while no strangers to sailing, are competing in the Cup for the first time. Team budgets range from $30 million to over $200 million. The largest budgets may be daunting to the smaller teams, but are no guarantor of success—the leaders, technology, and sailors' execution on the water will ultimately determine the next Cup winner.

Exhibit 7.2. AC Management

AC Management was the first separate management entity created for an America's Cup competition and is generally charged with augmenting each team's investment. AC Management acts as an industry representative, promoting the sport and the events as a whole, and also runs the sailing regattas that serve to qualify all challengers for the ultimate right to face the defending champion. In the recent past, the "defender" team and its home sailing club planned and oversaw the regattas—an arrangement that might be viewed as the equivalent of having U.S. major-league baseball umpires on the payroll of a particular team. Having AC Management run the qualifiers was intended to decrease the inherent bias of the old system, as well as to manage the appearance of such arrangements to worldwide spectators.

found a leadership infusion. In the background of these high-profile dramas, less experienced teams jockeyed to get to the next level. Mascalzone Latino tempered any disadvantage of a relatively young roster through shared leadership, building spirit, and levering expertise by distributing responsibility throughout the team. By contrast, Areva Challenge's general manager pondered whether a directive, highly involved style would best pull together her diverse team. Other teams sought to make a good showing for their sponsors. For instance, Luna Rossa was bankrolled by Prada and charged with raising their international profile. Yet other teams competed for national pride, such as Desafio Espanol's mission to make a good showing for Spain, the host country of the America's Cup finals in Porto Valencia.

Niccolo believed that team leadership—how it was used to define team roles, empower team members, and structure the team—was one of the most important, yet underrated determinants of the 32nd Cup champion. There were no cookie-cutter solutions, no leadership style that could guarantee success in winning the Cup, or any other team goals. However, by the end of the Cup finals it was clear that some teams were led into the competition more effectively than others. There are many ways to be a leader, and the America's Cup competition reveals a variety of team leadership approaches and styles.

Team Lessons

1. Identify Team Goals and Resources

To effectively lead a team, it is essential to understand its overall purpose, cascading goal system, and full complement of human and other resources available to their pursuit. As noted above, teams came to the Cup with different issues and intentions. For the most part, teams were competitive and focused. When asked why they joined a team, or their personal aims, the leaders' answers were invariably clear and consistent: "To win the Cup." However, when pressed to further elaborate or to give their best projection of the final team rankings, their responses became more nuanced and precise.

First, typically, leaders would describe relative state of team finances, technology, equipment, and personnel. Although not all teams disclosed the specifics of their budgets, it was common knowledge within the port that several teams were funded to the tune of $90 million, $120 million, or even well over $200 million over a three-year cycle, while others limped by on $30 million or less. Top teams such as Alinghi and Luna Rossa had two new specially designed boats with two full crews, allowing within-team competition while testing variations in hulls, sails, tactics, and other technology. Lesser-endowed teams, including Areva and Shosholoza, might have one boat recycled from the last Cup competition, perhaps refurbished but not up to the latest standards. Crew member specialties, experience, and growth potential were often discussed, especially in how well they performed together under pressure.

After outlining the team resources, leaders analyzing their teams' likely outcome would then connect the resource overview to the expectation of stakeholders who were important to the team. In some cases, such as Luna Rossa, this was a sponsor; Prada credited their investment in the prior America's Cup with a large increase in their share of the Asian clothing market. Walking in the Luna Rossa team shop of Porto Valencia—each team had one and even Shosholoza offering a few bright t-shirts and other apparel—it was clear that their image included more than a bit of expensive style. For others such as Team China, their home government was behind their sailing venture, with an expectation of good technical sailing with potential for success in future Cups, but no awards in this cycle. Still other teams sought to raise awareness of sailing in their home while setting their sights on a showing in the semi-finals, as they knew that most teams would be eliminated in the march to the one-on-one Finals series.

A realistic and nuanced conception of team goals and resources is a necessary step in preparing to lead a team. The vignettes that follow this section further describe the interaction of these in America's Cup teams.

2. Examine Leadership Styles, Beliefs, and Fit

> "At bottom, becoming a leader is synonymous with becoming yourself. It's precisely that simple, and it's also that difficult."
>
> —Warren Bennis

Leaders vary not only in their properties and processes, as discussed above, but also in their beliefs about themselves, their team members, and how they should function as leaders. As Bennis implies in the quote above, a first step to becoming a good leader is to understand one's own capabilities, perspectives, preferences, and limitations. Such a personal inventory will help leaders to be authentic and circumspect with regard to their influence on others. It also identifies probable best fits with particular team characteristics and goals, as well as identifying clear areas for leadership growth.

Another important aspect to understand personal leadership is to consider one's beliefs about team members and how a leader should function. For instance, teams are often discussed as vehicles for empowerment, with members monitoring and giving feedback to one another within their task purview, while external leaders provide vision, direction, and resources before stepping back to let the experts do their work (Manz & Sims, 1987). However, both leaders and team members must be suitably oriented for such empowerment to occur.

It may be, for example, that a leader's willingness to engage in empowering actions may be dependent on his or her implicit beliefs about the ability of others to learn and grow, termed the leader's "implicit personality theory" (IPT; Dweck & Leggett, 1988). Leaders who believe that their team members are finished products are termed to have an "entity" IPT. A leader with this view is less likely to invest time or other resources in team members, other than what is strictly needed to address task behavior, because it isn't believed that the members can benefit or grow. Leaders with an "incremental" IPT, on the other hand, believe that others are capable of growth and independent positive action, so are more likely to spend effort in training, guiding, and otherwise devoting resources to team members. Team members may become empowered collectively in response to the leader's actions, or through increased motivation of individual members in response to their perceptions of the leader's beliefs (Chen, Kirkman, Kanfer, Allen, & Rosen, 2007; Pearce, Gallagher, & Ensley, 2002).

In the vignettes, consider each leader's demonstrated beliefs and actions, along with the probable reaction of the team members and the effect on team performance outcomes. There is considerable difference both in what each leader believed about the team and in how he or she went about the task of leadership.

3. Create a Structure and Process That Leverages the Team's Strengths

Team structures may vary widely in the manner of their design and interaction. Some teams operate with a strict hierarchical structure, with little flexibility of roles or decision-making procedures. Typically, such structures are most effective when there is clear expertise, authority, urgency, or other limitations that make distributed decision making unnecessary or unwieldy. Other teams are built with more distributed power and decision structures. This configuration can vary widely, such as in the case of clear subteam leaders who interact as a collection of equals, versus a more egalitarian arrangement with cross-functional roles. Within America's Cup teams, expert roles may be based on, for instance, knowledge of hull design, sailing tactics, fundraising, marketing, or legal maneuvering (e.g., Conner's understanding of the rules in the 1989 challenge gave his team a distinct advantage; see Exhibit 7.1).

A team's process of interaction and operation should also be carefully considered by team leaders. Communication, for example, could vary on relative formality, frequency, direction, and mode. Such communication choices will pair with the team structure to form the experience of each member, including his or her interpersonal interactions and resultant satisfaction with other members and potentially other team outcomes. While team structure and process choices may be influenced by preferences of team leaders, there are also likely to be effects of other factors, such as size of the team, amount of time available to make decisions, and the aforementioned expertise. These choices are inevitably linked to team performance and member outcomes, as will be illustrated further in the vignettes.

4. Coach for Peak Performance at the Right Time

Teams cycle in accordance with internal rhythms, goals, and external factors that punctuate the experience of the members. As such, the performance of real-world teams must be modulated over time, an important challenge for team leaders. A growing body of work has modeled and tested the temporal, or time-oriented, process of team performance. Early research tracked performance with group dynamics, developing as member roles and norms progress through stages of forming, storming, norming, and performing, a more synergistic operational mode (Tuckman, 1965). Gersick (1988) changed the focus of team performance to be more coincident with the environment, postulating that externally set tasks punctuate a team's equilibrium through deadlines and intermediary targets, such that task-oriented behavior is more likely to occur close to those deadlines. These two influential models, while seemingly at odds, may instead be characterized as describing different processes (Seers & Woodruff, 1997). Tuckman's stage model illustrates the life span development of a group, while Gersick's punctuated equilibrium explains the group's task pacing.

It seems probable that the temporal aspects of team performance, pacing tasks and modulating peak cycles, would be important levers for a team leader to manipulate. While our understanding of how teams respond to their environment is growing, the role of the leader is not entirely clear. There are indications of some areas in which leaders can effectively influence team task pacing and team performance, however. It may be that team leaders can influence task pacing directly through goal setting, for instance. This would include clarifying goals, connecting to team resources, and giving feedback on progress toward completion and deviance from the optimal course. Less directly but related would be the modeling role of leaders, who through their complacency or urgency are likely to affect the temporal mood of the team. Additionally, team leaders may fill the role of boundary spanners from their teams to other actors in the environment, such as within-organizational governing units, partners along a supply chain, or competitors in the external environment. This role may be especially critical in multi-team systems (DeChurch & Marks, 2006) as a mechanism for modulating precisely timed behaviors and output among the sub- or coordinating teams. Certainly, as leaders consider how to motivate long-term, real-world teams, they would find it valuable to plan for periods of peak performance and times for gathering strength, skill, or other resources. America's Cup teams modulated their temporal peaks in a variety of ways, such as the German team's wakeboarding behind their sailboat or the contingent of teams who arranged a race in Dubai during a lull—lifting boats, crew, and all 7,000 kilometers away. These and other performance shocks were used by leaders seeking to find peaks where the teams could most use them.

5. Build in Feedback, Acknowledge Wins, and Plan for the Future

A good leader understands that teams are evolving, ongoing entities that thrive on information about their progress, praise for their accomplishments, and direction for their next steps. The manner in which leaders communicate these messages will vary according to the lessons discussed so far—the team's specific goals, structure, processes, temporal orientation, and the leader's own beliefs about how to relate to the team. Feedback can be direct and frequent, blunt, detailed, and to the point, if this fits with the team and its norms. Conversely, other teams will benefit most from feedback administered at preplanned points of goal completion, time, or team development. This feedback might focus on broad themes or big ideas rather than specifics. The key is that the leader and team are on the same page, communicating through whatever mechanistic or organic process best suits their goals, resources, and context. It is also important to have a sense for the team's future plans or to allow the team to develop plans if appropriate. Not only do individual team members appreciate having plans for themselves, but the presence of an ongoing team entity may assist in retaining valued employees while keeping their attention on the next set of organizational goals.

America's Cup Team Vignettes

The following four team vignettes—Silvio Arrivabene of Mascalzone Latino Capitalia, Dawn Riley of Areva Challenge, Chris Dickson of BMW Oracle, and Grant Simmer of Alinghi—illustrate the five lessons discussed above, each to varying degrees and in its own ways. The illustrations are not meant as ideal representations; instead, they are a picture of real leaders coping with complex situations in the high-demand, high-performance arena of international yachting races.

Silvio Arrivabene at Mascalzone Latino Capitalia: Structuring Leadership

Silvio Arrivabene knew he had a tough challenge ahead of him. At thirty, he was one of the youngest managers in the America's Cup competition. His team Mascalzone Latino Capitalia had adequate resources, but could not match some of the giants in the regatta whose budgets topped $100 million US. There was a big gap—in money, talent, and other resources—between his team and what many were calling the "Big Four": the defending Cup winner, Alinghi, and challengers BMW Oracle, Luna Rossa, and TNZ. Mascalzone had some great personnel, signed several great sailors, and had good designers working for them. The only hole left to fill was his team management. The pressure was on him to make his first big decision for the team. Did he need managers who could drive and direct or ones who could facilitate and motivate? Was there any in-between? Silvio stated:

> "I believe you have to lead by example. There is no other way to get it, especially long-term . . . To get the motivation out of the people, you have to get your hands dirty, like everybody else."
>
> —Silvio Arrivabene

Arrivabene had been brought in after several other managers had been fired. Although the reasons for the changes were entirely clear, the team was clearly not performing well under the previous managers. Silvio had a formidable challenge ahead of him, and he believed it would be important to strike some sort of balance managing the team. The sailors should have some input on what the team was doing—and if something wasn't working, they were the first ones to notice. They were all world-class professionals at the top of their game (including Arrivabene himself), competing against the best from all over the world. Empowering his team could bring them together, give them each a purpose in the organization, and help them focus over the long four-year campaign. However, like any other business manager, he thought it appropriate to build some level of control into the structural relationships of the organization. Sponsors were paying a lot of money for them to sail the boats, and he wanted the team to be successful.

Silvio had several directions in which he could take Mascalzone, but he needed the proper fit for his young, ambitious, and talented team. He was smart enough to realize that leading a team was a matter of clearing the path from aspirations to objectives, reducing obstacles, and leveraging resources. Showing team members the relationship among these elements was one important step. Next, he would have to empower each team member to do what he or she did best—from the sailors on the boat to the critical support functions such as boat builders and marketing staff. If everyone knew his or her job and was trusted to do it with the available resources, the team could perform at the highest levels when the time came to race. After all, at this level of competition, everyone on the team was an expert.

> "All of the people in the restricted group that we're talking about are specialists in their own field, way more than me. . . . There is a boat builder and I just helped him to lay down the carbon, which is something I don't know anything about. I put on a pair of gloves and he said, 'Hold this for me.' . . . This way, I try to see what they are seeing."
>
> —Silvio Arrivabene

Syndicates such as Emirates Team New Zealand (TNZ), Cup winners in 1995 and 2000, had success with a relatively "flat" management structure. Tasks from team practice scheduling to design innovation decisions are taken care of by team members according to expertise, rather than positional authority. Silvio believed that emulating this structure would allow his enthusiastic crew to shine and decided to build an organizational culture where everyone—designers, sailors, even maintenance workers—were all welcome to contribute their opinions to the operation. But how could he make the ideal a reality? Did the competitive environment of the

Cup, combined with a relatively junior team, mean that members would be looking to one manager to act decisively?

Other teams had tried to copy the TNZ structure with varying success. It seemed that the team had to be prepared for this type of transition; they had to be ready to assume leadership themselves. Alinghi, the Swiss team, was having some success in using a relatively flat structure. Members of other teams who had aped the TNZ system have complained that there was not enough structure or managerial action. Even teams that encourage members to offer suggestions might be stymied by a maze of committees, procedures, and reporting relationships. Decisions that depend on multiple persons gathering in assorted meetings to reach agreement tend to stymie progress and team development. The process also often meant delays while area experts made their decisions, leading to last-minute scheduling and its attendant stress on those wondering what they would be doing in the coming week, or even to the day. Team members are devoting a large amount of time—up to four years with some teams—to accomplish one major event. They can't afford to be set back, as the next chance to be on an AC team may not come.

Silvio contemplated how to empower and inspire his team members, sharing his vision but giving them room to develop their own skills. His work was cut out for him.

Dawn Riley at Areva Challenge: Leadership in Transition

Dawn Riley had a tough decision to make about her Areva team roster. As general manager, she was faced with the choice of cutting herself from the sailing crew to devote all her efforts to managing the larger, overall team or to maintain two roles. Should she stay onboard, manage from the shore, or attempt both together? Riley had pulled off that dual role for another team in 2003, but was finding Areva to be a bit more demanding of her time. Areva was a small team, with less than a quarter of the budget of spending leader BMW Oracle, yet it faced the rough waters as any of the teams vying for the Cup. In order to close the gap, they would have to perform perfectly on the water—and the pressure was on Riley to put together the best crew to do it.

As something of a pioneer in the sport, Riley was known for advocating the position that simple competence, not gender or even past wins, is criteria enough for making an AC team roster. She had personally broken the barrier by serving in the physically demanding pit of the boat (not the relatively clean job of navigator or skipper) of the eventual Cup winner, America3. Further, she headed the first open-trial coed team in the 2000 America's Cup race.

> "I was the CEO, I had put in my own money, my life savings, raised the money, found a great partner, who put up the bulk of the private funds, good sailors all the way around. It was all good."
>
> —Dawn Riley

Even with as much support as she'd had in and out of racing circles for her competence-based approach, Riley was aware that in practice AC racing was still predominantly a men's club. Even her own achievements weren't without what others might consider to be limitations. It had been fifteen years since she served in America3's pit throughout the Challenger trials, only to be left off the boat in the AC finals. Her Cup win came as part of the larger team, but she knew that her role had been prescribed by those who didn't think a woman belonged in the boat when it came to crunch time.

Riley didn't doubt that she still had skills enough to contribute as a member of the sailing crew, but did being on the crew detract from her ability to lead the larger team? Both practical and symbolic issues factored in. First, her managerial duties wouldn't allow her sufficient time to train for the physical and mental demands of the sailing crew, at least not to her exacting professional standards. Every day she would be beaconing priorities through her actions. Inevitably, a crew member needed help with his or her own development, the design guys would need input on a hull improvement, or a potential donor would want a meeting. Where would she draw the line?

Second, her natural position on the boat wasn't one with physical or symbolic oversight of the crew, such as a navigator or skipper. Instead, Riley had earned her career berth in the trenches, operating from the pit of the boat where sails and other equipment were hoisted to respond to the fast-moving conditions. Everyone on the boat could influence the team's performance—even the "pitman" often called out the starts and timing—but in a practical sense, visibility would be limited and concentration directed by the physical efforts involved. Would the crew look to the pit for decisions because the general manager was the pitman? Dawn knew that she could make it work, but would it be the best choice for Areva?

In addition to the decisions about personnel for Areva, a team sponsored by France's state nuclear power company, Riley's position as general manager would hold further challenges. For instance, this was the first French team to welcome "Anglos," much less to be managed by an American, and there were multiple national culture barriers for team members to overcome. Riley discovered early on that she would need to accommodate different ideas about work scheduling. First, she was accustomed to requiring her teams to attend early-morning workouts. However, 7 a.m. was too early for her European employees. They preferred a later workout schedule, so Riley had to work that in to an already bulging schedule. In true American style, she found some extra time by scheduling the day's rundown meeting during breakfast, but was soon conquered by the French palate and respect for mealtime conversation. This team was teaching her new lessons, but as the members also respected her stature and accomplishments in the field, they wanted her to take them somewhere that they hadn't yet been.

Another issue that couldn't be ignored was their relative lack of resources. As a smaller team with a limited budget, they did not have the luxuries of Alinghi and BMW Oracle, with their large shore crews and seemingly boundless equipment. They also only had one boat, on which any testing of designs and modifications must be done. If the vessel was undergoing modifications, or in need of repair, the team would not be sailing that day!

> "You see that all the teams with two boats are in front, and the teams with one boat are in the second half of the ranking . . . We ran out of money in 2004, and the winter, basically we stopped all operations, sailing [and] construction of the boats."
>
> —Dimitri Nicolopoulos, Areva

Riley could manage these issues; all it took was careful planning, time, and communication. Perhaps she should just focus on the larger team issues and leave the sailing to others. However, there was something to be said for leading from the boat—modeling the way to win, reducing the separation from those who were most critical to the actual racing. In either arena, Riley would admit to having trouble micromanaging—focusing too much on small problems, like daily schedule changes, instead of seeing the big picture. Add to that a late-arriving boat, keel design troubles, and budget problems, this team had significant challenges that teams like Alinghi didn't have to fathom.

Pondering these issues, Riley considered whether she should transition from crew to professional manager or to lead from her position on the boat. In either case, should she be the first to dirty her hands or leave the jobs to the people she hired to do them? Were these issues of role and functions related to her own leadership style? Could she learn a new role?

Chris Dickson at BMW Oracle: Leadership from the Top

Chris Dickson was an accomplished sailor and skipper, a seasoned America's Cup veteran, and an experienced leader. Cementing his reputation sailing with the New Zealand teams of the 1990s, Dickson demonstrated a fierce determination and commanding presence to augment his formidable seamanship. At BMW Oracle, Chris Dickson was in charge of everything involved with the team. "Dicko," as he was commonly (sometimes affectionately) called from a distance, was also an early entrant among the class of America's Cup mercenaries, eschewing country allegiances to find a team that would match both his particular leadership style and his desire to win. Larry Ellison had hired him to be solely in charge of his $270 million team for the 2007 Cup.

On the sailboat, Dickson was the skipper, in charge of the helm and the crew alike. His authority went far beyond that, however. Virtually every BMW Oracle team decision went through Dickson, whether falling into the bailiwick of the designers, shore crew, or sailors on the boat. He held decision-making authority and veto power. Some viewed this arrangement as the equivalent of a NASCAR driver or an NFL quarterback running the entire business operation of the team. Perhaps not surprising to anyone who has run a tight ship in his or her day, there were advantages to such a system. Since all BMW Oracle team members knew that Dickson was in charge, they did not have to go through channels to find the answers they needed. For example, before the Louis Vuitton qualifying trials began, several of the BMW Oracle crew commented on how refreshing it was to have a clear line of authority and strict organizational structure—the schedule was set from the top and everyone knew who to go to when direction was needed.

Such a concentration of power is not, however, without drawbacks. The America's Cup teams were filled with people—sailors, designers, boat builders, and others—who were at the top of their professions. No one person, no matter how talented or driven, could win the Cup on his own. The Cup promoted a team environment in which members were expected to achieve excellence through intrinsic motivation and monitor their own progress toward self-set goals in line with the team mission. If their ability to make their own decisions was limited, even in their own areas of expertise, their performance could well be compromised.

There are further challenges inherent in such top-down systems that go beyond team empowerment. In BMW Oracle's system, there was no one to critique the man at the top, no powerful advisory structure or "board of directors." Having one person saddled with operational control of each area can hinder progress simply due to the need to clear decisions through a busy person. A designer forced to wait an extra day for Dickson's decision on a necessary adjustment could delay the project, costing the team a day of practice. Even suspect decisions couldn't be questioned unless the performance of the team on race day made it painfully obvious that a change in leadership was needed.

Only Larry Ellison, the billionaire software developer who represented the team sponsors, could act contrary to Dickson's wishes. Ellison chose to let his charismatic leader have free reign, however, and even pulled himself from his former position of sharing the boat's helm for major races. After great success in the Acts leading to the final series to determine the Cup

Challenger, suddenly BMW Oracle foundered in a few demanding races. The crew, highly talented though they were, seemed to be shaken by the development, losing confidence in Dickson as cracks appeared in his armor. Soon the collapse of the team was so widely accepted that the news media openly speculated on Dickson's removal. Eventually, Ellison pulled Dickson off the boat late in the Challenger series, where teams contested for the right to face the defending champion Alinghi in a one-on-one series.

Removing such a strong leader so suddenly and completely left the BMW Oracle team foundering on the water. The crew didn't respond well to their new skipper, losing their final two races. Despite being ranked as one of the top challengers for almost three years, BMW Oracle exited early in the semi-finals, taking just one race in a seven-race series from lower-ranked Luna Rossa. In terms of race results, top-down organizational leadership didn't seem to help BMW Oracle's team in 2007. It remained to be seen what the team thought of the system after they were sent home.

> "While Dickson may be respected, he is hardly 'loved' by his employees. When he goes one way, they go the other, so it is hard to imagine them digging deep for someone so disliked." Scuttlebutt 2349 (online sailing newsletter), May 22, 2007

Grant Simmer at Alinghi: Shared Goals, Shared Leadership

Grant Simmer, general manager of the Alinghi team, rode the team chase boat as it eased its way back into the small harbor in Valencia. His sailing team was returning from the clinching race of the 2007 America's Cup; he was watching rather than in his old position on the crew. Team New Zealand had given them a good challenge, but Alinghi won in the end, controlling their races and holding position on the water. While TNZ experienced equipment failures, the defending champion kept an even keel. Alinghi stayed with a sailing crew that had been painstakingly constructed over the past three years, rather than letting even the mistakes of its rival dictate the course. The win gave Simmer—finally—a few moments to reflect on the steps the organization had taken to bring the team to this level and his role in the process.

As the cup Defender, the pressure was on Simmer and his team to ensure that they protected what they had won in 2003. As early as 2004, it became apparent that it would not be easy. Russell Coutts, the undisputed team leader and helmsman of the boat, parted ways with Team Alinghi soon after Valencia was chosen for the race venue. Coutts' personality and vision had imbued the team, and his docksiders would be difficult to fill. However, unlike BMW Oracle's last-minute disruption when Dickson left the team, when Coutts departed there were leagues to go before the 2007 finals. Simmer knew that time not only healed wounds, but also was a critical resource for teams in transition—"time to allow us to prepare, to get as strong as possible . . . obviously time is more critical than money." Given enough time, team Alinghi could not only plan a direction, but could groom the talent on the team and enact a strategy that fit their composition.

But what direction should Alinghi chart? One obvious choice would be to keep the organizational structure intact, simply filling the vacancy at the top with another strong leader. This idea, however, was dismissed almost as soon as it was described. Alinghi had a strong team culture that had grown throughout their championship run to the 2003 Cup, and it didn't rely just on Coutts anymore, if it ever did.

Alinghi's management brain trust decided to let the team's own actions determine the course. Soon after Coutts' departure, they constructed a "flat" management structure that gave each functional area of the team the ability to not only make its own decisions, but to also encourage each to weigh in on the traditionally closely held domain of other units. To accomplish this transition, Simmer knew that it wasn't enough to merely tell members of Team Alinghi that they were "empowered." He had to plan for it, structure the team to fit the organizational goals system, open communication channels among various factions, reward initiative, and—critically, for a team used to a strong leader—have the top managers know when to stay out of the way.

> "I've got to let them win by some of us sitting on the sideline, in a sense waiting until they fight the battle themselves. We are pretty open within the team . . . communicating in a team environment and not in a business departmental-type structure."
>
> —Grant Simmer

One tactic Alinghi used was to frequently stage internal competitions, but with rotating unit memberships, with the idea that team cohesion will build through a common purpose of winning, rather than rivalry between the subteams. Other tactics included having an "open mike" session at the end of weekly staff meetings, where any team member could raise an issue, whether in his or her functional area or not. This was in stark contrast to most strategy meetings across Cup teams, typically either restricted to department-level managers or tightly scripted to deliver a message, rather than encourage feedback.

The media would have plenty to write about in the months following Coutts' exit, questioning whether Alinghi would succeed without their former leader, especially as no other dominant character emerged from the team. Within their own circles, however, team members just grew more confident in themselves and their ability to master their role within the larger goal structure. As Simmer put it, "This time is more of a business-model way. We have departments and different people responsible in different areas."

Alinghi had successfully defended its hold on the America's Cup, taking the finals from Team New Zealand in very convincing fashion. While gear breakdowns and bad luck seemed to plague TNZ, bringing about frustration and conflict, Alinghi was simply self-possessed. Every team member, in the boat and on shore, knew his or her place, and the team was determined to sail its own race. While there were many factors leading to their victory, their shift from a dominant personality to a shared sense of leadership meant that each team member truly owned the victory.

Lessons Forward

The teams of the America's Cup can be a challenging trial for a leader, with a wealth of lessons for those who follow the action.

Embedded within the five broad lessons discussed are numerous intricacies and points to ponder. While the route may seem clear to those reading in the cold light of the next day, decisions made in the murky present are difficult to get right. Even good choices can be turned aside by the competing factors of goals, resources, styles, and temporal constraints.

BMW Oracle had a strong leader operating in a very clear, tight hierarchy. Their sailors were among the best in the world, the boat design was cutting-edge, and the system was working very well—until it derailed. Was it the fault of Chris Dickson, or was he merely the fall guy at the helm? One truism on the water was that the weather on any given day, or series of days, could work against a hull that would be perfect for slightly different weather conditions. The timing of Dickson's—or the team's—collapse couldn't have been worse. Regardless of their leading edge in the earlier Acts, they didn't perform when they needed to move on. Of course, it could be argued that the real breakdown of BMW Oracle was a failure to prepare the team for such hardships, which may be almost inevitable in a multiyear cycle.

Meanwhile, Areva worked at which leadership structure would be best, with Dawn Riley eventually determining to lead from the shore, for the most part anyway. This decision may have been as much precipitated by her injury in an automobile accident as anything else, which on its own was a shock to the team's equilibrium. Riley was an engaging, forthright, and determined leader who made communication and hard work priorities on her watch. In the end, her team didn't fare particularly well, finishing the Round Robin cycle ahead of only Teams China, Germany, and +39, none of which was expected to be competitive. It could be that the French team's difficulties were attributable more directly to funding shortages than leadership, but perhaps the leader was too focused on her boat-shore dilemma than more external boundary spanning needed to find support for the team.

Mascalzone and Alinghi pursued similarly distributed structures but with different goals, gaining success at disparate levels. While it's likely Silvio Arrivabene never realistically could win the 32nd America's Cup, his team made some very impressive showings in the Acts and Louis Vuitton rounds. He had a very young team, but he believed that they could grow and he could mature with them as a leader. His style was that of a participative leader, getting to know his team and getting his hands dirty.

Alinghi's shore leader, Grant Simmer, planned and designed a structure and process, persuaded his team to buy in, set it in motion, then assigned himself to a background role in the operation. While he was always present, the team members were at the forefront, discussing team issues across functional lines, as needed, to be their best. Perhaps he sought to embody the teachings of the Lao-Tse, the legendary founder of Taoism circa 6th century BCE, who said:

> "The wicked leader is he who the people despise,
> "The good leader is he who the people revere,
> The great leader is he who the people say, 'We did it ourselves.'"
>
> —Lao-Tse, Taoist founder

In any case, Simmer seemed very attuned to the goals, resources, and rhythms of the Alinghi team. Of all the team managers to whom I spoke, Simmer had the most unique response to the question: "What is your goal?" replying that it was simply "to build brand." He saw Alinghi as more than just a sailing team, or even more than a $100-million venture, but rather as a vehicle for creating something greater. Perhaps that is the last lesson here: to see more in your team than they know they are themselves.

References and Further Reading

Bass, B.M. (1990). *Bass and Stodgill's handbook of leadership: Theory, research, and managerial applications.* New York: The Free Press.

Bennis, W.G. (1989). *On becoming a leader.* Reading, MA: Addison-Wesley.

Chen, G., Kirkman, B., Kanfer, R., Allen, D., & Rosen, B. (2007). A multilevel study of leadership, empowerment, and performance in teams. *Journal of Applied Psychology, 92,* 331–346.

DeChurch, L.A., & Marks, M.A. (2006). Leadership in multi-team systems. *Journal of Applied Psychology, 91,* 311–329.

Dweck, C.S., & Leggett, E.L.A. (1988). A social-cognitive approach to motivation and personality. *Psychological Review, 95*, 256–273.

Gersick, C.J.G. (1988). Time and transition in work teams: Toward a new model of group development. *Academy of Management Journal, 31*(1), 9–41.

Greenleaf, R.K. (1970). *The servant as leader.* Indianapolis, IN: Robert K. Greenleaf Center.

Hackman, J.R. (1987). The design of work teams. In J. Lorsch (Ed.), *Handbook of organizational behavior* (pp. 315–342). Englewood Cliffs, NJ: Prentice Hall.

Hackman, J.R., & Wageman, R. (2005). A theory of team coaching. *Academy of Management Review, 30*, 269–287.

Kirkman, B.L., & Rosen, B. (1999). Beyond self-management: Antecedents and consequences of team empowerment. *Academy of Management Journal, 42*, 58–74.

Kozlowski, S.W.J., Gully, S.M., Salas, E., & Cannon-Bowers, J.A. (1996). Team leadership and development: Theory, principles, and guidelines for training leaders and teams. In M. Beyerlein, D. Johnson, & S. Beyerlein (Eds.), *Advances in interdisciplinary studies of work teams: Team leadership, Vol.* 3 (pp. 251–289). Greenwich, CT: Elsevier Science/JAI Press.

Manz, C.C., & Sims, H.P. (1987). Leading workers to lead themselves: The external leadership of self- managing work teams. *Administrative Science Quarterly, 32*, 106–129.

Manz, C.C., & Sims, H.P. (1991). Super leadership: Beyond the myth of heroic leadership. *Organizational Dynamics, 19*(4), 18–35.

Manz, C.C., & Sims, H.P. (1995). *Business without bosses: How self-managing teams are building high-performing companies.* Hoboken, NJ: John Wiley & Sons.

Pearce, C.L., Gallagher, C.A., & Ensley, M.D. (2002). Confidence at the group level of analysis: A longitudinal investigation of the relationship between potency and team effectiveness. *Journal of Occupational and Organizational Psychology, 75*(1), 115–119.

Seers, A., & Woodruff, S. (1997). Temporal pacing in task forces: Group development or deadline pressure? *Journal of Management, 23*(2), 169–187.

Strauss, A., & Corbin, J. (1998). *Basics of qualitative research: Techniques and procedures for developing grounded theory* (2nd ed.). Thousand Oaks, CA: Sage.

Tuckman, B.W. (1965). Developmental sequence in small groups. *Psychological Bulletin, 65*(6), 384–399.

Zaccaro, S.J., Rittman, A.L., & Marks, M.A. (2001). Team leadership. *The Leadership Quarterly, 12*(4), 451–483.

Part Four

The Organizational Context

CHAPTER EIGHT

Virtual Teams

The How To's of Making "Being Virtually There" Successful

Debra J. Cohen and Alexander Alonso
Society for Human Resource Management

Introduction

SoftCo, a bi-coastal company with an established office in Philadelphia, opened a facility in Oregon. The Philadelphia office has 750 employees and the Portland Oregon office has two hundred employees on the way up to 350. Fifty employees are in the field working remotely, scattered around the United States and Europe. As the company, a high-tech software firm, grows, its founding president, Valentina, knew that in order to increase sales and synergy there needed to be more interaction with the two primary offices and the field staff; and there needed to be more innovation. She sent a memo to the executive staff instructing them to form a cross-functional virtual team with three employees from each coast and three from the field to brainstorm new ideas. She went on to say that the team had great latitude for setting its own agenda, processes, and structure. Her only expectation was to have a report in three months.

Three months later, she received a report that analyzed employee attitudes at the two locations and offered a set of recommendations about how to improve the working relationships among the one thousand employees of SoftCo. Valentina sat back in her chair and was dumfounded that she had not received what she was looking for—a set of innovative ideas about how to improve their products, ideas for new products, and novel ideas about how to bring their products to market to increase sales and market share.

The nine employees who had been assigned to work on the team were glad to have the assignment over. And, had it not been for John, who finally volunteered to collect all their individual ideas and put them together in a report, they might not have finished at all. Nine of SoftCo's best employees had been tagged for this assignment and, while each was happy to assist the company, they found themselves at a loss as to what to do. The first two conference calls had focused on trying to gain clarity on what Valentina really expected, how to move forward, what processes to use, why they had each been selected for the assignment, and who was to do what. John was frustrated by the lack of progress and finally offered to pull together everyone's ideas so that the deadline would not be missed.

How do organizations prevent this type of failure from occurring? Virtual teams have become a way of corporate life. They occur in the same town, across the country, and around the world. Some virtual teams have been quite successful, while others have failed like the one in the SoftCo example above. Some fail without even realizing it. There has been a great deal of research focused on understanding how teams of all types and, in particular, how virtual teams form, survive and succeed (Martins & Schilpzand, 2011; Tannenbaum, Mathieu, Salas, & Cohen, in press). It is well documented that having clear objectives, focused leadership, continuous communication, and effective technology to facilitate productivity are among the top factors for success (Wallace & Hinsz, 2010). The key is in adapting processes that allow teams to thrive in a face-to-face environment to the realities of virtual work.

A virtual team can be defined as one that engages individuals who are geographically dispersed and that engages them across time, location, and organizational boundaries. Organizations use virtual teams for a variety of reasons. These reasons have changed and evolved somewhat over time but are fairly straightforward. A targeted poll of 335 HR professionals indicated that 41 percent *consciously* use virtual teams. In today's competitive and economically challenged environment, organizations want to include talent in different locations and wish to boost collaboration among employees in geographic locations; minimizing costs and improving productivity are highly desired as well.

Poor planning, training, leadership, attitude, and rapport are reasons why virtual teams fail (SHRM, 2011). It is not as simple as switching from face-to-face teams to virtual teams without thinking carefully and planning purposefully. Like any team, you must have specific goals and objectives, and it may be that even greater clarity is needed in virtual teams because the ability to clarify them before, during, or after meetings is lost or curtailed. As in the SoftCo example, there was no designated leader, there were no clear or agreed-on objectives and, while the employees had a positive attitude at the outset toward helping the organization, their attitudes had waned by the end of the assignment—perhaps contributing to a disappointing outcome for the president.

A virtual team is like a car. The parts may come from many different manufacturing facilities, perhaps even different areas of the world. In the end, the parts must be assembled to work together in order to be effective and move forward. The driver of the team/car needs to be able to trust that the brakes will work or that the windshield wipers and lights will operate when necessary. Similarly, if team leaders and team members do not trust that work will occur when promised, the team/car may not be engaged properly. A team/car that is not engaged properly has a greater likelihood of breaking down and failing than one that is well built and well maintained. Virtual teams may have a more difficult time building trust than traditional teams because of the lack of face-to-face interaction. In fact, when asked, HR professionals noted that developing trust among team members was first in a list of the top five most successful behaviors for on-time traditional face-to-face teams, whereas brainstorming solutions for problems or issues was top for the most successful behaviors of virtual teams.

While there was great overlap in the responses cited, another salient difference is that respondents thought coordinating the tasks of the team during initiatives or projects was among the top five successful behaviors for virtual teams, but not for traditional face-to-face teams. The reverse was true of respondents about traditional face-to-face teams. This finding shows that virtual teams have a harder time establishing trust or seeing the need for

Table 8.1. Most Successful Behaviors for Virtual and Traditional Teams

Top five most successful behaviors for virtual teams in your organization	*The top five most successful behaviors for on-time/traditional face-to-face teams in your organization*
1. Brainstorming solutions for problems or issues	1. Developing trust among team members
2. Setting goals for team initiatives or projects	2. Setting goals for team initiatives or projects
3. Developing plans for team initiatives or projects	3. Brainstorming solutions for problems or issues
4. Coordinating the tasks of the team during initiatives or projects	4. Developing plans for team initiatives or projects
5. Designing strategy for the team	5. Designing strategy for the team

Source: 2011 SHRM Poll on Virtual Teams.

trust in order to have the team be successful, whereas traditional teams spend less time in coordinating the tasks of the team or in seeing that this is a necessary ingredient for success compared to developing trust among members. See Table 8.1 for the detailed results.

In exploring the most challenging behaviors for virtual teams compared to traditional face-to-face teams, the SHRM poll again revealed many similarities and a few important differences. The salient difference was that, consistent with the previous finding, developing trust among team members was the top challenge for virtual teams and only the fifth challenge (tied with maintaining team morale during initiatives or projects) for traditional teams. Establishing team norms for process and performance was in the top five for traditional teams, but not for virtual teams. On the other hand, virtual teams are noted to have monitoring the performance of other team members as a top challenge, whereas traditional teams are not indicated as having the same challenge. Given that virtual teams are more focused on coordination and planning than are traditional teams, it may not be surprising that traditional teams have more difficulty establishing team norms for process and planning. Nor is it surprising that monitoring the

Table 8.2. Most Challenging Behaviors for Virtual and Traditional Teams

Top five most challenging behaviors for virtual teams in your organization	*The top six most challenging behaviors for on-time/traditional face-to-face teams in your organization*
1. Developing trust among team members	1. Resolving relationship or personality conflicts during initiatives or projects
2. Resolving relationship or personality conflicts during initiatives or projects	2. Resolving task or information conflicts during initiatives or projects
3. Resolving task or information conflicts during initiatives or projects	3. Developing trust among team members
4. Monitoring the performance of other team members	4. Establishing team norms for process and performance
5. Maintaining team morale during initiatives or projects	5. Designing strategy for the team
	6. Maintaining team morale during initiatives or projects

Source: 2011 SHRM Poll on Virtual Teams.

performance of other team members is an issue for virtual teams. Table 8.2 shows the results from this poll question.

There are different types of teams; some are used formally, while others are used informally. During a recent SHRM poll, HR managers indicated virtual teams are used most often as project teams, followed by top management teams. Given some of the challenges virtual teams experience and some of the reasons why they are formed in the first place, it makes sense that the primary capacity in which virtual teams are used is temporary in nature and that members represent different functions. Quality control teams are the least likely to be used in a virtual team setting. This also makes a great deal of sense because quality control may be something that organizations believe needs to be accomplished in a face-to-face manner.

Beyond the behaviors displayed by teams and team members and beyond the types of teams, respondents to the poll were asked to identify the top three challenges to the success of virtual teams. "Building team relations" was cited as the top challenge. This is

Table 8.3. Challenges to Virtual Team Success

Building team relations	51 percent
Time differences	49 percent
Distribution of work	32 percent
Leadership	25 percent
Differences in cultural norms	26 percent
Multidisciplinary expertise conflicts	24 percent
Technology barriers	21 percent
Team composition	18 percent
Overexertion	16 percent
Language	10 percent

Source: 2011 SHRM Poll on Virtual Teams.

consistent with the previous results regarding behaviors. The next two challenges that topped the list reflect the environmental issues of time differences and decisions that are made about the distribution of work. Table 8.3 shows all ten challenges to the success of virtual teams in terms of the priorities identified by HR professionals. It is interesting to note that language, overextension, technology barriers, and multidisciplinary expertise conflicts were all cited as a challenge less than 25 percent of the time.

Striving for Success

How can an organization or responsible manager determine whether a virtual team is in danger of being ineffective? Table 8.4 identifies key factors that have to be managed and the issues included in each, and poses a series of questions that can be asked to help determine the readiness of the team and the potential for success or failure. This same series or subset of questions can be used for each team an organization creates and at various points throughout the operation of a virtual team. Given that virtual teams place different emphasis on planning and preparation than traditional teams that emphasize team interactions, it is important to recognize how team processes are adapted from traditional to virtual team settings. This entails examining the formality,

Table 8.4. Factors and Questions Leading to Team Success

Factors to Manage	*Issues*	*Questions to Ask*
People: Team Composition	Geographic Locations Skills Attitudes Cultural Differences Leadership Familiarity	How geographically dispersed are the teams; how many locations and time zones are included? Do team members have existing relationships with one another; are some more familiar than others? Will the virtual team have similar skill sets or will they be fairly divergent? Are the team members likely to have a positive attitude or will there be issues to be dealt with in advance? Will there be significant cultural differences among the team members, including working styles, values, norms, and so forth? What steps can be taken to ensure cohesion among the team members? Are team members likely to trust one another from the beginning or will steps need to be taken to ensure that trust develops among the members? Are there any barriers to building trust? Will the team be self-managed or has a leader been designated or in need of being designated? Is there a mechanism for resolving conflicts and for monitoring performance?

Continued

Table 8.4. Continued

Factors to Manage	*Issues*	*Questions to Ask*
Purpose: Team Objective	Complexity Problem Solving or Decision Making Innovation Clarity	How complex is the assignment for the team and how much interaction needs to take place with others inside and outside the organization? The more boundaries the task crosses, the more complex it is likely to be to accomplish. Is the purpose of the team to solve a problem for the organization, a client, something else, or is the purpose of the team broader, for example, to develop something for the organization or to make a decision about an organizational issue? Is the objective to create something innovative to help the organization or a client but not specifically related to problem solving? How clear is the purpose of the team? Where has the assignment originated and is there agreement as to the primary objectives and processes by which to accomplish the objectives? How will coordination of the tasks occur and be maintained throughout the duration of the team?
Technology	Communication Tools Shared Work Site Collaborative Tools Technological Support	Does everyone on the team have access to the same level and type of technology, both hardware and software? What communication tools are available, and do all virtual team members know how to use them effectively? Have shared worksites or collaborative tools been used previously, and is everyone comfortable in using them effectively? Does everyone have the same level of technological savvy or the same access to tech support should he or she need it to effectively participate? What mechanisms for brainstorming solutions will be most effective for this team configuration?

Task Complexity	Cost Uncertainty Duration Interdependence	What is the budget to complete the task(s), and are there sufficient resources for the team to feel empowered to complete the task as requested? Is there a clear path or approach to the task or is there some ambiguity as to how the objective will be accomplished? The greater the uncertainty, the more time it may take to develop an appropriate plan. Is there a planned duration for task accomplishment or is it open-ended? Behavior may be positively or negatively affected if the duration is uncertain. Will team members share information and work closely together or will they work independently or sequentially to perform the assigned task(s)? Has a strategy for the team been designed or will the team design this strategy at the outset?
Logistics	Face-to-Face Meeting Structure Reporting Fluidity Behavior	Is an initial face-to-face meeting feasible or advisable? Have norms for behavior been set or is there an expected code of conduct for participants? Will team members come and go on a regular basis? The more fluid the team, the more there is a need for a cohesive force to maintain momentum. Does the team have an identified structure and clear leadership designated? Who will the team report to and what is expected in the way of outcomes (reports, presentations, etc.) What sort of advance training is necessary, and how will all team members complete the training?

frequency, and function of team dynamic processes as they relate to the traditional and virtual settings. Prior to applying these factors, some preliminary questions must be considered to determine the parameters of the team to which the factors will be applied. Is the team permanent (long-term) or is it temporary?

- What is the anticipated duration of the team if temporary? (*Note:* A temporary team that is established for a long period of time may need to be evaluated differently.)
- Will the entire team be virtual or will some subsets be meeting face-to-face?
- How large will the team be in terms of members?
- How critical is the task or objective of the team to the organization?

Once the parameters for the team are known, the factors and questions in Table 8.4 can be applied to help determine what needs to be done to ensure that the team is successful. Every team is different and every situation is different. Because of this, this type of proactive and advance analysis should be done routinely for any virtual team that is created. There may be different emphasis or slightly different issues if the team is a project team versus a top management team versus an action team. The key is in ensuring that team processes can thrive in a virtual environment and understanding the parameters, which may be more complex for virtual teams, is critical.

The use of teams is ubiquitous and, although virtual teams are a more recent addition to the team landscape, they too have been used for decades. Technology has made virtual teams easier and has no doubt increased the use of such teams. As the SHRM poll indicates, technology is less of an issue than are people and behaviors. A 2007 report from the Center for Creative Leadership indicated that, 95 percent of the time, people participate in more than one team at a time (Martin & Bal, 2007). This makes sense given the proliferation of all types of teams and the fact that project teams are the most commonly formed teams. Even when teams are not totally virtual, more than half the time the members are geographically dispersed. As a result, it may be that there are face-to-face teams that must also deal with characteristics of virtual teams. These "hybrid" teams may need to account for and accommodate multiple types of dynamics.

Taking SoftCo as an example, it may be that members of the leadership team reside in both Philadelphia and Portland, and perhaps even in the field. The leadership team may meet face-to-face on a regular basis, making them resemble a traditional team, yet there are bound to be virtual meetings as well that encompass all or part of the team. Hybrid team formats such as these must have processes that allow them to thrive in both face-to-face interactions as well as in virtual interactions. The factors and questions identified in Table 8.4 will assist in ensuring success. Other recent trends, besides the proliferation of articles, books, and research, include the creation of technical solutions to aid in information-sharing and collaboration. These tools allow for team members and co-workers, virtual or not, to more easily share data and to do so in a more sustainable, convenient and "green" fashion.

So how did we get here and where do we need to go? The next section explores the nature of challenges encountered by virtual teams when using team processes—virtual and otherwise—and then we will identify tips for improving teamwork and suggest strategies for adapting virtual team processes to meet contemporary needs.

Review of Team Processes, Virtual and Otherwise

The findings of our poll indicate a need to focus on teamwork, specifically virtual team processes, to ensure success. Improving virtual team performance requires an analysis of virtual teamwork and processes. First, we will provide an overview of teamwork concepts and processes. Second, we will compare processes for virtual teams with those for traditional teams. Finally, we will demonstrate recent trends in teamwork among virtual teams.

Teamwork and Processes

Teamwork has been studied extensively over the past forty years. Specifically, team research has revolved around two primary areas: (1) explaining team performance and (2) understanding the mechanisms that lead to team performance. The first area focuses primarily on defining the realm of team performance and how it can be assessed. The second area is analogous to understanding how various components of the team and their interactions lead to team effectiveness. To use an analogy, the body of research in teams resembles the anatomy of car engines. There are numerous outputs from a car engine, including speed, acceleration, horsepower, fuel efficiency, and exhaust. Each of these represents a different criterion for car engine performance. In team research, there are myriad outputs.

The second and more important part of an engine focuses on the combustion or what it takes to make it perform effectively. To ensure effective teamwork in any context, we must examine team performance, as well as what it takes to perform effectively as a team. From a classical perspective this entails an investigation of the input-process-output systems model for teams (McGrath, 1984). McGrath posited that team outcomes (aka outputs) were a function of the inputs brought by team members and the dynamic processes required for completion of their tasks. The study of these dynamic processes ranges far and wide, with numerous researchers offering their perspectives on everything from the types of processes, the temporal nature of the processes, and the relative impact of the processes on team outcomes like performance and team orientation (Baker, Gustafson, Beaubien, Salas, & Barach, 2003; Campion, Medsker, & Higgs, 1993; Stevens & Campion, 1994; Fleishman & Zaccaro, 1992; Marks, Zaccaro, & Mathieu, 2000; Salas, Dickinson, Converse, & Tannenbaum, 1992; Salas, Sims, & Burke, 2005). This research suggests that teamwork is defined by a set of interrelated coordination, communication, and cognitive processes that support one's teammates, objectives, and mission (Baker, Gustafson, Beaubien, Salas, & Barach, 2003; Cannon-Bowers, Tannenbaum, Salas, & Volpe, 1995; Salas, Dickinson, Converse, & Tannenbaum, 1992; Salas, Bowers, & Cannon-Bowers, 1995). This body of research has yielded a significant evidence-base for a set of core team processes that directly impact team performance and other outcomes in interdependent task settings (Marks, Mathieu, & Zaccaro, 2001; Salas, Sims, & Burke, 2005; Salas, Rosen, Burke, Nicholson, & Howse, 2007). The critical aspects of teamwork include: cognition, planning, coordination, and communication. Based on an extensive review of the team and virtual team literature, we have identified nine major processes critical to virtual teams.

1. Team Leadership

Leadership is a critical process related to planning and effective team performance. Leaders impact team effectiveness by facilitating team actions and by making sure that teams have all the necessary resources to perform. Facilitation of team actions often involves activities like ensuring that team actions are understood by all and that changes in information are shared by team members. In addition, leaders must also provide team members the appropriate human and material resources (e.g., team members with proper skills) to perform. Facilitation of team actions results in the development of a shared mental model among the team, while managing resources ensures that teams can be adaptable.

Virtual teams, like traditional teams, thrive on leadership. However, unlike traditional teams, virtual teams appear to engage in more leadership behaviors during the formation stage. This is evident from the development of formal protocols for a variety of team interactions.

2. Mutual Performance Monitoring

Mutual performance monitoring is the process of actively scanning and assessing the performance of your team members to mitigate the potential for error. Typically, mutual performance monitoring is based upon a degree of cross-monitoring seen primarily in action teams (Marks, Sabella, Burke, & Zaccaro, 2002). Mutual performance monitoring requires situation assessment as described by Salas and colleagues (2007), where elements of the "situation" are assessed to gain or maintain an accurate awareness or understanding of the situation in which the team is functioning. The process of monitoring a situation results in a greater degree of situation awareness that, if communicated to others, will cultivate a mutual understanding of the current course of action when treating patients (i.e., shared mental model) (Marks, Mathieu, & Zaccaro, 2001).

Virtual teams engage in mutual performance monitoring like traditional teams do. However, mutual performance monitoring is carried out differently through task assistance and communication in virtual teams. This is, in large part, because virtual teams are not co-located and do not necessarily work at the same time.

3. Backup Behavior

Backup behavior is considered critical to the social and task performance aspects of teams and involves helping other team members to perform their tasks. Backup behavior can typically range from simple task assistance and helping team members adjust plans for completing tasks (adaptive supportive behaviors) (Salas, Rosen, Burke, Nicholson, & Howse, 2007). Critical behaviors for backup behavior can include conflict resolution, task assistance, and verbal feedback, all of which yield greater team adaptability in changing situations and environments.

Backup behavior is perhaps the most distinct process between virtual and traditional teams. In traditional teams, backup behavior is more frequent because virtual teams do not necessarily engage in mutual performance monitoring (a prerequisite for backup behavior). However, virtual teams do have a commonly ignored potential to engage in backup behavior because certain intellectual and developmental tasks allow for the performance monitoring through evaluation of products and progress.

4. Adaptability

Adaptability represents a team's ability to adjust actions and plans according to recurring evaluation of team effectiveness and efficiency. This process is considered critical to team performance because it represents primal evidence that the team is evaluating its actions and making systematic changes based upon their assessment. Further, adaptability provides evidence of recognized need among team members for a different course of action. Researchers such as Rico, Sánchez-Manzanares, Gil, and Gibson (2008) posit that adaptive behaviors among teams provide evidence of more effective coordination. Salas, Rosen, Burke, Nicholson, and Howse (2007) argue that adaptive behaviors represent a clear form of team support behaviors and indicate, by extension, some critical team orientation markers.

Adaptability is often easy for virtual teams, as opposed to traditional teams. This is largely because virtual teams engage in planning and process evaluation activities much more than traditional teams do. When engaging in planning, virtual teams are often evaluating their progress toward goals and determining how to adapt their work to meet revised demands.

5. Shared Mental Models

The process of monitoring a situation may lead to greater situation awareness on the part of an individual team member; however, in isolation, it is possible that the individual misinterpreted cues or placed too much emphasis on one piece of information and therefore chose an inappropriate action. The act of sharing and discussing information gained from situation monitoring provides the opportunity to gather more information about the situation and helps cultivate a mutual understanding of the current situation. This mutual understanding has many possible names, but is commonly referred to as shared or team mental models.

Shared mental models are defined as organized knowledge structures of relevant facts and relationships about a task or situation that are commonly held by members of a team. Mohammed and Dumville (2001) identified several constructs studied by various disciplines that are similar to the concept of shared mental models in their effort to further the empirical link between shared mental models and team outcomes.

The basic premise regarding the relationship of shared mental models and teamwork is that team effectiveness will improve if team members have a shared understanding of the situation. Currently, there are many papers postulating the theoretical impact of shared mental models on team effectiveness; however, there is little empirical evidence substantiating this relationship due to the difficulty of measuring this cognitive construct at the group level. Nonetheless, the theoretical, empirical, and anecdotal evidence suggests that team members who possess shared mental models yield teams that have members who can anticipate one another and fill in as needed to ensure continuity of performance.

Virtual teams have a very hard time developing shared mental models relative to traditional teams. This occurs because traditional teams have common language and experiences as a function of their collocation. Virtual teams must engage in more formal planning to develop a shared understanding of the task at hand and how best to approach it.

6. Problem Identification

Problem identification is the ability to define problems and articulate goals for resolving the team problem. Specifically, problem identification or diagnosis is an acknowledged precursor process to articulating plans and developing a course of action for teams (Salas, Rosen, Burke, Nicholson, & Howse, 2007). Typically, teams engage in problem identification by conducting individual assessments of the challenges that lie ahead. Individual assessments will consist of an understanding of the problem, including perceptions of criticality and consequences for not acting accordingly. Then, teams will engage in evaluation of the individual assessments to build consensus about the problem. After consensus is reached, teams will begin the process of brainstorming for solutions. This signifies the transition from planning to plan execution.

For virtual teams, this is the most common process-based activity. Traditional teams do not engage in this activity as often as virtual teams do. The primary reason for this is a focus on task rather than relationship or team interaction issues. The unfortunate side effect of this focus is a lack of trust.

7. Plan Execution

Plan execution is the process by which teams establish and execute plans for team actions. The process typically begins with brainstorming resulting from the evaluation of a problem. Following brainstorming, teams will engage in a second round of consensus building designed to ensure agreement on the plan. The next phase of this process focuses on executing the plan and engaging in coordinated actions for attaining the team's objectives. Implicit in the team's ability to execute critical plans is their ability to monitor their progress toward goals (Marks, Mathieu, & Zaccaro, 2001).

Like problem identification, virtual teams engage in plan execution more often than traditional teams do. Like problem identification, virtual teams suffer from a lack of trust because they focus on the execution of the plan more than on team engagement issues.

8. Communication

Effective teamwork can only be attained if there is good communication among team members. Researchers have noted that good communication is a function of two critical sub-skills: exchanging information and consulting with others (Cannon-Bowers, Tannenbaum, Salas, & Volpe, 1995). Information exchange was defined by such behaviors as closed-loop communication, information sharing, procedural talk, and volunteering and requesting information. Consulting with others consisted of effective influence, open exchange of relevant interpretations, and evaluative interchange (Cannon-Bowers, Tannenbaum, Salas, & Volpe, 1995). Good communication among team members facilitates the development of mutual trust and shared mental models enabling teams to adapt quickly to changing situations.

Virtual teams are most effective when they engage in structured communication. They differ greatly from traditional teams who have the option for informal communication without jeopardizing plan execution. For optimal effectiveness, virtual teams must ensure avenues for all types of communication. In many cases, virtual teams fail because they assume their team is temporary and that there will be no spillover from their engagement in the virtual work.

9. Mutual Trust

Trust among team members is a critical cog of team processes in high risk and high interdependence situations (Salas, Sims, & Burke, 2005; Webber, 2002). Trust among team members represents an acknowledgement of accountability for coordinated actions. Trust among team members also provides direct evidence that individuals are aware of the shared consequences for failure. Trust among team members enables more direct communication and fosters specific protocols for coordination. Trust among team members enables individuals to engage in proactive evaluation and monitoring without fear. Mutual trust among team members serves as the key lever for renewed engagement in team activities.

Mutual trust is the single biggest challenge for virtual teams. Virtual teams often ignore the importance of mutual trust because they assume their engagement is temporary. However, virtual teams, if successful, are often called upon to take on new tasks or engagements. Thus, their focus should be on developing mutual trust. At the very least, they should attempt virtual activities that would enhance mutual trust. This is a process that traditional teams concentrate on and build more quickly.

Together, these nine processes serve as the meat grinder by which team performance and orientation are achieved. Teams are composed with a series of critical organizational, individual, and contextual inputs in mind. The team is provided a task and must use the collective meat grinder to create an output. The degree to which these processes are dynamic and successfully practiced directly affects a team's output. For virtual teams, this equation is no different. The key processes are the same, but the relative importance varies.

In the next section, we will examine challenges to teamwork in the virtual team context and provide tips for adapting team processes to overcome challenges in the virtual team context.

Challenges to Virtual Teamwork

Challenges to effective virtual teamwork fall into two categories: (1) logistical challenges and (2) process challenges. Logistical challenges deal primarily with scheduling and problems with technology. Process challenges deal primarily with teamwork and the interactions among team members. Next, we highlight the prominent challenges to teamwork and identify how team process can play a role in overcoming them.

Table 8.5. Common Process Challenges for Virtual Teams

Techno-literacy—at least on some level—is required, as is the equipment, both soft and hard, to use it.
Lack of engagement—without face-to-face proximity, some participants may feel that they do not have to contribute.
Absence of appropriate training and development experiences.
Difficulty scheduling when crossing multiple and/or wider time zones—flexibility may not be enough.

Source: 2011 SHRM Poll on Virtual Teams.

In our recent poll of HR managers, six major challenges were identified as detrimental to the effectiveness of virtual teams (SHRM, 2011). Table 8.5 summarizes these challenges.

Techno-Literacy

Techno-literacy is defined as the level of technological systems savvy held by virtual team members. Users of virtual teams highlighted techno-literacy challenges as the biggest obstacle to success. Technology enables virtual teamwork. However, it often hinders as much as it enables. Overcoming potential technology challenges requires relative techno-literacy from team members. The adaptability of a team often serves as a lever to ensure that teams succeed in spite of technological problems. Often, virtual teams are most adaptable when they have contingencies for technological problems. Therefore, virtual teams are best suited to engage in two primary team processes more frequently when met with a technological challenge—adaptability and planning.

Lack of Engagement

The lack of face-to-face proximity can often diffuse team accountability. This is most evident in the waning of communication and input from disengaged team members. Symptoms of lack of engagement include diminished communication and interest in providing input. This is a clear departure from traditional co-located teams where disengagement is not as easily hidden. To overcome this challenge, team processes, especially communication and leadership, need to be increased in frequency and formality. Team leaders can play a large role in monitoring the communication among team members in a virtual setting. First, they can serve as role models and even go as far to develop prescriptive communication protocols. Second, they can hold all team members accountable to a relative standard. Third, team leaders can work with team members to identify the best strategies for providing input. But the most obvious way to impact accountability is to require a greater degree of frequency when communicating among team members. Only team leaders have the authority to hold team members accountable. The frequency with which they engage in this behavior can have a direct impact on frequency and quality of communication among team members.

Absence of Training and Preparation

It has been established that problem identification is key to success as a virtual team. One part of problem identification is conducting a training needs assessment. Assuming a diverse virtual team composition, especially in global multinational corporations, we need to provide training. Often virtual teams fail because they do not focus on the formal processes they will engage in. They do not identify specific protocols for communication. They do not determine nor identify processes for when the team encounters challenges. They do not establish ways of measuring success. They do not assess accountability and establish mutual trust. These failures can be remedied through planning and training. Leadership plays a large role in setting the norms for the group. The communication of these norms requires a more formal concerted effort on the part of virtual team leaders.

Scheduling Flexibility

To this point, we have talked about the importance of adaptability for virtual teams. However, we have yet to address the most obvious function for adaptability—scheduling. The currency of communication in a virtual setting is meetings. Meetings are the easiest way to ensure a shared mental model. Unfortunately, working in virtual teams means that meetings will often take place outside the usual work schedule. Overcoming this challenge requires adaptability on the part of individual team members. This requires organizational flexibility, workplace flexibility, and intense team orientation. When asked how difficult it is to work in virtual teams, HR managers and practitioners indicated the lack of flexibility in scheduling as a common obstacle. The primary problems, according to HR managers, is a lack of mutual trust among team members and failure to perform tasks within allotted timeframes. Many also indicated a reduced team orientation when teams cannot schedule adaptively. Virtual teams that do succeed address this challenge through flexible schedules built to account for multiple perspectives. For example, virtual teams comprised of U.S.- and India-based staff often establish an alternating meeting schedule so that team members will meet twice a month. The first meeting occurs at a time convenient for India staff members while the second meeting occurs at a time convenient for U.S. staff members. This equitable model proves to be more successful than trying to find a time that is mutually convenient. Other approaches to overcoming this challenge include meeting through non-visual or non-auditory systems. Communication is improved when team members can explore blog-style methods for communication on a twenty-four-hour cycle.

Using Team Processes to Overcome Challenges

Tips for overcoming the challenges to virtual teamwork described above range from logistical and technology-based ones to process-based, team interaction–based ones. Some practical tips are provided in Table 8.6 that may help organizations be more consistent and get the most out of teams.

Of particular note in Table 8.6 are the strategies for overcoming typical team-formation and norm-setting problems. Specifically, team cohesion can be greatly affected by steps taken in the formation and planning phases. Take, for example, the formation of a virtual team to develop a new assessment for engineers. Several norms have to be established based on the roles within the team. An assessment development team calls for psychometricians, item writers, analysts, subject-matter experts, engineers, and

Table 8.6. Tips for Overcoming Process Challenges to Virtual Teamwork

Process Challenges	*Tips*
Challenges to mutual trust and team orientation	Build in networking time beyond the opening five minutes of a virtual meeting.
	Send a gift basket to virtual workers, particularly if there is a face-to-face component who will have coffee and bagels or lunch.
	Send any gifts or "thank you's" given in the room to onsite participants to virtual participants as well.
	Use free e-mail e-cards to express appreciation and camaraderie.
Challenges to problem identification and plan development	Send paper materials (charts, PPT, reports, etc.) in advance.
	Establish technology demands well in advance.
	Establish specific protocols and responsibilities for communication during formation.
Challenges to team formation and norm setting	Take and post pictures of all team participants to help build stronger relationships.
	Hold a face-to-face kick-off meeting or periodic face-to-face meetings if feasible.
	Ask team members what they want in the way of interaction and how they think they can build a relationship with other team members; check in periodically to see how the team feels about their cohesion and trust as a team.
	If appropriate, use personality tests, such as Predictive Index or Myers-Briggs, to help people gain insight into the different personalities of people involved.
Challenges to communication	Use live cameras in a room or attached to individual work stations if feasible.
	Use specific protocols and technology systems (intranets and blogs) expanding the work cycle.

Source: Unpublished presentation by Debra J. Cohen.

administrators. This virtual team must establish protocols for item development and review. They must establish proper channels of communication for security and efficiency. They must establish mutual trust that each subgroup will be accountable and deliver as promised. This requires that the team develop mutual trust by repeated completion of tasks on time. Each strategy suggested for team cohesion serves as a means of celebrating the team's diversity and success.

In the next section, we offer guidance for exploring the virtual teamwork issues for tomorrow. Then we conclude with three guiding principles for defining your virtual team endeavors.

Virtual Teamwork Issues for Tomorrow

The issues affecting virtual teamwork are always changing. Although numerous factors play a role in making virtual teams successful, a select few lead to its ever-changing state:

- *Technology is always changing and advancing.* The media available to virtual teams is always growing. Social media was born of systems for communication like e-mail and the Internet. The fact that technology is always changing means that tools for working virtually are always changing. Hardware continues to advance such that cameras and digital voice systems are commonplace. This makes seeing someone in Bangladesh possible twenty-four hours a day. Similarly, software systems like Skype are advancing, making virtual communication inexpensive and reliable. The big questions are: What technology or system will be next? Will there be new virtual reality systems for ensuring virtual work in design teams? Will there be new systems specifically designed to provide virtual teamwork templates? Will there be a place for older systems and software to ensure effective integration of virtual teams across multiple platforms? Will all teams use the same technology? Most people will be members of more than one team. How easy or difficult will it be for team members to adapt from one team process to another if the technology tools are different or used in a different way? All these questions need to be addressed by virtual teams. The key will be adaptability and proper problem identification.

- *Trust has to come more quickly and strategies must be developed for building it.* Mutual trust just doesn't come naturally for a variety of cultural and political reasons. Virtual teams must work even harder than traditional teams to develop mutual trust. Researchers and practitioners alike must focus their efforts on strategies for building trust. Ideally, the emphasis will be on core team tasks that trigger trust. Some viable strategies include conducting kickoff meetings in face-to-face formats and using basic team-building activities. Basically, research should focus on examining how small successes affect perceptions of accountability and mutual trust.
- *"Virtual" needs to be better defined.* As virtual work changes, so will the way organizations use virtual teams. The nature of virtual will continue to change, and more types of activities will be completed in virtual ways. As the workplace changes, so will virtual work. As a result, it is incumbent upon practitioners to define what constitutes virtual work. As technology improves, virtual work teams will take on new roles and different types of projects. What we refer to as virtual work and virtual teams may be very different in coming years. For example, a project team located across one state may no longer be referred to as a virtual team. Health care action teams, which are traditionally thought of as non-virtual teams, may take on tasks like diagnosis and treatment from a virtual perspective. The lines around the virtual world are narrowing and expanding at once. The key will be to define what constitutes virtual work and how teams engage in virtual activities.

Conclusion

Virtual teams have been around for decades. The work that can be accomplished virtually is ever-expanding. Despite their ubiquitous nature, virtual teams fail in large part because of the failure to engage in dynamic team processes. Virtual teams often fail to develop a shared mental model of team communication, plans, and roles. Virtual teams often fail to develop an understanding of how formal, frequent, and functional common teamwork behaviors should be. Because of this, effective teamwork is never truly achieved. Recent research indicates numerous obstacles, both logistic and process-based. Remediation strategies ranging from trust-building to communication-based initiatives do exist.

The key to unlocking the potential of virtual teams lies in three principles:

- Know the composition of the virtual team and its charge.
- Build trust above all else to ensure effectiveness.
- Focus on the three Fs of team process dynamics (formality, frequency, and function) when deciding how teams will interact with one another.

Challenges to teamwork will always exist, but virtual teams can overcome them with the proper focus on team processes. As workplace flexibility increases in importance, there will be a greater need and desire to improve virtual team processes. Moreover, the increasingly competitive landscape and global nature of today's business environment demand greater attention to these issues. Like a car that is taken on an extended road trip, a virtual team must be prepared for the journey and must pause along the way to refuel, recharge the driver, and energize the passengers.

References and Further Reading

Baker, D.P., Gustafson, S., Beaubien, J.M., Salas, E., & Barach, P. (2003). *Medical teamwork and patient safety: The evidence-based relation.* Washington, DC: American Institutes for Research.

Blickensderfer, E.L., Cannon-Bowers, J.A., & Salas, E. (1997). Theoretical bases for team self-corrections: Fostering shared mental models. In M.M. Beyerlein, D.A. Jackson, & S.T. Beyerlein (Eds.), *Advances in interdisciplinary studies of work teams* (4th ed., pp. 249–279). Greenwich, CT: JAI Press.

Campion, M.A., Medsker, G.J., & Higgs, A.C. (1993). Relations between work group characteristics and effectiveness: Implications for designing effective work groups. *Personnel Psychology, 46,* 823–851.

Cannon-Bowers, J.A., & Salas, E. (1998). *Making decisions under stress: Implications for individual and team training.* Washington, DC: American Psychological Association.

Cannon-Bowers, J.A., Tannenbaum, S.I., Salas, E., & Volpe, C.E. (1995). Defining competencies and establishing team training requirements. In R.A. Guzzo, E. Salas, & Associates (Eds.), *Team effectiveness and decision-making in organizations* (pp. 333–380). San Francisco: Jossey-Bass.

DeChurch, L.A., & Marks, M.A. (2003). Teams leading teams: Examining the role of leadership in multi-team systems. An unpublished doctoral dissertation.

Fleishman, E.A., & Zaccaro, S.J. (1992). Toward a taxonomy of team performance functions. In R.W. Swezey & E. Salas (Eds.), *Teams: Their training and performance.* Orlando, FL: Academic Press.

Keyton, J., & Beck, S.J. (2008). Team attributes, processes, and values: A pedagogical framework. *Business Communication Quarterly, 71,* 488–504.

Klein, G., & Pierce, L.G. (2001). Adaptive teams. Unpublished work.

Klimoski, R., & Mohammed, S. (1994). Team mental model: Construct or metaphor? *Journal of Management, 20,* 403–447.

Kozlowski, S.W., Gully, S.M., Nason, E.R., & Smith, E.M. (1999). Developing adaptive teams: A theory of compilation and performance across levels and time. In D.R. Ilgen & E.D. Pulakos (Eds.), *The changing nature of performance: Implications for staffing, motivation, and development* (pp. 240–292). San Francisco: Jossey-Bass.

Kraiger, K., Ford, J.K., & Salas, E. (1993). Application of cognitive, skill-based and affective theories of learning to new methods of training evaluation. *Journal of Applied Psychology, 78,* 311–328.

Marks, M.A., Mathieu, J.E., & Zaccaro, S.J. (2001). A temporally based framework and taxonomy of team processes. *Academy of Management Review. 26,* 356–376.

Marks, M.A., Sabella, M.J., Burke, C.S., & Zaccaro, S.J. (2002). The impact of cross-training on team effectiveness. *Journal of Applied Psychology, 87,* 3–13.

Marks, M.A., Zaccaro, S.J., & Mathieu, J.M. (2000). Performance implications of leader briefings and team-interaction training for team adaptation to novel environments. *Journal of Applied Psychology, 85*, 971–986.

Marta, S., Leritz, L.E., & Mumford, M.D. (2005). Leadership skills and the group performance: Situational demands, behavioral requirements, and planning. *Leadership Quarterly, 16*, 97–120.

Martin, A., & Bal, V. (2007). The state of teams. *A CCL research white paper.* Greensboro, NC: Center for Creative Leadership.

Martins, L.L., & Schilpzand, M.D. (2011). Global virtual teams: Key developments, research gaps, and future directions. In A. Joshi, H. Liao, & J.J. Martocchio (Eds.), *Research in personnel and human resources management* (Vol. 30, pp. 1–72). Bingley, UK: Emerald Group Publishing Limited.

Mathieu, J.E., Heffner, T.S., Goodwin, G.F., & Salas, E. (2000). The influence of shared mental models on team process and performance. *Journal of Applied Psychology, 85*, 273–283.

Mathieu, J.E., Maynard, M.T., Taylor, S.R., Gilson, L.L., & Ruddy, T.M. (2007). An examination of the effects of organizational district and team contexts on team processes and performance: A meso-mediational model. *Journal of Organizational Behavior, 28*, 891–910.

McGrath, J.E. (1984). *Groups: Interaction and performance.* Englewood Cliffs, NJ: Prentice Hall.

McIntyre, R.M., & Salas, E. (1995). Measuring and managing for team performance: Emerging principles from complex environments. In R.A. Guzzo, E. Salas, & Associates (Eds.), *Team effectiveness and decision making in organizations* (pp. 9–45). San Francisco: Jossey-Bass.

Mohammed, S., & Dumville, B.C. (2001). Team mental models in a team knowledge framework: Expanding theory and measure across disciplinary boundaries. *Journal of Organizational Behavior, 22*, 89–103.

Moon, H., Hollenbeck, J.R., Humphrey, S.E., Ilgen, D.R., West, B., Ellis, A.P.J., & Porter, C.O.L.H. (2004). Asymmetric adaptability: Dynamic team structures as one-way streets. *Academy of Management Journal, 47*, 681–695.

Mumford, M.D., Zaccaro, S.J., Harding, F.D., Jacobs, T.O., & Fleishman, E.A. (2000). Leadership skills for a changing world: Solving complex social problems. *Leadership Quarterly, 11*, 11–35.

Qui, J., Zhang, Z., & Liu, L.A. (2011). Cultural processes in teams: The development of team mental models in heterogeneous work teams. In A.K. Leung, C. Chiu, & Y. Hong (Eds.), *Cultural processes: A social psychological perspective* (pp. 172–187). New York: Cambridge University Press.

Rice, D.J., Davidson, B.D., Dannenhoffer, J.F., & Gay, G.K. (2007). Improving the effectiveness of virtual teams by adapting team processes. *Computer Supported Cooperative Work: The Journal of Collaborative Computing, 16*, 567–594.

Rico, R., Sánchez-Manzanares, M., Gil, F., & Gibson, C. (2008). Team implicit coordination processes: A team knowledge-based approach. *Academy of Management Review, 33*, 163–184.

Salas, E., Bowers, C.A., & Cannon-Bowers, J.A. (1995). Military team research: 10 years of progress. *Military Psychology, 7*, 55–75.

Salas, E., Burke, C.S., & Stagl, K.C. (2004). Developing teams and team leaders: Strategies and principles. In R.G. Demaree, S.J. Zaccaro, & S.M. Halpin (Eds.), *Leader development for transforming organizations.* Mahwah, NJ: Lawrence Erlbaum Associates.

Salas, E., Dickinson, T.L., Converse, S.A., &, Tannenbaum, S.I. (1992). Toward an understanding of team performance and training. In R.W. Swezey & E. Salas (Eds.), *Teams: Their training and performance* (pp. 3–29). Norwood, NJ: Ablex.

Salas E., Rosen, M.A., Burke, C.S., Nicholson, D., & Howse, W.R. (2007). Markers for enhancing team cognition in complex environments: The power of team performance diagnosis. *Aviation Space Environmental Medicine, 78 (5, Suppl.)*, B77–85.

Salas, E., Rozell, D., Mullen, B., & Driskell, J.E. (1999). The effect of team building on performance: An integration. *Small Group Research, 30*, 309–329.

Salas, E., Sims, D.E., & Burke, C.S. (2005). Is there a "big five" in teamwork? *Small Group Research, 36*, 555–599.

Salas, E., Sims, D.E., & Klein, C. (2004). Cooperation and teamwork at work. In C.D. Speilberger (Ed.), *Encyclopedia of applied psychology*. San Diego, CA: Academic Press.

SHRM. (2011). *Poll on virtual teams.* Alexandria, VA: Society for Human Resource Management.

Smith-Jentsch, K.A., Salas, E., & Baker, D.P. (1996). Training team performance-related assertiveness. *Personnel Psychology, 49,* 909–936.

Stevens, M., & Campion, M. (1994). The knowledge, skill, and ability requirements for teamwork: Implications for human resource management. *Journal of Management, 20,* 503–530.

Tannenbaum, S.I., Mathieu, J.E., Salas, E., & Cohen, D.J. (in press). Teams are changing: Are research and practice evolving fast enough? *Industrial and Organizational Psychology: Perspectives on Science and Practice.*

Tesluk, P., Mathieu, J.E., Zaccaro, S.J., & Marks, M. (1997). Task and aggregation issues in the analysis and assessment of team performance. In M.T. Brannick, E. Salas, & C. Prince (Eds.), *Team performance assessment and measurement: Theory, methods, and applications* (pp. 197–224). Mahwah, NJ: Lawrence Erlbaum Associates.

Volpe, C.E., Cannon-Bowers, J.A., Salas, E., & Spector, P.E. (1996). The impact of cross training on team functioning: An empirical investigation. *Human Factors, 38,* 87–100.

Wallace, D.M., & Hinsz, V.B. (2010). Teams as technology: Applying theory and research to model macrocognition processes in teams. *Theoretical Issues in Ergonomics Science, 11,* 359–374.

Webber, S.S. (2002). Virtual teams: A meta-analysis. Presented at Academy of Management Conference, Denver, Colorado.

CHAPTER NINE

Trust and Conflict at a Distance

How Can I Improve Relational Outcomes in Distributed Work Groups?

Jeanne Wilson
The College of William and Mary

How Can I Improve the Way My Distributed Group Works Together?

It's hard enough to achieve positive interpersonal relationships in traditional groups. But now managers are faced with the challenges of getting their far-flung employees to trust and cooperate with each other. Distributed work groups, virtual teams, global product development groups, departments of telecommuting employees—all of these groups present challenges for managers who need members of these groups to share critical information, build on each others' ideas, and reach consensus. The pressure on managers is particularly acute because these groups are often formed explicitly to optimize diverse points of view and expertise—making their success contingent on developing trust and effectively managing conflict. For these reasons, building trust and managing conflict are often cited by both scholars and practitioners as the biggest challenges in virtual work (Hinds & Bailey, 2003; Lipnack & Stamps, 1997; Thomas & Bostrom, 2010; Zaccaro & Bader, 2003; Zeffane & Connell, 2003). Fortunately, partly as a result of these concerns, there is a substantial body of research that can be marshaled to advise managers. In this review I will use the accumulated research evidence to avoid both the naïve optimism and uninformed skepticism that sometimes characterize popular treatments of virtual work.

This review focuses on virtual teams but covers any interdependent group of people working toward a common goal while separated by geographic distance, time, and/or location (O'Leary & Cummings, 2007). By some accounts these conditions are becoming as common as co-located work (Cordery, Soo, Kirkman, Rosen, & Mathieu, 2009; Morello, 2005; Staples & Webster, 2007; Wright & Drewery, 2006). This advice covers a broad range of distributed work, including global virtual teams such as those at Buchman Laboratories that form and disband on a project basis. These teams consist of employees who are culturally diverse, geographically dispersed, and who operate across different time zones and even different organizational boundaries. It also includes more permanent virtual teams such as the telecommunications R&D teams at Texas Instruments, whose members are spread across California, France, and Japan to achieve a twenty-four-hour workday. While these teams are geographically, culturally, and temporally dispersed, all of the members come from the same organization (Shin, 2005).

This review focuses on interpersonal relations in distributed work because, by many accounts, it's more challenging than the technical aspects of virtual work (Gratton, 2007). Managers may feel they are caught in a paradox. Developing trust and cooperation are thought to require close face-to-face contact to manage, and yet they seem to be particularly important in relationships where close face-to-face contact is not possible. Fortunately, research has generated an ample amount of data about how distributed groups can achieve positive relationships (Walther, 2009).

Basic Principle: Social Information

Virtual groups are often thought to be at a disadvantage due to distance, their reliance on technology, and increased uncertainty about team members' local contexts (Brandl & Neyer, 2009). However, several theories describe how the acquisition and processing of social information in these groups enable trust to form and conflict to be effectively managed (Carlson & Zmud, 1999; Lea & Spears, 1992; Walther, 1992). Furthermore, these theories argue that distant team members adapt communication technology to fit their social needs in working at a distance.

These models assume that people are driven to develop social relationships, regardless of their mode of interaction (such as electronic or face-to-face). In all cases, people test their assumptions about others over time, refine their impressions, and adjust their relational communication. It's just that the acquisition and use of social information may be different in distributed work. One difference is that it can take longer to accumulate social information about team members at a distance using technology-mediated communication (Walther, 1992). Another difference is that, in the absence of individuating information about distant team members, impressions may be more heavily based on group or social identity (Lea & Spears, 1992; Walther 1996). A final difference is that some team members can wring more social information out of communications using supposedly impoverished technologies as a result of their experience (with each other or with the technology) (Carlson & Zmud, 1999).

So, for example, if the Acme Corporation sets up a product redesign team composed of members of its Product Engineering group who happen to be spread out across Mumbai, Paris, Tokyo, and Atlanta, these theories suggest that the members will use the social cues that are available to them (we are all Acme engineers). This social identity will convey further social information (we are competent, we share the same engineering language, we are focused on the same goals) which will enable trust to form and the potential for conflict to be minimized.

Of course, there are multiple ways to acquire and process social information in distributed work and thus multiple routes to trust and cooperation. Different theories focus on different means of acquiring and processing social information. For managers, this equifinality means that there are multiple levers that can be used to help virtual teams acquire and use social information to their advantage.

Mechanisms That Affect Social Information in Distributed Groups

There are multiple factors that affect the extent to which virtual groups acquire and process social information. All of these have been shown to affect the development of trust and the trajectory of conflict in these groups. In this section, I review three conditions that affect the acquisition and processing of social information, which have in turn been shown to influence trust and conflict in distributed groups.

Develop Group Identity

Group identity represents team members' sense of oneness with the group and has a cognitive component (sense of belonging), an affective component (emotional attraction), and a behavioral component (joint effort toward a common goal) (Ashforth & Mael, 1989; Webster & Wong, 2008). Group identity serves as a kind of shorthand for social information in groups. Members of the in-group are assumed to be more trustworthy, predictable, and cooperative (Dawes & Thaler, 1988). People within group boundaries express more positive affect and trust (Brewer & Kramer, 1985; Shapiro, Sheppard, & Cheraskin, 1992) and elicit cooperative rather than competitive behavior (Brewer & Brown, 1998; Schopler & Insko, 1992).

Indeed, when members of virtual teams have a shared team identity they have lower levels of conflict (Hobman, Bordia, Irmer, & Chang, 2002; Lea & Spears, 1992; Hinds & Mortensen, 2005; Mortensen & Hinds, 2001) and higher levels of trust (Davenport & Daellenbach, 2011; Jarvenpaa, Knoll, & Leidner, 1998; Wilson, 2001).

Allow for Time and Familiarity

Familiarity refers to the knowledge group members have about each other. Familiarity with specific others is thought to be important to the development of trust and cooperation because it makes the partners' behavior more predictable, and the partners experience less anxiety and uncertainty about what the other will do (Brandl & Neyer, 2009; Valley, Neale, & Mannix, 1995). Zack (1994) found that, as time goes on and members of virtual teams become more familiar with each other, technology mediated communication does not hinder team processes. Similarly, Alge, Wiethoff, and Klein (2003) found that teams with an established history are able to use electronic means of communicating just as effectively as face-to-face. Hinds and Mortensen (2005) found that distance did not affect conflict in virtual groups because team members developed shared familiarity and shared processes. Many studies have confirmed that prior familiarity aids in the maintenance of distant interpersonal relationships (Kraut, Patterson, Lundmark, Kiesler, Mukopadhyay, & Scherlis, 1998; Latane, Liu, Nowak, Bonevento, & Zheng, 1995; Van den Bulte & Moenaert, 1998). There is also evidence from studies of research collaborations that once a collaboration has begun there is no difference between distant and proximal relationships in the likelihood of continuing to collaborate or in satisfaction with the collaboration (Kraut, Galegher, & Egido, 1990).

Research also shows that, over time, in groups without the benefit of prior familiarity, group members acquire social information and develop trust and cooperation. A meta-analysis showed that with extended interactions virtual groups achieve effective relational communication patterns and results (Walther, Anderson, & Park, 1994). People interacting at a distance adapt their use of technology to achieve familiarity with distant partners (Walther & Parks, 2002).

Build Relationships via Frequent Communication

Another way to acquire social information in the absence of prior familiarity is through frequent communication with distributed team members. Frequent communication has been found to moderate the effects of distribution on conflict (Cramton, 2001; Hinds & Mortensen, 2005; Metiu, 2006) and trust (Burgoon, Bonito, Ramirez, Dunbar, Karadeen, & Fischer, 2002; Jarvenpaa, Knoll, & Leidner, 1998; Maznevski & Chudoba, 2000; Nesdale & Todd, 1998). In a study of globally distributed development teams, being central in the communication network led to being central in the trust network, which in turn led to higher performance (Sarker, Ahuja, Sarker, & Kirkeby, 2011).

Examples and Evidence from Practice

Deep bonds are certainly possible for people who work at a distance. Familiarity and frequent communication with others can lead to surprising levels of closeness between people who have never met. In a study of distributed account teams in a financial services company, one of the account managers established a very close relationship with a vice president at the team's customer site, in spite of the fact that the two had never met. In an interview, the account manager mentioned that she was not going to ask this client contact to review a report that day because she knew that the client was experiencing the adverse effects of chemotherapy. The account manager revealed that she knew all about her client's breast cancer, even though these two had never met in person. The disclosures had begun on e-mail when the account manager happened to mention that she was visiting her sister in the hospital. The client (a vice president of HR at a major corporation) asked in the return e-mail, "Oh, what's wrong?" and the account manager disclosed that her sister had a form of skin cancer. The client revealed her own struggles with breast cancer in a phone call shortly thereafter (Wilson, 2001).

Group Identity

When there are subgroups within the virtual team, subgroups significantly increase the risk of conflict (Gibbs, 2009). This was apparent in a study of a geographically distributed software team with subgroups on the West Coast of the United States and in Bangalore, India (Metiu 2006). In this case, low levels of identification between the subgroups led to misinterpretations and negative attributions about the others' performance. The presence of subgroups fueled suspicions about the other subgroup's work:

> "They [the Indian engineers] want to make sure they have work to do, but they have less of a stake in the product and are less concerned with the end product. How do they feel about things

that fail? [Do they say] I don't really care if this fails: I move on to another project?" (Metiu, 2006; p. 425)

The conflict between the two subgroups was exacerbated by status differences between the U.S. subgroup and the subgroup of programmers in India. Even when the Indian developers traveled to the West Coast site and were co-located with their U.S. counterparts, the physical proximity did not improve relations. At a lunch for the team, the Indian developers sat at one table and the U.S. developers sat at another table (Metiu, 2006). The team never developed a shared identity, conflicts persisted, and in the end resulted in the move of all code ownership to the United States. The researcher concluded "the problem in distant collaboration is less rooted in communication tools' lack of sophistication than it is in in-group and out-group categorizations and the lack of desire to work cooperatively with a remote site" (Metiu, 2006, p. 433).

Time and Familiarity

Leaders' familiarity with remote employees can enable them to maintain strong relationships, as this quote from a leader of virtual teams demonstrates:

> "I call [my colleague] two or three times a week. She was sick last week and I sent her home. [ ] Because I know this person. Just by listening to her voice over the phone, I thought she was about to pass out. She was green over the phone so imagine her in person! [ ] Before she gets to an emotional point where she won't be able to take it anymore, I have to be on top of things. You have to be very proactive because in a traditional group you can easily see if someone is not feeling well." (Virtual team leader from Dube & Robey, 2008, p. 19)

Another leader of virtual teams at Alcoa makes a similar point about the effects of time on relationships at a distance:

> "On improving trust and familiarity among members over time and the practices that led to this trust, certainly over time people have started to feel more comfortable. They come to know the

> rewards of sharing knowledge over time and certainly are much more open in discussions." (Cordery, Soo, Kirkman, Rosen, & Mathieu, 2009, p. 211)

Frequency of Communication

As noted earlier, frequency of communication may matter more than the medium used to communicate. At Nokia, the preferred communication tool was text messaging, whereas at BP norms about e-mail and acceptable reply times eased virtual teamwork (Gratton, 2007). In all cases, frequent and responsive communication is particularly important in helping virtual teams establish trust and minimize conflict:

> "When you are working with people you never see, you can develop trust, but you must respond to that person. Follow through. If you tell them that you are going to get back to a customer, get back to them." (member of a virtual team at Sabre. Kirkman, Rosen, Gibson, Tesluk, & McPherson, 2002, p. 69)

Some members of virtual teams learn to communicate frequently with their distant team members through experience:

> "We maintained contact religiously every week through conference calls. Some weeks we did this just to make sure we were maintaining the beat. But there is always something new." (from interview with virtual team member; Dube & Robey, 2009, p. 12)

When frequent and regular communication breaks down, it can leave open the possibility for misunderstanding and conflict, as this example from a virtual programming team illustrates:

> "Rob is a computer programmer in San Diego who works for a virtual team that designed and creates computer programs for accounting companies. Rob and his teammates work on different parts of the project. Once Rob finishes the programming of his part, he e-mails it to Kelly in Boston, who integrates Rob's with her own work and e-mails it again to the project manager who is in charge of the team. Kelly has become tired of fixing [little mistakes Rob makes], and has started to change his work without

notifying him. Rob recently found from an e-mail with the project manager that Kelly changed his work without his permission. [ ] He insists that he cannot trust Kelly and does not want to work with her anymore. [ ] Both of them avoid communicating." (Shin, 2005. p. 339)

Myths and Misconceptions

So much has been written about virtual work that there are bound to be some misconceptions that circulate and persist, even in the face of evidence to the contrary. In this section I address three practices and beliefs that defy mounting evidence: the necessity of face-to-face meetings, the superiority of "rich" communication media, and avoidance of complete dispersion.

Belief: Face-to-Face Meetings Are Necessary to Build Trust and Reduce Conflict in Virtual Work

A popular version of this belief is that all virtual groups must start with a face-to-face kickoff meeting. There is no doubt that members of virtual groups often report that face-to-face meetings are vital (Dube & Robey, 2008). This is a popular lay theory (Lipnack & Stamps, 1997). However, just because people prefer something doesn't mean that it is effective. This is not unlike comforting medicines. For instance, over-the-counter cough syrup has been shown to be no better than a placebo, yet it remains quite popular (Schroeder & Fahey, 2002).

There isn't even a guarantee that if you hold face-to-face meetings it will improve the *satisfaction* of the group. Some research suggests that it may be better to not start with face-to-face meetings because virtual teams develop trust by task-oriented exchanges first (Avolio & Kahai, 2003; Hart & McLeod, 2003) and that early face-to-face meetings may be an annoyance (Gratton, 2007).

The accumulated research evidence indicates that other forms of interaction can, under certain conditions, substitute for face-to-face interaction. One condition that reduces the need for face-to-face meetings is time (Driskell, Radtke, & Salas, 2003). Within a span of a few interactions, trust levels in virtual groups are the same as those that started with a face-to-face meeting (Wilson, Straus, & McEvily, 2006; Walther, 1995; Walther & Burgoon, 1992; Webster & Wong, 2008). Bos, Olson, Gergle, Olson, and Wright (2002) found that cooperation and trust in groups using video-conference or audio-conferencing rose to face-to-face levels within a few interactions but that this was not true for groups who interacted only by text (a condition that is rare in organizational groups). In a meta-analysis of the effects of time and technology-mediated communication on relational development in groups, Walther, Anderson, and Park (1994) found that positive interpersonal relations occurred in computer-mediated groups with extended interactions.

Another condition that reduces the need for face-to-face meetings is familiarity. Prior contact or familiarity (whether face-to-face or otherwise) is sufficient to produce trust and effective communication patterns in virtual groups (Alge, Wiethoff, & Klein, 2003; Burke & Chidambaram, 1995; Wilson, 2001; Zack, 1994). Van den Bulte and Moenaert (1998) examined the effects of relocating R&D teams to a separate facility. Reducing the distance between R&D teams increased the amount of communication among R&D professionals. Although the move dramatically increased the distances between R&D personnel and professionals in marketing and operations, the increased distances did not adversely affect the communication across these functions—perhaps because the individuals in these functions had already established some level of familiarity. Dube and Robey (2008) also describe the members of one virtual team who had worked together before, which allowed them to trust each other and share knowledge effectively, without the need for face-to-face meetings. Similarly, the expectation of future interaction has been shown to be a better predictor of relational communication in virtual groups than the use of technology alone (Matheson & Zanna, 1990; Walther, 1994) and to generally result in more cooperative behavior (Heide & Miner, 1992).

Similar results have been obtained for conflict (Hobman, Bordia, Irmer, & Chang, 2002 Hinds & Mortensen, 2005;). Hinds & Mortensen (2005) found that neither the use of technology nor the frequency of face-to-face meetings was associated with conflict in their study of R&D teams in a multinational organization.

Belief: It Is Always Best to Use the "Richest" Communication Medium Available

This belief or practice is probably related to faith in face-to-face meetings. If managers can't arrange face-to-face meetings, they try to come as close to the face-to-face experience as possible, investing in expensive videoconferencing systems and other technological solutions. When virtual groups have no choice over what media they use, plain text conferencing achieves as much psychological closeness as groups using multi-cue communication systems or face-to-face meetings (Walther & Bazarova, 2008). In some cases, the use of asynchronous communication media may even reduce conflict because competitive behavior is less apparent when communicating using technology (Montoya-Weiss, Massey, & Song, 2001).

Leaders of parallel global virtual teams at Alcoa summed this up:

> "Teleconferences are the dominant mode of communication. We rarely use net-meetings. We had a couple of videoconferences but they tend to be very awkward and difficult. [ ] as a regular communication tool videoconferences are more trouble than they are worth." (Cordery, Soo, Kirkman, Rosen, & Mathieu, 2009, p. 210)

Belief: Conflict Is Highest in Completely Dispersed Groups

Managers may believe that having only one member of a virtual group at each site is the worst possible arrangement. Many worry about isolation and the need for a co-located colleague (Cooper & Kurland, 2002; Kurland & Egan, 1999). But research shows that teams composed solely of isolates (1–1–1–1–1–1) do better than those with partially distributed groups (2–2–2) (Cramton & Hinds, 2005; Huang & Ocker, 2006; O'Leary & Mortensen, 2010; Polzer,

Crisp, Jarvenpaa, & Kim, 2006; Webster & Wong, 2008). Geographic isolates don't trigger the social categorization processes that can disrupt team dynamics. In fact, creating collocated groups under assumptions of "strength in numbers" is likely to do more harm than good (Jarman, 2005; O'Leary & Mortensen, 2010; Panteli & Davison, 2005). Imbalance in partially distributed groups may also result in minority sites feeling less influence and engagement with the larger group (O'Leary & Cummings, 2007; Ocker, Huang, Benbunan-Fich, & Hiltz, 2011).

The accumulated research evidence suggests that managers may be worrying about the wrong things. The threats to trust and cooperation in distributed work seem to have less to do with face-to-face meetings and technology and more to do with the subgroup structure of the groups. The interesting question is whether managers and members of virtual work groups are prepared to set aside ideology in the face of data. Just as the use of pills and surgery persists against medical evidence partly because they are potent symbols of healing power, holding face-to-face meetings may be a potent symbol that management cares about the group. But our faith in these symbols can blind us to truths. Voltaire wrote, "The art of medicine consists of amusing the patient while nature cures the disease." Perhaps the art of managing virtual teams involves distracting the team while time enables the development of trust and cooperation.

Implementation

Based on the available research evidence, what should managers do to improve trust and conflict in distributed groups? In Table 9.1 I have organized advice in four areas: the design of the teams, selection of members, training of the teams, and facilitation or leadership of the teams.

Designing Virtual Teams

Ironically, much of the literature treats virtual teams as if their pattern of dispersion is preordained or fixed (Siebdrat, Hoegl, & Ernst, 2009). "Virtual team design has so far been treated as an afterthought" (Powell, Piccoli, & Ives, 2004, p. 15) by both

Table 9.1. Managing Virtual Teams to Promote Trust and Cooperation

Virtual Team Design
Avoid subgroups or faultlines by location.
Promote empowerment and autonomy.
Encourage teams to develop norms and structure.
Selection for Virtual Teams
Openness to experience improves virtual team performance.
Members with prior familiarity and experience working at a distance can aid in virtual team development.
Training and Support for Virtual Teams
Provide training in the use of technology, virtual meetings, and respect for differences.
Provide structural assurance in the form of organizational support and performance management.
Leadership and Facilitation
Leaders should develop shared identity and promote frequent communication.
Create norms for responsiveness.
Promote disclosure in a psychologically safe environment.

researchers and practitioners. The fact is that teams can be explicitly designed to optimize their performance. In particular, the research on faultlines in virtual groups suggests that these teams should be designed, whenever possible, to avoid creating subgroups at different locations. If this is unavoidable, then it is particularly important to avoid creating inadvertent faultlines. The worst possible configuration for conflict and trust in distributed teams is to have all of the engineers at one location and all of the marketing people at another. These kinds of faultlines are especially problematic if one subgroup has more power than the other (Huang & Ocker, 2006; Metiu, 2006). If functional faultlines are unavoidable, members who are familiar with each other should be spread across sites, or roles should be assigned to cut across subgroups (to reduce within-site in-group effects).

In addition to planning the geographic configuration of the teams, virtual groups should be designed with empowerment in mind. Evidence shows that virtual teams perform better with more autonomy, and this can be designed into the teams' task from the beginning (Kirkman, Rosen, Gibson, Tesluk, & McPherson, 2002; Orlikowski, 2002; Robey, Khoo, & Powers, 2000; Vickery, Clark, & Carlson, 1999). The benefits of empowerment or autonomy have also been upheld in a meta-analysis of telecommuting relationships (Gajendra & Harrison, 2007). It is, however, important to note that empowerment does not mean lack of structure. Structures that the teams devise with help from their experienced members and leaders or explicit training can be helpful in enabling coordination across distance.

Selecting for Virtual Teams

There has been some preliminary work on individual differences that improve performance in virtual teams. For instance, openness to experience has been shown to be important in the decision-making performance of virtual teams. Teams can actually benefit from technology-mediated communication as long as they have one very open member or several members with above-average openness (Colquitt, Hollenbeck, Ilgen, LePine, & Sheppard, 2002). Openness has also been shown to improve team performance on computer-assisted tasks when the team is dealing with diversity (Homan, Hollenbeck, Humphrey, van Knippenberg, Ilgen, & Van Kleef, 2008). Openness to experience is also similar to telecooperative attributes that have been cited as important in virtual teams (propensity to trust and intercultural skills) (Hertel, Konradt, & Voss, 2006; Kirkman, Rosen, Gibson, Tesluk, & McPherson, 2002; Siebdrat, Hoegl, & Ernst, 2009).

When possible it will improve virtual teams' chances for success if they can be staffed with some members who are familiar with each other, but perhaps not so many that it reduces the prospects for innovation (Cummings & Kiesler, 2008; Dube & Robey, 2008; Gratton, 2007; Wilson, 2001). It also helps to have members with some experience working at a distance (Powell, Piccoli, & Ives, 2004). Of course, in the absence of such experience, there is some evidence that a realistic job preview of virtual work can help candidates select out of a role which may be a poor fit (Kirkman, Rosen, Gibson, Tesluk, & McPherson, 2002).

If the organization has limited degrees of freedom in selecting team members for virtual work (for instance, when particular members must be chosen for their technical skill), training and leadership guidance can help teams avoid known pitfalls in distributed work (Cramton, 2001).

Providing Training and Support

The skills required to work effectively in virtual teams may not come naturally to most people, and cooperation with distant team members may require more mindful attention (Kock, 2004). In spite of the need, most organizations have not figured out how to prepare their employees for distributed work. Randomized surveys of members of the Society for Human Resource Management indicate that only about one-third of the organizations provide training for virtual team members and leaders, and of those that do, only 7 percent rated their current efforts as "very effective" or "extremely effective" (Rosen, Furst, & Blackburn, 2006). Fortunately, training in technology-mediated interactions can improve trust, lower conflict, and increase performance (Kirkman, Rosen, Gibson, Tesluk, & McPherson, 2002; Rice, Davidson, Dannenhoffer, & Gay, 2007; Salas, Cooke, & Rosen, 2008; Staples & Webster, 2007; Tullar & Kaiser, 2000; Warkentin & Beranek, 1999). In one study Warkentin and Beranek (1999) compared virtual groups with and without training over time. Virtual groups that were trained in virtual meeting processes, techniques for sharing information, and including other members exhibited significantly more trust, were significantly more open in expressing ideas, and performed better than virtual groups without the training. Surveys of organizations engaged in virtual team training show that those who report the most effective training offer more modules on "sensitivity to cultural differences" and "creation of a team charter and mission statement" (Rosen, Furst, & Blackburn, 2006). Whenever possible, training for distributed work should be staged in such a way so that some training occurs *before* the group becomes entrained on ineffective routines and before subgroup categorizations have set in and become resistant to intervention (Fiol &

O'Connor, 2005); and then additional training occurs when the team has developed sufficient trust to encourage the transfer of the training (Kirkman, Rosen, Tesluk, & Gibson, 2006).

One virtual team leader from the aerospace industry described the importance of training in virtual teams this way:

> "Before you get on a team at our company we go through a whole training process about the expectations of being on a team so that everyone speaks the same language and knows the lingo of teams before getting on one. It's also very, very important to define your boundaries and conflict resolution upfront because we've all been on teams where you hit that imaginary brick wall and then you get that curve when it goes down. Either the team makes it through that crisis or you hit that brick wall and disperse." (Gibson & Cohen, 2003, p. 314)

An organization with well-developed selection, training, and reward practices may also confer a certain level of structural assurance to members of virtual groups (McKnight, Cummings, & Chervany, 1998). If the organization effectively selects, trains, and manages the performance of its employees, members of distributed groups will feel that they can rely on their distant colleagues, comfortable in the knowledge that their colleagues are competent and that any violations will be handled promptly and effectively. This increases the willingness of members of distributed teams to be vulnerable, share knowledge, and generally cooperate with distant colleagues they have never personally met.

Improving Leadership and Facilitation

Virtual groups can be coached into effective interaction patterns that improve group relations and performance. Research evidence highlights the importance of familiarity, group identity, and frequent communication in the management of trust and conflict in distributed groups (Rocco, Finholt, Hofer, & Herbsleb, 2000). Ironically, these results come at a time when trends in organizations seem likely to produce lower levels of familiarity (through declining levels of tenure) and lower levels of group identity (as employees are increasingly likely to be assigned to multiple teams simultaneously).

Contact (face-to-face or otherwise) in the absence of a strong shared identity does not increase trust and cooperation or reduce conflict (Cramton & Hinds, 2005; Metiu, 2006; Pettigrew, 1998). Therefore, one of the first goals for leaders of virtual groups is to build a shared identity. Fortunately, organizational practices for increasing group identity are already quite well-known. Increasing task and reward interdependence, identifying competing groups, and providing a team name or other team identifiers all work to increase team identity. Some other effective practices from virtual teams with high levels of group identity include having all-team conference calls to provide updates on client activity and creating opportunities for all team members to interact with the client. Distance is not, in and of itself, a barrier to group identity (Wilson, 2001). In addition to creating a shared group identity, leaders of virtual groups need to ensure that they do not inadvertently create in- and out-groups based on members' proximity to the leader (Cascio & Shurygailo, 2003; Ocker, Huang, Benbunan-Fich, & Hiltz, 2011).

Once a shared identity has been established, high levels of communication early in the life of virtual teams will help foster trust and reduce conflict (Jarvenpaa & Leidner, 1999). In particular, creating a psychologically safe communication environment can mitigate the potential negative effects of virtuality (Gibson & Gibbs, 2006). Leaders of virtual groups should focus on facilitating regular, detailed, and prompt communication among team members (Avolio & Kahai, 2003; Golden, Veiga, & Dino, 2008; Kayworth & Leidner, 2002). There is some evidence that, in communications between members of virtual groups, delayed responses may have particularly severe consequences for lower-status partners (Sheldon, Thomas-Hunt, & Proell, 2006). Lower-status members of distributed teams risk having their contributions misperceived or devalued with delayed responses. In addition, it appears that the effect of leaders' communication behavior on team performance may be stronger the more dispersed (or virtual) the teams are (Cummings, 2008; Purvanova & Bono, 2009). Leaders can also encourage team members to agree on norms or procedures, which helps reduce uncertainty associated with working at a distance (Massey, Montoya-Weiss, & Hung, 2003; Montoya-Weiss, Massey, & Song, 2001; Tan & Thoen, 2000; Walther & Bunz, 2005).

It cannot be reinforced enough: frequent communication about the task improves virtual team functioning (Avolio & Kahai, 2003; Iacono & Weisband, 1997; Mathieu, Heffner, Goodwin, Salas, & Cannon-Bowers, 2000; Walther & Bunz, 2005; Weisband & Atwater, 1999).

> "I think trusting someone in a virtual team is linked directly to their work ethic. It is task first. The trust has been built through the task-based relationship that has evolved." (quote from Sabre in Kirkman, Rosen, Gibson, Tesluk, & McPherson, 2002, p. 69)

Furthermore, being responsive to distant team members, overtly acknowledging receipt of messages (Cramton, 2001), and keeping them informed of schedules and absences results in higher levels of trust (Jarvenpaa & Leidner, 1999).

Some of the ways leaders can promote familiarity in the absence of prior working relationships include a structured program of information disclosures between distant partners (Erez, 2010). If virtual group members have not worked together before, exchanging social information can substantially improve trust and cooperation (Cascio & Shurygailo, 2003; Jarvenpaa & Leidner, 1999; Walther & Bunz, 2005; Zheng, Bos, Olson, & Olson, 2001). Being asked to reveal information to a partner improves the outcomes in negotiation even in the absence of a shared group identity (Moore, Kurtzberg, Thompson, & Morris, 1999). Asking team members who have not interacted with each other previously to exchange information about themselves improves their ratings of each others' benevolence, integrity, and ability (Jarvenpaa, Knoll, & Leidner, 1998).

Conclusion

Virtual teams have the potential to offer greater flexibility, responsiveness, and diversity of perspectives than traditional groups (Jarvenpaa, Knoll, & Leidner, 1998) Walther & Bunz, 2005). But realizing this potential is contingent on effectively managing trust and conflict. Despite claims that trust and conflict are impossibly difficult to manage in virtual groups (Handy, 1995), this chapter has offered evidence that accommodations can be made to reverse that claim (Walther & Bunz, 2005).

References and Further Reading

Alge, B.J., Wiethoff, C., & Klein, H.J. (2003). When does the medium matter? Knowledge-building experiences in decision-making teams. *Organizational Behavior and Human Decision Processes, 91*, 26–37.

Ashforth, B., & Mael, F. (1989). Social identity theory and the organization. *Academy of Management Review, 14*, 20–39.

Avolio, B.J., & Kahai, S.S. (2003). Adding the E to e-leadership: How it may impact your leadership. *Organizational Dynamics, 31*, 325–338.

Axtell, C.M., Fleck, S.J., & Turner, N. (2004). Virtual teams: Collaborating across distance. *International Review of Industrial and Organizational Psychology.*

Blackburn, R., Furst, S., & Rosen, B. (2003). Building a winning virtual team: KSA's, selection, training and evaluation. In C.B. Gibson & S.G. Cohen (Eds.), *Virtual teams that work* (pp. 95–120). San Francisco: Jossey-Bass.

Bos, N., Olson, J., Gergle, D., Olson, G., & Wright, Z. (April, 2002). Effects of four computer-mediated communications channels on trust development. *CHI Proceedings.* Minneapolis, Minnesota.

Brandl, J., & Neyer, A.K. (2009). Applying cognitive adjustment theory to cross-cultural training for global virtual teams. *Human Resource Management, 48*, 341–353.

Brewer, M.B., & Brown, R.J. (1998). Intergroup relations (pp. 554–594). In D.T. Gilbert, S.T. Fiske, & G. Lindzey (Eds.), *Handbook of social psychology.* Hoboken, NJ: John Wiley & Sons.

Brewer, M., & Kramer, R. (1985). The psychology of intergroup attitudes and behavior. *Annual Review of Psychology, 36*(1), 219–243.

Burgoon, J., Bonito, J., Jr., Ramirez, A., Dunbar, N., Karadeen, K., & Fischer, J. (2002). Testing the interactivity principle: Effects of mediation, propinquity, and verbal and nonverbal modalities in interpersonal interaction. *Journal of Communication, 52*, 657–677.

Burke, K., & Chidambaram, L. (1995). Developmental differences between distributed and face-to-face groups in electronically supported meeting environments: An exploratory investigation. *Group Decision and Negotiation, 4*(3), 213–233.

Carlson, J.R., & Zmud, R.W. (1999). Channel expansion theory and the experiential nature of media richness perceptions. *Academy of Management Journal*, pp. 153–170.

Cascio, W.F. (2000). Managing a virtual workplace. *Academy of Management Executive, 14*, 81–90.

Cascio, W.F., & Shurygailo, S. (2003). E-leadership and virtual teams. *Organizational Dynamics, 31*, 362–376.

Cheshin, A., Rafaeli, A., & Bos, N. (2011). Anger and happiness in virtual teams: Emotional influences of test and behavior on others' affect in the absence of non-verbal cues. *Organizational Behavior and Human Decision Processes, 116*, 2–16.

Colquitt, J.A., Hollenbeck, J.R., Ilgen, D.R., LePine, J.A., & Sheppard, L. (2002). Computer-assisted communication and team decision-making: The moderating effect of openness to experience. *Journal of Applied Psychology, 87*, 402–410.

Connaughton, S.L., & Shuffler, M. (2007). Multinational and multicultural distributed teams: A review and future agenda. *Small Group Research, 38*, 387–412.

Cooper, C.D., & Kurland, N.B. (2002). Telecommuting, professional isolation, and employee development in public and private organizations. *Journal of Organizational Behavior, 23*, 511–532.

Cordery, J., Soo, C., Kirkman, B., Rosen, B., & Mathieu, J. (2009). Leading parallel global virtual teams: Lessons from Alcoa. *Organizational Dynamics, 38*, 204–216.

Cramton, C.D. (2001). The mutual knowledge problem and its consequences for dispersed collaboration. *Organization Science, 12*, 346–371.

Cramton, C.D., & Hinds, P.J. (2005). Sub-group dynamics in internationally distributed teams: Ethonocentrism or cross-national learning? *Research in Organizational Behavior, 26*, 231–263.

Cummings, J.N. (2008). Leading groups from a distance: How to mitigate consequences of geographic dispersion. In S. Weisband (Ed.), *Leadership at a distance* (pp. 33–50). Mahwah, NJ: Lawrence Erlbaum Associates.

Cummings, J.N., & Kiesler, S. (2008). Who collaborates successfully? Prior experience reduces collaboration barriers in distributed interdisciplinary research. *Proceedings of the ACM 2008 Conference on Computer Supported Cooperative Work*. San Diego, California.

Curseu, P.L., Schalk, R., & Wessel, I. (2008). How do virtual teams process information? A literature review and implications for management. *Journal of Managerial Psychology, 23,* 628–652.

Daft, R.L., & Lengel, R.H. (1984). Information richness: A new approach to managerial behavior and organizational design. *Research in Organizational Behavior, 6,* 191–233.

Daft, R.L., & Lengel, R.H. (1986). A proposed integration among organizational information requirements, media richness, and structural design. *Management Science, 32,* 554–571.

Davenport, S., & Daellenbach, U. (2011). Belonging to a virtual research centre: Exploring the influence of social capital formation processes on member identification in a virtual organization. *British Journal of Management, 22,* 54–76.

Dawes, R., & Thaler, R.H. (1988). Anomalies: Cooperation. *The Journal of Economic Perspectives,* pp. 187–197.

Driskell, J.E., Radtke, P.H., & Salas, E. (2003). Virtual teams: Effects of technological mediation on team performance. *Group Dynamics, 7,* 297–323.

Dube, L., & Robey, D. (2009). Surviving the paradoxes of virtual teamwork. *Information Systems Journal, 19,* 3–30.

Erez, M. (2010). Culture and job design. *Journal of Organizational Behavior, 31,* 389–400.

Fiol, C., & O'Connor, E. (2005). Identification in face-to-face, hybrid and pure virtual teams: Untangling the contradictions. *Organization Science, 16*(1), 19–32.

Gajendra, R.S., & Harrison, D.A. (2007). The good, the bad and the unknown about telecommuting: Meta-analysis of psychological mediators and individual consequences. *Journal of Applied Psychology, 92,* 1524–1541.

Gibbs, J.L. (2009). Dialetics in a global software team: Negotiating tensions across time, space, and culture. *Human Relations, 62,* 905–935.

Gibson, C.B., & Cohen, S.G. (2003). *Virtual teams that work.* San Francisco: Jossey-Bass.

Gibson, C.B., & Gibbs, J.L. (2006). Unpacking the concept of virtuality: The effects of geographic dispersion, electronic dependence, dynamic structure and national diversity on team innovation. *Administrative Science Quarterly, 51,* 451–495.

Golden, T.D., Veiga, J.F., & Dino, R.N. (2008). Impact of professional isolation on teleworker job performance and turnover intentions: Does time spent teleworking, interacting face-to-face, or having access to communication-enhancing technology matter? *Journal of Applied Psychology, 93,* 1412–1421.

Gratton, L. (2007, June 16). Working together when apart. *The Wall Street Journal.*

Fiol, C.M., & O'Connor, E.J. (2005). Identification in face-to-face, hybrid and pure virtual teams: Untangling the contradictions. *Organization Science, 16,* 19–32.

Handy, C. (1995). Trust and the virtual organization. *Harvard Business Review, 73*(3), 40–49.

Hart, R.K., & McLeod, P.L. (2003). Rethinking team building in geographically dispersed teams. *Organizational Dynamics, 31,* 352–361.

Heide, J.B., & Miner, A.S. (1992). The shadow of the future: Effects of anticipated future interaction and frequency of contact on buyer-seller cooperation. *Academy of Management Journal, 35,* 265–291.

Hertel, G., Konradt, U., & Voss, K. (2006). Competencies for virtual teamwork: Development and validation of a web-based selection tool for members of distributed teams. *European Journal of Work and Organizational Psychology, 15,* 477–504.

Hill, N.S., Bartol, K.M., Tesluk, P.E., & Langa, G.A. (2009). Organizational context and face-to-face interaction: Influences on the development of trust and collaborative behaviors in computer-mediated groups. *Organizational Behavior and Human Decision Processes, 108,* 187–201.

Hinds, P.J., & Bailey, D.E. (2003). Out of sight out of sync: Understanding conflict in distributed groups. *Organization Science, 14,* 615–632.

Hinds, P.J., & Mortensen, M. (2005). Understanding conflict in geographically distributed teams: The moderating effects of shared identity, shared context and spontaneous communication. *Organization Science, 16,* 290–307.

Hobman, E.V., Bordia, P., Irmer, B., & Chang, A. (2002). The expression of conflict in computer-mediated and face-to-face groups. *Small Group Research, 33,* 439–465.

Homan, A.C., Hollenbeck, J.R., Humphrey, S.E., van Knippenberg, D., Ilgen, D.R., & Van Kleef, G.A. (2008). Facing differences with an open mind: Openness to experience, salience of intragroup differences, and performance of diverse work groups. *Academy of Management Journal, 51,* 1204–1222.

Huang, H., & Ocker, R. (2006). Preliminary insights into the in-group/out-group effect in partially distributed teams: An analysis of participant reflections. *Proceedings of the 2006 ACM SIGMIS CPR Conference on Computer Personnel Research,* pp. 264–272.

Iacono, C., & Weisband, S. (1997, January). Developing trust in virtual teams. *Proceedings of the Thirtieth Hawaii International Conference on System Sciences, 2,* 412–420.

Jarman, R. (2005). When success isn't everything: Case studies of two virtual teams. *Group Decision and Negotiation, 14,* 333–354.

Jarvenpaa, S.L., Knoll, K., & Leidner, D.E. (1998). Is anybody out there? Antecedents of trust in global virtual teams. *Journal of Management Information Systems, 14,* 29–64.

Jarvenpaa, S., & Leidner, D. (1999). Communication and trust in global virtual teams. *Organization Science, 10,* 791–815.

Kayworth, T.R., & Leidner, D.E. (2002). Leadership effectiveness in global virtual teams. *Journal of Management Information Systems, 18,* 7–40.

Kirkman, B.L., Rosen, B., Gibson, C.B., Tesluk, P.E., & McPherson, S.O. (2002). Five challenges to virtual team success: Lessons from Sabre Inc. *Academy of Management Executive, 16,* 67–79.

Kirkman, B.L., Rosen, B., Tesluk, P.E., & Gibson, C.B. (2006). Enhancing the transfer of training proficiency in geographically distributed teams. *Journal of Applied Psychology, 91,* 706–716.

Kock, N. (2004). The psychobiological model: Towards a theory of computer-mediated communication based on Darwinian evolution. *Organization Science, 15*, 327–348.

Kraut, R.E., Galegher, J., & Egido, C. (1990). Patterns of contact and collaboration in scientific research. In J. Galegher, R. Kraut, & C. Egido (Eds.), *Intellectual teamwork* (pp. 111–145). Mahwah, NJ: Lawrence Erlbaum Associates.

Kraut, R.E., Patterson, M., Lundmark, V., Kiesler, S., Mukopadhyay, T., & Scherlis, W. (1998). Internet paradox: A social technology that reduces social involvement and well-being? *American Psychologist*, pp. 1017–1031.

Kurland, N.B., & Egan, T.D. (1999). Telecommuting: Justice and control in the virtual organization. *Organization Science, 10*, 500–513.

Kurland, N.B., & Cooper, C.D. (2002). Manager control and employee isolation in telecommuting environments. *Journal of High Technology Management, 13*, 107–126.

Latane, B., Liu, J.H., Nowak, A., Bonevento, M., & Zheng, L. (1995, August). Distance matters: Physical space and social impact. *Personality and Social Psychology Bulletin, 21*(8), 795–805.

Lea, M.T., & Spears, R. (1992). Paralanguage and social perception in computer-mediated communication. *Journal of Organizational Computing, 2*, 321–341.

Lipnak, J., & Stamps, J. (1997). *Virtual teams: Reaching across space, time, and organizations with technology.* Hoboken, NJ: John Wiley & Sons.

Malhotra, A., Majchrzak, A., Carman, R., & Lott, V. (2001). Radical innovation without co-location: A case-study at Boeing-Rocketdyne. *MIS Quarterly, 25*, 229–249.

Malhotra, A., Majchrzak, A., & Rosen, B. (2007). Leading virtual teams. *Academy of Management Perspectives, 21*, 60–69.

Martins, L., Gilson, L., & Maynard, M.T. (2004). Virtual teams: What do we know and where do we go from here? *Journal of Management, 30*, 805–835.

Massey, A.P., Montoya-Weiss, M.M., & Hung, Y.-T. (2003). Because time matters: Temporal coordination in global virtual project teams. *Journal of Management Information Systems, 19*(4), 129–155.

Matheson, K., & Zanna, M.P. (1990). Computer-mediated communications: The focus is on me. *Social Science Computer Review, 8,* 1–12.

Mathieu, J.E., Heffner, T.S., Goodwin, G.F., Salas, E., & Cannon-Bowers, J.A. (2000). The influence of shared mental models on team process and performance. *Journal of Applied Psychology, 85,* 273–283.

McKnight, D.H., Cummings, L.L., & Chervany, N.L. (1998). Initial trust formation in new organizational relationships. *Academy of Management Review, 23,* 473–490.

Maznevski, M., & Chudoba, K. (2000). Bridging space over time: Global virtual team dynamics and effectiveness. *Organization Science, 11*(5), 473–492.

Metiu, A. (2006). Owning the code: Status closure in distributed groups. *Organization Science, 17,* 418–435.

Montoya-Weiss, M., Massey, A., & Song, M. (2001). Getting it together: Temporal coordination and conflict management in global virtual teams. *Academy of Management Journal, 44*(6), 1251–1262.

Moore, D.A., Kurtzberg, T.R., Thompson. L.L., & Morris, M.W. (1999). Long and short routes to success in electronically mediated negotiations: Group affiliations and good vibrations. *Organizational Behavior and Human Decision Processes, 77,* 22–43.

Morello, D. (2005). *The human impact of business IT: How to avoid diminishing returns* (Research Report G00125740). Stamford, CT: Gartner.

Mortensen, M., & Hinds, P.J. (2001). Conflict and shared identity in geographically distributed teams. *International Journal of Conflict Management, 12,* 212–238.

Nesdale, D., & Todd, P. (1998). Intergroup ratio and the contact hypothesis. *Journal of Applied Social Psychology, 28*(13), 1196–1217.

Ocker, R.J., Huang, H., Benbunan-Fich, R., & Hiltz, S.R. (2011). Leadership dynamics in partially distributed teams: An exploratory study of the effects of configuration and distance. *Group Decision and Negotiation, 20,* 273–292.

O'Leary, M.B., & Cummings, J. (2007). The spatial, temporal, and configurational characteristics of geographic dispersion in teams. *MIS Quarterly, 31,* 433–452.

O'Leary, M.B., & Mortensen, M. (2010). Go (con)figure: Subgroups, imbalance, and isolates in geographically dispersed teams. *Organization Science, 21,* 115–131.

Orlikowski, W. (2002). Knowing in practice: Enacting a collective capability in distributed organizing. *Organization Science, 13*(3), 249–273.

Panteli, N., & Davison, R.M. (2005). The role of subgroups in the communication patterns of global virtual teams. *IEEE Transactions on Professional Communication, 48,* 191–200.

Pettigrew, T.F. (1998, February). Intergroup contact theory. *Annual Review of Psychology, 49,* 65–85.

Polzer, J.T., Crisp, C.B., Jarvenpaa, S.L., & Kim, J.W. (2006). Extending the faultline model to geographically dispersed teams: How colocated subgroups can impair group functioning. *Academy of Management Journal, 49,* 679–692.

Powell, A., Piccoli, G., & Ives, B. (2004). Virtual teams: A review of current literature and directions for future research. *The DATA BASE for Advances in Information Systems, 35,* 6–36.

Purvanova, R., & Bono, J. (2009). Transformational leadership in context: Face-to-face and virtual teams. *The Leadership Quarterly, 20*(3), 343–357.

Rice, D.J., Davidson, B.D., Dannenhoffer, J.F., & Gay, G.K. (2007). Improving the effectiveness of virtual teams by adapting team processes. *Computer Supported Cooperative Work, 16,* 567–594.

Robey, D., Khoo, H.M., & Powers, C. (2000). Situated learning in cross-functional virtual teams. *IEEE Transactions on Professional Communication, 43,* 51–66.

Rocco, E., Finholt, T.A., Hofer, E.C., & Herbsleb, J.D. (2000). Presentation at the European Academy of Management: Out of sight, short of trust. Barcelona, Spain.

Rosen, B., Furst, S., & Blackburn, R. (2006). Training for virtual teams: An investigation of current practices and future needs. *Human Resource Management, 45,* 228–247.

Salas, E., Cooke, N.J., & Rosen, M.A. (2008). On teams, teamwork, and team performance: Discoveries and developments. *Human Factors, 50,* 540–547.

Sarker, S., Ahuja, M., Sarker, S., & Kirkeby, S. (2011). The role of communication and trust in global virtual teams: A social network perspective. *Journal of Management Information Systems, 28,* 273–309.

Schopler, J., & Insko, C.A. (1992). The discontinuity effect in interpersonal and intergroup relations: Generality and mediation. In W. Stoebe & M. Hewstone (Eds.), *European Review of Social Psychology, 3* (pp. 121–151). Chicester, England: John Wiley & Sons.

Schroeder, K., & Fahey, T. (2002). Should we advise parents to administer over the counter cough medicines for acute cough? Systematic review of randomised controlled trials. *Archives of Disease in Childhood, 86,* 170–175.

Siebdrat, F., Hoegl, M., & Ernst, H. (2009). How to manage virtual teams. *Sloan Management Review, 50,* 63–68.

Shapiro, D., Sheppard, B., & Cheraskin, L. (1992). Business on a handshake. *Negotiation Journal, 8,* 365–377.

Sheldon, O.J., Thomas-Hunt, M.C., & Proell, C.A. (2006). When timeliness matters: The effect of status on reactions to perceived time delay within distributed collaborations. *Journal of Applied Psychology, 91,* 1385–1395.

Shin, Y. (2005). Conflict resolution in virtual teams. *Organizational Dynamics, 34,* 331–345.

Staples, D.S., & Webster, J. (2007). Exploring traditional and virtual team members' best practices: A social-cognitive theory perspective. *Small Group Research, 38,* 60–97.

Staples, D.S., & Webster, J. (2008). Exploring the effects of trust, task interdependence and virtualness on knowledge sharing in teams. *Information Systems Journal, 18,* 617–640.

Tan, A.-H., & Thoen, W. (2000). A logical model of trust in electronic commerce. *Electronic Markets, 10*(4), 258–263.

Ter Bush, R.F. (2006). *Proceedings of the 39th Hawaii International Conference on System Sciences:* Silence, attribution accuracy and virtual environments: Implications for developers and facilitators.

Thomas, D.M., & Bostrom, R.P. (2010). Vital signs for virtual teams: An empirically developed trigger model for technology adaptation interventions. *MIS Quarterly, 34,* 115–142.

Tullar, W., & Kaiser, P. (2000). The effect of process training on process and outcomes in virtual groups. *Journal of Business Communication, 37,* 408–427.

Valley, K., Neale, M., & Mannix, E. (1995). Friends, lovers, colleagues, strangers: The effects of relationships on the process and outcome of dydadic negotiations. *Research on Negotiation in Organizations, 5,* 64–94.

Van de Bulte, C., & Moenaert, R.K. (1998). The effects of R&D team co-location on communication patterns among R&D, marketing, and manufacturing. *Management Science, 44*(11, Part 2), S1–S18.

Vickery, C.M., Clark, T.D., & Carlson, J.R. (1999). Virtual positions: An examination of structure and performance in ad hoc workgroups. *Information Systems Journal, 9,* 291–312.

Walther, J.B. (1992). Interpersonal effects in computer-mediated interaction: A relational perspective. *Communication Research, 19,* 52–90.

Walther, J.B. (1994). Anticipated ongoing interaction versus channel effects on relational communication in computer-mediated interaction. *Human Communication Research, 20,* 473–501.

Walther, J.B. (1995). Relational aspects of computer-mediated communication: Experimental observations over time. *Organization Science, 6,* 186–203.

Walther, J.B. (1996, February). Computer-mediated communication: Impersonal, interpersonal, and hyperpersonal interaction. *Communication Research, 23*(1), 3–43.

Walther, J.B. (2009). Computer-mediated communication and virtual groups: Applications to interethnic conflict. *Journal of Applied Communication Research, 37,* 225–238.

Walther, J.B., Anderson, J.F., & Park, D.W. (1994). Interpersonal effects in computer-mediated interaction: A meta-analysis of social and anti-social communication. *Communication Research, 21,* 460–487.

Walther, J.B., & Bazarova, N.N. (2008). Validation and application of electronic propinquity theory to computer-mediated communication in groups. *Communication Research, 35,* 622–645.

Walther, J.B., Boos, M., & Jonas, K.J. (2002). *Proceedings of the 35th Hawaii Conference on Systems Sciences:* Misattribution and attributional redirection in distributed virtual groups.

Walther, J.B., & Bunz, U. (2005). The rules of virtual groups: Trust, liking, and performance in computer-mediated communication. *Journal of Communication, 55*, 828–846.

Walther, J.B., & Burgoon, J.K. (1992). Relational communication in computer-mediated interaction. *Human Communication Research, 19*(1), 50–88.

Walther, J.B., & Parks, M.R. (2002). Cues filtered out, cues filtered in: Computer-mediated communication and relationships. In M.L. Knapp & J.A. Daly (Eds.), *Handbook of interpersonal communication* (pp. 529–563). Thousand Oaks, CA: Sage.

Wakefield, R.L., Leidner, D.E., & Garrison, G. (2008). A model of conflict, leadership and performance in virtual teams. *Information Systems Research, 19*, 434–455.

Warkentin, M., & Beranek, P.M. (1999). Training to improve virtual team communication. *Information Systems Journal, 9*, 271–289.

Webster, J., & Wong, W.K.P. (2008). Comparing traditional and virtual group forms: Identity, communication and trust in naturally occurring project teams. *International Journal of Human Resource Management, 19*, 41–62.

Weisband, S., & Atwater, L. (1999). Evaluating self and others in electronic and face-to-face groups. *Journal of Applied Psychology, 84*(4), 632.

Wilson, J.M. (2001). The development of trust in distributed groups. Unpublished doctoral thesis. Pittsburgh, PA: Carnegie Mellon University.

Wilson, J.M., Straus, S., & McEvily, B. (2006). All in due time: The development of trust in computer-mediated and face-to-face teams. *Organizational Behavior and Human Decision Processes, 99*(1), 16–33.

Wright, N.S., & Drewery, G.P. (2006). Forming cohesion in culturally heterogenous teams: Differences in Japanese, Pacific Islander and Anglo experiences. *Cross Cultural Management, 13*, 43–53.

Zaccaro, S.J., & Bader, P. (2003). E-leadership and the challenges of leading e-teams: Minimizing the bad and maximizing the good. *Organizational Dynamics, 31*, 377–387.

Zack, M. (1994). Electronic messaging and communication effectiveness in an ongoing work group. *Information and Management, 6*(4), 231–241.

Zeffane, R., & Connell, J. (2003). Trust and HRM in the new millenium. *International Journal of Human Resource Management, 14,* 3–11.

Zheng, J., Bos, N., Olson, J.S., & Olson, G.M. (2001). Trust without touch: Jump-start trust with social chat. *Proceedings from the Computer Human Interaction Conference* (pp. 293–294).

Zolin, R., Hinds, P.J., Fruchter, R., & Levitt, R. (2004). Interpersonal trust in cross-functional, geographically distributed work: A longitudinal study. *Information and Organization, 14,* 1–26.

CHAPTER TEN

Teamwork Improvement in Health Care

A Decade of Lessons Learned Every Organization Should Know*

Sandra A. Almeida, MD, LLC, MPH
Healthcare Consulting

Heidi King, MS, FACHE, CMC, CPPS
Office of the Assistant Secretary of Defense (Health Affairs), TRICARE Management Activity

Mary L. Salisbury, MSN, RN
The Cedar Institute, Inc.

Introduction

This chapter presents the lessons learned from TeamSTEPPS® (**T**eam **S**trategies and **T**ools to **E**nhance **P**erformance and **P**atient **S**afety), a medical team performance improvement training program and a national keystone effort to save thousands of

*This publication was prepared by Booz Allen Hamilton under contract to TRICARE Management Activity, Department of Defense (DoD) Contract No. W81XWH-08-D-0025, Task Order No. 0015. The views herein are those of the authors and are not to be construed as official or as reflecting the views of TRICARE Management Activity or the Department of Defense.

patient lives annually by eliminating preventable medical errors. Developed by the Department of Defense (DoD) in collaboration with the Agency for Healthcare Research and Quality (AHRQ), it has gained international recognition as the gold standard for building a culture of teamwork and safety across the global health care system. In the ten-year journey from TeamSTEPPS' development to its current worldwide footprint across both military and civilian health care systems, much was learned about what makes team training work—specifically what leads to transfer of newly learned teamwork knowledge and skills to the job and the resultant desired improvements in team performance.

A foundational lesson learned was that scientifically designed training curricula and instructional strategies alone rarely lead to implementation and sustainment of newly learned team behaviors. Success is also highly dependent on several more complex organizational variables such as trainee preparation and a supportive work environment. The recommendations and practical tips presented in this chapter focus on those organizational variables ("success factors") and what leaders and practitioners can do—before, during, and after training delivery—to structure their team performance improvement initiatives for success. Although the information presented was primarily generated from practical experience and evaluation efforts focused on TeamSTEPPS initiatives within the U.S. Military Health System (MHS), feedback from the civilian health care industry indicates that the findings are not unique to the MHS. In fact, decades of research have increasingly demonstrated that similar organizational factors are pivotal to success, regardless of the industry or targeted outcome, of any broad-based organizational improvement initiative—including workforce training and development (Baldwin & Ford, 1988; Brinkerhoff & Montesino, 1995; Burke & Hutchins, 2008; Grossman & Salas, 2011; Salas & Cannon-Bowers, 2001; Salas, Tannenbaum, Kraiger, & Smith-Jentsch, 2012); diffusion of innovations (Greenhalgh, Robert, MacFarlane, Bate, & Kyriakidou, 2004; Helfrich, Weiner, McKinney, & Minasian, 2007; Rogers, 1962, 2003); and adoption and sustainment of human resource and management best practices (Garman, McAlearney, Harrison, Song, & McHugh, 2011).

Background

In 1999 the Institute of Medicine (IOM), the distinguished scholars who provide advice to the nation on matters of medicine and health, released a landmark report that shocked the public and changed the face of medical practice forever. *To Err Is Human: Building a Safer Health System* (Kohn, Corrigan, & Donaldson, 2000) made national headlines by declaring that preventable medical errors cost an estimated 98,000 lives and $17 billion to $29 billion annually, making errors a leading cause of death in America and a major contributor to escalating health care costs. The IOM identified human fallibility in the context of poorly designed health care systems as the cause of these errors, and recommended that all health care organizations "establish interdisciplinary team training programs for providers that incorporate proven methods of team training" as one of the foundational strategies to eliminate preventable patient harm across the nation.

A rapidly growing body of evidence provided further support for the IOM's team training recommendation. Medical databases consistently identified ineffective communication among medical teams as a leading cause of preventable medical errors and patient harm throughout the health care system (Dunn, Mills, Neily, Crittenden, Carmack, & Bagian, 2007; The Joint Commission, 2007). Over twenty years of research and experience in other high-risk industries, such as aviation and nuclear power, showed that team-based collaboration and communication had a positive effect on organizational safety, and that individuals could develop teamwork competencies through carefully designed team training programs (Salas, Tannenbaum, Kraiger, & Smith-Jentsch, 2012). Studies also were emerging in the medical literature that demonstrated a similar positive impact of improved team performance on the quality, safety, and cost-effectiveness of health care delivery, including fewer medical errors (Morey, Simon, Jay, Wears, Salisbury, Dukes, & Berns, 2002), lower hospital lengths of stay (Friedman & Berger, 2004), and reduced patient mortality (Wheelan, Burchill, & Tilin, 2003).

Despite the criticality of medical team coordination and communication for safe patient care, few health professions' educational curricula included teamwork training, and few medical practices integrated teamwork principles. Team training became a priority focus for the DoD when Congress, through the 2001 Floyd D. Spence National Defense Authorization Act (NDAA), mandated that the DoD implement medical team training across the MHS and continue investments in research and development efforts aimed at improving teamwork in health care. In response to the IOM's call to action, and catalyzed by the NDAA of 2001, the DoD Patient Safety Program, within the Office of the Chief Medical Officer at TRICARE Management Activity, and AHRQ partnered with the vision of developing and rapidly diffusing an evidence-based training program that would equip all health care professionals across the nation and the DoD with the teamwork competencies essential for delivery of safe, quality care.

The Evidence Base for TeamSTEPPS®

The Scientific Evolution

TeamSTEPPS is the result of a multi-year research and development program sponsored by the DoD Patient Safety Program in collaboration with AHRQ. This section presents a brief summary of the historical development and expansive scientific basis of TeamSTEPPS; comprehensive reviews have been published elsewhere (Alonso, Baker, Holtzman, Day, King, Toomey, & Salas, 2006; King, Battles, Baker, Alonso, Salas, Webster, Toomey, & Salisbury, 2008).

TeamSTEPPS' development was initiated in January 2003 when DoD and AHRQ convened a national panel of researchers, clinicians, medical educators, human factors specialists, and leading experts in team performance, training, and evaluation. The panel identified core competencies for medical teams and developed a roadmap for the creation of TeamSTEPPS (King, Battles, Baker, Alonso, Salas, Webster, Toomey, & Salisbury, 2008). Initial strategies that provided evidence-based guidelines for TeamSTEPPS included a comprehensive literature review on the relationship between teamwork and patient safety (Baker, Gustafson, Beaubien, Salas, & Barach, 2005) and an extensive independent evaluation of three of the DoD's early medical team training programs: MedTeams®; Medical Team Management; and Dynamics Outcome Management© (DOM) (Baker, Beaubien, & Holtzman, 2006).

Based on this foundational work, the DoD-AHRQ expert team determined that, although there were many strengths to the three early programs and the aviation industry's Cockpit Resource Management (CRM) team training model on which they were all based, the programs did not leverage state-of-the-art science or instructional strategies. The team therefore concluded that it was necessary to create one standardized medical team training system (TeamSTEPPS) that would incorporate the most current research and best practices from across multiple fields including team performance, adult learning, human error prevention, training evaluation, and organizational change (Alonso, Baker, Holtzman, Day, King, Toomey, & Salas, 2006; King, Battles, Baker, Alonso, Salas, Webster, Toomey, & Salisbury, 2008). This expansive multidisciplinary body of science informed the creation of TeamSTEPPS, an evidence-based comprehensive team training system designed to provide health care organizations with the structures and processes critical to produce high-performing medical teams that optimize the use of information, people, and resources to achieve the best clinical outcomes for every patient, every time . . . ultimately leading to an organizational culture of safety.

Curriculum Core Content and Instructional Framework

Figure 10.1 presents the TeamSTEPPS instructional framework. At its center are four evidence-based core team competency sets—leadership, situation monitoring, mutual support, and communication—teamwork skills that can be trained. At the corners of the framework are team performance, knowledge, and attitudes—the anticipated outcomes resulting from proficiency in the core competencies. For each of the four competency sets, TeamSTEPPS provides a set of simple tools and strategies learners may use to gain proficiency in each competency area as well as put the competencies into practice in their work environments (Table 10.1).

Training Course Delivery

The TeamSTEPPS training delivery model is grounded in adult learning theory and the science of team training (Salas & Cannon-Bowers, 2001). It incorporates well-tested interactive instructional

Figure 10.1. The TeamSTEPPS® Instructional Framework

strategies and tools, such as case studies, vignettes, videos, role plays, practice, and feedback. During training, emphasis is placed on defining the four core team competencies, demonstrating the tools and strategies, and providing learners an opportunity to practice the skills.

The TeamSTEPPS® Three-Phased Organizational Change Approach

TeamSTEPPS is not just a training course, but rather a training system aimed at producing sustained team behavior changes that will ultimately transform an organization to a culture of safety. TeamSTEPPS can be implemented at any level of a health care organization—within a work unit, clinic, or throughout the entire facility. Regardless of the level at which it is implemented, TeamSTEPPS is most effectively trained and integrated

Table 10.1. TeamSTEPPS® Competencies, Skills, and Related Tools

Teamwork Competencies	*Behaviors and Skills*	*Tools and Strategies*
Leadership Ability to direct and coordinate, assign tasks, motivate team members, resource, and facilitate optimal team performance.	Clarify team member roles; provide performance expectations; engage in team events (e.g., brief, huddle, debrief); facilitate team problem solving.	Resource Management Delegation Brief Huddle Debrief
Situation Monitoring Ability to develop common understandings of the team environment and apply appropriate strategies to accurately monitor teammate performance; maintain a shared mental model	Anticipate and predict each other's needs through cross-monitoring the actions of fellow team members; provide feedback early, which allows a team member to self-correct; establish a safety net; watch each other's backs.	Situation Awareness Cross-Monitoring Step I'm Safe
Mutual Support Ability to anticipate other team members' needs through accurate knowledge, and shift workload to achieve balance during high periods of workload or pressure.	Correct deficiencies in workload distribution through shifting of responsibilities to underutilized team members; give and receive constructive and evaluative feedback; resolve conflict; advocate and assert.	Task Assistance Feedback Advocacy and Assertion Two-Challenge Rule CUS DESC Script Collaboration
Communication Ability to effectively exchange information among team members, irrespective of the medium.	Communicate critical information through structured communication techniques; ensure information conveyed is understood through follow-up and acknowledgement.	SBAR Call-Out Check-Back Handoff I Pass the Baton

Based on data from Baker, Gustafson, Beaubien, Salas, and Barach, 2005.

through an ongoing partnership between TeamSTEPPS Masters (expert TeamSTEPPS trainers and consultants, either internal or external to the organization) and an internal organizational change team consisting of an executive sponsor, front-line champions, and other key stakeholders who will drive the initiative at the local level. A TeamSTEPPS initiative occurs in three continuous phases of clear leadership and well-known organizational change principles and actions (Kotter & Rathgeber, 2006) (Figure 10.2).

During Phase I (Assessment), TeamSTEPPS Masters partner with the organization's Change Team and determine whether the site (work unit, clinic, or facility) is ready for a TeamSTEPPS initiative. The Change Team defines the desired outcome, "the aim(s)" of their TeamSTEPPS initiative, and begins to formulate a plan for achieving it. They also assess whether the site has the necessary leadership support, information base, and resources in place to support the initiative.

Phase II is the Planning-Training-Implementation segment of the initiative. It begins with developing the TeamSTEPPS Action Plan—a written report detailing exactly what an organization or work group intends to do during the initiative. The Change Team then conducts TeamSTEPPS training, implements the plan, and begins measurements to determine whether they are achieving their TeamSTEPPS aim(s), and if not, why not.

The goal of Phase III (Sustainment) is to sustain and spread improvements in team performance, clinical processes, and outcomes resulting from the initiative. During this phase, front-line users integrate teamwork skills and tools into daily practice; provide ongoing coaching and team learning; continually monitor team behaviors, organizational barriers to change, and initiative impact; and, for larger facilities, begin efforts to spread the initiative beyond the initial site.

Field-Testing and Subject-Matter Expert Input

TeamSTEPPS was field-tested over an eighteen-month period spanning twenty-four facilities, including both DoD and civilian health care organizations. It was created over more than two years, across multiple health care settings, with input from hundreds of

Figure 10.2. The TeamSTEPPS® Phased Approach

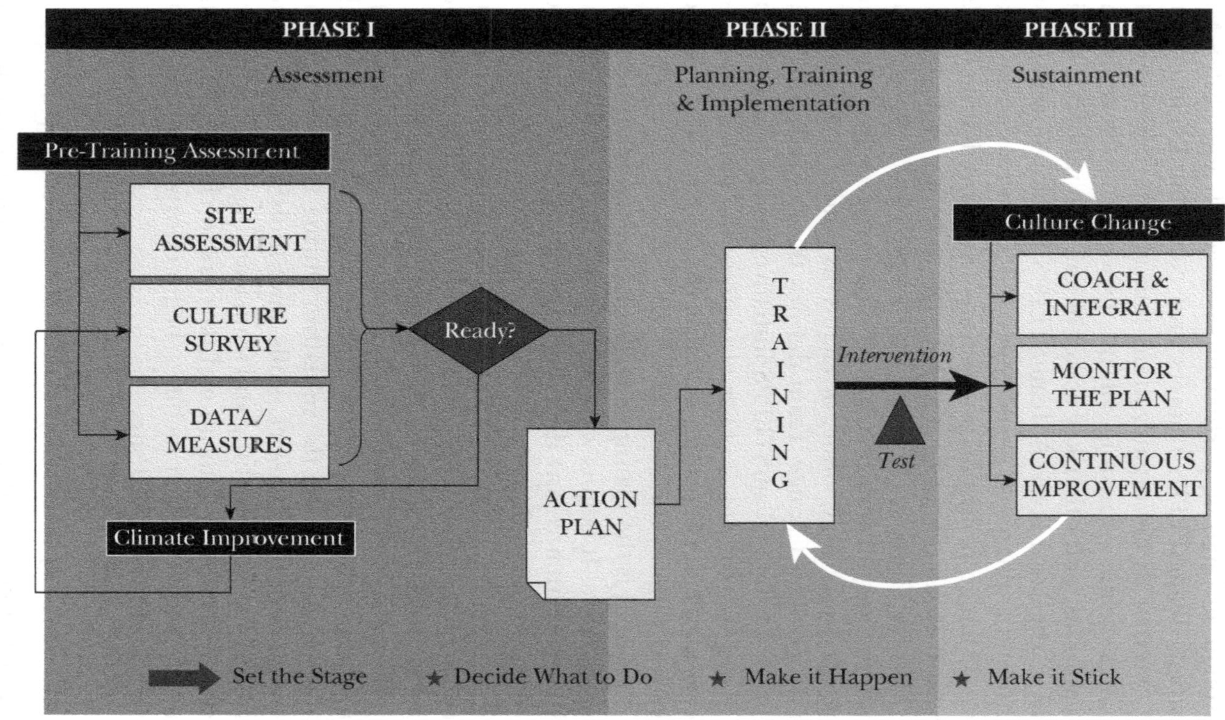

subject-matter experts and users, including patient and family advocates; patient care providers; health care leaders; researchers; human factors specialists; educators; and social, industrial, and organizational psychologists.

TeamSTEPPS® Today, a Systems Solution: Lessons Learned About Drivers of Success

Despite a rigorous scientific foundation and rich field-testing, TeamSTEPPS continues to evolve to this day; and the current program is as much a product of trial-and-error and practical user feedback as systematic science-based design. When TeamSTEPPS launched in 2006, the initial focus was on the training event. However, it quickly became apparent that course delivery was the easy part. Course evaluations showed that trainees liked the training, considered it relevant to their work, found the tools easy to use, and intended to use the new skills on the job. However, early TeamSTEPPS impact evaluations showed disappointing results: although there were pockets of excellence, few organizations were implementing TeamSTEPPS in the work environment. Getting trained facilities to promote transfer of newly learned TeamSTEPPS skills to the job, produce team behavior changes, and then sustain them was far more complex than delivering a well-designed training curriculum.

The DoD Patient Safety Program TeamSTEPPS evaluation team started asking TeamSTEPPS Masters and front-line practitioners, "Is it working? If so, why? If not, why not?" The answers were consistent, regardless of the staffing situation, work tempo, or health care setting (including the combat medical support arenas): implementing and sustaining TeamSTEPPS was highly dependent on characteristics of the work environment and organizational culture. It was at this point that the focus began broadening beyond the training event to include the full systems solution approach on which TeamSTEPPS was built; and evaluation efforts began shifting away from answering "Does it work" toward "How do we make it work?"

The TeamSTEPPS lessons learned reflect well-established training transfer models—specifically that training success requires appropriate trainee characteristics, well-designed training, and a work environment that fosters training transfer (Baldwin & Ford, 1988; Grossman & Salas, 2011). DoD TeamSTEPPS evaluations and user feedback indicated that trainee characteristics and training design elements were in place for successful training transfer, but at many facilities the work environment and organizational culture failed to encourage the consistent use of team behaviors on the job. The recognition that complex organizational variables, such as leadership support, learning culture, and front-line "champions," are key predictors of success is increasingly emerging in the training transfer (Baker, Day, & Salas, 2006; Blume, Ford, Baldwin, & Huang, 2010; Kotter & Rathgeber, 2006; Salas & Cannon-Bowers, 2000, 2001; Salas, Almeida, Salisbury, King, Lazzara, Lyons, Wilson, Almeida, & McQuillan, 2009; Salas, Tannenbaum, Kraiger, & Smith-Jentsch, 2012) and organizational performance improvement (Garman, McAlearney, Harrison, Song, & McHugh, 2011; Helfrich, Weiner, McKinney, & Minasian, 2007) literature. An understanding of these variables and the strategies for their optimization is critical to the success of a teamwork training effort.

Through over six years of feedback from TeamSTEPPS Masters (at DoD, Service, and facility levels), facility Change Teams, and front-line practitioners, several lessons were learned about organizational barriers to team training transfer and strategies to create a supportive work environment and organizational climate. The lessons learned are summarized below in ten evidence-based organizational "success factors" with practical tips organizations may use to structure their team performance improvement initiatives for success. Success factors are grouped by the time period when the respective transfer solutions should primarily be applied—before or after the training event. However, virtually all of these transfer remedies take time to establish within an organization; therefore planning and initial implementation should begin early in the pre-training phase. In addition, most of the success factors play a role across all phases of the training process—before, during, and after the training event. For example, it is critical to engage leadership support before training and maintain it through to long-term sustainment of team behavior changes. The recognition that organizational influencers of training transfer typically are not time-bound is aligned with the growing systems perspective on transfer (Broad, 2005; Burke & Hutchins, 2008).

Success Factors Applied Before Training Delivery

Success Factor 1: Align the Initiative with the Organization's Mission, Vision, and Values

> "The main thing [in succeeding] is to keep the main thing, the main thing."
>
> —Jim Barksdale, CEO, Netscape

Organizations exist to deliver on their missions—to accomplish what they are designed to do. To do this, all actions undertaken must align to hit targeted goals. "Where consistently goals fail to achieve, the organization does not survive" (Labovitz & Rosansky, 1997). Upon close examination, these failed settings are rife with multiples of stand-alone, unfocused initiatives that did not contribute to the overall mission to ensure "the main thing." No matter their worth, unaligned, stand-alone initiatives waste resources—time, money, precious human capital, and organizational good will. Unlinked to mission or vision, rogue initiatives confuse the workforce and, although elements may remain, they characteristically fall by the wayside. Establishing a history of failed initiatives gives rise to the dynamic "if we lie low long enough, this too shall pass," and typically, pass they do. Enough of these failed initiatives can lead an organization to its destruction.

The number of initiatives undertaken by an organization matters less than how well each works together to provide mission clarity and/or facilitate its achievement. More than slogans or corporate speak, alignment ensures the rapid deployment of strategy at the front line where safe, high-quality outcomes reliably occur (Labovitz & Rosansky, 1997).

Alignment and promotion of multiple organizational quality and safety improvement initiatives is, in fact, a common and foundational reason that TeamSTEPPS is brought into a health care organization. Before TeamSTEPPS training occurs, the organization's leaders and front-line champions assess how the organization's mission and goals could be better achieved with improved team performance. The organization's TeamSTEPPS initiative is then customized to optimize the organization's strategic plan for improving quality and safety of patient care at the frontline.

Alignment also promotes long-term sustainment of the teamwork improvement initiative. Clear links between the initiative and the organization's mission, goals, and values ensure an organizational commitment to making the initiative work. When aligned, the initiative receives:

- Status as a critical element of the organization's strategic plan for success;
- Budget line-item positioning, including dedicated resources;
- High visibility and scorecard status; and
- Trust as a reliably strong plank in the platform of quality and safety.

TeamSTEPPS provides the education and planning processes necessary for executive sponsors, champions, and Change Team members to partner, align, tailor, and structure all team-driven strategies such that they optimize the organization's ability to deliver on its mission and attain its "main thing."

Success Factor 2: Provide Organizational Support

Alignment informs the selection of the TeamSTEPPS executive sponsor, who then seeks out front-line champions and Change Team members. Change Team members are chosen for their passion, strong leadership skills, and ability to prepare the unit, clinic, or facility for a teamwork improvement initiative.

It is the ongoing front-line experience of TeamSTEPPS that, unless this inter-professional, cross-organizational support is present, staff commitment and compliance do not occur, and only small, if any, gains in performance and safety are appreciated. Without short- and long-term organizational support, a teamwork improvement initiative is at high risk of failure. There is disagreement on the calculus to figure the cost of failure, but there is agreement that the cost is great.

Success Factor 3: Engage Leadership at All Levels

A common reported characteristic of a successful TeamSTEPPS initiative is active, visible participation of leadership at all levels, including executive leadership, managers, supervisors, and front-line clinical leaders. What leaders say and do can heavily influence employees' perceived value of teamwork and their motivation to learn teamwork skills and use them on the job. Therefore, success of a team performance improvement effort is highly dependent on sustained active leadership support and participation throughout the initiative, beginning early in the pre-training phase.

A key role of boards and executive leaders is to communicate to all employees the importance of the team training initiative to the organization's mission and goals. They should actively demonstrate their commitment to team training by devoting time, attention, and resources to team training interventions and by holding staff members accountable for progress toward specified team training goals.

Supervisors, managers, and senior practitioners direct front-line operations and heavily influence the opinions and actions of their entire staff. A common finding across the MHS was that front-line clinicians did not implement TeamSTEPPS if they perceived ambivalence or lack of support from their supervisors or clinical "thought leaders." Supervisors may effectively demonstrate support in multiple ways, including modeling trained behaviors, communicating positive messages about teamwork, and providing positive reinforcement for observed teamwork behaviors among staff members (Tannenbaum & Yukl, 1992). Positive reinforcements, such as verbal praise, team awards, and public recognition, should immediately follow the new team behaviors in order to increase the likelihood that behaviors will be repeated in the future (McConnell, 2005). If supervisors wait too long to provide reinforcements, new behaviors will occur infrequently and ultimately disappear.

The pivotal role of leadership engagement is not unique to TeamSTEPPS' success. Studies of organizational improvement initiatives consistently identify leadership support as a key predictor of success—including diffusion of innovations (Greenhalgh, Robert, MacFarlane, Bate, & Kyriakidou, 2004; Helfrich, Weiner, McKinney, & Minasian, 2007), workforce development (Blume, Ford, Baldwin, & Huang, 2010; Salas, Tannenbaum, Kraiger, & Smith-Jentsch, 2012), and adoption of human resources best practices (Garman, McAlearney, Harrison, Song, & McHugh, 2011).

Time dedicated to engaging leadership prior to launching a team training initiative is well spent. The DoD TeamSTEPPS program uses multiple strategies to solicit leadership support and active participation. Awareness-building was integrated into existing leadership meetings and educational programs. A leadership forum was established to allow leaders to discuss ideas and share practical strategies for promoting team-based care. Prior to launching a TeamSTEPPS initiative, TeamSTEPPS Masters partner with the site's leaders to ensure they understand the program, the essential roles they play, and the strategies they may use to structure their organizations for success. Supervisor and front-line leaders are also encouraged to actively participate in TeamSTEPPS initiatives as coaches, Change Team members, instructors, and key contributors to the TeamSTEPPS action plan and local evaluation efforts.

Success Factor 4: Prepare for Training

With executive sponsors and champions in place, organizational Change Teams (at the unit, clinic, or facility level) are established to facilitate all three phases of the TeamSTEPPS initiative, using a project management and organizational change approach. During Phase I, activities are conducted to prepare the staff for training as well as structure the work environment to support a successful team initiative. Phase I comprises about two-thirds of the early initiative effort and accounts for approximately 20 percent of why the initiative "takes" (Salas, Wilson, Lazzara, King, Augenstein, Robinson, & Birnbach, 2008).

If the TeamSTEPPS effort is initiated at the front line (vice–top leadership), the executive leadership must be briefed during Phase I and offered the opportunity to consider whether the proposed teamwork improvement effort aligns with the organization's mission and values. If leadership concurs that alignment exists, an executive sponsor is chosen and a local Change Team established. From this point forward, leadership and the Change Team work collaboratively to support the assessment, planning, and initiative rollout processes. The Change Team partners with health care team members as well as patient advocate groups to ensure that the teamwork initiative includes opportunities to engage and improve the patient experience. A high driver of a successful initiative is that all involved have clear roles, responsibilities, accountability, and a shared commitment to (1) the organization, (2) their peers and patients, and (3) the broader community they serve.

Selection of units or clinics for TeamSTEPPS training is based on an information-driven assessment of needs and readiness. Change Teams and champions also use assessment data to prepare staff members for training by demonstrating the importance and relevance of a teamwork initiative to their jobs, safe patient care, and achievement of optimal patient outcomes. To further facilitate adoption, build good will, and prepare for training, the Change Team initiates a communication campaign using round-table town-hall meeting-like settings to disseminate information to stakeholders, answer questions, and establish positive expectations.

Success Factor 5: Create a Plan

Equipped with a self-assessment, organizational data, and a preliminary aim for the TeamSTEPPS initiative, the organization's executive sponsor and Change Team members attend a highly interactive TeamSTEPPS Train-the-Trainer course. Throughout the course, TeamSTEPPS Masters facilitate learning of the full TeamSTEPPS system using proven team training instructional strategies such as role playing and table-top demonstrations. The course concludes with a "teach-back" session. This "see one, do one, teach one" method serves to establish the sense of urgency necessary for the Change Teams to return to their organizations and immediately carry out the roll-out plan. The Train-the-Trainer course provides Change Teams with practice-based experience in teaching team fundamentals, designing and managing an effective innovation and diffusion of change process, and developing an action plan for the entire TeamSTEPPS initiative.

The action planning process begins with the team analyzing their own performance assessment information and identifying their strengths and weaknesses around which the action plan will focus. Ideally, the team undertakes a ten-step information-driven process to develop the action plan, including prioritizing targets at which to aim their TeamSTEPPS intervention(s), developing a communication strategy to keep all stakeholders engaged, and identifying metrics to determine whether the aims were achieved.

The action plan also includes strategies for ongoing coaching support. Each team is assigned a TeamSTEPPS Master Trainer as its coach who will facilitate Change Team discussions at mutually agreed-on times during the post-training phase. The coaching sessions are intended to facilitate progression of the team's action plan by identifying barriers, generating solutions, and building in accountability.

Success Factors Applied After Training Delivery

Success Factor 6: Facilitate Application of Trained Teamwork Skills on the Job

Training transfer refers to the extent to which trainees apply their newly learned knowledge, skills, and attitudes (KSAs) on the job; and much has been written about this topic (Blume, Ford, Baldwin, & Huang, 2010; Grossman & Salas, 2011; Salas, Tannenbaum, Kraiger, & Smith-Jentsch, 2012). One of the most important lessons learned from TeamSTEPPS was the necessity to create, *before* conducting TeamSTEPPS training, a work environment that would facilitate training transfer. Early TeamSTEPPS training evaluations consistently showed that trainees liked the training, felt it was relevant to their work, had confidence in their teamwork skills, and intended to use them on the job; however, most did not. The TeamSTEPPS experience largely reflected what the training experts had documented: training transfer and sustainment of new behaviors require that organizations provide trainees ample opportunities to use their learned KSAs on the job, encourage and reinforce those behaviors, and hold resistors accountable. Thus, in addition to preparing for the training event itself, organizations must also establish an organizational climate that will facilitate the generalization, application, and maintenance of trained KSAs in the work environment.

Job supervisors play a major role in training transfer. They can encourage it by role modeling, providing feedback, setting goals and performance expectations, ensuring trainees have time to practice newly learned skills, and establishing rewards and accountability systems. Peers can also greatly impact training transfer by observing one another and providing peer-to-peer coaching and feedback.

Success Factor 7: Engage Champions to Drive Implementation

Clinical champions, usually at least one physician and nurse, are carefully selected by the organization to help drive the TeamSTEPPS initiative at the front line. Sometimes they are self-selected, and may even bring the concept of TeamSTEPPS to the executive suite for consideration. As early adopters, they often gain awareness of teamwork and its power to improve outcomes through journals, discussions with peers, or learning sessions offered by professional organizations. Their curiosity and passion for learning are recognized and typically held in high regard by their peers. Champions are early adopters of change who are often dissatisfied with the *status quo.* They are individuals others watch and consider well-informed thought-leaders and trend-setting, cutting-edge, team members. Champions are the individuals "first to come to mind" when seeking out project leaders. Characteristically, they are respected, amicable, positive, influential informal leaders and solution-providers interested in ever-improving the experience of care for providers and patients. Their history of investing their own time and professional talent to thoroughly investigate and bring evidence-based, data-driven "good-fit" solutions to their colleagues generates staff trust in new initiatives.

As strong diffusers of information and innovators of change, TeamSTEPPS champions are carefully chosen to act on behalf of the organization and to take an active role in leading the communication campaign. They ensure all staff members' questions and the "what's-in-it-for-me" are answered, communicating the value and relevance of improved teamwork for the bottom line—the patients with whom the teams are entrusted. Champions role model TeamSTEPPS behaviors, customize the tools and strategies to best meet the needs of their team members and patients, and act as coaches and "cheerleaders" for adoption. Champions maintain a "can-do" and "whatever-it-takes" attitude. Particularly in the military, where organizations may lose champions due to transfers or deployments, TeamSTEPPS encourages champions to engage in succession planning—to build workforce capacity by identifying and mentoring motivated junior staff to become the next champions of team-based care and patient safety.

Success Factor 8: Prepare the Organization for Continuous Learning on the Job

It is estimated that only 7 to 9 percent of skill acquisition comes from formal training (Tannenbaum, 1997), and nearly 90 percent of classroom learning is lost within thirty days in the absence of additional performance support or coaching (Snipes, 2005). Continuous learning on the job is therefore essential to the success of any training effort. Reports from TeamSTEPPS Masters and front-line users clearly indicate that follow-on learning opportunities are necessary for successful implementation and sustainment of teamwork skills learned through TeamSTEPPS training events. Trainees need ongoing coaching, mentoring, performance support tools and resources, and opportunities to practice and further develop their skills.

Prior to conducting team training, successful organizations establish mechanisms to reinforce newly learned teamwork skills and foster continuous learning on the job. On-the-job coaching and feedback are two of the most effective strategies. It is important to carefully select coaches (supervisors, front-line champions, and/or peers) and train them on effective feedback and coaching techniques. Another effective, but underused, strategy for ongoing learning is the team debrief (Hackman & Wageman, 2005; Salas, Tannenbaum, Kraiger, & Smith-Jentsch, 2012). During a debrief, teams identify what they did well and what could be improved, thereby reinforcing positive team behaviors and self-correcting poor team performance. Teams can use debriefs as a learning tool after any event that requires them to apply their newly learned team competencies—either on the job or in a training event. Newly learned teamwork skills will quickly decay in the absence of practice, so it is essential that organizations provide trainees ample opportunities to use their newly learned teamwork skills, either through normal work practices or formal periodic training programs. Finally, organizations can provide continuous learning through various performance support resources such as job aids, communities of learning, and related virtual learning opportunities.

Success Factor 9: Establish Partnerships and Collaborations

Inter- and intra-organizational partnerships, networks, and collaborations are important facilitators of TeamSTEPPS adoption, sustainment, and spread for multiple reasons. They are an ongoing source of support and continuous learning for facilities, providing mechanisms for sharing ideas, lessons learned, and resources, as well as for containing costs. As channels through which facilities may broadly communicate their stories of how team-based care improved patient outcomes, these networks accelerate the spread of TeamSTEPPS within and across organizations, influencing slow adopters to likewise engage. Networks and collaboratives show similar positive influential effects on organizational adoption of human resource best practices (Garman, McAlearney, Harrison, Song, & McHugh, 2011) and diffusion of innovations.

TeamSTEPPS uses multiple strategies to establish these mutually supportive relationships, including formal inter-agency partnerships, an annual meeting collaborative, listservs, websites, and a web-based community of learning. Since 2003, the DoD has also sponsored a technical expert panel with international broad-based stakeholder representation, including professional associations, health care oversight and regulatory agencies, academia, practitioners, and research communities. This inter-professional and cross-agency approach fosters a shared commitment to a common mission, enabling widespread transformational change across the global health care system. With the National Implementation of TeamSTEPPS, an AHRQ-DoD collaborative project supported by federal funding, numerous hospitals and health care delivery systems have learned from each other and continue to partner at multiple levels to advance patient safety through team-based care.

Success Factor 10: Measure the Effectiveness of the Team Training Program

Organizations potentially waste time and resources when they engage in any training or performance improvement effort without conducting evaluations. Measurement, in addition to answering the core question of whether the training or improvement initiative positively impacted the health care organization, provides several other meaningful benefits including promotion of buy-in from key leaders and frontline staff, generation of employee enthusiasm, identification of training deficiencies and opportunities for continued improvement, and validation of the training program's value. Measurement is consistently cited as a critical component of any successful organizational training (Salas et al., 2009; Salas, Tannenbaum, Kraiger, & Smith-Jentsch, 2012) or performance improvement initiative (Garman, McAlearney, Harrison, Song, & McHugh, 2011; Helfrich, Weiner, McKinney, & Minasian, 2007); and TeamSTEPPS is no exception.

A key lesson learned from TeamSTEPPS was that measurement can be used not only to show impact of team training but to drive implementation and sustainment. To do so, evaluation must answer three questions:

- Did training work?
- If it did . . . why?
- If not . . . why not?

The only meaningful way to do that is to evaluate training effectiveness on multiple levels—trainee motivation to learn, trainee reactions, learning, transfer of trained skills to the job (behavior change), organizational results, return on investment, and, perhaps most importantly, organizational barriers and enablers to success (the answers to why it did or did not work). Therefore, measurement should occur during all phases of the training initiative—before, during, and after training delivery. Multi-level evaluations will help identify what components of the training initiative are successful, what areas require modification, and what organizational barriers must be addressed. Ongoing measurements of teamwork behavior change, and organizational barriers and enablers to those changes, are the most important for driving implementation and sustainment. In fact, assessing organizational barriers and enablers *before* training occurs is an essential step toward ensuring the work environment is structured for successful training transfer and long-term sustainment of improved team performance.

Because it is easiest and least expensive, most organizations assess only lower levels of training effectiveness, such as trainee reactions, typically using surveys to measure whether trainees liked the training or found it relevant to their work. However, positive trainee reactions are not related to transfer of trained skills to the job or to organizational impact (Goldstein & Ford, 2002); so higher-level assessments are essential to show team training effectiveness as well as to drive implementation. The importance of multi-level evaluations is clearly reflected in the scientific literature on training evaluation (Kirkpatrick & Kirkpatrick, 2010; Weaver, Salas, & King, 2011) and organizational change (Kotter & Cohen, 2002). Although multi-level evaluations require organizational time and commitment, they are a key driver of a successful team training initiative. Careful initiative planning and alignment of team training aims with organizational goals and values make multi-level team training measurements both feasible and meaningful to all stakeholders.

Implications for the Future of Health Care Team Training

Since Baldwin and Ford's (1988) early work on training transfer, there has been an explosion of research across multiple professional fields and industries to broaden our understanding of how organizational factors influence training transfer, diffusion of innovations, and adoption of best practices. This vast body of literature and the TeamSTEPPS lessons learned suggest that advances in medical team performance will necessitate that leaders are educated about these factors and that front-line Change Teams are restructured to include not only clinical thought leaders but also skilled project managers and improvement science practitioners.

Scientific evidence indicates that some organizational factors, such as leadership support, are ubiquitous and enduring predictors of success (Grossman & Salas, 2011). However, the more practical aspects of how to create a supportive organizational climate and the conditions under which specific transfer solutions apply are still largely unknown (Burke & Hutchins, 2008; Grossman & Salas, 2011). These unknowns are relevant across industries, including health care. Additionally, health care is a complex industry, in a near-constant state of dynamic flux. It is unknown how changing system variables, such as growing fiscal constraints, increasingly complex patients, expanding electronic information systems, and a progressively more technologically savvy workforce, will affect the role organizational success factors play—which ones matter or the strategies for putting them in place. There is a great need for additional research in these areas within the context of improvement science.

Conclusion

TeamSTEPPS is an evidence-based training program aimed at eliminating preventable medical errors and patient harm by improving performance of health care teams. In the short six-year period since its public release in 2006, TeamSTEPPS has achieved a worldwide footprint and international recognition as the gold standard for building a culture of teamwork and safety across the global health care system. Many factors attributed to the enormous success of TeamSTEPPS, including a curriculum design grounded in the sciences of training, evaluation, and organizational change; careful attention to user feedback; and ongoing multi-level effectiveness evaluations aimed at answering "Is it working, and if so, why . . . and if not, why not?" A foundational lesson learned was that scientifically designed training curricula and instructional strategies alone rarely lead to implementation and sustainment of newly learned team behaviors. Additional key drivers of success are related to the work environment and organizational climate.

This chapter presented a summary of ten action-oriented organizational factors that TeamSTEPPS Masters (TeamSTEPPS expert trainers and consultants) and front-line users identified as critical to successful implementation and sustainment of team performance improvement initiatives across widely diverse health care settings within the MHS (Table 10.2). The MHS TeamSTEPPS lessons learned reflect what was described decades ago and is now increasingly emerging in the training transfer and organizational performance improvement literature: success is highly dependent not only on well-designed training curricula and instructional

Table 10.2. Tips for Creating a Successful Organizational Climate for Team Training

Success Factor	*Tips and Timing*
1. Align the initiative with the organization's mission, vision, and values.	*Review and use only the best evidence available.* Visibly, clearly, map team behaviors, tools, and strategies to the mission. Develop consensus on goal alignment among all stakeholders. Focus on transportable team behaviors. Innovate where possible. Adapt when necessary. Communicate in one-on-one staff discussions to map and link the *"What do I do, what is my role?"* and the *"What's-in-it-for-me?"* Role model and send the single message that teamwork matters to caregivers and the patients they serve. *Timing:* Alignment is a dynamic process that applies pre-training but must be monitored and ensured throughout the initiative.

Continued

Table 10.2. Continued

Success Factor	*Tips and Timing*
2. Provide organizational support.	Solicit support from all stakeholders across the organization. Provide adequate resources, including budget, materials, personnel, time, and training space. Resources must be specific, irrevocable, in place, and dedicated to the long-term mission. Establish an organization-wide communication campaign, including town hall, walking rounds, and one-on-one communications to disseminate information and gain commitment. Build in support such as policies, procedures, and practices that align with the initiative goals and establish a supportive work climate. Lead by example: set an expectation for role modeling and mentoring from the executive suite to front-line leaders. Hold all accountable for achieving team training and safety goals. Promote involvement of all stakeholders from executive leadership to front-line caregivers, e.g., discuss in walking rounds, attend team debriefs, observe teams in action. Show leadership support, dedication, and involvement, e.g., attend team briefs/debriefs, follow-up problem tracking/solving, breakdown of identified team performance barriers. Create policies and procedures that facilitate building workforce capacity in patient safety, quality, and partnering. Some examples include: Job descriptions that address patient safety and quality core competencies Workforce education and training programs that target the patient safety and quality and partnering competencies *Timing:* Training should not occur until supports are in place. Support must be monitored, evaluated, and adjusted throughout the phases and stages of teamwork.

3. Engage leadership at all levels.	Communicate to leaders, from the executive suite to the front line, the importance of teamwork for the organization and the pivotal role they play in ensuring team training success. Provide leadership practical strategies for promoting implementation and sustainment of the teamwork initiative. Actively engage supervisors and front-line leaders as team training instructors, coaches, mentors. Ask leaders to provide input for the team initiative action plan and evaluation metrics. Feed back evaluation results to leaders in a meaningful way. *Timing:* It is critical to engage leadership support before training and maintain it through to sustainment of the team behavior changes.
4. Prepare for training.	Brief leadership and determine the "good fit." Appoint an executive sponsor. Establish a Change Team and consumer advocate partnership. Determine the unit or clinic that will be trained first. Communicate, communicate, communicate to all stakeholders: Providers and staff Consultancy Ancillary departments Union and contracting agencies Within-network transfer facilities. Set the expectations for high performance and good outcomes. Train the Change Team *Timing:* Preparations for training are specific to initial, new employee and renewal or refresher phases of education.

Continued

Table 10.2. Continued

Success Factor	*Tips and Timing*
5. Create a plan.	Develop a detailed action plan including measurable aims, teamwork tools and strategies, roles and responsibilities, a communication campaign, training plan, and evaluation processes. Include an evaluation strategy with defined metrics. Use reflection and debriefs to assess progress toward initiative aims. Leverage TeamSTEPPS coaching partnerships. *Timing:* The TeamSTEPPS action plan is developed during the pre-training and training phases and then carried out throughout the initiative.
6. Facilitate application of trained teamwork skills on the job.	Provide trainees ample opportunities to practice their learned teamwork skills: on the job and/or through periodic training. Ensure minimal delay between training delivery and trainees' opportunity to use the new skills on the job. Ensure supervisors reinforce new team behaviors on the job, e.g., through rewards, feedback, role-modeling, setting goals and performance expectations. Establish accountability system for resistors. Encourage peer-to-peer coaching and feedback. *Timing:* Although these factors are put in place after training, they must be planned, and in some cases developed, during the early pre-training phases.

7. Engage champions to drive implementation.	Choose the "go-to" staff. Provide champions with TeamSTEPPS lessons learned and turn them loose to innovate. Ensure champions are provided executive and administrative support. Remember that champions are talented as communicators and innovators, but not necessarily as maintainers and sustainers. *Timing:* It is essential to engage champions in the pre-training and training phase and then to send them out to gather information and formulate thoughts on ways to innovate further.
8. Prepare the organization for continuous learning on the job.	Select and train supervisors, front-line champions, and/or peers to act as coaches post-training. Implement team debriefs to reinforce positive team behaviors and self-correct poor team performance. Provide trainees ample opportunities to practice newly learned teamwork skills, either through normal work practices or formal periodic training programs. Minimize the delay between training and opportunity to use newly learned skills on the job. Ensure trainees have access to other performance support resources such as job aids, communities of learning, and related virtual learning opportunities. *Timing:* Although these factors are put in place after training, they must be planned, and in some cases developed, during the early pre-training phases.

Continued

Table 10.2. Continued

Success Factor	*Tips and Timing*
9. Establish partnerships and collaborations.	Establish inter- and intra-organizational networks, collaborations, and partnerships to share ideas, lessons learned, and resources, e.g., formal inter-organizational partnerships, meeting collaboratives, expert panels, listservs, learning networks, websites, web-based communities of learning.
	Timing: These factors are planned and sometimes initially implemented prior to training. They stay in effect post-training, typically strengthening over time as they are embedded in the work of improving team performance.
10. Measure the effectiveness of the team training program.	Assess training on multiple levels (trainee motivation, reactions, learning, behavior change, organizational results, return on investment).
	Monitor behavior change on the front line and associated organizational barriers and enablers to drive implementation and sustainment.
	Involve leaders, supervisors, front-line staff in metric selection and evaluation plan development.
	Balance scientific rigor with feasibility; use existing metrics if possible.
	Feed back results in a timely manner and in a meaningful way to all stakeholders.
	Timing: These factors are put into place as an element of preparation, are strengthened, and remain in place across the phases of implementation and sustainment. The factors are strengthened as they become embedded in the work of improving teamwork performance over time.

strategies, but on several more complex organizational variables, such as leadership support, organizational culture, and front-line "champions." An understanding of these variables and the strategies for their optimization is critical to the success of any organizational team training effort. By considering these factors—before, during, and after team training delivery—leaders will conserve precious resources, optimize training time, and structure their organizations for a successful team performance improvement initiative.

References

Alonso, A., Baker, D.P., Holtzman, A., Day, R., King, H.B., Toomey, L., & Salas, E. (2006). Reducing medical error in the Military Health System: How can team training help? *Human Resource Management Review, 16*, 396–415.

Baker, D.P., Beaubien, J.M., & Holtzman, A.K. (2006). *DoD medical team training programs: An independent case study analysis.* AHRQ Publication No. 06–0001. Rockville, MD: Agency for Healthcare Research and Quality. (Prepared by the American Institutes for Research under Contract No. 282-98-0029, Task Order No. 54.)

Baker, D.P., Day, R., & Salas, E. (2006). Teamwork as an essential component of high-reliability organizations. *Health Services Research, 41*(4 Pt 2), 1576–1598.

Baker, D.P., Gustafson, S., Beaubien, J., Salas, E., & Barach, P. (2005). Medical teamwork and patient safety: The evidence-based relation. Literature review (Contract No. 282–98–0029, Task Order #54 to the American Institutes for Research). AHRQ Publication No. 05–0053. Rockville, MD: Agency for Health Care Research and Quality.

Baldwin, T.T., & Ford, J.K. (1988). Transfer of training: A review and directions for future research. *Personnel Psychology, 41*, 63–104.

Blume, B.D., Ford, J.K., Baldwin, T.T., & Huang, J.L. (2010). Transfer of training: A meta-analysis review. *Journal of Management, 36*, 1065–1105.

Brinkerhoff, R.O., & Montesino, M.U. (1995). Partnerships for training transfer: Lessons from a corporate study. *Human Resource Development Quarterly, 6*(3), 263–274.

Broad, M.L. (2005). *Beyond training transfer: Engaging systems to improve performance.* San Francisco: Pfeiffer.

Burke, L.A., & Hutchins, H.M. (2008). A study of best practices in training transfer and proposed model of transfer. *Human Resource Development Quarterly, 19*(2), 107–128.

Dunn, E.J., Mills, P.D., Neily, J., Crittenden, M.D., Carmack, A.L., & Bagian, J.P. (2007). Medical team training: Applying crew resource management in the Veterans Health Administration. *Joint Commission Journal on Quality & Patient Safety, 33*(6), 317–325.

Friedman, D.M, & Berger, D.L. (2004). Improving team structure and communication: A key to hospital efficiency. *Archives of Surgery, 139,* 1194–1198. Retrieved from http://archsurg.com.

Garman, A.N., McAlearney, A.S., Harrison, M.I., Song, P.H., & McHugh, M. (2011). High-performance work systems in health care management, part 1: Development of an evidence-informed model. *Health Care Management Review, 36,* 201–213.

Goldstein, I.L., & Ford, J.K. (2002). *Training in organizations: Needs assessment, development, and evaluation* (4th ed.). Belmont, CA: Wadsworth.

Greenhalgh, T., Robert, G., MacFarlane, F., Bate, P., & Kyriakidou, O. (2004). Diffusion of innovations in service organizations: Systematic review and recommendations. *The Milbank Quarterly, 82*(4), 581–629.

Grossman, R., & Salas, E. (2011). The transfer of training: What really matters. *International Journal of Training and Development, 15,* 103–120.

Hackman, J.R., & Wageman, R. (2005). A theory of team coaching. *Academy of Management Review, 30*(2), 269–287.

Helfrich, C.D., Weiner, B.J., McKinney, M.M., & Minasian, L. (2007). Determinants of implementation effectiveness: Adapting a framework for complex innovations. *Medical Care Research and Review, 64*(3), 279–303.

King, H.B., Battles, J., Baker, D.P., Alonso, A., Salas, E., Webster, J., Toomey, L, & Salisbury, M. (2008). TeamSTEPPS™: Team strategies and tools to enhance performance and patient safety. In K. Henriksen, J.B. Battles, M.A. Keyes, & M.L. Grady (Eds.), *Advances in patient safety: New directions and alternative approaches* (Vol. 3: Performance and Tools, pp. 5–20). Rockville, MD: Agency for Health care Research and Quality (US).

Kirkpatrick, J.D., & Kirkpatrick, W.K. (2010). *Training on trial: How workplace learning must reinvent itself to remain relevant.* New York: American Management Association.

Kohn, L.T., Corrigan, J.M., & Donaldson, M.S. (Eds.). (2000). *To err is human: Building a safer health system.* Committee on Quality of Health Care in America, Institute of Medicine. Washington, DC: National Academy Press.

Kotter, J., & Cohen, D.S. (2002). *The heart of change: Real-life stories of how people change their organization.* Boston: Harvard Business School Press.

Kotter, J., & Rathgeber, H. (2006). *Our iceberg is melting: Changing and succeeding under any conditions.* New York: St. Martin's Press.

Labovitz, G., & Rosansky, V. (1997). *The power of alignment.* Hoboken, NJ: John Wiley & Sons.

McConnell, C.R. (2005). Motivating your employees and yourself: How different is the manager from the staff? *Health Care Manager, 24*(3), 284–292.

Morey, J.C., Simon, R., Jay, G.D., Wears, R.L., Salisbury, M., Dukes, K.A., & Berns, S.D. (2002). Error reduction and performance improvement in the emergency department through formal teamwork training: Evaluation results of the MedTeams project. *Health Services Research, 37,* 1553–1581.

Rogers, E.M. (1962). *Diffusion of innovations* (1st ed.). New York: The Free Press.

Rogers, E.M. (2003). *Diffusion of innovations* (5th ed.). New York: The Free Press.

Salas, E., Almeida, S.A., Salisbury, M., King, H.B., Lazzara, E.H., Lyons, R., Wilson, K.A., Almeida, P.A., & McQuillan, R. (2009) What are the critical success factors for team training in health care? *Joint Commission Journal on Quality and Patient Safety, 35,* 398–405.

Salas, E., & Cannon-Bowers, J. (2000). Design training systematically. In E.A. Locke (Ed.), *The Blackwell Handbook of Principles of Organizational Behavior* (pp. 43–59). Malden, MA: Blackwell.

Salas, E., & Cannon-Bowers, J. (2001). The science of training: A decade of progress. *Annual Review of Psychology, 52,* 471–499.

Salas, E., Tannenbaum, S.I., Kraiger, K., & Smith-Jentsch, K. (2012). The science of training and development in organizations: What matters in practice. . . . *Psychological Science in the Public Interest, 13*(2), 74–101.

Salas, E., Wilson, K.A., Lazzara, E.H., King, H.B., Augenstein, J S., Robinson, D.W., & Birnbach, E.J. (2008). Simulation-based training for patient safety: Ten principles that matter. *Journal of Patient Safety, 4,* 3–8.

Snipes, J. (2005, September). Blended learning: Reinforcing results. *Chief Learning Officer,* pp. 1–6.

Tannenbaum, S.I. (1997). Enhancing continuous learning: Diagnostic findings from multiple companies. *Human Resource Management, 36,* 437–452.

Tannenbaum, S.I., & Yukl, G. (1992). Training and development in work organizations. *Annual Review of Psychology, 43,* 399–441.

The Joint Commission. (2007, September 13). Report of audio conference *The Joint Commission 2007 National Patient Safety Goals.* Available at www.jointcommission.org.

Weaver, S.J., Salas, E., & King, H.B. (2011). Twelve best practices for team training evaluation in health care. *The Joint Commission Journal on Quality and Patient Safety, 37,* 341–349.

Wheelan, S.A., Burchill, C.N., & Tilin, F. (2003). The link between teamwork and patients' outcomes in intensive care units. *American Journal of Critical Care, 12,* 527–534.

CHAPTER ELEVEN

Why Teamwork Matters

Enabling Health Care Team Effectiveness for the Delivery of High-Quality Patient Care

Joanne Lyubovnikova
Aston University
Michael A. West
Lancaster University

Providing health care is a complex task, especially for certain disorders such as chronic depression, cancer care, or accident and emergency admissions. Many interventions therefore require

---

Team-based working is widely advocated as the optimal work design for improving patient safety and reducing medical error in health care services (Bosch et al., 2009). Given the complex, high-stakes environment in which health service organizations operate, teams can synthesize different knowledge, skills, and resources to deliver high-quality and timely care to patients. And indeed, research suggests that effective teamwork is associated with improved patient safety and reduced medical errors in hospital settings (Baker, Day, & Salas, 2006; Heinemann & Zeiss, 2002; Manser, 2009). Other studies link team working in primary health care with lower hospitalization rates (Sommers, Marton, Barbaccia, & Randolph, 2000) and in operating theatres with lower error rates (Sexton, Thomas, & Helmreich, 2000). The link between teamwork and clinical outcomes has been demonstrated across a range of contexts including intensive care units, operating rooms, nursing homes, accident and emergency departments, maternity suites, and surgical wards (Salas et al., 2009). The imperative for effective teamwork is also consistently emphasized by health care policymakers (Department of Health, 2010; The Joint Commission, 2009).

health care professionals from different disciplinary backgrounds to combine unique skills and knowledge to provide effective and timely care. This interaction between human fallibility and the undertaking of complex and often highly stressful health care tasks inevitably leads to some degree of error (Sharit, 2006). The challenges facing health care organizations are therefore not only clinical but also organizational, specifically with regard to how to develop and sustain effective team-based working which spans professional, hierarchical, and organizational boundaries (Richardson, West, & Cuthbertson, 2010) as well as reducing medical error.

In addition to the arguments about the benefits of team working in health care, there are two further reasons for focusing on this topic in this sector. First, health care is an increasingly important slice of national economies because of major demographic, technological, and behavioral changes. Increasing scientific and technological advancement is enabling the provision of new forms of care for formerly untreatable illnesses; there are new challenges because of increases in obesity and long-term conditions such as diabetes and asthma; the increasing longevity of populations means that the requirements for health care are increasing; and the nature of health problems is changing with disorders of old age becoming more prevalent. The proportion of GDP taken up by health care activities is high and increasing (in the United States it is around 17.4 percent of GDP, in the United Kingdom 9.8 percent; OECD Health Statistics, 2011). Second, health care as a sector in which to undertake research has been relatively neglected by industrial and organizational (I/O) psychologists. We have the potential to make great contributions from our discipline to improving health care around the world, but this potential has not yet been realized.

The purpose of this chapter is to synthesize and clarify how our understanding of teams and teamwork in I/O psychology and research on teamworking in health care has contributed to the delivery of effective patient care. We also examine the factors that predict the effectiveness of teams in health care. The chapter is intended to delineate current and future challenges that face teams working in health care and to provide recommendations for practitioners for improving the effectiveness of health care teams. We begin by outlining the context of health care teams—their typical composition and task characteristics as well as the nature of outcome measures at the individual, team, and organizational level. We then review what we know about facilitating high performance in health care teams—key processes important for overcoming the complex challenges health care teams face, as well as some specific interventions and practical guidelines that have shown to enable team effectiveness. Finally, we conclude with some of the key challenges that researchers must grapple with to ensure that I/O psychology will achieve its potential contribution in developing and improving health care delivery via effective team-based working in the future.

The Context and Characteristics of Health Care Teams

Health care includes a wide range of activities, from the delivery of care in the community for patients with chronic or acute mental health problems; the provision of primary health care services including referrals to secondary care, the management of long-term illnesses such as diabetes, and the treatment of minor depression, anxiety, and other ailments and injuries; secondary care in hospitals ranging from the treatment provided in Accident and Emergency to the long-term treatment of cancer; other health care such as hospice care for terminally ill patients; and ancillary care provided by, for example, ambulance services. Teamwork is central to the provision of effective care in all of these contexts. Complex day-to-day tasks, conflicting objectives and missions, a highly diverse professional workforce, and a demanding external environment are all salient features of health care organizations (Ramanujam & Rousseau, 2006). However, it is important to remember that health care systems are highly context specific. There are major differences between countries in how health care systems are organized and delivered, with some heavily privatized and others based largely on public provision (Schoen, Osborn, Doty, Bishop, Peugh, & Murukutla, 2007). Nevertheless, the fundamental importance of teamwork to health care delivery appears consistent across these contexts.

So what do health care teams look like and how are they composed? Given the complex nature of health service delivery both nationally and internationally, health care teams come in a wide variety of shapes, forms, compositions, and functions, all of which can impact outcomes. In order to outline a typology for health care teams, we adopt the organizing framework proposed by Hollenbeck, Beersma, and Shouten (2012), which identifies three underlying dimensions that can be used to describe work teams: *skill differentiation, temporal stability,* and *authority differentiation.*

First, skill differentiation describes the extent to which members of a team have specialist knowledge, expertise, or functional capabilities, that would make it difficult to interchange team member roles or substitute team members (Hollenbeck, Beersma, & Shouten, 2012). In the context of health care teams, some may be described as unidisciplinary, such as a group of pediatric nurses working together in a hospital ward. Such teams have low levels of skill differentiation, as all team members hold similar functional knowledge and carry out parallel clinical tasks. However, due to increasing levels of medical knowledge, skill specialization, and requirements for interdependence in today's health services (Nembhard & Edmondson, 2006), the use of interdisciplinary health care teams is becoming increasingly commonplace. Interdisciplinary (also referred to as multiprofessional/crossdisciplinary) teams are composed of members from a range of different occupational groups and disciplines with high levels of knowledge and skill differentiation. Interdisciplinary teamwork involves close collaboration between two or more health care professionals who work interdependently to make shared decisions regarding patient-centered goals and deliver health care in an integrated (rather than sequential) way (Jansen, 2008). Such functionally diverse teams are thought to optimize patient, staff, and organizational outcomes by capitalizing on their larger pool resources (different knowledge, perspectives, and skills) to deliver high-quality health care (Edmondson, Roberto, & Watkins, 2003; Xyrichis & Ream, 2008).

The second dimension proposed by Hollenbeck, Beersma, and Shouten (2012) is temporal stability, which refers to the extent to which a team has a history and is likely to remain intact in the future. The specific type of task work that a health care team is responsible for delivering is key in determining both team composition and longevity. Some health care teams may have a long history of working together and are characterized by a high level of temporal stability. For example, members of a community mental health team from the same organization could work together on an ongoing basis for a number of years with only minimal turnover in team membership. Membership stability is argued to facilitate the development of shared mental models regarding both task and teamwork processes (Hackman, 2002; Mathieu, Heffner, Goodwin, Salas, & Cannon-Bowers, 2000). Indeed, membership stability has also been shown to have beneficial effects on emergent states such as team psychological safety, which in turn impacts team performance and safety-related outcomes in health care (Edmondson, 1996, 1999; Pisano, Bohmer, & Edmondson, 2001). In contrast, a team of specialists from different health care organizations might come together to work as a "one shot" team for just a couple of hours on a highly novel surgical procedure. Temporal stability is therefore very low as team members are unlikely to work together again in future.

The third team descriptor Hollenbeck, Beersma, and Shouten (2012) propose concerns authority differentiation, referring to the degree to which decision-making power lies with the team as a whole or individual members/subgroups who occupy leadership roles. The existence of differential autonomy and status due to entrenched professional hierarchies in medicine is ubiquitous. Many interdisciplinary health care teams have clearly appointed leaders (typically members in senior clinical positions) and therefore lie at the top end of the authority differentiation continuum, whereas unidisciplinary health care teams tend to have lower levels of authority differentiation. Research has shown that a hierarchical authority structure, in combination with a culture deeply rooted in individual professional autonomy and poor communication, can create barriers to establishing a safe culture in health care teams (Leape & Berwick, 2005). Indeed, perceptions of individual autonomy may decrease as decisions become shared and responsibility is diffused throughout the team (Kirkman & Rosen, 1999).

The Science of Health Care Teams

Much of the existing theory and research on the functioning of health care teams has been structured around the traditional Input-Process-Output (IPO) framework of team effectiveness (Cohen & Bailey, 1997), the general premise being that the input-output relationship is influenced by the interactions that occur between team members, defined as team processes. Over the years, a handful of both generic and context-specific models of health care team effectiveness have been proposed. These include the Integrated Team Effectiveness Model (ITEM; Lemieux-Charles & McGuire, 2006) and the Intensive Care Unit Team Performance Framework (Reader, Flin, Mearns, & Cuthbertson, 2009). In the following sections of this chapter, we first consider the most important and well-researched outcomes of health care teams at the individual, team, and organizational level. We then consider six key team processes involved in the delivery of health care that have been shown to predict these outcomes.

Outcomes in Health Care Teams

As in other sectors, the outcomes of teamwork in health care can be conceptualized at three principal levels: *individual, team,* and *organizational.*

Individual Level Outcomes

Individual level outcomes include team member satisfaction, performance, commitment, engagement, and health and well-being. The delivery of health care is in general stressful and hazardous for staff. Mistakes can harm patients and staff, leading to illness and injury. If the team is effective, positive, and supportive, team members are more likely to be satisfied with the team environment. This is particularly important when team members are working in a context characterized by pain and suffering (Richardson, West, & Cuthbertson, 2010). Research in health care has consistently shown that a heavy workload and a hostile environment are associated with lower levels of job satisfaction and higher intentions to leave the job (Hetlevik & Hunskår, 2004; Kaarna,

2004). Furthermore, a longitudinal national survey among general practitioners in England found that job satisfaction was the main factor predicting intention to quit (Sibbald, Bojke, & Gravelle, 2003), with similar results being found among nurses (Murrells, Clinton, & Robinson, 2005).

In a recent meta-analysis, Richter, Dawson, and West (2011) found that the implementation of teamworking across thirty-five health care studies had a positive effect on employee attitudes, and that this effect was significantly greater than in twenty-three non–health care studies. Membership in well-structured teams, which show clarity in team and individual goals, meet regularly, and recognize diverse skills of their members, is associated also with reduced stress among health care team members (Carter & West, 1999). In a study of four hundred health care teams, including primary health care, acute hospital care, and community mental health teams, Borrill, West, Shapiro, and Rees (2000) found, for all types of health care teams, that better team functioning was associated with better mental health; the clearer the team's objectives, the higher the level of participation in the team, the greater the emphasis on quality, and the higher the support for innovation in the team, the better the mental health of team members. In a study of 65,142 respondents in acute/specialist National Health Service (NHS) hospitals across England, Buttigieg, West, and Dawson (2011) found that those in well-structured teams had the highest levels of job satisfaction and the least intention to leave their jobs. Analysis suggested that these differences in mental health could be accounted for by the higher levels of social support and role clarity experienced by those who work in clearly defined teams. Those working in teams also reported greater cooperation among all staff and clearer feedback from their organizations on staff performance. The findings therefore suggest that team membership buffers individuals from the effects of organizational climate and conflict. Conversely, poor teamworking has been associated with increased sickness and absence in doctors (Kivimaki, 2001).

Violence against health care staff is a widespread threat and endemic in reality. The effectiveness of the team in protecting the individual from violence affects both satisfaction and well-being (Borrill, West, Shapiro, & Rees, 2000; Buttigieg, West, & Dawson,

2011; Carter & West, 1999). In a study of 3,465 U.S. emergency nurses, 25 percent reported experiencing physical violence more than twenty times in the previous three years (Gacki-Smith, Juarez, Boyett, Homeyer, Robinson, & MacLean, 2009). Similarly, 11 percent of UK NHS staff reported experiencing physical violence from patients (or their caregivers and relatives) in the previous year (Care Quality Commission, 2010a). These figures are higher (at 15 percent) among front-line staff and among all staff in mental health (18 percent) and ambulance (26 percent) services. Effective teamwork can reduce or buffer the effects of physical violence by providing consistent and high-quality patient care via clearly stipulated team objectives, role clarity, effective team coordination, and supportive team member relationships (Buttigieg, West, & Dawson, 2011; Carter & West, 1999; Mickan & Rodger, 2005).

"Needle stick injuries" caused by hypodermic needles and "sharps" injuries (caused by sharp instruments) can also prove serious for staff. Within the English NHS, 14 percent of staff reported suffering work-related injuries and illness in 2009 (Care Quality Commission, 2010a). However, teams that adhere to protocols and reinforce safe practices are less likely to expose individual members to hazardous processes affecting their health and well-being (McKee, West, Flin, Grant, Johnston, & Jones, 2010). In summary, research suggests that the processes and functioning of health care teams have a significant impact on both performance and affective outcomes of team members.

Team Level Outcomes

Team level outcomes include the quality of health care the teams provide and patient satisfaction. Health care quality incorporates the effectiveness of the health care, safety, and the patient's experience (Borrill, West, Shapiro, & Rees, 2000; Poulton & West, 1999). Health care effectiveness is the extent to which care leads to cure, recovery, effective disease management (in the case of long-term conditions), or appropriate support in the case of interventions for non-pathological situations such as obstetric care. Patient satisfaction is important because patients have a right to expect that their experience should be an important consideration in health care team performance. Factors that influence patient satisfaction include the extent to which they are kept informed about their treatments; are involved in decisions about their care; are presented with treatment options over which they can have control; and whether their dignity is protected in a respectful atmosphere (Duggirala, Rajendran, & Anantharaman, 2008).

Medical errors are another important outcome at the team level. In the United States, research suggests that between 44,000 and 98,000 patients die each year from preventable errors, making this the eighth most common cause of death. In one study, clinical staff reported that error is important but is difficult to discuss, with only one-third of staff reporting that errors are handled appropriately in their hospitals (Sexton, Thomas, & Helmreich, 2000). Often this is because of poor team working and status hierarchies, resulting in unwillingness to point out errors to senior staff (Nembhard & Edmondson, 2006). Research also suggests that ineffective teamwork and communication leading to medical errors and patient harm constitute between 43 percent and 70 percent of medical malpractice claims in the United States. A study of 193 critical prescribing incidents revealed that over one-third were team-related problems such as hierarchical structure, adhering to prescribing etiquette (not challenging poor practice), not questioning other team members' practices or decisions, and ignoring hospital regulations and best practice in the interests of team relationships (Lewis & Tully, 2009).

Other team level outcomes include the extent to which health care teams develop new and improved ways of providing patient care (Fay, Borrill, Amir, Haward, & West, 2006; King, Chermont, West, Dawson, & Hebl, 2007). Such innovations include the intentional application of new ways of working or new forms of care that lead to greater effectiveness of care, higher levels of safety, improved patient experience, reduced costs or higher levels of productivity.

Quality of inter-teamworking is also an important team outcome measure in health care. As is reflected in the wider team literature, much of the existing research into improving health care team effectiveness has focused on intra-team processes and dynamics. However, health care teams do not operate in an organizational vacuum. They exist as part of a complex team network, constantly coordinating with neighboring teams and other agencies to discuss treatment goals and ensure that patients flow smoothly through various care pathways. When multiple teams cooperate together effectively, the performance of the entire organization may exceed the sum of individual teams (DeChurch & Zaccaro, 2010). Inter-teamworking is therefore crucial in the delivery of high-quality health care, and errors are far more likely to occur if one team does not properly communicate with another; even if in isolation, both teams are highly effective. Thus, the primary health care team must be able to manage referral processes to hospitals effectively, ensuring that patients have access to the specialist hospital services they may need. Within hospitals, the handover of staff between shifts is a critical time for ensuring continuity of care and the coordination of teams providing different aspects of care (Miller, Scheinkestel, Limpus, Joseph, Karnik, & Venkatesh, 2009), such as A & E teams working effectively with the radiography department. Research has highlighted the importance of the role of boundary spanners in promoting intergroup effectiveness in health care teams (Richter, Scully, & West, 2005). Boundary spanning behavior occurs when certain team members interact and exchange information with members of other organizational groups. However, such behaviors may be counterproductive when health care teams are operating under conditions of competitive interdependence. For example, if neighboring health care teams are competing over financial resources or trying to reduce their patient caseloads, boundary spanners may purposely withhold important information or withdraw instrumental support from surrounding teams. Teams may therefore focus all of their energy toward the achievement of team-level objectives at the expense of inter-team effectiveness and organizational performance. Given the ongoing scarcity of resources in many publicly funded health care organizations across the world, inter-team competition is a major threat to both organizational effectiveness and patient safety. Health care organizations should therefore seek to create a culture of cooperative interdependence and collaboration between teams, emphasizing the shared nature of a superordinate goal focused on the delivery of high-quality care and patient safety. Indeed, Ross, Rink, and Furne (2000) found a lack of focus on patient care among primary care nursing teams in England during an evaluation of an organizational change promoting teamwork.

Overall, effective team working in health care settings can lead to significantly improved team-level outcomes due to a shared understanding of treatment goals and knowledge of patient status, improved decision making, continuity of care, better communication, and decreased medical errors (Campbell, Hann, Hacker, Burns, Oliver, Thapar, Mead, et al., 2001; Morey, Simon, Jay, Wears, Salisbury, Dukes, & Berns, 2002; West & Borrill, 2005; Wiegmann, ElBardissi, Dearani, Daly, & Sundt, 2007).

Organizational Level Outcomes

The quality of teamworking in health care organizations relates to aggregate levels of patient satisfaction, quality of care, effective use of resources, staff absenteeism, staff turnover, and hospital financial performance (West, Dawson, Admasachew, & Topakas, 2011). There is evidence, too, that the quality of teamworking is among the best predictors of patient mortality in hospitals. A recent report, based on eight years of data gathering with an average of 200,000 responses per year from more than three hundred health care organizations in the UK, revealed important conclusions about organizational outcomes in health care (West & Dawson, 2011). The report concluded that "By giving staff clear direction, good support and treating them fairly and supportively, health care leaders create cultures of engagement, where dedicated staff in turn can give of their best in caring for patients" (p. 3). Further, the analysis of the data showed this can be achieved by:

- Focusing on the quality of patient care;
- Ensuring that all staff and their teams have clear objectives;
- Supporting staff via enlightened human resource management (HRM) practices such as effective appraisal and high-quality training;
- Creating positive work climates;
- Building trust; and
- Ensuring teamworking is effective.

Indeed, West, Borrill, Dawson, Scully, Carter, Anelay, Patterson, et al. (2001) investigated the link between hospital HRM practices and patient mortality and found a significant negative relationship between teamworking and mortality. Results demonstrated that in hospitals where over 60 percent of staff reported working in formal teams, mortality was around 5 percent lower than would be expected, even after controlling for other factors that might influence the results (such as previous mortality rates, number of doctors per one hundred beds, variations in local health profiles, hospitals, and income). Teamworking in health care has also been linked to reduced hospitalization and costs. By comparing primary health care teams with physician care across eighteen private U.S. practices, Sommers, Marton, Barbaccia, & Randolph (2000) found that the use of primary health care teams was associated with lowered hospitalization rates and reduced physician visits. The use of primary health care nursing teams in England was also linked to reduced duplication of efforts, streamlined patient care, and the more cost-effective use of specialist skills (Ross, Rink, & Furne, 2000). Research therefore suggests that effective team-based working in health care is associated with a number of significant safety- and efficiency-related outcomes at the organizational level.

Team Processes for Ensuring Health Care Team Performance

What then are some of the key teamwork processes involved in the delivery of health care? Here we consider six of the most cited: *team objectives, participation, conflict management, reflexivity, diversity, management,* and *leadership.*

Team Objectives

A substantial amount of research demonstrates the importance of team objectives to the effectiveness of health care (and other) teams. For example, in Spain, primary care teams with clear goals performed better on patient-perceived quality and patient satisfaction than did those without (Goñi, 1999). Agreement on team objectives is often reached through a superordinate goal focused on patient needs (Headrick, Wilcock, & Batalden, 1998). However, few health care teams appear to set clear objectives, resulting in a lack of clarity about team purpose, thereby making interdependent working highly challenging.

Borrill, West, Shapiro, and Rees (2000) found that, among their sample of primary care and community mental health care teams, team processes predicted team effectiveness. Results showed that quality of teamworking was powerfully related to team effectiveness; the clearer the team's objectives, the higher the level of participation in the team, the greater the emphasis on quality, and the higher the support for innovation in the team, the more effective the team. These dimensions of team working predicted self-ratings of effectiveness in both community mental health and primary health care teams, and also predicted external expert ratings of team effectiveness and innovation. In a study of sixty-eight primary health care teams, Poulton and West (1999) concluded that clarity of and commitment to team objectives were the single best predictors of team effectiveness, as rated by managers. Similar findings were also reported by Cashman, Reidy, Cody, & Lemay (2004), who found that common team objectives improved team functioning. Finally, research evidence from a longitudinal study of top management teams of hospitals (West & Anderson, 1996) provides further support for the proposition that clarity of and commitment to team goals are associated with high levels of team innovation. In turn, the consequences of lack of clarity about team objectives are poorer health care, lower patient satisfaction, and poorer health outcomes.

Participation

Health care teams must share information about patients effectively in order to be able to deliver integrated collaborative care and consistent communication to the patient and to enable effective decision making regarding diagnosis and treatment (Smith & Cole, 2009). Yet much evidence suggests these processes are often not well managed, particularly at handover when shifts change or when patients are referred on to other teams for the next stage of their care. Bond, Cartilidge, Gregson, Philips, Bolam, and Gill (1985) found little inter-professional collaboration in primary health care teams in their study of 309 paired professionals. West and Poulton (1997) examined primary health care team functioning in sixty-eight practice teams and found that on four dimensions of team functioning (clarity of objectives, participation, commitment to quality, and support for innovation) primary health care teams scored significantly lower than the other (non-health care) team types. West and Slater (1996), in a separate study of primary health care teams, reported that potential benefit was not being realized, with less than one in four health care teams building effective communication and teamworking practices.

Another barrier to teamworking is that health care comprises a wide range of stakeholders (health care professional groups, hospitals, health authorities, patients, caregivers, voluntary groups) each with their own aims, objectives, and priorities. In addition, there is considerable variation in philosophies of care among professional groups (Toon, 1994) and different approaches and perspectives on what is considered quality of care (Maxwell, 1992). One consequence of this is that health care can be judged as more or less effective depending upon the criteria adopted by the particular stakeholder, or the philosophy of care espoused by a certain professional group. As Smith and Cole (2009, p. 167) argue: "mutual respect, confidentiality, responsiveness, empathy, effective listening, and communication among all clinical team members are necessary for promoting teamwork and shared decision making." They advocate that commitment, competence, communication, coordination, and agreement on common goals for patients are necessary for effective health care teamwork.

Conflict Management

As in other settings, conflict within teams can be highly detrimental to team performance in health care (De Dreu & Weingart, 2003). Typically, there are conflicts within and between professional staff groups (doctors, nurses, and radiologists, for example) and between agencies. Teams that exhibit inter-professional rivalries and schisms are less likely to have interaction processes that encourage the sharing of knowledge and skills, instead protecting professional identities by hoarding knowledge to the detriment of patient care. Indeed, a qualitative study of sixteen Canadian hospitals revealed that disagreement between professionals over patient treatment goals was the most common source of conflict in the ICU (Danjoux Meth, Lawless, & Hawryluck, 2009).

Team members in health care also have disagreements with management over competing criteria of health care delivery, such as the conflict between an emphasis on quality of care versus throughput of patients. Typically, this manifests as a tension between targets set by managers and the quality of interaction processes with patients. Such professional rivalries exacerbate status differences, reducing the effectiveness of teams and increasing the stress experienced by team members. Given that stress has been linked to efficacy of health care provided (AbuAlRub, 2004), it is crucial that health care team conflict be managed in a constructive manner. Again, this can be achieved through emphasizing a superordinate goal focused on quality of patient care. Such goals create conditions of cooperative outcome interdependence, and thus facilitate psychological safety, pro-social motivation, and trust within a team (De Dreu, 2007).

Reflexivity

Health care teams that take time out to review their objectives, strategies, and processes and make changes accordingly are more effective in their functioning than those which do not (Carter & West, 1998). Reflexivity is particularly important for interdisciplinary health care teams working in complex high-stakes environments, as it enables them to understand whether the way in which they are currently working corresponds with patient needs, emerging challenges, and external conditions. Reflexive teams can also build self-awareness and monitor how members coordinate with one another, and are therefore more likely to recognize areas that need attention and development, implementing improvement plans accordingly (Tjosvold, Tang, & West, 2004).

However, one of the challenges for health care teams is a widespread perception of high workload that does not permit teams to take time out to review performance and how it can be improved. A study of 250 health care team members by Wiles and Robison (1994) found that three-quarters reported not having regular team meetings, with most professionals only meeting each other if there was a specific problem to be resolved. Similar findings were also reported by Field and West (1995). Consequently, many teams continue to pursue goals and targets that may no longer be appropriate for their context, such as reducing the time taken with each patient, as opposed to spending necessary time with appropriate patients, as well as taking time out to reflect on their performance. Research on intensive care teams, for example, reveals relatively low levels of reflexivity (Miller, Scheinkestel, & Joseph, 2009), despite evidence that nurses would prefer regular post-crisis feedback sessions to reflect on performance with other health care professionals (Piquette, Reeves, & Leblanc, 2009). Indeed, there is clear evidence that teams that do take time out to review performance are associated with better individual and organizational outcomes (West, Dawson, Lyubovnikova, & Carter, 2012; Widmer, Schippers, & West, 2009).

Diversity Management

Health care teams are highly diverse on a number of functional and demographic dimensions. Due to the interdisciplinary nature of many health care teams, functional diversity mainly comes in the form of occupational grouping; a community mental health team, for example, typically comprises a consultant psychiatrist, a clinical psychologist, several mental health nurses, an occupational therapist, a social worker, and a number of nursing support workers. By virtue of this functional diversity, health care teams are also often characterized by entrenched status inequities based on professional groupings or disciplines. Such status hierarchies are detrimental to open communication and information-sharing across professional groups, which can in turn inhibit decision-making quality, innovation, and ultimately the quality of patient care provided (Edmondson, 2003). For example, low-status groups such as nursing assistants or administrative staff may have difficulty speaking up to high-status groups such as physicians, whose views are given more weight and attention. Furthermore, research has shown that team member status can inhibit participation in decision-making and team meetings (Molyneux, 2001; Rutherford & Mcarthur, 2004), which has serious implications for team learning and effectiveness. Mitchell, Parker, Giles, and White (2010) also found evidence that in inter-professional health care teams, team members tend to operate in uni-professional silos in which attempts to share information across professional boundaries are often unsuccessful. Nevertheless, our own research has found that primary health care teams high in professional diversity judged their overall effectiveness to be higher, and judged their effectiveness in relation to patient-focused care also to be higher (Borrill, West, Shapiro, & Rees, 2000). After controlling for team size, the analysis also revealed that more professionally diverse teams introduced more innovations focused on improving quality of patient care, thus supporting the information/decision-making perspective on team diversity (van Knippenberg & Schippers, 2007).

Gender segregation is also salient, as some professional disciplines remain dominated by certain genders (O'Lynn, 2004). For example, females make up 87 percent of nurses and health care assistants in NHS organizations across England, whereas 60 percent of medical and dental consultants are male (Care Quality Commission, 2010b). As the population of Western industrialized countries is increasingly populated by different ethnic and racial backgrounds, cultural diversity is another major source of diversity in health care teams (Dreachslin, Hunt, & Sprainer, 2000). According to theory on work group diversity, surface-level diversity such as gender and ethnicity has the potential to be a source of both social categorization and/or enhanced information processing and decision making (van Knippenberg & Schippers, 2007), depending on how team processes are managed. Our recent findings from a study involving 135 community-based adult mental health teams across eleven English NHS organizations revealed that teams that rated themselves as most effective were those that reported a culture of inclusiveness, learning, and respect between different professional groups; a culture that was primarily facilitated via effective team leadership (West, Alimo-Metcalfe, Dawson, El Ansari, Glasby, Hardy, et al., 2012). This leads us to the final team process under consideration.

Leadership

This brief review of the outcomes, contexts, and process challenges that face health care teams speaks to the need for effective leadership of such teams. And the evidence suggests that leadership (as in other contexts) makes a significant difference to the performance of health care teams. Researchers have consistently pointed to the importance of leadership in determining the effectiveness of teams over the last ten years while suggesting that, particularly in health services, leadership is often poor (Ovretveit, 2002; Plsek & Wilson, 2001). West (2003) analyzed ratings of leadership in a sample of 3,447 respondents from ninety-eight primary health care teams, 113 community mental health teams, and seventy-two breast cancer care teams. He examined the extent to which team members were clear about who the leader of the team was, since there is often uncertainty about who occupies the leader role due to inter-professional boundary disputes and status incongruities. The results revealed that leadership clarity is associated with clear team objectives, high levels of participation, commitment to excellence, and support for innovation. These team processes consistently predicted team innovation across all three samples. Where there was conflict about leadership within the team, both team processes and outcomes were poor. Such conflicts are not unusual in health care, where leadership is often determined on the basis of professional background rather than leadership ability or network centrality. Thus, doctors sometimes assume the role of leader, even when their expertise in an area is less than that of other members of the team. Only one-third of primary health care teams and one-tenth of community mental health teams reported having a single clear leader, and in nearly half of primary health care teams, members reported that a number of people led the team. In addition, lack of clear leadership predicted poorer mental health among team members.

Leadership in health services is important, not just at the team level, but at the organizational level too. In a study involving 17,949 employees from eighty-six hospitals, Shipton, Armstrong, West, and Dawson (2008) examined the relationship between leadership effectiveness and hospital performance, taking into account external quality measures and the number of patient complaints. The results revealed that leadership style was associated with both quality of care, clinical governance, and patient complaints. The relationships were mediated by the climate for quality of care within the hospitals. These results offer insight into how non-clinical leadership may foster performance outcomes for health care organizations, and that the quality of care provided by health care teams is influenced both by team leaders and senior leaders within the organization.

Practical Measures of Health Care Team Effectiveness

In order to understand baseline performance, enhance patient care, and justify resources invested in team training, the measurement of teamwork is becoming increasingly paramount to health care organizations (O'Leary, Sehgal, Terrell, & Williams, 2011). However, given the vast array of medical conditions that health care teams treat, the focus and outcomes of different team tasks, and the unique specialist skills that different health care professionals bring to a team from each respective discipline, it could be argued that a generalist all-encompassing measure of health care team effectiveness is unlikely to be found. A number of researchers have therefore developed unique scales that focus on a particular health care domain. For example, Temkin-Greener, Gross, Kunitz, and Mukamel (2004) developed a survey instrument for assessing the performance of interdisciplinary teams in long-term-care settings. Based on an existing theoretical model, their scale consists of six key dimensions: leadership, communication, coordination, conflict management, team cohesion, and perceived unit effectiveness. Similarly, Upenieks, Lee, Flanagan, and Doebbeling (2010) developed the Health Care Team Vitality Instrument (HTVI), a four-factor instrument for assessing the vitality of nursing teams.

Alternatively, Andersen, Jensen, Lippert, Østergaard, and Klausen (2010) used techniques from crew resource management to develop behavioral markers for multi-professional resuscitation team performance. Another example is a twenty-seven-item questionnaire scale developed for measuring the effectiveness of community mental health teams (CMHTs; Rees, Stride, Shapiro,

Richards, & Borrill, 2001). However, due to a large amount of restructuring the mental health services in the English NHS over the past decade, we recently proposed a new scale for CMHT effectiveness (West, Alimo-Metcalfe, Dawson, El Ansari, Glasby, & Hardy, 2012), which was developed based on Productivity Measurement and Enhancement System (ProMES; Pritchard, Harrell, DiazGranados, & Guzman, 2008). ProMES requires all key stakeholders, including representatives from each type of CMHT (for example, early intervention, crisis resolution) and professional group (for example, clinical psychologist, occupational therapist), as well as patients and caregivers, to first define what effective teamworking looks like in the context of mental health, before extracting these themes and operationalizing them to form a psychometric scale. Stakeholders remain involved throughout the process, scrutinizing themes, cognitively testing items, and refining the final item list. Overall, this approach to measure development involves participation from a wide group of stakeholders and therefore generates a high level of construct and face validity. We therefore recommend this as a useful and valid method for the development of new team performance measures in other domains of health care in the future.

Recommendations for Improving Health Care Team Effectiveness

So what practical steps can be taken to promote the effectiveness of health care teams? Baker, Amodeo, Krokos, Slonin, & Herrera, (2010) propose three basic strategies by which the effectiveness of teamwork can be enhanced: training interventions; team member competencies; and the team task environment. In reality, the most optimal approach is to implement a combination of these strategies, which are together adapted to fit the unique organizational culture and clinical setting (O'Leary, Sehgal, Terrell, & Williams, 2011). Nevertheless, each of these strategies will now be discussed in turn, drawing upon empirical evidence in order to provide practical guidance for practitioners looking to improve the effectiveness of health care teams.

First, the most common strategy in the context of health care is to provide training interventions that aim to develop teamwork behaviors and competencies. Most training programs aim to improve interdisciplinary team effectiveness via inter-professional training, general teamwork training, participative action research, or programs based on crew resource management techniques. A major team training program developed by the Agency for Health Care Research and Quality (AHRQ) is TeamSTEPPS (Team Strategies and Tools to Enhance Performance and Patient Safety). TeamSTEPPS is a publicly available resource kit that aims to develop effective teamwork skills to health care professionals based around four key competencies; communication, leadership, mutual support, and situation monitoring (Baker, Amodeo, Krokos, Slonim, & Herrera, 2010). The AHRQ found improvements in teamworking processes following implementation of the program, specifically in relation to better communication and greater intra-team respect (Ferguson, 2008). A similar UK-based intervention is the Aston Team Facilitation Programme (ATFP; Aston Organisation Development, 2003), which is widely used in English NHS organizations. The ATFP consists of five one-day workshops held at one-month intervals that enable teams to assess and develop their effectiveness. Each workshop is focused on improving a specific area of team effectiveness, such as developing a team identity, agreeing on shared objectives, and increasing participation. Another widely used and more generic approach is the use of standardized communication tools such as SBAR (situation, background, assessment, recommendation) to improve team communication and patient safety (Leonard, Graham, & Bonacum, 2004).

So what evidence is there that such interventions actually work? Morey, Simon, Jay, Wears, Salisbury, Dukes, and Berns (2002) conducted a quasi-experimental study to show that a formal teamwork training intervention significantly improved the quality of team behaviors and reduced clinical error rates in emergency department teams, although no differences were found in patient satisfaction between experimental and control groups. In a review of forty-eight interventions, tools, and training to improve teamwork in health care, Buljac-Samardzic, Dekker-van Doorn, van Wijngaarden, and van Wijk (2010) found that, although many studies report positive associations with teamwork skills, processes, and clinical outcomes (Makary et al., 2007; Salas, DiazGranados,

Weaver, & King, 2008), some found only moderate effects (Cooley, 1994) and others no effects at all (Nielsen, Goldman, Mann, Shapiro, Marcus, & Pratt, 2007). Nevertheless, Clark (2009) argues that using any number of teamwork development programs in health care organizations will have a positive impact on staff empowerment and satisfaction while, in turn, improving patient safety, lowering staff turnover, and therefore reducing costs.

Given the somewhat scattered evidence on the effectiveness of teamworking interventions (Buljac-Samardzic Dekker-van Doorn, van Wijngaarden, & van Wijk, 2010), Salas, DiazGranados, Weaver, and King (2008) developed eight evidence-based principles in an effort to improve the success and effectiveness of future team training programs in health care. These are summarized in Exhibit 11.1.

The second strategy by which the effectiveness of health care teams can be enhanced focuses on individual competencies

Exhibit 11.1. Eight Principles for Designing Team Training Programs

Principle 1: Identify critical teamwork competencies and use them to underpin the content of the training program.
Principle 2: Emphasize the importance of teamwork over task work, and design for teamwork to improve team processes.
Principle 3: Accept that one size does not fit all—let organizational resources and desired team-based learning outcomes guide the training process.
Principle 4: Team training must go beyond task exposure—provide hands-on, guided practice.
Principle 5: Ensure that training is relevant to transfer environment using simulation-based training.
Principle 6: Provide descriptive, timely, and relevant feedback.
Principle 7: Evaluate training beyond reaction data, looking at clinical outcomes, individual learning, and impact on behavior.
Principle 8: Use performance management and coaching to reinforce desired teamwork behaviors.

Adapted from Salas, DiazGranados, Weaver, and King, 2008.

(Baker, Day, & Salas, 2006). A balance must be struck between selecting team members who have the correct technical knowledge, skills, and abilities (KSAs) for the task at hand (for example, ensuring a surgical team must include at least one anesthetist and scrub nurse) and selecting team members who have KSAs for teamwork. Stevens and Campion (1994) identified several specific KSAs for teamwork, including communication, collaborative problem solving, conflict resolution, goal setting, planning, and coordination, all of which are crucial for enabling team effectiveness.

Finally, teamwork can be enhanced by examining the contextual environment in which it occurs and adjusting workflow, structure, and/or task conditions accordingly (Campion, Medsker, & Higgs, 1993). This may involve reengineering structural interdependence within a team, increasing task interdependence between professional groups, or making cooperative outcome interdependence more explicit through team goals and reward structure (De Dreu, 2007; Wageman, 1999). The context within which teams are embedded must ultimately support team-based working through an appropriate reward system, information system, and education system (Hackman, 2002).

Based on lessons learned from empirical research with health care teams, we have extrapolated a number of key recommendations for practitioners trying to develop and improve health care team effectiveness, summarized in Exhibit 11.2.

Future Challenges for Health Care Team Research

Having provided an overview of the key team processes that enable health care team effectiveness, as well as a brief consideration of the impact of team training interventions, in this section we move on to outline the future challenges that I/O psychologists researching health care teams face in terms of extending knowledge in this important area. We begin by considering the thorny and central problem of what a *real* health care team is, and the consequences of authentic and pseudo team membership. We then consider the emerging phenomenon of multiple team membership and how this can be managed in the complex environment of health care.

Exhibit 11.2. Practical Recommendations for Promoting Health Care Team Effectiveness

Recommendations	Tips for Implementation	Supporting Literature
Make Team Goals Explicit	Ensure health care teams have clear shared goals, which all team members agree on and are committed to. This will facilitate a collective team orientation whereby team members will be incentivized to work closely and interdependently.	(Grumbach & Bodenheimer, 2004; Piquette, Reeves, & Leblanc, 2009; Salas, Rosen, & King, 2007; West, Dawson, Lyubovnikova, & Carter, 2012)
Establish Team Leadership	Clear and effective team leadership is crucial for ensuring the appropriate distribution of work, the establishment of clear team goals and team member roles, the constructive management of team conflict, and the development of collective trust and team potency.	(Künzle, Kolbe, & Grote, 2010; Reader, Flin, Mearns, & Cuthbertson, 2009; Richardson, West, & Culbertson, 2010)
Provide Role Clarity	Each team member should have a clear understanding of his or her unique role within the team and how this contributes to the achievement team goals. However, roles should encompass a degree of flexibility enabling team members to adapt quickly during crises and to compensate for one another if necessary.	(Clay-Williams & Braithwaite, 2009; Firth-Cozens, 2001; Leggat, 2007; Mickan & Rodger, 2000, 2005; Miller, Scheinkestel, Limpus, Joseph, Karnik, & Venkatesh, 2009)

Recommendations	Tips for Implementation	Supporting Literature
Take Time Out for Reflexivity	Teams should designate some regular time for team reflexivity (at least every month, and certainly after a critical incident) in which team members meet together and reflect on performance. Teams should openly discuss mistakes, errors, and incidents and formulate specific actionable solutions about how they will adapt future team processes to improve effectiveness.	(Carter & West, 1998; De Dreu, 2007; Fay, Borrill, Amir, Haward, & West, 2006; Mickan & Rodger, 2000; Widmer, Schippers, & West, 2009)
Train KSAs for Teamwork	Team members should not only develop their unique clinical skills and expertise via continued professional development, but should also receive training in essential KSAs for teamwork, such as communication, collaborative problem solving, adaptability, and mutual performance monitoring.	(Baker, Day, & Salas, 2006; Burke, Salas, Wilson-Donnelly, & Priest, 2004; Leggat, 2007; Stevens & Campion, 1994)

Continued

Recommendations	Tips for Implementation	Supporting Literature
Ensure Stability in Team Membership	Where possible, ensure that team membership remains relatively stable over time so that team members can develop social cohesion and shared mental models over team tasks. This will enable team members to anticipate one another's specific needs, recognize strengths and weaknesses, share knowledge, learning, and experience, and, over time, build a climate of trust and psychological safety.	(Bushe & Chu, 2011; Hackman, 2002; Hirst, 2008; Mathieu, Heffner, Goodwin, Salas, & Cannon-Bowers, 2000; O'Leary, Sehgal, Terrell, & Williams 2011)
Encourage Effective Inter-Team Working	Identify and empower certain team members to act as boundary spanners, to communicate regularly with other teams and external agencies, cooperating with them to ensure that information and knowledge is not lost in the cracks between team and organizational boundaries.	(Richter, West, Van Dick, & Dawson, 2006; Richter, Scully, & West, 2005)

Authentic Team Membership

Given the human inclination to seek membership of structured and stable groups, the apparent lack of research into the concept and consequences of team membership in research and theory represents an important gap in the team literature. Here we consider how "authentic" team membership can be defined as a means of sharpening our focus on the nature of teams in health care organizations.

Health care teams are composed of multiple team members with varying degrees of specialist skills, scope for autonomy, and temporal stability. However, simply calling groups of health care professionals "teams" and structuring their work according to a team-based design is not necessarily a recipe for team effectiveness and patient safety (Baker, Day, & Salas, 2006). Given the indiscriminate use of the term "team" in organizations today, we are often uncertain about which individuals constitute real team members and which individuals are simply other organizational members who interact more or less closely with a team (West & Lyubovnikova, 2012), which has hindered the exploration of the teamwork concept (Xyrichis & Lowton, 2008). This becomes even more challenging in the context of high reliability organizations such as health care organizations, given the unique complexity of health care teams and the hazardous environment within which they work (Andreatta, 2010). Indeed, our recent findings from the NHS national staff survey suggest that, although over 90 percent of staff report that they work in a team, only just over half of these staff report that their team has clear shared objectives, works closely and interdependently, and reviews its effectiveness on a regular basis—all fundamental team characteristics (West, Dawson, Lyubovnikova, & Carter, 2012).

We therefore argue that there is a conceptual difference between being a member of a team with real team characteristics (an "authentic" team) or a team that is a team in name only (a "pseudo" team), and that a focus on authentic and pseudo team membership offers a unique approach to identifying the presence or absence of real teamworking in organizations. Indeed, checking whether team members report their teams as having the qualities of a real team (shared team objectives, task interdependence, team self-regulation) allows us to more accurately establish whether real teams exist. Further, by clearly defining what constitutes authentic team membership and distinguishing this from pseudo team membership, researchers can begin to disentangle the effects that authentic and pseudo teamworking can have for individuals and the organizations to which they belong. Such an approach enables us to pose important new questions regarding the nature of outcomes of teamworking in health care. What are the consequences for individuals of authentic and pseudo team membership? Is pseudo team membership associated with greater conflict, more errors, or poor decision making? And what are the implications for health care organizations and for organizational performance of varying proportions of employees having authentic or pseudo team membership? Does having a higher proportion of staff working in authentic teams lead to higher levels of innovation, improved patient safety, and effectiveness? We suggest that the study of team membership, as a theoretical concept, can help us make progress in understanding the differences between authentic and pseudo teamworking in the health care context. We also suggest that such an approach will enable us to answer important questions much more precisely than heretofore about the effects of real teamworking at individual, team, and organizational levels of analysis.

Multiple Team Membership

A second key challenge for future research on the effectiveness of health care teams is the notion of multiple team membership, and the consequences this can have for both staff and patient outcomes. In health care organizations, it is becoming increasingly common for people to be members of more than one team at any one time. Given the multitude and diversity of tasks that health care organizations must undertake, multi-teaming enables individual expertise, knowledge, and resources to be redistributed across multiple team tasks to maximize productivity and learning (O'Leary, Mortensen, & Woolley, 2011). But what impact does this have on individual and team performance and the quality of care provided to patients? Research on multitasking provides a foundation for thinking about how task swapping and task interruption can have cognitive costs that impact individual performance. For example, research has shown that individual responses are slower and typically more prone to error immediately after a task switch (Monsell, 2003), suggesting that health care professionals who regularly switch between several teams may not perform as effectively as those working with just one or two teams. Indeed, the more teams an individual belongs to, the more he or she has to divide his or her cognitive resources and attention, and the longer it takes to reengage with the task and members of any one team. As was recently theorized by O'Leary, Mortensen, and Woolley (2011), although the initial relationship between moderate levels of multiple team membership and performance may be positive (through focusing team member attention on the task at hand and balancing workload across teams), holding an increasing number of team memberships could begin to have a detrimental effect on individual and team productivity. This is because individuals who belong to a greater number of teams may struggle to cope with competing work demands from their respective teams, impacting on the productivity and work flow of fellow team members, as well as leading to a poor utilization of time. Although high levels of variety of multiple team membership may have positive effects on individual learning and creativity, both individual and team productivity are likely to suffer due to the frequent switching between the different "working spheres" of each team (O'Leary, Mortensen, & Woolley, 2011).

Nevertheless, multiple team membership has become an inherent part of teamworking in health care, and therefore managers need practical advice on how to best distribute and manage health care professionals across teams to ensure that both staff and patient outcomes are optimized. Therefore, future research should explore the impact that multiple team membership has on both staff and patient outcomes. Although very little empirical research has so far explored this area, one solution could be to ensure that each individual has one or two clearly identifiable "home teams"—those in which they spend the greatest proportion of their time. This would allow health care professionals to develop more salient group affiliations and thus a positive sense of social identity (Tajfel & Turner, 1986). In turn, this positive self-definition enables individuals to internalize group goals and become intrinsically motivated to act in terms of their group membership, rather than according to what is individually rewarding (Ellemers, De Gilder, & Haslam, 2004). A positive social identity has also been shown to have a beneficial impact on individual health and well-bring (Haslam, Jetten, Postmes, & Haslam, 2009), as well as team performance (van Leeuwen, van Knippenberg, & Ellemers, 2003). However, new research in the unique context of health care teams is needed to explore these propositions further.

Conclusion

Given the multifaceted, diverse, and complex environment of health care organizations, coupled with the imperative to provide safe, consistent, and high-quality patient care, effective interdisciplinary teamworking in health care is a necessity. We believe our discipline has much to offer to the health care industry and that our theoretically based interventions can transform the effectiveness of health care teams. The consequent impact upon patient care and organizational effectiveness and efficiency are potentially enormous. Here is an area in which I/O psychology can make a profound difference and save lives by enhancing the effectiveness of health care both nationally and internationally.

References

AbuAlRub, R.F. (2004). Job stress, job performance, and social support among hospital nurses. *Journal of Nursing Scholarship, 36*(1), 73–78.

Andersen, P.O., Jensen, M.K., Lippert, A., Østergaard, D., & Klausen, T.W. (2010). Development of a formative assessment tool for measurement of performance in multiprofessional resuscitation teams. *Resuscitation, 81*(6), 703–711.

Andreatta, P.B. (2010). A typology for health care teams. *Health Care Management Review, 35*(4), 345–354.

Aston Organisation Development. (2003). *Aston Team Facilitation Programme.* Farnham, Surrey, UK: Aston Organization Development.

Baker, D.P., Amodeo, A.M., Krokos, K.J., Slonim, A., & Herrera, H. (2010). Assessing teamwork attitudes in health care:

Development of the TeamSTEPPS teamwork attitudes questionnaire. *Quality and Safety in Health Care, 19*(6), 1–4.

Baker, D.P., Day, R., & Salas, E. (2006). Teamwork as an essential component of high-reliability organizations. *Health Services Research, 41*(4 Pt 2), 1576–1598.

Bond, J., Cartilidge, A.M., Gregson, B.A., Philips, P.R., Bolam, F., & Gill, K.M. (1985). *A study of interprofessional collaboration in primary health care organisations.* Report No. 27, vol.2. Newcastle upon Tyne: Health Care Research Unit, University of Newcastle upon Tyne.

Borrill, C., West, M.A., Shapiro, D., & Rees, A. (2000). Team working and effectiveness in the NHS. *British Journal of Health Care Management, 6*(8), 364–371.

Bosch, M., Faber, M., Cruijsberg, J., Voerman, G.E., Leatherman, S., Grol, R.P.T.M., Hulscher, M., et al. (2009). Review article: Effectiveness of patient care teams and the role of clinical expertise and coordination: A literature review. *Medical Care Research and Review: MCRR, 66*(6 Suppl), 5S–35S.

Buljac-Samardzic, M., Dekker-van Doorn, C.M., van Wijngaarden, J.D.H., & van Wijk, K.P. (2010). Interventions to improve team effectiveness: A systematic review. *Health Policy, 94*(3), 183–195.

Burke, C.S., Salas, E., Wilson-Donnelly, K., & Priest, H. (2004). How to turn a team of experts into an expert medical team: Guidance from the aviation and military communities. *Quality & Safety in Health Care, 13*(suppl 1), i96–104.

Bushe, G.R., & Chu, A. (2011). Fluid teams. *Organizational Dynamics, 40*(3), 181–188.

Buttigieg, S.C., West, M.A., & Dawson, J.F. (2011). Well-structured teams and the buffering of hospital employees from stress. *Health Services Management Research, 24*(4), 203–212.

Campbell, S.M., Hann, M., Hacker, J., Burns, C., Oliver, D., Thapar, A., Mead, N., et al. (2001). Identifying predictors of high quality care in English general practice: Observational study. *British Medical Journal, 323*(7316).

Campion, M.A., Medsker, G.J., & Higgs, A.C. (1993). Relations between work group characteristics and effectiveness: Implications for designing effective work groups. *Personnel Psychology, 46*(4), 823–847.

Care Quality Commission. (2010a). Reports, surveys and reviews. Retrieved from www.cqc.org.uk/aboutcqc/howwedoit/engagingwithproviders/nhsstaffsurveys/staffsurvey2009.cfm.

Care Quality Commission. (2010b). NHS staff survey 2010. Retrieved from http://webarchive.nationalarchives.gov.uk/20110718105843/.

Carter, A.J., & West, M.A. (1999). Sharing the burden: Teamwork in health care settings. In J. Firth-Cozens & R. Payne (Eds.), *Stress in health professionals: Psychological causes and interventions.* Chichester, UK: John Wiley & Sons.

Carter, S.M., & West, M.A. (1998). Reflexivity, effectiveness, and mental health in BBC-TV production teams. *Small Group Research, 29*(5), 583–601.

Cashman, S., Reidy, P., Cody, K., & Lemay, C. (2004). Developing and measuring progress toward collaborative, integrated, interdisciplinary health care teams. *Journal of Interprofessional Care, 18*(2), 183–196.

Clark, P.R. (2009). Teamwork. Building healthier workplaces and providing safer patient care. *Critical Care Nursing, 32*(3), 221–231.

Clay-Williams, R., & Braithwaite, J. (2009). Determination of health-care teamwork training competencies: A Delphi study. *International Journal for Quality in Health Care, 21*(6), 433–440.

Cohen, S.G., & Bailey, D.E. (1997). What makes teams work: Group effectiveness research from the shop floor to the executive suite. *Journal of Management, 23*(3), 239–290.

Cooley, E. (1994). Training an interdisciplinary team in communication and decision-making skills. *Small Group Research, 25*(1), 5–25.

Danjoux Meth, N., Lawless, B., & Hawryluck, L. (2009). Conflicts in the ICU: Perspectives of administrators and clinicians. *Intensive Care Medicine, 35*(12), 2068–2077.

De Dreu, C. K.W. (2007). Cooperative outcome interdependence, task reflexivity, and team effectiveness: A motivated information processing perspective. *Journal of Applied Psychology, 92*(3), 628–638.

De Dreu, C.K.W., & Weingart, L.R. (2003). Task versus relationship conflict, team performance, and team member satisfaction: A meta-analysis. *Journal of Applied Psychology, 88*(4), 741–749.

DeChurch, L.A., & Zaccaro, S.J. (2010). Perspectives: Teams won't solve this problem. *Human Factors: The Journal of the Human Factors and Ergonomics Society, 52*(2), 329–334.

Department of Health. (2010). The NHS Constitution. The NHS belongs to us all. Retrieved from www.nhs.uk/choiceintheNHS/Rightsandpledges/NHSConstitution/Pages/Overview.aspx

Dreachslin, J.L., Hunt, P.L., & Sprainer, E. (2000). Workforce diversity: Implications for the effectiveness of health care delivery teams. *Social Science & Medicine, 50*(10), 1403–1414.

Duggirala, M., Rajendran, C., & Anantharaman, R.N. (2008). Patient-perceived dimensions of total quality service in health care. *Benchmarking: An International Journal, 15*(5), 560–583.

Edmondson, A.C. (1996). Learning from mistakes is easier said than done: Group and organizational influences on the detection and correction of human error. *Journal of Applied Behavioral Science, 32*(1), 5–28.

Edmondson, A.C. (1999). Psychological safety and learning behavior in work teams. *Administrative Science Quarterly, 44*(2), 350.

Edmondson, A.C. (2003). Speaking up in the operating room: How team leaders promote learning in interdisciplinary action teams. *Journal of Management Studies, 40*(6), 1419–1452.

Edmondson, A.C., Roberto, M.A., & Watkins, M.D. (2003). A dynamic model of top management team effectiveness: Managing unstructured task streams. *The Leadership Quarterly, 14*(3), 297–325.

Ellemers, N., De Gilder, D., & Haslam, S.A. (2004). Motivating individuals and groups at work: A social identity perspective on leadership and group performance. *Academy of Management Review, 29*(3), 459–478.

Fay, D., Borrill, C., Amir, Z., Haward, R., & West, M.A. (2006). Getting the most out of multidisciplinary teams: A multi-sample study of team innovation in health care. *Journal of Occupational and Organizational Psychology, 79*(4), 553–567.

Ferguson, S.L. (2008). TeamSTEPPS: Integrating teamwork principles into adult health/medical-surgical practice. *Medsurg Nursing: Official Journal of the Academy of Medical-Surgical Nurses, 17*(2), 122–125.

Field, R., & West, M.A. (1995). Teamwork in primary health care. 2. Perspectives from practices. *Journal of Interprofessional Care, 9*, 123–130.

Firth-Cozens, J. (2001). Cultures for improving patient safety through learning: The role of teamwork. *Quality in Health Care: QHC, 10*(Suppl II), ii26–31.

Gacki-Smith, J., Juarez, A.M., Boyett, L., Homeyer, C., Robinson, L., & MacLean, S.L. (2009). Violence against nurses working in US emergency departments. *Journal of Nursing Administration, 39*(7/8), 340–349.

Goñi, S. (1999). An analysis of the effectiveness of Spanish primary health care teams. *Health Policy, 48*(2), 107–117.

Grumbach, K., & Bodenheimer, T. (2004). Can health care teams improve primary care practice? *Journal of the American Medical Association, 291*(10), 1246–1251.

Hackman, J.R. (2002). *Leading teams. Setting the stage for great performances.* Boston: Harvard Business School Press.

Haslam, S.A., Jetten, J., Postmes, T., & Haslam, C. (2009). Social identity, health and well-being: An emerging agenda for applied psychology. *Applied Psychology, 58*(1), 1–23.

Headrick, L.A., Wilcock, P.M., & Batalden, P.B. (1998). Continuing medical education: Interprofessional working and continuing medical education. *British Medical Journal, 316*(7133), 771–774.

Heinemann, G.D., & Zeiss, A.M. (2002). A model of team performance. In G.D. Heinemann & A.M. Zeiss (Eds.), *Team performance in health care* (pp. 28–42). Boston: Springer.

Hetlevik, O., & Hunskår, S. (2004). The length of the patient list, waiting lists, workload and job satisfaction among general practitioners in Bergen. *Tidsskr Nor Laegeforen, 124*(6), 813–815.

Hirst, G. (2008). Effects of membership change on open discussion and team performance: The moderating role of team tenure. *European Journal of Work and Organizational Psychology, 18*(2), 231–249.

Hollenbeck, J.R., Beersma, B., & Shouten, M.E. (2012). Beyond team types and taxonomies: A dimensional scaling conceptualization for team description. *Academy of Management Review, 37*, 82–106.

Jansen, L. (2008). Collaborative and interdisciplinary health care teams: Ready or not? *Journal of Professional Nursing, 24*(4), 218–227.

Kaarna, M. (2004). The progress of reforms: Job satisfaction in a typical hospital in Estonia. *International Journal for Quality in Health Care, 16*(3), 253–261.

King, E.B., Chermont, K., West, M., Dawson, J.F., & Hebl, M.R. (2007). How innovation can alleviate negative consequences of demanding work contexts: The influence of climate for innovation on organizational outcomes. *Journal of Occupational and Organizational Psychology, 80*(4), 631–645.

Kirkman, B.L., & Rosen, B. (1999). Beyond self-management: Antecedents and consequences of team empowerment. *Academy of Management Journal, 41*(1), 58–74.

Kivimaki, M. (2001). Sickness absence in hospital physicians: Two-year follow-up study on determinants. *Occupational and Environmental Medicine, 58*(6), 361–366.

Künzle, B., Kolbe, M., & Grote, G. (2010). Ensuring patient safety through effective leadership behaviour: A literature review. *Safety Science, 48*(1), 1–17.

Leape, L.L., & Berwick, D.M. (2005). Five years after "to err is human": What have we learned? *Journal of the American Medical Association, 293*(19), 2384–2390.

Leggat, S.G. (2007). Effective health care teams require effective team members: Defining teamwork competencies. *BMC Health Services Research, 7*(1), 17.

Lemieux-Charles, L., & McGuire, W.L. (2006). What do we know about health care team effectiveness? A review of the literature. *Medical Care Research and Review, 63*(3), 263–300.

Leonard, M., Graham, S., & Bonacum, D. (2004). The human factor: The critical importance of effective teamwork and communication in providing safe care. *Quality & Safety in Health Care, 13,* (Suppl 1), i85–90.

Lewis, P.J., & Tully, M.P. (2009). Uncomfortable prescribing decisions in hospitals: The impact of teamwork. *Journal of the Royal Society of Medicine, 102*(11), 481–488.

Makary, M.A., Mukherjee, A., Sexton, J.B., Syin, D., Goodrich, E., Hartmann, E., Rowen, L., et al. (2007). Operating room briefings and wrong-site surgery. *Journal of the American College of Surgeons, 204*(2), 236–243.

Manser, T. (2009). Teamwork and patient safety in dynamic domains of health care: A review of the literature. *Acta anaesthesiologica Scandinavica, 53*(2), 143–151.

Mathieu, J.E., Heffner, T.S., Goodwin, G.F., Salas, E., & Cannon-Bowers, J.A. (2000). The influence of shared mental models on team process and performance. *The Journal of Applied Psychology, 85*(2), 273–283.

Maxwell, R.J. (1992). Dimensions of quality revisited: From thought to action. *Quality in Health Care, 1*(3), 171–177.

McKee, L., West, M.A., Flin, R., Grant, A., Johnston, D., & Jones, M. (2010). *Understanding the dynamics of organisational culture change: Creating safe places for patients and staff.* Final report. NIHR Service Delivery and Organisation Program.

Mickan, S.M., & Rodger, S.A. (2000). Characteristics of effective teams: A literature review. *Australian Health Review, 23*(3), 201–208.

Mickan, S.M., & Rodger, S.A. (2005). Effective health care teams: A model of six characteristics developed from shared perceptions. *Journal of Interprofessional Care, 19*(4), 358–370.

Miller, A., Scheinkestel, C., & Joseph, M. (2009). Coordination and continuity of intensive care unit patient care. *Human Factors, 51*(3), 354–367.

Miller, A., Scheinkestel, C., Limpus, A., Joseph, M., Karnik, A., & Venkatesh, B. (2009). Uni- and interdisciplinary effects on round and handover content in intensive care units. *Human Factors, 51*(3), 339–353.

Mitchell, R., Parker, V., Giles, M., & White, N. (2010). Review: Toward realizing the potential of diversity in composition of interprofessional health care teams: An examination of the cognitive and psychosocial dynamics of interprofessional collaboration. *Medical Care Research and Review, 67*(1), 3–26.

Molyneux, J. (2001). Interprofessional teamworking: What makes teams work well? *Journal of Interprofessional Care, 15*(1), 29–35.

Monsell, S. (2003). Task switching. *Trends in Cognitive Sciences, 7*(3), 134–140.

Morey, J.C., Simon, R., Jay, G.D., Wears, R.L., Salisbury, M., Dukes, K.A., & Berns, S.D. (2002). Error reduction and performance improvement in the emergency department through formal teamwork training: Evaluation results of the MedTeams Project. *Health Services Research, 37*(6), 1553–1581.

Murrells, T., Clinton, M., & Robinson, S. (2005). Job satisfaction in nursing: Validation of a new instrument for the UK. *Journal of Nursing Management, 13*(4), 296–311.

Nembhard, I.M., & Edmondson, A.C. (2006). Making it safe: The effects of leader inclusiveness and professional status on psychological safety and improvement efforts in health care teams. *Journal of Organizational Behavior, 27*(7), 941–966.

Nielsen, P.E., Goldman, M.B., Mann, S., Shapiro, D.E., Marcus, R.G., & Pratt, S.D. (2007). Effects of teamwork training on adverse outcomes and process of care in labor and delivery: A randomized controlled trail. *Obstetrics & Gynecology, 109*(1), 48–55.

OECD Health Statistics. (2011). Statistics from A to Z. Retrieved from www.oecd.org/document/0,3746,en_2649_201185_46462759_1_1_1_1,00.html.

O'Leary, K.J., Sehgal, N.L., Terrell, G., & Williams, M.V. (2011). Interdisciplinary teamwork in hospitals: A review and practical recommendations for improvement. *Journal of Hospital Medicine, 7*(1), 48–54.

O'Leary, M.B., Mortensen, M., & Woolley, A.W. (2011). Multiple team membership: A theoretical model of its effects on productivity and learning for individuals and teams. *Academy of Management Review, 36*(3), 461–478.

O'Lynn, C.E. (2004). Gender-based barriers for male students in nursing education programs: Prevalence and perceived importance. *The Journal of Nursing Education, 43*(5), 229–236.

Ovretveit, J. (2002). Quality collaboratives: Lessons from research. *Quality and Safety in Health Care, 11*(4), 345–351.

Piquette, D., Reeves, S., & Leblanc, V.R. (2009). Interprofessional intensive care unit team interactions and medical crises: A qualitative study. *Journal of Interprofessional Care, 23*(3), 273–285.

Pisano, G.P., Bohmer, R.M.J., & Edmondson, A.C. (2001). Organizational differences in rates of learning: Evidence from the adoption of minimally invasive cardiac surgery. *Management Science, 47*(6), 752–768.

Plsek, P.E., & Wilson, T. (2001). Complexity, leadership, and management in health care organisations. *British Medical Journal, 323,* 746–749.

Poulton, B.C., & West, M.A. (1999). The determinants of effectiveness in primary health care teams. *Journal of Interprofessional Care, 13*(1), 7–18.

Pritchard, R.D., Harrell, M.M., DiazGranados, D., & Guzman, M.J. (2008). The productivity measurement and enhancement system: A meta-analysis. *Journal of Applied Psychology, 93*(3), 540–567.

Ramanujam, R., & Rousseau, D.M. (2006). The challenges are organizational not just clinical. *Journal of Organizational Behavior, 27*(7), 811–827.

Reader, T.W., Flin, R., Mearns, K., & Cuthbertson, B.H. (2009). Developing a team performance framework for the intensive care unit. *Critical Care Medicine, 37*(5), 1787–1793.

Rees, A., Stride, C., Shapiro, D., Richards, A., & Borrill, C. (2001). Psychometric properties of the Community Mental Health Team effectiveness questionnaire (CMHTEQ). *Journal of Mental Health, 10*(2), 213–222.

Richardson, J., West, M.A., & Cuthbertson, B.H. (2010). Team working in intensive care: Current evidence and future endeavours. *Current Opinion in Critical Care, 16*(6), 643–648.

Richter, A., Dawson, J.F., & West, M.A. (2011). The effectiveness of teams in organizations: A meta-analysis. *The International Journal of Human Resource Management, 13,* 1–21.

Richter, A., Scully, J., & West, M.A. (2005). Intergroup conflict and intergroup effectiveness in organizations: Theory and scale development. *European Journal of Work and Organizational Psychology, 14*(2), 177–203.

Richter, A., West, M.A., Van Dick, R., & Dawson, J.F. (2006). Boundary spanners' identification, intergroup contact, and effective intergroup relations. *Journal of Applied Psychology, 49*(6), 1252–1269.

Ross, F., Rink, E., & Furne, A. (2000). Integration or pragmatic coalition? An evaluation of nursing teams in primary care. *Journal of Interprofessional Care, 14*(3), 259–267.

Rutherford, J., & Mcarthur, M. (2004). A qualitative account of the factors affecting team-learning in primary care. *Education for Primary Care, 15*(3), 9.

Salas, E., Almeida, S.A., Salisbury, M., King, H.B., Lazzara, E.H., Lyons, R., Wilson, K.A., et al. (2009). What are the critical success factors for team training in health care? *Joint Commission Journal on Quality and Patient Safety, 35*(8), 398–405.

Salas, E., DiazGranados, D., Weaver, S.J., & King, H.B. (2008). Does team training work? Principles for health care. *Academic Emergency Medicine, 15*(11), 1002–1009.

Salas, E., Rosen, M.A., & King, H.B. (2007). Managing teams managing crises: Principles of teamwork to improve patient safety in the emergency room and beyond. *Theoretical Issues in Ergonomics Science, 8*(5), 381–394.

Schoen, C., Osborn, R., Doty, M.M., Bishop, M., Peugh, J., & Murukutla, N. (2007). Toward higher-performance health systems: Adults' health care experiences in seven countries. *Health Affairs, 26*(6), 717–734.

Sexton, J.B., Thomas, E.J., & Helmreich, R.L. (2000). Error, stress, and teamwork in medicine and aviation: Cross sectional surveys. *British Medical Journal (Clinical research ed.), 320*(7237), 745–749.

Sharit, J. (2006). Human error. In G. Salvendy (Ed.), *Handbook of human factors and ergonomics.* Hoboken, NJ: John Wiley & Sons.

Shipton, H., Armstrong, C., West, M.A., & Dawson, J. (2008). The impact of leadership and quality climate on hospital performance. *International Journal for Quality in Health Care, 20*(6), 439–445.

Sibbald, B., Bojke, C., & Gravelle, H. (2003). National survey of job satisfaction and retirement intentions among general practitioners in England. *British Medical Journal, 326*(7379), 22.

Smith, J.R., & Cole, F.S. (2009). Patient safety: Effective interdisciplinary teamwork through simulation and debriefing in the neonatal ICU. *Critical Care Nursing Clinics of North America, 21*(2), 163–179.

Sommers, L.S., Marton, K.I., Barbaccia, J.C., & Randolph, J. (2000). Physician, nurse, and social worker collaboration in primary care for chronically ill seniors. *Archives of Internal Medicine, 160*(12), 1825–1833.

Stevens, M.J., & Campion, M.A. (1994). The knowledge, skill, and ability requirements for teamwork: Implications for human resource management. *Journal of Management, 20*(2), 503–530.

Tajfel, H., & Turner, J.C. (1986). The social identity theory of the intergroup behaviour. In S. Worchel & W.G. Austin (Eds.), *Psychology of intergroup relations.* Chicago: Nelson-Hall.

Temkin-Greener, H., Gross, D., Kunitz, S.J., & Mukamel, D. (2004). Measuring interdisciplinary team performance in a long-term care setting. *Medical Care, 42*(5), 472–481.

The Joint Commission. (2009). Patient safety goals. Retrieved from www.jointcommission.org/standards_information/npsgs.aspx.

Tjosvold, D., Tang, M.M.L., & West, M. (2004). Reflexivity for team innovation in China: The contribution of goal interdependence. *Group & Organization Management, 29*(5), 540–559.

Toon, P.D. (1994). *What is good general practice? A philosophical study of the concept of high quality medical care.* Occasional paper (Royal College of General Practitioners), *65*(i–viii), 1–55.

Upenieks, V.V., Lee, E.A., Flanagan, M.E., & Doebbeling, B.N. (2010). Health care team vitality instrument (HTVI): Developing a tool assessing health care team functioning. *Journal of Advanced Nursing, 66*(1), 168–176.

van Knippenberg, D., & Schippers, M.C. (2007). Work group diversity. *Annual Review of Psychology, 58*, 515–541.

van Leeuwen, E., van Knippenberg, D., & Ellemers, N. (2003). Continuing and changing group identities: The effects of merging on social identification and ingroup bias. *Personality & Social Psychology Bulletin, 29*(6), 679–690.

Wageman, R. (1999). Task design, outcome interdependence, and individual differences: Their joint effects on effort in task-performing teams (commentary on Huguet et al., 1999). *Practice, 3*(2), 132–137.

West, M.A. (2003). Leadership clarity and team innovation in health care. *The Leadership Quarterly, 14*(4–5), 393–410.

West, M.A., Alimo-Metcalfe, B., Dawson, J.F., El Ansari, W., Glasby, J., Hardy, G., et al. (2012). *Effectiveness of multi-professional team working (MPTW) in mental health care.* Final report. NIHR Service Delivery and Organization Program.

West, M.A., & Anderson, N.R. (1996). Innovation in top management teams. *Journal of Applied Psychology, 81*(6), 680–693.

West, M.A., & Borrill, C.S. (2005). The influence of team working. In J. Cox, J. King, A. Hutchinson, & P. McAvoy (Eds.), *Understanding doctors' performance.* Oxford: Radcliffe Publishing.

West, M.A., Borrill, C.S., Dawson, J.F., Scully, J., Carter, M., Anelay, S., Patterson, M., et al. (2001). The link between the management of employees and patient mortality in acute hospitals. *The International Journal of Human Resource Management, 13*(8), 1299–1310.

West, M.A., & Dawson, J.F. (2011). NHS staff management and health service quality. Retrieved from www.dh.gov.uk /health/2011/08/nhs-staff-management/

West, M.A., Dawson, J.F., Admasachew, L., & Topakas, A. (2011). NHS staff management and health service quality: Results from the NHS staff survey and related data. Retrieved from www.dh.gov.uk/health/2011/08/nhs-staff-management/

West, M.A., Dawson, J.F., Lyubovnikova, J., & Carter, M. (2012). 24-Karat or fool's gold? Consequences of authentic and pseudo team membership in health care organizations. Manuscript under review.

West, M.A., & Lyubovnikova, J. (2012). Real teams or pseudo teams? The changing landscape needs a better map. *Industrial and Organizational Psychology, 5*(1), 25–28.

West, M.A., & Poulton, B.C. (1997). A failure of function: Teamwork in primary health care. *Journal of Interprofessional Care, 11*(2), 205–216.

West, M.A., & Slater, J.A. (1996). *The effectiveness of teamworking in primary health care.* London: HEA Publishing.

Widmer, P., Schippers, M., & West, M.A. (2009). Recent developments in reflexivity research: A review. *Psychology of Everyday Activity, 2*(2), 2–11.

Wiegmann, D.A., ElBardissi, A.W., Dearani, J.A., Daly, R.C., & Sundt, T.M. (2007). Disruptions in surgical flow and their relationship to surgical errors: An exploratory investigation. *Surgery, 142*(5), 658–665.

Wiles, R., & Robison, J. (1994). Teamwork in primary care: The views and experiences of nurses, midwives and health visitors. *Journal of Advanced Nursing, 20*(2), 324–330.

Xyrichis, A., & Lowton, K. (2008). What fosters or prevents interprofessional teamworking in primary and community care? A literature review. *International Journal of Nursing Studies, 45*(1), 140–153.

Xyrichis, A., & Ream, E. (2008). Teamwork: A concept analysis. *Journal of Advanced Nursing, 61*(2), 232–241.

CHAPTER TWELVE

Rethinking Team Diversity Management*

Evidence-Based Strategies for Coping with Diversity Threats

Mirko Antino

Universidad Complutense de Madrid

Ramón Rico

Universidad AutonOma de Madrid

Miriam Sánchez-Manzanares

Universidad Carlos III de Madrid

Dora C. Lau

Chinese University of Hong Kong

Introduction

In a web design company, a four-person team (Team A) works on the development and maintenance of interactive web pages for money transactions. Two members are women, Karen and Susan, in their twenties, with an educational background in art and both with master's degrees in web design; while the other two are men, Paul and Simon, thirty-nine and forty-four years old, with IT and telecommunication engineering training and specializing in

*Our research was supported in part by grant PI10/01272 from the FIS Instituto de Salud Carlos III.

Table 12.1. Team A Composition

Team A	*Member 1*	*Member 2*	*Member 3*	*Member 4*
Name	Karen	Susan	Paul	Simon
Gender	Female	Female	Male	Male
Age	24	27	39	44
Educational Background	Art and web design	Art and web design	IT	Telecom. engineering
Religion	Atheist	Agnostic	Observant	Observant
Hobby	Volleyball	Poker	Golf	Windsurfing

programming. The composition of the department is shown in Table 12.1.

The four teammates used to work together with excellent results, combining common knowledge, skills, and abilities (KSAs) (all team members share basic programming and web design skills) as well as specific technical KSAs (the men possess more complex programming skills, whereas the women have more experience in creative tasks and design tools). The team has a great history of collaboration. When starting a new project, they usually meet for planning purposes with the supervisor, who explains the project and organizes the task to fulfill its goals. In the first phase all teammates discuss the web-page architecture; second, the two designers prepare the graphics of the homepage without introducing the logo, which is usually prepared by the IT experts; third, the telecommunication engineer constructs the programming architecture of the page; and finally, they assemble the parts and run different usability tests.

However, this time, after exchanging opinions about planning a new project, the team experienced a tense situation—a strong debate started. First, Karen and Susan disagreed with Paul and Simon regarding the amount of resources spent on design and programming. Later, Paul and Simon frequently talked in private about the company's recent policies to recruit more female employees and expressed concerns about whether they could keep their jobs. At the same time, Karen and Susan went for tea together frequently to discuss the recent promotion of a male manager. In public or private, stable subgroups form and the team of four seldom agree. Unfortunately, team conflict often aligns with the subgroup boundary. This event dramatically affected the team's functioning, creating an atmosphere of mistrust and conflict among the team members. The team drastically reduced its performance and its members were no longer happy working together.

The former situation is quite common in organizations nowadays where *diverse* teams are frequently in charge of developing innovative products, making important decisions and improving efficiency. Since diversity has become a fact of organizational life, understanding its impact on team functioning has become one of the main challenges for organizational theory and practice (Guzzo & Dickson, 1996). Existing research shows that diversity effects are elusive (van Knippenberg & Schippers, 2007) and has both positive and negative effects on team process and performance (Williams & O'Reilly, 1998), highlighting the important consequences that diversity comports for day-to-day work in organizations.

Since 1998 a new approach has been adopted, considering that team members simultaneously differ on several attributes (such as gender, educational background, and nationality) and that the combinations of correlated diversity dimensions yield a basis for subgroup differentiation (that is, *team faultlines,* Lau & Murnighan, 1998). In the example above, the team presents a strong faultline with two likely subgroups: one subgroup consists of Karen and Susan, both in their twenties, female, and artistic, while Paul and Simon, both older males and programming-oriented, belong to another subgroup. We may expect a clear division between the subgroups, especially when relevant issues arise.

From a managerial perspective, this change of approach presents important implications as it involves rethinking previous assumptions on team diversity. We contend that, without such rethinking, it is difficult for today's leaders to know when and how to respond to workplace diversity-related issues (such as subgroup divisions on a team). Despite the significant work done so far, faultline literature has devoted little effort to synthesizing and disseminating the lessons learned over more than a decade of research.

To address that gap, this chapter is devoted first to explaining the effects of team faultlines on team performance, summarizing the key points in a clear framework; and second, to proposing different managerial strategies based on empirical evidence. These strategies will be illustrated and contextualized (using the Team A example) below the proposed framework. In doing so, we briefly introduce faultline literature in connection with team diversity research. We continue by explaining how team faultlines operate and their implications for team leaders. Then we propose different managerial strategies to manage team faultlines, reviewing for each of them the supporting empirical evidence and outlining its implications in practice. Finally, we integrate such strategies in our framework and briefly discuss some implications concerning the macro contexts in which teams are embedded.

The Theory of Faultlines

From Team Diversity to Team Faultlines

The key question in diversity research is when (in the presence of what conditions) and how (through what mechanisms) differences between team members (usually in terms of gender, age, ethnicity, tenure, personality, educational or functional background) affect team processes and performance. For instance, following a traditional approach, researchers might examine the effect of gender or educational background differences on team performance by comparing heterogeneous teams (like Team A) and homogeneous teams. Using this approach, different dimensions of diversity have been investigated, generating mixed results (van Knippenberg & Schippers, 2007). On the one hand, diversity has been described as a potential value for teams, because diverse teams generally possess more heterogeneous knowledge and perspectives to solve tasks. On the other hand, diversity has been negatively related to team processes and performance, because of subgroup divisions that create "we versus they" distinctions, leading to interpersonal tensions and conflict that impair normal team functioning.

One of the reasons for such mixed results is the way in which team diversity has been conceptualized and measured. Traditionally, researchers have analyzed the effects of a particular diversity dimension in isolation (for example, gender), without considering the potential interactions among different diversity dimensions (such as age or ethnicity). To overcome this limitation, recent studies have proposed more refined models of team diversity. The point is that team members differ simultaneously in different attributes, such as gender, race, or age, and that diversity can be analyzed as combinations of correlated dimensions of diversity that yield a clear basis for differentiation between subgroups. Based on this premise, Lau and Murnighan (1998) proposed the concept of *faultlines* in the diversity literature, referring to them as "hypothetical dividing lines that may split a group into subgroups based on one or more attributes" (p. 328). When team members share an attribute with one or more of their teammates, they may align themselves on the basis of that attribute. For example, this is particularly evident when male-majority companies try to balance the distribution by recruiting new female applicants, thus forming a faultline between older males and younger females in the organizations. Moreover, common workplace characteristics such as working in a joint venture (Li & Hambrick, 2005) or a global virtual setting (Polzer, Milton, & Swann, 2002) bring new and relevant diversity dimensions to the team, which could be sufficient to generate subgroup divisions in faultline teams. For those reasons, leaders must be aware of being continually challenged by faultline-based fractures, especially taking into account that team members differ on a variety of dimensions. Therefore, faultlines can be considered as a basic characteristic of team structure.

For instance, in Team A, Karen and Susan are similar to each other in age, gender, and educational background. They tend to team up together against Paul and Simon. Conflict along the fracture line is frequent and intense, and sometimes they are hesitant to share information across this front, and team decisions are often made under such conditions. Innovative team ideas are scarce because of the intense atmosphere between members. Although they are concerned with the team situation, they do not know how to change it.

Faultlines are potentially present in every team structure and can easily damage team functioning. But how do faultlines concretely influence team functioning? How does *subgrouping* affect team performance? To answer these questions, first we delve into the psychological mechanisms that are the basis of subgroup divisions. Then we describe the team processes directly affected by team faultlines, which can explain the faultlines-performance relation. Thus, we lay the foundation of why and how different managerial strategies work.

The Psychology of Faultlines

The faultline perspective explores how aligned dimensions of diversity can degenerate into subgroup fractures, with serious implications for team functioning. The key psychological mechanism behind the subgroup divisions is called *categorization,* and it accounts for the individual's tendency to transform continuous variables into discrete classes (Tajfel, Billig, & Bundy, 1971). For example, age is clearly a continuum variable between an individual's birth and death. Within the variable age, people create mutually exclusive categories through social conventions, such as reaching majority or adulthood versus minority or underage. Similarly, a categorization process within Team A could create two exclusive categories of young (Karen and Susan) versus old (Paul and Simon). These categories are only meaningful within the team because in other teams Paul and Simon could be part of a *young* category in relation to older people. More than sixty years of research on intergroup relations shows that the creation of categories has important consequences for three main reasons (Brewer, 1999). First, in our example, Susan perceives that she has more in common with Karen, as part of the *young* category (her *in-group*), than with Paul and Simon, as members of the *old* category (her *out-group*). Technically, this is called the *intergroup accentuation principle.* Second, Susan would have more trust in Karen because they belong to the same category. This is called the *favoritism principle.* Third, Karen and Susan will tend to feel in competition with Paul and Simon, therefore perceiving a negative relation with the *old* subgroup. This is called the *social competition principle.*

The above three principles of categorization are considered the bases of the preference and affinity for one's in-group over out-group (called *intergroup bias*) that can explain the negative consequences of subgrouping in diverse teams. Nevertheless, diversity-based categorization only happens when the diversity dimensions are accessible and salient for individuals. Specifically, three circumstances favor categorization (Oakes, Haslam, & Turner, 1994): (1) *comparative fit*: the degree to which the categorization is related to actual differences between team members—thus, it is more likely that a *young-old* categorization will occur in Team A than in a team where all the members are twenty-five years old; (2) *normative fit*: the extent to which the categorization is meaningful for the team members—a *young-old* categorization is more meaningful in a football team, where age is a key factor for performance, than in an administrative team, where age might not be relevant; (3) *cognitive accessibility*: how easily team members perceive the differences among them and how quickly they come to mind—race-based categories would become very accessible during a conference on racism.

If the three circumstances are satisfied (Turner, Hogg, Oakes, Reicher, & Wetherell, 1987), diverse teams are likely to experience internal fractures. In a work setting, where teammates constantly interact, categorization could occur just because an element (called a *trigger*, Chrobot-Mason, Ruderman, Weber, Ohlott, & Dalton, 2007) of the team task or context stimulates the recognition of differences between the team members. Such a trigger is an activation mechanism that may have its origin in everyday work, acting as a cue and generating subgroup dynamics (Jehn & Bezrukova, 2010). Building on this theory, Lau and Murnighan (1998) argue that faultlines will remain latent until the team task or context, containing faultline-relevant elements, activates the salience of similarities and differences.

In reference to our example, possible triggers could be:

1. A well-known entertainment company requires the implementation of its online-poker web page and contacts the web design company, which assigns the work to the team. Within the team the two men are religious and do not approve of gambling and games like poker, whereas one woman is a member of a poker

club and an expert player. A simple comment like "poor people who spend a lot of time and money on those things" could start a conflictive discussion in which the men's subgroup would defend its position in contraposition to the women's subgroup.

2. The supervisor decides to allocate a performance bonus differentiated by organizational tenure. When this issue comes up, the team reorganizes itself into subgroups where organizational tenure is clearly associated with age (aligned with gender and educational background). Again, this could start a conflictive contraposition between the two subgroups.

In summary, in faultline teams (even in those considered high-performing teams), subgroup divisions can appear at any moment, threatening team functioning. But how do faultlines specifically harm team performance? In the following subsection we focus on two team processes that explain the negative impact of faultlines on team performance: information elaboration and team conflict.

Information Elaboration in Faultline Teams

Diversity leads to high performance only when team members are able to combine and build on each other's ideas. Team members' diverse knowledge and perspectives need to be shared within the team, but a simple exchange of information and perspectives is not enough; this information needs to be discussed and integrated into a team-level product, such as a decision or a solution. This is defined as information elaboration—the exchange, discussion, and integration of task-relevant information and perspectives (van Knippenberg, De Dreu, & Homan, 2004). Without information elaboration, teams are not able to exploit their potential and will perform poorly. Studies have shown that diverse teams with high integration and cohesion have great levels of information processing (Harrison, Price, Gavin, & Florey, 2002). By comparison, in faultline teams where salient differences among the members create subgroup fractures, information elaboration can be drastically reduced. In such situations, individuals are less willing to share ideas and engage in communications with diverse others; interactions between subgroups become reduced, creating fewer opportunities for communication and sharing diverse knowledge (Mesmer-Magnus & DeChurch, 2009). This directly affects the quantity of shared information and thus the quality of information available for team-level elaboration. Moreover, people tend to reduce communication and elaboration within each subgroup because they expect to agree with in-group members, and raising discrepant views could violate those expectations. This effect impairs the active processing of information (Petty & Cacioppo, 1986) and thus the quality of information elaboration at the team level.

In summary, information elaboration is a crucial process for faultline teams, especially for those teams performing complex tasks that require information processing, creativity, and collaborative decision-making (Rico, Sánchez-Manzanares, Antino, & Lau, 2012). However, the presence of faultlines and potential subgroup fractures also constantly threatens the elaboration of diverse information (consequently, team performance) because of possible conflicts, as explained in the next subsection.

Team Conflict in Faultline Teams

Besides the information elaboration challenges, in strong faultline teams different subgroups are likely to form coalitions (Stevenson, Pearce, & Porter, 1985), and their members are prone to experience intense team conflict, defined as disagreements over interpersonal or work-related issues (Jehn, Northcraft, & Neale, 1999; Thatcher & Patel, 2011). The perceived similarity among subgroup members leads to a comparison between in-groups and out-groups, increasing conflict between the subgroups (Hogg, Turner, & Davidson, 1990). The desire to differentiate from other subgroup leads subgroup members to oppose the ideas proposed by out-subgroup members. Thus, teams drastically reduce information elaboration since comments are interpreted as criticism rather than constructive feedback (Lau & Murnighan, 2005). Moreover, the desire to remain distinct from and superior to out-subgroup members may contribute to a common subgroup view of task goals but a differential view across subgroups (Brewer, 1999). This favors internal subgroup competition, reinforcing the conflict and reducing performance.

In summary, team faultlines increase the occurrence of team conflict that can significantly reduce information elaboration and performance (Thatcher & Patel, 2011). This statement again points to the need for an active management of team faultlines in order to prevent or reduce harming team conflict.

The Management of Faultlines

Faultline Teams, Implications for Managers

Figure 12.1 summarizes how team faultlines impact on team performance outcomes. In a nutshell, with proper management strategies, the detrimental effects of strong faultline teams will be under control or minimized, ensuring low conflict and high performance through high levels of information elaboration. However, objective dimensions of diversity can be the basis for social categorization, starting from a trigger when certain conditions are present (comparative fit, normative fit, and cognitive accessibility). Social categorization leads to intergroup biases and augments team conflict; under such conditions faultlines negatively affect performance through the interruption of information elaboration.

Adopting the faultlines perspective implies a new way of viewing and assessing team diversity, but what are the implications for managers? The first step for leaders is recognizing the presence of faultlines within their teams. Specifically, two aspects must be considered: (1) *faultline strength* or the degree of alignment among team members across several attributes (Thatcher, Jehn, & Zanutto, 2003). For instance, based on the examples in Table 12.2, Team 5 presents high diversity but no possible alignments among diversity dimensions. In turn, Team 2 presents strong faultlines where race and function crosscut; (2) *faultline distance* refers to the extent to which subgroups diverge as a result of accumulated differences between subgroups (Bezrukova, Jehn, Zanutto, & Thatcher, 2009). Team 6a presents the same diversity configuration as Team 6b, but the faultline distance in Team 6b is greater, given that its members have higher age differences.

Figure 12.1. Faultline-Performance Framework

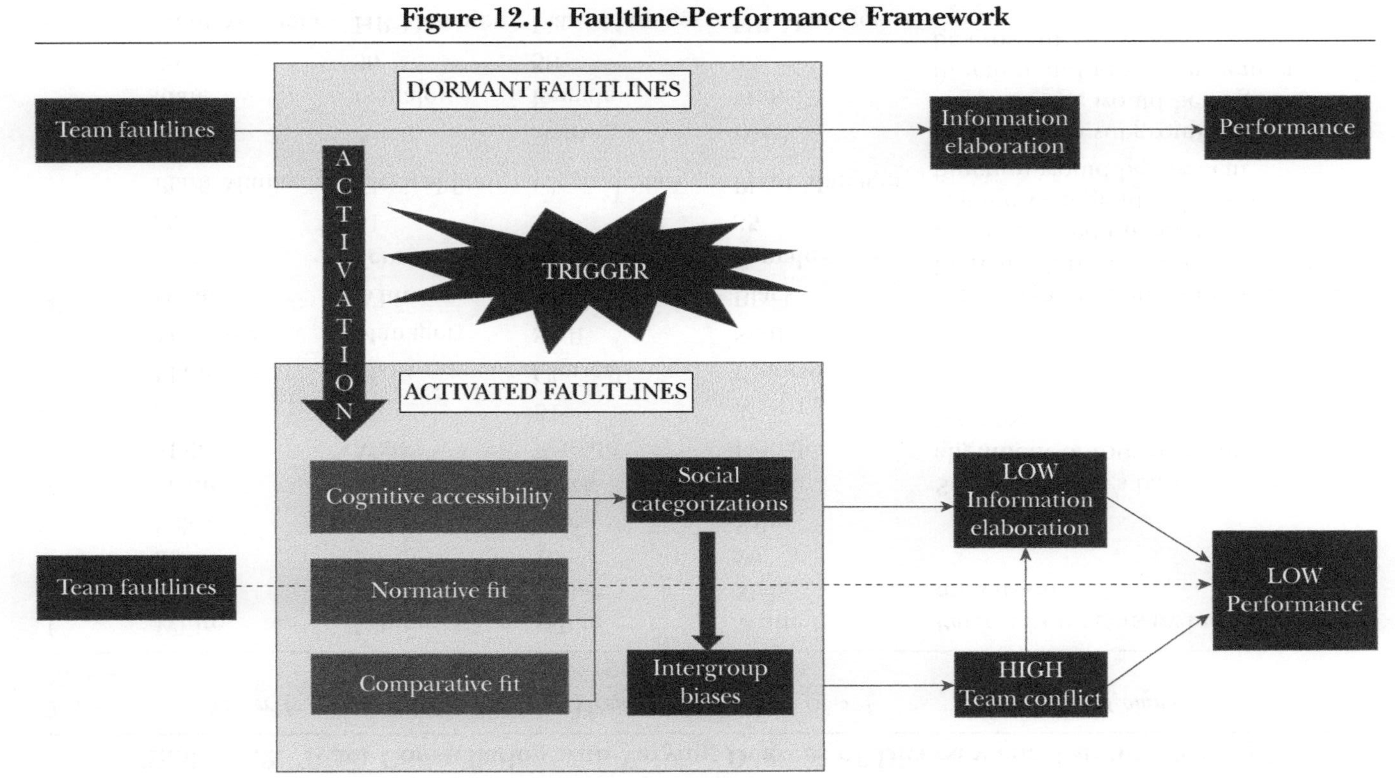

Table 12.2. Team Constellation with Varying Degrees of Diversity and Faultline Strength

Team Number	*Member 1*	*Member 2*	*Member 3*	*Member 4*	*Comments*
1	White Male 20 Sales	White Male 20 Sales	White Male 20 Sales	White Male 20 Sales	Perfect homogeneity in four diversity dimensions
2	White Male 50 Plant Manager	White Male 55 Plant Manager	Black Female 31 Clerical Staff	Black Female 35 Clerical Staff	Strong faultlines based on the alignment of four diversity dimensions
3	White Male 50 Plant Manager	White Female 31 Clerical Staff	Black Male 55 Clerical Staff	Black Female 35 Plant Manager	Same degree of attribute diversity as in Team 2. In this case a subgroup fracture based on age would be aligned with gender, but race and function would be crosscut
4	White Male 60 Plant Manager	Asian Female 30 HR Manager	White Female 58 Plant Manager	Black Male 35 HR Manager	In this case a subgroup fracture based on age would be aligned with function and race; only gender would be crosscut

5	Asian	White	Black	Asian	Almost maximal diversity
	Female	Male	Female	Male	For a group of four, all team members are unique, except gender, and alignment cannot be found
	20	30	65	50	
	Unskilled	Supervisor	Executive	Machinist	
6a	White	White	Black	Black	Strong faultlines with perfect bipolarity with even subgroup sizes, i.e., 2 vs. 2
	Male	Male	Female	Female	
	20	20	40	40	
	Sales	Sales	Manager	Manager	
6b	White	White	Black	Black	Stronger faultline width than for Team 6a, given that the separation of age is higher: 20 vs. 60 years
	Male	Male	Female	Female	
	20	20	60	60	
	Sales	Sales	Manager	Manager	
6c	White	White	White	Black	Team with strong faultlines, with bipolarity but with different subgroup sizes, i.e., 3 vs. 1
	Male	Male	Male	Female	
	20	20	20	40	
	Sales	Sales	Sales	Manager	

Source: Teams 1–6 are based on Trezzini (2008, p. 344), who in turn adapted the groups from Lau and Murnighan (1998, p. 330).

A regular monitoring of the team is necessary (especially in large teams with frequent rotation) for team leaders to act either in a preventive way before subgroup fractures occur, or in a palliative way when the team is experiencing an *activated* faultline situation with all the associated detrimental effects on team functioning (this will be discussed later in this chapter). Subgrouping attributes may be observable, such as gender and race, or unobservable, such as personality, values, and hobbies. Managers need to know their team members well and be aware of both observable and unobservable differences. Once team faultlines have been diagnosed, team leaders can act in two alternative ways. On the one hand, they can operate at the *structural level*, by providing structural components to the team such as the design of work or the definition of team composition, as described in the functional leadership literature (Hackman, 2002). This allows the management of task roles, task design, and other elements that are essential for some strategies we will discuss later (the management of contextual elements, crosscutting, the management of goal structure, the combination of crosscutting and goal structure, and the management of task autonomy). On the other hand, leaders can operate at the *relational level* by managing motivation and persuading team members to adopt new values, attitudes, and goals, as described in the relational leadership literature (Hogg, Martin, & Weeden, 2004). This allows the management of team awareness of distributed knowledge and team diversity beliefs.

We next classify all the evidence-based strategies in two general categories according to the two described levels: *structure level managerial strategies* and *relational level managerial strategies*. For each proposed strategy we will provide different "put in practice" suggestions as well as a short conceptual explanation according to the faultline-performance framework (see Figure 12.1). Finally, we will describe when the leaders should intervene, considering the different stages of faultline functioning.

Structural Level Managerial Strategies

Management of Contextual Elements

Context refers to the situational setting in which workplace phenomena occur. Joshi and Roh (2009) found that the effect of diversity on team functioning partially depends on some industry and occupational characteristics. Some industry and occupational characteristics may increase the salience of particular attributes. For instance, in high-tech industries, older programmers will often be the targets of negative stereotypes, and age faultlines are easy to form in this industry (Joshi & Roh, 2009).

Sometimes, organizational human resource policies may have strong impact on faultline formation. For instance, when organizations try to correct the intra-organizational gender imbalance by recruiting a large proportion of female applicants within a short period of time, this creates a natural faultline of senior male versus junior female employees. Awareness among organizational decision-makers becomes crucial in designing human resource policies.

At the management level, those elements of the context that are under the direct control of leaders may represent important management tools in faultline teams in order to enhance the team's performance. In Team A, leaders could reduce the formality of meetings (for example, in terms of behavior, clothing, speech) by organizing the team meetings in informal settings, such as during a meal in a specific room with a catering service or in a restaurant. Empirical evidence shows that informality in team meetings allowed greater attention to entrepreneurial issues in strong faultline teams, leading to a better understanding and acceptance of the different perspectives within the team (Tuggle, Schnatterly, & Johnson, 2010).

Other contextual elements to manipulate may be the seating arrangement and the differentiation of work materials such as chairs or gadgets (Homan, van Knippenberg, Van Kleef, & De Dreu, 2007; Rico, Sánchez-Manzanares, Antino, & Lau, 2012). In our case, team members could be seated at a round work table, mixing up the two subgroups and thus lowering the sensation of physical separation and division. This strategy could act at different levels, for example, enabling cognitive accessibility to different diversity dimensions or preventing the intergroup bias in a situation of categorization.

Takeaway

Leaders can easily manage contextual elements to reduce potential differentiating elements.

Crosscutting Strategies

Crosscutting refers to a situation in which members of a subgroup are the same in one attribute but differ in others, regardless of how the subgroups are formed. To crosscut Team A, the team leader could divide the team into two subgroups (Karen and Simon versus Paul and Susan) and crosscut memberships by assigning similar tasks to the subgroups, such as making a rough draft of the web page instead of all working together or generating a brief report based on a preliminary market investigation on poker web pages. Another way to crosscut the team could be hiring a female programmer who would share gender with Karen and Susan and specific skills with Paul and Simon.

The idea in this strategy is to make social categorization more difficult by crossing different diversity dimensions, such as age, gender, or educational background. When subgroup members share some salient attributes with out-subgroup members, there is cross-subgroup alignment of attributes, and the overlapping of attributes should break down the distinctive "us" versus "them" division (Bettencourt, Molix, Talley, & Eubanks, 2007; Brewer, 1999). This cross-subgroup alignment of relevant attributes reduces the subgroup identification and thus the faultlines' strength. Specifically, social categorization becomes more complex and decreases the distinction between in-group and out-group (Turner, Hogg, Oakes, Reicher, & Wetherell, 1987).

Empirically, Sawyer, Houlette, and Yeagley (2006) revealed that crosscutting strategies reduce team faultlines' strength, enhance information sharing, and improve decision making.

Takeaway

To cross membership reduces the occurrence of subgroup divisions.

Goal Structure Management: Introduction of Superordinate Goals

Creating a team-level common goal increases the salience of the team identity (Hornsey & Hogg, 2000). In Team A the team leader could introduce a common goal by offering a team bonus based on the quality of the web page, which is a team product. The functioning of this strategy is based on the assumption that within-group differences become less salient in the presence of situational or structural factors that emphasize the team as a whole (Brown & Turner, 1981). This means that the original in-group/out-group distinction diminishes when both subgroups are included in a new inclusive group (through the introduction of a superordinate goal) that encompasses previously separated groups.

The introduction of superordinate goals extends the benefits of in-group favoritism to former out-group members, transforming the "we-they" categorizations into a unique "we" categorization (Brown & Turner, 1981; Sherif, 1958). In the presence of a common goal, team members tend to decrease the distinction between personal and category welfare (that is, *goal transformation*; De Cremer & Van Vugt, 1999), augmenting cooperative expectations (that is, *goal amplification*; Wit & Wilke, 1992). The superordinate goal strategy could impede subgroup bias either before or after the occurrence of categorization.

Empirical evidence described by Homan, Hollenbeck, Humphrey, van Knippenberg, Ilgen, and Van Kleef (2008) found that teams where the reward structure pointed to a superordinate identity (team rewards) performed better than teams where reward structure converged with diversity. This result indicates that the presence of a superordinate identity can help to overcome some of the negative consequences of team faultlines.

Takeaway

A common goal creates a new overarching team identity.

Combining Crosscutting and Superordinate Goal Strategies

Crosscutting and superordinate goal strategies should be combined to effectively manage team faultlines (Rico, Sánchez-Manzanares, Antino, & Lau, 2012). In Team A, after crosscutting task roles, the team leader could introduce a superordinate goal by manipulating the reward system. The logic of combining both strategies is that in a divided team both strategies work at the categorization level, reducing intergroup bias: while crosscutting lowers the boundaries of the perceived categories, a superordinate goal will include precedent boundaries in a bigger and more inclusive superordinate categorization.

Different lines of research provide empirical evidence and theoretical development in this vein. Allport (1954) pointed out that, for a contact to be effective in reducing intergroup conflict, a common goal is one prerequisite feature. More recently, Vescio, Judd, and Kwan (2004) evidenced that crosscutting lowered categorization, but was not sufficient to significantly reduce intergroup bias. Coherently, Brewer (1999) suggested an integrated perspective by crosscutting social categories and involving the presence of a salient superordinate level of categorization.

Rico, Sánchez-Manzanares, Antino, and Lau (2012) combined both strategies in an experimental setting, studying teams with strong and activated faultlines. They found that teams with crosscut task roles (but not aligned task roles) performed better when they worked in the superordinate goal condition rather than in the subgroup goal condition. This positive interaction effect could be explained through the augmentation of information elaboration. These results clearly indicate that the combination of both management strategies is recommended in cases of teams with activated faultlines.

Takeaway

Effectively bridging of activated faultlines requires combining crosscutting members and setting common goals.

Managing Team Task Autonomy

Task autonomy is a key task design feature for managing faultlines (Rico, Molleman, Sánchez-Manzanares, & Van der Vegt, 2007). Task autonomy refers to the degree of freedom a team has to set goals, plan work, and decide on best work methods and timing (Rico, Molleman, Sánchez-Manzanares, & Van der Vegt, 2007). Low levels of task autonomy indicate that the task is structured and the team has no need to organize it. However, high task autonomy requires teams to participate often in decision making in order to manage task-related issues. In Team A, the leader could set certain levels of task autonomy during the first briefing. In addition, the leader may organize other meetings and further adjust the levels of task autonomy several times, discussing the organization of the task.

We consider task autonomy as a facilitator of social categorization because of its effect on cognitive accessibility (the more interaction is needed, the higher the cognitive accessibility of the diversity dimensions). Empirical support is offered by Rico, Molleman, Sánchez-Manzanares, and Van der Vegt (2007), who found that in teams with weak faultlines, task autonomy is conducted to increase decision quality, whereas in teams with strong faultlines, task autonomy exacerbates the negative effects of faultlines on team performance. In these teams, more intensive communication and frequent interaction among members could make diversity attributes salient, creating competing subgroups and thus reducing decision-making quality. Based on this evidence, team leaders should actively manage the level of task autonomy in their teams. For example, the leader's pre-briefings and feedback during task performance increase task autonomy (Marks, Zaccaro, & Mathieu, 2000).

Takeaway

Matching the level of team autonomy with group faultline strength: team autonomy increases team performance when faultlines are weak, but decreases it when faultlines are strong.

Relational Level Managerial Strategies

Managing Team Diversity Beliefs

Diversity beliefs are beliefs about the value of being diverse for a team to function (van Knippenberg & Haslam, 2003). Diversity beliefs may lead people to respond more favorably to work team diversity by influencing judgments about the appropriateness of the composition of the team in relation to the task. In Team A, the leader could foster team members' pro-diversity beliefs by reinforcing learning from diversity (Ely & Thomas, 2001). Moreover, the team leader could communicate in the initial team meeting his strong belief in the value of diversity by explaining how task performance can benefit from different perspectives and knowledge. In addition, as suggested by Homan, van Knippenberg, Van Kleef, and De Dreu (2007), leaders could redirect diversity training to work on feelings about diversity itself (rather than focus on different others) to make the team members aware of the potential value of being a member of a diverse team. Another way to stimulate pro-diversity beliefs is the recruitment and selection of appropriate newcomers holding beliefs of this kind.

The logic behind this managerial strategy is that in faultline teams pro-diversity beliefs may lead team members to actively solicit new information and perspectives from fellow members because of positive values associated with diverse knowledge and perspectives. Based on that reasoning, we believe that pro-diversity beliefs could impede intergroup bias, even in the presence of certain categorizations.

van Knippenberg, Haslam, and Platow (2004) empirically supported those affirmations, showing that team identification in diverse teams depends on the levels of diversity beliefs. When individuals believed that diversity was beneficial for the task, diversity was positively related to team identification. Similarly, Homan, van Knippenberg, Van Kleef, and De Dreu (2007) found that informational diverse teams performed better when they held pro-diversity beliefs rather than pro-similarity beliefs.

Takeaway

Considering diversity beliefs when crafting a team will prevent the deleterious effects of strong faultlines.

Managing Team-Distributed Information Awareness

The awareness of team-distributed information refers to the knowledge of who knows what within a team. In Team A, the team members could be invited to voice and discuss their areas of expertise relevant to the team project during the first meeting. This would allow them to delve into the expertise of each member and to update the awareness of team-distributed information. A high awareness of team-distributed information can prevent intergroup bias in faultline teams for different reasons. If team members have a deep knowledge of who knows what, categorization will become more complex because of less cognitive accessibility, since they posed a large amount of information for each team member. Moreover, this could involve an appreciation of knowledge differences, as long as those differences are useful for the team functioning, therefore reducing normative fit.

Empirical studies show that teams in which members are informed about others' areas of expertise exchange more unique information (that is, information possessed by only one of the team members) and make higher-quality decisions than teams in which members are not informed (Stasser, Stewart, & Wittenbaum, 1995). Similarly, van Ginkel and van Knippenberg (2008) observed that teams reflecting on their distribution of diverse knowledge have greater understanding of the task. We can conclude that, to stimulate the effective use of diverse informational resources, it is important to actively build knowledge of who knows what, for example, through reflection (van Ginkel & van Knippenberg, 2008). Specifically, reflection sessions at certain points of the task could favor a climate of information sharing and pro-diversity.

Takeaway

Increasing understanding (or awareness) of who knows what in the team (or others' task-relevant information) will prevent strong faultline negative effects.

When Should Leaders Intervene?

Now that we have described different managerial strategies, we want to focus on when the interventions should take place. As explained above, team leaders must regularly monitor their teams to identify the presence and the state (dormant versus activated) of faultlines. Depending on the diagnostic, leaders can act on the different stages of the functioning of faultlines.

First, team leaders can *prevent the occurrence of faultlines.* Given that faultlines are formed based on team composition, team leaders can directly manipulate the composition of their teams in order to avoid faultline situations. This can be achieved through accurate recruitment and applying crosscutting strategies, thus impeding the formation of faultlines within the team structure or bridging the precedent for faultline through new incomers.

Second, team leaders can *prevent faultline activation.* Once they recognize that faultlines are present in their teams, team leaders have to act in order to avoid the activation mechanism. At this stage, strategies that can be used are the management of contextual elements, crosscutting, the management of goal structure, associating team task autonomy levels to faultline strength, and the management of pro-diversity beliefs. All these strategies are directly linked to faultline-related attributes and could prevent the activation of existing faultlines by impeding categorization or avoiding intergroup bias.

Third, team leaders can act in a palliative way by *managing activated faultlines.* This is the most complicated stage of management whereby team leaders have to act to reduce team conflict and guarantee appropriate levels of information elaboration. In this case the most powerful strategy could be the combination of crosscutting and superordinate goal strategies. Other strategies aimed at enhancing greater information elaboration also could be used, depending on the severity of the situation, but there is still little empirical evidence in this direction.

To help our readers to schematize all the provided information, we have summarized the proposed intervention strategies in Table 12.3, describing when (during which faultline stages) and how (through what level of intervention in the faultline performance relation) leaders can employ them.

At this point, and before concluding, we want to share with our readers a final consideration. Recent research indicates that the effects of diversity may be contingent with broader contextual settings, such as an occupational context, that are not directly under the team leader's control. For instance, Joshi and Roh (2009) found that in occupations dominated by male or white

Table 12.3. Intervention Strategies for Faultline Stages

Put in Practice How to Manage Team Faultlines		Theory Faultline Evolution Stage		
Managerial strategy	**Practical recommendations**	**Prevention of faultline formation or occurrence**	**Prevention of faultline activation**	**Management of activated faultlines**
Managing team context *Reduction of potential differentiating elements*	Team leaders can **reduce the formality of meeting** by choosing an external place to meet, organizing a dinner with "simple" food, maybe with some music, in general, all those elements that reduce the formality of the setting. Another important aspect is the **reduction of possible differentiation elements**. For example, leaders should choose the same color of work materials (or crosscut it respect to the diversity dimensions). Leaders should break possible subgroup formation by forcing the seating arrangement. Furthermore, different companies are beginning to decorate their halls with **elements of different cultures**, for example, the flags of all the countries of origin of their employees. These contextual elements also help the construction of a positive pro-diversity value.		Prevents intergroup bias, enabling cognitive accessibility	

Continued

Table 12.3. Continued

	Put in Practice How to Manage Team Faultlines	Theory Faultline Evolution Stage		
Managerial strategy	**Practical recommendations**	**Prevention of faultline formation or occurrence**	**Prevention of faultline activation**	**Management of activated faultlines**
Crosscutting *Reduction of the occurrence of subgroup divisions*	To crosscut a team, leaders have different options. First, they can **organize the task in different subtasks**, so that not the entire team has to work on it. In this way, they can create different subgroups and crosscut membership by assigning similar tasks to the subgroups (men and women, young and older people, etc.). Another way to crosscut the team could be through the **hiring process**, taking into account those diversity elements that are at the basis of internal subgroups.	Eliminates potential alignments through direct intervention on team composition	Reduces categorization, lowering comparative fit	

Superordinate goals *Creation of a new overarching team identity*	One of the possible ways to set a common goal is the introduction of a **team-level bonus**; for example, offering a team bonus based on the quality of team-level output. Similarly, part of the **salary** could be transformed into a bonus, **depending on the quality of the teamwork**. Different companies are employing this system with regard to project teams, assessing the teamwork skills at the end of each project. This could reinforce the perception of a common goal within a team. Another way could be the fixation of a **bonus for the best team of each company's department**. This could emphasize a sense of pertinence to the team against other teams and create a common goal related to the bonus. This last strategy could create inter-team conflict, so it is not recommended when inter-team collaboration is required.	Reduces intergroup biases through a new inclusive categorization	(In combination with crosscutting) Lowers precedent categorization boundaries and includes precedent boundaries in a new inclusive categorization
Matching task autonomy with faultline strength *High autonomy with weak faultlines, low autonomy with strong faultlines*	A team leader can **reduce task autonomy** by setting the degree of freedom that the team has to decide goals, plan work, and decide on best work methods and timing. When high task autonomy is required, leaders should monitor the team and organize different meetings and further adjust the levels of task autonomy several times, discussing the organization of the task and thus monitoring the possible occurrence of subgroup divisions.	Reduces categorization, lowering cognitive accessibility	

Continued

Table 12.3. Continued

Put in Practice How to Manage Team Faultlines		Theory Faultline Evolution Stage		
Managerial strategy	**Practical recommendations**	**Prevention of faultline formation or occurrence**	**Prevention of faultline activation**	**Management of activated faultlines**
Pro-diversity beliefs *Prevention of the deleterious effects of strong faultlines*	Leaders should improve teammates' beliefs about the value of being diverse for a team to function. The first step will be to **openly communicate their strong belief in the value of diversity** by explaining how task performance can benefit from different perspectives and knowledge. Moreover, leaders can **reinforce learning from diversity** through specific meetings where they highlight effective solutions that diverse teams created thanks to their diversity. In addition, leaders could redirect **diversity training to work on feelings about diversity** to make the team members aware of the potential value of being a member of a diverse team. Leaders can also pay attention to pro-diversity beliefs during the **recruitment and selection** phase, choosing newcomers with strong pro-diversity beliefs. Another way is to **promote diversity in a broader context**. For instance, many companies organize regular thematic meals where typical food from different countries is served and the employees take the floor to talk about their countries.		Reduces normative fit and impedes intergroup bias in the presence of categorization	

Awareness of team-distributed information *Prevention of strong faultline negative effects, increasing reflexivity*	Leaders should reinforce teammates' knowledge of who knows what within the team. This should be done on an ongoing basis to ensure adequate updating of task-relevant knowledge. For example, at the beginning of decision-making the team can **review each member's area of expertise**, especially relevant for the task at hand. Another way could be through **role playing**, where members have to solve a simulated task using other teammates' technical skills. This would oblige them to make explicit their knowledge of who knows what. Finally, team members could include areas of expertise, as well as some personal information (e.g., hobbies) in a personal or team web page.	Reduces categorization, lowering cognitive accessibility and normative fit

employees, gender and ethnic diversity had more negative effects on performance. To this regard, Bezrukova, Thatcher, Jehn, and Spell (2011) found that the negative relationship between faultlines and performance was reversed when both the team and the organization were output-oriented. These results suggest a broader level of intervention (for example, at the department level or organizational level), for example, through formal socializations tactics whereby group members are forced to share common learning with other groups in their department or organization. At the current state we encourage leaders to reflect on macro-contextual elements, even if they are not under their direct control.

Final Considerations and Conclusion

Nowadays, organizations are increasingly dependent on diverse teams, and their leaders are continually called to deal with the potentially negative consequences of faultlines. Thus, team leaders must have the ability to understand, predict, and effectively manage faultlines. Departing from this statement, our first goal with this chapter was to offer some essential theoretical notions to allow practitioners to understand the phenomenon of faultlines. In doing so, we explained how faultlines lead to subgroup fractures if activated and why this situation is associated with high conflict and low information elaboration. Then we described different managerial strategies to deal with faultlines, explaining their level of intervention in the faultline-performance relation.

It is important to consider that team faultline literature is recent and growing and that there are still many facets to uncover; for example, many of the proposed management strategies have to be tested in applied organizational settings and in conditions of activated faultlines. Also, the role of macro-contextual elements is still uncovered.

Despite such limitations, faultline research is generating promising results (for a recent review, see Thatcher & Patel, 2011). Notwithstanding the big threat that faultlines represent for team performance, the literature offers various management tools that allow us to look at faultline teams with more optimism.

Based on current research, we have explained how leaders can prevent the occurrence of faultlines in their teams by turning (widely diffused) mindless recruiting into an occasion for efficient management. In addition, leaders can operate at different levels to either prevent faultline activation or manage them to reduce their effects.

In conclusion, our challenge in this chapter was to contribute by linking faultline research to different management strategies that can be effective in counteracting the potential deleterious effects of faultlines on work teams. While far from complete and conclusive, we would like to believe that this piece represents a step forward in this respect. It is our hope that team leaders, team members, and practitioners in general find our approach useful.

References

Allport, G.W. (1954). *The nature of prejudice.* Reading, MA: Addison-Wesley.

Bettencourt, B., Molix, L., Talley A., & Eubanks, P. (2007). Numerical representation and cross-cut role assignments: Majority members' responses under cooperative interaction. *Journal of Experimental Social Psychology, 43,* 553–564.

Bezrukova, K., Jehn, K.A., Zanutto, E.L., & Thatcher, S.M.B. (2009). Do workgroup faultlines help or hurt? A moderated model of faultlines, team identification, and group performance. *Organization Science, 20,* 35–50.

Bezrukova, K., Thatcher, S.M., Jehn, K.A., & Spell, C.S. (2011, July 11). The effects of alignments: Examining group faultlines, organizational cultures, and performance. *Journal of Applied Psychology.*

Brewer, M. (1999). The psychology of prejudice: In-group love or out-group hate? *Journal of Social Issues, 55,* 429–444.

Brown, R., & Turner, J.C. (1981). Interpersonal and intergroup behaviour. *Intergroup behaviour,* pp. 33–65.

Chrobot-Mason, D., Ruderman, M., Weber, T., Ohlott, P., & Dalton, M. (2007). Illuminating a cross-cultural leadership challenge: When identity groups collide. *The International Journal of Human Resource Management, 18,* 2011–2036.

De Cremer, D., & Van Vugt, M. (1999). Social identification effects in social dilemmas: A transformation of motives. *European Journal of Social Psychology, 29,* 871–893.

Ely, R.J., & Thomas, D.A. (2001). Cultural diversity at work: The effects of diversity perspectives on work group processes and outcomes. *Administrative Science Quarterly, 46,* 229–273.

Guzzo, R., & Dickson, M. (1996). Teams in organizations: Recent research on performance and effectiveness. *Annual Review of Psychology, 47,* 307–338.

Hackman, J.R. (2002). *Leading teams: Setting the stage for great performances.* Boston: Harvard Business School Press.

Harrison, D.A., Price, K. Gavin, J., & Florey, A. (2002). Time, teams, and task performance: Changing effects of surface and deep-level diversity on group functioning. *The Academy of Management Journal, 45,* 1029–1045.

Hogg, M.A., Martin, R., & Weeden, K. (2004). Leader-member relations and social identity. In D. van Knippenberg & M.A. Hogg (Eds.), *Leadership and power: Identity processes in groups and organizations* (pp. 18–33). London: Sage.

Hogg, M.A., Turner, J.C., & Davidson, B. (1990). Polarized norms and social frames of reference: A test of the self-categorization theory of group polarization. *Basic and Applied Social Psychology, 11,* 77–100.

Homan, A.C., Hollenbeck, J.R., Humphrey, S.E., van Knippenberg, D., Ilgen, D.R., & Van Kleef, G.A. (2008). Facing differences with an open mind: Openness to experience, salience of intragroup differences, and performance of diverse work groups. *Academy of Management Journal, 51,* 1204–1222.

Homan, A.C., van Knippenberg, D., van Kleef, G., & De Dreu, C. (2007). Bridging faultlines by valuing diversity: Diversity beliefs, information elaboration, and performance in diverse work groups. *Journal of Applied Psychology, 92,* 1189–1198.

Hornsey, M., & Hogg, M. (2000). Intergroup similarity and subgroup relations: Some implications for assimilation. *Personality and Social Psychology Bulletin, 26,* 65–93.

Jehn, K., & Bezrukova, K. (2010). The faultline activation process and the effects of activated faultlines on coalition formation, conflict, and group outcomes. *Organizational Behavior and Human Decision Processes, 112,* 24–42.

Jehn, K., Northcraft, G., & Neale, M. (1999). Why differences make a difference: A field study of diversity, conflict, and performance in workgroups. *Administrative Science Quarterly, 44,* 741–763.

Joshi, A.A., & Roh, H. (2009). The role of context in work team diversity research: A meta-analytic review. *Academy of Management Journal, 52,* 599–627.

Lau, D., & Murnighan, J. (1998). Demographic diversity and faultlines: The compositional dynamics of organizational groups. *The Academy of Management Review, 23,* 325–340.

Lau, D., & Murnighan, J. (2005). Interactions within groups and subgroups: The effects of demographic faultlines. *Academy of Management Journal, 48,* 645–659.

Li, J., & Hambrick, D. (2005). Factional groups: A new vantage on demographic faultlines, conflict, and disintegration in work teams. *The Academy of Management Journal, 48,* 794–813.

Marks, M.A., Zaccaro, S.J., & Mathieu, J.E. (2000). Performance implications of leader briefings and team-interaction training for team adaptation to novel environments. *Journal of Applied Psychology, 85,* 971–986.

Mesmer-Magnus, J.R., & DeChurch, L.A. (2009) Information sharing and team performance: A meta-analysis. *Journal of Applied Psychology, 94,* 535–546.

Oakes, P.J., Haslam, S.A., & Turner, J.C. (1994). *Stereotyping and social reality.* Malden, MA: Blackwell.

Petty, R., & Cacioppo, J. (1986). *Communication and persuasion: Central and peripheral routes to attitude change.* New York: Springer.

Polzer, J., Milton, L., & Swann, J.W. (2002). Capitalizing on diversity: Interpersonal congruence in small work groups. *Administrative Science Quarterly,* 296–324.

Rico, R., Molleman, E., Sánchez-Manzanares, M., & Van der Vegt, G.S. (2007). The effects of diversity faultlines and team task autonomy on decision quality and social integration. *Journal of Management, 33,* 111–132.

Rico, R., Sánchez-Manzanares, M., Antino, M., & Lau, D. (2012). Bridging team faultlines by combining task role assignment and goal structure strategies. *Journal of Applied Psychology, 97,* 407–420.

Sawyer, J.E., Houlette, M.A., & Yeagley, E.L. (2006). Decision performance and diversity structure: Comparing faultlines in convergent, crosscut, and racially homogenous groups. *Organizational Behavior and Human Decision Processes, 99,* 1–15.

Sherif, M. (1958). Superordinate goals in the reduction of intergroup conflict. *The American Journal of Sociology, 63,* 349–356.

Stasser, G., Stewart, D.D., & Wittenbaum, G.M. (1995). Expert roles and information exchange during discussion: The importance of knowing who knows what. *Journal of Experimental Social Psychology, 31,* 244–256.

Stevenson, W.B., Pearce, J.L, & Porter, L.W. (1985). The concept of "coalition" in organization theory and research. *Academy of Management Review, 10*(2), 256–268.

Tajfel, H., Billig, C., & Bundy, M.R. (1971). Social categorization and intergroup behavior. *European Journal of Social Psychology, 1,* 149–177.

Thatcher, S.M.B., Jehn, K., & Zanutto, E. (2003). Cracks in diversity research: The effects of diversity faultlines on conflict and performance. *Group Decision and Negotiation, 12,* 217–241.

Thatcher, S.M.B., & Patel, P.C. (2011, June 20). Demographic faultlines: A meta-analysis of the literature. *Journal of Applied Psychology.*

Trezzini, B. (2008). Probing the group faultline concept: An evaluation of measures of patterned multi-dimensional group diversity. *Quality & Quantity, 42,* 339–368.

Tuggle, C.S., Schnatterly, K., & Johnson, R.A. (2010). Attention patterns in the boardroom: How board composition and processes affect discussion of entrepreneurial issues. *Academy of Management Journal,* (*3*), 550–571.

Turner, J.C., Hogg, M., Oakes, P., Reicher, S., & Wetherell, M. (1987). *Rediscovering the social group: A self-categorization theory.* Oxford: Blackwell.

van Ginkel, W.P., & van Knippenberg, D. (2008). Group information elaboration and group decision making: The role of shared task representations. *Organizational Behavior and Human Decision Processes, 105*, 82–97.

van Knippenberg, D., De Dreu, C., & Homan, A. (2004). Work group diversity and group performance: An integrative model and research agenda. *Journal of Applied Psychology, 89*, 1008–1022.

van Knippenberg, D., & Haslam, S.A. (2003). Realizing the diversity dividend: Exploring the subtle interplay between identity, ideology, and reality. In S.A. Haslam, D. van Knippenberg, M.J. Platow, & N. Ellemers (Eds.), *Social identity at work: Developing theory for organizational practice* (pp. 61–77). New York and Hove, UK: Psychology Press.

van Knippenberg, D., Haslam, S.A., & Platow, M.J. (2004, April). Unity through diversity: Value-in-diversity beliefs as moderator of the relationship between work group diversity and group identification. Paper presented at the Society for Industrial and Organizational Psychology 19th Annual Conference, Chicago, Illinois.

van Knippenberg, D., & Schippers, M. (2007). Work group diversity. *Annual Review of Psychology, 58*, 515–541.

Vescio, T., Judd, C., & Kwan, V. (2004). The crossed-categorization hypothesis: Evidence of reductions in the strength of categorization, but not intergroup bias. *Journal of Experimental Social Psychology, 40*, 478–496.

Williams, K.Y., & O'Reilly, C.A. (1998). Demography and diversity in organizations. *Research in Organizational Behavior, 20*, 77–140.

Wit, A.P., & Wilke, H.A.M. (1992). The effect of social categorization on cooperation in three types of social dilemmas. *Journal of Economic Psychology, 13*, 135–151.

CHAPTER THIRTEEN

High Performance in Temporally Separated Team Work

J. Alberto Espinosa

Kogod School of Business, American University

Overview

Prior research has discussed and investigated how global teams bridge multiple boundaries (distance, time, culture) that separate members and impact the coordination of their work. Several studies suggest that temporal boundaries (time zones) present more coordination challenges than any of the boundaries. These challenges increase exponentially as teams grow larger, more locations and time zones are included, and temporal distances are larger. Yet, it remains the most under-studied team boundary in the literature. In order to fill this gap, my research with multiple colleagues at various institutions in the last decade has focused on understanding the main challenges and best practices associated with work coordination when members are temporally separated by time zones. In this chapter I summarize key findings from our research in this area, with a particular focus on effective work coordination for high team performance.

Introduction

In this chapter I discuss the main challenges teams face when coordinating work across when they are temporally dispersed (across time zones) and the best practices identified through almost a decade of research in this area. Temporal distance refers to the difference in work schedules among collaborators, which occur primarily, but not exclusively, due to time zone differences. Temporal distance can also happen with things like schedule differences, holiday schedules, and mobile work, among other things. Work has become highly globalized in the last several years with team members typically spread across multiple locations and time zones. These global teams need to bridge multiple internal boundaries (geographic, time zones, language, culture, etc.) to get the job done (Espinosa, Cummings, Wilson, & Pearce, 2003; Lu, Chudoba, Wynn, & Watson-Manheim, 2003; Orlikowski, 2002; Watson-Manheim, Chudoba, & Crowston, 2002). Why is it important to understand coordination issues across temporal distance in particular? Because it is not only one of the least understood and least studied global boundary, but it is also the one boundary that unequivocally affects team synchronous and asynchronous interaction patterns. My colleague Erran Carmel and I discuss this in depth in our book about coordination across time zones (Carmel & Espinosa, 2011). My work in this area started after hearing during our research interviews about the severe challenges global team members face when collaborating across time zones.

This can represent substantial problems for technical project teams in which members' task activities are highly interdependent, thus requiring substantial coordination (Van de Ven, Delbecq, & Koenig, 1976), which has been documented in global technical tasks like software development (Herbsleb & Grinter, 1999a) and found to be important for virtual team success (Cohen & Alonso, 2013). However, the very presence of these team boundaries not only reduces the range of coordination mechanisms available to team members, but also makes it more difficult to employ available tools and mechanisms, thus making them less effective. When team members are separated by time and distance, their interaction is largely mediated by leaner communication and information technologies (DeSanctis & Poole, 1997; Drucker, 1993), which reduces the benefits of co-presence (frequent and spontaneous interaction, availability of contextual reference, presence awareness, workspace awareness, etc.) and same-time synchronous interaction. Time differences affect coordination outcomes and tend to increase coordination costs.

While much has been written about coordination in global teams (Carmel, 1999; Herbsleb & Grinter, 1999b; Herbsleb, Mockus, Finholt, & Grinter, 2001) and geographically dispersed teams in general (Armstrong & Cole, 2002; Cramton, 2001; Hinds & Bailey, 2003; Kiesler & Cummings, 2002; Majchrzak, Rice, Malhotra, King, & Ba, 2000; McDonough, Kahn, & Barczak, 2001; Olson & Olson, 2000; Powell, Piccoli, & Ives, 2004; Van den Bulte & Moenaert, 1998), there has been very little research that has differentiated the specific effects of the individual boundaries. Spatial separation due to geographic dispersion often co-varies with other boundaries (temporal, cultural), thus making it difficult to isolate the effects of a particular boundary in prior research. We are particularly interested in better understanding the effects of temporal distance on coordination outcomes and team performance. A prior review of the virtual team literature identified the role of time in virtual teams as an important area of research, which has not been adequately investigated (Powell, Piccoli, & Ives, 2004), and some of our recent studies have confirmed this (Espinosa, Lee, & DeLone, 2006). Erran Carmel and I (2004b) also articulated and proposed a conceptual model that describes how time separation affects coordination costs, but very little empirical work has been done to validate this model or the effects of time coordination on other outcomes.

This was the motivator for my collaborators and me to research this complex aspect of global work. In the last several years, my collaborators and I have conducted various conceptual and empirical studies with collaborators from multiple institutions, including early conceptual work on the basic foundations of temporally separated work (Carmel, Espinosa, & Dubinsky, 2010; Espinosa & Carmel, 2003, 2004a, 2004b); interview studies with technical project team members at a global semi-conductor manufacturing company (Espinosa & Pickering, 2006); studies of time separation in the context of multiple global boundaries (Espinosa, Lee, & DeLone, 2006; Lee, DeLone, & Espinosa, 2006); an interview study at Infosys at Bangalore, India (Carmel, 2006); survey studies with technical project team members at a global semi-conductor manufacturing company (Cummings, Espinosa,

& Pickering, 2009; Espinosa, Cummings, & Pickering, 2006; Espinosa, Cummings, & Pickering, 2012); and experiment studies simulating time zone difference in computer labs (Espinosa, Nan, & Carmel, 2007; Nan, Espinosa, & Carmel, 2009). My discussions in this chapter focus on challenges and best practices associated with achieving effective work coordination and high team performance in temporally separated work and are based on these various studies. The chapter is organized around the overarching themes that have emerged from our empirical findings.

Throughout this chapter, we discuss and make reference to a number of constructs. These constructs are summarized in Table 13.1.

The Role of Team Coordination

Collaborating in temporally separated environments is not always difficult. It all depends on the time pressures of the task and the associated dependencies among task activities. For example, if a team of eight experts is working on a collaborative document, like a manual or procedural handbook, and each of the areas of expertise is fairly independent from the others, then the experts can be widely dispersed and work fairly independently. Each contributor can edit his or her own section at his or her own pace, more so when the deadlines are fairly loose. Conversely, a team of eight software developers working on a single product with time-to-market pressures, using agile methods, will have very tightly coupled dependencies with each other, thus making it more difficult to work when the team members are temporally separated. Why? Because member and task dependencies need to be managed and the ability to do it effectively is hampered when there are temporal boundaries among members. The management of task dependencies is precisely what work coordination is all about (Malone, 1987; Malone & Crowston, 1990), that is, tightly coupled dependencies among task activities require substantial coordination, whereas relatively independent task activities require little or no coordination.

The organizational literature suggests two primary types of coordination (March & Simon, 1958; Thompson, 1967; Van de Ven, Delbecq, & Koenig, 1976): (1) mechanistic (by plan, by

Table 13.1. Summary of Main Constructs

Construct	*Definition*	*Reference*
Team Coordination	Management of dependencies among task activities	(Malone, 1987; Malone & Crowston, 1990)
Mechanistic Coordination	Coordination by plan or by program—most effective for most routine dependencies	(March & Simon, 1958; Thompson, 1967; Van de Ven, et al., 1976)
Organic Coordination	Coordination by mutual adjustment, by feedback or through communication—most effective for less predictable dependencies	(March & Simon, 1958; Thompson, 1967; Van de Ven, Delbecq, & Koenig, 1976)
Implicit Coordination	Coordination based on unspoken assumptions about what others are likely to do—largely based on team cognition	(Cannon-Bowers & Salas, 2001; Wittenbaum & Stasser, 1996)
Global Boundary Complexity	Number of information cues about global boundaries (e.g., types of boundaries; number of boundaries for each type; member distribution across boundaries) that team members need to process to work with each other	(Campbell, 1988; Wood, 1986)
Temporal Separation Complexity	The complexity of the temporal context of the team across time zones, which is based on the temporal configuration parameters like number of time zones, maximum time zone span, member distribution across time zones, and team size	(Espinosa, Cummings, & Pickering, 2006; Espinosa & Pickering, 2006)

Table 13.1. Continued

Construct	*Definition*	*Reference*
Follow-the-Sun	A round-the-clock work rotation method aimed at reducing project duration, in which the knowledge product is owned and advanced by a production site and is then handed off at the end of each work day to the next production site several time zones west	(Carmel & Espinosa, 2011; Carmel, Espinosa, & Dubinsky)
Time Shifting	Shifting of work schedules to increase the work time overlap between sites in different time zones	(Carmel & Espinosa, 2011)
Synchronous Interaction	Real-time or same-time interaction with frequent turns among speakers and relatively simultaneous communication (e.g., face-to-face, telephone)	(Dennis, Fuller, & Valacich, 2008)
Asynchronous Interaction	Non-real-time or different-time interaction with infrequent turns among speakers and time delays in obtaining responses (e.g., e-mail)	(Dennis, Fuller, & Valacich, 2008)
Conveyance	Transmission of information from one member to another	(Dennis, Fuller, & Valacich, 2008)
Convergence	Developing a shared understanding of the meaning of the information exchanged	(Dennis, Fuller, & Valacich, 2008)

program, by task organization), which involves processes, mechanisms, and tools aimed at managing the most predictable and routine dependencies among task activities. Examples of mechanistic coordination include things like routines, procedures, schedules, calendars, specifications, and project documents, among many others. Even mundane things like traffic lights and currency are some forms of mechanistic coordination. Managers should coordinate mechanistically as much as possible because, once developed and implemented, mechanistic coordination is very cost-effective, particularly when team communication is difficult, as in the case of temporally separated teams, organic (by communication, by feedback, by mutual adjustment), which involves team interaction and communication aimed at the least predictable and non-routine aspects of the task. For example, one can coordinate a conference meeting using things like meeting programs, room scheduling, web postings, and so on for all known programmed activities. But if there is a major snowstorm or power loss the day before, or some other disrupting event, all involved will need to engage in high volumes of communication to address the non-routine nature of the situation. Managers should be cautious about organic coordination. Organic coordination is less efficient in the short term in the sense that meetings divert member attention from the focal task. On the other hand, frequent interaction and communication help team members get to know each other and foster common ground and shared knowledge, which, as I discuss below, are important for implicit coordination. In addition, research has found that when organic coordination happens spontaneously and informally, it can be most effective (Kraut & Streeter, 1995).

The team cognition literature suggests a third form of coordination, which is implicit based on unspoken assumptions team member make about what others are likely to do (Wittenbaum & Stasser, 1996). There are many forms of team cognition discussed in the literature (Cannon-Bowers & Salas, 2001), but they are all based on some form of knowledge similarity or overlap that members have about each other and their respective tasks. A few examples of this include: team mental models or knowledge members share about the task and each other, which helps them anticipate future task and member activities (Cannon-Bowers,

Salas, & Converse, 1993; Klimoski & Mohammed, 1994); collective mind or heedful interrelating among team members (Weick, 1993); and transactive memory—knowing who knows what in the team, which helps acquire, manage, and access specialized knowledge when needed (Wegner, 1995). Developing implicit coordination in teams can take a long time through organic coordination in the form of frequent interaction and communication. As others in this book recommend (Cohen & Alonso, Chapter 8), managers are encouraged to organize team meetings early in the project for members to get to know each other to foster implicit coordination.

Studies have shown that all types of coordination are important. While mechanistic coordination is generally effective to manage predictable aspects of the task, studies have shown that mechanistic coordination is also very important in temporally separated task environments because communication is impaired (Espinosa, Cummings, & Pickering, 2012). Similarly, implicit coordination based on team cognition is also a very effective way to coordinate things in geographically dispersed environments because it makes the limited communication among team members more effective (Espinosa, Slaughter, Kraut, & Herbsleb, 2007). Furthermore, in complex, multi-disciplinary, long-term task environments, team cognition becomes a self-fueling mechanism that not only improves coordination, but makes organic and mechanistic coordination more effective, which further strengthens team cognition (that is, self-fueling) (Espinosa, Armour, Boh, & Clark, 2012). Managers should strive to help the team develop team cognition through joint training, visits to each other's sites, and frequent communication. This will not only foster effective implicit coordination, but will also make mechanistic and organic coordination more effective. In sum, work, coordination is a key factor in temporally dispersed work, and in many empirical studies coordination is the mediator variable between temporal or spatial distance and team performance outcomes.

Global Boundary Complexity

One of the difficulties in understanding how a particular boundary may affect work outcomes or team performance is that most global boundaries correlate highly, thus making it difficult to tease out the effect of one or the other. Teams who are spatially separated are often temporally and culturally separated too. So how can we be sure that the observed effects in a research study are due to time zone differences, geographic distance, or language misunderstandings? Many studies have struggled trying to find the effect of one boundary while controlling for others (Cummings, Espinosa, & Pickering, 2009; Espinosa, Cummings, & Pickering, 2012; Espinosa, Nan, & Carmel, 2007). This is not an easy problem to resolve because not controlling for various boundary effects creates omitted variable bias problems (the effect of omitted variables is picked up by the included variables), whereas including various boundary control variables creates problems with multi-collinearity.

One solution being explored to address this issue has to do with the concept of "global boundary complexity" (Lee, DeLone, & Espinosa, 2007). The idea behind this concept is that it is less important to understand the effect of one particular boundary than the combined effect that all boundaries have collectively over coordination costs and coordination success. For example, prior research has studied the effect of "faultlines" or the simultaneous co-existence of multiple boundaries between sites, which create deep divisions between team members, making them extremely difficult to bridge when working together (Lau & Murnighan, 1998; Polzer, Jarvenpaa, Crisp, & Kim, 2006). Our global boundary complexity concept builds upon the faultline concept, extending it to multi-site contexts in which there may be various degrees of faultiness between any two sites, which will drive the complexity of the entire task context. For example, in a team operating in multiple locations, two sites like New York and Bangalore will have deep faultlines due to geographic distance, time zone, cultural, and maybe even organizational differences. Members from these two sites will need to bridge all these differences to communicate and coordinate effectively. Conversely, two sites like New York and Miami will have mainly geographical distance boundaries to bridge. Such faultline analysis is useful when working in two sites, but it becomes more difficult for managers to apply faultline concepts to manage teams in multiple sites. For example, what is the "faultiness" of a team operating in the three locations above, that is, New York, Miami, and Bangalore? I recommend that managers analyze all boundaries represented in a team and evaluate the overall boundary complexity in their task environments, because it is this complexity that will drive coordination effectiveness and costs.

Tasks become more complex when the number of information cues necessary to carry out the task increases and when the relationship between these cues becomes more interdependent and dynamic (Campbell, 1988; Wood, 1986). Thus, boundary complexity can be viewed as the number of cues team members need to process to work effectively across all present boundaries, for example, how many cultures are represented, how many locations team members are in, how many time zones are covered, how many people we have in each location and how widely dispersed they are among these locations, how team membership in those locations is changing over time, etc. We are conducting studies to develop a composite measure of these factors to represent the complexity of a team boundary, which may become a better predictor of coordination costs, challenges, and outcomes. My recommendation to managers is to evaluate the overall boundary complexity of their teams based on the factors discussed above and make managerial decisions to bring this complexity down as much as possible. For example, if a team has deep cultural, distance, time zone, and organizational boundaries among many locations, with many cultures, time zones, and organizations represented, and team members are widely distributed across these boundaries, it may become close to impossible to coordinate task activities. In such a case, task activities should be assigned to sites in such a way that task activity dependencies are maximized within each site and minimized across sites, which will bring coordination costs down.

Temporal Separation Complexity

While the concept of global boundary complexity is appealing, its development and implementation are not so simple. Take temporal boundaries alone. When we started studying the effects of time zones, we started with very simple conceptual models, which quickly escalated in complexity as we identified more factors involved. Take, for example, a single task involving two temporally separated team members, one making a task request (R) and one producing the requested task (P). We used this very simple model in our initial conceptual work on coordination across time zones (Espinosa & Carmel, 2003, 2004b). A simple fine-grained model like this helped us develop a very nuanced understanding of the coordination costs associated with a single task unit. However, most real teams involve multiple team members in multiple time zones. Even within the simple dyadic model, the timing of the task request, how long it takes to carry it out, and the timing of the task completion can make a big difference. If the task request is made during the work time overlap period, then R and P can communicate and discuss things. If the task request is made during the non-overlap period, P may not be able to clarify issues until the next day. Similarly, if the task takes many days, then time zones may not get in the way, but if the task takes only an hour or two, time zones can have an impact. Finally, if the task is completed during the non-overlap period, one may need to wait until the next day to obtain and discuss the results.

Now, let's complicate things further. Once we take the dyad model into a full team model, we need to look into a number of additional variables: team size; geographical configuration (north-south, east-west, scattered, etc.; Espinosa, Cummings, & Pickering, 2006; Espinosa & Pickering, 2006); member distribution across time zones (evenly, unevenly, core dominant site, etc.); number of time zones represented; and maximum time zone difference spanned by the team (Cummings, Espinosa, & Pickering, 2009; Espinosa, Cummings, & Pickering, 2012). Any of these variations will sharply complicate any predictive research model. The recommendation for managers is to keep the temporal separation complexity to a minimum. Working across time zones often requires substantial time shifting, but radical time shifts requiring members to work at odd hours leads to burnout and dissatisfaction in the long term (Carmel & Espinosa, 2011). Simpler temporal separation configurations are always more effective because coordination costs and the cognitive load to keep track of time zone information associated with the task are reduced.

Time Zone Coordination Tactics

In an interesting study conducted at InfoSys, my colleague Erran Carmel found that global outsourcing firms, which have developed expertise at working across very large time-zone-span environments, have adopted solutions that have worked well, including developing a twenty-four-hour culture of work in which employees have all the resources and training to work at any hour of the day; time flexibility, that is, willingness to time-shift work at various hours or even longer hours; twenty-four-hour work environment, supporting workers' ability to work at all hours with things like food, transportation, gymnasiums, and sleeping rooms; liaisons, creating human bridges or liaisons between locations, who often shift their schedules and have cultural similarity with the counterpart liaison on the other site, which fosters effective communication; allocation, that is, tasks carefully allocated to locations to minimize task dependencies across sites; status reporting to reduce coordination errors across sites; periodic real-time meetings; escalation protocols with standard protocols in place to handle issues when they arise; methodology-embedded technology suites, that is, high reliance on specialized and integrated tools to facilitate communication and workflow across sites; and awareness technologies, tools to acquire up-to-date information about what is going on with time zone calendars, instant messengers, mobile texting, presence awareness tools, and so forth.

Temporal Distance and Calendar Efficiencies

Is temporal distance good or bad? For some work, temporal distance creates communication barriers that are difficult to bridge, thus causing delay. However, if we view the global task environment as a collection of task requestors and task producers, and if we view task delays from the perspective of task requestors, who depend on task producers, then the time that task producers spend on the task while the requestor is sleeping (due to time zone differences) can actually reduce delay. This is the theme of our book with Erran Carmel, *I'm Working While They're Sleeping* (Carmel & Espinosa, 2011). The question is, does handing off work at the end of one's work day to sites in different time zones accelerate or delay the task? We developed the conceptual foundations to understand these issues and conducted some preliminary empirical analysis in a study of the "follow-the-sun" practice (Carmel, Espinosa, & Dubinsky, 2010). In this study we defined follow-the-sun as "a round-the-clock work rotation method aimed at reducing project duration, in which the knowledge product is owned and advanced by a production site and is then handed off at the end of each work day to the next production site several time zones west." It is important to note that this is very different in concept from simple "round-the-clock" work, typical of help desks and other support services. In follow-the-sun one site works on a knowledge or digital product and then hands off the product to the next site at the end of the day.

Two key concepts that emerged from this research, which help us understand whether follow-the-sun is beneficial for a particular task, are calendar efficiencies and coordination costs. We proposed in our study that the objective of follow-the-sun is to explicitly increase production speed or reduce task duration, and that calendar efficiencies are at the heart of this. For example, in a manufacturing plant, production volume can be increased by adding shifts. The whole idea with time shifts in manufacturing is that physical plant facilities contain very costly resources that are not effectively utilized when they sit idle overnight because several production hours are wasted. Adding shifts creates what we call "calendar efficiencies," which basically means producing more in the same calendar time. This is precisely the driver for follow-the-sun, except that we are not shifting time around a manufacturing plant, but the actual digital product being produced, which can be digitally transported to other sites at a negligible cost. Calendar efficiencies in follow-the-sun can double or even triple the production of an eight-hour shift in a given day. However, how much additional production is gained will be dependent on the amount of time spent on coordinating the hand-off. Just as nursing shifts require some overlapping time between shifts to debrief the next team, follow-the-sun requires some time for hand-off coordination. This is where the coordination costs come into play.

The best way to understand the role of coordination costs in "follow the sun" is to think of, say, three subteams that will collaborate on the production of a digital product. What is more cost-effective? To put all three subteams to work in parallel in the same location? Or to arrange the subteams sequentially across time zones and hand off the work from site to site? The former requires a fair amount of lateral communication and integration, which will have a substantial coordination overhead, which we call "within-site" coordination costs. The latter requires a fair amount of hand-off coordination from site to site, which we call "cross-site" coordination costs. In a nutshell, follow-the-sun is more efficient if all within-site coordination costs plus cross-site coordination costs associated with hand-offs are smaller than the total within-site coordination costs associated with a single production site. The efficiency of the hand-off process is a key factor that will shift the scale in one direction or another. The implication for managers is that, generally, hand-off efficiency, and thus the attractiveness of follow-the-sun, increases with simpler products, more predictable production processes, and more effective team communication. Also, the attractiveness of single-site production diminishes in favor of follow-the-sun as teams become larger because coordination costs grow exponentially with team size (Brooks, 1995), for example, a single team of thirty members in one site will have exponentially more within-site coordination costs than a team with three subteams of ten members.

Temporal vs. Spatial Distance

While global teams work across multiple boundaries (Orlikowski, 2002), the two most salient boundaries in global team research are temporal and spatial (Cummings, Espinosa, & Pickering, 2009; Espinosa, Cummings, & Pickering, 2012). Understanding the specific effects of one isolated from the other is very difficult because these boundaries generally co-exist. At the same time, the nature of spatial distance varies widely from the nature of temporal distance. Consider these examples: spatial distance is symmetric (that is, the distance from A to B is the same as from B to A), whereas temporal distance is not (that is, one side is ahead of the other); spatial distance cannot be easily measured (Is it binary? Travel time? Physical distance?), whereas temporal distance is mathematically precise (that is, two sites are X hours apart);

spatial distance can be easily bridged with technology, whereas temporal distance cannot; spatial distance does not necessarily change the pattern of team interaction, whereas temporal distance dictates the pattern of communication, that is, synchronous versus asynchronous; and timing of the workflow is not so critical with spatial separation, whereas workflow has to be carefully planned with temporal separation. It is this dichotomy—that spatial and temporal distance correlate so much, while being so very different in nature—that has made the study of temporal distance effects not only so challenging, but also so interesting and necessary.

We conducted a qualitative study at a large semi-conductor manufacturing company specifically aimed at learning about work coordination challenges across spatial and temporal distance (Espinosa & Pickering, 2006). Our interview protocols were specifically designed to differentiate and contrast the two. Our study found that geographic configurations (north-south, east-west, evenly dispersed, unevenly dispersed, etc.) make a big difference on coordination challenges. More specifically, consistently with prior research (Espinosa & Carmel, 2003; Orlikowski, 2002; Watson-Manheim, Chudoba, & Crowston, 2002), we found that coordination challenges escalate rapidly as the number of time zones represented in a team increase. We also found that prior experience working with team members helped cope with coordination challenges across time zones.

One interesting thing we learned is that, while theory tells us when mechanistic, organic, or implicit coordination is most effective, team members selected their coordination processes, mechanisms, and tools based on personal preferences. No systematic criteria for using one or the other emerged from our interviews. The preferred mode of synchronous and asynchronous communication was telephone and electronic mail, respectively, but there was no particular preference of one over the other. Some members preferred the telephone and some preferred electronic mail, irrespective of whether there was work time overlap or not. One important implication for managers is that, while this finding may seem trivial, it points to the need for education and training for global workers about effective coordination practices across temporal distance.

With respect to mechanistic coordination, most participants discussed the use of: centralized process, project, or product documents to access process, project, or product information; task organization arrangements, for example, division of labor, redundant roles across sites, relocation of personnel, meeting schedules, and special procedures to deal with time zones; and use of special collaboration tools, such as SharePoint™, Outlook™ shared calendar, shared drives, software tools, and so forth. Team members also used various types of implicit coordination mechanisms, such as: task awareness (knowledge of who has done what with respect to the task and when) and transactive memory (knowing who knows what in the team).

Interestingly, most participants felt that their work was well coordinated or somewhat coordinated. While co-located team members were more coordinated than distant members, and distant members were more coordinated than time-separated members, the difference was very small in their perceptions. This is perhaps due to the fact that corporate pressures and competitiveness require most projects to be successful, but as we discuss later, coordination effectiveness in time-separated contexts was only achieved with substantial additional coordination costs. So, while time proximity reduces the effort necessary to coordinate, this doesn't necessarily mean that teams will be better coordinated in the end. It appears that when the coordination barriers imposed by time separation are removed, teams experience other problems (such as meeting overload, working on multiple projects, production losses, and too many one-on-one face-to-face meetings, which reduce available production time).

While most projects were successfully coordinated in our study, time separation required a substantial amount of additional effort by team members. This effort was materialized in several forms, including extraordinary effort required to schedule meetings; adjusting and extending work schedules to increase overlap time between sites; the need to work from home and be available almost around the clock; creating redundancies and overlapping responsibilities between sites; additional meetings and training sessions at the beginning of the project; the need for special and more rigorous work processes, task organization, and team interaction routines; and the need to obtain additional information and more details up-front before meetings. These findings are consistent with prior research (DeLone, Espinosa, Lee, & Carmel, 2005), but we also found that this additional effort required is greatly increased as more time zones are involved in a project. Whereas a team with only two time zones can make adjustment to work practices and schedules to cope with reduced overlapping times, this becomes a monumental challenge when team members are spread out across several time zones. In one account, participants shifted their schedules so much that co-located team members rarely saw each other (co-located time separation).

In the end, team members put a lot of extra effort to succeed. One lesson for managers from these findings for coordination researchers is that we may not be able to observe variance in coordination effectiveness between co-located, spatially separated, and temporally separated teamwork when teams have strong pressures to succeed. But we should then see great variance in effort. Therefore, studies that look exclusively at coordination success or coordination costs may provide an incomplete picture and we may need to analyze both. Related to this, the majority of participants indicated that time separation led to higher coordination costs in the form of increased delay. Almost half of the participants indicated that having to repair misunderstandings across time zones had a severe impact on delay and that it took up to an extra day in response time for a misunderstanding to be noticed and corrected, which is not the case in same-time-zone contexts. A few participants also indicated that such misunderstandings often led to rework. At the same time, most participants, when asked to contrast outcomes with same-time-zone distributed work and co-located work, clearly suggested that when work overlap was maximized it was easier to coordinate the work and that coordination costs were lowered. An important implication for managers facing substantial time-zone differences within a team is to adopt time shifting strategies that will create some amount of work time overlap when the whole team can meet synchronously.

We learned from our interviews that most participants had experience working globally and had therefore made adjustments to cope with spatial separation. Furthermore, the availability of synchronous collaboration tools like web data conferencing, social networking, and mobile texting reduced the relevance of spatial distance as a critical factor. Furthermore, team members enjoyed most of the benefits of co-location (presence awareness, spontaneous interaction, task awareness, and rich communication media). In essence, distance separation was not a big problem for work coordination at this company. Time separation, on the other hand, did present monumental challenges to these teams. One reason for this was that the range of available coordination mechanisms narrowed when team members were separated by distance or time. Geographically separated teams have fewer coordination mechanisms available than co-located teams, and temporally separated teams have fewer coordination mechanisms available than teams in the same time zone. Furthermore, as more time zones were represented in a team, the coordination challenges increased and it became more difficult to find a window of time for team members to communicate synchronously.

Because synchronous communication options are reduced, asynchronous communication and mechanistic coordination become more predominant with temporal separation. Team members can still communicate synchronously, but this requires long work hours, widespread schedule shifts, and substantial effort planning meetings. The amount of effort required to plan synchronous meetings with team members in multiple time zones is daunting; therefore, tasks are coordinated mechanistically to a large extent. The most popular mechanistic coordination devices in our study were shared documents, rigorous procedures and routines, substantial task organization, well-organized workflows, and redundant roles across different sites. Meeting team members in person before the project started was also very effective to get to know each other, to get trained jointly on global teamwork, and to carefully define and adopt procedures, all of which had a positive effect on team coordination across temporal distance. Such practices fostered effective implicit coordination in teams. And as we pointed out earlier, there was a lot of time shifting to create work time overlap among team members who had to interact frequently.

Transactive memory (knowing who knows what) (Wegner, 1995) was most important for our participants when working across temporal distance. Simply knowing where expertise resided and being able to tap into this expertise when needed was helpful, which is consistent with prior findings on the effects of "expertise coordination" (Faraj & Sproull, 2000). Task awareness (knowing who has done what and when) was the second-most-often mentioned cognitive mechanism, followed by presence awareness (knowing who is around and when, and knowing where and when to find team members). A few members also mentioned that shared knowledge about the task or the team is important with colleagues in other time zones, and a few of these also discussed the importance of shared beliefs (common vision, shared goals). However, most participants reported that, while these mechanisms are always important, this knowledge can be more easily acquired when team members are co-located. Therefore, an important implication for managers has to do with the importance of meeting in person before the project starts or at periodic times throughout the project duration.

Dyad-Level Findings

Studying dyads in temporally separated teams is important because a time zone difference is dyadic in nature, that is, it is the temporal distance between two locations. I have argued in my research that how teams coordinate their work across global boundaries is better understood when we view teams not as a collection of individuals but as a collection of dyads. Team members have individual attributes (knowledge, feelings, expertise, motivation), but any two individuals will also have relational attributes (friendship, affection, communication frequency, friendship, shared knowledge, etc.). Dyads have been studied extensively in research involving rational roles (Barley, 1986, 1990), that is, how one individual relates to another, and in social network research (Borgatti & Cross, 2003; Krackhardt, 1988; Sparrowe, Liden, Wayne, & Kraimer, 2001).

For example, understanding the coordination delays associated with every pair in the team, and how this delay is affected by the temporal distance separating the two members, can go a long way in explaining how a team operates. In one particular survey study at a large semi-conductor manufacturing team, we collected individual, dyadic, and team-level data, resulting in two separate empirical studies (Cummings, Espinosa, & Pickering,

2009; Espinosa, Cummings, & Pickering, 2012). The impetus for doing this resided in the fact that some aspects of teamwork are better understood at the individual level (such as expertise, motivation, time employed by the organization), others at the dyad level (such as communication volume, shared knowledge, temporal distance), and yet others at the team level (such as mechanistic coordination tools adopted, project outcomes).

In the first survey study conducted with dyadic data (Cummings, Espinosa, & Pickering, 2009), we investigated how temporal and spatial coordination affected coordination delay, and how this effect was influenced by synchronous and asynchronous communication. This was the first study to systematically evaluate differences among spatial and temporal boundaries and, more importantly, to examine how these differences affect the success of communication technologies in helping reduce coordination delay. We formulated a relational model of coordination delay, thereby tapping into the practical problems faced by pairs of globally distributed project members. Our study found that both spatial and temporal boundaries were associated with coordination delays. We also found that synchronous (for example, web conferencing) and asynchronous communication (for example, e-mail) helped reduce coordination delays for pairs of members who had overlapping work hours, regardless of their temporal distance. Our results showed that just having a small amount of overlap in work hours among sites was enough to help members take greater advantage of communication technologies.

In contrast, we found that, for pairs who did not have overlapping work hours, the use of communication technology did not help reduce delay. Thus, temporal boundaries appear to be more difficult to cross with communication technologies when there is no window of opportunity for synchronous interaction, more so than with spatial boundaries. Our study also found that spatial and temporal boundaries did not directly affect project performance, but they did so indirectly through coordination delay. Therefore, our study concluded that temporal boundaries were a major hindrance to the effective employment of agile methodologies (such as scrum) because coordination delay decreased the ability of project members to be flexible and agile in their work. However, our study concluded that if temporally separated members have some work time overlap, they may be in a better position to use agile methods and make effective use of communication tools. This is consistent with other research showing that tactics such as taking into account time zones when scheduling meetings, making them short and frequent, and temporarily staggering work time may help project members bridge time zones through synchronous communication (Sarker & Sarker, 2009). However, our study also shows that even asynchronous communication is more effective with some work time overlap.

Finally, consistent with our interview study above, our dyad survey also found that prior experience working with each other helped reduce coordination delays, suggesting that shared experiences that members have had during prior projects can reduce coordination delays across temporal distance. In addition, we found that member dependencies were also helpful for reducing coordination delays. While prior research argues that dependencies require coordination to be managed, our study suggested that this necessary coordination eventually helps reduce delay. In sum, managers are encouraged to view their teams as a collection of dyads. They should then analyze each dyad for geographical distance; time zone difference (or work time overlap); dependencies on each other; communication frequency, by type (synchronous versus asynchronous); friendship; knowledge of each other; and knowledge of each other's tasks, among other things. Based on this analysis, managers should decide on an effective time-shifting strategy to create work time overlap windows for dyads with more tightly coupled dependencies.

Team Level Findings

In the second survey study with team level data and individual level data aggregated to the team level (Espinosa, Cummings, & Pickering, 2012) from the same company, we investigated the effects of temporal separation on team coordination and team performance, differentiating these effects from those of spatial separation. The primary factors we analyzed were spatial separation among team members (as a control) and two aspects of time separation: number of time zones (a team with members in Washington, D.C., Paris, and Bangalore has three time zones) and maximum time zone differences spanned by the team (the same team has a time zone span of 10.5 hours). We also accounted for other factors that could affect team coordination and team performance, such as team size, project length, project priority, project resources, and communication tool use.

Our study found that the maximum time zone difference spanned by the team led to more coordination problems, which led to lower team performance. But the negative effect of time zone span on team performance was fully mediated by coordination problems. We also found that task organization—a form of mechanistic coordination—helped reduce coordination problems, thus helping to offset those associated with large time zone spans. It is interesting to compare these findings with the dyad level. Any two members can coordinate their work across time zones by communicating, but general task organization is necessary for the full team to operate effectively in geographically dispersed contexts. Similar to our interview study, we found that none of the geographic configuration variables predicted the use of mechanistic coordination processes or tools. Again, global team members appear to select a mix of coordination processes based on personal preferences rather than geographic configuration. Once again, this suggests that simple training on how to use mechanistic coordination effectively may yield substantial benefits. Interestingly, team communication did not help reduce coordination problems. In our dyad study we found that team communication helped reduce coordination delays in dyads, but in contrast, the team level study does not show that general team communication helps alleviate general team coordination problems. Conversely, mechanistic coordination in the form of task organization, which is not applicable to the dyad level, has the strongest effect on team level coordination outcomes. Our results from this study suggest that team members should communicate selectively in pairs as needed to resolve any coordination delay issues with their peers, but for the team's coordination as a unit, task organization is fundamental.

Naturally, coordination problems can be reduced by selecting locations that minimize the time zone difference spanned by the team, but often this is not feasible, in which case organizing project tasks can more effectively help reduce coordination problems. Often, managers gravitate toward technological solutions to bridge spatial and temporal boundaries, but our findings suggest that managers should strive to identify and implement sound task organization practices, like division of labor and process rigor, which may be more effective and also help reduce the need to communicate, which is more difficult across large temporal distances.

The Role of Interaction Synchronicity

Of all our research studies of coordination in temporally separated work, our experimental study may offer the most interesting insights into how temporal distance affects team performance. In this study, participants worked in dyads completing a digital task in the computer lab. The task was a map drawing task in which one team member acted as a map designer—the task requestor—who described the map to be drawn, and the other as a map maker—the task producer—who drew the maps from the designer's instructions. We simulated fifteen-minute working days and created four conditions of temporal separation. We used an overlap index (O'Leary & Cummings, 2007) indicating the fraction of work time overlap the dyad had—full overlap, large partial overlap (two-thirds or ten minutes), small partial overlap (one-third or five minutes), and no overlap. Participants were assigned randomly to these four conditions. The dyad teams were given training and twelve maps to produce. We measured speed—process performance—based on the number of maps completed by the team and quality or accuracy—product performance—based on the number of correct elements drawn in the correct positions. We conducted the study in three separate phases.

In the first phase, participants worked on a simple task involving only a few drawing elements necessary to produce the maps. We found that larger temporal separation (less work time overlap) was associated with lower product quality (that is, accuracy). Interestingly, we found that small amounts of temporal separation reduced speed, but larger temporal separation actually increased speed, with the highest speed attained with no work time overlap at all, that is, a "U" shaped curve (Espinosa, Nan, & Carmel, 2007). We attributed this result to two factors. First, teams with full overlap can work effectively because of their ability to communicate synchronously, and the introduction of small amounts of temporal separation breaks the fluidity of this interaction, therefore reducing speed. However, synchronous interaction can be distracting when members are communicating frequently, diverting time that could be devoted to the task. As more temporal separation is introduced, team members can work without interruption, therefore increasing their speed. The second factor has to do with the simplicity of the task. If the task is very simple, then the task requestor can easily batch instructions, which can then be easily and unambiguously interpreted by the map designer during non-overlapping times. Because there is little miscommunication, temporal separation helps them work faster. After finding this result, we speculated that modifying the task such that it required more intense and frequent communication to resolve issues would accentuate the detrimental effects of temporal separation. This led us to design Phases 2 and 3 of the experimental study in which we manipulated the task by making it more complex and more equivocal, respectively (Nan, Espinosa, & Carmel, 2009).

In Phase 2 we made the task more complex by using the exact same maps to be drawn (to make performance outcomes comparable), but increased substantially the number of possible map elements given to the map producer. A task becomes more complex when it requires more information cues to complete it (Campbell, 1988; Wood, 1986). We anticipated that task complexity would require more frequent interactions to clarify issues and repair miscommunication and would, therefore, be more affected by temporal separation. In Phase 3 we made the task more equivocal (Dennis & Kinney, 1998), that is, the framework for information interpretation to carry out the task is less clear, leading to different views and interpretations of the task. We accomplished this in two ways. First, there were two designers whose job was to develop and agree on specific instruction to give to a fictitious map-maker to draw the maps (the maps were later drawn by external experiment assistants, based on the instructions produced by the team). Second, we introduced information asymmetries by providing some map elements uniquely to each member and some that were common to both members, such that no map descriptions could be completed accurately without exchanging information.

In both cases, the complex and equivocal tasks, speed increased monotonically and quality decreased monotonically with increased temporal separation. Thus, our conclusion at that time was "temporal separation is good for speed but bad for quality" (Nan, Espinosa, & Carmel, 2009). However, this was a very simplistic conclusion because we knew that real teams make tradeoffs between speed and quality, depending on the reward system and the specific goals of the task. For example, a software development team working on an air traffic control system will most likely have quality and zero defects as their ultimate goals. On the other hand, a software team developing products with critical time-to-market demands may be more concerned about speed. In our study, we made speed and quality equally important by offering performance bonuses based on both. We suspect that varying the performance incentives in favor of either speed or quality may give us different results. With this doubt in our minds, we then searched for better theoretical explanations for our results, which led to a complete reanalysis of our data. The theory we found most useful for our analysis is "media synchronicity theory" (Dennis, Fuller, & Valacich, 2008). According to this theory, media can be relatively synchronous (a telephone) or asynchronous (electronic mail); team members can appropriate the technology to make their interactions more synchronous (chatting back and forth using electronic mail) or more asynchronous (leaving voice mail); asynchronous communication is more effective to convey (transmit) new information, whereas synchronous communication is more effective to converge on the meaning of that information.

With media synchronicity theory as our explanatory framework, we investigated how temporal separation and task type affected the interaction synchronicity of the team and how this, in turn, affected performance. Because we captured more than twenty thousand chat entries in the communication logs we recorded during the experiments, we were able to measure the interaction synchronicity of the communication and how much of it was used for conveyance (task instructions) and convergence (discussions, clarifications). We are not finished analyzing the data, but our preliminary results suggest that temporal separation per se is not the issue, but how temporal separation alters the synchronicity of the team interaction. The team's interaction synchronicity then influences how much conveyance and how much convergence take place in the team communication. Interestingly, our preliminary results suggest that effective conveyance may help speed, whereas effective convergence may help quality.

In sum, while this study is still under way, our preliminary results suggest that we need to focus more on the synchronous and asynchronous nature of the team communication, more so than on temporal separation per se. The implication for managers is that interaction synchronicity appears to be at the heart of effective work coordination and team performance in time-separated task environments. Time zone separation does not appear to be a problem for simpler tasks that require a fair amount of information to be exchanged because team members can convey this information asynchronously in an effective manner. Conversely, time zone separation presents more substantial challenges when the task is equivocal, requiring a fair amount of convergence on the meaning of the information exchanged, thus benefitting from more synchronous interaction. Collaborators may work largely asynchronously because they are in different time zones, because their schedules don't match, or because they are highly mobile. Interaction synchronicity can be altered with effective practices and tools like time-shifting, twenty-four-hour availability, and mobile communications. In the end, it is the team's interaction patterns that will determine the effectiveness of their work coordination, rather than the temporal distance per se. Nevertheless, temporal distance is naturally the strongest predictor of (reduced) synchronicity, thus the importance of studying it.

Concluding Remarks

In this chapter I have provided an overview of the various aspects of effective work coordination in temporally dispersed teams, informed by my research with various colleagues and other related research in this area. Collaboration across temporal distance is still not well understood, and it continues to pose a substantial challenge for global teams. While my collaborators and I have been studying various aspects of temporally dispersed work for almost a decade, there is still so much we need to learn in this field. In sum, task coordination is a key aspect of temporally separated knowledge work when task activities are highly interdependent. The various arrangements of dyads in a global task context lead to global team boundary complexity, making it difficult to tease out the individual boundary effect. But in the end, what matters is the complexity of the collaboration environment resulting from the presence of these various boundaries. Temporal separation alone is a very complex issue because of the many factors that may affect how teams work together: geographic configuration (north-south; east-west; widely/evenly distributed; widely/unevenly distributed); number of time zones covered; the number of team members in each time zone; the maximum time zone difference spanned by the team; etc. But temporal distance is not necessarily a bad thing and it can actually be advantageous for speed if work is organized around the clock in a follow-the-sun if calendar efficiencies are achieved by minimizing the cross-site coordination costs associated with hand-offs from site to site.

Team communication is also very important in temporally dispersed teams, but this communication has its strongest effect on coordination delay within dyads. Coordination delay increases when dyads have temporal boundaries. Communication helps reduce these delays, but only when team members have some work time overlap. When team members have no work time overlap, communication, either synchronous or asynchronous, doesn't seem to help much, so managers are advised to implement time-shifting strategies to create some work time overlap between dyads that collaborate more frequently. At the team level, task organization and other forms of mechanistic coordination are most effective, whereas general team communication does not seem to have an effect.

Finally, managers are advised to look for ways to alter the team's interaction synchronicity to fit the particular needs of the task. Temporal distance affects the interaction synchronicity (that is, more temporal distance leads to more asynchronous interaction), but while temporal distance may not be so easily manipulated, synchronicity can be altered with practices like time shifting, twenty-four-hour availability, use of liaisons, and use of mobile communications. More asynchronous interaction is generally effective for conveyance and speed, whereas more synchronous interaction is generally effective for convergence and quality.

References

Armstrong, D.J., & Cole, P. (2002). Managing distances and differences in geographically distributed work groups. In P. Hinds & S. Kiesler (Eds.), *Distributed work* (pp. 187–215). Cambridge, MA: MIT Press.

Barley, S. (1986). Technology as an occasion for structuring: Evidence from observations of CT scanners and the social order of radiology departments. *Administrative Science Quarterly*, pp. 78–108.

Barley, S. (1990, March). The alignment of technology and structure through roles and networks. *Administrative Science Quarterly, 35*, 61–103.

Borgatti, S.P., & Cross, R. (2003). A relational view of information seeking and learning in social networks. *Management Science, 49*(4), 432–445.

Brooks, F. (1995). *The mythical man-month: Essays on software engineering* (anniv. ed.). Reading, MA: Addison-Wesley.

Campbell, D.J. (1988). Task complexity: A review and analysis. *Academy of Management Review, 13*(1), 40–52.

Cannon-Bowers, J.A., & Salas, E. (2001). Reflections on shared cognition. *Journal of Organizational Behavior*, *22*(2), 195–202.

Cannon-Bowers, J.A., Salas, E., & Converse, S. (1993). Shared mental models in expert team decision-making. In J. Castellan (Ed.), *Individual and group decision-making: Current issues* (pp. 221–246). Mahwah, NJ: Lawrence Erlbaum Associates.

Carmel, E. (1999). *Global software teams.* Upper Saddle River, NJ: Prentice Hall.

Carmel, E. (2006). Building your information systems from the other side of the world: How Infosys manages time zone differences. *MIS Quarterly Executive, 5*(1), 43–53.

Carmel, E., & Espinosa, J.A. (2011). *I'm working while they're sleeping: Time zone separation challenges and solutions.* Washington, DC: Nedder Stream Press.

Carmel, E., Espinosa, J.A., & Dubinsky, Y. (2010). Follow-the-sun: Workflow in global software development: Conceptual foundations. *Journal of Management Information Systems, 27*(1), 17–37.

Cohen, D.J., & Alonso, A. (2013). Virtual teams: The how to's of making "being virtually there" successful. In E. Salas, S. Tannenbaum, D. Cohen, & G. Lathum (Eds.), *Developing and enhancing high performance teams.* San Francisco: Pfeiffer.

Cramton, C.D. (2001). The mutual knowledge problem and its consequences for dispersed collaboration. *Organization Science, 12*(3), 346–371.

Cummings, J., Espinosa, J.A., & Pickering, C. (2009). Crossing spatial and temporal boundaries in globally distributed projects: A relational model of coordination delay. *Information Systems Research, 20*(3), 420–439.

DeLone, W., Espinosa, J.A., Lee, G., & Carmel, E. (2005). Bridging global boundaries for IS project success. Paper presented at the 38th Hawaiian International Conference on System Sciences, Big Island, Hawaii.

Dennis, A.R., Fuller, R.M., & Valacich, J.S. (2008). Media, tasks, and communication processes: A theory of media synchronicity. *MIS Quarterly, 32*(3), 575–600.

Dennis, A.R., & Kinney, S.T. (1998). Testing media richness theory in the new media: The effects of cues, feedback, and task equivocality. *Information Systems Research, 9*(3), 256–274.

DeSanctis, G., & Poole, M.S. (1997). Transitions in teamwork in new organizational forms. In B. Markovsky (Ed.), *Advances in group processes* (Vol. 14, pp. 157–176). Greenwich, CT: JAI Press.

Drucker, P.J. (1993). *Concept of the corporation.* Piscataway, NJ: Transaction Publishers.

Espinosa, J.A., Armour, F., Boh, W.F., & Clark, M.A. (2012). A self-fueling coordination model for enterprise architecting effectiveness. Paper presented at the 45th Hawaiian International Conference on System Sciences, Maui, Hawaii.

Espinosa, J.A., & Carmel, E. (2003, May). Modeling coordination costs due to time separation in global software teams. Paper presented at the Global Software Development Workshop, International Conference on Software Engineering (ICSE), Portland, Oregon.

Espinosa, J.A., & Carmel, E. (2004a). The effect of time separation on coordination costs in global software teams: A dyad model. Paper presented at the 37th Hawaiian International Conference on System Sciences, Big Island, Hawaii.

Espinosa, J.A., & Carmel, E. (2004b). The impact of time separation on coordination in global software teams: A conceptual foundation. *Journal of Software Process: Practice and Improvement, 8*(4), 249–266.

Espinosa, J.A., Cummings, J., & Pickering, C. (2012). Time separation, coordination, and performance in technical teams. *IEEE Transactions on Engineering Management, 59*(1), 91–103.

Espinosa, J.A., Cummings, J.N., & Pickering, C. (2006). Your time zone or mine? Geographic configurations, global team coordination, and project outcomes. Paper presented at the Academy of Management Conference, Atlanta, Georgia.

Espinosa, J.A., Cummings, J.N., Wilson, J.M., & Pearce, B.M. (2003). Team boundary issues across multiple global firms. *Journal of Management Information Systems, 19*(4), 157–190.

Espinosa, J.A., Lee, G., & DeLone, W. (2006). Global boundaries, task processes and IS project success: A field study. *Information, Technology and People, 19*(4), 345–370.

Espinosa, J.A., Nan, N., & Carmel, E. (2007, August 27–30). Do gradations of time separation make a difference in performance? A first laboratory study. Paper presented at the Second IEEE International Conference on Global Software Engineering, Munich, Germany.

Espinosa, J.A., & Pickering, C. (2006). The effect of time separation on coordination processes and outcomes: A case study. Paper presented at the 39th Hawaiian International Conference on System Sciences, Poipu, Kauai, Hawaii.

Espinosa, J.A., Slaughter, S.A., Kraut, R.E., & Herbsleb, J.D. (2007). Team knowledge and coordination in geographically distributed software development. *Journal of Management Information Systems, 24*(1), 135–169.

Faraj, S., & Sproull, L. (2000). Coordinating expertise in software development teams. *Management Science, 46*(12), 1554–1568.

Herbsleb, J.D., & Grinter, R.E. (1999a). Architectures, coordination, and distance: Conway's law and beyond. *IEEE Software, 16*(5), 63–70.

Herbsleb, J.D., & Grinter, R.E. (1999b, September/October). Splitting the organization and integrating the code: Conway's law revisited. Paper presented at the International Conference on Software Engineering, Los Angeles, CA.

Herbsleb, J.D., Mockus, A., Finholt, T., & Grinter, R.E. (2001, May). An empirical study of global software development: Distance and speed. Paper presented at the 23rd International Conference on Software Engineering (ICSE), Toronto, Canada.

Hinds, P.J., & Bailey, D.E. (2003). Out of sight, out of synch: Understanding conflict in distributed teams. *Organization Science, 14*(6), 615–632.

Kiesler, S., & Cummings, J.N. (2002). What do we know about proximity in work groups? A legacy of research on physical distance. In P. Hinds & S. Kiesler (Eds.), *Distributed work* (pp. 57–80). Cambridge, MA: MIT Press.

Klimoski, R.J., & Mohammed, S. (1994). Team mental model: Construct or metaphor. *Journal of Management, 20*(2), 403–437.

Krackhardt, D. (1988). Predicting with networks: Nonparametric multiple regression analysis of dyadic data. *Social Networks, 10*, 359–381.

Kraut, R.E., & Streeter, L.A. (1995). Coordination in software development. *Communication of the ACM, 38*(3), 69–81.

Lau, D., & Murnighan, J.K. (1998). Demographic diversity and faultlines: The compositional dynamics of organizational groups. *Academy of Management Review, 23*(2), 325–340.

Lee, G., DeLone, W., & Espinosa, J.A. (2006). Ambidextrous coping strategies in globally distributed software development projects. *Communications of the ACM, 49*(10), 35–40.

Lee, G., DeLone, W., & Espinosa, J.A. (2007). Ambidexterity and global IS project success: A theoretical model. Paper presented at the 40th Hawaiian International Conference on System Sciences, Big Island, Hawaii.

Lu, M., Chudoba, K.M., Wynn, E., & Watson-Manheim, M.B. (2003). Understanding virtuality in a global organization: Toward a virtuality index. Paper presented at the International Conference on Information Systems, Seattle, Washington.

Majchrzak, A., Rice, R.E., Malhotra, A., King, N., & Ba, S. (2000). Technology adaptation: The case of a computer-supported inter-organizational virtual team. *MIS Quarterly, 24*(4), 569–600.

Malone, T. (1987). Modeling coordination in organizations and markets. *Management Science, 33*(10), 1317–1332.

Malone, T., & Crowston, K. (1990). What is coordination theory and how can it help design cooperative work systems? Paper presented at the Computer Supported Collaborative Work Conference, Los Angeles, California.

March, J., & Simon, H.A. (1958). *Organizations.* Hoboken, NJ: John Wiley & Sons.

McDonough, E.F., Kahn, K., & Barczak, G. (2001). An investigation of the use of global, virtual, and co-located new product development teams. *Journal of Product Innovation Management, 18*(2), 110–120.

Nan, N., Espinosa, J.A., & Carmel, E. (2009). Communication and performance across time zones: A laboratory experiment. Paper presented at the International Conference on Information Systems, Phoenix, Arizona.

O'Leary, M.B., & Cummings, J.N. (2007). The spatial, temporal, and configurational characteristics of geographic dispersion in teams. *MIS Quarterly, 31*(3).

Olson, G.M., & Olson, J.S. (2000). Distance matters. *Human-Computer Interaction, 15*(1), 139–179.

Orlikowski, W. (2002). Knowing in practice: Enacting a collective capability in distributed organizing. *Organization Science, 13*(3), 249–273.

Polzer, J.T., Jarvenpaa, S., Crisp, C.B., & Kim, W.Y. (2006). Extending the faultline model to geographically dispersed teams: How co-located subgroups can impair group functioning. *Academy of Management Journal, 46*(4), 679–692.

Powell, A., Piccoli, G., & Ives, B. (2004). Virtual teams: A review of current literature and directions for future research. *Data Base for Advances in Information Systems, 35*(1), 6–36.

Sarker, S., & Sarker, S. (2009). Exploring agility in distributed information systems development (ISD) teams: An interpretive study in an off-shoring context. *Information Systems Research, 20*(3), 440–461.

Sparrowe, R.T., Liden, R.C., Wayne, S.J., & Kraimer, M.L. (2001). Social networks and the performance of individuals and groups. *Academy of Management Journal, 44*(2), 316–325.

Thompson, J. (1967). *Organizations in action.* New York: McGraw-Hill.

Van de Ven, A.H., Delbecq, L.A., & Koenig, R.J. (1976). Determinants of coordination modes within organizations. *American Sociological Review, 41*(2), 322–338.

Van den Bulte, C., & Moenaert, R. (1998). The effects of R&D team co-location on communication patterns among R&D, marketing, and manufacturing. *Management Science, 44*(11), S1–S18.

Watson-Manheim, M.B., Chudoba, K., & Crowston, K. (2002). Discontinuities and continuities: A new way to understand virtual work. *Information, Technology and People, 15*(3), 191–209.

Wegner, D. (1995). A computer network model of human transactive memory. *Social Cognition, 13*(3), 319–339.

Weick, K. (1993). The collapse of sensemaking in organizations: The Mann Gulch disaster. *Administrative Science Quarterly, 38*(4), 628–652.

Wittenbaum, G.M., & Stasser, G. (1996). Management of information in small groups. In J.L. Nye & A.M. Brower (Eds.), *What's social about social cognition?* (pp. 3–27). Thousand Oaks, CA: Sage.

Wood, R.E. (1986). Task complexity: Definition of the construct. *Organizational Behavior and Human Decision Processes, 37*(1), 60–82.

Part Five

The Assessments, Applications, and Interventions for Teams

CHAPTER FOURTEEN

Designing, Delivering, and Evaluating Team Training in Organizations*

Principles That Work

Megan E. Gregory, Jennifer Feitosa, Tripp Driskell, and Eduardo Salas

Department of Psychology, Institute for Simulation and Training, University of Central Florida

William Brandon Vessey

EASI/Wyle, NASA Johnson Space Center

Today, teams are ubiquitous in the workplace. While teams can be beneficial in that they allow for better utilization of expertise and management of workload (Smith-Jentsch, Campbell, Milanovich, & Reynolds, 2001), when teams fail, the consequences can be disastrous. For example, failed teamwork has been an alleged cause of tragedies such as the failed Hubble telescope (Ellis, 2006) and friendly fire in the military (Rafferty, Stanton, & Walker, 2010). Furthermore, the majority of aviation accidents involve

*The work presented here was supported by funding from the National Aeronautics and Space Administration (NASA; Grant# NNX09AK48G). The views expressed in this work are solely those of the authors and not those of NASA or the University of Central Florida.

human error (Helmreich, 2000), with many of these being teamwork errors. Finally, in the health care arena, Risser and colleagues (1999) found that more than half of deaths and permanent disabilities that occurred due to error in eight hospitals could have been avoided by better teamwork. In addition, they reported that improved teamwork can save hospitals about $345,000 per 100,000 emergency department visits. Because teamwork in organizations is so advantageous, and the costs associated with unsuccessful teamwork can be high, it is valuable to properly train teams.

Why should an organization care about team training? Teams do not automatically know how to work well together. In order for organizational teams to best utilize their resources, teams must be trained, and this team training only works when it is designed, delivered, and implemented well. The purpose of this chapter, therefore, is to explain the science behind team training. Our goal is to translate the science into practical tips and guidelines that can be utilized by practitioners. This science is backed up by research on teams, training, and team training. As previously stated, teamwork can improve performance of work teams and can prevent some adverse outcomes. But to improve teamwork, team training must be grounded in science (see Salas & Cannon-Bowers, 2001). What follows is a list of ten principles that should be followed to maximize the impact of a team training program.

In this chapter, we provide an overview of the team training process and describe actions that should be done before, during, and after team training in order to maximize its effectiveness. We also provide checklists of steps that can be taken to properly develop, implement, and evaluate a team training program in any organization. These are the things that all practitioners should know before implementing a team training program.

Teamwork and Team Training

Before describing how to implement team training, we must first discuss the goals of team training. What is team training? It has been defined as "a set of instructional strategies and tools aimed at enhancing teamwork knowledge, skills, processes, and performance" (Tannenbaum, Salas, & Cannon-Bowers, 1996, p. 516).

Teamwork can more succinctly be described as three facets: attitudes (such as cohesion or trust), behaviors (such as back-up behavior), and cognitions (such as shared mental models) (Salas, Rosen, Burke, & Goodwin, 2008). Furthermore, Salas, Shuffler, Thayer, Bedwell, and Lazzara (2012) have introduced a list of what they consider to be key team processes ("cognitive, verbal, and behavioral activities," Marks, Mathieu, & Zaccaro, 2001, p. 357) and emergent states ("cognitive, motivational, and affective *states* of teams," Marks, Mathieu, & Zaccaro, 2001, p. 357) that affect team outcomes: cooperation, conflict, coordination, communication, coaching, and cognition. We will later go on to define these terms and describe when and how they should be used in a team training program.

Principles for Team Training

Following, we provide ten scientifically derived principles that should be followed before, during, and after team training in order to ensure a solid team training design and to maximize effectiveness. After each sub-section, we provide a checklist that briefly summarizes the principles and recommendations. Additionally, considering the overlap in some of these principles, we provide a chart (see Figure 14.1) to illustrate the approximate beginning and end of them over time. Some of these principles are most vital during specific phases of team training, while others maintain their importance throughout the entire process. Thus, while many principles overlap and cross phases, for purposes of organization, we have laid out this chapter by placing principles in what we consider to be their *most* appropriate spot.

Before Team Training

The majority of the work in implementing a team training program occurs *before* the team training ever begins. The principles provided in this sub-section facilitate the creation of a solid team training design. Processes such as preparing the climate for learning, creating conditions for teamwork, and conducting a team needs analysis are vital components of team training design.

Figure 14.1. A Temporal Display of the Principles of Team Training

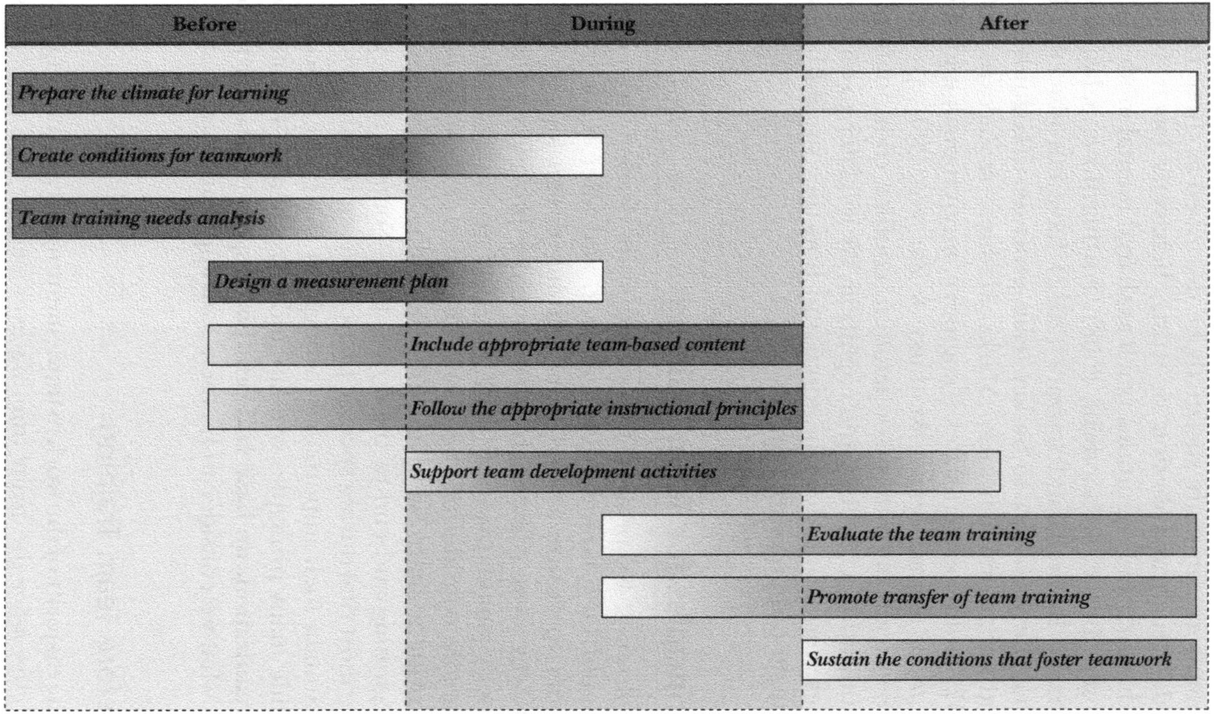

Before | During | After

Prepare the climate for learning

Create conditions for teamwork

Team training needs analysis

Design a measurement plan

Include appropriate team-based content

Follow the appropriate instructional principles

Support team development activities

Evaluate the team training

Promote transfer of team training

Sustain the conditions that foster teamwork

Principle 1. Prepare the Climate for Learning

(cf. Cannon-Bowers, Salas, & Milham, 2000; Colquitt, LePine, & Noe, 2000; Quiñones, 1997; Salas, Burke, & Cannon-Bowers, 2002; Salas, Tannenbaum, Kraiger, & Smith-Jentsch, 2012; Swezey & Salas, 1992). In order to achieve a smooth development and implementation of a team training program, the right climate has to be in place before any logistics of the training begin. Organizational climate can be defined as the perception of the organizational practices, procedures, and norms within the organization (Denison, 1990). These practices, procedures, and norms should be aligned with the training goals. For instance, Quiñones (1997) identified three categories that can maximize training outcomes: (1) involvement of trainees in the decision to participate, (2) an organization that supports learning, and (3) framing the training as a procedure that is valued by the organization. We will briefly review each of these components of learning climate below.

First, involving employees in the decision to participate in the team training program is important in order to allow them to feel that their voices have been heard. However, one should be cautious when implementing a policy of voluntary attendance in training. Some employees may erroneously extrapolate from such a policy that there is a lack of organizational support toward the training. On the other hand, it is also important that trainees not view the team training program as an unappealing mandatory assignment or another unnecessary training program. Rather, the team training program should be framed as an opportunity to make work a more positive environment. With this in mind, Salas, Tannenbaum, Kraiger, and Smith-Jentsch (2012) specified that striving for a balance between voluntary and mandatory attendance is often the best way to go. This balance may help build trainees' motivation prior to the team training. Trainee motivation has been empirically shown to improve positive attitudinal change, learning acquisition, learning retention, and the likelihood of transitioning acquired competencies to the transfer environment (cf. Salas & Cannon-Bowers, 2001, p. 479). In general, there are two types of motivation: intrinsic and extrinsic. Intrinsic, or internal, motivation refers to motivation that is derived from an individual or team's intrinsic interest in a task. According to Markus and Zajonc (1985), an intrinsically motivated task is one in which individuals are "challenged by it and sets up internal standards of excellence and success" (p. 205). In addition, Colquitt and colleagues (2000) found that training motivation is impacted by situational characteristics. This later finding refers to the second type of motivation, extrinsic motivation, or motivation manifested from external factors such as incentives. The importance of trainee motivation has been stressed throughout all phases of the training program and in both the pre- and post-training environments (Salas & Cannon-Bowers, 2001). Because of this importance of trainee motivation throughout the team training lifecycle, this principle's importance crosses the entire spectrum of time (see Figure 14.1). In other words, a positive learning climate should be present before, during, and after training.

F.H. Allport (as cited in Markus & Zajonc, 1985) suggests that, taken as a whole, motivational forces primarily come in the form of goals, needs, incentives, and attitudes. A team training program should aim to increase both intrinsic (goals, needs, attitudes) and extrinsic (incentives) motivation, with an emphasis on the former. In fact, Ryan and Deci (2000) stated that interventions that increase intrinsic motivation are by and large more favorable than those aimed at increasing extrinsic motivation. There are many ways an organization can implement motivation inducement strategies within team training programs. Perhaps the most scientifically substantiated strategy is goal setting. Goal setting—especially in the case that the goals are specific and challenging—has been shown to increase intrinsic motivation and performance (cf. Locke & Latham, 1990). Moreover, goal-setting has also been shown to increase the transfer of learning through directing attention, increasing effort, enhancing persistence, and by indirectly leading to the use of previously or newly acquired knowledge and strategies (Locke & Latham, 2002). Taylor, Russ-Eft, and Chan (2005) note that goal-setting strategies should include the establishment of both proximal and distal goals for applying the competencies acquired during training. However, this is not to say that increasing extrinsic motivation is not also important. External motivation for team training can be enhanced through the provision of individual and team incentives for both participating in the team training and for using trained behaviors on the job.

In addition, framing the training as a procedure that is valued by the organization is another fundamental step toward building the appropriate learning climate. In order to further show that the team training is valued by the organization, consider displaying positive and accurate signals about the training (Cannon-Bowers, Rhodenizer, Salas, & Bowers, 1998). Specifically, the organization should build accurate expectations about the training. Furthermore, buy-in should be obtained from supervisors, leaders, and potential trainees. These goals can be achieved by distributing tools prior to training, such as advance organizers, preparatory information, and pre-practice briefs (Salas, Tannenbaum, Kraiger, & Smith-Jentsch, 2012). Clarity is key here because it will facilitate the understanding of the team training content and help the trainees to value it. Furthermore, allowing trainees to participate in setting goals may allow them to feel heard (that is, employee voice) as well as to become more involved and committed to the training.

Thus, these actions are part of the foundation for a successful learning climate and should be maintained across time in order to reinforce the desired team processes and behaviors.

Principle 2. Create Conditions for Teamwork

(cf. Blume, Ford, Baldwin, & Huang, 2010; Ford, Quiñones, Sego, & Sorra, 1992; Rouiller & Goldstein, 1993; Smith-Jentsch, Salas, & Brannick, 2001). Beyond the initial buy-in that includes framing the training as an opportunity, the organization should develop an environment that will not only encourage the training, but also provide trainees with a positive climate for transfer of what is learned during the team training. The process of setting up the environment to allow team training to transfer back to the organization should be initiated before the training even begins. If careful preparation does not take place at this stage, organizations may find themselves conducting team training programs that have no impact on the organization's bottom line. In other words, if the team training does not transfer relevant behaviors back to the job, it is unlikely that the organization will see any results.

Consequently, a supportive organizational climate includes providing teams with the opportunity to display those trained behaviors and rewarding team behaviors used on the job. This will influence whether trainees will actually use the content of the training (that is, teamwork competencies) on the job. Ways to facilitate this behavioral transfer include showing that the organization values teamwork (Sims, Salas, & Burke 2005), providing team-level rewards, and encouraging the development of team-level goals (Cannon-Bowers, Salas, & Milham, 2000). Hence, we highlight the use of relevance within the team training and pilot testing scenarios as the main goals within this principle.

Some steps can be taken in order to ensure that a team training program is focused on behaviors that are relevant to the job. Of course, the team needs analysis (Principle 3) is an integral part of this process. However, the principles of psychological fidelity and transfer appropriate processing are also important. Psychological fidelity, defined as a training environment that prompts the psychological processes that are used on the job (Kozlowski & DeShon, 2004), has been found to facilitate learning (Bowers & Jentsch, 2001), and can improve the effectiveness of a training program (Kozlowski & DeShon, 2004). Psychological fidelity can be created in any simulation context, even within simple role plays. The idea is that the scenario should *feel* real to the participant. This does not mean that the training environment has to *look* like the real environment (physical fidelity). It is important to note that psychological fidelity differs from physical fidelity, which is a training environment that is physically similar to the job environment. Physical fidelity is not always necessary; in fact, psychological fidelity may be more beneficial. Furthermore, attempting to create physical fidelity can be "costly, time-consuming, and inefficient" (Kozlowski & DeShon, 2004, p. 4).

Transfer appropriate processing (TAP) is similar to psychological fidelity in that it involves trainees participating in processes similar to those that they would engage in on the job. However, a distinction can be made in that psychological fidelity involves the training environment, while TAP involves actual actions that are done by trainees during the training. An example of TAP during training is that of error management training, wherein trainees are encouraged to make and cognitively work through errors (Keith & Frese, 2008), as they would on the job.

Once scenarios are designed according to cognitive processes on the job, they should be pilot-tested to assess their focus on teamwork. In other words, the entire scenario should be run to ensure that it proceeds smoothly and that the objectives uncovered in the team task analysis are met (Beard, Salas, & Prince, 1995). As recommended by Beard and colleagues, participants in the pilot-test should have similar levels of training and experience. There should be enough participants to allow for role players as well as observers. This allows for evaluation of clarity and catching errors in materials, instructions, timing, and scenarios. For instance, the training literature emphasizes the importance of focusing trainees' attention toward an expert model (e.g., Smith-Jentsch, Cannon-Bowers, Tannenbaum, & Salas, 2008; Taylor, Russ-Eft, & Chan, 2005). This can clearly delineate what the training intent is and allow for trainees to keep a cognitive representation of the course. Piloting the scenarios can help identify gaps within the training design that would have been inhibitory to the transfer of desired behaviors to the work environment.

Principle 3. Conduct a Team Needs Analysis

(cf. Arthur, Edwards, Bell, Villado, & Bennett, 2005; Baker, Salas, & Prince, 1991; Blickensderfer, Cannon-Bowers, Salas, & Baker, 2000; Bowers, Baker, & Salas, 1994; Goldstein, 1991; Salas & Cannon-Bowers, 2000; Salas & Cannon-Bowers, 2001; Schraagen, Chipman, & Shalin, 2000; Swezey & Salas, 1992). Similar to any type of training, one of the most vital steps in establishing a successful team training program should be conducting a thorough training needs analysis. One may argue that this should be the first step in any training program; however, we do not foresee this step being successful and informative if there is not buy-in from subject-matter experts (SMEs) before the needs analysis begins. That is to say, if SMEs do not perceive the team training to be useful or important, they will likely not provide relevant information during the team training needs analysis. A training needs analysis involves the assessment of organizational, task, and person needs prior to implementing a training program (Arthur, Bennett,

Edens, & Bell, 2003). In other words, this process aims to identify what, how, and who the training should consist of. These steps are congruent with Baldwin and Ford's (1988) model, which considers work environment (organizational analysis), training design (task analysis), and trainee characteristics (person analysis) to be inputs to training. However, for team training, there are slight differences. A *team* task analysis needs to be conducted (Baker, Salas, & Prince, 1991; Salas & Cannon-Bowers, 2000) in order to uncover tasks that the *teams* perform. Thus, one must consider the interdependencies among trainees and their knowledge, skills, and abilities (KSAs). Below, we will briefly explore these three steps: (1) organization, (2) task, and (3) person needs analyses for team training.

First, the *organization analysis* refers to the degree to which the organization supports the training. This can be informative in identifying whether the organizational environment has characteristics that will likely facilitate or hinder the effectiveness of a team training program. Is the organization sending a message that this training matters? Will the organization reward those who participate in training and who display the trained teamwork processes on the job?

Second, the *team task analysis* entails the identification of specific tasks that are essential for teamwork. Team task analysis identifies tasks related to KSAs that can be developed through team training. In other words, a team task analysis reveals what interdependent tasks teams perform on the job, how critical they are to the job, and how difficult they are to perform and to learn (Baker, Salas, & Prince, 1991; Salas & Cannon-Bowers, 2001). One may conduct a team task analysis by first conducting a task analysis and then determining which tasks are team-oriented (that is, require coordination in order to be accomplished; Salas & Cannon-Bowers, 2000). The goal of this team task analysis is to uncover which teamwork processes are important for the organization and the specific jobs, thus, which teamwork processes and states should be included in team training.

Third, the *person analysis* looks at both who should be trained and what the characteristics of these trainees are. Which teams need to undergo team training? What kinds of teams are these? What are the characteristics of team members? Answers to these questions will guide the design of the team training. For example,

Towler and Dipboye (2001) found that a combination of organized lectures and inexpressive trainers actually led to *lower* problem-solving skills for trainees who were high in mastery goal orientation. Hence, knowing trainees' characteristics can help shape training delivery method. Furthermore, a person analysis may also identify actions that an organization can take prior to the team training to increase its effectiveness. Specifically, team aptitude should be measured (Cannon-Bowers, Salas, & Milham, 2000). Additionally, motivation is an important individual difference that should be captured in a person analysis. Intrinsic motivation implies individual differences. For example, a meta-analytic integration conducted by Colquitt, LePine, and Noe (2000) indicated that training motivation is influenced by individual characteristics such as cognitive ability, self-efficacy, age, and conscientiousness.

Thus, we warrant that the assessment of precursors of learning and motivation should not be taken for granted. In addition, providing remedial pre-training to enhance collective efficacy and to raise collective orientation before training is highly linked to the effectiveness of the training (Cannon-Bowers, Salas, & Milham, 2000).

The overall goal of the team needs analysis is to develop clear objectives, goals (both outcome-oriented and process-oriented; Smith-Jentsch, Cannon-Bowers, Tannenbaum, & Salas, 2008), and a team mission (Salas & Cannon-Bowers, 2000; Swezey & Salas, 1992). The development of these objectives, goals, and mission will assist throughout the team training process, including during both the design and the evaluation of a team training program. In order to reinforce these objectives, goals, and team missions, it is important to be as unambiguous and specific as possible. Utilizing advance organizers can assist with this effort (Cannon-Bowers, Salas, & Milham, 2000). Furthermore, it is worth repeating that the success of a team training needs analysis depends on the extent to which buy-in has previously been obtained from the SMEs who will provide information during the needs analysis.

Principle 4. Design a Measurement Plan

(cf. Guttentag & Struening, 1975; Holt, Boehm-Davis, & Beaubien, 2001; Rosen, Salas, Wilson, King, Salisbury, Augenstein, Robinson, & Birnbach, 2008; Swezey & Salas, 1992). Evaluation measures should be developed before the training begins. These measures should align with the results of team needs analysis. This is consistent with the recommendations from the ADDIE model, which consists of steps involving generic analysis, design, development, implementation, and evaluation (see Allen, 2006, for an overview). This model has identified those core elements as common to a number of instructional processes, but more importantly, it places evaluation in the center of the model connecting to all other core elements. This highlights the importance of measurement within the training context.

Furthermore, some have emphasized that the implementation of measures needs to be "purposeful, planned, and systematic" (Russ-Eft & Preskill, 2005, p. 72). In order to achieve such standardization, we recommend searching for the most reliable and valid measurement tools. As Rosen and colleagues (2008) point out, the number one "best practice" for team performance measurement is to ground measurement tools in theory. Beyond the psychometric properties of the measures, the results of measurement should be explicit and allow management to understand trainees' performance, which in turn can be used as a meaningful way to provide diagnostic feedback.

In addition to selecting and developing measures before the training, trainees should be evaluated prior to the team training. This has two main purposes: (a) to assess trainees' individual differences and (b) to collect their baseline measure of potential teamwork competencies. By assessing trainees' individual differences, one can determine potential issues with collective efficacy, trainees' goal orientation, and perceived organizational support (see Principles 1 and 2). As previously mentioned, an intervention to raise these crucial predictors of effective team training can increase the likelihood of positive outcomes (Cannon-Bowers, Salas, & Milham, 2000). Thus, it is beneficial to know whether such an intervention should be conducted. Furthermore, baseline measures are essential tools that allow for the comparison between teamwork competencies prior to training and after training. Measuring this change is extremely important in order to assess training effectiveness. Another way that training effectiveness can be assessed is by comparing the knowledge, skills, and abilities (KSAs) of those who attended the training versus those who did not attend. Either way, choosing a measurement plan is an issue that must be addressed prior to inception of the training program. However, we must reiterate that evaluation is an ongoing process; therefore, we will discuss its role after training as well.

Table 14.1 provides a checklist of the aforementioned steps that should be taken before the inception of a team training program.

During Team Training

The work does not stop once the team training program has begun. In this section, we discuss best practices for the use of team-based content, delivery methods (that is, information, demonstration, and practice), strategy, and development activities. The science behind the principles presented within this section is grounded in the extant theories of learning (behaviorism, constructivism, cognitivism, etc.) and motivation (drive theory, arousal theory, incentive theory, etc.), as well as their derivatives.

Principle 5. Include Appropriate Team-Based Content

(cf. Salas, Burke, & Cannon-Bowers, 2002; Salas, Shuffler, Thayer, Bedwell, & Lazzara, 2012). The main objective of a team training program is enhancing teamwork ("behavioral, cognitive, and attitude skills needed to communicate, interact, and coordinate tasks effectively with other team members"; Salas, Burke, & Cannon-Bowers, 2002, p. 240). Thus, while it is important that trainees be proficient at the task, attempting to teach teamwork before teaching taskwork (that is, the skills needed to complete the task; Salas, Burke, & Cannon-Bowers, 2002) is not advisable. Instead, training on taskwork should precede the team training. In other words, participants in a team training program should be proficient at the work task *before* engaging in the team training component (Salas, Burke, & Cannon-Bowers, 2002; Salas & Cannon-Bowers, 2000). This can ensure the best bang for an organization's buck when attempting to improve employee teamwork skills. Furthermore, task proficiency becomes even more important during the practice stage of team training, wherein the scenarios gradually increase in complexity.

Table 14.1. Checklist for Team Training—Before

Step	*Considerations*	*Outcome*
I. Team Training Design		
□ Prepare climate for learning	Is the climate for learning continuous and constant rather than sporadic? Do trainees understand the purpose of the training? Do all members of the organization see the alignment between the benefits of the team training and the organization's mission?	The team training is valued and understood by trainees, supervisors, and stakeholders.
□ Involve trainees in the decision to participate	Do trainees have voice? Is team training framed as an opportunity instead of a mandatory assignment or punishment? Are trainees intrinsically motivated to participate in the training? Are teams and trainees given input into the training?	Trainees feel involved in the decision to participate and thus more engaged in training.
□ Organizational support for learning	Are trainees extrinsically motivated to participate in the team training? Are objectives, goals, and mission stated in a clear, accurate, and specific manner? Does the organization have incentives and a reward system in place to support learning?	Trainees will perceive the importance of learning to the organization.

Table 14.1. Continued

Step	*Considerations*	*Outcome*
I. Team Training Design		
□ Obtain buy-in	Are the stakeholders convinced about the benefits of the training? Do supervisors show their support toward the team training? Do job incumbents want to attend the team training? Are there preparatory information and pre-practice debriefings available to employees?	Trainees learn more and value the team training.
□ Create conditions for teamwork	Is the team training designed around cognitive processes of the team when on the job? Is the organizational climate going beyond learning and targeting the desired team behaviors? Are stakeholders and supervisors becoming familiar with team training goals?	The team training is designed to maximize transfer.
□ Create relevance	Is the team training realistic? Does the training environment prompt the team processes that are used on the job? Do the scenarios require teams to engage in tasks and processes similar to those on the job?	Team training is designed with psychological fidelity and transfer appropriate processing.
□ Pilot-test to ensure focus on teamwork	Are all trainees proficient at all tasks? Have materials been piloted? Is the team training designed? Are supervisors included in the developmental process?	This ensures that the team training program achieves its objective, focusing on teamwork.

Continued

Table 14.1. Continued

Step	*Considerations*	*Outcome*
I. Team Training Design		
□ Conduct a team needs analysis	Are all three analyses (organizational, team task, person) conducted thoroughly?	The basis for design, implementation, and evaluation of the team training emerges.
□ Organizational analysis	Does the organization have policies in place that may support the team training (a rewards system that targets the team, encouragement of use of trained behaviors, etc.)? Does the organization have barriers that may impede team training effectiveness (for example, team training not valued by supervisors)?	Barriers to the team training and/or transfer of training are revealed. Policies and procedures that may support the team training and transfer are understood.
□ Team task analysis	What is the purpose and goal of each team? How do teams achieve their goals? Which tasks are done by one team member, and which tasks require interdependence?	The tasks that teams perform on the job are clarified, including which tasks are interdependent, how important each task is, and how difficult each task is.

Table 14.1. Continued

Step	*Considerations*	*Outcome*
I. Team Training Design		
□ Person analysis	What teams (formal and informal) are considered part of the organization? Who is on each team? Are all team members proficient on the tasks? What are the strengths, weaknesses, and individual needs of each team member?	Who is on the team and their strengths and weaknesses are revealed.
□ Design a measurement plan	Are evaluation tools grounded in theory? Are evaluation tools meaningful?	Evaluation tools are in place and ready to be utilized during and after team training.
□ Link measures to needs analysis results	Were measurement tools designed after results of team training needs analysis? Are measures valid and reliable?	Meaningful measures are designed and aligned with training goals.
□ Measure at multiple times	Is there a way to compare trainees' knowledge, skills, and attitudes before and after the training? Are there measures assessing trainees' characteristics (for example, goal orientation and collective orientation) that can hinder training benefits?	Baseline evaluations are conducted, and low scores in key constructs may be properly remediated before team training.

As previously stated, Salas, Shuffler, Thayer, Bedwell, and Lazzara (2012) have proposed six team competencies: cooperation, conflict, coordination, communication, coaching, and cognition. Each of these competencies may have a place in a team training program. Below, we briefly review each of them.

Cooperation involves the "attitudes, beliefs, and feelings of the team that drive behavioral action" (Salas, Shuffler, Thayer, Bedwell, & Lazzara, 2012, p. 8). Some of the specific attitudes that fall under the umbrella of cooperation, and that can be included in a team training program, are: collective efficacy (the team's belief that it can be effective; Katz-Navon & Erez, 2005; Zaccaro, Blair, Peterson, Zazanis, & Maddux, 1995), mutual trust (a shared belief that all team members will perform their roles and protect the team; Bandow, 2001; Salas, Sims, & Burke, 2005), and psychological safety (a shared feeling that it is safe to take risks; Edmondson, 1999).

Conflict, defined as the discrepancies or incompatibilities among members of a group (Jehn & Bendersky, 2003), includes both task conflict (disagreements about tasks that the team performs; Jehn, 1995) and relationship conflict (interpersonal disagreements among members of the team; Jehn, 1995). Some conflict management strategies can be taught during team training, including preemptive conflict management (preventing or managing conflict before it occurs) and reactive conflict management (working through conflict once it has occurred; Marks, Mathieu, & Zaccaro, 2001).

Coordination involves utilizing the behavioral processes necessary to transform team resources into outcomes (Sims & Salas, 2007). Coordination can be implicit, wherein team members have a shared understanding of each member's role and of the task, thus allowing them to anticipate the needs of other team members (Rico, Sánchez-Manzanares, Gil, & Gibson, 2008). In addition, coordination may be explicit, wherein team members overtly plan and communicate. Both implicit and explicit coordination can be addressed in team training. Implicit coordination may be increased by facilitating the development of a shared understanding of the task and of team member roles and responsibilities. Furthermore, team adaptation and coordination training (Entin & Serfaty,

1999) is a team training strategy that teaches trainees to use all available resources in order to improve coordination.

Communication has been defined as "the exchange of information between a sender and a receiver" (Salas, Wilson, Murphy, King, & Salisbury, 2008, p. 335). According to these authors, communication is most effective when it is open, accurate, and concise. Additionally, they say that communication is more likely to be utilized in team environments that are perceived to be psychologically safe. Team training can enhance communication by teaching trainees about the use of information exchange protocols, wherein communication is structured in order to facilitate effective use and recall. Furthermore, effective communication should be closed-loop; in other words, team members should confirm that a message was received, and should check that it is accurate (Baker, Salas, King, Battles, & Barach, 2005).

Coaching, also known as leadership, involves establishing goals and setting a direction to accomplish these goals (Fleishman, Mumford, Zaccaro, Levin, Korotokin, & Hein, 1991). Coaching behaviors do not necessarily have to be displayed by a formal team leader; rather, they may be exhibited by anyone on the team, or even people external to the team. Coaching increases team performance by enhancing use of effective processes and states (Zaccaro, Rittman, & Marks, 2001).

Finally, *cognition* is a shared understanding among team members (Klimoski & Mohammed, 1994). It is beneficial for team members to share knowledge on the roles of each team member, the environment, and the task. When teams possess this shared understanding, they are better able to coordinate and communicate (Cannon-Bowers & Salas, 1998), as well as solve problems (Salas, Rosen, Burke, & Goodwin, 2008). Team training strategies such as cross-training, wherein team members learn the roles and tasks of their fellow team members, are a way in which cognition can be increased in teams (Cannon-Bowers, Salas, Blickensderfer, & Bowers, 1998).

Which of these competencies to focus on should be decided by referring back to the results of the team needs analysis? In other words, which competencies matter most for the team(s) that will be trained? Of these, which have room for improvement?

The answers to these questions will guide the team training strategy that is used. Furthermore, they should guide the design of the scenarios in simulation-based training, wherein the scenario should be designed so that a critical event occurs that allows the competency in question to be displayed.

Principle 6. Incorporate the Appropriate Instructional Strategy (cf. Arthur, Bennett, Edens, & Bell, 2003; Littrell & Salas, 2005; Salas & Cannon-Bowers, 1997, 2000, 2001; Salas & Priest, 2005; Sims, Salas, & Burke, 2005). A comprehensive team training program provides teams with four principal components: information, demonstration, practice, and feedback (Salas & Cannon-Bowers, 1997, 2000). In this section we will describe the three methods of training delivery (information, demonstration, and practice), while deferring our discussion on feedback for a later section.

Information. Information-based methods refer to the conventional practice of providing trainees with material that they are to passively learn. Common types of information-based methods include slide presentations, training packets, advanced organizers, and lectures. While this type of content delivery method is not the pièce de résistance of team training, it does serve to provide learners with a baseline of declarative knowledge and a road map of forthcoming events. Advanced organizers, for instance, can assist trainees in developing accurate individual and team mental models by guiding learning. Moreover, additional information presented during training can help develop mental models of both taskwork and teamwork behaviors. The primary advantages of information-based methods for organizations are their ease of delivery, ease of application, relative low costs, and effectiveness when combined with other methods of delivery. Weaver, Rosen, Salas, Baum, and King (2010) note that, when used in isolation (without other methods of content delivery), information-based training methods have nominal impact on team training effectiveness. Thus, information-based training methods are best employed in conjunction with more active methods of content delivery.

Demonstration. Beyond the provision of information, demonstration-based methods have been used to augment team training effectiveness. Demonstration-based methods are grounded in social learning theory (Bandura, 1977) and behavior modeling training (Sorcher & Goldstein, 1972), and have been shown to be effective training methods (Taylor, Russ-Eft, & Chan, 2005). As the name implies, a demonstration is a method by which a trainee or a team of trainees is able to observe specific taskwork and teamwork behaviors presented by models (for example, instructors, actors, etc.). Specifically, trainees are exposed to a team of models engaging in an example of task performance. These demonstrations convey the identified team competencies (coordination, communication, cooperation, etc.) through the behaviors they exhibit. Demonstrations are an especially flexible means of training. For instance, demonstration-based training methods can be presented in person, through video, or through simulations. Moreover, they represent a cost-effective means of training that can easily be integrated with other training delivery methods. The content of the demonstrations is identified during the team needs analysis. Also, the delivery of demonstrations during team training should reflect both good and bad examples of team competencies. Specifically, a successful demonstration should portray how to, and how not to, exercise teamwork behaviors.

Practice. Team training programs that fail to afford trainees the opportunity to practice competencies are seriously lacking. Practice-based methods have by and large become the sine qua non of comprehensive team training programs. Intuitively, when teams are given the opportunity to practice targeted competencies, learning should be enhanced. Although the age-old adage "practice makes perfect" may not be unconditionally correct, empirical evidence clearly illustrates its benefits for team training outcomes (Salas, DiazGranados, Klein, Burke, Stagl, Goodwin, & Halpin, 2008). However, as previously alluded to, practice by itself is inadequate. For instance, practicing incorrect behaviors or practicing without direction can be unproductive or, worse, counterproductive. Thus, practice-based methods employed within team training programs should be guided. As Salas and colleagues (2002) describe, guided practice fosters team training by ensuring that teams practice the relevant team competencies identified by the researcher and/or the organization. This enables the most efficient use of practice time and thus saves organizations time, money, and resources.

Two widely used practice-based training methods of considerable interest for organizations are role play and simulation. Practice activities such as these afford learners the opportunity to practice learned behaviors in a safe and secure learning environment (Salas, Wilson, Priest, & Guthrie, 2006), which can benefit both trainees and instructors alike. Role-play activities entail teams taking on specific roles determined by an instructor or script and adapting their behaviors in order to accommodate these roles. In simulations, teams practice learned and/or observed behaviors in settings or situations designed to simulate real-world task environments. In each of these approaches, teams observe, process, and perform target behaviors in a controlled environment, enhancing the likelihood that these behaviors will transfer to work settings.

While an ideal team training program would include all of these methods, we recognize that this is not always possible given an organization's logistics and resources. There are specific benefits to each approach and, therefore, we advise keeping in mind the ultimate goal of the team training program when deciding which method(s) to use. An information-based approach (such as lectures) can provide a good foundation for learning the basics of teamwork, while demonstration- and practice-based (such as simulation) approaches can help teams better understand and learn how to use the skills, which may increase the likelihood that trainees will actually use the skills on the job. To help organizations choose which method(s) is(are) right for them, we have broken down each method by its importance, resource-intensiveness, benefits, and drawbacks in Table 14.2. It is important to note that, for each method of training, materials will need to be created, purchased, or adapted. There are many free (for example, TeamSTEPPS®) or commercially available team training materials; however, one must adapt these materials in accordance with the team needs analysis conducted (see Principle 3). If appropriate material does not exist, it should be created.

In addition to instructional methods, there are also many different strategies that can be employed when conducting team training. Here we briefly describe three commonly used strategies: team coordination training, cross-training, and guided team

Table 14.2. Pros and Cons of Delivery Methods of Team Training

Method	*Types*	*Effectiveness*	*Resources Required*	*Benefits*	*Drawbacks*
Information	—	Should always be used	Some/ More	Provides baseline knowledge and a mental model; ease of delivery; low cost; effective; ease of application	Best employed in conjunction with other methods
	Lectures	Effective	Some	Simple to create; not resource-intensive	Can be ineffective if speaker is inexpressive
	Slide presentations	Effective	Some	Facilitates immediate learning	Can be perceived as uninteresting
	Handouts (workbooks, advanced organizers, packets)	Effective	More	Facilitates development of a shared mental model	Can be slightly resource-intensive
Demonstration	—	More effective	More	Flexible; cost-effective	Best employed with information- and practice-based methods

Continued

Table 14.2. Continued

Method	*Types*	*Effectiveness*	*Resources Required*	*Benefits*	*Drawbacks*
	Multimedia (like video)	More effective	More	Can foster a shared mental model; easy to use if material already exists	Can be resource-intensive if creation of multimedia is required
	In person (live skit, presentation of behavior)	More effective	More	Can foster a shared mental model; may be less resource-intensive versus multimedia	Less consistency (versus multimedia)
Practice	—	Most effective	More/ Most	Enhances transfer of training. Especially useful for infrequent and/or dangerous tasks	If not guided, can lead to unproductive or counterproductive outcomes
	Role play	Most effective	More	Cost-effective	Can be difficult to implement with a large number of trainees; requires training of "actors"
	High-fidelity simulation	Most effective	Most	Realistic	Expensive

self-correction. These strategies are described in order to facilitate the reader's understanding of team training and should not be seen as a complete list of all team training strategies. (For a more comprehensive list of team training strategies, see Salas & Priest, 2005; Salas, Weaver, Rosen, & Gregory, 2012; Sims, Salas, & Burke, 2005.) Furthermore, these are not one-size-fits-all approaches. That is to say, one should not choose a team training strategy and attempt to adapt it to an organization. Rather, the team needs analysis should guide the strategy. In other words, the objectives, goals, and team mission uncovered earlier should drive the team training strategy that is to be chosen. The results of the person, team task, and organizational analyses will help to tailor the team training strategy to the unique strengths, weaknesses, and needs of the organization. With these caveats in mind, we move on to describing a few of the many team training strategies.

Team coordination training (Entin & Serfaty, 1999; Salas & Cannon-Bowers, 1997), also known as team coordination and adaptation training, is based on the idea that team members have a shared mental model (SMM), that is, shared knowledge. This SMM allows team members to anticipate each other's needs and actions in order to increase performance by allowing for more effective communication. Furthermore, the training teaches team members to adjust their coordination strategies. This team strategy has commonly been employed in the aviation industry, where it is a component of crew resource management (CRM) training. Meta-analytic evidence for the effectiveness of team coordination training is promising (see Salas, DiazGranados, Klein, Burke, Stagl, Goodwin, & Halpin, 2008).

Cross-training (Cannon-Bowers, Salas, Blickensderfer, & Bowers, 1998; Volpe, Cannon-Bowers, Salas, & Spector, 1996), which is also based on SMM theory, entails training the team members on each other's roles. This strategy may help mitigate the decrement in team performance when one or more team members turn over. It can also facilitate communication and coordination amongst the team. Empirical evidence for cross-training has been mixed (see Salas, Nichols, & Driskell, 2007; Salas et al., 2008).

Guided team self-correction training (Smith-Jentsch, Cannon-Bowers, Tannenbaum, & Salas, 2008) involves teams briefing and debriefing around a training or performance event. During these briefings and debriefings, team members discuss both processes and outcomes of the event in order to increase team processes and team performance. Self-correction training has enjoyed decent meta-analytic effect sizes (see Salas, Nichols, & Driskell, 2007).

Here we have briefly described three team training strategies in order to help illustrate the concept of team training to the reader. However, it is worth repeating that there are many other strategies that are described elsewhere and, thus, this is not a comprehensive list.

Principle 7. Support Team Development Activities

(cf. Smith-Jentsch, Cannon-Bowers, Tannenbaum, & Salas, 2008). An important step in promoting the acquisition of teamwork KSAs and transfer of training is the provision of feedback. Feedback is a vital component during demonstration- and practice-based methods of training delivery, wherein feedback promotes a better understanding of what individuals and teams are doing well and where there is room for improvement. Additionally, feedback can be provided as part of team debriefings (also known as after-action reviews [AAR]), whether formal (such as in "team dimensional training"; see Smith-Jentsch, Zeisig, Acton, & McPherson, 1998) or informal. The following section will describe the principles of feedback provision, as well as provide an explanation of feedback activities.

First and foremost, feedback must be accurate. Inaccurate feedback can reinforce undesired behaviors, prevent teams from forming accurate mental models, and subsequently stymie knowledge and skill acquisition. Second, feedback should be delivered in a timely manner (preferably after task performance). Third, feedback should focus on team processes (what individuals and teams did during the practice) instead of outcomes (Smith-Jentsch, Zeisig, Acton, & McPherson, 1998). Fourth, it is important that feedback be appropriate. It should be clear, concise, and constructive (task-focused instead of person-focused). In other words, a positive environment should be fostered. Finally, both constructive positive and negative feedback should be provided.

In addition to meeting the aforementioned criteria, two types of feedback should be present in a team training program. Within each of these types of feedback, two levels should be addressed: individual and team. Individual feedback refers to the provision of feedback that reflects an individual's taskwork and teamwork behaviors. Feedback at the team level refers to feedback that centers on team processes and performance. Both instructor and intra-team feedback should be present. Given that the instructor has ample knowledge of the training content, he or she should provide guidance and feedback that helps develop declarative, procedural, and strategic knowledge acquisition. Practice activities, for instance, enable the provision of direct feedback regarding individual and team performance, which allows team members to gain information about their behaviors and how, if necessary, to modify them (Murthy, Challagalla, Vincent, & Shervani, 2008). Additionally, training programs with automated instruction (virtual environments, serious games, computer-based simulations) must also implement direct feedback regarding task performance. Beyond feedback given by the instructor, it is also important that teams engage in intra-team with feedback, that is, team members providing each other with feedback throughout the training program. For example, during practice scenarios intra-team feedback can help individuals, as well as teams, learn the most effective means to complete a task. This also helps individuals and teams develop accurate mental models (Smith-Jentsch, Salas, & Brannick, 2001) that can aid in the transfer of training.

In addition, post-performance feedback exercises are equally important. Team debriefings can be carried out by a training instructor or by the teams themselves. In short, the objective of debriefing sessions is to constructively diagnose both positive and negative team performance, with the ultimate goal being to improve future performance. For example, if a team identifies a deficiency in team performance, they would then diagnose underlying causes, develop lessons learned, and cultivate a strategy for improving performance (Beaubien & Baker, 2004). Moreover, these post-performance feedback sessions should focus on teamwork over taskwork behaviors.

Debriefings can also occur on the job after an event. This is especially useful for action teams such as teams in the health care industry. For example, a surgical team might conduct a debriefing at the end of a surgery, discussing issues such as communication, distribution of workload, and any errors that may have occurred or that were avoided. While not a substitute for the inclusion of debriefings in a team training program, these routine debriefings may provide informal, on-the-job training that can enhance future team performance.

Team debriefings are frequently employed as methods for team building and have been empirically demonstrated to enhance teamwork mental models, teamwork processes, and team performance outcomes (Smith-Jentsch, Cannon-Bowers, Tannenbaum, & Salas, 2008). In a meta-analytic integration of 111 effect sizes from forty-six independent samples in thirty-one studies on individual and team debriefings, Tannenbaum and Cerasoli (2013) found a significant positive effect between debriefing and performance ($d = .67$). This resulted in roughly a 25 percent increase in performance over a control condition. Findings were comparable when examining individual and team debriefings in isolation, resulting in effect sizes of $d = .71$ (or 26 percent) and $d = .66$ (or 25 percent), respectively. The authors concluded that to improve team performance, team debriefings should be conducted with teams, adopting a team focus during the sessions, and to measure the performance at the team level. However, as Smith-Jentsch, Cannon-Bowers, Tannenbaum, and Salas (2008) note, merely providing teams the opportunity to debrief does not guarantee success. Specifically, they argue that team debriefings need to be structured and guided in order to improve the likelihood of their effectiveness. The empirical data supporting team debriefings is clear: they work. (See Table 14.3 for a checklist of considerations during team training.)

After Team Training

Once the team training program has been completed, there is still more that should be done. In fact, the principles in this section are perhaps the most important part of a team training's effectiveness, because what happens after the training can make or break a training program. In other words, if the organizational climate does not continue to support the team training, then the skills learned in training will not transfer back to the job. We also discuss sustainment of skills learned during team training.

Table 14.3. Checklist for Team Training—During

Step	*Considerations*	*Outcome*
II. Team Training Implementation		
Include appropriate team-based content	Were team competencies to be included in team training chosen by considering results of the team needs analysis?	Training focuses on team competencies that are important to the team and that have room for improvement.
Incorporate the appropriate instructional strategy	Are instructors trained on how to present materials? Are instructional materials being used? Is the learning environment congruent with training needs analysis? Was the strategy chosen by considering results of the team needs analysis? Does the chosen strategy get at the team competency(ies) of interest?	Selected and developed methods of instructional delivery are executed. Training utilizes a strategy that makes sense for the team and for the team competencies that are to be trained.
Information	Is baseline knowledge provided in materials? Is informational material coherent? How are materials expected to be used throughout training? Does information provide trainee(s) with specific expectations?	Trainees are provided with useful informational materials.

Continued

Table 14.3. Continued

Step	*Considerations*	*Outcome*
II. Team Training Implementation		
Demonstration	Are relevant KSAs demonstrated? How many persons does demonstration require? Are there enough? Are examples of "right" and "wrong" strategies or behaviors demonstrated?	Instructor (or instructional system) presents demonstrations of identified KSAs to trainees.
Practice	Is practice *guided*? Does practice require alternate resources? Is practice individual or at a team level? Does practice follow scheduled procedures?	Trainees practice the KSAs taught during training.
Support team development activities	Is feedback accurate? Is feedback timely? Does feedback focus on processes (instead of outcomes)? Is feedback appropriate (task-focused versus person-focused, clear, constructive)? Is both positive and negative feedback given? Is both individual and team feedback given? Is both instructor and intra-team feedback given?	Teams learn what they did correctly and what can be improved upon. Teams learn to debrief themselves, both during training and on the job.

Furthermore, we discuss how to evaluate team training in order to assess whether training was effective or not. We recommend the use of multi-level evaluations (reactions, learning, behavior, and results) and consider the implications of each level below.

Principle 8. Evaluate the Team Training

(cf. Alvarez, Salas, & Garofano, 2004; Brannick, Salas, & Prince, 1997; Kirkpatrick, 1959; Kraiger, Ford, & Salas, 1993; Salas, Burke, & Cannon-Bowers, 2002; Salas, Fowlkes, Stout, Milanovich, & Prince, 1999). The evaluation of training is crucial for an effective team training program, and this is an ongoing effort. As we mentioned in our discussion of Principle 4, crucial steps such as detailing the measurement plan should happen before the training even begins. Furthermore, assessment of teamwork behaviors during the training can provide information about team processes and learning. However, the bulk of the evaluation occurs after training. A well-rounded way to evaluate team training program is by using Kirkpatrick's (1959) levels of training evaluation, which include reactions, learning, behavior, and results. This framework has been used for more than four decades to investigate training effectiveness. The earlier levels (reactions and learning) are precursors of later levels. However, it should be emphasized that positive outcomes in one level do not necessarily yield positive outcomes on subsequent levels. We will now briefly discuss these levels.

Reactions refer to trainees' attitudes toward the training. This includes not only how enjoyable they judged the training to be, but also how useful they perceived the training to be. It has been shown that reactions can influence the subsequent levels, but it is not sufficient to guarantee results. Reactions are often assessed immediately after the training. *Learning*, on the other hand, refers to the maximum performance (what trainees "can do" as opposed to what they "will do"; Klehe & Anderson, 2007) change during the training. In other words, it is simply what the trainees have learned, a measure of declarative knowledge. It is important to consider learning as knowledge-, skill-, and attitudinal-based (Kraiger, Ford, & Salas, 1993). Learning should be assessed during the training, but with measures of pre- and post-training in order to capture the changes. It is important to point out that sometimes there may be a delayed effect on learning (Keith & Frese, 2008). Even if learning shows only slight improvements, behavioral transfer may still occur.

Behavioral transfer refers to trainees' typical performance (the "will do"; Klehe & Anderson, 2007) on the job. The main difference between learning and behavior evaluation is that the former could be assessed in an artificial environment (training context), whereas the latter focuses on what the trainee chooses to demonstrate on the job (communication, leadership skills, etc.). *Results* refer to the measures of effectiveness of a training program. Results take into consideration external variables that go beyond trainees' control and will later feed into utility (such as the cost-benefit ratio). The assessment of results occurs after all the previous levels are assessed.

The caveat that differentiates team training evaluation from individual training evaluations is the focus on teamwork, as opposed to the sole emphasis on specific trainees' taskwork skills. Here are three crucial recommendations that will allow for a more thorough evaluation of team training effectiveness: (a) develop tools that assess team processes and outcomes, (b) measure individual as well as team-level data, and (c) appraise the performance at multiple points of time (Salas, Burgess, & Cannon-Bowers, 1995; Salas & Cannon-Bowers, 2000; Salas & Cannon-Bowers, 2001; Sims, Salas, & Burke, 2005). Furthermore, the evaluation should go beyond the trainees' performance by evaluating leadership, overall team performance, and training content (Swezey & Salas, 1992). In addition to providing insight as to the effectiveness of the team training, a careful evaluation can help to determine whether the team training program is out-of-date or otherwise has to be modified before continued use in the organization. Consequently, evaluation is a crucial step before, during, and after team training.

Besides ascertaining the extent to which the team training was effective, there are other reasons why evaluation of team training is important. For example, an evaluation provides feedback about the training and trainees' performance, including whether certain trainees and/or teams require remediation training. The general goal of remediation is twofold. First, it is intended to "fill in" whatever deficiencies in knowledge are present for individuals and teams after training. Second, remediation training is meant to bolster existing knowledge gained from the team training program. However, diagnosing the need for remediation training is impractical without proper performance appraisals. In other words, data are required to identify who needs training and what type of training they need. Remediation, if necessary, should be conducted directly following a team training program. Additionally, the focus on remediation should be on teamwork behaviors and can be provided to both individuals and teams, depending on performance diagnostics and organizational resources.

Principle 9. Promote Transfer of Team Training

(cf. Baldwin & Ford, 1988; Burke & Hutchins, 2007; Grossman & Salas, 2011; Holton & Baldwin, 2000; Tracey, Tannenbaum, & Kavanagh, 1995). Transfer of team training is a major concern that can hinder positive outcomes to the organization, even when trainees have learned the content of team training. Some consider transfer to have both generalization (bringing trained skills back to the job) and maintenance (long-term retention and use of trained skills) components (Baldwin & Ford, 1988; Blume, Ford, Baldwin, & Huang, 2010). Considering the importance of both components, we will target generalization first and focus on maintenance and sustainability of team training outcomes later, as we believe these two components are crucial and deserve their own principles.

First, trainees must have learned from the training before they are able to transfer to the work environment. In other words, learning is a precursor of transfer. The focus now goes beyond the motivation to learn and targets the motivation trainees have to transfer the learned skills. There are certain strategies that can help to bridge the gap between learning and transfer. For instance, the use of transfer appropriate processing during the training and self-regulation can lead to adaptive transfer (Bell & Kozlowski, 2008; also see Principle 2). According to these authors, simulating cognitive processes that will be required of the trainees on the job during training and teaching them to manage their own activities are important training design elements. Consequently, when trainees engage in the right processes and activities, the same opportunities should be available on the job to increase the likelihood of transfer. However, learning will not necessarily lead to transfer.

Second, supervisors play a key role in ensuring that the behaviors learned in team training are actually used on the job (Colquitt, LePine, & Noe, 2000; Smith-Jentsch, Campbell, Milanovich, & Reynolds, 2001). Therefore, if the team training is to be taken seriously by trainees and the behaviors are to be transferred back to the job, buy-in from supervisors is also necessary. One way in which one can increase the likelihood of transfer is by including supervisors in the training, because supportive leadership is related to supportive organizational climate (Taylor, Russ-Eft, & Chan, 2005). In a similar vein, one study found that supportive leaders were empirically shown to increase the application of learned skills in the team task under typical performance (Smith-Jentsch, Campbell, Milanovich, & Reynolds, 2001). However, once again, the supervisor buy-in is not the only focus and does not guarantee that desired behaviors will be applied on the job.

Based on Baldwin and Ford's model, Grossman and Salas (2011) have identified cognitive ability, self-efficacy, motivation, perceived utility of training, behavioral modeling, error management, realistic training environments, transfer climate, support, opportunity to perform, and follow-up as the most important precursors of a successful transfer of training. Consequently, we would like to highlight the importance of the last few precursors, those that are set specifically by the organization. There should be a reward system in place to reinforce the repetition of teamwork behaviors (also see Principle 1). For instance, Cannon-Bowers, Salas, and Milham (2000) specifically call for team-level rewards and team-level goals to increase the focus on teamwork, which in turn shows that the organization values those behaviors. Even though these steps all help promote transfer, the climate for teamwork should have been set prior to the inception of the team training program (see Principle 1). Furthermore, we warrant attention to an organizational climate (environmental favorability) that encourages transfer in order to assure an effective team training program as a whole. Therefore, a climate for teamwork should start by creating the conditions for teamwork (see Principle 2) and shift to the promotion of transfer of team training in order to increase the likelihood of transfer.

Principle 10. Sustain the Conditions to Foster Teamwork (cf. Ford, Quiñones, Sego, & Sorra, 1992; Rosen et al., 2008). In this section, we discuss the aforementioned maintenance phase of training transfer. Specifically, we discuss how training results can continue to be beneficial via two means: (a) organizational support and (b) refresher training.

Organizational support has been found to have a moderate effect on trainee reactions (Sitzmann, Brown, Casper, Ely, & Zimmerman, 2008). Furthermore, organizations that show support for team training may facilitate maintenance and sustainment of the team skills learned in training. Organizations can show this support and, thus, continuously encourage use of the trained skills by providing: cues to remind trainees of what they learned in the team training program, opportunities to use the trained skill incentives for using trained skills, and feedback on the trained skills (Ford, Quiñones, Sego, & Sorra, 1992; Quiñones, 1995; Rouiller & Goldstein, 1993; Tracey, Tannenbaum, & Kavanagh, 1995). While these recommendations are similar to some previous principles, the distinction here is that these policies and procedures should remain in place *continuously and over time.*

An illustration of how the organization can show support over time and how employees can see that the organization values teamwork is team developmental activities (see Principle 7 for details). By implementing systematic debriefing meetings, employees will be reminded of teamwork competencies and desired knowledge, skills, and attitudes that were once learned during the team training program. These debriefings could occur after specific events or at predetermined timeframes. The advantage of this technique is its low cost, coupled with its positive impact. In other words, as Tannenbaum and Golhaber-Fiebert (2013) highlighted, debriefings are simple and powerful tools, but underutilized.

In addition, trainees should not be expected to elicit trained behaviors just following the training, but at all times. Thus, policies should be in place to convey the message that those behaviors are expected, perhaps by using a reward system or providing the aforementioned cues. If resources permit, refresher training should be employed to sustain the teamwork behaviors learned during training. Refresher training is a distal type of training reinforcement strategy provided to trainees at predetermined intervals (such as every six months or yearly) after a comprehensive team training program. The aim of refresher training is twofold. First, it is meant as a retraining tool that can enhance team competencies, especially when degradation in acquired team KSAs occurs. Second, it is meant to highlight the importance of teamwork in organizations and further promote the use of teamwork in the organizational environment. Refresher training can be delivered via a comprehensive team training program or by way of a watered-down—yet still scientifically robust—version of the comprehensive program. It is important to note, however, that determining the delivery of refresher training can be accomplished in two ways. First, as previously mentioned, refresher training can be delivered at a predetermined time identified by the organization. Second, an organization can undergo performance appraisals after training to decide whether a refresher course is necessary. Refresher training should follow the science of team training, as outlined throughout this chapter.

Table 14.4 provides a checklist of the steps that should be taken after a team training program has been implemented.

Conclusion

We have outlined the process and some team training strategies and have touched on steps that should be taken before, during, and after any organizational team training program in order to maximize its effectiveness. We hope these principles will be used by the practitioner interested in developing a team training program. Because implementing such a program can be resource-intensive, care should be taken to ensure that these steps are followed throughout so as not to compromise the success of the program. While it may be tempting to gloss over some of these steps, we urge the reader to carefully consider that just one missed step can compromise an entire team training program. Therefore, it is well worth investing the resources to ensure a robust team training program.

Table 14.4. Checklist for Team Training—After

Step	*Considerations*	*Outcome*
III. Team Training Evaluation		
Perform a thorough evaluation of training	Were the evaluation measures aligned with results from team needs analysis? How effective was the training?	Training's influence on trainees' reactions, learning, behavior, and results is uncovered.
Assess reactions	Did trainees enjoy the training? Did trainees see the training as a useful intervention?	The extent to which trainees perceived the training to be enjoyable and useful is revealed.
Assess learning	Did trainees learn new skills? Did trainees improve their knowledge? Did trainees have any attitudinal change?	The extent to which trainees' learning has improved cognitively, attitudinally, and behaviorally is revealed.
Assess behavior	Were trainees able to transfer what was learned from the training to the work environment? Was there a supportive climate that allowed targeted behaviors to be repeated?	The extent to which trained behaviors have transferred to the job is revealed.
Assess results	Did the organization improve after training employees? What types of organizational level consequences emerged from the training?	Team training's impact on organizational outcomes—such as return on investment—is revealed.
Promote transfer of team training	Did trainees learn the material during training? Is the organization and leadership encouraging the use of trained behaviors?	Trained behaviors are utilized on the job.

Continued

Table 14.4. Continued

Step	*Considerations*	*Outcome*
III. Team Training Evaluation		
Ensure that learning has occurred	Was there a positive change in teamwork knowledge, skills, and attitudes when comparing results from before and after training?	Trainees have the foundation necessary to transfer.
Ensure there is supportive leadership	Are leaders supportive of training? Did supervisors participate in the training with the subordinates? Are leaders and/or supervisors expecting trainees to elicit trained behaviors?	There is a shared perception among employees regarding importance of training to the organization.
Sustain the conditions that foster teamwork	Does the organization show support by providing cues, opportunities, incentives, and feedback? Is refresher training provided on a regular basis?	The content of the team training is reinforced and sustained over time.
Reward teamwork	Are the team behaviors being framed as something the organization values? Are there opportunities for trainees to display trained behaviors? Is the organization continually rewarding team behavior?	Trainees continue to perceive added value and expectations to elicit teamwork behaviors.
Assess long-term transfer	Is there a predetermined time to measure whether trainees are still demonstrating desired teamwork behaviors?	Whether or not refresher training is required is revealed.

References and Further Reading

Allen, W.C. (2006). Overview and evolution of the ADDIE training system. *Advances in Developing Human Resources, 8*(4), 430–441.

Alvarez, K., Salas, E., & Garofano, C.M. (2004). An integrated model of training evaluation and effectiveness. *Human Resource Development Review, 3*(4), 385–416.

Arthur, W.R., Bennett, W.R., Edens, P.S., & Bell, S.T. (2003). Effectiveness of training in organizations: A meta-analysis of design and evaluation features. *Journal of Applied Psychology, 88*(2), 234–245.

Arthur, W., Edwards, B.D., Bell, S.T., Villado, A.J., & Bennett, W. (2005). Team task analysis: Identifying tasks and jobs that are team based. *Human Factors, 47,* 654–669.

Baker, D.P., Salas, E., King, H.B., Battles, J., & Barach, P. (2005). The role of teamwork in the professional education of physicians: Current status and assessment recommendations. *Joint Commission Journal on Quality and Patient Safety, 31,* 185–202.

Baker, D.P., Salas, E., & Prince, C. (1991, April). Team task importance: Implications for conducting team task analysis. Paper presented at the sixth annual meeting of the Society for Industrial and Organizational Psychology. St. Louis, Missouri.

Baldwin, T.T., & Ford, J.K. (1988). Transfer of training: A review and directions for future research. *Personnel Psychology, 41*(1), 63–105.

Bandow, D. (2001). Time to create sound teamwork. *Journal for Quality and Participation, 24,* 41–47.

Bandura, A. (1977). Self-efficacy: Toward a unifying theory of behavioral change. *Psychological Review, 84,* 191–215.

Beal, D.J., Cohen, R.R., Burke, M.J., & McLendon, C.L. (2003). Cohesion and performance in groups: A meta-analytic clarification of construct relations. *Journal of Applied Psychology, 88*(6), 989–1004.

Beard, R.L., Salas, E., & Prince, C. (1995). Enhancing transfer of training: Using role-play to foster teamwork in the cockpit. *The International Journal of Aviation Psychology, 5,* 131–143.

Beaubien, J.M., & Baker, D.P. (2004). The use of simulation for training teamwork skills in healthcare: How low can you go? *Quality & Safety in Heath Care, 13,* 151–156.

Bell, B.S., & Kozlowski, S.W.J. (2008). Active learning: Effects of core training design elements on self-regulatory processes, learning, and adaptability. *Journal of Applied Psychology, 93,* 296–316.

Blickensderfer, E., Cannon-Bowers, J.A., Salas, E., & Baker, D.P. (2000). Analyzing knowledge requirements in team tasks. In S. Chipman, V. Shalin, & J.M. Schraagen (Eds.), *Cognitive task analysis* (pp. 431–447). Mahwah, NJ: LEA.

Blume, B.D., Ford, J.K., Baldwin, T.T., & Huang, J.L. (2010). Transfer of training: A meta-analytic review. *Journal of Management, 36,* 1065–1105.

Bowers, C.A., Baker, D.P., & Salas, E. (1994). Measuring the importance of teamwork: The reliability and validity of job/task analysis indices for team-training design. *Military Psychology, 6,* 205–214.

Bowers, C.A., & Jentsch, F. (2001). Use of commercial, off-the-shelf, simulations for team research. In C. Bowers & E. Salas (Eds.), *Advances in human performance and cognitive engineering research* (pp. 293–317). Mahwah, NJ: Lawrence Erlbaum Associates.

Brannick, M., Salas, E., & Prince, C. (Eds.). (1997). *Team performance assessment and measurement: Theory, methods, and applications.* Mahwah, NJ: Lawrence Erlbaum Associates.

Burke, L.A., & Hutchins, H.M. (2007). Training transfer: An integrative literature review. *Human Resource Development Review, 6*(3), 263–296.

Cannon-Bowers, J.A., Rhodenizer, L., Salas, E., & Bowers, C.A. (1998). A framework for understanding pre-practice conditions and their impact on learning. *Personnel Psychology, 51,* 291–320.

Cannon-Bowers, J.A., & Salas, E. (1998). Team performance and training in complex environments: Recent findings from applied research. *Current Directions in Psychological Science, 7,* 83–87.

Cannon-Bowers, J.A., Salas, E., Blickensderfer, E., & Bowers, C.A. (1998). The impact of cross-training and workload on team functioning: A replication and extension of initial findings. *Human Factors, 40,* 92–101.

Cannon-Bowers, J., Salas, E., & Milham, L. (2000). The transfer of team training: Propositions and guidelines. *Advances in Developing Human Resources: Managing and Changing Learning Transfer Systems in Organizations, 8,* 63–74.

Colquitt, J.A., LePine, J.A., & Noe, R.A. (2000). Toward an integrative theory of training motivation: A meta-analytic path analysis of 20 years of research. *Journal of Applied Psychology, 85,* 678–707.

Denison, D.R. (1990). *Corporate culture and organizational effectiveness.* Oxford, England: John Wiley & Sons.

Edmondson, A. (1999). Psychological safety and learning behavior in work teams. *Administrative Science Quarterly, 44*(2), 350–383.

Ellis, A.P.J. (2006). System breakdown: The role of mental models and transactive memory in the relationship between acute stress and team performance. *Academy of Management Journal, 49,* 576–589.

Entin, E.E., & Serfaty, D. (1999). Adaptive team coordination. *Human Factors, 41,* 312–325.

Fleishman, E.A., Mumford, M.D., Zaccaro, S.J., Levin, K.Y., Korotokin, A.L, & Hein, M.B. (1991). Taxonomic efforts in the description of leader behavior: A synthesis and functional interpretation. *The Leadership Quarterly, 2*(4), 245–287.

Ford, J.K., Quiñones, M.A., Sego, D.J., & Sorra, J.S. (1992). Factors affecting the opportunity to perform trained tasks on the job. *Personnel Psychology, 45*(3), 511–527.

Goldstein, I.L. (1991). Training in work organizations. In M.D. Dunnette & L.M. Hough (Eds.), *Handbook of industrial and organizational psychology* (2nd ed., Vol. 2, pp. 507–620). Palo Alto, CA: Consulting Psychologists Press.

Grossman, R., & Salas, E. (2011). The transfer of training: What really matters. *International Journal of Training and Development, 15,* 103–120.

Gulley, S.M., Devine, D.J., & Whitney, D.J. (1995). A meta-analysis of cohesion and performance: Effects of level of analysis and task interdependence. *Small Group Research, 26,* 497–520.

Guttentag, M., & Struening, E.L. (1975). *Handbook of evaluation research* (Vol. 2). Thousand Oaks, CA: Sage.

Helmreich, R.L. (2000). On error management: Lessons from aviation. *British Medical Journal, 320,* 781–785.

Holt, R.W., Boehm-Davis, D.A., & Beaubien, J.M. (2001). Evaluating resource management training. In E. Salas, C. Bowers, & E. Edens (Eds.), *Improving teamwork in organizations: Applications of resource management training* (pp. 165–188). Mahwah, NJ: Lawrence Erlbaum Associates.

Holton, E.F., III, & Baldwin, T.T. (2000). Making transfer happen: An action perspective on learning transfer systems. In E.F. Holton, S.S. Naquin, & T.T. Baldwin (Eds.), *Managing and changing learning transfer systems: Advances in developing human resources, 8* (pp. 1–6). San Francisco: Berrett-Koehler.

Jehn, K.A. (1995). A multimethod examination of the benefits and detriments of intragroup conflict. *Administrative Science Quarterly, 40*(2), 256–282.

Jehn, K.A., & Bendersky, C. (2003). Intragroup conflict in organizations: A contingency perspective on the conflict outcome relationship. *Research in Organizational Behavior, 25,* 187–242.

Katz-Navon, T.Y., & Erez, M. (2005). When collective and self-efficacy affect team performance: The role of task interdependence. *Small Group Research, 36*(4), 437–465.

Keith, N., & Frese, M. (2008). Effectiveness of error management training: A meta-analysis. *Journal of Applied Psychology, 93,* 59–69.

Kirkpatrick, D. (1959). Techniques for evaluating training programs. *Journal of the American Society for Training and Development, 13*(11), 3–9.

Klehe, U., & Anderson, N.R. (2007). Working hard and working smart: Motivation and ability during typical and maximum performance. *Journal of Applied Psychology, 92,* 978–992.

Klimoski, R., & Mohammed, S. (1994). Shared mental model: Construct or metaphor? *Journal of Management, 20,* 403–437.

Kozlowski, S.W.J., & DeShon, R.P. (2004). A psychological fidelity approach to simulation-based training: Theory, research and principles. In S.G. Schiflett, L.R. Elliott, E. Salas, & M.D. Coovert (Eds.), *Scaled worlds: Development, validation and applications* (pp. 75–99). Burlington, VT: Ashgate.

Kraiger, K., Ford, J.K., & Salas, E. (1993). Application of cognitive, skill-based, and affective theories of learning outcomes to new methods of training evaluation. *Journal of Applied Psychology, 78*(2), 311–328.

Littrell, L.N., & Salas, E. (2005). A review of cross-cultural training: Best practices, guidelines, and research needs. *Human Resource Development Review, 4*(3), 305–334.

Locke, E.A., & Latham, G.P. (1990). *A theory of goal setting & task performance.* Englewood Cliffs, NJ: Prentice Hall.

Locke, E.A., & Latham, G.P. (2002). Building a practically useful theory of goal setting and task motivation: A 35-year odyssey. *American Psychology, 9,* 705–717.

Marks, M.A., Mathieu, J.E., & Zaccaro, S.J. (2001). A temporally based framework and taxonomy of team processes. *Academy of Management Review, 26,* 355–376.

Markus, H., & Zajonc, R.B. (1985). The cognitive perspective in social psychology. In G. Lindzey & E. Aronson (Eds.), *Handbook of social psychology* (3rd ed., pp. 137–230). New York: Random House.

Murthy, N.N., Challagalla, G.N., Vincent, L.H., & Shervani, T.A. (2008). The impact of simulation training on call center agent performance: A field-based investigation. *Management Science, 54,* 384–399.

Quiñones, M.A. (1995). Pretraining context effects: Training assignment as feedback. *Journal of Applied Psychology, 80*(2), 226–238.

Quiñones, M.A. (1997). Contextual influences: On training effectiveness. In M.A. Quiñones & A. Ehrenstein (Eds.), *Training for a rapidly changing workplace: Applications of psychological research* (pp. 177–199). Washington, DC: American Psychological Association.

Rafferty, L.A., Stanton, N.A., & Walker, G.H. (2010). The famous five factors in teamwork: A case study of fratricide. *Ergonomics, 53,* 1187–1204.

Rico, R., Sánchez-Manzanares, M., Gil, F., & Gibson, C. (2008). Team implicit coordination processes: A team knowledge-based approach. *The Academy of Management, 33*(1), 163–184.

Risser, D.T., Rice, M.M., Salisbury, M.L., Simon, R., Jay, G.D., & Berns, S.D. (1999). The potential for improved teamwork to reduce medical errors in the emergency department. *Annals of Emergency Medicine, 34,* 373–383.

Rosen, M.A., Salas, E., Wilson, K.A., King, H.B., Salisbury, M., Augenstein, J.S., Robinson, D.W., & Birnbach, D.J. (2008). Measuring team performance in simulation-based training: Adopting best practices for healthcare. *Simulation in Healthcare, 3,* 33–41.

Rouiller, J.Z., & Goldstein, I.L. (1993). The relationship between organizational transfer climate and positive transfer of training. *Human Resource Development Quarterly, 4*(4), 377–390.

Russ-Eft, D., & Preskill, H. (2005). In search of the holy grail: Return on investment evaluation in human resource development. *Advances in Developing Human Resources, 7*(1), 71–85.

Ryan, R.M., & Deci, E.L. (2000). Self-determination theory and the facilitation of intrinsic motivation, social development, and well-being. *American Psychologist, 55*(1), 68–78.

Salas, E., Burgess, K.A., & Cannon-Bowers, J.A. (1995). Training effectiveness techniques. In J. Weiner (Ed.), *Research techniques in human engineering* (pp. 439–471). Englewood Cliffs, NJ: Prentice Hall.

Salas, E., Burke, C.S., & Cannon-Bowers, J.A. (2002). What we know about designing and delivering team training: Tips and guidelines. In K. Kraiger (Ed.), *Creating, implementing, and managing effective training and development: State-of-the-art lessons for practice* (pp. 234–259). San Francisco: Jossey-Bass.

Salas, E., & Cannon-Bowers, J.A. (1997). Methods, tools, and strategies for team training. In M.A. Quiñones & A. Ehrenstein (Eds.), *Training for a rapidly changing workplace: Applications of psychological research* (pp. 249–279). Washington, DC: American Psychological Association.

Salas, E., & Cannon-Bowers, J.A. (2000). The anatomy of team training. In S. Tobias & J.D. Fletcher (Eds.), *Training and retraining* (pp. 312–338). New York: Macmillan.

Salas, E., & Cannon-Bowers, J.A. (2001). The science of training: A decade of progress. *Annual Review of Psychology, 52,* 471–499.

Salas, E., DiazGranados, D., Klein, C., Burke, C.S., Stagl, K.C., Goodwin, G.F., & Halpin, S.M. (2008). Does team training improve team performance? A meta-analysis. *Human Factors, 50*(6), 903–933.

Salas, E., Fowlkes, J.E., Stout, R.J., Milanovich, D.M., & Prince, C. (1999). Does CRM training improve teamwork skills in the cockpit? Two evaluation studies. *Human Factors, 41*(2), 326–343.

Salas, E., Nichols, D.R., & Driskell, J.E. (2007). Testing three team training strategies in intact teams: A meta-analysis. *Small Group Research, 38*, 471–488.

Salas, E., & Priest, H.A. (2005). Team training. In N. Stanton, A. Hedge, K. Brookhuis, E. Salas, & H. Hendrick (Eds.), *Handbook of human factors and ergonomics methods* (pp. 44.1–44.7). Boca Raton, FL: CRC Press.

Salas, E., Rosen, M.A., Burke, C.S., & Goodwin, G.F. (2008). The wisdom of collectives in organizations: An update of the teamwork competencies. In E. Salas, G.F. Goodwin, & C.S. Burke (Eds.), *Team effectiveness in complex organizations* (pp. 39–79). New York: Taylor & Francis.

Salas, E., Shuffler, M.L., Thayer, A.L., Bedwell, W.B., & Lazzara, E.H. (2012). Teamwork. Manuscript submitted for publication.

Salas, E., Sims, D.E., & Burke, C.S. (2005). Is there a "big five" in teamwork? *Small Group Research, 36*(5), 555–599.

Salas, E., Tannenbaum, S.I., Kraiger, K., & Smith-Jentsch, K.A. (2012). The science of training and development in organizations: What matters in practice. *Psychological Science in the Public Interest, 13*, 74–101.

Salas, E., Weaver, S.J., Rosen, M.A., & Gregory, M.E. (2012). Team training for patient safety. In P. Carayon (Ed.), *Handbook of human factors and ergonomics in health care and patient safety* (pp. 627–647). Boca Raton, FL: CRC Press.

Salas, E., Wilson, K.A., Murphy, C.E., King, H.B., & Salisbury, M. (2008). Communicating, coordinating, and cooperating when lives depend on it: Tips for teamwork. *Joint Commission Journal on Quality and Patient Safety, 34*, 333–341.

Salas, E., Wilson, K.A., Priest, H.A., & Guthrie, J. (2006). Design, delivery, and evaluation of training systems. In G. Salvendy (Ed.), *Handbook of human factors and ergonomics* (3rd ed.; pp. 472–512). Hoboken, NJ: John Wiley & Sons.

Schraagen, J.M., Chipman, S.F., & Shalin, V.J. (2000). *Cognitive task analysis.* Mahwah, NJ: LEA.

Sims, D.E., & Salas, E. (2007). When teams fail in organizations: What creates teamwork breakdowns? In J. Langan-Fox, C.L. Cooper, & R.J. Klimoski (Eds.), *Research companion to the dysfunctional workplace: Management challenges and symptoms* (pp. 302–318). Cheltenham, UK: Edward Elgar.

Sims, D.E., Salas, E., & Burke, C.S. (2005). Promoting effective team performance through training. In S.A. Wheelan (Ed.), *The handbook of group research and practice* (pp. 407–425). Thousand Oaks, CA: Sage.

Sitzmann, T., Brown, K.G., Casper, W.J., Ely, K., & Zimmerman, R.D. (2008). A review and meta-analysis of the nomological network of trainee reactions. *Journal of Applied Psychology, 93,* 280–295.

Smith-Jentsch, K.A., Campbell, G.E., Milanovich, D.M., & Reynolds, A.M. (2001). Measuring teamwork mental models to support training needs assessment, development, and evaluation: Two empirical studies. *Journal of Organizational Behavior, 22,* 179–194.

Smith-Jentsch, K.A., Cannon-Bowers, J.A., Tannenbaum, S.I., & Salas, E. (2008). Guided team self-correction: Impacts on team mental models, processes, and effectiveness. *Small Group Research, 39,* 303–327.

Smith-Jentsch, K.A., Salas, E., & Brannick, M.T. (2001). To transfer or not to transfer? Investigating the combined effects of trainee characteristics, team leader support, and team climate. *Journal of Applied Psychology, 86,* 279–292.

Smith-Jentsch, K.A., Zeisig, R.L., Acton, B., & McPherson, J.A. (1998). Team dimensional training: A strategy for guided team self-correction. In J.A. Cannon-Bowers & E. Salas (Eds.), *Making decisions under stress: Implications for individual and team training.* Washington, DC: American Psychological Association.

Sorcher, M., & Goldstein, A.P. (1972). A behavior modeling approach in training. *Personnel Administration, 35,* 35–41.

Swezey, R.W., & Salas, E. (1992). Guidelines for use in team-training development. In R.W. Swezey & E. Salas (Eds.), *Teams: Their training and performance* (pp. 219–245). Norwood, NJ: Ablex.

Tannenbaum, S.I., & Cerasoli, C.P. (2013). Do team and individual debriefs enhance performance? A meta-analysis. *Human Factors: The Journal of Human Factors and Ergonomic Society, 55,* 231–245.

Tannenbaum, S.I., & Goldhaber-Fiebert, S. (2013). Medical team debriefs: Simple, powerful, and underutilized. In E. Salas & K. Frush (Eds.), *Improving patient safety through teamwork and team training.* (pp. 249–256). New York: Oxford University Press.

Tannenbaum, S.I., Salas, E., & Cannon-Bowers, J.A. (1996). Promoting team effectiveness. In M.A. West (Ed.), *Handbook of work group psychology* (pp. 503–529). West Sussex, England: John Wiley & Sons.

Taylor, P.J., Russ-Eft, D.F., & Chan, D.W.L. (2005). A meta-analytic review of behavior modeling training. *Journal of Applied Psychology, 90,* 692–709.

Towler, A., & Dipboye, R.L. (2001). Effects of trainer expressiveness, organization, and trainee goal orientation on training outcomes. *Journal of Applied Psychology, 86,* 664–673.

Tracey, J., Tannenbaum, S.I., & Kavanagh, M.J. (1995). Applying trained skills on the job: The importance of the work environment. *Journal of Applied Psychology, 80*(2), 239–252.

Volpe, C.E., Cannon-Bowers, J.A., Salas, E., & Spector, P.E. (1996). The impact of cross-training on team functioning: An empirical investigation. *Human Factors, 38,* 87–100.

Weaver, S.J., Rosen, M.A., Salas, E., Baum, K.D., & King, H.B. (2010). Integrating the science of team training: Guidelines for continuing education. *The Journal of Continuing Education in the Health Professions, 30*(4), 208–220.

Zaccaro, S.J., Blair, V., Peterson, C., Zazanis, M., & Maddux, J.E. (Eds.). (1995). *Self-efficacy, adaptation, and adjustment: Theory, research, and application. The Plenum series in social/clinical psychology* (pp. 305–328). New York: Plenum Press.

Zaccaro, S., Rittman, A., & Marks, M. (2001). Team leadership. *The Leadership Quarterly, 12,* 451–483.

CHAPTER FIFTEEN

Conducting Team Debriefings That Work*

Lessons from Research and Practice

Scott I. Tannenbaum, Rebecca L. Beard, and Christopher P. Cerasoli
Group for Organizational Effectiveness, Inc.

Teams are an inherent part of organizational life. Companies use them extensively and individuals can expect to spend a significant part of their careers as members of various teams, often participating in multiple teams simultaneously (Tannenbaum, Mathieu, Salas, & Cohen, 2012). Given the increasingly ubiquitous presence of teams, we need to find scientifically tested, practical, cost-effective ways to improve team effectiveness, build teamwork skills and capabilities, and enhance the teaming experience. This chapter examines team debriefings, a simple, inexpensive technique that holds great promise for addressing these key team needs.

The chapter is organized around a series of fundamental questions about debriefings. Throughout, we draw upon relevant scientific findings as well as our experience working with teams to address these questions. First, we define debriefings, explaining why practitioners have good reason to consider their use. Second,

*This work was supported, in part, by funding from NASA (Grant # NNX-11AR22G). All opinions expressed herein are, however, strictly those of the authors and not those of NASA.

we consider when debriefing can be used and by whom. Third, we examine the effectiveness and outcomes of debriefings, exploring both whether and why they tend to be effective. Next, we introduce common pitfalls and obstacles to effective implementation of debriefings. Finally, we share lessons learned from our experience, offer some practical tips, and conclude with future directions for research and practice.

What Is a Debriefing and Why Should We Care?

We start by acknowledging that there is no such thing as the perfect team. Teams are comprised of humans with distinct personalities, experiences, limitations, quirks, and expertise. In addition, teams operate in complex organizations and often face shifting demands and requirements. Thus, to achieve or maintain excellence, even the best teams must continually learn and adapt in order to thrive.

Certainly, selecting team members properly is a good start. A team that is composed of the right mix of people is more apt to work well together. Yet historically, people are hired not for teamwork skills but for individual skills. In addition, there are many constraints that prohibit optimal team composition (cf., Mathieu, Tannenbaum, Donsbach, & Alliger, Chapter 16 in this book). Given these limitations, we cannot rely solely on effective team composition to ensure team effectiveness; some team development is needed.

Unfortunately, simply being on a team together does not mean team members will learn to work well together. Experience alone does not ensure team success (Kim, 1997; Littlepage, Robison, & Reddington, 1997) and organizations vary dramatically in the rate at which they learn from experience (Pisano, Bohmer, & Edmonson, 2001). A method is needed to accelerate team learning, helping teams apply what they learn from their past experiences when they face subsequent challenges.

Debriefing, sometimes referred to as an after-action review, is a technique that is specifically designed to promote learning from experience (Ellis & Davidi, 2005). During a debriefing, team members: (a) reflect upon a recent experience, (b) discuss what happened, (c) identify lessons learned and opportunities for improvement, and (d) plan for the future. They attempt to build a common understanding (of priorities, roles, goals, or how to handle certain situations) or a "shared mental model" (Mesmer-Magnus & DeChurch, 2009) and establish agreements to ensure future success. A debriefing includes both a backward glance at a prior performance episode and a forward look at how the team wants to work together in the future. Debriefings are often conducted in thirty minutes or less, with some as short as five minutes and others that last over an hour (for example, those completed after a lengthy simulated training experience).

The U.S. military has conducted debriefing sessions for more than forty years (Morrison & Meliza, 1999), and recently teams in other sectors have started conducting them more frequently as well. Compared with other team development interventions such as team building and team training, debriefings are typically less expensive, less time-consuming, and easier to deploy. Moreover, as we show later, research strongly indicates that they are an effective approach. As such, a fundamental premise of this chapter is that organizations would benefit from using well-conducted debriefings more regularly.

When Can Debriefings Be Conducted and Who Can Use Them?

When to Conduct Them

A debriefing can be conducted after any team experience, for example, at the conclusion of a work shift, meeting, or training exercise; at any point during a project; or after any team "action" or performance episode. All available team members typically participate in a debriefing, which can be led by the team leader, or by a facilitator, consultant, coach, or instructor. Below we describe six types of debriefings. This typology is not exhaustive, but instead describes six of the most prevalent or potentially valuable types of debriefings. The first four take place with intact teams and are graphically depicted in Figure 15.1. The last two involve participants who then return to or move on to other teams, and these are graphically depicted in Figure 15.2. Table 15.1 summarizes the six different types of debriefs, which are differentiated by their focus on work or training, whether lessons

Figure 15.1. Alternative Types of Debriefings—Application to Same Team

Debriefing Type 1: Debriefing a work experience

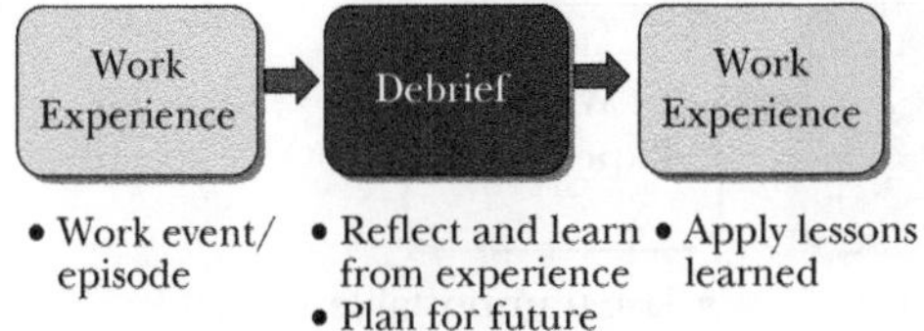

Debriefing Type 2: Ongoing debriefing of work experiences

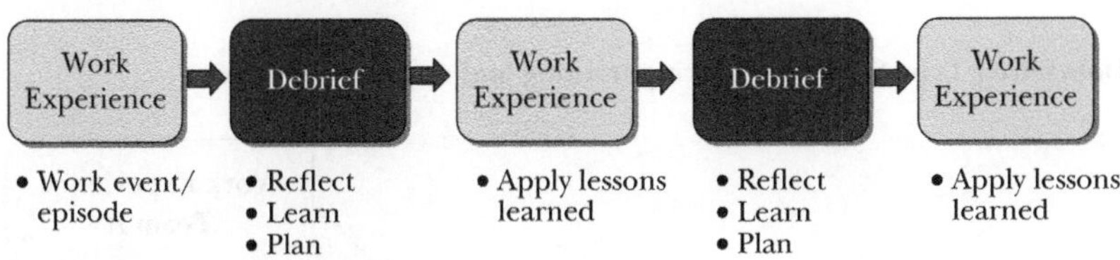

Debriefing Type 3: Debriefing a training experience

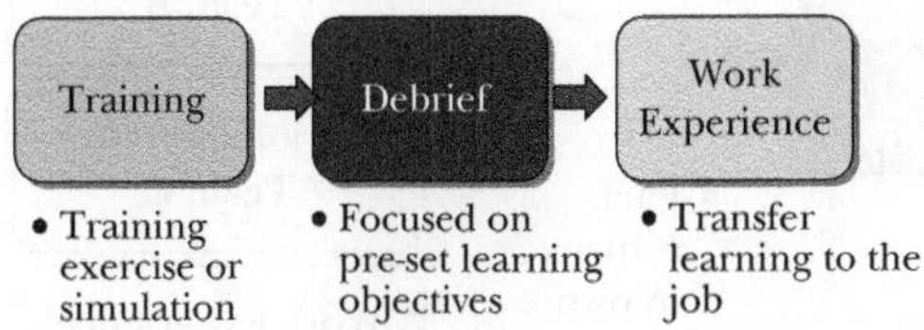

Debriefing Type 4: Debriefing a training experience with follow-up debriefing at work

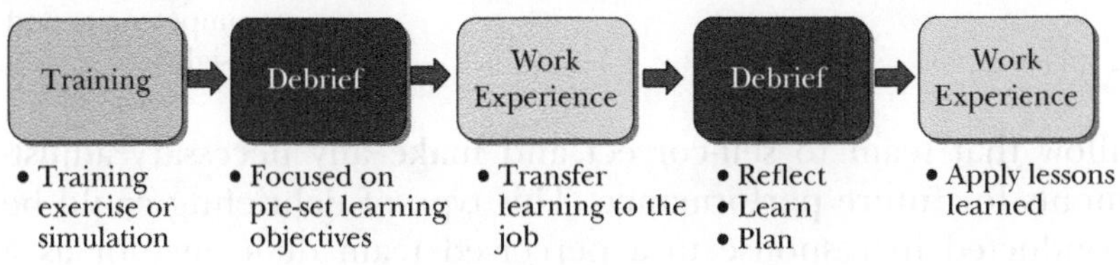

learned are applied to the same or different teams, and by their primary intent.

Debriefing Type 1

When conducted after a single on-the-job work experience with an intact team, a *one-time* work debriefing is typically intended to

Figure 15.2. Alternative Types of Debriefings—Application to Different Team

Debriefing Type 5. Debrief with one team and apply to another team

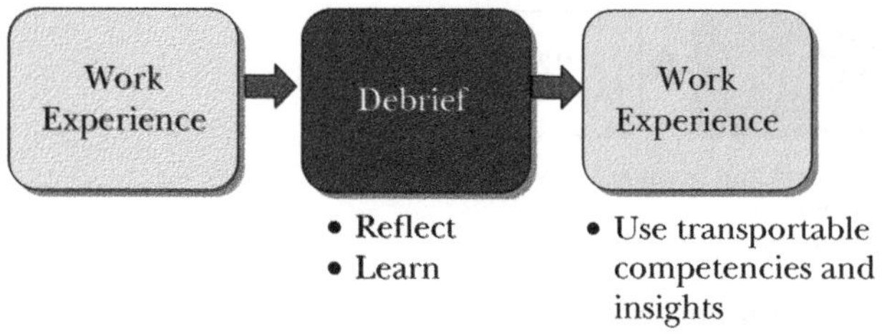

Debriefing Type 6. Debrief during training and apply to new teams

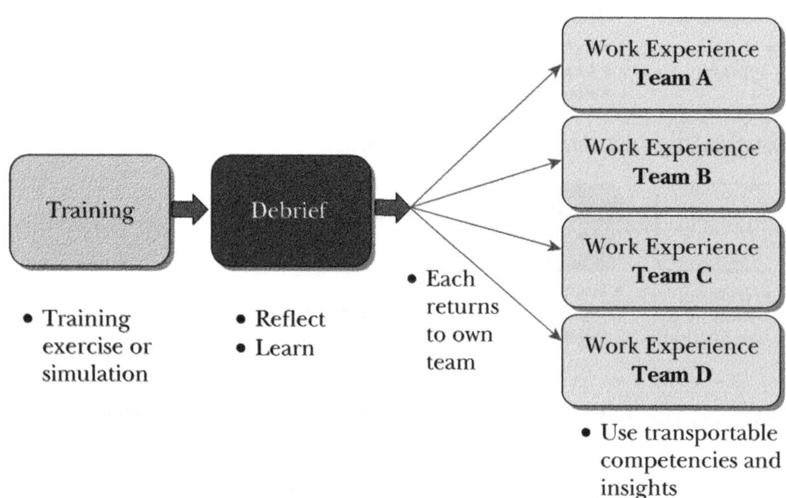

allow that team to self-correct and make any necessary adjustments for future performance. This type of debriefing could be conducted in response to a perceived team deficiency or as a follow-up to a meaningful work experience, one that provides a good learning opportunity. Debriefing Type 1 refers to a one-time or targeted debriefing of a particular work experience and is intended to allow the team to reflect on that experience, learn from it, and plan for immediate team self-corrections as needed. For example, after instituting a new procedure, a team might conduct a one-time debriefing to reflect on how well they are

Table 15.1. Six Types of Team Debriefings

Debriefing Type	*Focus*		*Apply Lessons to Same Team?*	*Intent*	*Example*
	Work Exp	*Training Exp*			
Intact Teams					
One-time debriefing of work experience	Yes	No	Yes	Allow team to self-correct	A service team debriefs one month after the introduction of a new service offering
Ongoing debriefing of work experiences	Yes	No	Yes	Enhance and maintain team effectiveness	A restaurant crew periodically debriefs at the end of its shift
Debriefing of training experience	No	Yes	Yes	Maximize learning from the training experience	A medical team debriefs after a simulated surgery
Debriefing of training experience with follow-up debriefing at work	Yes	Yes	Yes	Maximize transfer or application of trained skills to the job	A sales team debriefs after a training exercise and again after a sales presentation to a real prospect

Continued

Table 15.1. Continued

Debriefing Type	*Focus*		*Apply Lessons to Same Team?*	*Intent*	*Example*
	Work Exp	*Training Exp*			
Non-Intact Teams					
Debriefing of work experience applied to other teams	Yes	No	No	Enable individuals to apply lessons learned to future teams	A project team debriefs at the end of the project and team members each go on to other projects
Debriefing of training experience, participants from different teams	No	Yes	No	Build transportable competencies that individuals can use with their "home" teams	Debriefing a group of leaders after a training exercise so they can each apply a new team problem-solving approach with their own work team

using it and identify whether any adjustments are needed to enhance their use of the procedure.

Debriefing Type 2

Alternatively, a work team may choose to conduct *ongoing* on-the-job debriefings. In Debriefing Type 2, teams periodically debrief after work experiences or after a specified period of time has transpired as a way to ensure they stay on track and maintain strong performance. In such a case, debriefing becomes part of a repeatable work–debrief–work–debrief cycle. For example, a team might conduct a debriefing at the end of a work shift, try to apply lessons learned from the debriefing over the next several days, and then debrief again at the end of a shift the following week, repeating the cycle. Whether as a one-time event or as part of an ongoing cycle, the goal of most on-the-job debriefings with intact teams is to allow them to make the real-time adjustments that enhance their effectiveness as well as reinforce what they are doing well so they can sustain that effectiveness.

Debriefing Type 3

Debriefings can also be used in conjunction with team training. In Debriefing Type 3, debriefings are conducted after a team training activity or simulation (for example, after a simulated police SWAT team exercise). Debriefings conducted after a training experience tend to be more focused than those conducted after a work experience. Unlike a work experience, a training scenario can be carefully controlled to ensure specified challenges will arise, so a post-exercise debriefing discussion can focus on pre-established learning objectives to maximize the acquisition of specific insights during training.

Debriefing Type 4

Less frequently, training and work debriefings are combined (Debriefing Type 4). In such cases, a debriefing is conducted during training and then again as a planned follow-up on the job to reinforce and ensure that transfer of training occurs. For example, during a sales team training program, a team conducts a debriefing following a practice sales presentation, and then after returning to the job they would debrief after a real sales presentation. In both the training and on-the-job debriefings, a primary focus would be on the targeted skills and behaviors covered in the training.

Debriefing Type 5

In the debriefing types described above, the team that participated in the debriefing together went on to apply the lessons learned from their debriefing as an intact team. However, in some circumstances, participants will move on to or return to different teams. For example, in Debriefing Type 5, a team would debrief a work experience together but then the individual team members would move on to other team assignments (ideally carrying on the lessons learned). An example of this would be a team debriefing conducted at the conclusion of an IT implementation project, after which the team disbands and its members move on to other project teams. In such a case, the intent of the debriefing is to enable individuals to learn from the team's experience and then transport those lessons learned to future teams, in essence pollinating organizational learning.

Debriefing Type 6

Debriefing Type 6 occurs when a group of individuals debrief together during training but then return to (or are assigned to) their own teams after training. In other words, the training is not conducted with intact teams that will remain together after training. This can occur when leaders from various teams are brought together for leadership training and participate in team training exercises that conclude with a debriefing. In such a case, the goal is to help ensure that the individuals who participate in the debriefing build transportable team competencies and insights that they can then use with their own teams.

Although we specified six distinct types of team debriefings, it is possible to envision hybrids as well, for example by combining Debriefing Types 2 and 5. In such a case, an intact team would debrief and immediately apply what they learned to their team (Type 2), and then, as team members transition to other team assignments, each would attempt to transport what he or she learned from those prior team debriefings to a new team (Type 5).

Who Participates

It is quite likely that you have participated in a debriefing, at least an informal one. If you have ever been part of a group that discussed how a project was progressing, reviewed a recent customer meeting with a few of your colleagues, or "replayed" a key moment from a game with members of your sports team, you have participated in an informal debriefing of sorts. But many teams also conduct more systematic debriefings.

Teams that operate in high-risk environments often debrief. As noted earlier, the armed services have conducted structured "after-action reviews" for more than forty years. In fact, good military leaders and trainers are expected to conduct debriefings to ensure learning occurs. Debriefing has also been an integral component of aviation and aerospace training efforts (Rogers, 2007). Similarly, in the medical world, where teamwork breakdowns are among the most common cause of patient safety problems (Institute of Medicine, 1999), teams are increasingly conducting Type 3 and Type 6 debriefings during training (Fanning & Gaba, 2007), although there is the potential for greater use of Types 1 and 2 after real patient cases or work shifts (Tannenbaum & Goldhaber-Fiebert, 2013). Thus, it should not be surprising that teams that operate in high-risk environments rely on being able to debrief. A mistake by a medical, firefighting, police, aerospace, power plant, drilling, or military team can have serious, even lethal consequences. Therefore, they must use the most effective ways available to build high-reliability teams.

In recent years, the use of debriefings has broadened because their utility is not limited to high-risk teams. In fact, any team with members who must interact and rely on each other to accomplish their "mission" and who share performance episodes can debrief. In particular, situations in which a specific performance episode can be examined, such as a team assignment, sales call, safety effort, project launch, patient case, service experience, product development, or even a team meeting, would be prime candidates for real-world debriefing. There is also the opportunity to apply team debriefing techniques as a periodic team learning and collective reflexivity tool that goes beyond the review of a single, discrete performance episode (Felipe Gomez & Ballard, 2011).

There are many examples of teams and organizations that have employed debriefings, including high-risk teams such as firefighters (Allen, Baran, & Scott, 2010) and emergency room nurses (Cronin & Andrews, 2009), as well as a variety of more common management, sales, retail, and project teams (Kinni,

2003). Teams that are geographically dispersed, cross-cultural, and/or cross-functional are also strong candidates for debriefing, as those teams often face additional challenges to maintaining a common perspective and aligned view for operating as a team. Examples of other "lower-risk" teams that have debriefing include:

- Management teams
- Project teams (for example, technology, quality enhancement, change management teams)
- Retail teams (for example, restaurant, bank, hotel)
- Sales teams
- Sports teams
- Student teams
- Production/manufacturing teams
- Customer service teams
- R&D teams (for example, new product teams)
- Consultant teams

Do Debriefings Work and, If So, Why?

As debriefings become more prevalent and organizations consider adopting them or expanding their use, practitioners ask *do* they work and researchers want to know *why* and *how* they work. Answers to the first question can help us decide *whether* to conduct them, while answers to the research questions can provide insights about *how* to conduct them effectively.

The Efficacy of Debriefings

To determine their effectiveness, we recently conducted a meta-analysis that examined both team and individual debriefings (Tannenbaum & Cerasoli, 2013). Based on results from more than thirty studies, the meta-analysis revealed that debriefing improves performance by 20 to 25 percent on average. Across a number of different types of configurations and situations, their efficacy appears quite robust. Similar results were seen for team and individual debriefings, across simulated and real settings, and for medical and non-medical participants. Pragmatically, a 20 percent plus improvement is quite encouraging for an inexpensive intervention that requires little time to conduct (the average debriefing time reported in the meta-analysis was about eighteen minutes). Thus, not only are they typically quite effective, but they appear to be efficient as well.

Desired Improvements from Debriefing

Overall, there is a strong evidentiary base in support of debriefing. To understand why it works, we first consider what someone might want a well-executed team debriefing to accomplish. Table 15.2 contains a set of "desired improvements/changes" from debriefing. Some of these improvements are cognitive in nature, while others are behavioral. Because different teams have distinct needs, each debriefing may uncover different opportunities for improvement. Regardless, improvements can occur at three levels: individual team members, the team leader, and the team as a whole. Note that when we refer to the team leader in this context, we are talking about the head of the team, not necessarily the person who is facilitating.

Individual cognitive, attitudinal, and behavioral improvements. At the individual team member level, an effective debriefing could

Table 15.2. Desired Improvements/Outcomes from Debriefings

Level	*Desired Improvements/Outcomes*	
	Cognitive	*Behaviors*
Individual team members	Knowledge/awareness (self, team, situational) Attitudes (teammates, teaming, trust, collective efficacy) Motivation	Teamwork behaviors (e.g., backup behaviors, communications) Taskwork behaviors
Team leader	All individual level cognitions Insights about team (e.g., needs)	Teamwork and taskwork behaviors Leadership behaviors Removal of obstacles
Team	Shared mental models/ common understanding (e.g., cue-strategy) Role clarity Team climate	Teamwork behaviors (e.g., implicit coordination) Performance

yield several cognitive improvements. For example, after discussing a recent performance episode, a team member might develop greater self-awareness ("I didn't realize that I was handling that too slowly"), greater knowledge of team members ("Joe knows more about that piece of equipment than anyone else on the team"), or improved situational awareness ("I didn't realize we were that far behind schedule"). A debriefing can also help fill information gaps and increase a team member's knowledge about a variety of factors, including, for example, the team leader's priorities.

A debriefing may also have a positive effect on a team member's attitude or motivation. By reflecting on a recent performance episode, comparing observations, and discussing concerns with teammates, a team member may change his or her attitude about another person on the team. By identifying and eliminating obstacles to performance, team members can develop a greater sense of collective efficacy or confidence that the team will be able to perform effectively in the future (Jex & Gudanowksi, 2006). Similarly, team members who are on a team that successfully self-corrects and works together better should view the team experience more positively and could approach future teaming assignments with greater enthusiasm than individuals who participated in a dysfunctional team (Tesluk & Mathieu, 1999).

Debriefing could help individuals identify where specific behavioral changes are needed. They are often intended to enhance teamwork behaviors such as providing effective backup or clearer communications, so a team member can become a better team player by learning which teamwork behaviors he personally needs to change. A debriefing could also provide a team member with task-related information that could help her do her job better, resulting in improved taskwork behaviors.

Team leader cognitive, attitudinal, and behavioral improvements. Team leaders who participate in debriefings could benefit at the individual level in similar ways. In addition, they may acquire insights about the team that can help them be more effective leaders (for example, clarifying the type of situations in which the team will need greater guidance and direction from them). An interesting additional benefit that we sometimes see is that debriefings help reveal tangible obstacles to team performance, such as lack of resources, that the team leader can attempt to rectify.

Team-level cognitive, attitudinal, and behavioral improvements. At the team level, lingering misunderstandings or disagreements can lead to distrust and team conflict (De Dreu & Weingart, 2003). Uncovering and correcting misunderstandings during a debriefing can improve a team's interpersonal processes, and ultimately help create a better team climate. Debriefings are also ideally suited for helping teams develop shared mental models (SMMs) about the team, the task, and the work environment. Teams that have a shared mental model possess a common understanding, for example, about what to do when a particular problem arises (that is, cue-strategy associations) or who is responsible for filling in when a particular team member is unavailable (cf., Mohammed & Dumville, 2001). A shared mental model extends beyond any one team member's knowledge and reflects a team's collective understanding or shared awareness. Teams that possess shared mental models can better anticipate needs and exhibit greater implicit coordination and improved performance (DeChurch & Mesmer-Magnus, 2010).

Ultimately, at the team level, we want teams that debrief to learn and make adjustments that result in better performance. That could mean making better decisions, being more efficient or more productive, reducing errors, or enhancing quality. The mix of cognitive and behavioral improvements noted above can enhance team readiness and subsequently team performance.

Other desirable improvements. Thus far, our discussion about potential benefits has focused extensively on debriefing stable, intact teams (Types 1 through 4). However, team membership is often quite dynamic (Hirst, 2009). Team members often leave or are reassigned and new people may join a team in progress. In such cases, debriefing can be a helpful tool for assimilating new team members because team members share information, clarify expectations, and align their mental models while debriefing.

Moreover, participating in a team debriefing may help individual participants develop some transportable team competencies (Cannon-Bowers, Tannenbaum, Salas, & Volpe, 1995). For instance, if a debriefing heightens a person's awareness of what is needed to succeed in team settings, she may be able to apply some of that awareness when she participates on other teams (see Debriefing Types 5 and 6). Moreover, as noted before, if debriefing resolves a few teamwork problems, a team member should find his time with that team to be more enjoyable and, as a result, he may take a more positive attitude about "teaming" in future teams. While research is needed to confirm this, we would speculate that debriefing should build some transportable competencies and generate positive affect that individuals can transport with them to future team assignments.

Relevant Theory

In the prior section, we specified a set of desired outcomes from debriefing and suggested that it produces consistent improvements in team performance because it promotes learning from experience and team self-correction. But what is the theoretical rationale to explain why debriefing enhances team learning and self-correction? As noted earlier, experience alone does not ensure team learning. We posit that six key functions take place during debriefings that increase the likelihood of learning and team self-correction. These functions include: reflection, self-explanation, data verification, and feedback (Ellis & Davidi, 2005), as well as information sharing and goal setting/action planning. In practice, these six functions are not discrete, distinct phenomena. Some may overlap and occur simultaneously, but collectively they are what enable debriefing to yield desired results. For simplicity's sake, these six functions can be collapsed into three categories: (a) reflection and self-explanation, (b) data verification, feedback, and information sharing, and (c) goal setting and action planning. We explore these below.

Reflection and self-explanation. According to Barmeyer (2004), "in the heart of all learning lies the way in which experience is processed, in particular, the critical reflection of the experience" (p. 580). Marsick and Volpe (1999) noted that reflection involves looking back on what occurred, measuring the results against desired outcomes, and assessing the consequences. It is difficult to learn from experience if the appropriate connections are not made between action and outcome.

Reflection can involve asking key questions (Brooks, 1999) to help sort through and make sense of one's experiences or perhaps reframe a problem. During this process, individuals may challenge some implicit assumptions and revise existing mental models or form new ones. Reflection can also guide subsequent actions ("Let's try that next time and see how it works"), and it provides the opportunity to learn from mistakes and reduce the likelihood of similar mistakes recurring (Cannon & Edmondson, 2001; West 1996).

While reflection is the process of determining *what* happened, knowledge of the past is not sufficient for change. In order to begin to propose steps to improve team function, individuals must understand *why* certain events transpired. Self-explanation involves a conscious attempt to make sense of one's experiences, which can involve self-critiquing or recognizing why something is working or not working (Schon, 1987). It is this actively driven, deeper understanding that enables individuals, leaders, and teams to suggest potential improvements.

Data verification, feedback, and information sharing. A debriefing session is a specified time for reflection and a place where data can be verified against personal beliefs, enabling individuals as well as the team collectively to "recalibrate" as needed (Ellis & Kruglanski, 1992). For knowledge-type tasks that have an objectively correct solution, teams that possess multiple perspectives and can verify data against one another tend to make better decisions (Stasser & Titus, 1985). For judgment-type tasks, decision-making quality and performance may improve if individuals can share with one another their rationale for arriving at a particular decision (Kerr, MacCoun, & Kramer, 1996). In any case, when individuals can verify either their observed data or personal judgment processes with others, they can calibrate and align their mental models of the situation, which leads to superior performance (Mesmer-Magnus & DeChurch, 2009).

Debriefing also provides a relatively safe forum for feedback that can emanate from team members, a team leader, a trainer or facilitator, or even from the task itself. Feedback provides individuals with information needed to learn appropriate lessons from their experiences and can influence future actions (Balzer, Doherty, & O'Connor, 1989).

Debriefing is also designed to promote information sharing among team members. During a well-conducted debriefing, questions are posed of the team that elicit information from team members that can provide insights into a wide array of performance-relevant variables such as work processes, individual preferences, situational cues, etc. Such structured information sharing can also open up avenues for ongoing, informal sharing as information deficiencies are uncovered and information-sharing habits are formed. There is strong meta-analytic evidence that information sharing is an important enabler of team performance (Mesmer-Magnus & DeChurch, 2009).

Goal setting/action planning. Finally, well-conducted debriefing yields forward-looking agreements in the form of goals or action plans. Teams that establish agreements about how they want to work together tend to be more focused and motivated to implement self-corrections. Individuals who vocalize commitments in front of others are more likely to take action on them (Hollenbeck, Williams, & Klein, 1989). As noted earlier, while feedback is critical for learning, alone it does not always improve performance (Kluger & DeNisi, 1996). When feedback is combined with goal setting, it is far more likely to enhance performance (Bandura & Cervone, 1983; Locke, Frederick, Lee, & Bobko, 1984). Thus, the establishment of agreements, plans, and goals is a key element for debriefing effectiveness.

Theoretical summary. Debriefing provides a bounded opportunity for teams to reflect upon and interpret their experiences, share and verify information and feedback, and agree on plans and goals. As shown in Figure 15.3, we propose that the debriefing functions described above enables team members to enhance their knowledge and awareness, and more clearly specify their intent to operate as a team. In turn, this prepares them to demonstrate improved individual behaviors and teamwork processes, which subsequently yields better team performance. As teamwork processes have been increasingly shown to be a key mediator of team performance (Marks, Mathieu, & Zaccaro, 2001), there is good reason to believe that team performance gains attributable to debriefing operate through improved team processes. Figure 15.3 also suggests that because being on a team with good teamwork is an emotionally positive experience (as is being on a team

Figure 15.3. How Debriefing Works: Proposed Framework

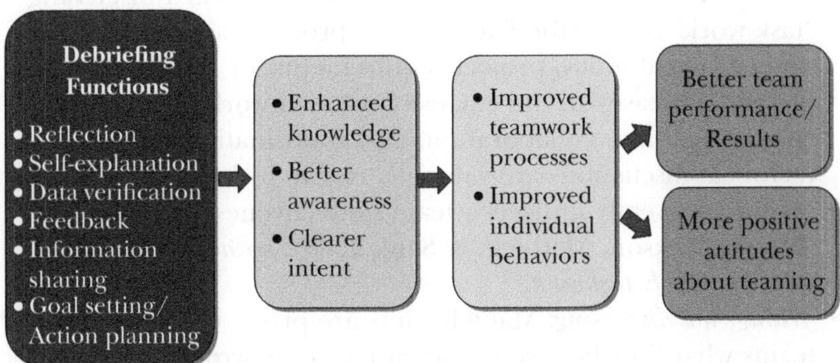

that is able to adjust and self-correct), individuals develop a more positive attitude toward working in teams in the future.

In summary, there is strong evidence that debriefing works, and there is a logical theoretical foundation for why. Moreover, because debriefing participants discuss actual work experiences (or at least work-relevant simulated experiences), team members are apt to perceive the debriefing process as highly salient, which has been found to heighten motivation to learn (Ames, 1992).

What Are the Most Common Debriefing Pitfalls and Obstacles to Success?

We have observed many debriefings, and some are clearly more effective than others. The way a debriefing is structured and conducted can affect how well it works. Few team leaders (and for that matter, few instructors and facilitators) have been trained on how to debrief. And unfortunately, simply having good interpersonal skills and technical competence does not ensure that a person will lead an effective debriefing (Dismukes, Jobe, & McDonnell, 2000). Based on our observations as well as the extant literature, we have identified six common pitfalls that can interfere with debriefing effectiveness.

- *Too much focus on "task work."* Leaders are often promoted into their positions because of their task expertise, so many are less comfortable discussing teamwork issues than taskwork issues. Thus, most leaders tend to gravitate toward discussing "task work" issues (the features of a product, a weapon system's capabilities, project requirements, or the nature of a patient's disease) to the exclusion of teamwork issues such as communication, collaboration, and coordination. While technical discussions are valuable, research shows that teamwork greatly impacts a team's effectiveness (LePine, Piccolo, Jackson, Mathieu, & Saul, 2008), so *address teamwork and not simply taskwork.*

- *Telling, not discussing.* Many leaders are prone to "telling" their teams what they believe the team has done wrong (or right) and fail to involve the team members in diagnosing team effectiveness and establishing team action plans. Since a leader can't see and know everything, if team members do not have the chance to reflect upon their experiences and offer their perspectives, subsequent actions may be based on incomplete information. Moreover, personal and active engagement produces a different type of insight than do more passive experiences (Kozlowski & Salas, 2010; Ron, Lipshitz, & Popper, 2002). When a leader simply tells his or her team what to do, team members are less likely to "own" and commit to those action plans. Instructors and other content experts who lead debriefings can also be prone to "talking at" teams, in part because that may fit their perceptions of their role and their greater expertise. However, learners who are guided toward self-discovery have better developmental experiences than those who are simply given answers (Eddy, D'Abate, Tannenbaum, Givens-Skeaton, & Robinson, 2006), so *actively involve team members and ensure their participation.*
- *Improper or insufficient focus.* Teams can spend too much time discussing issues they do not really need to discuss. For example, we have seen teams spend 90 percent of an unstructured debriefing talking about a relatively unimportant issue or one they didn't really need to discuss. This "spinning" can be very frustrating to participants and, when excessive, can discourage a team from debriefing in the future. Experiential learning is by definition a less structured

approach to personal development than is classroom learning, so an unguided debriefing ("Hey, let's talk about what happened") can wander somewhat aimlessly. Some researchers have suggested that organizations can help provide much needed structure to experiential learning through the use of various tools and processes (Lohman, 2000; Marsick, Volpe, & Watkins, 1999). So *provide enough structure to assure the team covers meaningful issues as efficiently as possible.*

- *No clear agreements or future plans.* We have observed teams engage in a healthy discussion about what happened in a recent performance episode, but then fail to establish any agreements about what they intend to do in the future. While discussing past experiences without action planning may be interesting, it is less likely to result in sustained or improved team performance. As noted earlier, feedback is more powerful when combined with goal setting (Locke, Frederick, Lee, & Bobko, 1984). So *debriefings should lead to agreements about future actions,* which could include agreements to continue doing those things that are working.
- *Not allocating sufficient time.* Without prompting, most teams do not naturally debrief in a structured way. Moreover, teams that do sometimes fail to schedule ample time. Not surprisingly, lack of time (Noe & Wilk, 1993) and time-related pressures have been found to be common inhibitors to developmental and informal learning activities (Lohman, 2000). Pragmatically, debriefing competes with many other demands on a team's time, and debriefing is rarely a "required" team activity. Yet we would suggest that a well-conducted debriefing is often more beneficial than almost any other activity a team could complete in a similar timeframe. So *allocate ample time to debrief.*
- *Too evaluative or threatening.* We have seen debriefings that feel more like performance reviews or inquisitions than developmental opportunities. The way a debriefing is described and conducted can convey that it is either: (a) a safe opportunity to explore prior work and acknowledge where changes would be beneficial or (b) a place where team

members will be judged and evaluated. People act differently when they feel they are being judged; they are more apt to become defensive and explain away problems and less likely to share information and acknowledge concerns. In fact, perceived purpose (judgmental versus developmental) has been shown to have a significant impact on the accuracy and acceptance of feedback (Jawahar & Williams, 1997). So *debriefings should be primarily developmental in intent rather than judgmental or evaluative.*

Lessons Learned: Levers and Tips to Promote Effective Team Debriefings

Several lessons learned emerge from our experience with and research on team debriefing. Below, we focus on four key leverage points for ensuring debriefing effectiveness: structure, preparation, discipline, and information quality. These levers can be "pulled" in several ways, and we believe that addressing them is the key to maximizing the benefits that can be attained.

Structure. The first lever for debriefing success is structure. A debriefing is more likely to accomplish desired outcomes when it provides participants with ample structure and a logical process. Simply getting together to discuss "how things are working" is OK, but unlikely to yield consistently positive results. Almost all of the debriefings in the meta-analysis we conducted (Tannenbaum & Cerasoli, 2013) employed at least moderate structure. Lack of structure can lead to circuitous discussions ("spinning") and make the group feel that they wasted time. While debriefing need not be tightly choreographed, a modest amount of structure can help a team stay focused and on track. In general, we would advocate employing a debriefing process that, at a minimum, includes the following elements:

- *Introduction.* The process should begin with an appropriate introduction to and framing of the debriefing that describes the purpose of the session and how it will be conducted, including any general ground rules. This helps set appropriate expectations and clarifies that the intent is non-punitive (that is, developmental rather than evaluative).

- *Reflection and Discussion.* Typically, a structured debriefing will include a general question or two that encourages participants to reflect on and describe the focal experience, for example, asking what happened and how that compares to what they expected. Additional probes or diagnostic questions can guide the team through a healthy discussion, such as what went well, what challenges they faced, why things happened as they did, and what they could have done differently. In addition, it helps to have questions available to guide the team to specifically consider teamwork-related issues to prevent them from focusing strictly on taskwork issues.
- *Agreement/Action Planning.* The structure should include ample time to clarify lessons learned, confirm understanding, and reach agreements about how the team intends to work together going forward. Action plans can include agreements to make adjustments as a team or as individuals, as well as to continue doing things that have been working.

In our experience, a properly structured debriefing can allow a person who is not an expert in what the team does to lead the discussion. For example, we have led debriefings with medical teams despite having no medical expertise. Also, when the debriefing will be conducted as part of training (Types 3, 4, and 6), then greater structure is typically called for, because the training has been designed to provoke certain decision points or challenges, and the discussion probes can be even more targeted. (See Rosen, Salas, Tannenbaum, Pronovost, and King [2012] for more on structuring debriefings during simulation-based team training.)

Preparation. The second lever for debriefing success is preparation, and in particular the preparation of the team leaders or facilitators. As noted earlier, leaders and experts can have some natural tendencies that run contrary to optimal design (for example, taskwork focus, telling rather than encouraging self-discovery, evaluative/judgmental tone). While it might seem that anyone with good interpersonal skills will naturally lead an effective debriefing (Dismukes, Jobe, & McDonnell, 2000), preparation is a key lever. In our experience a little preparation appears to greatly improve debriefing effectiveness.

Ideally, we would suggest training leaders and facilitators how to conduct effective debriefings. For example, we were involved in a project that focused on team training in the U.S. Navy (Tannenbaum, Smith-Jentsch, & Behson, 1998). As part of this effort we watched untrained commanding officers (COs) lead debriefings. All of the COs were highly experienced leaders, but some were clearly better debriefing facilitators than others. We identified a few of the key behaviors that influenced debriefing effectiveness, such as leaders acknowledging their own mistakes, allowing team members to reflect and offer their views before telling the team what they thought, not punishing team members who acknowledged concerns, and guiding the team to discuss a few key teamwork challenges. Teams led by leaders who were subsequently trained to conduct effective debriefings outperformed other teams by 40 percent (Smith-Jentsch, Cannon-Bowers, Tannenbaum, & Salas, 2008). Thus, it is apparent that employing a few key facilitation techniques can greatly enhance debriefing efficacy.

Some companies are trying to build this capability. For example, at Lenovo, the world's second largest producer of PCs, they train their managers in what their chairman calls "fu pan" or replaying the chessboard (Salter, 2012). Unfortunately, providing debriefing training to all team leaders, project leaders, trainers, and facilitators can be difficult. For example, as medical schools continue to add better team simulation capabilities, a challenge they face is scaling up the debriefing skills of the instructors (Tannenbaum & Goldhaber-Fiebert, 2013). So while training is advocated, when that is not feasible, at a minimum it can help to provide leaders with tools that provide them with some basic guidance and advice. For example, we have used simple tip sheets that outline the debriefing process and provide a handful of tips similar to those covered in the Navy leadership study. In a subsequent section, we provide advice and tips that can be used when preparing people to lead effective debriefings.

Discipline. Most teams do not naturally debrief. Without prompting or encouragement, leaders may not know that they should debrief, may forget to do so, or may feel that their teams don't have the time. Therefore, the third lever is simply developing the discipline to debrief. In some organizations, this is accomplished by identifying a few "debriefing champions." These are individuals who understand the value of debriefing, who will conduct them, and who will encourage others to do the same. In essence this lever is about developing the culture and habit of allocating time for debriefing until it is an expected and natural part of working as a team. For example, a project team could schedule a short team debriefing for the end of every second team meeting or a work team might establish a monthly team debriefing that focuses on a recent work experience. Alternatively, a leader might identify three types of team experiences that are worthy of debriefing and let the team know that when one of these experiences arises, they can expect to participate in a team debriefing shortly thereafter. Interestingly, we have observed that, once leaders have led a few effective debriefings, it often becomes part of their leadership toolkit and they will conduct them with any of the teams they lead.

Information quality. The fourth lever for debriefing effectiveness is information quality, specifically the nature of the information that is shared. As an extreme example, if a team were to perform a task wearing blindfolds and earplugs, it would be difficult for them to conduct a subsequent debriefing because they would not have much useful feedback to share. Primary sources of information are the perceptions and recollections of team members and the team leader. Observations from non-participants (for example, trainers during a training debriefing) and data that emerges from the task itself (productivity, quality, or sales data) are other possible information sources.

There are a few options for helping ensure that there is reasonably good quality information to share. We know that the greater the length of time that transpires after an event, the more difficult it is for individuals to recall details about the event (Schmolck, Buffalo, & Squire, 2000). So one way of enhancing information quality is to conduct debriefings fairly close in time to the performance of interest. When there will be a substantial time lag, it could be beneficial to provide team members and/or the leader with a simple way of recording observations and insights (perhaps a notepad or diary) (DeNisi & Williams, 1988).

In controlled team simulations (in aviation, military, aerospace, and medical training), video recording devices and other performance capturing tools are being used to allow a trainer to "play back" an episode to refresh the team's memory. While the research evidence isn't yet clear about when video may be beneficial (Beaubien & Baker, 2003), the intent behind any recording device is to improve the quality of the information available.

Perhaps the three most universally applicable solutions for improving information quality are to (1) let team members know in advance that a debriefing will be conducted and what will be discussed (so they are more alert to and aware of events as they occur); (2) create an environment during the debriefing in which participants are comfortable admitting concerns, mistakes, and uncertainties (because an unwillingness to acknowledge issues may create the biggest decline in information quality); and (3) reduce the aforementioned time lag by scheduling debriefings closer to performance episodes. These three solutions do not require investment in technology and can be applied in any of the six types of debriefs.

The good news is that information quality need not be perfect to stimulate a healthy and constructive debriefing. However, employing a few of the tactics noted above can help enhance information quality when necessary.

We conclude with a list of lessons learned for organizations and for facilitators.

Advice for Organizations

- *Debriefing works*—Encourage your team leaders, project leaders, trainers, and managers to debrief. Promote the value of allocating time to periodically reflect and learn from recent experiences.
- *Tools and processes help*—Provide team leaders with a set of tools and processes that can help them structure debriefings in a manner that promotes learning. Ensure your process covers teamwork as well as taskwork.
- *Train facilitators to lead debriefings*—Any team leader can be a debriefing "facilitator" and so can your human resource professionals, quality consultants, and learning professionals.

Teach them how to conduct effective debriefings. Embed debriefing tips into manager and leader training. Have your internal consultants model effective debriefing techniques.

Tips for Leaders: The Right Mindset

- *Participants first, you second.* When it is time for reflection and critique, let the team go first. Avoid telling too much or too soon, as either tends to result in less learning.
- *Look back, then forward.* Reflection and critique (back), then specific action plans (forward).
- *Ask and pause.* Let silence be your friend.
- *What's right, not who is right.* Avoid finger-pointing or chastising.
- *All aboard.* When possible, try to involve all relevant team members in some way.
- *Be the navigator, not the driver*—unless they aren't driving properly!
- *Reinforce and thank.* Reinforce what they did well. Thank people when they acknowledge mistakes.

What Does the Future Hold for Debriefing?

We anticipate that as various professions, companies, and team leaders learn more about debriefing, we will see a significant increase in its use in a wide range of industries and settings. The tipping point will occur when debriefing becomes a natural, expected part of participating in a team, similar to the way developing a team charter has become a fairly standard launching point for most project teams. We can envision a time when team members and leaders naturally think, "Of course, it's time to debrief."

Debriefing is also a fruitful area for future research. To date, most of the studies conducted can be thought of as "efficacy" studies to assess how well they work. There is now ample evidence to suggest that debriefing works quite well, so future research should help us understand why and how. Research should address questions such as:

- When are the best times to debrief? How frequently should teams debrief?
- When is facilitation required? What are the best ways to prepare facilitators and team leaders?
- Which debriefing tools and techniques enhance team performance or success and under what circumstances?
- How should technology be used?
- Can debriefing with one team yield benefits for future teams and, if so, how can we encourage that?

We are hopeful that future research on debriefing can yield tangible advice and techniques for debriefing and provide insights into general team dynamics. In the meantime, we end this chapter with a reminder of our fundamental premise: *organizations would benefit from debriefings more regularly.* We hope the chapter has provided an impetus and a few ideas for doing so.

References and Further Reading

Allen, J.A., Baran, B.E., & Scott, C.W. (2010). After-action reviews: A venue for the promotion of safety climate. *Accident Analysis and Prevention, 42,* 750–757.

Ames, C. (1992). Classrooms: Goals, structures, and student motivation. *Journal of Educational Psychology, 84,* 261–271.

Balzer, W.K., Doherty, M.E., & O'Connor, R. (1989). Effects of cognitive feedback on performance. *Psychological Bulletin, 106,* 410–433.

Bandura, A., & Cervone, D. (1983). Self-evaluative and self-efficacy mechanisms governing the motivational effects of goal systems. *Journal of Personality and Social Psychology, 45,* 1017–1028.

Barmeyer, C.I. (2004). Learning styles and their impact on cross-cultural training: An international comparison in France, Germany, and Quebec. *International Journal of Intercultural Relations, 28,* 577–594.

Beaubien, J.M., & Baker, D.P. (2003). Post-training feedback: The relative effectiveness of team- versus individual-led debriefs. *Proceedings of the 47th Annual Meeting of the Human Factors and Ergonomics Society,* Denver, Colorado.

Brooks, A.N. (1999). Critical reflection as a response to organizational disruption. *Advances in Developing Human Resources, 1,* 66–79.

Cannon, M.D., & Edmondson, A.C. (2001). Confronting failure: Antecedents and consequences of shared beliefs about failure in organizational workgroups. *Journal of Organizational Behavior, 22,* 161–177.

Cannon-Bowers, J.A., Tannenbaum, S.I., Salas, E., & Volpe, C.E. (1995). Defining team competencies: Implications for training requirements and strategies. In R. Guzzo & E. Salas (Eds.), *Team effectiveness and decision making in organizations* (pp. 333–380). San Francisco: Jossey-Bass.

Cronin, G., & Andrews, S. (2009). After-action reviews: A new model for learning. *Emergency Nurse, 17,* 32–35.

De Dreu, C.K., & Weingart, L.R. (2003). Task versus relationship conflict, team performance, and team member satisfaction. *Journal of Applied Psychology, 88,* 741–749.

DeChurch, L.A., & Mesmer-Magnus, J.R. (2010). Measuring shared team mental models: A meta-analysis. *Group Dynamics, 14,* 1–14.

DeNisi, A.S., & Williams, K.J. (1988). Cognitive approaches to performance appraisal. *Research in Personnel and Human Resources Management, 6,* 109–155.

Dismukes, R.K., Jobe, K.K., & McDonnell, L.K. (2000). Facilitating LOFT debriefings: A critical analysis. In R.K. Dismukes & G.M. Smith (Eds.), *Facilitation in aviation training and operations* (pp. 13–25). Aldershot, UK: Ashgate.

Eddy, E.R., D'Abate, C.P., Tannenbaum, S.I., Givens-Skeaton, S., & Robinson, G. (2006). Key characteristics of effective and ineffective developmental interactions. *Human Resource Development Quarterly, 17,* 59–84.

Ellis, S., & Davidi, I. (2005). After-event reviews: Drawing lessons from successful and failed experience. *Journal of Applied Psychology, 90,* 857–871.

Ellis, S., & Kruglanski, A.W. (1992). Self as an epistemic authority: Effects on experiential and instructional learning. *Social Cognition, 10,* 357–375.

Fanning, R.M., & Gaba, D.M. (2007). The role of debriefing in simulation-based learning. *Simulation in Healthcare: The*

Journal of the Society for Simulation in Healthcare, 2, 115–125.

Felipe Gomez, L., & Ballard, D.I. (2011). Communication for change: Transactive memory systems as dynamic capabilities. *Research in Organizational Change and Development, 19,* 91–115.

Hirst, G. (2009). Effects of membership change on open discussion and team performance: The moderating role of team tenure. *European Journal of Work and Organizational Psychology, 18,* 231–249.

Hollenbeck, J.R., Williams, C.R., & Klein, H.J. (1989). An empirical examination of the antecedents of commitment to difficult goals. *Journal of Applied Psychology, 74,* 18–23.

Institute of Medicine. (1999). *To err is human: Building a safer health system.* Washington, DC: National Academy Press.

Jawahar, I.M., & Williams, C.R. (1997). Where all the children are above average: The performance appraisal purpose effect. *Personnel Psychology, 50,* 905–925.

Jex, S.M., & Gudanowksi, D.M. (2006). Efficacy beliefs and work stress: An exploratory study. *Journal of Organizational Behavior, 13,* 509–517.

Kerr, N.L., MacCoun, R.J., & Kramer, G.P. (1996). Bias in judgment: Comparing individuals and groups. *Psychological Review, 103,* 687–719.

Kim, P.L. (1997). When what you know *can* hurt you: A study of experiential effects on group discussion and performance. *Organizational Behavior and Human Decision Processes, 69,* 165–177.

Kinni, T. (2003). Getting smarter every day: How can you turn organizational learning into continual on-the-job-behavior? *Harvard Management Update, 8,* 1–4.

Kluger, A.N., & DeNisi, A. (1996). The effects of feedback interventions on performance: A historical review, a meta-analysis, and a preliminary feedback intervention theory. *Psychological Bulletin, 119,* 254–284.

Kozlowski, S.W.J., & Salas, E. (Eds.). (2010). *Learning, training, and development in organizations.* New York: Routledge.

LePine, J.A., Piccolo, R.E., Jackson, C.L., Mathieu, J.E., & Saul, J.R. (2008). A meta-analysis of teamwork processes: Tests of a multidimensional model and relationships with team effectiveness criteria. *Personnel Psychology, 61*, 273–307.

Littlepage, G., Robison, W., & Reddington, K. (1997). Effects of task experience and group experience on group performance, member ability, and recognition of expertise. *Organizational Behavior and Human Decision Processes, 69*, 133–147.

Locke, E.A., Frederick, E., Lee, C., & Bobko, P. (1984). Effect of self-efficacy, goals, and task strategies on task performance. *Journal of Applied Psychology, 69*, 241–251.

Lohman, M.C. (2000). Environmental inhibitors to informal learning in the workplace: A case study of public school teachers. *Adult Education Quarterly, 50*, 83–101.

Marks, M.A., Mathieu, J.E., & Zaccaro, S.J. (2001). A temporally based framework and taxonomy of team processes. *Academy of Management Review, 26*, 356–376.

Marsick, V.J., & Volpe, M. (1999). The nature and need for informal learning. *Advances in Developing Human Resources, 1*, 1–9.

Marsick, V.J., Volpe, M., & Watkins, K.E. (1999). Theory and practice of informal learning in the knowledge era. *Advances in Developing Human Resources, 1*, 80–95.

Mathieu, J.E., Tannenbaum, S.I., Donsbach, J.S., & Alliger, G.M. (2012). Achieving optimal team composition for success. Chapter 16 in E. Salas, S.I. Tannenbaum, D.J. Cohen, & G. Latham (Eds.), *Developing and enhancing high-performance teams.* San Francisco: Pfeiffer.

Mesmer-Magnus, J.R., & DeChurch, L.A. (2009). Information sharing and team performance: A meta-analysis. *Journal of Applied Psychology, 94*, 535–546.

Mohammed, S., & Dumville, B.C. (2001). Team mental models in a team knowledge framework: Expanding theory and measurement across disciplinary boundaries. *Journal of Organizational Behavior, 22*, 89–106.

Morrison, J.E., & Meliza, L.L. (1999). *Foundations of the after action review process* (Special Report 42). U.S. Army Research Institute for the Behavioral and Social Sciences.

Noe, R.A., & Wilk, S.L. (1993). Investigation of the factors that influence employees' participation in development activities. *Journal of Applied Psychology, 78*, 291–302.

Pisano, G.P., Bohmer, R.M.J., & Edmondson, A.C. (2001). Organizational differences in rates of learning: Evidence from the adoption of minimally invasive cardiac surgery. *Management Science, 47,* 752–768.

Rogers, D.G. (2007). Sustaining NASA's safety culture shift. *RADECS 2007 Proceedings of the 9th European Conference on Radiation and Its Effects on Components and Systems, 645,* 38–41.

Ron, N., Lipshitz, R., & Popper, M. (2002). How organizations learn: Post-flight reviews in an F-16 fighter squadron. *Organization Studies, 27,* 1069–1089.

Rosen, M.A., Salas, E., Tannenbaum, S.I., Pronovost, P., & King, H.B. (2012). Simulation-based training for teams in health care: Designing scenarios, measuring performance, and providing feedback. In P. Carayon (Ed.), *Handbook of human factors and ergonomics in health care and patient safety* (pp. 573–594). Boca Raton, FL: CRC Press.

Salas. E., DiazGranados, D., Klein, C., Burke, C.S., Stagl, K.C., Goodwin, G.F., & Halpin, S.M. (2008). Does team training improve team performance? A meta-analysis. *Human Factors: The Journal of the Human Factors and Ergonomics Society, 50,* 903–933.

Salter, C. (2012). Protect and attack. *Fast Company, 161,* 116–121.

Schmolck, H., Buffalo, E.A., & Squire, L.R. (2000). Memory distortions develop over time: Recollections of the O.J. Simpson trial verdict after 15 and 32 months. *Psychological Science, 11,* 39–45.

Schon, D. (1987). *Educating the reflective practitioner.* San Francisco: Jossey-Bass.

Smith-Jentsch, K.A., Cannon-Bowers, J.A., Tannenbaum, S.I., & Salas, E. (2008). Guided team self-correction: Impacts on team mental models, processes, and effectiveness. *Small Group Research, 39,* 303–327.

Stasser, G., & Titus, W. (1985). Pooling of unshared information in group decision making: Biased information sampling during discussion. *Journal of Personality and Social Psychology, 48,* 1467–1478.

Tannenbaum, S.I., & Cerasoli, C.P. (2013). Do team and individual debriefs enhance performance? A meta-analysis. *Human*

Factors: The Journal of Human Factors and Ergonomics Society, 55, 231–245.

Tannenbaum, S.I., & Goldhaber-Fiebert, S. (2013). Medical team debriefs: Simple, powerful, underutilized. In E. Salas & K. Frush (Eds.), *Improving patient safety through teamwork and team training* (pp. 249–256). New York: Oxford University Press.

Tannenbaum, S.I., Mathieu, J.E., Salas, E., & Cohen, D.J. (2012). Teams are changing: Are research and practice evolving fast enough? *Industrial and Organizational Psychology: Perspectives on Science and Practice, 5,* 2–24.

Tannenbaum, S.I., Smith-Jentsch, K.A., & Behson, S.J. (1998). Training team leaders to facilitate team learning and performance. In J.A. Cannon-Bowers & E. Salas (Eds.), *Decision making under stress: Implications for training and simulation* (pp. 247–270). Washington, DC: American Psychological Association.

Tesluk, P.E., & Mathieu, J.E. (1999). Overcoming roadblocks to effectiveness: Incorporating management of performance barriers into models of work group effectiveness. *Journal of Applied Psychology, 84,* 200–217.

West, M.A. (1996). Reflexivity and work effectiveness: A conceptual integration. In M.A. West (Ed.), *Handbook of work group psychology* (pp. 555–579). Chichester, UK: John Wiley & Sons.

CHAPTER SIXTEEN

Achieving Optimal Team Composition for Success*

John E. Mathieu
University of Connecticut

Scott I. Tannenbaum, Jamie S. Donsbach, and George M. Alliger
Group for Organizational Effectiveness, Inc.

Consider the following situation. You are responsible for a cross-functional product development team. The team is about to lose Donna, who is from operations, has good product knowledge, is an average team builder, and was always available to take on new work. The pool of replacements includes:

Sam from operations, who has great product knowledge, but limited availability;
Jack from marketing, who has modest product knowledge, is a great team builder, and is completely available;
Mary from operations, who has great product knowledge, is available, but is considered arrogant and has some bad blood with current members; and

**Author Note*: This work was supported, in part, by a grant awarded to the authors from NASA (Grant #NNX11AR22G), in part by the U.S. Army Research Institute (#W91WAW-08-C-0021), and in part by a grant awarded to the first author by the Connecticut Center for Entrepreneurship and Innovation. All opinions expressed herein are, however, strictly those of the authors and not necessarily those of the sponsoring organizations.

Alex from IT, who has little project knowledge, is available, and has great leadership skills.

Who would you choose? Notice that if you favor a "replacement in kind" from operations, the choice reduces to Sam versus Mary. And between them, it comes down to greater availability (Mary) versus avoiding potentially dysfunctional interpersonal relations (Sam). Alternatively, if you are willing to forego having great product knowledge and representing operations, Jack and Alex become viable candidates. Between them, deciding factors would be the premiums on adding team building versus leadership skills to the team, and the relative value of marketing versus IT department representation. The choice is not easy or straightforward. And it may be more complicated still. Suppose that your organization values demographic diversity and Alex would add significantly to the mix—but you already have a representative from the IT unit on the team. How would your decision be swayed if: (1) others on the team possessed limited (or high) product knowledge; (2) the team was currently functioning well (or was experiencing substantial conflict); and (3) the team had a culture of shared leadership (or was suffering from a leadership vacuum)? What if your decision had to be made quickly? Most team composition decisions are similar to the scenario just outlined, in that they are far more complex than they appear on the surface. And although research and practice have addressed team membership dynamics for years and many different approaches and models exist, there is a dire need for integration and guidance for practice.

We have four primary objectives for this chapter. First, we provide a brief overview of different types of team composition decision situations. These range from a relatively simple but still challenging single member replacement situation, such as the one described above, to vastly more complex situations such as reconfiguring numerous current and new employees into multiple teams. Second, we highlight four different models or strategies for composing team membership that have been advanced in the literature and suggest a synthesis. Third, we outline four different types of constraints or external factors that impact such decisions. Finally, we conclude with guidelines for practice based on these various factors.

From the onset, we note that we have been studying and helping organizations to manage team composition issues for many years. We recently conducted structured interviews with twenty-one team composition experts (SMEs) from private- and public-sector organizations. They were all considered to be team staffing experts by their respective organizations. On average, they had over fifteen years of experience staffing a wide variety of team types. Several representative quotes from those interviews are included throughout this chapter. Our experience is that everyone appreciates the importance of "getting the right people on the team"—yet many struggle with doing so. Our hope is that this chapter helps to address those concerns.

> "If you don't have the right mix of people, the team is dead from the start."
>
> —CEO, Large Insurance Company

Introduction

Organizational leaders worldwide recognize the tremendous benefits of effective teamwork. As such, organizations across sectors and a myriad of industries have designed their tasks and workforce around teams (Ilgen, Hollenbeck, Johnson, & Jundt, 2005; Kozlowski & Ilgen, 2006; Mathieu, Maynard, Rapp, & Gilson, 2008). Kozlowski and Bell (2003, p. 334) defined teams as collectives "who exist to perform organizationally relevant tasks, share one or more common goals, interact socially, exhibit task interdependencies, maintain and manage boundaries, and are embedded in an organizational context that sets boundaries, constrains the team, and influences exchanges with other units in the broader entity." The key elements of this definition are that, in order to have a team, members must have some shared goal and some degree of interdependence. In addition, real teams operate in a context that has implications for their functioning. Although team success is ultimately contingent upon a variety of factors, research and practice suggest that placing the right mix of people on a team sets the stage for effective team outcomes. Specifically, the mix of knowledge, skills, abilities, and other characteristics

(KSAOs) of team members contributes significantly to their team's level of effort, their coordination, and ultimately to their team's performance (Bell, 2007; Ilgen, 1999). For example:

> "If you cannot optimize the composition of your teams, you are just not going to have the best impact that you can have. The leader's job is to get the team to be the best it can be. If you don't obtain optimal composition, it is like having a 500 horsepower car on the snow!"
>
> —Director of Business Performance, Financial Institution

Although today's leaders place a premium on understanding how to best staff teams, the task of forming a team remains a challenging one. Leaders must simultaneously consider how members' attributes align with position requirements, compared to those of other teammates' and to the team KSAO distributions. This is a cognitively complex and challenging task that often leads to sub-optimal team composition decisions. Team staffing errors can result in poor team performance and often create the need to make costly corrections to team membership well into a team's mission. Research suggests that by considering team-level characteristics in addition to individual characteristics, a leader should be able to build more effective teams (Devine & Philips, 2001; Stevens & Campion, 1994). Unfortunately, these team-level factors are often overlooked in traditional team member selection models.

Types of Team Composition Decisions

During our interviews we asked SMEs to describe specific team staffing situations they had encountered. We had them "think aloud" and explain the process used for making the decision and the kinds of constraints placed on staffing decisions in a natural operational environment. Based on their responses and our review of the team composition literature, we identified six different types of team composition decisions that are shown in Table 16.1. The first three listed involve decisions relevant to *existing*

Table 16.1. Types of Team Composition Decisions

Types of Teams	*Decision Type*	*Description*	*Example*
Existing Teams	Single Member Replacement	Assigning a replacement member to a single team	*"I had to replace a leader on a single off-shore oil rig. The previous leader was promoted."*
	Multiple Member Replacement	Assigning multiple replacement members to a single team	*"I had to reorganize a team after I had promoted a number of people. I had to back-fill their positions and reorganize."*
	New Member Distribution	Assigning new members to multiple teams	*"We partnered with a local university and filled the additional plant positions with a group of new graduates."*
New Teams	Single Team Formation	Assigning all members to a new team	*"I had to build a new helo [combat helicopter] crew."*
	Multiple Team Formation	Assigning all members to multiple new teams	*"I was tasked with filling hundreds of positions within multiple departments of a new store."*
	Reconfiguration	Assigning or re-assigning multiple members to multiple teams	*"We had to form new teams with members from previously warring competitors."*

teams, whereas the latter three concern decisions about the formation of *new teams.* The examples listed in the right column come from our interviews.

The simplest form of composition decision involves the *(re) placement of a single individual on a single team.* Typically, these decisions are in the context of *replacing a person* who has left for whatever reason, but they could also be in terms of adding a member to address deficiencies or increased work demands. Herein the decision often boils down to whether it is most advantageous to seek a "replacement in kind"—essentially a clone of the leaving member—or whether the team would benefit from a different kind of individual. If a replacement in kind is sought, then we have a traditional situation of seeking a replacement who possesses the most similar KSAO profile as the leaver, weighted by which of those factors are deemed to be most important. If the situation calls for a different kind of person, then not only do individuals' KSAOs come into play, but questions concerning the balance or mix of member attributes on the team rise in importance.

The second type of decision, *multiple member replacement*, simultaneously adds greater complexity and opportunities to the situation. On one hand, rather than searching for a single replacement, the challenge is increased in magnitude by the number of replacements needed. On the other hand, shortcomings in any one placement might be compensated for by strengths in another. For example, if one of the departing members possessed both high product knowledge and leadership skills, and the replacement candidate with the highest product knowledge is not a leader, then perhaps the second replacement member might be selected based more highly on leadership attributes than would otherwise be the case.

The third type of decision, *new personnel distribution*, overlays a multiple team consideration atop the multiple member type decision. Examples of this type of situation could include allocating a new state police officer academy graduating class to geographical regions throughout the state. Many of those allocations are likely to be replacements for officers who have left the ranks for whatever reason, whereas others might be to build up a force in response to growing needs in some area. These decisions not only involve assigning one or more new members to existing teams, but also call into question the relative importance of the distribution of human capital. In other words, at a more strategic level, one must consider whether it is preferable to have roughly equal capability across teams versus whether it is important to staff some "super-star teams" at the expense of having some below-average teams. In many industries it is preferable to have a high degree of across-team homogeneity for consistent functioning or service. In other instances, it is important to have some elite teams for deployment in special circumstances (for example, police officer SWAT teams, forensic accounting teams for high-value clients facing litigation). It is also possible to envision the requirement that different teams be strong in different constellations of KSAOs (for example, police officers in one region of the state need good drug interdiction capabilities, while officers in another part of the state focus more on patrol and security).

The three remaining decision types deal with forming new teams. Whereas the decisions involving member placement(s) into existing teams amount to optimizing the "fitting in" of new members, new team formation questions start with a blank slate. This simultaneously relaxes constraints associated with the mix of who is already on the team, while adding substantial complexity in terms of the myriad of potential member combinations and how they should be compared. In the *single-team formation situation,* implicitly one would seek the optimal combination of members for the specific team (for example, constituting a new project team). In the *multiple-team formation* situation, we again need to consider the strategic advantage of forming comparatively good teams versus composing some elite and some weaker teams. Again, the advantage of these situations versus merely allocating new members to one or more existing teams is that there is greater flexibility to orchestrate different combinations of members. But, of course, that flexibility brings with it enormous complexity in terms of deciding what kinds of balances are most appropriate, both within and between teams.

Finally, there are *reconfiguration* scenarios where, for example, one or more organizations are reassigning members to new teams. These situations not only involve the typical team-building and development challenges associated with constituting new teams, but they also occur in the context of numerous other factors. For example, is the new configuration being done to exploit a growing market share and future opportunities, or is the organization retrenching and struggling for survival? Is the change providing new growth opportunities for members or are their jobs at risk? Is the reconfiguration the result of a conciliatory merger or a hostile takeover? The relative emphasis on employee KSAOs, the distribution of employees both within and across teams, the importance of having comparable versus elite teams, and so forth, will all hang in the balance and be quite important.

Models of Team Composition

Team composition research focuses on the attributes of team members, and the impact of the combination of such attributes on processes, emergent states, and ultimately outcomes. Team composition research has a rich history dating back over half a century (see Heslin, 1964, and Mann, 1959, for early reviews). The extant literature indicates that team processes and effectiveness are impacted by aspects of group composition such as members' skills, job and organizational experiences, and group heterogeneity as a whole (Mathieu, Maynard, Rapp, & Gilson, 2008). Yet, challenges concerning how to best understand and index team composition and how to model its influences continue to plague the field (Arrow & McGrath, 1995; Ilgen, 1999; Ilgen, Hollenbeck, Johnson, & Jundt, 2005; Kozlowski & Bell, 2003; Morgan & Lassiter, 1992).

Kozlowski and Klein (2000) describe composition processes as relatively simple combination rules, such as average team member characteristics, as representing a higher-level construct such as team human capital. Diversity indices are also compositional in nature, as they represent the higher-level construct as a variance of members' individual characteristics. An important point to note about compositional models is that all lower-level entities are presumed to be comparable and weighted equally in the construction of the higher-level construct. In contrast, "in compilation models, the higher-level phenomenon is a complex combination of diverse lower-level contributions" (Kozlowski & Klein, 2000, p. 17). In other words, compilation describes a situation where the higher-level construct is something different from a mere descriptive statistic of members' attributes. For example, team performance may be unduly influenced by the least (or most) competent individual member.

Table 16.2. Four Models of Team Composition Effectiveness

	Individual Focus	*Team Focus*
Individual Models	**Traditional Personnel—Position Fit Model** *Position-Specific KSAOs* Cognitive Ability Psychomotor Ability Conscientiousness	**Personnel Model with Teamwork Considerations** *Team Generic KSAOs* Organizing Skills Cooperativeness Team Orientation
Team Models	**Relative Contribution Model** *Relative KSAOs* Weakest Member Highest Leader Propensity Cooperativeness of Most Central Person	**Team Profile Model** *KSAO Distributions* Average Experience Functional Diversity Team Requisite KSAO

Historically, work on team composition has essentially progressed along two different streams. First, there are individual-based models that have either a focus on individuals and job requirements or on members' generic team-related KSAOs. Second, there are team-based models that adopt a comparative or "relative contribution" view of individual members' KSAOs or consider more complex combinations or team profiles of KSAOs. In general, individual-based models consider each position opening separately, while team-based models consider individuals' contributions to the overall mix or profile of the team. Table 16.2 depicts these different approaches, which are detailed below.

Traditional Personnel—Position Fit Model

The first stream of team composition models (the first row in Table 16.2) derives from the application of traditional individual-focused personnel psychology or human resource (HR) frameworks. These approaches are based on the assumption that one seeks to optimize the fit between individuals' KSAO profiles and the positions or roles they occupy. The upper left quadrant of Table 16.2 refers to the position-fit model. Based on a thorough job analysis, the relative importance of various dimensions or tasks assigned to any given position is identified, and the individual KSAOs that are important for performing those tasks is specified and used for staffing decisions (McCormick, 1979; Stevens & Campion, 1994). In short, this model assumes that when higher-quality people are in each team position, the team as a whole will be more successful. For example, Cooke, Kiekel, Salas, Stout, Bowers, and Cannon-Bowers (2003) demonstrated that team effectiveness was enhanced to the extent the members possessed valuable team knowledge related to the positions that they occupied. Naturally, this model also assumes that there are distinguishable and fairly fixed positions in a team that individuals can be aligned with.

Personnel Model with Teamwork Considerations

With the advent of team-based organizations, the KSAOs considered in the traditional model have been extended to include team-relevant competencies (Hirschfeld, Jordan, Field, Giles, & Armenakis, 2006; Stevens & Campion, 1994). Cannon-Bowers and colleagues (1995) discussed team-generic competencies as ones that would be universally valuable across team situations.

> "I typically look for how the person will fit with the team, someone who is flexible (can fill other roles when needed), someone with certain skills (e.g., interpersonal) and experience, and whether they can fill existing skill gaps on the team. . . . I also look for people to be able to back-up one another."
>
> —Director of Workforce Development, large credit union

Along these lines, Baker, Salas, and Cannon-Bowers (1998) submitted that individuals' competencies in terms of providing feedback, cooperating, communication, promoting team morale, adaptability, accepting feedback, and coordinating their efforts with others are generic and beneficial across teams. Mumford, Van Iddekinge, Morgeson, and Campion (2008) developed measures of individuals' task, social, and boundary spanning knowledge and demonstrated them to be predictive of individuals' team-oriented behaviors. Elsewhere, we discuss the development and validation of measures of six different *team role experience and orientations* (that is, TREO—organizer, innovator, doer, challenger, team builder, and connector) and illustrate their correlations with peer ratings of individuals' contributions to team effectiveness (Mathieu, Tannenbaum, Kukenberger, Donsbach, Alliger, & Salas, 2009). Other research has suggested that average member teamwork orientation enhances effectiveness (e.g., Bell, 2007; Harris & Barnes-Farrell, 1997; Jung & Sosick, 1999; Watson, Johnson, & Merritt, 1998). The underlying assumption of this personnel teamwork model is that team effectiveness is enhanced to the extent to which members all possess generic team-related competencies.

Team Profile Model

The approach to the consideration of team composition focuses attention at the team level and includes team profile and relative contribution models (the second row in Table 16.2). Several approaches have considered team composition in terms of summary indices of members' characteristics. This team-profile approach (bottom right box in Table 16.2) indexes composition in terms of descriptive statistics of members' KSAOs. The key feature of these approaches is that team members' KSAOs are considered collectively rather than in terms of individuals' position fit. For example, researchers have employed indices of *central tendency,* such as average member tenure, task-related knowledge, agreeableness, and conscientiousness (Barrick, Stewart, Neubert, & Mount, 1998; Devine & Philips, 2001) as predictors of team effectiveness. Other researchers have focused on the *diversity* of member attributes, such as functional backgrounds, demographics, or personalities (Jackson, Brett, Sessa, Cooper, Julin, & Peyronnin, 1991). With these approaches, each member's characteristics contribute to a distribution feature that is indexed at the team level. Recent reviews have indicated that diversity effects vary as a function of both the nature of variables (for example, demographics versus task-related KSAOs), and time (for example, team formation versus maturity), as well as other factors (see Bell, Villado, Lukasik, Belau, & Briggs, 2011). Implicit in such an approach is that all members' scores will be treated equally as these summary indices are derived. In other words, no members or positions that individuals occupy are viewed as any more (or less) important than others.

An extension of this team-focused and team-level approach is to consider whether some key attribute is present or absent or exists to a certain degree in a team. For example, it may be critical that one or more members assume leadership responsibilities in an empowered team. Another example may be that someone in the team must know the technical aspects of a task or be fluent in a particular language. The unifying theme is that having a particular member attribute present (or absent) somewhere in the team will be particularly advantageous (or detrimental) for team functioning. However, these attributes are not necessarily part of any given position—they just have to be available somewhere in the team. This notion is also not limited to single members or characteristics. For example, it might be that at least 50 percent of the team needs to know a certain language in order for the team to coordinate its efforts with host nation members in a multicultural context.

Relative Contribution Model

Some team-based approaches have advanced the notion that overall team performance depends more on the characteristics of certain members than others. This approach, which represents a compilation model (Kozlowski & Klein, 2000), has often been referred to as the relative or selected score approach. Based mostly on the work of Steiner (1972), these studies have considered attributes such as the competencies of the weakest or strongest member, or the emotional stability of the most neurotic member (Halfhill, Nielsen, Sundstrom, & Weilbaecher, 2005; LePine, Hollenbeck, Ilgen, & Hedlund, 1997). In this sense, given the nature of the task interdependencies, particular individuals can carry or undermine the entire team effort.

> "Currently, the team staffing decision processes here don't consider the composition of the existing team. However, we probably should."
>
> —Vice President of Human Resources,
> Consumer Products Company

More recently, Ellis, Bell, Ployhart, Hollenbeck, and Ilgen (2005) argued that the knowledge levels of members who occupy more critical team roles would exhibit higher correlations with team outcomes than would the knowledge levels of members who occupy less critical roles. Depending on the situation, such focal attributes could be anything from the physical fitness of certain members, to the leadership qualities of someone in a certain position. In effect, this most recent approach advocates a network style model to the study of team composition (Bell, 2007). The critical point here is that, rather than treating all members the same (as is done in the individual models and the team profile model), the competencies of different (more critical) members should be weighted differently. Such weights will depend on the nature of the different positions or roles that individuals may occupy in a team, along with the interrelationships among positions. For example, Humphrey, Morgeson, and Mannor (2009) argued that the competencies of "core" team members would be more predictive of team outcomes than would those of peripheral members. They found support for this hypothesis using eighteen years of data about professional baseball players and their teams' performances.

Synthesis of the Models

> "I don't use formal metrics to evaluate my team staffing decisions. I'm more of a process/results person. I look at how effective the team is."
>
> —Lieutenant Colonel, United States Air Force

> "We have a lot of formal metrics that measure team productivity (e.g., the number of jobs filled), customer satisfaction. We also, more informally, gauge how much the team members like each other and talk to each other."
>
> —Client Manager for IT Staffing, Large Insurance Company

Although the importance of getting teams right from the start is widely recognized, few organizations have processes or systems in place to make composition decisions ahead of time, as exemplified in the quotes above. Most rely on assessing how well teams are functioning after the fact. But given the different models and their implications, how should one proceed? We advocate an integrated approach that incorporates elements of each model. Whether implemented via management intuition or through an elegant formalized algorithm, the following approach that integrates individual- and team-based models can be taken. First, to the extent that an organization has a team-based design, team-generic skills (*personnel model with teamwork considerations*) will be advantageous for all employees. Given that individuals will likely work simultaneously on multiple teams and team memberships will likely be fluid over time, having employees with good generic teamwork skills will enhance human capital and the ability to deploy them quickly to different teams. Second, to the extent that there are designated positions in a team, the *traditional personnel-position fit model* is beneficial. While we fully acknowledge that a team of experts does not necessarily translate into an expert team (Burke, Salas, Wilson-Donnelly, & Priest, 2004), to the extent that individuals are well suited and capable for the positions that they occupy, the team will have greater resources to draw upon and be more likely to be successful. Even if there are not designated team positions per se (that is, perhaps an empowered team design or a parallel-team arrangement), important team roles exist and will emerge over time (such as task organizer, team builder, boundary spanner). To the extent that the individuals who come to occupy such roles have the competencies to perform them, the team is more likely to be successful.

Moving beyond individuals' fit in positions or roles and their generic teamwork KSAOs, any team composition can also be indexed in terms of the *team profile* and *relative contribution models.* For example, adding a member who fits a particular position well also has implications in terms of extreme team scores and distributions. Recall that from our opening example of the people who were available, Mary possessed the most product knowledge and would not alter the functional or gender diversity of the team. But she would be the most arrogant member of the team and has a history of demonstrating poor team-generic skills. In contrast, Jack has only modest product knowledge but high team generic skills. Adding him to the team would also alter gender and functional diversities—for better or for worse. Alternatively, perhaps someone else on the team already has strong team-building skills, but there is a leadership vacuum in the team. If that were the case, then perhaps Alex (who has even less product knowledge than Jack) would be preferable, because he brings leadership talents to the table. Ultimately, who is the best candidate comes down to a question of the relative importance of position-specific KSAOs, versus team-generic KSAOs, versus relative KSAOs, versus KSAO distributions. And since each and every team member contributes scores that fold into those four models, therein lie the key and the challenge.

To determine who would be the best person to add to the team, one needs to specify the relative importance of those four sets of variables (position fit, teamwork considerations, relative position contributions, team profile). For instance, if a team has limited position interdependence, then there is likely to be a higher emphasis on the traditional personnel-position fit model. Alternatively, to the extent that the organization places a high value on demographic or functional diversity, then team profiles or configurations that maximize scores along those lines would be preferred. In short, we are advocating a balanced scorecard style approach whereby decision-makers must first articulate the relative priority of different concerns along the four models. Then various team compositions can be indexed along the various attributes, scored, weighted, and compared. Such an approach is scalable beyond the individual replacement scenario up through the complete reconfiguration situation. The decisions involving multiple team compositions would also need to consider whether the goal is to have teams that are fairly comparable or have some elite teams. Clearly, the approach that we described—simultaneously consider individual, team, and organizational factors—can feel like a daunting task. In the next section we introduce several common constraints that limit the options available to decision-makers and therefore potentially simplify the decision space.

Team Composition Decision Constraints

In an ideal world, a decision-maker responsible for composing teams would have full information available about all team openings, a complete human resource information system available with candidates' KSAO scores already banked, a full information optimization routine written and ready to apply, and abundant time and resources available to make decisions. But no one lives in that ideal world. Various constraints limit the discretion that decision-makers can exercise.

> "I often didn't get my top picks because the person's commander wouldn't let them go, or the personnel system wouldn't let me have them."
>
> —Retired Commander, United States Air Force Weapons School

> "The biggest constraint for me is availability of personnel."
>
> —Major, United States Marine Corps

> "Cost considerations were a major factor. They wanted a team with global experience; however it is expensive to move candidates to New Jersey from other parts of the world."
>
> —Senior Director, Global Pharmaceutical Company

Table 16.3 lists various sources of constraints that limit decision-makers' ability to optimize team compositions. Naturally the *availability* of candidates is a prime consideration. Not only must candidates be available when the need arises, but they also must be willing to take the position if offered and not be overly committed to other assignments. And therein lies the dilemma: the most valuable individuals will be the ones who are overly subscribed (to multiple projects) and stretched thin. Organizations find it difficult to anticipate when various team staffing challenges will occur and to monitor when the most appropriate

Table 16.3. Constraints on Team Composition Decisions

Availability of Candidates
When are candidates available for assignments?
How many teams are people currently members of?
Timing Associated with Making Composition Decisions
Can one anticipate when composition decisions need to be made?
How much time do you have to make a decision?
Information Issues
Are team and tasks sufficiently scoped to determine composition emphases?
Is applicable information available for all candidates or does it need to be gathered?
Costs
What are the costs associated with candidate search and decision making?
What are the relative costs associated with different forms of decision errors?

people will become available. To the extent that such contingencies are not anticipated and compensated for, situations will arise for which critical team staffing needs cannot be met (or are met suboptimally) because key players are assigned elsewhere—or complications arise as star players are over-assigned or pulled from some teams and assigned to new ones.

A related concern deals with *timing* issues. If team staffing needs can be anticipated, decision-makers can better schedule and align the availability of suitable members. Continually operating in a reactive fashion to the latest staffing crisis inevitably leads to stress and suboptimal decisions. Even if composition needs can be anticipated, if managers are not given sufficient time to make such decisions, they certainly won't be able to exploit available information and maximize their choices. In short, "timing crises" inevitably lead to rushed decisions that fail to consider the range of team composition issues and often emerge later in the form of dysfunctional team processes and functioning.

Similar to any complex organizational decision, complete *information* for making team composition choices is typically lacking. When information about various team positions, roles, and demands is not known a priori, decision-makers are forced to rely on generic assumptions and member qualifications. When information about candidates is lacking, it is hard to assess position fit, and when information about existing team members is lacking, it is hard to assess overall team fit. When salient candidate information is available to decision-makers, whether that comes via a formal database or familiarity with candidates, they are in a position to make better informed decisions. In most cases, however, information is incomplete, which suggests decision-makers will make suboptimal choices based more on their implicit theories and personal interactions with candidates, than on sound member-team fit.

And finally, there are *costs* associated with any decision, including ones concerning team composition. First, there are costs involved in the decision itself, such as gathering candidate information and integrating it. This takes time, which can clearly have cost implications. Second, and perhaps more importantly, there are costs associated with different decision errors. Typically, the lament is that "we don't have time for such decisions" and "we can't afford to delay, gather data, and make more formalized assignments!" But what are the implications if we place the wrong mix of members on a team? How costly will it be to deal with process loss and dysfunctions that result? What are the costs of wasting a talented individual on a dysfunctional team? What are the implications for future teaming and retention if members have a positive experience versus a miserable one? Far too often, in our experience, managers focus on the visible costs associated with making decisions over the hidden costs of decision mistakes.

In summary, decision-makers often face one or more constraints when trying to make a team composition decision. Preferred candidates may be unavailable and decisions may need to be made quite quickly with imperfect data and a limited budget. From a strategic HRM perspective, such limitations should be recognized and managed to the extent possible to minimize their impact.

A Recommended Approach for Practitioners

"I first identify the core team lead. I then work with the management team—those that represent our seven functional disciplines (e.g., design, clinical, marketing)—to select the other team members. Generally, the managers of each functional discipline decide who to assign from their function, but I give some input."

—Senior Director, Medical Equipment Company

"I first consider the mission complexity and visibility. I start by filling the flight lead and the critical positions. I first ask: Who is available? What kind of experience do they have? Time dictates the extent to which we can consider other factors in our (team staffing) decisions. If we have time, we definitely think about things like whether guys can work together, or if they should be doing something else."

—Lieutenant Colonel, United States Air Force

Given the complexity of team composition dynamics and the prevalence of numerous constraints, it is not surprising that decision-makers often rely on heuristics such as "choose the most [position] qualified people" or "I need people who are team players." Short of a full-information system and abundant resources, what practical advice can we provide? Table 16.4 describes a practical seven-step process or heuristic for composing teams. For each step, the table contains key questions, along with a few tips or considerations when answering the questions. The process draws from the four types of team composition models and recognizes the common constraints. It can be used when you need to make a fairly quick decision with limited data, although having additional time and information increases the probability of success.

Step 1 is to ground the decision by *describing the team*. First, identify the positions on the team (each position is one "slot" for one person). Consider whether any of the positions are particularly important for team performance because, given limited time and resources, those are positions that should receive the greatest

Table 16.4. Recommendations for Application

Step	*Tips*
Step 1. Describe the Team	
What are the **positions** on the team? Are any particularly **critical** for team success?	Begin by considering the nature and mission of the team and clarifying the positions on the team. If this is an existing team, it may be a good time to determine whether all existing positions will remain the same or whether a change is needed. Identify any positions that are particularly critical, because those are often worthy of additional time and resources when recruiting and assessing candidates. For example, the team leader position often merits extra attention, as do positions that others must rely on for support, information, decisions, expertise, etc.
How much will team members interact with and need to **rely** on each other for the team to be successful, versus each person simply doing his or her own job well?	If team members need to interact with and rely on one another extensively, then teamwork competencies will likely be very important. If team members work quite independently, then you can focus more attention on finding the candidates who are best equipped to do their own jobs.
Who are the **existing** members of the team?	If there are existing team members, or if some individuals have been designated as members of the team, consider their strengths and limitations. This will help you clarify any new or additional capabilities that the team may need in Step 2.
Step 2. Clarify Requirements	
What are the **position-specific** requirements for the open position(s)?	For each open position, identify the knowledge, skills, abilities, and other attributes (KSAOs) that are needed to be able to perform the position effectively. Consider whether any of the position-specific KSAOs are more important than others, so if tradeoffs are required, you can prioritize KSAO requirements.

Continued

Table 16.4. Continued

Step	*Tips*
Are there any **team-level** requirements?	Find any skills or capabilities that must exist somewhere on the team, but not necessarily in a particular position. For example, do you need someone on the team who has experience working with a particular senior leader or who speaks a specific language, regardless of the position? Given the profiles of current team members, are there any competency gaps that must be filled somewhere on the team?
	Are there any "groups" that need to be adequately represented? For example, do certain divisions, functional areas, or regions need to be on the team?
	Determine whether you need people on the team who are good "team players" and, if so, whether one or two are adequate, or if everyone on the team needs to be at least somewhat team-oriented.
	Specify which positions on the team need a designated "back-up" person who can fill in for the primary person in that position.
Are there any **organizational requirements** or preferences to consider (e.g., developmental assignments, seeking greater diversity)?	Determine other organizational needs that should be considered. For example, is there an expectation that being assigned to the team will provide a developmental opportunity for someone? Is it important that the team have sufficient diversity?
Looking **across the position, team, and organizational requirements,** are any of these more important than the others?	Identify the relative importance of the position-specific, team, and organizational requirements.
	Clearly distinguish requirements ("must have") from preferences ("nice to have"). This will help you prioritize alternative solutions.

Table 16.4. Continued

Step	*Tips*
Step 3. Establish the Candidate Pool	
Who is **eligible** for the team? Who is potentially **available** and **willing** to join?	Trim the candidate pool based on candidate eligibility and availability. If possible, do this before assessing candidates to avoid wasting resources evaluating individuals who are unavailable.
Are there any particular candidates who **must be on the team** (i.e., placement on the team is mandatory)?	Determine any individuals who must be on the team and whether they need to fill a particular position or can be assigned "somewhere" on the team. Locking people into positions early in the composition process reduces the number of decisions you need to make later, but may also limit some of your options.
What other **constraints** to team membership are there?	For example, perhaps it is known that two of the candidates cannot work well together. Or perhaps you need to "save" the strongest candidate for a position so she can fill an opening on another team that is about to be launched. Decide whether these constraints are firm or could be relaxed if needed.
Step 4. Assess Candidates	
What are the candidates' **individual** position-specific competencies?	In some instances, it is feasible and worthwhile to assess candidates against each position-specific competency requirement. However, in other cases it may only make sense to assess candidates' overall position fit or readiness.
What are the candidates' **team- and organization-**relevant competencies and attributes?	If you identified any team-level or organization-level requirements in Step 2, assess how the candidates compare against those requirements. For example, if each region must be represented on the team, gather information about the home region of each candidate. If you specified that the team will need several people who are good team players, assess the teamwork competencies of the candidates.

Continued

Table 16.4. Continued

Step	*Tips*
How well would the candidates "**fit**" with existing team members?	Compare the candidates' capabilities to those of the existing team members. See whether any of the candidates will fill a capability gap or create an "overload" in any particular area.
Step 5. Tentatively Assign Candidates	
What is a logical way to **assign** a candidate to each open position?	With the information about requirements, current team members, candidates, and constraints in mind, tentatively assign candidates to open positions. If there are multiple openings, begin by trying to meet any non-negotiable requirements and address the most critical needs first. For example, if you have identified two key positions on the team, begin by tentatively placing candidates into those positions. This step and Steps 6 and 7 should be iterative, where you tentatively assign candidates, assess the overall team composition, make adjustments as needed, and assess overall fit until you are comfortable with the team's composition.
Step 6. Assess the Proposed Team Composition	
Is each **position** filled with a person who has at least the basic qualifications to perform (or quickly learn) the position? Do the most **important** positions have high-quality candidates assigned to them?	Sometimes tradeoffs will be needed. For example, you may not be able to fill each position with the person who technically is the best fit (e.g., in the case where the "best" candidates for two positions cannot be on the team together because they dislike one another). Nonetheless, try to ensure that each position is filled by a qualified individual and that the most critical positions take precedence.

Table 16.4. Continued

Step	*Tips*
Are **team-level requirements**, if any, met?	For example, if you specified that the team needed representatives from different functions, check to ensure the proposed solution meets that requirement. Consider how likely it is that the team as configured will be able to work well together (assuming collaboration will be important). Would the candidates as assigned fill any known capability gaps?
Does the proposed "solution" comply with all known **constraints**? Will it satisfy specified **organizational** needs?	Ensure that the composed team complies with unchangeable constraints and mandatory requirements. If you specified organizational needs, confirm that those requirements would be met as well.
Step 7. Adjust the Proposed Membership and/or Plan Compensatory Actions	
Do we need to **adjust** the team composition before finalizing our decision?	If the tentative solution from Step 6 doesn't appear to be ideal, you may want to adjust membership and then compare the alternative solutions. Examine each potential team composition "solution," and rank them according to how well they meet the requirements (by revisiting the questions in Step 6).
Should we plan any **compensatory** actions to mitigate team composition limitations (e.g., training, coaching, and other forms of support)?	After establishing the team's composition, it often makes sense to take actions to help ensure team success. For example, a new team member may need training; a newly formed team may benefit from a planning session; etc. Specify any actions that are needed to help build the team's effectiveness. In some cases, these actions will target a known deficiency, while in others they may simply be the application of a good team development practice.

attention or, in some cases, be filled first with other positions being filled around them.

Contemplate how much team members will need to rely on each other to be successful. As we noted earlier, in teams with high task interdependence, teamwork becomes more critical, which suggests a need to consider and place at least some importance on candidates' team generic KSAOs as well as how well they "fit" with one another (described further under Step 2). In contrast, if the positions are quite independent, you can employ more of a traditional personnel model, simply looking for the best candidate to fill each position. Finally, if the decision involves changing members of an intact team, it helps to think about the team members who will remain on the team. What are their strengths? What deficiencies are there on the team?

With the nature of the team in mind, Step 2 is to *clarify requirements,* including: (a) position-specific requirements; (b) team-level requirements (e.g., skills needed on the team but not a particular position, certain groups that need to be "represented" on the team, team member cooperativeness, and backup requirements); and (c) organizational requirements or preferences (e.g., we want to use this assignment to build a new leader's skill set or we want the team to have a diverse makeup). Decision-makers should then consider the relative priority of the requirements. Overall, this step is about clarifying the target and at least contemplating requirements beyond those associated with doing a particular job on the team and prioritizing the importance of these requirements, which reflects the balanced scorecard feature that we noted earlier. Getting this step right lays a solid foundation and makes all the subsequent steps easier.

Step 3 is to *establish the candidate pool.* This can range from generating a quick list of targeted candidates to job posting or conducting an external search to uncover possible team members. During this step it is important to consider candidate availability (whether their workload allows them to participate on a project team or whether they are willing to relocate) as well as any other constraints (for example, we want to save a really strong candidate for a forthcoming team assignment or we require a particular person to be on the team in some capacity).

Once the pool has been identified, the next step (Step 4) is to *assess the candidates.* The type of assessment will be based on the previously identified requirements, so sometimes the candidate assessment will focus almost strictly on technical skills, while in other cases it will also include teamwork competencies and how well prospective team members will "fit" with existing team members or fill key team needs. This assessment can be rigorous and data-driven (for important decisions when time and resources allow) or quick and subjective. As with all selection decisions, having good data and a rigorous process will likely result in higher validity, but we recognize that, when forming a quick project team, a rigorous assessment of the candidates may not always be feasible.

Based on the assessment, Step 5 is to *tentatively assign candidates* to the team. Depending on the type of team composition decision, this could be one person joining an existing team, forming a team from scratch, etc. In any case, this step involves the preliminary, tentative assignment of candidate(s) to positions. Prior to making the final decision, Step 6 is to *examine the proposed team composition*. Assuming this is the team, would the requirements established earlier be met? Are any of the proposed candidates not fully ready to perform the position they have been tentatively assigned to fill? Are there any shortages or surpluses of skills or capabilities on the team? Are there any collaboration challenges that are likely to emerge given this mix of people? Do we have enough people who are "team players"? Do we have too many people who are difficult to work with? Do we have enough team members who can be counted on and are reliable? In short, this stage amounts to a face or judgmental validity check where one gauges the extent to which the proposed composition feels right along a myriad of dimensions.

Finally, Step 7 is to *make any adjustments* as needed and/or *plan compensatory actions* to mitigate concerns. If the proposed team composition appears to fully address all needs, then proceed. But in some cases, upon reflection it may become apparent that the proposed team composition is not ideal.

If so, it may make sense to compare alternative team configurations, changing individual members or entire configurations. In such a case, you would compare the various "solutions" and rank them based on how well they meet the requirements specified in Step 2.

Sometimes you may need to establish a plan to remediate remaining concerns. For example, that might mean pairing an inexperienced team leader with a coach; providing training to a team member to offset a known skill deficiency; or facilitating a meeting with the team to clarify their mission and roles if the team is composed of people who have not worked on this type of team before. In some cases, it could even make sense to redesign particular team tasks or positions to offset a potential shortcoming.

Whereas remedial efforts of this nature can help address potential shortcomings in team composition, they also signal that a suboptimal composition may have been constituted to begin with. To be clear, we fully realize that there is no such thing as guaranteed team synergy by simply putting together the right mix of people. Sometimes, given the candidate pool, a fully qualified team cannot be formed. And even the best of teams struggle at times and require help. But to be equally clear, defaulting to a decision process of "who is available" or "who can do this job well" without considering the overall composition of the team is courting failure. Remedial efforts are costly and less effective once the team has established a pattern of struggling. It is worth attending to the composition issues from the beginning, for example, applying a mindset such as the one embedded in the seven-step process.

Additional Considerations for Research and Application

Our focus has been on how to best allocate employee human talent to enhance team effectiveness. And while we consider this to be a primary driver of organizational competitiveness, we recognize that there are additional goals that should be considered. For example, it is very tempting to over-commit your most talented employees. If team effectiveness is important, then you want to have your best players on the team. But this logical strategy has hidden costs. First, over-committing your most talented employees will stress and burn them out. It may well have the unintended consequence of driving your best human resources out of the organization. Furthermore, if your star employees are the ones who are always called upon, you may fail to develop future stars. In other words, if you do not develop your bench by giving people "stretch" assignments, you become vulnerable because your star employees may not be available for important assignments in the future. Failing to do so also sends an implicit message that only your star members' efforts are valued. The larger issue is that team composition has to be viewed from the perspective of the larger human resource system. Not only do teams have to be optimally staffed for effectiveness (within and across teams), but teaming assignments serve larger human resource purposes by constituting vehicles for informal learning, cross-training, morale boosting, and a variety of other purposes.

While there is an emerging science of team composition, clearly many challenges lie ahead. For example, research should address which combinations, of which models, under what circumstances, best predict effective team composition. Second, we have discussed team composition as though it is a static variable, but team membership changes over time. Consequently, questions as to the relative benefits or detriments of changing team composition should be overlaid on the current approach. Moreover, individuals are typically members of multiple teams in many organizations. How does multiple team membership influence individual members? Are there benefits in terms of knowledge sharing and transfer through multiple memberships? Is there a tipping point beyond which multiple memberships become dysfunctional for individuals and teams alike? In short, not only should future research consider the complex combinations of multiple composition models outlined above, but it should also consider dynamic factors and alternative work arrangements, and how they enhance or undermine team composition effects.

As described in our discussion of constraints, a challenge associated with applying a team optimization process or system is the amount of information and other resources that can come into play when making a decision. In a traditional personnel selection scenario, more complete information on the position requirements and individual candidate capabilities result in better predictions about the best candidate(s) for the position. But the time required to accurately specify the position requirements and conduct comprehensive and valid assessments of a large pool of job candidates is non-trivial. The proposed approach layers additional information requirements and assessments onto those of a traditional selection decision (for example, team-level requirements, relative importance weights). Although the evaluations can be quick and subjective rather than rigorous and data-driven, gathering and organizing even quick assessment data can be challenging when it is required for the position and team. Also, when making decisions about existing teams, assessments of current team members are needed in addition to assessments of candidates.

In summary, team composition issues are simultaneously very simple and very complex. Team composition is straightforward in that team-based organizations benefit from emphasizing team-generic competencies throughout their HRM system. It really is that simple. Team composition is complex, however, in that achieving optimal team compositions is a daunting task, as each member simultaneously adds to the generic team skills, position competencies, extreme scores, and distributional properties of KSAOs in the team. In this chapter we have provided some recommendations that we believe may be helpful for decision-makers faced with such responsibilities. Whether managers are relying on their instincts, or whether they are applying well-informed algorithms, to the extent that they specify a priori the relative priority of scores derived from the four different models and consider team composition in the context of a larger HRM system, their efforts will be rewarded with greater organizational effectiveness.

References and Further Reading

Arrow, H., & McGrath, J.E. (1995). Membership dynamics in groups at work: A theoretical framework. *Research in Organizational Behavior: An Annual Series of Analytical Essays and Critical Reviews, 17,* 373–411.

Bell, S.T. (2007). Deep-level composition variables as predictors of team performance: A meta-analysis. *Journal of Applied Psychology, 92*(3), 595–615.

Bell, S.T., Villado, A.J., Lukasik, M.A., Belau, L., & Briggs, A.L. (2011). Getting specific about demographic diversity variables and team performance relationships: A meta-analysis. *Journal of Management, 37*(3), 709–743.

Barrick, M.R., Stewart, G.L., Neubert, M.J., & Mount, M.K. (1998). Relating member ability and personality to work-team processes and team effectiveness. *Journal of Applied Psychology, 83*, 377–391.

Baker, D.P., Salas, E., & Cannon-Bowers, J.A. (1998). Team task analysis: Lost but hopefully not forgotten. *The Industrial-Organizational Psychologist, 35*, 79–83.

Burke, C.S., Salas, E., Wilson-Donnelly, K., & Priest, H. (2004). How to turn a team of experts into an expert medical team: Guidance from the aviation and military communities. *Quality Safety Health Care, 13*(1), 96–104.

Cannon-Bowers, J.A., Tannenbaum, S.I., Salas, E., & Volpe, C.E. (1995). Defining team competencies and establishing team training requirements. In R. Guzzo & E. Salas (Eds.), *Team effectiveness and decision making in organizations.* San Francisco: Jossey-Bass.

Cooke, N.J., Kiekel, P.A., Salas, E., Stout, R., Bowers, C., & Cannon-Bowers, J.A. (2003). Measuring team knowledge: A window to the cognitive underpinnings of team performance. *Group Dynamics: Theory Research and Practice, 7*(3), 179–199.

Devine, D.J., & Philips, J.L. (2001). Do smarter teams do better: A meta-analysis of cognitive ability and team performance. *Small Group Research, 32*(5), 507–532.

Ellis, A.P.J., Bell, B.S., Ployhart, R.E., Hollenbeck, J.R., & Ilgen, D.R. (2005). An evaluation of generic teamwork skills training with action teams: Effects on cognitive and skill-based outcomes. *Journal of Applied Psychology, 58*(3), 641–672.

Halfhill, T., Nielsen, T.M., Sundstrom, E., & Weilbaecher, A. (2005). Group personality composition and performance in military service teams. *Military Psychology, 17*(1), 41–54.

Harris, T.C., & Barnes-Farrell, J.L. (1997). Components of teamwork: Impact on evaluations of contributions to work team effectiveness. *Journal of Applied Social Psychology, 27*(19), 1694–1715.

Heslin, R. (1964). Predicting group task effectiveness from member characteristics. *Psychological Bulletin, 62*, 248–256.

Hirschfeld, R.R., Jordan, M.H., Feild, H.S., Giles, W.F., & Armenakis, A.A. (2006). Becoming team players: Team members' mastery of teamwork knowledge as a predictor of team task proficiency and observed teamwork effectiveness. *Journal of Applied Psychology, 91*(2), 467–474.

Humphrey, S.E., Morgeson, F.P., & Mannor, M.J. (2009). Developing a theory of the strategic core of teams: A role composition model of team performance. *Journal of Applied Psychology, 94*, 48–61.

Ilgen, D.R. (1999). Teams embedded in organizations—Some implications. *American Psychologist, 54*(2), 129–139.

Ilgen, D.R., Hollenbeck, J.R., Johnson, M., & Jundt, D. (2005). Teams in organizations: From IPO models to IMOI models. *Annual Review of Psychology, 56*, 517–543.

Jackson, S.E. (1992). Team composition in organizational settings: Issues in managing an increasingly diverse workforce. In S. Worchel, W. Wood, & J.A. Simpson (Eds.), *Group process and productivity*. Thousand Oaks, CA: Sage.

Jackson, S.E., Brett, J.F., Sessa, V.I., Cooper, D.M., Julin, J.A., & Peyronnin, K. (1991). Some differences make a difference: Interpersonal dissimilarity and group heterogeneity as correlates of recruitment, promotion, and turnover. *Journal of Applied Psychology, 76*, 675–689.

Jung, D.I., & Sosik, J.J. (1999). Effects of group characteristics on work group performance: A longitudinal investigation. *Group Dynamics: Theory, Research, and Practice, 3*, 279–290.

Kozlowski, S.W.J., & Bell, B.S. (2003). Work groups and teams in organizations. In W. Borman, D.R. Ilgen, & R. Klimoski (Eds.), *Comprehensive handbook of psychology: Industrial and organizational psychology* (Vol. 12, pp. 333–375): Hoboken, NJ: John Wiley & Sons.

Kozlowski, S.W.J., & Ilgen, D.R. (2006). Enhancing the effectiveness of work groups and teams. *Psychological Science, 7*, 77–124.

Kozlowski, S.W.J., & Klein, K.J. (2000). A multi-level approach to theory and research in organizations: Contextual, temporal, and emergent processes. In K.J. Klein & S.W.J. Kozlowski (Eds.), *Multilevel theory, research, and methods in organizations* (pp. 3–90). San Francisco: Jossey-Bass.

LePine, J.A., Hollenbeck, J.R., Ilgen, K.R., & Hedlund, J. (1997). Effects of individual differences on the performance of hierarchical decision-making teams: Much more than g. *Journal of Applied Psychology, 82*, 803–811.

Mann, R.D. (1959). A review of the relationship between personality and performance in small groups. *Psychological Bulletin, 56*(4), 241–270.

Mathieu, J., Maynard, M.T., Rapp, T., & Gilson, L. (2008). Team effectiveness 1997–2007: A review of recent advancements and a glimpse into the future. *Journal of Management, 34*(3), 410–476.

Mathieu, J.E., Tannenbaum, S.I., Kukenberger, M., Donsbach, J.S., Alliger, G.E., & Salas, E. (2010). The development of the team role experience and orientation (TREO) measure. Working paper. Albany, NY: Group for Organizational Effectiveness.

McCormick, E.J. (1979). *Job analysis: Methods and applications.* New York: AMACOM.

Morgan, B.B., Jr., & Lassiter, D.L. (1992). Team composition and staffing. In R.W. Swezey & E. Salas (Eds.), *Teams: Their training and performance* (pp. 75–100). Norwood, NJ: Ablex.

Mumford, T.V., Van Iddekinge, C.H., Morgeson, F.P., & Campion, M.A. (2008). The team role test: Development and validation of a team role knowledge situational judgment test. *Journal of Applied Psychology, 93*(2), 250–267.

Steiner, I.D. (1972). *Group processes and productivity.* New York: Academic Press.

Stevens, M.J., & Campion, M.A. (1994). The knowledge, skill, and ability requirements for teamwork: Implications for human resource management. *Journal of Management, 20,* 503–530.

Watson, W.E., Johnson, L., & Merritt, D. (1998). Team orientation, self-orientation, and diversity in task groups: Their connection to team performance over time. *Group & Organization Management, 23*(2), 161–188.

CHAPTER SEVENTEEN

How, When, and Why You Should Measure Team Performance

Kimberly A. Smith-Jentsch,
Mary Jane Sierra,
and Christopher William Wiese
University of Central Florida Department of Psychology

As the prevalence of team-based work designs continues to grow, the degree to which organizational success depends on team performance is rapidly increasing (Devine, Clayton, Philips, Dunford, & Melner, 1999). As a result, the measurement of team performance is also becoming increasingly important to organizations. This is the case because measuring team performance contributes to enhancing it, as well as to enhancing organizational performance itself. It could be said, in fact, that team performance measurement is the first step toward performance improvement within organizations.

Team performance measurement (TPM) has the potential to increase team performance and to benefit organizations in multiple ways. Its ultimate value to an organization, however, is determined by the quality of the TPM methods employed. The quality of TPM, in turn, hinges upon a number of key factors. In this chapter, we review the many valuable functions that TPM can serve within organizations and identify the primary factors which must be taken into consideration to ensure that TPM efforts serve their intended purpose.

Why Measure Team Performance?

Team performance measurement efforts have the potential to benefit organizations in multiple ways. There are four primary functions that TPM can serve. First, TPM allows organizations to provide teams with performance feedback. Such feedback can be used to increase the motivation of teams to perform, as well as team performance itself (for example, Chen & Kanfer, 2006; DeShon, Kozlowski, Schmidt, Milner, & Weichmann, 2004; Kluger & DeNisi, 1996; Pritchard, Harrell, DiazGranados, & Guzman, 2008). Second, TPM allows organizations to distribute rewards fairly (for example, pay, benefits) to teams based on their performance. Such performance-based compensation can also be used to increase the motivation and performance of teams (for example, Akdere & Yilmaz, 2006; DeMatteo, Eby, & Sundstrom, 1998). Third, TPM allows organizations to monitor team performance and diagnose team performance problems. Such information can be used to assess team training needs and to make additional decisions about a team's future (for example, whether the team should be disbanded or promoted). Lastly, TPM can serve to help organizations evaluate the effectiveness of various human resource (HR) policies, procedures, and tools (Wildman, Bedwell, Salas, & Smith-Jentsch, 2011). Specifically, TPM can aid in the validation of team selection and composition methods, team training methods, team feedback systems, and team reward systems.

In order for TPM to fulfill its potential to benefit an organization by serving one or more of the above functions, it must be conducted in a manner that is appropriate given its intended purpose. Thus, the quality of TPM ultimately determines its usefulness. The quality of TPM itself is determined by the decisions made when an organization is faced with three unavoidable questions: namely, *what* aspect of team performance should be measured, *how* should team performance be measured, and *when* should team performance be measured?

Because there are many aspects of team performance that can be measured, many ways to measure each, and many times at which team performance can be measured, the decisions facing organizations are by no means simple ones. In addition, the consequences of incorrect decisions during the TPM process are by no means minor. Measuring team performance requires the investment of valuable organizational resources (for example, money, manpower). Failing to measure the correct aspect of team performance or doing so using an inappropriate method or at the wrong time will ultimately reduce an organization's return on its investment into TPM, thereby resulting in wasted resources. Further, TPM systems that are incorrectly designed and/or implemented may even serve to harm organizations. This may occur if such systems are perceived by organizational members as being inappropriate, ineffective, or unjust. Moreover, because an invalid TPM system is likely to provide inaccurate information about team performance to organizational decision-makers, such systems may result in poor team performance-related decisions and, ultimately, the misallocation of organizational resources (for example, training dollars). Because of the risks associated with making incorrect decisions during the TPM process, the remainder of this chapter outlines the factors that organizations should consider when determining which aspects of team performance to measure, how to measure them, and when to conduct TPM.

What Should Be Measured?

Before measuring team performance, organizations must first make decisions about which aspect or aspects of team performance to measure. Because team performance has multiple components, these decisions are not necessarily easy ones. As such, the following section will detail the different aspects of team performance, outline factors that organizations should consider when determining which aspects to measure, and provide recommendations for measuring each.

There are multiple aspects of team performance that can be assessed during TPM. The first choice that an organization must make is whether to measure team performance outcomes, team performance processes, or both. *Team outcome measures* assess the products or results of a team's efforts. In other words, they indicate *what* the team achieves. Team performance outcomes can be measured in terms of how fast, how efficiently, or how well a team met its objectives. Some examples include sales dollars, customer satisfaction, accidents, wasted materials, airport take-offs and landings per hour, and military casualties. *Team process measures,* on the other hand, assess the actions taken by team members during and between team performance episodes. In other words, they indicate what team members do during team performance or *how* the team achieves what it does (that is, how the team achieves performance outcomes). Team performance processes can be further divided into taskwork- and teamwork-oriented processes. *Taskwork processes* are the actions performed by individual team members to accomplish their role-specific tasks. These often involve team member interactions with technology, data, or customers. Some examples of taskwork processes include maintaining altitude (for an aircrew member), taking blood pressure readings (for a medical team member), and interpreting a radar scope (for a military team member). *Teamwork processes* are the actions performed by team members to coordinate or interact with one another. Some examples of teamwork processes include information exchange, error-correction, offering assistance, and providing guidance to another team member (Morgan, Salas, & Glickman, 1993; Smith-Jentsch, Johnston, & Payne, 1998).

As compared to team performance processes, organizations more often measure team performance outcomes. This is largely due to the fact that team outcomes appear, on their surface, to be more objective. In addition, they are generally easier to measure. This does not mean that it is always best to measure team outcomes in lieu of measuring team processes, however. In fact, team outcome measures are often less appropriate for and useful to organizations as compared to team performance measures. One reason for this is that, oftentimes, outcome measures are contaminated by factors other than team performance (Borman, 1991). Although team outcomes do vary as a function of team members' actions, they can also be heavily affected by factors outside of the team's control (Smith-Jentsch, Johnston, & Payne, 1998). Thus, outcome measures are most useful when an organization is interested in identifying how factors external to the team (for example, policies, procedures, or environmental features) impact team performance rather than determining how a team's own characteristics or behaviors (for example, a team's level of knowledge or skill) impact their performance.

To the degree that the external factors that impact team outcomes can be identified and controlled, outcome measures can be very useful to organizations. They are especially useful when an organization is interested in comparing the performance of multiple teams to one another or to some predefined criterion (for example, sales needed in order to make a profit). For instance, the performance of a sales team can be compared to that of other sales teams operating in similarly affluent areas (since affluence of potential customers is a factor external to the team that may greatly impact sales team performance outcomes). If such external factors are not taken into consideration, however, and organizations still proceed with using only outcomes to compare teams' performance, negative consequences may result. This is especially true if TPM is conducted to determine reward distribution among teams. Specifically, teams are likely to perceive the TPM strategy (and thus reward distribution) as being biased and unfair, which, in turn, is likely to decrease their motivation to perform.

A focus on team performance outcomes may also result in negative consequences when an organization uses TPM for the purpose of providing teams with performance feedback (for example, to increase their motivation and performance). Feedback that is based solely on measurements of team performance outcomes may be useful in motivating teams to work *harder* because it tells them how close/far they are from achieving their desired outcomes, but such feedback does not provide teams with the information they need to work *smarter* because it does not tell them *how* to improve their performance processes to achieve those outcomes. Therefore, feedback based solely on team outcome measures (that is, with no regard to team process measures) is not likely to improve team performance. If team members do not possess the necessary skills or knowledge to improve their own performance without being given information about *how* to improve it, then they will not benefit from outcome-focused performance feedback (Dorsey, Russell, Keil, Campbell, Van Buskirk, & Schuck, 2009). In fact, outcome-focused feedback may only serve to frustrate and demotivate such teams because it will make them want to perform better without telling them how to. In addition to these issues, there is often a delay between the time that team performance processes occur and the time that team performance outcomes are realized as a result of those processes. Therefore, feedback based on outcome data alone may not accurately reflect the health and status of their current team performance processes. As a result, such feedback may cause teams to adjust aspects of their performance processes that are no longer broken or to ignore existing problems in their performance processes that have not yet had an impact on their outcomes.

Unlike team outcome measures, team process measures allow an organization to pinpoint particular areas of team performance (specific processes) that are in need of improvement. Therefore, performance feedback based on team process measures tells teams *how* to improve their performance to achieve desired outcomes (Kluger & DeNisi, 1996). Further, because team processes are not as likely as team outcomes to be heavily impacted by factors outside the team's control, team process measures are less prone to contamination by extraneous factors. As a result, team process measures allow organizations to determine the degree to which a team's outcomes are simply a matter of luck, or other factors outside the team's control, by comparing them to team outcome measures. Information obtained from team process measures can be extremely useful to organizations. Such information may be used to redesign workflow, identify a need for additional team members (or a reduction in team members), identify a need to shift team membership, or modify team training. Further, because measures that assess taskwork processes provide organizations with different information than measures that assess teamwork processes (Morgan et al., 1993), it is important for organizations to utilize both. Measuring both types of team processes enables organizations to identify the precise types of interventions necessary to exact the greatest improvements in team performance outcomes. Based on this, we offer four recommendations regarding which aspects of team performance should be measured.

- *Recommendation 1:* Whenever possible, identify and account for factors outside of a team's control that significantly bias *team outcome measures,* especially when using TPM to distribute rewards.

- *Recommendation 2:* Data from *team outcome measures* should be used for motivational purposes only when team members possess the knowledge and skills to perform their roles effectively and not when they need developmental assistance in order to improve their performance.
- *Recommendation 3:* Data from *team process measures* should be used to determine training needs, to provide developmental feedback, to inform work redesign efforts, and to identify problems with team composition/staffing.
- *Recommendation 4:* Both *measures of taskwork and teamwork* should be used in order to determine the appropriate target for remedial training (that is, weak links or the team as a whole).

How Should Team Performance Be Measured?

Before measuring team performance, organizations must make decisions about *how* to measure it. Because team performance can be measured using multiple rating sources and multiple rating formats, these decisions are not easy ones. The following section will detail the different rating sources and formats available, outline factors that organizations should consider when determining which sources and formats to use, and provide recommendations for using each.

Rating Sources

An organization has many options when deciding who will be the *source* of team performance information. Information regarding team processes and outcomes can be obtained from a number of different sources. These include sources such as automated systems (for example, latency data), outside observers, supervisors, and even team members themselves. Each source of team performance information may be more or less useful to organizations depending on the intended purpose of the TPM system. Further, each source comes with both advantages and disadvantages that organizations must consider before deciding how to obtain team performance information.

For organizations interested in measuring team processes, team performance information gathered from team members themselves may be particularly useful. Team member ratings are especially useful when organizations wish to collect team process data over long periods of time. Compared to individuals outside of the team, team members have a greater number of opportunities to make relevant observations of team processes during any given period of time (Brannick, Roach, & Salas, 1993; Tesluk, Mathieu, Zaccaro, & Marks, 1997) and are able to make such observations during their entire tenure with the team. Further, they are more likely to be aware of the behavioral intentions and assumptions of team members and are, therefore, better able to provide organizations with information that is helpful for understanding *why* specific actions were engaged in. Such information is useful in that it may be used to inform team training, among other HR functions. There is a downside to using team members as sources of team performance information, however. Specifically, team members' performance ratings are likely to be distorted by self-serving biases (Tesluk et al., 1997) and are, therefore, likely to be inflated to some degree. There are some steps organizations can take to enhance the accuracy of team performance information collected directly from team members, however. For example, team member ratings are likely to be most accurate when they are collected for developmental purposes only and when team members themselves are made aware of the intended purpose of TPM (Jawahar & Williams, 1997; Heidemeier & Moser, 2009).

Supervisors or leaders may also be a particularly useful source for team performance information when organizations are interested in measuring team processes. As with information provided by team members, however, performance information provided by supervisors/leaders may be distorted in a self-serving manner (Hogan & Shelton, 1998). This may be especially likely if supervisors/leaders believe that their team performance ratings are going to be used to determine the distribution of rewards among team members and/or leaders within the organization. In addition to this significant disadvantage, there are several advantages to using supervisor and leader ratings.

For instance, given their status and experience, those responsible for supervising or leading teams may be more likely than team members (as well as other sources) to have a good understanding of the organization's normative standards for team performance. As such, team performance ratings provided by supervisors/leaders may be more meaningful because they are informed by information regarding organizational expectations for team performance as well as information regarding the performance of other teams within the organization. Despite this, there are additional disadvantages to collecting team performance information from supervisors/leaders. Namely, supervisors typically have fewer observations of team performance to inform their performance ratings than do team members themselves (Cascio & Aguinis, 2011). This, of course, results from the fact that they often do not spend as much time with the team as team members do. Moreover, when a supervisor or team leader *does* have an opportunity to observe team performance, he or she is often unable to gather information about the team's typical "everyday" performance behaviors. This is the case because team members are likely to perform to their fullest potential in response to the supervisor's/leader's presence.

In other words, supervisors and team leaders may see only what teams are capable of doing when they are trying their best (maximum performance) and not what teams typically do when they are unaware their performance is being observed (typical performance; Klehe & Anderson, 2007; Sackett, Zedeck, & Fogli, 1988). Therefore, team performance information provided by supervisors/leaders may be based on their incomplete knowledge of team performance in general and especially the team's *typical* performance.

Observers from outside the organization may also be useful sources for organizations interesting in obtaining information about team performance processes. As is true with supervisors/leaders, however, the presence of outside observers during team performance (whether it be on-the-job or during simulation activities) is likely to increase team members' motivation to perform to their full potential (Klehe & Anderson, 2007). Information about team performance gathered from outside observers may not be indicative of a team's typical performance. Despite the disadvantage that gathering team performance information from outside observers shares with gathering such information from supervisors/leaders, looking to outside observers for team performance information has some advantages.

The primary advantage of utilizing outside observers is that such individuals are not as likely as supervisors, leaders, and team members to provide information about team performance that is biased and self-serving (Wildman et al., 2011). This is a result of the fact that outside observers are less likely to have a vested interest in teams performing well, allowing them to be more objective when observing and evaluating team performance. An additional factor that organizations must consider when deciding whether to use outside observers as a source of team performance information is the relative utility of doing so. Because outside observers must be purposefully brought into settings where they would not otherwise be present, relying on them for team performance information may not be as cost-effective as relying on supervisors, leaders, and team members, who do not usually need to be repositioned in order to provide information about team performance.

Finally, information regarding team processes, as well as team outcomes, can also be obtained from sources capable of gathering it unobtrusively. Such sources include electronic communication records and written documents. As the prevalence of computer-mediated communication continues to increase (Baltes, Dickson, Sherman, Bauer, & LaGanke, 2002), these automated sources are becoming rich wells of team performance information in organizations. Utilizing automated sources for collecting team performance information has a number of important advantages. First, these sources are less likely than any other to provide information regarding team performance that is biased (self-serving). Further, because these sources are unobtrusive and often part of the team's daily work, their presence is less likely than other sources (supervisors, leaders, outside observers) to have an impact on team performance. Therefore, information gathered from these sources is more likely than that obtained from many other sources to be indicative of a team's typical performance. Further, because of the role they are likely to play in the team's daily work, these sources have the ability to collect a large amount of team performance information on a regular basis. In addition, because it is likely to reduce the number of man-hours required for TPM, utilization of these sources has the potential to be a highly cost-effective method for collecting information about team performance processes and outcomes. Along with the many advantages they afford, these sources also come with disadvantages. Specifically, these sources may not be the most appropriate for, or even capable of, collecting certain type of team performance information (for example, information that is only observable to human raters). As a result, the information these sources provide to organizations regarding team performance may be incomplete.

Based on what is known about the most valuable uses for, as well as the advantages and disadvantages of, each potential source of team performance information, we offer three recommendations for organizations interested in initiating a TPM system.

- *Recommendation 5: Supervisors or outside observers* can provide useful ratings of a team's capability to perform team processes at "maximum performance."
- *Recommendation 6: Team members* themselves can provide useful ratings of typical team processes, particularly when such ratings are being used for developmental purposes and the team members are aware of this.
- *Recommendation 7: Unobtrusive sources* of data on team processes and outcomes (for example, logs from shared online workspaces, recordings) are useful as a measure of teams' more typical performance.

Rating Formats

Just as there are many rating sources, there are multiple rating formats available to organizations interested in initiating a TPM system. There are four primary rating formats that rating sources can use to assess team performance. These include checklists, frequency scales, latency/deviation metrics, and subjective rating scales. While numerous variations of these formats exist, an exhaustive description of these is beyond the scope of this chapter. In general, however, each assessment format possesses

Exhibit 17.1 Sample Checklist for a Restaurant Team

Sample Restaurant Performance Checklist

Restaurant Name: _______________ **Date:** ________
Assessment Start Time: __________
Assessment End Time:___________

Instructions

Please check the box next to each action as it is completed by the team.

- ☐ Server took customer's order
- ☐ Server delivered order to kitchen
- ☐ Kitchen prepared customer's order
- ☐ Kitchen notified server order was completed
- ☐ Server delivered order to customer

characteristics that make it more or less appropriate for measuring team performance during certain team tasks. As such, we describe the characteristics associated with each format and make recommendations for their use based on the team tasks for which they are most appropriate.

Checklists provide raters of team performance with a list of actions that must be performed and/or a list of objectives that must be achieved by a team (see Exhibit 17.1; Krokos, Baker, Alonso, & Day, 2009). Checklists simply require raters to indicate whether or not the team performed each necessary action (for example, opening a valve) and/or whether or not the team achieved each necessary objective (for example, solving a problem) listed on the checklist. Because checklists must be developed prior to team performance, this format can only be used to assess team processes when team tasks are highly proceduralized, so that actions (and ideally the order of those actions) can be identified ahead of time. Checklists are particularly useful when a team's errors of omission (failing to complete necessary actions) are considered to be more important than errors of commission (completing unnecessary actions) since necessary actions are specified in advance whereas unnecessary ones are not. Raters themselves only need to determine whether or not an action was completed and *not* whether the absence of an action was an error. As such, checklists are relatively easy for raters of team performance to complete.

Frequency scales provide team performance raters with descriptions of necessary performance behaviors/actions (for example, offering assistance) and/or outcomes (for example, sales) and ask them to indicate the number of times the team completed each action and achieved each outcome (see Exhibit 17.2; Krokos et al., 2009). One limitation of frequency scales is that their validity is highly dependent on the clarity and specificity of the definitions provided for each action and outcome. Further, although frequency scales are useful for providing organizations with information regarding the number or amount of times a team accomplished an action or outcome, they do not take into account the quality of that action or outcome. Thus, they are most appropriate for use when the quality of an action (for example, asking for assistance) or outcome (for example, sales) is not expected to vary significantly over time or across teams and the primary determinant of team performance is the quantity of such actions or outcomes.

Moreover, frequency scales have a significant advantage over checklists because there is no need for particular actions or outcomes (and the timing of those needs) to be specified prior to team performance. This is the case because frequency scales can be (and are often) completed by raters *after* team performance episodes. It is important to note, however, that because of memory limitations (Sackett & Tuzinski, 2001), raters may find it difficult to accurately report the frequency of a team's actions and outcomes over an extended period of time or when their cognitive resources are consumed by non-TPM activities. Therefore, frequency scales are most practical when the team performance observation period is short and when outside observers are used who can focus solely on TPM. For this reason, they may be most useful as part of simulation-based training and assessment efforts.

Latency/deviation-based formats may be used to assess the speed or accuracy of a team's performance (Krokos et al., 2009).

Exhibit 17.2 Sample Frequency for a Sales Team

Sample Sales Team Frequency Measure

Company Name: ____________ **Assessment Start Date: _____**
Assessment End Date: ______

Instructions

Please place a checkmark in the frequency column every time the team engages in a specific action.

Targeted Actions

Asking for Assistance—A team member asked another team member for support with completion of their job tasks or information concerning how to complete their job tasks.

Set Sales Goal—Teams gathered to establish the desirable number of sales to be attained within a sales period.

Made a Sale—Team members completed a transaction with a client which resulted in a sale of a product.

Met to Discuss Prospective Clients—Teams gathered to exchange information concerning new potential clients.

Action	Frequency
Asking for assistance	
Set sales goal	
Made a sale	
Met to discuss new prospective clients	

Examples of this type of format include units of time (for example, minutes until a customer is served) or physical distance (for example, miles from a target). Due to their nature, such measures are most appropriate when an automated system can be used to reliably capture this type of information with a high level of specificity and accuracy (for example, time stamps).

Subjective rating scales (see Exhibit 17.3) may be used to quantify the quality of a team's processes (for example, redistribution of workload) or outcomes (for example, innovation). These scales require raters to indicate the quality of a team's processes or outcomes by selecting a numbered option, out of a set (arranged along a continuum ranging from effective to ineffective processes and outcomes), that best describes the team's performance (Robbins & Judge, 2008). The number of scale points provided, varies, as does the specificity of the descriptions assigned to each scale point. For example, some scales (for example, behaviorally anchored rating scales, BARS) provide detailed descriptions for each scale point, whereas others may simply provide descriptions or anchors for the scale points at the ends of the continuum (Wildman et al., 2011).

Alternatively, raters may simply be provided with a definition of the process or outcome in question (for example, a definition of innovation) and then asked to rate the degree to which the team's process or outcome meets that definition. Because subjective rating scales allow raters to assess the quality of team processes and outcomes, they are most useful when team performance in a task depends mainly on the quality of the team's actions/outcomes and not their mere presence, absence, or quantity. Moreover, because their accurate completion requires an in-depth understanding of team processes and outcomes as well as extensive knowledge of what ineffective and effective team processes and outcomes look like, subjective rating scales are most appropriate for use with certain sources and with certain team tasks. Specifically, subjective rating scales are most appropriate for use when the raters of team performance are highly experienced or skilled in the task at hand. Further, these scales are most useful for measuring team processes and outcomes over longer periods of time, when impressions can be formed based on multiple observations.

Exhibit 17.3 Sample Rating Scale Measure for a Typical Team

Sample Rating Scale

Company Name: ________

Instructions

Please rate the team's effectiveness in the following areas using the scale provided, where 1 = Highly Ineffective and 7 = Highly Effective.

Dimension Definitions

Strategy Formulation—The planned actions or approaches the team specifies for achieving team goals and objectives.

Goal Specification—Identifying, prioritizing, assigning, and providing time and resource allocation parameters concerning the team's goals.

Coordination—Synchronization of interdependent actions with one another with respect to the order in which team actions are performed.

Conflict Management—Establishing preventative measures to counteract potential conflict as well as addressing and quelling conflict as it arises.

Backup Behavior—Verbally providing a teammate with feedback or coaching, aiding a teammate in accomplishing their tasks, and absorbing and completing the remainder of a teammate's task.

	Highly Ineffective						Highly Effective
1. Strategy Formulation	1	2	3	4	5	6	7
2. Goal Specification	1	2	3	4	5	6	7
3. Coordination	1	2	3	4	5	6	7
4. Conflict Management	1	2	3	4	5	6	7
5. Backup Behavior	1	2	3	4	5	6	7

Based on what is known about the four types of rating formats and their compatibility with various team tasks, we offer five recommendations.

- *Recommendation 8:* Use *checklists* to measure team performance when necessary actions (for example, procedural) or outcomes are predictable in advance and errors of omission are important.
- *Recommendation 9:* Use *frequency counts* to measure team performance processes or outcomes when the quantity of a particular action or outcome is what primarily distinguishes effective from ineffective teams and the quality of the action varies little (situations when more is always better).
- *Recommendation 10:* Use automated systems to provide inputs for *latency/deviation-based scales.*
- *Recommendation 11:* Whenever possible, *collect raw data* reflecting productivity (for example, sales, units produced) and efficiency (for example, amount of time or materials per unit) rather than chunking the data (for example, more than five, less than 50 percent).
- *Recommendation 12:* Use *subjective rating scales* (Likert-type or BARS) when the quality of an action or outcome is what primarily distinguishes effective from ineffective teams rather than the presence or absence or quantity of an action.

When Should Team Performance Be Measured?

Finally, before measuring team performance, organizations must decide *when* to measure it. Because team performance can be measured at multiple times, this decision is a substantial one. The following section will detail the different times at which team performance can be measured, outline factors that organizations should consider when determining at which times to measure team performance, and provide recommendations for measuring team performance at each point in time.

Measure Team Performance After Raters Have Been Trained

In order for team performance to be accurately measured, individuals responsible for rating team performance must first be trained to identify and differentiate among the processes and outcomes being measured (Cascio & Aguinis, 2011; Landy & Farr, 1980). There are a number of reasons for this. First, without a clear understanding of what they are to measure, raters may fail to observe relevant behaviors and outcomes because their attentional resources may not be dedicated to looking for them. Second, raters typically are not able to remember the specific details related to team performance over time. Instead, as they observe team performance, they use their pre-existing notions of performance to interpret what they observe and then they store those general interpretations into memory. As a result, instead of noticing and remembering specific details of team performance, raters tend to only notice and remember their general impressions of how effective or ineffective a team was (Woehr, 1992). Thus, although a rater (for example, supervisor, outside observer) may be present when a relevant process or outcome is demonstrated by a team, he or she may not realize the significance of the process or outcome at the time. As a result, the rater may not store that process or outcome into memory in a form that can be retrieved later when he or she is asked to make judgments about specific team performance categories. In sum, to be most effective, raters need to be trained to understand performance categories prior to observing team performance. This is true regardless of who provides the ratings (for example, team members, supervisors, outside observers).

- *Recommendation 13:* Measure team performance *after* raters receive training on how to identify and differentiate among the different targeted processes and outcomes.

Measure Team Performance on the Job or During Simulation-Based Exercises

Team performance may be measured either during on-the-job activities or during a simulation exercise that mimics on-the-job activities. There are reasons why an organization may benefit from measuring team performance during one or the other. Specifically, different aspects of team performance are more readily assessed during different activities.

Simulation exercises are particularly useful for measuring a team's processes that would normally occur in the context of rarely occurring and dangerous situations they may experience on the job (Dorsey et al., 2009). For example, simulation exercises are frequently used to measure the effectiveness of a team's response to emergency situations (for example, a terrorist attack). Simulations also allow multiple teams to be compared to one another on a level playing field, as the specific situations they face can be carefully controlled and made consistent across teams. Simulations can vary widely in terms of both their physical and psychological fidelity (Hays, 1980). Physical fidelity refers to the degree to which the materials, equipment, and environmental conditions mirror those in the on-the-job environment. On the other hand, psychological fidelity refers to the degree to which a simulation requires participants to engage in the same psychological processes (cognitive, behavioral) that they would on the job. Psychological fidelity in the context of TPM means that a simulation requires team members to engage in the same teamwork processes that they would in the actual work environment. Physical fidelity is primarily important if the purpose of team performance is to assess perceptual or psychomotor processes. Even during a simulation with high psychological fidelity, it is important to note that measures of team performance taken in this context are more likely to reflect a team's "maximum performance" and not their "typical performance" (Borman, 1991). This is because teams demonstrate what they "can do" when they are aware that they are being evaluated and are highly motivated to do their best, rather than what they typically "will do" when this is not the case (Klehe & Anderson, 2007).

Whereas TPM that occurs during simulation exercises is most likely to be indicative of a team's maximum performance, measurements of typical performance are best obtained from observers of on-the-job performance (Sackett et al., 1988). In order to obtain a reliable indicator of typical performance, team performance should be measured on the job at multiple times. Because multiple extraneous factors influence team performance at any given time, aggregation of multiple measures into an overall team performance measure is likely to be more representative of team performance than any single measurement. Measuring team performance at multiple times can also provide information regarding the trajectory of team performance (that is, whether it is declining or improving; Wildman et al., 2010). This information is quite valuable to organizational decision-makers who must make decisions about the future of the team (for example, decisions regarding disbanding, promoting, and training the team) based on their past performance as well as to HR system evaluators who are interested in assessing how changes in team performance correspond to the implementation of new HR strategies. Finally, multiple measurements allow organizations to identify time periods during which team performance was atypically high or atypically low so that the situational factors responsible for any anomalies in team performance may be identified. In this way, analysis of team performance trends can also inform decisions regarding job redesign, management style, or other factors outside of the team's control.

- *Recommendation 14:* Use simulation to measure team performance in critical, but rarely occurring, or dangerous/costly situations.
- *Recommendation 15:* Measure team performance on the job at multiple time intervals in order to obtain a more reliable indicator of "typical performance" and to identify performance trends.

Measure Team Performance Processes During Both Action and Transition Phases

Team performance processes can be thought of in terms of two distinct phases that alternate over time. These have been described as *action* phases, during which the team engages in activities that directly promote task accomplishment, and *transition* phases, during which the team reflects on prior action phases and plans for subsequent ones (see Table 17.1; Marks, Mathieu, & Zaccaro, 2001). Research has demonstrated that both types of processes uniquely contribute to team performance outcomes (LePine, Piccolo, Jackson, Mathieu, & Saul, 2008). Therefore, in order to fully assess team performance processes and to gain an accurate understanding of how likely the team is to achieve team

Table 17.1. Team Process Performance

Process Name	*Process Definition*
Transition Phase	
Mission Analysis Formulation and Planning	Understanding the task the team has undertaken as well as the resources at the team's disposal for completion of these goals
Goal Specification	Identifying, prioritizing, assigning, and providing time and resource allocation parameters concerning the team's goals
Strategy Formulation	The planned actions or approaches the team specifies for achieving team goals and objectives
Action Phase	
Monitoring Progress Toward Goals	Tracking progress toward goal attainment as well as sharing that progress with other team members
Systems Monitoring	Following and cataloging the status of team resources as they relate to objective completion
Team Monitoring and Backup Behavior	Verbally providing a teammate with feedback or coaching, aiding a teammate in accomplishing his or her tasks, and absorbing and completing the remainder of a teammate's task
Coordination	Synchronization of interdependent actions with one another with respect to the order in which team actions are performed
Interpersonal Phase	
Conflict Management	Establishing preventative measures to counteract potential conflict as well as addressing and quelling conflict as it arises
Motivation and Confidence Building	The promotion of a sense of overall confidence, motivation, and cohesion throughout the team
Affect Management	The fielding and regulation of the team's emotional responses (frustration, enthusiasm) during goal and objective progression

performance outcomes, team processes should be measured during both action and transition phases of team performance.

- *Recommendation 16:* Measure team processes during both transition and action phases of team performance.

Allow Time for Team Processes to Affect Outcomes

Any team-level intervention (for example, training, job redesign, team composition) is likely to impact team processes much more quickly than it is to impact team outcomes. This is the case because team processes occur before and ultimately lead to team outcomes (LePine et al., 2008). The length of time it takes for the outcomes of team processes to emerge varies as a function of the tasks performed. For instance, team processes observed for an aircrew or air traffic control team may affect outcomes within a matter of minutes or hours. However, the team processes that an advertising team engages in may not translate into performance outcomes for weeks or even months. Thus, when an organization wishes to measure the impact of any type of intervention on team performance outcomes, they must first consider how long it is likely to take for a change in team processes to impact team outcomes.

- *Recommendation 17:* Consider the *length of time* it takes processes to result in outcomes when planning to evaluate the impact of any team intervention.

Directions for Future Research

Team performance measurement provides organizations with information critical for sustaining effective team selection, composition, training, feedback, and compensation systems, as well as for facilitating effective organization decision making. The ultimate value of TPM to organizations, however, depends entirely on how well it is conceived of and executed. The quality of TPM, in turn, depends on what choices are made with regard to what aspect of team performance is measured, how it is measured, and when it is measured. For TPM to serve its intended purpose, these choices must be based on consideration of multiple factors likely to impact the degree to which different TPM strategies are effective under various conditions. Although we have already identified several of these factors based on our review of the extant literature, research dedicated to studying variables that are likely related to TPM effectiveness is scarce. This means that future research is needed to verify the proposed impact of the factors discussed in this chapter and to identify additional factors that influence the effectiveness of TPM strategies in general, as well as within specific situations and populations of some importance.

In addition to those already discussed, we believe that a number of other factors must also be considered by organizations interested in launching a TPM effort. First, organizations must consider the cost and practicality of various TPM strategies. For some organizations, it may not be practical or even feasible to utilize various TPM sources or methods or to measure team performance at certain times, frequencies, or intervals. Such limitations are likely to affect what aspect of team performance should be measured, how, and when. Therefore, exploration of how technology can be utilized to make TPM more practical and affordable for organizations may be a fruitful avenue for future research. Technology may be particularly helpful in the measurement of team performance, given the complexity of the phenomenon measured (for example, team processes) as well as the relative autonomy (and increasing prevalence) of self-managing teams (Alper, Tjosvold, & Law, 1998; Barker, 1993), compared to *individuals,* who are typically supervised more closely and whose performance is often less complex (and can, therefore, have their performance observed and assessed by human raters more easily). Increased utilization of technology to collect, manage, and store TPM information may come with costs, however (for example, reliability problems). Future research is needed to identify the ways in which technology can be most useful in TPM and to determine whether the costs of increased reliance on technology for TPM may outweigh its benefits.

In addition to practicality and utility concerns, organizations must also take into consideration the degree to which various TPM strategies suit organizational goals and values. As is true with any organizational initiative, in order for TPM to be successful, it must be aligned with an organization's mission and culture (Nenadál, 2008). Further, because aspects of it may also determine which TPM strategies are least/most acceptable to or valued by organizational members, the national culture within which an organization is embedded must also be considered (Wildman et al., 2011). For instance, if organizational members value playing an active role in organizational activities, it may be important for an organization to gather TPM information directly from team members. Also, it is important for future research to determine how organizational and national values and norms impact the degree to which various TPM strategies are utilized, accepted, and ultimately effective within organizations.

Even after careful decisions are made about which TPM strategy is best for an organization based on the factors described above, the work is not done. The next task is to ensure that the TPM strategy is executed properly, as incorrect implementation can often negate the value of prior correct decisions. There are a number of ways in which the implementation of TPM strategies can fall short but, due to its subjective nature, execution problems are most likely to occur during the team performance rating process. If TPM involves subjective ratings of team performance, special care must be taken to ensure the accuracy of those ratings. Performance ratings of all kinds (both individual and team) are prone to being affected by numerous rater biases and errors (for example, leniency, severity, and halo errors, gender bias, personal construct and implicit person theory-based biases; Borman, 1991; Heilman & Haynes, 2005; Heslin, Latham, & VandeWalle, 2005; Uggerslev & Sulsky, 2008), descriptions of which are beyond the scope of this chapter.

Fortunately, however, many rater errors and biases can be limited with various interventions involving the provision of specific information to raters (for example, information about a female member's contributions; Heilman & Haynes, 2005) and in-depth rater training (for example, frame of reference training, self-persuasion training; Heslin et al., 2005; Uggerslev & Sulsky, 2008). Organizations interested in launching a TPM effort should refer to relevant research to ensure that raters receive the proper information and training before making team performance ratings. Since most prior research on rater errors/biases has been conducted within the context of individual PM, however, future research should be dedicated to identifying errors/biases specific to TPM and to testing methods for preventing them (Heilman & Haynes, 2005).

Following the proper design and implementation of a TPM endeavor, an organization has yet more work ahead. Any change that occurs within an organization (for example, a change in team tasks) has the potential to impact the effectiveness and usefulness of an existing TPM strategy. As such, TPM strategies should be evaluated and revised continually to keep them in step with organizational changes. Further, in line with our previous suggestions, future research is needed to determine the specific impact of various organizational changes on the effectiveness of commonly used TPM strategies.

Finally, it is important to acknowledge that, in this chapter, we have discussed each aspect of team performance, method for measuring it, and time at which it can be measured as separate options for conducting TPM. In reality, however, it is common and often considered a "best practice" for organizations to measure multiple aspects of team performance in multiple ways at various times (Cascio & Aguinis, 2011). This often occurs and is typically most beneficial when TPM serves in multiple functions within an organization at once. Using TPM for multiple purposes yields a better return on the resources invested into TPM, but at the same time it yields a more complex TPM effort. These complex TPM efforts may be especially beneficial and even necessary in organizations comprised of multiple types of teams that vary widely in their nature and the tasks they complete.

Overall, because each TPM strategy comes with unique advantages and disadvantages, organizations can benefit from using multiple strategies simultaneously in order to maximize the advantages and limit the disadvantages of their overall TPM system. In addition to many benefits, complex TPM strategies may also have associated costs (for example, financial costs). Future research is needed to determine the relative costs and benefits of these complex TPM strategies, as compared to simpler ones. Further, research is needed to determine the relative costs and benefits of conducting TPM in general, as compared to *individual* PM.

Specifically, although TPM provides organizations with unique, useful information about team performance that individual PM does not yield (that is, information about performance attributable to synergy among individuals), the phenomenon measured during TPM is more complex and, therefore, potentially more costly to assess.

References and Further Reading

Akdere, M., & Yilmaz, T. (2006). Team performance based compensation plans: Implications for human resources quality improvement from agency theory perspective. *International Journal of Human Resources Development and Management, 6*(1), 77–91.

Alper, S., Tjosvold, D., & Law, K.S. (1998). Interdependence and controversy in group decision making: Antecedents to effective self-managing teams. *Organizational Behavior and Human Decision Processes, 74*(1), 33–52.

Atkins, P.W.B., Wood, R.E., & Rutgers, P.J. (2002). The effects of feedback format on dynamic decision making. *Organizational Behavior and Human Decision Processes, 88*(2), 587–604.

Baltes, B.B., Dickson, M.W., Sherman, M.P., Bauer, C.C., & LaGanke, J.S. (2002). Computer-mediated communication and group decision making: A meta-analysis. *Organizational Behavior and Human Decision Processes, 87*(1), 156–179.

Barker, J.R. (1993). Tightening the iron cage: Concertive control in self-managing teams. *Administrative Science Quarterly, 38*(3), 408-437.

Borman, W.C. (1991). Job behavior, performance, and effectiveness. In M.D. Dunnette & L.M. Hough (Eds.), *Handbook of industrial and organizational psychology* (Vol. 2, pp. 271–326). Palo Alto, CA: Consulting Psychologists Press.

Brannick, M.T., Roach, R.M., & Salas, E. (1993). Understanding team performance: A multimethod study. *Human Performance, 6*(4), 287–308.

Cascio, W.F., & Aguinis, H. (2011). *Applied psychology in human resource management* (7th ed.). Upper Saddle River, NJ: Prentice Hall.

Chen, G., & Kanfer, R. (2006). Toward a systems theory of motivated behavior in work teams. *Research in Organizational Behavior, 27*, 223–267.

Cooke, N., & Fiore, S.M. (2010). Cognitive science-based principles for the design and delivery of training. In S.W.J. Kozlowski & E. Salas (Eds.), *Learning, training, and development in organizations* (pp. 169–202). New York: Routledge.

DeMatteo, J.S., Eby, L.T., & Sundstrom, E. (1998). Team-based rewards: Current empirical evidence and directions for future research. In B.M. Staw & L.L. Cummings (Eds.), *Research in organizational behavior, vol. 20: An annual series of analytical essays and critical reviews* (pp. 141–183). Greenwich, CT: Elsevier Science/JAI Press.

DeShon, R.P., Kozlowski, S.J., Schmidt, A.M., Milner, K.R., & Wiechmann, D. (2004). A multiple-goal, multilevel model of feedback effects on the regulation of individual and team performance. *Journal of Applied Psychology, 89*(6), 1035–1056.

Devine, D.J., Clayton, L.D., Philips, J.L., Dunford, B.B., & Melner, S.B. (1999). Teams in organizations: Prevalence, characteristics, and effectiveness. *Small Group Research, 30*(6), 678–711.

Dorsey, D., Russell, S., Keil, C., Campbell, G.E., Van Buskirk, W., & Schuck, P. (2009). Measuring teams in action: Automated performance measurement and feedback in simulation-based training. In E. Salas, G.F. Goodwin, & C.S. Burke (Eds.), *Team effectiveness in complex organizations: Cross-disciplinary perspectives and approaches* (pp. 351–382). New York: Psychology Press.

Hays, R.T. (1980). Simulator fidelity: A concept paper (No. ARI-TR-490). Alexandria, VA: Army Research Institute for the Behavioral and Social Sciences.

Heidemeier, H., & Moser, K. (2009). Self–other agreement in job performance ratings: A meta-analytic test of a process model. *Journal of Applied Psychology, 94*(2), 353–370.

Heilman, M.E., & Haynes, M.C. (2005). No credit where credit is due: Attributional rationalization of women's success in male-female teams. *Journal of Applied Psychology, 90*(5), 905–916.

Heslin, P.A., Latham, G.P., & VandeWalle, D. (2005). The effect of implicit person theory on performance appraisals. *Journal of Applied Psychology, 90*(5), 842–856.

Hogan, R., & Shelton, D. (1998). A socioanalytic perspective on job performance. *Human Performance, 11*(2–3), 129–144.

Jawahar, I.M., & Williams, C.R. (1997). Where all the children are above average: The performance appraisal purpose effect. *Personnel Psychology, 50*(4), 905–925.

Klehe, U.C., & Anderson, N.R. (2007). Working hard and working smart: Motivation and ability during typical and maximum performance. *Journal of Applied Psychology, 92*(4), 978–992.

Kluger, A.N., & DeNisi, A. (1996). The effects of feedback interventions on performance: A historical review, a meta-analysis, and a preliminary feedback intervention theory. *Psychological Bulletin, 119*(2), 254–284.

Krokos, K.J., Baker, D.P., Alonso, A., & Day, R. (2009). Assessing team processes in complex environments: Challenges in transitioning research to practice. In E. Salas, G.F. Goodwin, & C.S. Burke (Eds.), *Team effectiveness in complex organizations: Cross-disciplinary perspectives and approaches* (pp. 383–410). New York: Psychology Press.

Landy, F.J., & Farr, J.L. (1980). Performance rating. *Psychological Bulletin, 87*(1), 72–107.

LePine, J.A., Piccolo, R.E., Jackson, C.L., Mathieu, J.E., & Saul, J.R. (2008). A meta-analysis of teamwork processes: Tests of a multidimensional model and relationships with team effectiveness criteria. *Personnel Psychology, 61*(2), 273–307.

Marks, M., Mathieu, J., & Zaccaro, S. (2001). A temporally based framework and taxonomy of team processes. *Academy of Management Review, 26*(3), 356–376.

Morgan, B.B., Jr., Salas, E., & Glickman, A.S. (1993). An analysis of team evolution and maturation. *The Journal of General Psychology, 120*(3), 277–291.

Nenadál, J. (2008). Process performance measurement in manufacturing organizations. *International Journal of Productivity and Performance Management, 57*(6), 460–467.

Pritchard, R.D., Harrell, M.M., DiazGranados, D., & Guzman, M.J. (2008). The productivity measurement and enhancement system: A meta-analysis. *Journal of Applied Psychology, 93*(3), 540–567.

Robbins, S.P., & Judge, T.A. (2008). *Organizational behavior* (13th ed., p. 752). Upper Saddle River, NJ: Prentice Hall.

Sackett, P.R., & Tuzinski, K.A. (2001). The role of dimensions and exercises in assessment center judgments. In M. London (Ed.), *How people evaluate others in organizations* (pp. 111–129). New York: Psychology Press.

Sackett, P.R., Zedeck, S., & Fogli, L. (1988). Relations between measures of typical and maximum job performance. *Journal of Applied Psychology, 73*(3), 482–486.

Smith-Jentsch, K.A., Johnston, J.H., & Payne, S.C. (1998). Measuring team-related expertise in complex environments. In J.A. Cannon-Bowers & E. Salas (Eds.), *Making decisions under stress: Implications for individual and team training* (pp. 61–87). Washington, DC: American Psychological Association.

Tesluk, P., Mathieu, J., & Zaccaro, S. (1997). Task and aggregation issues in the analysis and assessment of team performance. In M.T. Brannick, E. Salas, & C. Prince (Eds.), *Team performance assessment and measurement* (pp. 173–196). New York: Psychology Press.

Uggerslev, K.L., & Sulsky, L.M. (2008). Using frame-of-reference training to understand the implications of rater idiosyncrasy for rating accuracy. *Journal of Applied Psychology, 93*(3), 711–719.

Wildman, J.L., Bedwell, W.L., Salas, E., & Smith-Jentsch, K.A. (2011). Performance measurement at work: A multilevel perspective. In S. Zedeck (Ed.), *Handbook of industrial and organizational psychology, volume 1: Building and developing the organization* (pp. 303–342). Washington, DC: American Psychological Association.

Woehr, D.J. (1992). Performance dimension accessibility: Implications for rating accuracy. *Journal of Organizational Behavior, 13*(4), 357–367.

CHAPTER EIGHTEEN

Team Time Management

Psychological Insights for Timely Project Performance

Josette M.P. Gevers and Christel G. Rutte
Einhoven University of Technology, Netherlands

Speed and timeliness of work performance have become more important in organizations as a result of global competition, new technologies, and clients' raised expectations (Orlikowsky & Yates, 2002). Consequently, teams in organizations are increasingly facing temporal challenges to coordinate members' interdependent contributions in tightly scheduled projects. Finishing on time is an important measure of project success (Freeman & Beele, 1992), but a problematic issue for many teams. Time and again, project deadlines are put off or exceeded (Lientz & Rea, 2001). There is ample evidence of projects showing massive time overruns, be it in information technology (Moløkken & Jørgensen, 2003), product innovation (Gupta & Wilemon, 1990), or public construction works (Flyvbjerg, Holm, & Buhl, 2005). Delays can cause substantial damage to project owners; entering the market half a year behind schedule but within budget, for example, cuts high-tech innovation earnings 33 percent over a five-year period (Vesey, 1991). Consequently, the delivery of high-quantity and high-quality outputs past agreed-on deadlines mostly will not qualify as successful performance.

The increased salience of time and growing emphasis on rapid and timely performance in organizations are reflected in many theoretical and practical publications regarding the management of time as a scarce and valuable resource (for an overview, see Claessens, Van Eerde, Rutte, & Roe, 2007). Despite the omnipresence of teamwork arrangements, however, these publications predominantly focus on the individual employee. Far less systematic attention has been devoted to time management in teams. Organizational literature has shown a steady increase of interest in temporal issues, but only a few studies have been specifically devoted to issues of meeting deadlines in teams (Gersick, 1988, 1989; Gevers, Rutte, & Van Eerde, 2006; Gevers, Van Eerde, & Rutte, 2001, 2009; Waller, Giambatista, & Zellmer-Bruhn, 1999; Waller, Zelmer-Bruhn, & Giambatista, 2002). Most of these studies are of a descriptive rather than a prescriptive nature. Nevertheless, they bring forward two pivotal factors for teams working under deadline conditions: (1) the crucial role of attention to time in group pacing behavior and (2) the importance of a shared temporal perspective for synchronizing team task activity.

McGrath and O'Connor (1996) explained these factors as follows. In collaborative action, timeliness of performance requires both external and internal synchronization. On the one hand, team members need to structure their efforts to the deadline, i.e., they must find ways to anticipate what events and actions will take place and when they will occur to develop realistic schedules for meeting temporal goals. On the other hand, they must find ways to coordinate both the content and the timing of the actions of multiple individuals with one another, that is, they need to adapt to each other's actions in order to coordinate individual contributions. Synchronization of collective action may be complicated when temporal conflict occurs among team members due to, for example, differences in functional background (Yakura, 2002), differences in personal (Gevers & Peeters, 2009; Milliken & Martins, 1996) or temporal characteristics (Blount & Janicik, 2002; Mohammed & Nadkarni, 2011), or because employees experience conflicting pulls on their time use from working in multiple projects concurrently (O'Leary, Mortensen, & Willams Woolley, 2009). Unless managed effectively, mismatches in team members' temporal perspectives may seriously impede a group's ability to coordinate individual actions effectively, thereby endangering both the timeliness and the quality of performance (Mohammed & Nadkarni, 2011).

In this chapter, we will analyze the obstacles that teams face in regulating their collaborative efforts toward timely task completion, and present the evidence available in the scientific literature today for how teams may become better at meeting deadlines. Reviewing this literature, we work toward the development of a dynamic model of team time management that highlights what project members can do to build a shared temporal perspective within the team, thereby promoting synchronized action and a timely task completion. Most studies that we will discuss involve project teams or project groups (terms we will use interchangeably), that is, an interdependent collection of individuals whose primary function is to perform a complex task requiring a specific output (in the form of some product, plan, or decision) by some deadlines, after which they disband or move to another project (cf. Janicik & Bartel, 2003). These teams mostly operate under relatively high levels of autonomy, as members often come from different organizational departments and fields of expertise and need to be able to develop viable work approaches and effective ways of working together. We realize that, in the real world, these teams may be confronted with unrealistically tight deadlines, for example, when schedules and deadlines are based solely on strategic considerations. This is, however, not the type of situation we wish to analyze here. Rather, we will focus on teams working under conditions of tight, but realistic deadlines. Furthermore, we do not differentiate between the role of the project leader or manager and that of other members of the team. Although regulatory activities such as directing, guiding, and monitoring team action are often formalized as part of the project leader's or manager's role, in teams populated by highly educated knowledge workers it is typically expected that regular members also engage in these types of behaviors to regulate their own actions as well as those of the team as a whole. Also, to allow for general conclusions to be drawn, we will not take much notice of the specific nature of the work being performed, other than its temporal characteristics. Given the large variety of tasks represented in the literature that is being reviewed, we would say that the model we will ultimately propose is applicable to all time-limited, team-based project work, irrespective of the specific work setting.

Temporal Synchronization in Collaborative Action

Research on time in teams has emphasized the importance of temporal synchronization for effective team performance. Timely task accomplishment, in particular, requires a careful coordination of activities over time, that is, that the right person (or group) carries out the intended actions at the right time (Koslowski & Ilgen, 2006; McGrath & O'Connor, 1996). Occasionally, temporal synchronization may come about implicitly (Ancona & Chong, 1996; Ancona & Waller, 2007; McGrath & Kelly, 1986), but in many cases it requires at least a minimum amount of explicit attention to the combination of individual work efforts. In many organizations, temporal synchronization of teamwork is managed by means of schedules and deadlines that specify the exact time period allotted to the completion of the task. Projects are divided into phases with specified durations, tasks, and resources to communicate when it is most useful or appropriate to spend time to complete tasks. Schedules and deadlines may reduce temporal ambiguity and offer direction for the coordination of individual contributions, but cannot prevent that timelines are interpreted differently by individual organizational members (Yakura, 2002). Unfortunately, individual team members often do not perform tasks as given, but redefine project plans to better suit their personal preferences and perceived constraints and opportunities (Hacker, 2003; Roe, 1999), and come to work toward different objectives. Moreover, individual differences in how individuals perceive and use time may lead to differences in deadline salience and responses to progress feedback (Waller, Conte, Gibson, & Carpenter, 2001). Finally, differing views regarding the value of punctuality and adherence to deadlines may lead some members to exceed time limits instead of adjusting their pace to make sure that tasks are completed on time. Therefore, a first prerequisite for meeting deadlines is that team members internalize the meaning of schedules and deadlines to hold a shared perspective on what is needed to actually finish the task on time.

The Role of Shared Temporal Cognitions

In the early 1990s, much of the team literature emphasized the role of cognitive congruence in teamwork. According to this literature, effective team performance requires that important knowledge regarding taskwork and teamwork is shared among team members (Cannon-Bowers, Salas, & Converse, 1993; Klimoski & Mohammed, 1994; Rentsch & Hall, 1994; Wilke & Meertens, 1994). Not only should team members have shared knowledge regarding procedures, strategies, and actions necessary to perform the task, but they should also be informed about teammates' knowledge, skills, preferences, roles, and responsibilities. Additionally, it was suggested that team members should hold similar assumptions regarding key issues a team faces (Amason, 1996; Bliese & Halverson, 1998; Mohammed & Ringseis, 2001), including temporal issues (Bartel & Milliken, 2004; Farmer & Seers, 2004; Gevers, Rutte, & Van Eerde, 2004, 2006; Standifer & Bluedorn, 2006). In context of deadline work particularly, temporal synchronization requires that team members hold so-called shared temporal cognitions (Gevers, Rutte, & Van Eerde, 2004, 2006). Shared temporal cognitions represent congruence in team members' perceptions regarding the time-related aspects of executing collective tasks; it means that team members agree on the importance of meeting deadlines, on the allocation of tasks over time, and on the pace with which the team should work toward task accomplishment (Gevers & Peeters, 2009).

Gevers and colleagues (Gevers, Claessens, Van Eerde, & Rutte, 2009; Gevers & Peeters, 2009; Gevers, Rutte, Van Eerde, & Roe, 2005; Gevers, Rutte, & Van Eerde, 2006; Gevers, Van Eerde, & Rutte, 2009) performed a series of field studies into the antecedents and consequences of shared temporal cognitions. They found that, independent of the level of shared team cognitions and shared task cognitions, teams were more likely to meet deadlines when members had high levels of shared temporal cognitions in the early stages of the project and when shared temporal cognitions increased over the course of the project. These relationships were shown to be the result of a higher level of temporal synchronization established within the team, as well as a higher level of group potency or confidence among team members in the team's ability to be effective (Guzzo, Yost, Campbell, & Shae, 1993). Group potency was indeed identified in earlier studies as an important factor in getting groups to set and remain committed to difficult performance goals (Gully,

Incalcaterra, Joshi, & Beaubien, 2002) and a helpful quality for teams working under time pressure (Gevers, Van Eerde, & Rutte, 2001). Moreover, members of teams with higher levels of shared temporal cognitions were also found to be more satisfied with the team and its performance (Gevers & Peeters, 2009).

Although findings supported the proposed beneficial effects of shared temporal cognitions for team coordination, team motivation, and team performance, it should be noted that, in order for teams to meet deadlines, temporal cognitions should not only be shared, but should also be appropriate. In one of their studies, Gevers and colleagues (2006) found that shared temporal cognitions enhanced meeting deadlines when team members, on average, tended to start task activity early, but impeded meeting deadlines when members, on average, tended to put off work until the deadline was very close. It is important to realize that shared temporal cognitions may become dysfunctional in the sense that they impede rather than enhance timely performance when they promote unrealistic time estimates or when they undermine the importance of meeting deadlines. In that case, it may actually be important to invite some dissonance to the team. Think, for example, of a single time-conscientious team member in a team of otherwise deadline workers. This person's divergent perspective on time and how it should be used may stimulate the entire team to start task activities earlier and, thereby, considerably increase the likelihood of deadlines being met.

A third attribute that has been argued to determine the impact of shared temporal cognitions on team processes and performance concerns the extent to which members are aware that cognitions are being shared. In all of the studies reported above, team members were asked to indicate the extent to which they held common perspectives regarding the use of time in task accomplishment. This means that team members reporting shared cognitions were also aware of them. Not only does the awareness of shared cognitions strengthen team confidence, but it also affects how available information is being dealt with. For example, Van Ginkel and van Knippenberg (2008) found that groups with shared task cognitions that also realized they shared these cognitions processed available task information more thoroughly than groups that were not aware of their shared task cognitions. Moreover, the awareness of "sharedness" or, in fact, the lack of it, opens up the possibility for discussing deviants and taking action toward further temporal alignment.

Thus, we conclude that higher sharedness, appropriateness, and awareness of temporal cognition are associated with higher levels of synchronization and motivation among team members, which, in turn, contributes to higher levels of task progression and increased likelihood of a timely task completion. Before we go on to discuss how shared temporal cognitions may be established in teams, we will first address some of the impeding factors that may typically be found in project teams.

Threats to Shared Temporal Cognitions

In the literature so far, several impeding factors for shared temporal cognitions have been identified, mostly concerning differences in personal characteristics of team members. Conscientiousness, for example, reflects a personal tendency to feel responsible and to be organized, disciplined, and achievement-oriented and has emerged as the strongest and most consistent personality trait predicting individual performance (Barrick & Mount, 1991; Digman, 1990). Gevers and Peeters (2009) found that dissimilarity in conscientiousness was associated with lower levels of shared temporal cognition, which, in turn, hindered coordinated action between team members and, ultimately, deteriorated members' feelings of satisfaction with both the team and its performance. Shared temporal cognitions, their study showed, were more likely to exist in teams that were small, with high mean levels of conscientiousness, and little diversity in conscientiousness between members.

Differences in temporal characteristics also tend to instigate conflict and tension about time use in teams. People have been shown to differ in terms of time perspective (that is, being past-, present-, or future-oriented [Zimbardo & Boyd, 1999]), time urgency (general hurriedness and concern with the passage of time [Conte, Landy, & Mathieu, 1995]), polychronicity (the preference to engage in more than one task concurrently [Bluedorn, 2002]), and pacing styles (effort distribution tendencies in working toward deadlines [Gevers, Rutte, & Van Eerde, 2006]).

According to Mohammed and Nadkarni (2011), individuals, often unconsciously, carry these time-based individual differences into team settings where they may either enhance or inhibit team performance. On the one hand, temporal diversity may lead to a more balanced temporal perspective and effort distribution. On the other hand, individual temporal differences may create ambiguity and conflict among team members about pacing and scheduling activities, which may impede both the timeliness and quality of team output. Indeed, research done in this area suggests that, unless managed effectively, time-related individual differences impede a group's ability to pace and coordinate members' actions effectively (Mohammed & Nadkarni, 2011).

For example, time urgency diversity was found to be associated with higher levels of relationship conflict, as reflected in tension, animosity, and annoyance among team members, but only when team members failed to engage in effective teamwork behaviors, such as leadership, cooperation, and communication behaviors (Mohammed & Angell, 2004). Likewise, Thatcher and Patel (2010) found that higher levels of polychronic diversity resulted in process conflict and, thereby, reduced team performance and team satisfaction. Shared temporal cognition, however, mitigated these problems, because they helped team members to distribute tasks in accordance with members' polychronic orientations and to avoid conflict or frustration over temporal differences. Finally, in a recent study, Mohammed and Nadkarni (2011) showed that diversity in time urgency and pacing style was actually positively related to team performance when project leaders displayed high levels of temporal leadership and aided their team in structuring, coordinating, and managing the pacing of team task accomplishments.

In all, the empirical work available clearly confirms that individual (temporal) differences are a source of ambiguity and conflict and that shared cognitions and temporal synchronization are more difficult to establish in temporally heterogeneous teams. At the same time, though, effective management of these differences by team members or leaders appears to mitigate their deleterious effects on team functioning. According to Mohammed, Hamilton, and Lim (2009), the challenge for teams is therefore to "synergistically leverage temporal differences while minimizing the process losses that may be incurred" (p. 340). This requires that members "develop an awareness of their own temporal approach and actively manage temporal diversity to achieve temporal synchronization and high performance levels" (p. 340). We will now describe the regulatory mechanisms that have been shown to contribute to shared temporal cognitions and, hence, may also help to mitigate the deleterious effects of temporal heterogeneity in teams.

Advice for Practitioners on Team Composition

People differ in their temporal orientations. We would recommend composing a team wisely. Extreme differences in temporal orientation should be avoided, as this breeds conflict and wrecks team morale. Temporal heterogeneity could be beneficial to the team provided that it is managed effectively. Team members should know the differences in time orientations among members so that they can act upon it if necessary. If possible, the really time urgent tasks should be handed to team members who are time conscious. It is not necessary to compose a team only of members who are time conscious, because that could lead a team to jump to conclusions about a project too early. Having members in the team who like to think more thoroughly to arrive at better results is an asset. The right mix of team members is what counts. Some members should be time conscious, others content conscious. Make sure that all team members know each other's strengths and weaknesses and that this is appreciated.

Action Regulation Toward Meeting Deadlines

According to action regulation theory (Frese & Zapf, 1994), individuals and teams are more likely to obtain high performance levels when sequentially engaging in activities of task preparation (that is, orienting and planning), execution, evaluation, and adjustment (Arrow, Poole, Henry, Wheelan, & Mooreland, 2004; Hacker, 2003; Tschan, 2002). To achieve a common goal, a team first has to develop a common understanding of the task and prepare for action execution with a plan that describes what needs to be done, when, how, and by whom (preparation). When they know what to do, the team executes the planned actions (execution). As the task accomplishments progress, the monitoring and evaluation of action execution allow team members to determine whether they are moving sufficiently close to goal attainment (evaluation) and whether to continue as planned or whether adjustments to plans are required to complete the tasks (adjustment). Group performance is enhanced when task execution is regulated to conform with this so-called *ideal cycle of action regulation* (Tschan, 1995, 2002). Moreover, because ultimate goal attainment depends on a series of sub-goals to be fulfilled, the sequence of action regulation applies also to attaining sub-goals, resulting in a recurring sequence of preparation, execution, evaluation, and adaptation.

Communication is considered the central means for action regulation in teams (Von Cranach, Ochsenbein, & Valach, 1986), and communication about temporal issues and constraints is regarded as an essential part of action regulation for teams that perform complex tasks under deadline conditions (Gevers, Van Eerde, & Rutte, 2009). Although effective patterns of time allocation may emerge with little explicit discussion, individual temporal differences may create different expectations among team members, for instance regarding the flexibility or rigidity of deadlines or the pace at which subtasks should be completed, and may require that temporal issues are communicated explicitly. Several studies have indeed demonstrated that discussing time-related issues is important in regulating group pacing behavior (Janicik & Bartel, 2003; Mohammed & Nadkarni, 2011; Waller, Zellmer-Bruhn, & Giambatista, 2002). More specifically, Gevers, Van Eerde, and Rutte (2009) identified three mechanisms through which teams may pay explicit attention to time in the preparation, execution, evaluation, and adjustment of their task processes: temporal planning, temporal reminders, and temporal reflexivity. Each of these mechanisms was found to contribute to the establishment of shared temporal cognitions in teams and, thereby, help to mitigate the deleterious effects of temporal heterogeneity. In the following, we will review how these action regulation processes aid in establishing an effective temporal approach that allows teams to finish their tasks on time.

Temporal Preparation

The regulatory mechanism by which teams decide on a principal course of action for goal accomplishment is typically referred to as planning. It involves decision making about how team members will go about achieving their goal, discussion of expectations and task-related information, prioritization, and the assignment of roles and responsibilities to team members, while taking into account the situational and time constraints, team resources, member expertise, and changing nature of the environment (Marks, Mathieu, & Zaccaro, 2001). In planning, team members jointly conceptualize and understand the various components of their task, its purpose and meaning to the team, and how best to proceed with accomplishing the task (DeChurch & Haas, 2008). As such, planning serves multiple purposes, including providing direction and structure, allocating resources, synchronizing and sequencing action, and being prepared for changes through imagining alternative routes of action (Frese, Stewart, & Hannover, 1987). Mathieu and Rapp (2009) found that teams were more effective when they developed high-quality performance strategies (that is, deliberate task work plans with performance objectives, tactics, contingencies, and alternative courses of action) as well as high-quality team charters (agreement among members regarding how the team will work together). Although time-consuming, setting up well-articulated plans for dealing with both teamwork and task work aspects of team functioning was shown to pay off in terms of sustained levels of high performance over time.

Besides planning teamwork and taskwork, it has been shown important to pay explicit attention to temporal constraints in planning (Gevers, Van Eerde, & Rutte, 2001; Janicik & Bartel, 2003). Temporal planning involves consideration of how much time is available for goal accomplishment, how long it will take to accomplish certain tasks, and when they should be performed given dependencies among subtasks (Janicik & Bartel, 2003). Because it explicates how task activities are spread over time, temporal planning increases the degree to which team members understand each other's needs and requirements at specific points in time, which ultimately facilitates communication efficiency and temporal synchronization, especially during periods of high workload (Gevers, Van Eerde, & Rutte, 2001; Stout, Cannon-Bowers, Salas, & Milanovich, 1999).

Research shows that groups often rush into action without discussing strategic issues such as time use (Hackman, Brousseau, & Weiss, 1976; Tripoli, 1998; Weingart, 1992), while even modest attention to temporal constraints in the early stages of task execution consistently increases team members' attention to time in project execution (Janicik & Bartel, 2003). The early development of time awareness norms consistently heightens members' responsiveness to temporal information in the work context. Moreover, collaborative temporal planning offers the opportunity to become more familiar with team members' temporal characteristics and to "fit" them with the temporal constraints of the task. Also, team member familiarity contributes to increasingly synchronized patterns, with the positive consequence that delays, specifically unanticipated delays, decrease, and overall negative affect due to delays decreases accordingly (Harrison, Mohammed, McGrath, Florey, & Vanderstoep, 2003). Also, taking individual temporal differences into account when composing teams and planning task allocation helps to satisfy different goals (speed and quality; long- and short-term) and balance efforts over time (early, steady, and late pacing action), and facilitates a shared acceptance of temporal constraints (for example, everyone agrees on the individual contributions) and safeguards against temporal conflict (Mohammed & Nadkarni, 2011).

Advice for Practitioners on Temporal Planning

Planning is of great importance in a project, but a plan will only work when all team members agree with the plan, understand its importance, and feel committed to it. Asking every team member to give an estimate of the time needed to produce his or her deliverable and taking this into account in the planning can help to create this commitment. A kick-off meeting at the start of the project helps team members to understand the time plan and to develop a shared perspective on what is needed to meet the deadline. In making the time plan and deciding who is to do what, it is wise to take into account the time orientations of the various team members. Really time-critical parts of the project should be allocated as much as possible to team members who are time conscientious. Intermediate milestones and meetings to evaluate progress toward these milestones are helpful to keep all team members on the same time track. It is also important to make sure that all team members understand the mutual interdependencies in the team. Team members should not be hampered in their progress because they are waiting for a late deliverable from a colleague team member.

Temporal Evaluation

Once in action, the progression of time and task accomplishments provides team members with input for additional regulation in terms of reinforcement, reflection, and corrective action. Indeed, prior research has identified attention to time and task progress as an important prerequisite for adequate pacing of task accomplishments and, hence, for meeting deadlines (Gersick, 1988, 1989; Waller, Zellmer-Bruhn, & Giambatista, 2002). Being among the first to address the issue of temporal progression in work groups, Gersick (1988, 1989, 1994) showed that, when faced with a deadline, individuals and groups tend to use time and temporal milestones to guide their work and evaluate task progress. According to Gersick's work, transitions typically occur at the midpoint of the allotted time when a sense of urgency prompts intensive reflection among team members regarding task progress and a reevaluation and reassignment of tasks for the remainder of the time span. Researchers (Ancona & Waller, 2007; Okhuysen, 2001; Okhuysen & Waller, 2002; Waller, Zellmer-Bruhn, & Giambatista, 2002) later identified various other self-imposed and externally imposed interruptions (for example, instructions, interpersonal concerns, sudden deadline changes) that instigate a switch of attention in groups that offers members an opportunity to "stop and think," to evaluate progress, and to modify work strategies. For example, sudden deadline changes, independent of whether they involved an increase or decrease in temporal resources, caused groups to pay significantly more attention to time.

Attention to time may also elicit from sources within the team. Some individuals are simply more inclined to pay attention to time than others, and the presence of such an individual in a group may help groups pace their task activities. Time urgent individuals, for example, are more likely to voice concerns about time and timing, and their presence in a group was shown to increase a group's focus on their primary task, resulting in a steady progression through the subsequent phases of a decision-making task (Waller, Giambatista, & Zellmer-Bruhn, 1999). Thus, team members' utterances about time prevent teams from deviating from initial plans and falling behind schedule. Verbalizations of temporal concerns have also been shown to build and strengthen shared temporal cognition among team members during task execution. For example, the exchange of temporal reminders through which team members reminded each other of upcoming deadlines and urged one another to meet time limits helped to keep members on track. These temporal reminders, however, were helpful only in later stages of the collaboration. Early temporal reminders, it was argued, may cause teams to rush into implementation without establishing an adequate and shared understanding of the task situation, and unfamiliarity among team members in early project stages may inhibit the effectiveness of temporal reminders (for example, when aimed at the wrong person).

Thus, whereas temporal planning contributes to higher levels of shared temporal cognitions in early project stages, increased attention to time in the form of temporal reminders serves to further align temporal cognitions and regulate the pace of team activity.

Advice for Practitioners on Temporal Evaluation

Regular meetings to evaluate progress in the light of the various milestones are important to keep all team members on track. In these meetings temporal reminders can be given, either by the project leader or by time-conscious team members. Team members who are highly interdependent for their task progress should have meetings even more often, if not daily (for example, fifteen-minute stand-up meetings to inform each other of how things stand). It is important that team members are not judgmental when tasks agreed on are not finished due to unexpected problems. The purpose of the evaluation of progress or lack of progress should be to solve problems and, if necessary, to adapt the time plan of the project. If lack of progress leads to blaming, the risk is that team members will not be open about it, and this should be avoided. We recommend that teams and their leaders agree at the start of the project that, when time limits may be exceeded, this will be announced in a timely fashion so that plans can be changed, others can take over, or extra personnel can be hired.

Temporal Adaptation

Besides regulating an appropriate task pace during task execution to prevent a team from falling behind schedule, it is important that teams monitor task progress to recognize performance gaps and changes in circumstances that may endanger successful goal accomplishment. Monitoring team performance, evaluating task progress, and making reactive and non-scripted adjustments to task strategies are considered essential for team effectiveness (DeChurch & Haas, 2008; LePine, 2003; Marks, Mathieu, & Zaccaro, 2001). DeChurch and Haas (2008) examined three types of planning, two of which (deliberate planning and contingency planning) are enacted prior to team action, while the third (reactive planning) occurs during team action. Their findings showed that, although specifying a primary course of action and backup plan facilitated synchronized team action, reactive strategy adjustment in response to feedback or changes in the performance environment was the only planning activity that was also predictive of a team's final performance.

The extent to which team members collectively reflect upon a team's objectives, strategies, and internal processes and to which they adapt to current and anticipated endogenous or environmental circumstances has also been referred to as reflexivity (West, 1996). Reflexivity involves monitoring, reviewing, analyzing, and evaluating the effectiveness of team strategies and processes, exploring alternative courses of action for achieving goals, and implementing required changes in team activities (West, 1996). According to West, reflexivity helps teams to develop a more comprehensive and shared cognitive representation of their work, which enables them to be more adaptive to and more effective in the execution of their tasks, especially when operating in uncertain and dynamic circumstances.

So far, only a small number of studies have actually examined reflexivity in relation to meeting deadlines (Gevers, Van Eerde, & Rutte, 2001, 2009), and the findings suggest that reflexivity contributes to meeting deadlines, but no support was found for the assumption that reflexivity actually promotes shared temporal cognitions. Rather, the findings show a negative association between reflexivity and shared temporal cognitions, suggesting that team members engage in reflexivity when they experience a lack of temporal alignment to find out why things were not running smoothly. Also, reflexivity does not necessarily result in temporal adjustments. For example, when Waller and colleagues (2002) systematically changed deadlines (moving them closer or further away), groups with shortened deadlines did not exhibit a significant increase in task activity as compared to those with stable deadlines. Others, too, have shown that groups often tend to get stuck in habitual routines (Gersick & Hackman, 1990) and that they experience difficulties in adequately adapting their action patterns in response to performance feedback or changes in the task environment. Therefore, rather than relying on naturally occurring reflection, Gurtner and colleagues (2007) advocated the use of guided reflexivity. In their experimental study, guided reflexivity proved to be effective in helping teams to develop and implement adequate task adaptive strategies that resulted in more effective communication among team members as well as more similarity in their task cognitions. In all, these findings suggest that reflexivity is an important regulatory mechanism to ensure adequate team adaptation, although guidance is required.

Advice for Practitioners on Temporal Adaptation

What to do when plans cannot be met? This depends on the cause. If the cause is that the project is more difficult than anticipated, then all parties involved—project owners included—could negotiate an alternative time schedule. However, sometimes it will be necessary to simply speed up work processes, work overtime, or add extra personnel to the team. In that case, it is important to realize that, as with initial plans, consensus and commitment are crucial for such adaptations to succeed. Hence, similar steps as described earlier should be taken to ensure that the team acts in unity. If performance gaps stem from some team members showing dysfunctional time orientations, corrective action should concentrate on the individuals causing problems. In that case, the team leader and team members should more closely supervise and monitor these individuals to try to change their behavior for the better. Frequent informal contact among team members to check on task progress increases awareness of mutual dependencies and reinforces time awareness norms, which will help to motivate individuals to more closely adhere to the time plans so the team can finish the project on time.

A Dynamic Model of Team Time Management

The idea for this chapter originated from the observation that many teams fail to meet their deadlines, despite the fact that meeting deadlines is increasingly regarded as an important prerequisite for project success. Although the volume of work specifically devoted to temporal synchronization and meeting deadlines in collaborative action is limited, the evidence presented in the previous sections directly or indirectly contributes to our understanding of what it takes for teams to meet deadlines. The mechanisms and processes described provide the building blocks for a new model to guide teams in regulating their actions toward a timely project completion. Figure 18.1 presents the proposed model.

The model is based on the assumption that a team is established and that the task and the deadline are specified. With these

Figure 18.1. A Dynamic Model of Team Time Management

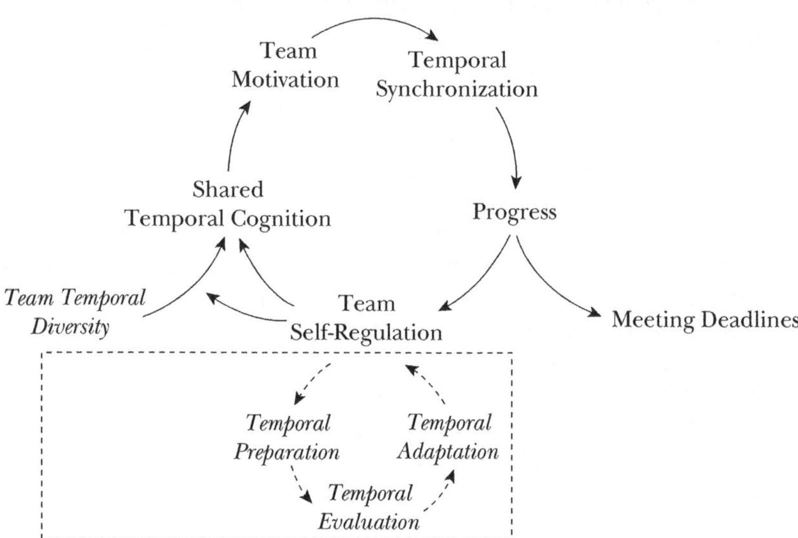

conditions given, the model depicts meeting deadlines in project teams as a dynamic process in which team members, despite their individual temporal differences, establish shared temporal cognitions either implicitly, when individual cognitions are congruent prior to group interaction, or explicitly though processes of action regulation. Shared temporal cognitions, in turn, enhance team motivation and facilitate temporal synchronization in team task execution, allowing the team to make progress in the direction of task completion. The progression of time and project accomplishments provides input for additional temporal regulation in terms of reflection and adaptive action. Eventually, the outcome of the process is a timely project completion, that is, meeting deadlines.

The rectangle at the bottom of Figure 18.1 indicates where team members and their managers can actually influence the team dynamics and project accomplishments. Besides considering individual temporal characteristics in team composition, temporal preparation (temporal planning), temporal evaluation (time monitoring and temporal reminders), and temporal adaptation (temporal reflexivity) are identified as important mechanisms in the regulation of work group activity. These action regulation mechanisms have a unique role in directing and controlling team processes toward a timely task completion and also help teams to overcome individual temporal differences.

It goes without saying that our model has been simplified, leaving out potential direct relationships or feedback loops among elements. Moreover, we have disregarded numerous complicating factors in modern team arrangements, such as virtual and multiple team membership, that we know are increasingly present in modern businesses and further complicate the temporal synchronization of members' efforts (Cummings & Haas, in press). Despite these shortcomings, we believe the model puts forward a couple of important insights that are meaningful for teams struggling to meet deadlines.

Practical Implications

A primary piece of advice for teams and their managers would be to devote time and energy to the development of shared cognitions within teams, not only about how to approach the task or how to organize the team, but also about the use of time in task execution. The research presented in this chapter suggests that shared temporal cognitions, in addition to shared task cognitions and shared team cognitions, enhance the ability of project teams to deal with problems of coordination and motivation that are often regarded as downsides of teamwork (Steiner, 1972). More specifically, shared temporal cognitions contribute to the temporal synchronization of team members' activities and also enhance team members' confidence in the abilities of the team, both of which are important prerequisites for teams facing time-pressured situations.

What, then, may teams and their managers do to establish shared temporal cognitions? First, the empirical evidence suggests that it would be helpful if teams engage in temporal planning after they have established clarity about project goals and circumstances. It may seem trivial to suggest that temporal planning helps teams to establish shared cognitions about their project, since it is often assumed to be common practice in projects.

However, research indicates that not all project teams automatically engage in planning and that, when they do, they do not always consider all the relevant aspects (Janicik & Bartel, 2003). In planning, the team should aim to fit task requirements and temporal characteristics of the team. In professional projects, planning and scheduling are often the responsibility of the team manager or team leader, but presenting team members with a cut-and-dried working schedule will often not be sufficient to establish shared temporal cognitions. Empirical evidence shows that team members are more likely to build a common perspective on task execution when they get the chance to participate in planning, for instance, by providing their personal estimates for work package duration, by discussing personal constraints and preferences, and by collectively figuring out the most efficient flow of work between team members.

Sure, collaborative planning may take up valuable time, but it is essential for safeguarding team members' commitment to the schedule, which eventually will resonate in schedule adherence and an increased likelihood that subtasks are actually completed on time. In addition, challenging group members to think about an effective flow of work will increase awareness of team members' interdependence and reduce the likelihood that individuals fail to pass on outputs that are accomplished earlier than scheduled, just because it is not in their personal interest (Leach, 1999).

In addition to planning, team members may build and consolidate shared temporal cognitions through the exchange of temporal reminders. Especially when the deadline draws near, it is beneficial when team members remind each other of important temporal milestones and urge one another to stick to the planning and finish subtasks on time. These temporal reminders may also be provided by the project manager when members themselves fail to engage in such activities (Mohammed & Nadkarni, 2011).

Finally, the evidence from the field highlights the importance of time monitoring and temporal adaptation. Teams need to closely monitor the progression of time and project accomplishment to be able to recognize dysfunctional use of time and adapt plans and actions in the service of timely project completion. However, research also suggests that teams may need guidance in effectively implementing adaptive strategies. In relation to this, we feel that it is justified to warn against inappropriate or dysfunctional shared temporal cognitions that may impede rather than foster meeting deadlines. Although team members with similar temporal characteristics are more likely to arrive at shared temporal cognitions quickly, diversity in temporal characteristics may enhance the adequacy of shared cognitions. Hence, our advice is to take temporal characteristics into consideration in decisions about team composition for time-critical projects. Putting together the ideal team with respect to time-related characteristics may not be feasible, but it may be beneficial to at least aim for a manageable level of temporal diversity.

Closing Comments

We have studied meeting deadlines in project teams from a team time management perspective, offering a central role to the concept of shared temporal cognitions in claiming that project teams are more likely to meet deadlines when they not only share a common perspective on the team and the task, but also on the temporal aspects of task performance, as this promotes both team motivation and temporal synchronization. For those interested in improving the timeliness of project performance, the available empirical evidence suggests that regulatory behavior in terms of temporal preparation, temporal evaluation, and temporal adaptation is crucial as a means to manage temporal diversity and to control and direct team processes toward meeting deadlines.

References

Amason, A.C. (1996). Distinguishing the effects of functional and dysfunctional conflict on strategic decision making: Resolving a paradox for top management teams. *Academy of Management Journal, 39*, 123–148.

Ancona, D., & Chong, C.L. (1996). Entrainment: Pace, cycle, and rhythm in organizational behavior. *Research in Organizational Behavior, 18*, 251–284.

Ancona, D.G., & Waller, M.J. (2007). The dance of entrainment: Temporally navigating across multiple pacers. In R. Hodson

& B. Rubin (Eds.), *Research in the sociology of work*. Amsterdam: Elsevier.

Arrow, H., Poole, M.S., Henry, K.B., Wheelan, S., & Mooreland, R.L. (2004). Time, change, and development: The temporal perspective on groups. *Small Group Research, 35*(1), 73–105.

Barrick M.R., & Mount, M.K. (1991). The big five personality dimensions and job performance: A meta-analysis. *Personnel Psychology, 44,* 1–26.

Bartel, C.A., & Milliken, F.J. (2004). Perceptions of time in work groups: Do members develop shared cognitions about their temporal demands? In E.A. Mannix, M.A. Neale, & S. Blount (Eds.), *Research on managing groups and teams: Time in group* (Vol. 6, pp. 87–109).

Bliese, P.D., & Halverson, R.R. (1998). Group consensus and psychological wellbeing: A large field study. *Journal of Applied Social Psychology, 28,* 563–580.

Blount, S., & Janicik, G.A. (2002). Getting and staying in-pace: The "in-synch" preference and its implications for work groups. *Research on managing groups and teams: Vol. 4. Toward phenomenology of groups and group membership* (pp. 235–266). New York: Elsevier Science.

Bluedorn, A.C. (2002). The human organization of time. *Temporal realities and experience.* Palo Alto, CA: Stanford University Press.

Claessens, B.J.C., Van Eerde, W., Rutte, C.G., & Roe, R.A. (2007). A review of the time management literature. *Personnel Review, 36,* 255–276.

Cannon-Bowers, J.A., Salas, E., & Converse, S. (1993). Shared mental models in expert team decision-making. In N.J. Castellan, Jr. (Ed.), *Individual and group decision making: Current issues* (pp. 221–246). Mahwah, NJ: Lawrence Erlbaum Associates.

Conte, J.M., Landy, F.J., & Mathieu, J.E. (1995). Time urgency: Conceptual and construct development. *Journal of Applied Psychology, 80,* 178–185.

Cummings, J.N., & Haas, M.R. (in press). So many teams, so little time: Time allocation matters in geographically dispersed teams. *Journal of Organizational Behavior.*

DeChurch, L.A., & Haas, C.D. (2008). Examining team planning through an episodic lens: Effects of deliberate, contingency, and reactive planning on team effectiveness. *Small Group Research, 39,* 542–568.

Digman, J.M. (1990). Personality structure: Emergence of the five-factor model. *Annual Review of Psychology, 41,* 417–440.

Farmer, S., & Seers, A. (2004). Time enough to work: Employee motivation and entrainment in the workplace. *Time & Society, 13,* 265–284.

Flyvbjerg, B., Holm, M.K.S., & Buhl, S.L. (2005). How (in)accurate are demand forecasts in public works projects? The case of transportation. *Journal of the American Planning Association, 71*(2), 131–146.

Freeman, M., & Beele, P. (1992). Measuring project success. *Project Management Journal, 23,* 8–17.

Frese, M., Stewart, J., & Hannover, B. (1987). Goal orientation and planfulness: Action styles as personality concepts. *Journal of Personality and Social Psychology, 52,* 1182–1194.

Frese, M.D., & Zapf, D. (1994). Action as the core of work psychology: A German approach. In H.C. Triandis, M.D. Dunnette, & L.M. Hough (Eds.), *Handbook of industrial and organizational psychology* (Vol. 4, pp. 271–340). Palo Alto, CA: Consulting Psychologists Press.

Gersick, C.J.G. (1988). Time and transition in work teams: Toward a new model of group development. *Academy of Management Journal, 31,* 9–41.

Gersick, C.J.G. (1989). Marking time: Predictable transitions in task groups. *Academy of Management Journal, 32,* 274–309.

Gersick, C.J.G. (1994). Pacing strategic change: The case of a new venture. *Academy of Management Journal, 37,* 9–45.

Gersick, C.J.G., & Hackman, J.R. (1990). Habitual routines in task-performing groups. *Organizational Behavior and Human Decision Processes, 47,* 65–97.

Gevers, J.M.P., Claessens, B.J.C., Van Eerde, W., & Rutte, C.G. (2009). Pacing styles, personality, and performance. In R.A. Roe, M.J. Waller, & S.R. Clegg (Eds.), *Time in organizational research* (pp. 80–102). New York: Routledge.

Gevers, J.M.P., & Peeters, M.A.G. (2009). A pleasure working together? The effects of dissimilarity in team member conscientiousness on team temporal processes and individual satisfaction. *Journal of Organizational Behavior, 30,* 379–400.

Gevers, J.M.P., Rutte, C.G., & Van Eerde, W. (2004). How work groups achieve coordinated action: A model of shared cognitions on time. In E.A. Mannix, M.A. Neale, & S. Blount (Eds.), *Research on managing groups and teams: Time in groups* (Vol. 6, pp. 67–85).

Gevers, J.M.P., Rutte, C.G., & Van Eerde, W. (2006). Meeting deadlines in work groups: Implicit and explicit mechanisms. *Applied Psychology: An International Review, 55,* 52–72.

Gevers, J.M.P., Rutte, C.G., Van Eerde, W., & Roe, R.A. (2005). Meeting deadlines in project teams: A longitudinal study on the effects of shared cognitions. Paper presented at the annual meeting of the Academy of Management, Honolulu, Hawaii.

Gevers, J.M.P., Van Eerde, W., & Rutte, C.G. (2001). Time pressure, potency, and progress in project groups. *European Journal of Work and Organizational Psychology, 10,* 205–221.

Gevers, J.M.P., Van Eerde, W., & Rutte, C.G. (2009). Team self-regulation and meeting deadlines in project teams: Antecedents and effects of temporal consensus. *European Journal of Work and Organizational Psychology, 18*(3), 295–321.

Gully, S.M., Incalcaterra, K.A., Joshi, A., & Beaubien, J.M. (2002). A meta-analysis of team efficacy, potency, and performance: Interdependence and level of analysis as moderators of observed relationships. *Journal of Applied Psychology, 87,* 819–832.

Gupta, A.K., & Wilemon, D.L. (1990). Accelerating the development of technology-based new products. *California Management Review, 32*(2), 24–44.

Gurtner, A., Tschan, F., Semmer, N.K., & Nägele, C. (2007). Getting groups to develop good strategies: Effects of reflexivity interventions on team process, team performance, and shared mental models. *Organizational Behavior and Human Decision Processes, 102,* 127–142.

Guzzo, R.A., Yost, P.R., Campbell, R.J., & Shea, G.P. (1993). Potency in groups: Articulating a construct. *British Journal of Social Psychology, 32,* 87–106.

Hacker, W. (2003). Action regulation theory: A practical tool for the design of modern work processes? *European Journal of Work and Organizational Psychology, 12,* 105–130.

Hackman, J.R., Brousseau, K.R., & Weiss, J.A. (1976). The interaction of task design and group performance strategies in determining group effectiveness. *Organizational Behavior and Human Performance, 16,* 350–365.

Harrison, D.A., Mohammed, S., McGrath, J.E., Florey, A.T., & Vanderstoep, S. (2003). Time matters in team task performance: Effects of member familiarity, entrainment, and task discontinuity on speed and quality. *Personnel Psychology, 56,* 633–669.

Janicik, G.A., & Bartel, C.A. (2003). Talking about time: Effects of temporal planning and time awareness norms on group coordination and performance. *Group Dynamics: Theory, Research, and Practice, 7,* 122–134.

Klimoski, R., & Mohammed, S. (1994). Team mental model: Construct or metaphor? *Journal of Management, 20,* 403–437.

Kozlowski, S.W.J., & Ilgen, D.R. (2006). Enhancing the effectiveness of work groups and teams. *Psychological Science in the Public Interest, 7,* 77–124.

Leach, L.P. (1999). Critical chain project management improves project performance. *Project Management Journal, 30*(2), 39–51.

LePine, J. (2003). Team adaptation and post-change performance: Effects of team composition in terms of members' cognitive ability and personality. *Journal of Applied Psychology, 88*(1), 27–39.

Lientz, B.P., & Rea, K.P. (2001). *Breakthrough technology project management.* London: Academic Press.

Marks, M.A., Mathieu, J.E., & Zaccaro, S.J. (2001). A temporally based framework and taxonomy of team processes. *Academy of Management Review, 26,* 356–376.

Mathieu, J.E., & Rapp, T.L. (2009). Laying the foundation for successful team performance trajectories: The roles of team charters and performance strategies. *Journal of Applied Psychology, 94*(1), 90–103.

McGrath, J.E., & Kelly, J. (1986). *Time and human interaction: Toward a social psychology of time.* New York: The Guilford Press.

McGrath, J.E., & O'Connor, K.M. (1996). Temporal issues in work groups. In M.A. West (Ed.), *Handbook of work group psychology* (pp. 25–52). Chichester, UK: John Wiley & Sons.

Milliken, F.J., & Martins, L.L. (1996). Searching for common threads: Understanding the multiple effects of diversity in organizational groups. *Academy of Management Review, 21,* 402–433.

Mohammed, S., & Angell, L. (2004). Surface- and deep-level diversity in workgroups: Examining the moderating effects of team orientation and team process on relationship conflict. *Journal of Organizational Behavior, 25,* 1015–1039.

Mohammed, S., Hamilton, K., & Lim, A. (2009). The incorporation of time in team research: Past, current, and future. In E. Salas, G.F. Goodwin, & C.S. Burke (Eds.), *Team effectiveness in complex organizations: Cross-disciplinary perspectives and approaches* (pp. 321–348). New York: Routledge Taylor and Francis Group.

Mohammed, S., & Nadkarni, S. (2011). Temporal diversity and team performance: The moderating role of team temporal leadership. *Academy of Management Journal, 54*(3), 489–508.

Mohammed, S., & Ringseis, E. (2001). Cognitive diversity and consensus in group decision making: The role of inputs, processes, and outcomes. *Organizational Behavior and Human Decision Processes, 85,* 310–335.

Moløkken, K., & Jørgensen, M. (2003). A review of surveys on software effort estimation. Paper presented at IEEE International Symposium on Empirical Software Engineering (ISESE 2003), Rome, Italy.

Okhuysen, G. (2001). Structuring change: Familiarity and formal interventions in problem-solving groups. *Academy of Management Journal, 44,* 794–808.

Okhuysen, G.A., & Waller, M.J. (2002). Focusing on midpoint transitions: An analysis of boundary conditions. *Academy of Management Journal, 45,* 1056–1065.

O'Leary, M.B., Mortensen, M., & Willams Woolley, A. (2009). Multiple team membership: A theoretical model of its effects on productivity and learning for individuals, teams, and organizations. Tepper School of Business, Paper 549.

Orlikowski, W.J., & Yates, J. (2002). It's about time: Temporal structuring in organizations. *Organization Science, 13*(6), 684–699.

Rentsch, J.R., & Hall, R.J. (1994). Members of great teams think alike: A model of team effectiveness and schema similarity among team members. In M.M. Beyerlein, D.A. Johnson, & S.T. Beyerlein (Eds.), *Advances in interdisciplinary studies of work groups: Vol. 1. Theories of self-managing work teams* (pp. 223–261). Greenwich, CT: Jai Press, Inc.

Roe, R.A. (1999). Work performance. A multiple regulation perspective. In G. Cooper & I.T. Robertson (Eds.), *International review of industrial and organizational psychology* (pp. 231–335). Chichester, UK: John Wiley & Sons.

Standifer, R., & Bluedorn, A. (2006). Alliance management teams and entrainment: Sharing temporal mental models. *Human Relations, 59*(7), 903–928.

Steiner, I.D. (1972). *Group processes and productivity.* New York: Academic Press.

Stout, R.J., Cannon-Bowers, J.A., Salas, E., & Milanovich, D.M. (1999). Planning, shared mental models, and coordinated performance: An empirical link is established. *Human Factors, 41,* 61–71.

Thatcher, S.M.B., & Patel, P.C. (2010). Managing polychromic diversity through shared cognitions and future temporal focus. Working paper.

Tripoli, A.M. (1998). Planning and allocating: Strategies for managing priorities in complex jobs. *European Journal of Work and Organizational Psychology,* 7, 455–476.

Tschan, F. (1995). Communication enhances small group performance if it conforms to task requirements: The concept of ideal communication cycles. *Basic and Applied Social Psychology, 17,* 371–393.

Tschan, F. (2002). Ideal cycles of communication (or cognitions) in triads, dyads, and individuals. *Small Group Research, 33,* 615–643.

Van Ginkel, W.P., & van Knippenberg, D. (2008). Group information elaboration and group decision making: The role of shared task representations. *Organizational Behavior and Human Decision Processes, 105*(1), 82–97.

Vesey, J.T. (1991). The new competitors: They think in terms of speed-to-market. *Academy of Management Executive, 5*(2), 23–33.

Von Cranach, M., Ochsenbein, G., & Valach, L. (1986). The group as a self-active system. *European Journal of Social Psychology, 16,* 193–229.

Waller, M.J., Conti, J.M., Gibson, C.B., & Carpenter, M.A. (2001). The effect of individual perceptions of deadlines on team performance. *Academy of Management Review, 26,* 586–600.

Waller, M.J., Giambatista, R.C., & Zellmer-Bruhn, M.E. (1999). The effects of individual time urgency on group polychronicity. *Journal of Managerial Psychology, 14,* 244–256.

Waller, M.J., Zellmer-Bruhn, M.E., & Giambatista, R.C. (2002). Watching the clock: Group pacing behavior under dynamic deadlines. *Academy of Management Journal, 45,* 1046–1055.

Weingart, L.R. (1992). Impact of group goals, task component complexity, effort, and planning on group performance. *Journal of Applied Psychology, 77,* 682–693.

West, M.A. (1996). Reflexivity and work group effectiveness: A conceptual integration. In M.A. West (Ed.), *Handbook of work group psychology* (pp. 555–579). Chichester, UK: John Wiley & Sons.

Wilke, H.A.M., & Meertens, R.W. (1994). *Group performance.* London: Routledge.

Yakura, E.K. (2002). Charting time: Timelines as temporal boundary objects. *Academy of Management Journal, 45,* 956–970.

Zimbardo, P.G., & Boyd, J.N. (1999). Putting time in perspective: A valid, reliable individual-differences metric. *Journal of Personality and Social Psychology, 77,* 1271–1288.

CHAPTER NINETEEN

Five Simple Processes That Improve High-Risk Team Effectiveness*

Michaela Kolbe

ETH Zurich, Switzerland

Introduction

In this chapter, five team processes that are essential for high-risk team effectiveness are presented. Building on evidence from micro-level observation studies in medicine and aviation, I will highlight that these teams are most effective when their members (1) *maintain high situation awareness* (Reader, Flin, & Cuthbertson, 2011), (2) *talk to the room* (Tschan, Semmer, Gurtner, Bizzari, Spychiger, Breuer, & Marsch, 2009; Waller & Uitdewilligen, 2008), (3) *engage in explicit reasoning* (Tschan et al., 2009), (4) *speak up* (Edmondson, 2003), and (5) *engage in closed-loop communication* (Salas, Sims, & Burke, 2005). Although these processes imply varying degrees of implicitness vs. explicitness (Kolbe, Burtscher, Manser, Künzle, & Grote, 2011), all of them are simple, straightforward, and easy to incorporate. Whereas much research on high-risk team effectiveness focuses on leadership, emphasizing

*I thank Bastian Grande, MD, Carl Schick, and Mona Weiss very much for their helpful comments on the examples from medicine, and Nadine Bienefeld-Seall, PhD, for her helpful comments on the examples from aviation.

the special role of the formal leader's behavior (Klein, Ziegert, Knight, & Xiao, 2006; Reader, Flin, & Cuthbertson, 2011; Tschan, Semmer, Gautschi, Hunziker, Spychiger, & Marsch, 2006), the acts of these five processes presented here can be performed by all team members, regardless of their hierarchical or functional position within the team. Training high-risk teams in using these processes offers possibilities for unburdening team leaders, sharing leadership, and enhancing team performance. I will also discuss evidence-based approaches for how the five processes can be put into practice by highlighting (a) the supporting role of the organization and the team leader (e.g., psychological safety and leader inclusive behavior as preconditions for speaking up, Nembhard & Edmondson, 2006), (b) interventions to help team members overcome their perceived awkwardness of communicating explicitly, and (c) interventions to help team members identify when switching from implicit to explicit processes is necessary. Overall, this chapter provides evidence-based best practices for five processes consisting of simple verbal and behavioral acts that enhance high-risk team effectiveness and complement best practices for team leaders and organizations.

High-Risk Team Specifics

Team literature is increasingly focusing on teamwork in high-risk environments (Kozlowski & Bell, 2003) such as health care, aviation, or offshore industries. These work contexts involve complexity, ambiguity, and consequential outcomes (Kozlowski, 2010). Work is performed by action teams, that is, teams in which members with specialized skills must improvise and coordinate their actions in order to perform intense (e.g., time-pressed, life-threatening), interdependent, and unpredictable tasks (Sundstrom, de Meuse, & Futrell, 1990). For example, in the trauma center of a university hospital, the ad-hoc trauma team is typically an ensemble of emergency physicians, anesthesiologists, surgeons of various disciplines, radiologists, and nurse specialists. They often have varying degrees of experience, may or may not have previously worked together, and by definition are tasked to effectively treat a seriously injured patient suffering from a polytrauma (life-threatening trauma). These action teams differ in a number of challenging ways from classic, long-term "real" teams. First, while real teams usually have membership stability and clear boundaries (Hackman, 2002), action team composition often varies (Klein, Ziegert, Knight, & Xiao, 2006). Second, although the temporal boundaries of long-term teams may also vary, action teams tend to have a short-term focus (Arrow, McGrath, & Berdahl, 2000). Third, while real teams can take time to team build and develop as a team, action teams have limited possibilities to do so—in many cases they must solve problems immediately upon formation.

Research has shown that high-risk teams realize safety via heedfulness and adaptiveness (Burke, Stagl, & Salas, 2006; Weick & Roberts, 1993), particularly with respect to leadership (Kozlowski, Watola, Jensen, Kim, & Botero, 2009; Künzle, Zala-Mezö, Kolbe, Wacker, & Grote, 2010), coordination (Grote, Kolbe, Zala-Mezö, Bienefeld-Seall, & Künzle, 2010; Kolbe, Burtscher, Manser, Künzle, & Grote, 2011; Riethmüller, Fernandez Castelao, Eberhardt, Timmermann, & Boos, 2012), and timing of actions (Tschan, Semmer, Gautschi, Hunziker, Spychiger, & Marsch, 2006; Tschan, Semmer, Hunziker, & Marsch, 2011; Waller, 1999). That is, looking at what members of high-risk teams do and how they do it reveals insights into best teamwork practices. The means by which team members work together to achieve meaningful outcomes has been referred to as team processes (Marks, Mathieu, & Zaccaro, 2001), nontechnical skills (Fletcher, McGeorge, Flin, Glavin, & Maran, 2002), and human factors or behavioral skills (Nestel, Walker, Simon, Aggarwal, & Andreatta, 2011). In the following section, I will focus on five team processes that are particularly essential for high-risk team effectiveness: situation awareness, talking to the room, explicit reasoning, speaking up, and closed-loop communication.

Five Simple (But Not Simplified) Team Processes

I chose these five team processes because: (1) although implementing these five team processes may seem difficult, the acts of which these processes consist of are actually simple and straightforward; (2) they can be performed by any team member, regardless of his or her hierarchical and functional position within the team; (3) they reflect the fact that the appropriate mixture of implicit as well as explicit behaviors can lead to high-risk team effectiveness; and (4) they represent mechanisms for managing both actions and information. This differentiation between action- versus information-management is becoming more and more acknowledged in the literature on team effectiveness, pointing out that teams do well when they coordinate not only actions but also information (Boos, Kolbe, & Strack, 2011; Kolbe, Burtscher, & Manser, in press; Kolbe, Burtscher, Manser, Künzle, & Grote, 2011; Minehart, Pian-Smith, Walzer, Gardner, Rudolph, Simon, & Raemer, 2012; Tschan, Semmer, Hunziker, & Marsch, 2011). By coordinating information, teams can develop resilience against inadequate exchange of information (Bogenstätter, Tschan, Semmer, Spychiger, Breuer, & Marsch, 2009; Mesmer-Magnus & DeChurch, 2009), insufficient evaluation of possible negative consequences of ego-based or predetermined decision preferences (Greitemeyer & Schulz-Hardt, 2003), and inappropriate integration of different information (Nijstad & Kaps, 2008). That is, coordinating information as well as actions within a team is crucial, and the processes I present here can be assigned to either one of these two coordination goals.

The second distinction I use is whether a process (action- or information-management) is either implicit or explicit. Explicitness entails resources being spent on the task of coordinating as such and is expressed in a purposeful, unambiguous manner, such as giving orders or relaying information upon request (Entin & Serfaty, 1999; Wittenbaum, Vaughan, & Stasser, 1998). In contrast, implicitness does not require extra resources but occurs based on a shared and correct understanding of the task requirements and the situation and relies on the correct anticipation of one another's actions and needs and on the respective behavior adjustment (Rico, Sánchez-Manzanares, Gil, & Gibson, 2008). The processes I present here vary in their degree of implicitness vs. explicitness. The overall framework, based on Kolbe et al. (2011), is presented in Figure 19.1.

My purpose is not to oversimplify teamwork in high-risk work environments. Being aware of the social challenges that can make it hard to perform them, I still aim to show that some of the most efficient team processes consist of acts that are simple in them-

Figure 19.1. The Five Team Processes Organized Along a Two-Dimensional Taxonomy

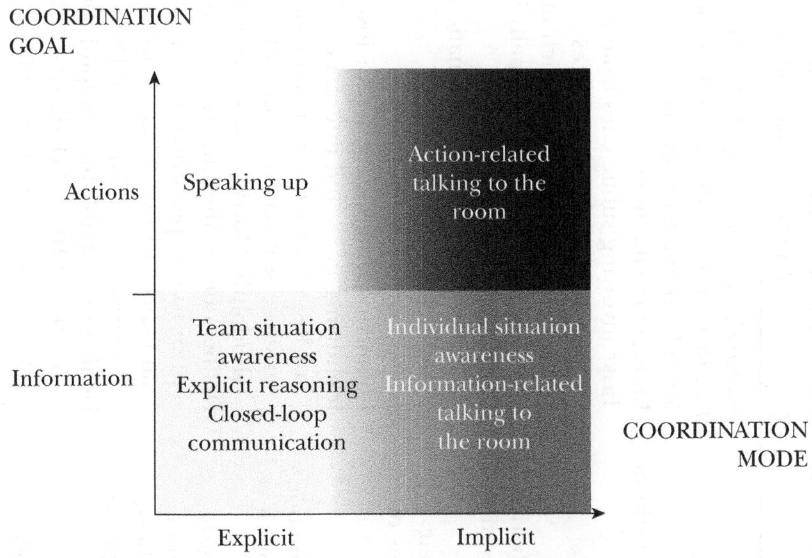

Source: Based on Kolbe, Burtscher, Manser, Künzle, and Grote, 2011.

selves, straightforward, and therefore easy to learn. They provide an opportunity for high-risk organizations to integrate low-key yet effective training interventions. It is plausible that the more members of an organization who are trained in performing these five team processes (for example, the complete staff of a trauma center), the more likely it will be that, when acting in teams, they will perform these processes when required and that dynamics can enfold that allow for synergy, resilience, and high performance. These real benefits of teamwork are ultimately required during high-risk situations, for example, when a pregnant polytrauma with a difficult airway is being brought into the trauma center.

The team processes I will present in the following section include behavioral, verbal, and cognitive aspects. Based on my experience in observational behavior research, I will concentrate on the observable verbal and behavioral aspects. Behavioral markers for all five processes can be found in Table 19.1.

Table 19.1. Five Team Processes, Examples for Behavioral Markers, and Practical Recommendations

Team Process	*Examples for Behavioral Markers*	*Practical Recommendations*
Situation Awareness (SA)	*Individual level:* Team members monitor the surrounding environment and their teammates Team members actively seek information without request Team members gather information from multiple sources Team members increase information gathering and monitoring in response to changes in situation Team members monitor the effects of their interventions and verbalize anticipations of their actions and of future events *Team level:* Team members actively cross-check information Team members provide information before it is requested Team members talk to the room and actively verbalize their assessments of the situation Team members observe other team members, identify mistakes, and speak up voicing their concerns Team members back each other up Team members use closed-loop communication Team members engage in explicit reasoning Team members demonstrate that they have an accurate understanding of each other's workload,	*Particularly required during* (Gaba, Howard, & Small, 1995; Reader, Flin, Mearns, & Cuthbertson, 2011): Multidisciplinary teamwork Emergency situations Tasks involving subtle cues from multiple dynamically changing sources Evolving situations during which management of one problem unintentionally leads to another problem Tasks involving specific information that has to be tracked *Improved via:* Identifying situational cues for losing SA Identifying intra- and interpersonal indicators for loss of SA ("fixation" via repeating an unsuccessful action again and again) (Rudolph, Morrison, & Carroll, 2009) Deliberately establishing shared understanding prior to task performance, e.g., via briefings and checklist use (Einav, Gopher, Kara, Ben-Yosef, Lawn, Laufer, & Donchin, 2010) Deliberately establishing helpful routines, such as "10s for 10min" (Rall, Glavin, & Flin, 2008) and "when you see something, say something" Applying heuristics Experience-based learning via after action review

Talking to the Room	*Information-related talking to the room:* Team members share information with the room at large Team members interpret information to the room at large *Action-related talking to the room:* Team members comment on their own current actions Does *not* include unspecific instructions such as "can someone start chest compressions?"	*Particularly required during:* Ambiguous situations of time pressure in which neither the relevant information nor its meaning is immediately obvious (Tschan et al., 2011; Waller & Uitdewilligen, 2008) Talking to the room can complement other coordination mechanisms but—particularly in emergency situations—not fully substitute them. In those situations it can, however, serve as trigger for explicit coordination. *Improved via:* Encouraging thinking aloud
Explicit Reasoning	Team members verbally seek and value informational and judgment input from other team members regardless of their status or member rank (Wilson, Burke, Priest, & Salas, 2005) Team members evaluate and summarize information (Grommes, 2000) Team members deliberately link utterances to work out logical conclusions based on either suppositional or actual information, for instance by using causal conjunctions such as *because* or *if-then* (Tschan et al., 2009) Team members provide information and opinion	*Particularly required during:* Problem solving and decision making in ambiguous situations (Tschan et al., 2009) Situations in which team members become fixated (Rudolph, Morrison, & Carroll, 2009) Interdisciplinary and multi-team cooperation and situations involving inexperienced team members *Only partly required during:* Situations in which information is easy to access, easy to interpret, and easy to transform into clear solution (Tschan et al., 2011) *Improved via:* Pairing advocacy and inquiry (Minehart et al., 2012)

Continued

Table 19.1. Continued

Team Process	*Examples for Behavioral Markers*	*Practical Recommendations*
Speaking Up	Team members verbalize their observations and concerns Team members express doubts regarding the correctness of a procedure, decision, or information Team members correct the task-relevant behavior of the other team members Team members ask for clarification Team members suggest alternative procedure Team members make explicit attempts to stop a potentially harmful behavior	*Particularly required:* Whenever a team member has doubts about the correctness of a behavior, decision or information or observes incidents that s/he considers harmful *Improved via:* Pairing advocacy and inquiry; using the two-challenge rule (Pian-Smith, Simon, Minehart, Podraza, Rudolph, Walzer, & Raemer, 2009) Avoiding aggressive communication and subtle hints Using standardized team timeouts to invite team members to voice potential concerns (Ginnett, 1993; World Alliance for Patient Safety, 2008) Inclusive leadership (Nembhard & Edmondson, 2006) Promoting psychological safety and establishing an organizational norm for speaking up (Edmondson, 1999; Liang, Farh, & Farh, 2012) Knowing each other's names and exploring what team members need from each other to feel at ease with speaking up Deliberately examining and dealing with barriers to speaking up

Closed-Loop Communication	Team members use standardized terminology and communication patterns Team members follow up with other team members to ensure that a message was received correctly Team members engage in confirming and cross-checking information	*Particularly required during:* Complex, dynamic, and ambiguous situations (Salas, Sims, & Burke, 2005) Interdisciplinary and multi-team cooperation (Bienefeld-Seall, 2012; Burke, Salas, Wilson-Donnelly, & Priest, 2004) *Improved via:* Practicing during routine procedures Making it a fundamental component of taskwork Avoiding de-coupling from actual actions

The first team process I present is *maintaining situation awareness*, a process that is particularly crucial for complex, ambiguous, and dynamic situations.

Maintaining Situation Awareness

Situation awareness (SA) is an individual's dynamic mental model of the current state of his or her environment (Wright, Taekman, & Endsley, 2004). It includes three processes: (1) perceiving the elements of the situation, (2) comprehending their meaning, and (3) projecting their status in the near future (Endsley, 1995). That is, SA is first and foremost a cognitive process. However, there is also an important behavioral aspect by which individuals and teams strive for situation awareness and to which I am referring here (Flin, Martin, Goeters, Hörmann, Amalberti, Valot, & Nijhuis, 2005; Reader, Flin, Lauche, & Cuthbertson, 2006; Salas, Sims, & Burke, 2005).

In order to obtain and maintain awareness of a situation, individuals monitor the surrounding system, monitor their teammates, gather information from multiple sources, and cross-check them (Burtscher, Kolbe, Wacker, & Manser, 2011; Gaba, Howard, & Small, 1995; Salas, Prince, Baker, & Shrestha, 1995). For example, during a surgical procedure, the anesthesiologist monitors the surgeon and the patient's vital signs, allowing the anesthesiologist to understand the meaning of a sudden drop in blood pressure. I consider this an implicit form of managing information (Figure 19.1). Team SA—the "degree to which every team member possesses the SA required for his or her responsibilities" (Endsley, 1995, p. 39)—on the other hand, is a process I consider to be explicit rather than implicit (Figure 19.1). Behavior required for achieving team SA is mainly verbal communication, such as sharing information and perspectives (Reader, Flin, Mearns, & Cuthbertson, 2011). For example, a routine, brief discussion between the anesthesiologist and surgeon prior to surgery can enhance their shared understanding of the patient's condition, of the planned procedure, and of the collective anticipation of potentially critical events. Team SA involves verbal communication as well as all of the four recommended teamwork behaviors

I describe below (talking to the room, explicit reasoning, speaking up, and closed-loop communication).

Benefits of Situation Awareness

Much has been written about the benefits gained from situation awareness. There is important evidence that situation awareness is positively related to high-risk team decision making (Endsley, 1995) and performance (Wright, Taekman, & Endsley, 2004). Looking particularly at the behavioral aspects of SA, team member monitoring has been considered crucial for keeping up-to-date and catching potential mistakes (Marks, Mathieu, & Zaccaro, 2001), particularly in dynamic work environments (Baker, Days, & Salas, 2006). In a recent study investigating teamwork patterns during actual inductions of general anesthesia, it was found that immediate consequences of team monitoring were speaking up, giving instructions, and providing unsolicited assistance—highlighting the importance of team monitoring for team adaptation, as it enables team members to recognize when their teammates need guidance or assistance (Kolbe, Künzle, Zala-Mezö, Burtscher, Wacker, Spahn, & Grote, 2010). However, in another recent study investigating simulated inductions of general anesthesia, it was found that team member monitoring was only beneficial when the team members had a shared and accurate team mental model prior to task performance (Burtscher, Kolbe, Wacker, & Manser, 2011)—indicating that monitoring works best in combination with shared cognition and that high-risk teams benefit from establishing a shared understanding before task performance. This shared cognition/understanding can be established during preoperational briefings and checklist use (Einav, Gopher, Kara, Ben-Yosef, Lawn, Laufer, & Donchin, 2010). For example, it was found that comprehensive surgical checklists applied during preoperative (and also intraoperative and postoperative) care lead to declined rates of postoperative complications (de Vries, Prins, Crolla, den Outer, van Andel, van Helden, Schlack, van Putten, Gouma, et al., 2010), presumably due to improved communication and more thorough planning, thereby reducing unnecessary distractions and errors in the operating room (Birkmeyer, 2010). Likewise, the use of surgical-crisis checklists is associated with significantly improved management of operating-room crises (Arriaga, Bader, Wong, Lipsitz, Berry, Ziewacz, Hepner, Boorman, Pozner, Smink, & Gawande, 2013).

Situations That Require Situation Awareness

Although situation awareness is a constant demand during teamwork in any high-risk environment, there are certain types of situations in which it is particularly called for.

First, team SA is particularly required during multidisciplinary teamwork. For example, during daily rounds in an intensive care unit (ICU) where multiple interdisciplinary ICU teams collaborate, team SA is likely to influence how team members will monitor the patient and anticipate patient progress, as each discipline harbors its own discrete set of monitoring routines and assumptions that may or may not be the same as other disciplines (Reader, Flin, Mearns, & Cuthbertson, 2011).

Second, SA is particularly needed in emergency situations. For example, surgical operations performed on an emergency basis and unplanned changes in the procedure were the two most important factors associated with an increased risk of retention of a foreign body (for example, a sponge) inside the patient after surgery (Gawande, Studdert, Orav, Brennan, & Zinner, 2003).

Third, subtle cues from multiple dynamically changing sources require SA (Gaba, Howard, & Small, 1995). Gaba and colleagues described a respective example in which the anesthesiologist was having difficulty opening the patient's mouth for intubation. Later on, he realized that heart rate, expired carbon dioxide level, as well as body temperature were increasing—indicating a malignant hypothermia—a very dangerous metabolic abnormality caused by anesthetics.

Fourth, so-called evolving situations, situations in which management of one problem unintentionally leads to another problem, also particularly require SA (for example, while inserting a catheter into the heart to monitor its activity and to administer drugs during surgery, the anesthesiologist accidentally punctures the lung, causing a tension pneumothorax as a critical event). And fifth, situations in which special knowledge elements have to be tracked, utilized, and monitored (for example, an expected difficult airway situation due to patient's special anatomic condition) require particular awareness.

Ways to Train Situation Awareness

Situation awareness is standard content of a variety of high-risk team trainings; for example, it is a long-established part of Crisis Resource Management (CRM) and simulation-based trainings (Rall & Gaba, 2005; Wright, Taekman, & Endsley, 2004). During these trainings, SA can be taught by temporarily freezing teamwork actions during the simulation scenario and reflecting about current individual and team SA (Endsley, 2000). Another option is to diagnose and reflect on gaps in shared knowledge by using a web-based diagnostic tool to ask individual team members after a simulated scenario questions with respect to taskwork and coordination, applying algorithms for automatically calculating knowledge gaps between the team members, and then discussing these gaps in the subsequent debriefing (Tannenbaum, 2010).

SA training should also address typical cues and triggers, not only for typical manifestations of critical events as well as guidelines on their management, but also for typical teamwork pitfalls. For example, CRM trainings offer the opportunity to discuss how to identify and react to situations when a team member is about to loose SA through fixation. Furthermore, SA training for high-risk teams should focus on team member roles and specific technical task competencies (Cannon-Bowers, Tannenbaum, Salas, & Volpe, 1995), on establishing heuristics (for example, routines in scanning instruments and environments), checklist procedures, systematic allocation of attention, re-evaluation schemes such as the ABCDE (airway, breathing, circulation, disability, environment) scheme for managing medical emergencies, and on fostering verbal communication according to task coordination requirements (for example, closed-loop communication, speaking up).

SA can also be fostered in daily practice before, during, and after team performance cycles. For example, prior to task performance, the above-mentioned checklist-based briefings (de Vries et al., 2010) can be used for establishing cross-check routines as well as for sharing mental models between different disciplines. During emergency situations, SA can be regained by applying the "10-seconds-for-10-minutes principle" (Rall, Glavin, & Flin, 2008): When in an emergency situation, do not rush into diagnosis and treatment but deliberately take a deep breath and a team timeout. Applying this principle can "defibrillate the team" and prevent fixation errors by giving the team the chance for rigorous problem definition and formal planning. After emergency situations, incidents, and complex operations, regular debriefings/after-action reviews can enhance both team inter- and intra-discipline SA.

In the following section I present the second recommended team process, which, among other advantages, can enhance team situation awareness: *talking to the room.*

Talking to the Room

Talking to the room describes undirected talk and sharing of relevant information with the room at large (Artman & Wærn, 1999; Tschan et al., 2009). It includes information having to do with general aspects of the task rather than specific instructions or plans (Tschan et al., 2011). I therefore consider it as implicit rather than explicit behavior, as it is performed in a spontaneous, intuitive style. Talking to the room can refer to information as well as actions. For example, during the management of an unexpected difficult intubation, a nurse may read the level of blood oxygen saturation shown on the anesthesia monitor aloud ("Oxygen saturation is down to 95 percent now."). I consider this interpreting and sharing of information as "information-related talking to the room" and therefore a form of information management. If the nurse would say, "I'm turning the alarm down" or "I'm calling the ICU," I would consider these verbal notifications on the performance of subtasks as "action-related talking to the room" and therefore a form of action management (Figure 19.1). The concept of talking to the room does not include unspecific—and usually ineffective—leadership instructions such as "Can someone start chest compressions?"

Benefits of Talking to the Room

The main benefit of talking to the room is its facilitation of collective sensemaking. By mentioning task-relevant information, the well-known potential possibility of not talking about meaningful information in teams (Stasser & Titus, 1985) can be handled, situation awareness can be enhanced, and the team mental model can continuously be updated. There is growing empirical evidence supporting this simple teamwork behavior. For example, Waller and Uitdewilligen (2008) analyzed the audio recordings of communication among the personnel of the Northeast Air Defense Sector of the United States (NEADS) during the 9/11 terrorist attacks. They found that talking to the room was helpful for realizing that the situation was not a training exercise but an actual hijacking and that the respective trained protocols were the appropriate response. Similarly, in a study on medical emergency-driven teams, Tschan and colleagues found that talking to the room facilitated finding the accurate diagnosis (Tschan et al., 2009).

Another benefit of talking to the room is its function for action management. For example, a nurse announces that he or she is going to fetch a tracheotomy set (a set of anesthesia devices for inserting a tracheostomy tube through an incision in the trachea, an invasive emergency procedure for securing the airway when no other airway management procedure had been successful). The doctor not only receives an update on the nurse's current mental model (that is, emergency tracheotomy is likely next step) but is also relieved of giving the respective instruction, which saves him or her time and cognitive resources for another subtask. In line with that reasoning, it was found for anesthesia teams that action-related talking to the room substituted more explicit (that is, more resource-intensive) forms of coordination (Kolbe, Künzle, Zala-Mezö, Burtscher, Wacker, Spahn, & Grote, 2010). Additionally, talking to the room can be a very tactful way for team members to mention their ideas or concerns without having to be very explicit and therefore risk embarrassing another team member (for example, as a member of a big trauma team, a first-year resident may say, "I am just going to auscultate the lung again to make sure we have equal breath sounds and that the tube is placed correctly").

Situations That Require Talking to the Room

Being a relatively new concept, there is not much research on when talking to the room is particularly important. In a very recent study, Tschan and colleagues compared two different tasks in emergency-driven medical teams. They found that talking to the room enhanced performance during an ambiguous diagnostic task (anaphylactic shock, a severe allergic reaction, when some of the symptoms are also typical for tension pneumothorax, a collapsed lung) but not during a resuscitation task (cardiac arrest). That finding indicates that talking to the room is particularly beneficial in ambiguous situations of time pressure in which neither the relevant information nor its meaning is immediately obvious. In these difficult situations, doctors are at risk of losing SA via becoming "vagabonding" (that is, generating a wide range of plausible diagnoses and jumping among them without verifying them properly), "stalled" (that is, having difficulties generating any diagnoses), or "fixated" (quickly establishing and remaining stuck on mainly one plausible but wrong diagnosis) in their problem-solving attempts (Rudolph, Morrison, & Carroll, 2009). Here, I think that talking to the room has the potential to trigger the team to start re-evaluating the situation more thoroughly, that is, to switch to a more explicit information coordination style (explicit reasoning).

Likewise, while action-related talking to the room may substitute for leadership behavior in routine situations (Kolbe et al., 2010), in non-routine situations it may serve as a trigger—but not as a substitute—for more explicit action coordination and initiate required leadership behavior. For example, upon occurrence of a cardiac arrest during induction of general anesthesia, the nurse may talk to the room, "I am going to call the attending," to which the resident may reply, "No, start chest compressions immediately."

Finally, there is the question of how much talking to the room is appropriate. Presumably, there is a curvilinear relationship between talking to the room and performance, which means that, while a certain amount of talking to the room is beneficial, too much or too little is detrimental. During post-simulation scenario debriefings of CRM training, I frequently hear team members expressing their concern about having possibly annoyed and distracted their teammates with their talking to the room. But I have never heard a respective complaint about being annoyed by someone's talking to the room. Quite the contrary: especially young doctors report perceiving nurses' talking to the room to be very helpful.

Ways to Train Talking to the Room

Talking to the room can very easily be implemented in early technical training by establishing both information- and action-related talking to the room behavior as integral parts of performing procedures. For instance, during regular simulation-based training (such as CRM courses), talking-to-the-room routines should be reinforced using video-based debriefings. Because talking to the room can be perceived by the sender as awkward or annoying and therefore avoided, debriefings allow for immediate feedback on the actual use of talking to the room. For example, I sometimes witness course participants' astonishment when realizing how quiet they were during task performance. These situations offer the possibility to discuss potential benefits and appropriate timepoints for talking to the room ("If you had known what she was doing in that situation, what do you think would have been different in your teamwork?").

I will now present the third team process: *explicit reasoning*.

Explicit Reasoning

Explicit reasoning describes a process of verbally relating different pieces of information to one another (Tschan et al., 2009). I consider explicit reasoning an explicit behavior of information management (Figure 19.1). Compared to talking to the room, which can involve only brief utterances that relay information or subtask updates (for example, "heart rate is going up"), explicit reasoning includes the deliberate linking of utterances to work out logical conclusions based on either suppositional or actual information, for instance, by using causal conjunctions such as *because* or *if-then* (Tschan et al., 2009), such as "I think the heart rate is going up because he feels pain." In other words, as talking to the room may include only an observation or statement, explicit reasoning involves eliciting of additional information among team members.

The importance of (individual) explicit reasoning is well described in the literature on diagnostic reasoning in clinical medicine (Bowen, 2006). Whenever teamwork is involved, explicit reasoning should exploit the synergistic aspect of teamwork by verbally seeking and valuing informational and judgment input from other team members, regardless of their status or member rank (Wilson, Burke, Priest, & Salas, 2005). For example, explicit reasoning can be enacted by simply inquiring "What do you think?" or "What is your idea?" and coherently discussing and summarizing the input's meaning within the team (Grommes, 2000). Ideally, it involves the pairing of two communication strategies: *advocacy*, verbalizing one's thinking, and *inquiry*, asking other team members what they think (Minehart et al., 2012; Rudolph, Simon, Rivard, Dufresne, & Raemer, 2007).

Benefits of Explicit Reasoning

The main benefit of explicit reasoning is its facilitation of collective sensemaking, problem solving, and decision making within the team (Minehart et al., 2012; Tschan et al., 2009). That is, it enhances the ability of teams to elicit their members' individually held knowledge/expertise, to use this knowledge/expertise for sensemaking, and to apply it for discriminating among any number of diagnostic explanations. For example, even simple mechanisms such as repeating and summarizing mentioned information or verbally listing the evidence present in a case were found to be positively associated with decision quality (Eva, 2004; Kolbe, Strack, Stein, & Boos, 2011). Similarly, investigating cockpit crew coordination during a simulated clean approach, Grote and colleagues (2010) found that explicit communication was generally important for good crew performance. Studying diagnostic accuracy in simulated ambiguous medical emergency situations, Tschan and colleagues (2009) found that teams displaying more explicit reasoning were more likely to find the correct diagnosis. Thus, while errors in clinical reasoning are frequently due to inappropriate cognitive processing (Graber, Franklin, & Gordon, 2005) and poor team information-management (Larson, Christensen, Franz, & Abbott, 1998) rather than insufficient team member knowledge, explicit reasoning among team members can support effectively sharing cognitions in high-risk teams.

Situations That Require Explicit Reasoning

Explicit reasoning is required during team problem solving and decision making in ambiguous situations (Larson, Christensen, Franz, & Abbott, 1998), for example, during difficult medical cases (Elstein & Schwartz, 2002) or ill-defined medical emergencies (Tschan et al., 2009). It can be particularly useful when team members become stalled or fixated during problem solving (Rudolph, Morrison, & Carroll, 2009). For example, a team member can initiate explicit reasoning when he or she realizes that his or her colleagues are engaging in "premature closure" (failing to consider further alternatives once an initial diagnose has been achieved, Graber, Franklin, & Gordon, 2005), which can happen due to false consensus (Ross, Green, & House, 1977) or preference-consistent (versus objective) evaluation of information (Greitemeyer & Schulz-Hardt, 2003). Explicit reasoning is also required in situations involving inexperienced team members or interdisciplinary and multi-team cooperation.

However, explicit reasoning is less likely required in situations when the information is easy to access, easy to interpret, and easy to transform into a clear solution. For example, a cardiac arrest—an easily diagnosable situation with task requirements prescribed by standardized guidelines—benefits from immediate action and leadership (Tschan et al., 2011). Resource investment of explicitly soliciting team members' individual information and opinions is likely not only unnecessary but will actually distract the team from task management. That is, looking at task coordination requirements and distinguishing whether actions or information should be coordinated are useful for predicting the effectiveness of teamwork behaviors such as explicit reasoning (Kolbe, Burtscher,

Manser, Künzle, & Grote, 2011; Tschan et al., 2011; see also Figure 19.1).

Ways to Teach Explicit Reasoning

Explicit reasoning can be taught as a fundamental problem-solving skill on both the individual and team level. Teaching around examples (Eva, 2004) and prompting learners to prioritize a list of diagnostic alternatives and explain their justifications are typical teaching examples of explicit reasoning (for an excellent summary, see Bowen, 2006). On the team level, simulation-based training can particularly focus on recognizing situational cues that call for explicit reasoning (for example, fixation error). For example, similar to team SA-training, during video-based debriefings the facilitator asks circular questions such as "How could you recognize whether your team colleague was fixated on one particular problem diagnosis?" "What could he need from you in that situation?" (Kolbe, Weiss, Grote, Knauth, Dambach, Spahn, & Grande, in press).

In the following section I describe the fourth recommended team process: *speaking up.*

Speaking Up

Speaking up refers to explicitly communicating task-relevant observations, requesting clarification, or explicitly challenging or correcting a task-relevant decision or a procedure. In her recent review on employee voice behavior, Morrison (2011) specified that voice behavior can have three distinct natures: suggestion-focused (such as voicing an idea how to improve a work process), opinion-focused (for example, expressing a point of view that differs from the one held by others), and problem-focused (for example, explicitly expressing concern about behaviors that could be harmful). It is particularly the latter type of voice behavior that is considered essential for preventing harm and ensuring high performance (Morrison, 2011). By its very nature, speaking up is an explicit teamwork behavior (Figure 19.1). I consider it action management rather than information management, because it mostly aims at challenging action procedures (for example, after double-checking with the patient chart a nurse realizes that the patient is allergic to cephalosporin [a certain class of antibiotics] and immediately calls "stop, don't administer the Cefazolin [an antibiotic of cephalosporin]!"). However, in some cases it may also serve information management (for example, "Are you sure that he has really no allergies?").

Benefits of Speaking Up

The main benefit of speaking up is that it can prevent harm. In aviation, there is particular evidence that a lack of speaking up (for example, the first officer deciding not to challenge the captain's potentially dangerous behavior) can have disastrous consequences (Jentsch & Smith-Jentsch, 2001). In a recent simulator study, Bienefeld-Seall (2012) looked at the positive consequences of speaking up. She observed that subordinate cockpit or cabin crewmembers who spoke up with their concerns and observations were able to mitigate errors made by their leaders. Those crewmembers who effectively spoke up significantly improved decision making and team performance.

In health care, speaking up is considered essential for preventing medical harm and ensuring good quality of care (Dwyer, 1994; Henriksen & Dayton, 2006). In a tragic example of a lack of speaking up leading to the death of a patient, a nurse observed very experienced senior anesthesiologists during the induction of general anesthesia unsuccessfully attempting to intubate a patient scheduled for a routine operation. After the patient had not been ventilated for several minutes, the nurse got a tracheotomy set but did not attract sufficient attention to this correct problem solution from the doctors to change their course of action (Reynard, Reynolds, & Stevenson, 2009). The evidence that speaking up can actually prevent such medical harm and facilitate taskwork is growing. For example, Edmondson (2003) found that the perceived ease of speaking up was correlated with the success of implementing a new technology for minimal invasive cardiac surgery. Furthermore, in a study of simulated anesthesia inductions involving several minor non-routine events, nurses' speaking up behavior and technical team performance were positively related (Kolbe, Burtscher, Wacker, Grande, Nohynkova, Manser,

Spahn, & Grote, 2012). This study also found that the immediate benefits of speaking up for team interaction were clarifications of the current procedure, team member monitoring, and initiations of changes in the procedure.

Situations That Require Speaking Up

In principle, speaking up is required whenever a team member has doubt or concern about the correctness of a behavior or observes incidents that he or she regards as harmful. It involves neither aggressive behavior (Jentsch & Smith-Jentsch, 2001) nor a disturbing habit of continuously questioning everything in every situation. The requirement is for straight-to-the-point, specific expressions of concern or requests for clarifications—in fast-paced high-risk teams caught up in the momentum of an incorrect procedure. In actuality, speaking up in such a situation is evidently easier said than done, given the evidence of the need to do it in previous life-threatening situations but nevertheless not done. The perceived threshold for speaking up may be high. In the following sections I suggest ideas that can help to ease the difficulties with speaking up.

Ways to Train Speaking Up

I consider three points essential for successful training of speaking up. First, the perceived barriers of speaking up should be examined and dealt with. There is a lot of empirical evidence showing the role of social influence: People decide not to speak up because they fear repercussion or social rejection (Bienefeld & Grote, 2012; Detert & Edmondson, 2011; Kobayashi, Pian-Smith, Sato, Sawa, Takeshita, & Raemer, 2006), feel resignation (Morrison, 2011), feel that the team's climate does not allow for voicing successfully (Morrison, Wheeler-Smith, & Kamdar, 2011), or fear of being wrong (Raemer, 2010). These barriers should be addressed explicitly. In line with this, psychological safety (Edmondson, 1999) should be promoted. This is challenging, because safety culture in general cannot be managed or regulated as such by any regulators but only affected through safety management measures, for example, safety-fostering routines and team trainings (Grote, 2012).

Second, speaking up should be explicitly initiated. In aviation, pre-flight debriefings offer an excellent possibility for the captain to set the stage and actively invite all crew members to speak up with observations or concerns should they occur (Ginnett, 1993). The leadership style associated with this attenuation of status difference—leader inclusiveness—was found to predict cockpit and cabin crewmembers' propensity to speak up (Bienefeld-Seall, 2012). In health care, the recently introduced WHO Surgical Safety Checklist offers a similar opportunity for a "time-out" during which not only the OR team has the chance to team up and to discuss anticipated critical patient issues before skin incision but the senior doctors can invite the team members to voice potential concerns (World Alliance for Patient Safety, 2008). This leader inclusive behavior can mitigate some of the above-mentioned perceived barriers to speaking up (Nembhard & Edmondson, 2006).

During simulation-based training, leader inclusiveness can be trained by combining the advocacy-inquiry technique (Rudolph, Simon, Rivard, Dufresne, & Raemer, 2007) with circular questions from the systemic-constructivist approach (Kolbe, Weiss, Grote, Knauth, Dambach, Spahn, & Grande, in press; Kriz, 2010). For example, during a post-scenario debriefing, the instructor may say: "In that situation my impression is that you are not OK with what he is doing, but I did not hear you saying it out loud" (advocacy): "What was on your mind?" (inquiry); or (*to another team member*): "What do you think she might have needed from you to speak up in that situation?" (circular question).

Further, based on empirical evidence indicating that speaking up in an earlier phase of teamwork is related to speaking up during later phases (Kolbe et al., 2012), speaking up early sets the stage for being more at ease and more likely to apply it later on. Accordingly, teams should be encouraged to become comfortable with speaking up early instead of waiting with the first attempt to speak up until a critical situation occurs.

Third, speaking up should be trained as a skill. This training should include simulation-based behavior role modeling (Smith-Jentsch, Salas, & Baker, 1996), metacognitive strategies for determining when to be assertive (Jentsch & Smith-Jentsch, 2001), and techniques for speaking up. An excellent example for a speaking-up technique is the "two-challenge rule" (challenge twice and, if that does not lead to success, get additional help) in which advocacy (for example, "I see that you plan to administer Cefazolin. In the patient chart I have read that she is allergic to cephalosporin") is combined with inquiry ("Can you clarify how to go on?") (Pian-Smith, Simon, Minehart, Podraza, Rucolph, Walzer, & Raemer, 2009; Rudolph, Simon, Rivard, Dufresne, & Raemer, 2007).

The final and fifth team process I recommend is the explicit communication pattern known as *closed-loop communication.*

Closed-Loop Communication

Closed-loop communication is a special form of content-checking, repeat-back communication. Optimally, it involves three steps: (1) the sender initiates a message, (2) the receiver acknowledges that he or she has received the message, and (3) the sender confirms or paraphrases to ensure that the intended message was received (Salas, Sims, & Burke, 2005). For example, in aviation, making sure who is flying an airplane is initiated by the captain's "my aircraft" and acknowledged by the first officer's "your aircraft." In medicine, during the management of a cardiac arrest, a doctor may ask a nurse to administer epinephrine, which—once administered—should be confirmed ("One milligram epinephrine given"). That is, team members use standardized communication patterns (Salas, Rosen, Burke, Nicholson, & Howse, 2007).

I consider closed-loop communication an explicit process for information management in teams (Figure 19.1). Closed-loop communication is a central coordinating mechanism in the "big five" model of general team competencies (Salas, Sims, & Burke, 2005). No other explicit communication mechanism better ensures that not only was the message received but that the content of the message was received as intended, giving the sender the opportunity to either correct what was originally said or correct its misinterpretation by the receiver. With respect to high-risk teams, it is a particularly well-established part of general guidelines for crisis management in teams (Burke, Salas,

Wilson-Donnelly, & Priest, 2004) and of special crisis resource management (CRM) principles, for example, in anesthesia (Rall & Gaba, 2005).

Benefits of Closed-Loop Communication

"Closing the loop" has a variety of benefits. First, it is a very simple way of ensuring that sent communications are heard and accurately understood and of preventing communication breakdowns (Salas, Sims, & Burke, 2005). That is, potential misunderstandings (receiving a different message than the sender intended to send) can be clarified before harm is done. During information overload in complex situations, closed-loop communication can be something like a secure communication channel and work as a shared language between different disciplines. Second, closed-loop communication promotes shared situation awareness (Wilson, Burke, Priest, & Salas, 2005). Third, research with military aviation crews has shown that closed-loop communication facilitates problem-solving processes (Bowers, Jentsch, Salas, & Braun, 1998).

Situations That Require Closed-Loop Communication

Closed-loop communication is required in complex, dynamic, and ambiguous situations (Salas, Sims, & Burke, 2005), for example, during the occurrence of non-routine events. It is particularly useful during interdisciplinary cooperation (for example, in ad hoc trauma teams consisting of specialists from disciplines), because each discipline has its own jargon, which increases the potential for miscommunication (Burke, Salas, Wilson-Donnelly, & Priest, 2004). In a similar vein, closed-loop communication has overall been associated with performance of multi-team systems, that is, networks of teams that interact directly and interdependently toward at least one shared goal (Marks, DeChurch, Mathieu, Panzer, & Alonso, 2005). For example, Bienefeld (2012) found that closed-loop communication was positively related to multiteam performance in cockpit and cabin crew collaborations.

Also, I consider closed-loop communication a communication strategy that can generally be established in high-risk teams' daily practice during routine procedures, with the idea that it is then well-learned and easy to perform in non-routine situations when it matters even more. However, in order to prevent closed-loop communication from becoming an automated, rote routine that is de-coupled from the actual behavior, it should always be mutually related to situation awareness.

Ways to Train Closed-Loop Communication

Like talking to the room, closed-loop communication can very easily be implemented in early technical training, being considered part of performing procedures. It is usually trained as procedural type communication and promoted through the use of standardized terminology (Burke, Salas, Wilson-Donnelly, & Priest, 2004). During regular simulation-based training, it should be refreshed using video-based debriefings. They allow for feedback on the actual use of closed-loop communication and for in-depth reflection on the proximate (for example, "What are your thoughts on why your closed-loop communication was beneficial in this particular situation?") and ultimate functions (for example, "Looking back at the beginning of your interaction, how did closed-loop communication help you to establish a safety-driven working routine?") of this particular behavior for safe team performance.

Outlook

The five processes presented in this chapter enhance the performance of high-risk teams. They vary with respect to implicitness versus explicitness (see Figure 19.1) (Kolbe, Burtscher, Manser, Künzle, & Grote, 2011)) and information versus action management purpose. My aim was not to oversimplify teamwork in high-risk work environments but to show that some of the most efficient team processes consist of acts that are simple in themselves, straightforward, and therefore relatively easy to learn—even speaking up—if their barriers are examined, if they are explicitly encouraged by the team leader, and if they are taught and acknowledged as a worthy team skill. I hope to have stimulated an increased attention to these five straightforward team processes by practitioners as well as more research on the functions, tasks requirements, and interrelations of these behaviors in experimental settings as well as "in the wild."

References

Arriaga, A.F., Bader, A.M., Wong, J.M., Lipsitz, S.R., Berry, W.R., Ziewacz, J.E., Hepner, D.L., Boorman, D.J., Pozner, C.N., Smink, D.S., & Gawande, A.A. (2013). Simulation-based trial of surgical-crisis checklists. *New England Journal of Medicine, 368*, 246–253.

Arrow, H., McGrath, J.E., & Berdahl, J.L. (2000). *Small groups as complex systems: Formation, coordination, development, and adaption.* Thousand Oaks, CA: Sage.

Artman, H., & Wærn, Y. (1999). Distributed cognition in an emergency co-ordination center. *Cognition, Technology and Work, 1*, 237–246.

Baker, D.P., Days, R., & Salas, E. (2006). Teamwork as an essential component of high-reliability organizations. *Health Services Research, 41*(1), 1576–1598.

Bienefeld, N. (2012). Leadership, boundary-spanning, and voice in high-risk multiteam systems. Dissertation, ETH Zurich, Switzerland.

Bienefeld-Seall, N., & Grote, G. (2012). Silence that may kill: When aircrew members don't speak up and why. *Aviation Psychology and Applied Human Factors, 2*(1), 1–10.

Birkmeyer, J.D. (2010). Strategies for improving surgical quality—Checklists and beyond. *New England Journal of Medicine, 363*, 1963–1965.

Bogenstätter, Y., Tschan, F., Semmer, N.K., Spychiger, M., Breuer, M., & Marsch, S.U. (2009). How accurate is information transmitted to medical professionals joining a medical emergency? A simulator study. *Human Factors, 51*, 115–125.

Boos, M., Kolbe, M., & Strack, M. (2011). An inclusive model of group coordination. In M. Boos, M. Kolbe, P. Kappeler, & T. Ellwart (Eds.), *Coordination in human and primate groups* (pp. 11–36). Heidelberg, Germany: Springer.

Bowen, J.L. (2006). Educational strategies to promote diagnostic reasoning. *New England Journal of Medicine, 355*, 2217–2225.

Bowers, C.A., Jentsch, F., Salas, E., & Braun, C. (1998). Analyzing communication sequences for team training needs assessment. *Human Factors, 40*, 672–679.

Burke, C.S., Salas, E., Wilson-Donnelly, K., & Priest, H. (2004). How to turn a team of experts into an expert medical team: Guidance from the aviation and military communities. *Quality and Safety in Health Care, 13*(Suppl 1), i96–i104.

Burke, C.S., Stagl, K.C., & Salas, E. (2006). Understanding team adaptation: A conceptual analysis and model. *Journal of Applied Psychology, 91*, 1189–1207.

Burtscher, M.J., Kolbe, M., Wacker, J., & Manser, T. (2011). Interactions of team mental models and monitoring behaviors predict team performance in simulated anesthesia inductions. *Journal of Experimental Psychology: Applied, 17*, 257–269.

Cannon-Bowers, J.A., Tannenbaum, S., Salas, E., & Volpe, C.E. (1995). Defining competencies and establishing team training requirements. In A. Guzzo & E. Salas (Eds.), *Team effectiveness and decision making in organizations* (pp. 333–380). San Francisco: Jossey-Bass.

de Vries, E.N., Prins, H.A., Crolla, R.M.P. H., den Outer, A.J., van Andel, G., van Helden, S.H., Schlack, W.S., van Putten, M.A.S., Gouma, D.J., et al. (2010). Effect of a comprehensive surgical safety system on patient outcomes. *New England Journal of Medicine, 363*, 1928–1937.

Detert, J.R., & Edmondson, A. (2011). Implicit voice theories: Taken-for-granted rules of self-censorship at work. *Academy of Management Journal, 54*, 461–488.

Dwyer, J. (1994). Primum non tacere. An ethics of speaking up. *Hastings Center Report, 24*(1), 13–18.

Edmondson, A. (1999). Psychological safety and learning behavior in work teams. *Administrative Science Quarterly, 44*, 350–383.

Edmondson, A.C. (2003). Speaking up in the operating room: How team leaders promote learning in interdisciplinary action teams. *Journal of Management Studies, 40*, 1419–1452.

Einav, Y., Gopher, D., Kara, I., Ben-Yosef, O., Lawn, M., Laufer, N., & Donchin, Y. (2010). Preoperative briefing in the operating room: Shared cognition, teamwork, and patient safety. *Chest, 137*, 443–449.

Elstein, A.S., & Schwartz, A. (2002). Clinical problem solving and diagnostic decision making: Selective review of the cognitive literature. *British Medical Journal, 324*, 729–732.

Endsley, M.R. (1995). Toward a theory of situation awareness in dynamic systems. *Human Factors, 37*, 32–64.

Endsley, M.R. (2000). Direct measurement of situation awareness: Validity and use of SAGAT. In M.R. Endsley & D.J. Garland (Eds.), *Situation awareness analysis and measurement* (pp. 147–174). Mahwah, NJ: Lawrence Erlbaum Associates.

Entin, E.E., & Serfaty, D. (1999). Adaptive team coordination. *Human Factors, 41*, 312–325.

Eva, K.W. (2004). What every teacher needs to know about clinical reasoning. *Medical Education, 39*, 98–106.

Fletcher, G.C.L., McGeorge, P., Flin, R.H., Glavin, R.J., & Maran, N.J. (2002). The role of non-technical skills in anaesthesia: A review of current literature. *British Journal of Anaesthesia, 88*, 418–429.

Flin, R., Martin, L., Goeters, K.-M., Hörmann, H.-J., Amalberti, R., Valot, C., & Nijhuis, H. (2005). Development of the NOTECHS (non-technical skills) system for assessing pilots' CRM skills. In D. Harris & H.C. Muir (Eds.), *Contemporary issues in human factors and aviation safety* (pp. 133–154). Aldershot, UK: Ashgate.

Gaba, D.M., Howard, S.K., & Small, S.D. (1995). Situation awareness in anesthesiology. *Human Factors, 37*(1), 20–31.

Gawande, A.A., Studdert, D.M., Orav, E.J., Brennan, T.A., & Zinner, M.J. (2003). Risk factors for retained instruments and sponges after surgery. *New England Journal of Medicine, 348*, 229–235.

Ginnett, R.C. (1993). Crews as groups: Their formation and their leadership. In E.L. Wiener, B.G. Kanki, & R.L. Helmreich (Eds.), *Cockpit resource management* (pp. 71–98). San Diego: Academic Press.

Graber, M.L., Franklin, N., & Gordon, R. (2005). Diagnostic error in internal medicine. *Archives of Internal Medicine, 165*, 1493–1499.

Greitemeyer, T., & Schulz-Hardt, S. (2003). Preference-consistent evaluation of information in the hidden profile paradigm: Beyond group-level explanations for the dominance of shared information in group decisions. *Journal of Personality and Social Psychology, 84*, 322–339.

Grommes, P. (2000). Contributing to coherence: An empirical study on OR-team-communication. In Minnick-Fox, Williams, & Kaiser (Eds.), *Proceedings of the 24th Penn Linguistics Colloquium* (pp. 87–98).

Grote, G. (2012). Safety management in different high-risk domains—All the same? *Safety Science, 50*, 1983–1992.

Grote, G., Kolbe, M., Zala-Mezö, E., Bienefeld-Seall, N., & Künzle, B. (2010). Adaptive coordination and heedfulness make better cockpit crews. *Ergonomics, 52*, 211–228.

Hackman, J.R. (2002). *Leading teams: Setting the stage for great performances.* Boston: Harvard Business School Press.

Henriksen, K., & Dayton, E. (2006). Organizational silence and hidden threats to patient safety. *Health Services Research, 41*, 1539–1554.

Jentsch, F., & Smith-Jentsch, K.A. (2001). Assertiveness and team performance: More than "just say no." In E. Salas, C.A. Bowers, & E. Edens (Eds.), *Improving teamwork in organizations. Applications of resource management training* (pp. 73–94). Mahwah, NJ: Lawrence Erlbaum Associates.

Klein, K.J., Ziegert, J.C., Knight, A.P., & Xiao, Y. (2006). Dynamic delegation: Shared, hierarchical, and deindividualized leadership in extreme action teams. *Administrative Science Quarterly, 51*, 590–621.

Kobayashi, H., Pian-Smith, M., Sato, M., Sawa, R., Takeshita, T., & Raemer, D. (2006). A cross-cultural survey of residents' perceived barriers in questioning/challenging authority. *Quality and Safety in Health Care, 15*, 277–283.

Kolbe, M., Burtscher, M.J., & Manser, T. (in press). Co-ACT—A framework for observing coordination behaviour in acute care teams. *BMJ Quality & Safety.*

Kolbe, M., Burtscher, M.J., Manser, T., Künzle, B., & Grote, G. (2011). The role of coordination for preventing harm in healthcare groups: Research examples from anaesthesia and an integrated model of coordination for action teams in healthcare. In M. Boos, M. Kolbe, P. Kappeler, & T. Ellwart (Eds.), *Coordination in human and primate groups* (pp. 75–92). Heidelberg: Springer.

Kolbe, M., Burtscher, M.J., Wacker, J., Grande, B., Nohynkova, R., Manser, T., Spahn, D., & Grote, G. (2012). Speaking-up is related to better team performance in simulated anesthesia inductions: An observational study. *Anesthesia & Analgesia, 115,* 1099-1108.

Kolbe, M., Künzle, B., Zala-Mezö, E., Burtscher, M.J., Wacker, J., Spahn, D.R., & Grote, G. (2010). The functions of team monitoring and "talking to the room" for performance in anesthesia teams. *Proceedings of the Human Factors and Ergonomics Society 54th Annual Meeting* (pp. 857–861). Santa Monica, California.

Kolbe, M., Strack, M., Stein, A., & Boos, M. (2011). Observing coordination in human group decision-making: MICRO-CO—A micro-analytical taxonomy for analysis of coordination mechanism in decision-making groups. In M. Boos, M. Kolbe, P. Kappeler, & T. Ellwart (Eds.), *Coordination in human and primate groups* (pp. 199–222). Heidelberg, Germany: Springer.

Kolbe, M., Weiss, M., Grote, G., Knauth, A., Dambach, M., Spahn, D.R., & Grande, B. (in press). TeamGAINS: A tool for structured debriefings for simulation-based team trainings. *BMJ Quality & Safety.*

Kozlowski, S.W.J. (2010). High-risk, extreme teams: Common themes and links to the literature. Paper presented at the 25th Annual Meeting of the Society for Industrial & Organizational Psychology, Atlanta, Georgia.

Kozlowski, S.W.J., & Bell, B.S. (2003). Work groups and teams in organizations. In D.R. Borman, D.R. Ilgen, & R.J. Klimoski (Eds.), *Handbook of psychology: Industrial and organizational psychology* (Vol. 12, pp. 333–375). London: John Wiley & Sons.

Kozlowski, S.W.J., Watola, D.J., Jensen, J.M., Kim, B.H., & Botero, I.C. (2009). Developing adaptive teams: A theory of dynamic team leadership. In E. Salas, G.F. Goodwin, & C.S. Burke (Eds.), *Team effectiveness in complex organizations: Cross-disciplinary perspectives and approaches (SIOP Frontier Series)* (pp. 113–155). New York: Taylor and Francis.

Kriz, W.C. (2010). A systemic-constructivist approach to the facilitation and debriefing of simulations and games. *Simulation & Gaming, 41,* 663–680.

Künzle, B., Zala-Mezö, E., Kolbe, M., Wacker, J., & Grote, G. (2010). Substitutes for leadership in anaesthesia teams and their impact on leadership effectiveness. *European Journal of Work and Organizational Psychology, 19,* 505–531.

Larson, J.R., Christensen, C., Franz, T.M., & Abbott, A.S. (1998). Diagnosing groups: The pooling, management, and impact of shared and unshared case information in team-based medical decision making. *Journal of Personality and Social Psychology, 75,* 93–108.

Liang, J., Farh, C.I.C., & Farh, J.-L. (2012). Psychological antecedents of promotive and prohibitive voice: A two-wave examination. *The Academy of Management Journal, 55*(1), 71–92.

Marks, M.A., DeChurch, L.A., Mathieu, J.E., Panzer, F.J., & Alonso, A. (2005). Teamwork in multiteam systems. *Journal of Applied Psychology, 90,* 964–971.

Marks, M.A., Mathieu, J.E., & Zaccaro, S.J. (2001). A temporally based framework and taxonomy of team processes. *Academy of Management Review, 26,* 356–376.

Mesmer-Magnus, J.R., & DeChurch, L.A. (2009). Information sharing and team performance: A meta-analysis. *Journal of Applied Psychology, 94,* 535–546.

Minehart, R.D., Pian-Smith, M.C.M., Walzer, T.B., Gardner, R., Rudolph, J.W., Simon, R., & Raemer, D.B. (2012). Speaking across the drapes: Communication strategies of anesthesiologists and obstetricians during a simulated maternal crisis. *Simulation in Healthcare, 7,* 166–170.

Morrison, E.W. (2011). Employee voice behavior: Integration and directions for future research. *The Academy of Management Annals, 5*(1), 373–412.

Morrison, E.W., Wheeler-Smith, S., & Kamdar, D. (2011). Speaking up in groups: A cross-level study of group voice climate and voice. *Journal of Applied Psychology, 96*(1), 183–191.

Nembhard, I.M., & Edmondson, A.C. (2006). Making it safe: The effects of leader inclusiveness and professional status on psychological safety and improvement efforts in health care teams. *Journal of Organizational Behavior, 27,* 941–966.

Nestel, D., Walker, K., Simon, R., Aggarwal, R., & Andreatta, P. (2011). Nontechnical skills: An inaccurate and unhelpful descriptor? *Simulation in Healthcare, 6*(1), 2–3.

Nijstad, B.A., & Kaps, S. (2008). Taking the easy way out: Preference diversity, decision strategies, and decision refusal in groups. *Journal of Personality and Social Psychology, 94,* 860–870.

Pian-Smith, M.C.M., Simon, R., Minehart, R.D., Podraza, M., Rudolph, J., Walzer, T., & Raemer, D. (2009). Teaching residents the two-challenge rule: A simulation-based approach to improve education and patient safety. *Simulation in Healthcare, 4,* 84–91.

Raemer, D.B. (2010). The clinician's response to challenging cases. In E. Yano, I. Kawachi, & M. Nakao (Eds.), *The healthy hospital: Maximizing the satisfaction of patients, health workers, and community* (pp. 27–32). Tokyo: Shinohara Shinsha.

Rall, M., & Gaba, D. (2005). Patient simulators. In R.D. Miller (Ed.), *Anesthesia* (Vol. 6, pp. 3073–3103). Philadelphia: Elsevier Churchill Livingstone.

Rall, M., Glavin, R., & Flin, R. (2008, September). The "10-seconds-for-10-minutes principle"—Why things go wrong and stopping them getting worse. *Bulletin of The Royal College of Anaesthetists,* (51), 2614–2616.

Reader, T.W., Flin, R., & Cuthbertson, B.H. (2011). Team leadership in the intensive care unit: The perspective of specialists. *Critical Care Medicine, 39,* 1683–1691.

Reader, T., Flin, R., Lauche, K., & Cuthbertson, B.H. (2006). Non-technical skills in the intensive care unit. *British Journal of Anaesthesia, 96,* 551–559.

Reader, T.W., Flin, R., Mearns, K., & Cuthbertson, B.H. (2011). Team situation awareness and the anticipation of patient progress during ICU rounds. *BMJ Quality & Safety,* 1035–1042.

Reynard, J., Reynolds, J., & Stevenson, P. (2009). *Practical patient safety.* Oxford, UK: Oxford University Press.

Rico, R., Sánchez-Manzanares, M., Gil, F., & Gibson, C. (2008). Team implicit coordination processes: A team knowledge-based approach. *Academy of Management Review, 33*(1), 163–184.

Riethmüller, M., Fernandez Castelao, E., Eberhardt, D., Timmermann, A., & Boos, M. (2012). Adaptive coordination development in student anaesthesia teams: A longitudinal study. *Ergonomics, 55*(1), 55–68.

Ross, L., Green, D., & House, P. (1977). The "false consensus effect": An egocentric bias in social perception and attribution processes. *Journal of Experimental Social Psychology, 13,* 279–301.

Rudolph, J.W., Morrison, J.B., & Carroll, J.S. (2009). The dynamics of action-oriented problem solving: Linking interpretation and choice. *Academy of Management Journal, 34,* 733–756.

Rudolph, J.W., Simon, R., Rivard, P., Dufresne, R.L., & Raemer, D.B. (2007). Debriefing with good judgement: Combining rigorous feedback with genuine inquiry. *Anesthesiology Clinics, 25,* 361–376.

Salas, E., Prince, C., Baker, D.P., & Shrestha, L. (1995). Situation awareness in team performance: Implications for measurement and training. *Human Factors, 37*(1), 123–136.

Salas, E., Rosen, M.A., Burke, C.S., Nicholson, D., & Howse, W.R. (2007). Markers for enhancing team cognition in complex environments: The power of team performance diagnosis. *Aviation Space and Environmental Medicine, 78,* B77–B85.

Salas, E., Sims, D.E., & Burke, C.S. (2005). Is there a "big five" in teamwork? *Small Group Research, 36,* 555–599.

Smith-Jentsch, K.A., Salas, E., & Baker, D.P. (1996). Training teams performance-related assertiveness. *Personnel Psychology, 49,* 909–936.

Stasser, G., & Titus, W. (1985). Pooling of unshared information in group decision making: Biased information sampling during discussion. *Journal of Personality and Social Psychology, 48,* 1467–1578.

Sundstrom, E., de Meuse, K.P., & Futrell, D. (1990). Work teams. Applications and effectiveness. *American Psychologist, 45,* 120–133.

Tannenbaum, S. (2010). Measuring and building shared cognitions and teamwork in applied settings. Paper presented at the 25th Annual SIOP Conference, Atlanta, Georgia.

Tschan, F., Semmer, N.K., Gautschi, D., Hunziker, P., Spychiger, M., & Marsch, S.U. (2006). Leading to recovery: Group performance and coordinative activities in medical emergency driven groups. *Human Performance, 19,* 277–304.

Tschan, F., Semmer, N.K., Gurtner, A., Bizzari, L., Spychiger, M., Breuer, M., & Marsch, S.U. (2009). Explicit reasoning, confirmation bias, and illusory transactive memory. A simulation study of group medical decision making. *Small Group Research, 40,* 271–300.

Tschan, F., Semmer, N.K., Hunziker, P.R., & Marsch, S.C.U. (2011). Decisive action vs. joint deliberation: Different medical tasks imply different coordination requirements. In V.G. Duffy (Ed.), *Advances in human factors and ergonomics in healthcare* (pp. 191–200). Boca Raton, FL: Taylor & Francis.

Waller, M.J. (1999). The timing of adaptive group responses to nonroutine events. *Academy of Management Journal, 42,* 127–137.

Waller, M.J., & Uitdewilligen, S. (2008). Talking to the room. Collective sensemaking during crisis situations. In R.A. Roe, M.J. Waller, & S.R. Clegg (Eds.), *Time in organizational research* (pp. 186–203). Oxford, UK: Routledge.

Weick, K.E., & Roberts, K.H. (1993). Collective mind in organizations: Heedful interrelating on flight decks. *Administrative Science Quarterly, 38,* 357–381.

Wilson, K.A., Burke, C.S., Priest, H.A., & Salas, E. (2005). Promoting health care safety though training high reliability teams. *Quality and Safety in Health Care, 14,* 303–309.

Wittenbaum, G.M., Vaughan, S.I., & Stasser, G. (1998). Coordination in task-performing groups. In R.S. Tindale, L. Heath, J. Edwards, E.J. Posavac, F.B. Bryant, Y. Suarez-Balcazar, E. Henderson-King, & J. Myers (Eds.), *Theory and research on small groups* (pp. 177–204). New York: Plenum Press.

World Alliance for Patient Safety. (2008). *World Health Organizations surgical safety checklist* (1st ed.). Geneva, Switzerland: World Health Organizations.

Wright, M.C., Taekman, J.M., & Endsley, M.R. (2004). Objective measures of situation awareness in a simulated medical environment. *Quality and Safety in Health Care, 13*(suppl 1), i65–i71.

Part Six

Summary

CHAPTER TWENTY

Enhancing the Practice of Teamwork in Organizations

Emerging Themes

Stephanie Zajac and Eduardo Salas
University of Central Florida

Teams have become a ubiquitous presence in organizations of all sizes. They are used not only to tackle tasks too large or complex for individuals, but also to overcome spatial boundaries and bring experts together. Effective teamwork has been cited as the reason behind positive organizational outcomes such as improved efficiency and innovation. While the benefits have been well-defined, there are also many challenges inherent to working in teams. Simply bringing together talented individuals does not guarantee success. Attention must be given to both the individual as well as organizational characteristics that exert an influence on the team processes.

The purpose of the current volume is to elucidate emerging themes arising from the changing nature of teamwork and to outline the compositional and contextual components that drive effective team performance. To fully realize the potential advantages of teamwork, we must first understand the fundamental elements behind effective team performance. The experts who have contributed to the current effort make it apparent that we have learned many lessons about what contributes to and detracts from successful teamwork. Valuable advice and practical guidelines have been provided regarding forming and managing a team, team processes and performance, and training. Below we delineate the major themes that emerged and how they contribute to our understanding of teamwork:

1. Clearly, teamwork does matter!
2. Break down barriers to intra- and inter-team coordination.
3. Consider composition variables when forming and managing teams.
4. Organizational conditions drive team performance.
5. The nature of teamwork is changing to include virtual distributed teams.
6. Team training must be scientifically grounded and systematically designed, delivered, implemented, and evaluated.
7. Teams are adaptable social entities.
8. Leadership matters!
9. Engage team members with a shared vision, clear mission, and compelling purpose.
10. There's still a lot to learn about teamwork.

1. Clearly, Teamwork Does Matter in Organizations!

Organizations can take several avenues to gain a competitive advantage, but people are the key to sustainable organizational performance. The evolving nature of work has given rise to complex, knowledge-based environments in which people (and their experience and skills) are the most crucial resource. In addition, technological advancements and a global marketplace have generated dynamic tasks that often necessitate the use of teams. While the right mix of skills and expertise is important, it is teamwork skills (for example, leadership, situation awareness) that present both the greatest challenge and the most potential for success. The good news is that these teamwork skills are *trainable* (Almeida, King, & Salisbury, Chapter 10).

As can be observed from the previous chapters, teamwork has been cited as the impetus behind essential performance outcomes across a variety of organizational domains, including increased patient safety in health care, lower error rates in aviation, and increased innovation in product development teams (Lyubovnikova & West, Chapter 11). While the benefits of teamwork have been clearly delineated in the literature, so have the disastrous and costly consequences of ineffective teamwork. Deficient teamwork has been cited as a potential reason for friendly fire in the military, unsuccessful disaster relief systems, and loss of patient life (Gregory, Feitosa, Driskell, Salas, & Vessey, Chapter 14). Organizations have recognized the salience of teamwork and have responded with team training initiatives that target vital team processes (for example, team strategies and tools to enhance performance and patient safety). The continuous outpour of attention that teamwork has received in both the academic and professional arenas indicates that, indeed, teamwork does matter!

2. Break Down Barriers to Intra- and Inter-Team Coordination

A recent meta-analytic review of frameworks targeting teamwork behaviors found that coordination was unequivocally critical to effective performance, and that task complexity and interdependency strengthen this relationship (Rousseau, Aube, & Savoie, 2006). Indeed, barriers to coordination are often cited as significant impediments faced by teams. Common obstacles include differing functional departments, disparate interpersonal and cultural orientations, and unclear strategies (Beer, Chapter 1). Curtis (Chapter 2) also purports that coordination breaks down when team processes are unclear or lack structure. Perhaps the most salient of these team processes is communication, which enables the behavioral components necessary to coordinate interdependent actions and work toward shared goals.

In order to facilitate coordination, organizational structures should be characterized by open, clear lines of communication (Beer, Chapter 1). Furthermore, communication should cross organizational boundaries that exist due to hierarchies, differences in expertise, and temporal and spatial distance. The key to obtaining open and honest communication lies in establishing trust among all team members (Meisinger, Chapter 6). This can be difficult to accomplish, especially when it requires members to openly express their divergent opinions to superiors, to show weakness, or to ask for help when necessary. Team interventions are commonly comprised of strategies aimed at communication, including speaking up to address observations or concerns and the use of closed-loop communication to ensure information was not only heard but understood (Kolbe, Chapter 19).

However, contextual restraints (such as time limitations) often limit the amount of explicit behaviors that a team can actively engage in and leave the team to rely on implicit coordination enabled by a shared understanding of the task, environment, and member roles and responsibilities. These shared mental models allow team members to anticipate each other's actions and needs and to provide assistance without having to be asked (Entin & Serfaty, 1999). In fact, it is often the correct combination of both explicit and implicit processes used to manage member actions and information that enables effective coordination (Kolbe, Chapter 19).

3. Composition Variables Influence the Management of Teams

Diversity in both surface- and deep-level composition variables can positively impact team performance, but only if it is managed appropriately. Individual differences in expertise and background provide for a greater range of perspectives, knowledge, skills, and abilities. This, in turn, can lead to the improved generation and evaluation of alternative solutions as well as innovation (Cannella, Park, & Lee, 2008). However, diversity can also give rise to emotional and interpersonal conflict, mistrust, and decreased morale (Pelled, Eisenhardt, & Xin, 1999; Gevers & Rutte, Chapter 18). As mentioned earlier by Antino, Rico, Sánchez-Manzanares and Lau (Chapter 12), diversity can instigate arguments over task priorities and division of resources, which ultimately hurts team performance. Fortunately, employees can be allocated to maximize team performance, and diversity can be managed so that its benefits are realized.

Managing the differences of individual team members is especially relevant within the context of knowledge intense work

(Curtis, Chapter 2). In fact, the right blend of knowledge, skill, and ability has been shown to influence both team-level effort and coordination across a range of teams (Mathieu, Tannenbaum, Donsbach, & Alliger, Chapter 16). In the current volume, Mathieu and colleagues put forth a detailed plan for forming teams, which includes: (1) describing the team (that is, critical positions, interdependence); (2) clarifying requirements at all organizational levels; (3) establishing a candidate pool of those who are eligible, available, and willing; and finally, (4) assessing the candidates based on their individual and team competencies. In addition, Antino and colleagues (Chapter 12) propose strategies that can be used to manage teams once their members are in place. Structural-level strategies (for example, managing task autonomy, creating superordinate goals) and relational-level strategies (such as managing motivation and emphasizing the importance of adopting new values and attitudes) can be put in place to manage both taskwork and teamwork processes.

4. Organizational Conditions Drive Team Performance

Organizational policies and procedures that are put in place without consideration of their effect on team functioning may actually end up being detrimental to performance. As can be noted from the previous chapters, this is especially true when policies are inconsistent, unclear, or unsupported by management (Curtis, Chapter 2; Rassouli, Chapter 3). In fact, numerous elements may influence a team's performance other than those related to team characteristics. For instance, without the adequate resources necessary (tools and knowledge) to fulfill task needs, a team will underperform, regardless of how well they function during task execution. Alternatively, if goals are unrealistic or unobtainable, teams will fall short, even if they are given the resources to perform well.

Therefore, it is imperative that evaluations of team performance consider contextual variables that are outside the control of the team in addition to team-level characteristics when measuring performance. As previously stated in the chapter by Smith-Jentsch and colleagues (Chapter 17), measures of performance outcomes are most useful when exploring elements external to the team. However, reliance on outcome measures alone for reward distribution and feedback interventions may be viewed as unfair, and subsequently cause team motivation to suffer. Therefore, organizations should strive to measure both team performance *and* outcomes in order to identify and parse out these external factors.

5. The Nature of Teamwork Is Changing to Include Virtual Distributed Teams and Teams of Teams

A global marketplace, coupled with technological advancements, has driven the increased emergence of teams formed across temporal and spatial boundaries. Globalization also escalates the demand for prompt delivery of products and services, and therefore requires that time be managed appropriately. In fact, it has been proposed that temporal boundaries are responsible for a significant amount of the coordination challenges that arise when managing interdependent tasks in distributed teams. Espinosa (Chapter 13) indicates that not only does temporal distance reduce the types of coordination methods available, but it makes those that are still possible harder to employ. For example, distributed members can use conference calls to explicitly communicate, but they may struggle to find a time that works across different time zones. The author proposes the disadvantages faced by these distributed teams can be mitigated in part by organizing meetings before a project begins to allow team members to become familiar with each other and to spend additional time planning and organizing. Other techniques that have proven effective are allowing distributed members to visit each other's sites and arranging schedules so there is a small amount of overlap in work hours.

Perhaps more salient than task-related constraints, virtual teams face teamwork challenges unique to distributed environments. In order to attain the benefits of diversity, teams must learn to adapt strategies accordingly. The promotion of intra-team trust and conflict resolution is paramount to achieving success in virtual teams. However, these teams lack the face-to-face interactions that foster trust and positive interpersonal relationships. This lack of collaboration and social information regarding other team members hinders the development of critical teamwork skills (Cohen & Alonso, Chapter 8; Wilson, Chapter 9). Fortunately, strategies can be put in place to cultivate a sense of team identity and familiarity. In forming teams, it is advantageous to select members who possess the individual characteristic "openness to experience" or who have had previous experience in distributed teams. If possible, choose those who have had previous experience working together. Organizational support can be provided by delivering the proper training, facilitating frequent communication, and monitoring the team to track goal attainment (Wilson, Chapter 9).

6. Team Training Works, But Must Be Scientifically Grounded and Systematically Designed, Delivered, Implemented, and Evaluated

Team training *works*. Science had provided us with the evidence to support this claim; the relationship between training and performance holds across a variety of domains including military operations, aviation, business, and health care (Driskell, Lazzara, Salas, King, & Battles, 2012). In a recent meta-analysis conducted by Salas and colleagues (2008), team training was shown to have a significant, positive relationship across a variety of contexts with critical cognitive, affective, process, and performance outcomes. However, it's not that simple. Training effectiveness is contingent upon the way the program is designed, delivered, and implemented (Salas, Tannenbaum, Kraiger, & Smith-Jentsch, 2012). Furthermore, training is not accomplished through a single event. It represents a complex initiative with organizational variables that need to be addressed before, during, and after the actual training takes place. As pointed out by Almeida and colleagues (Chapter 10), scientifically designed training curricula alone are unlikely to lead to sustained learning and use of learned behaviors on the job.

Organizations spend billions of dollars each year to train their employees, and there are several ways to maximize the benefits gained from these training investments. Gregory and colleagues

(Chapter 14) assert that one of the first steps to successfully implementing a training program is to create a climate for learning. This means buy-in must be obtained from all levels of the organizational hierarchy, with management expressing both commitment to the training initiative as well as the individual and organizational value of training. A needs analysis should be conducted to determine *what* and *who* to train and to ensure that training objectives are linked to the organizational requirements and goals.

Another key component of training programs is the development of valid performance measurement criteria used to evaluate the program's effectiveness (Smith-Jentsch, Sierra, & Wiese, Chapter 17). Typically, evaluation is aimed at measuring whether training objectives (that is, cognitive, skill-based, and affective learning outcomes) were achieved and whether learning affected on-the-job performance (Kraiger, Ford, & Salas, 1993). Evaluation not only helps in identifying the value of training to the organization, but can also be used to identify the best training strategies and inform future iterations of the training program.

One training intervention that is easy to implement, yet represents a highly effective way to ensure continued learning, is the team debriefing. Debriefings can be designed to target a diverse set of taskwork and teamwork competencies. During a debriefing, teams reflect on previous performance episodes through techniques such as instructor feedback and self-explanation. In fact, a recent meta-analysis suggests that debriefings can increase team performance by approximately 20 to 25 percent when properly executed (Tannenbaum & Cerasoli, 2013). Team coordination and adaptation training is another valuable training intervention that has received a great deal of support in the literature. In fact, according to Driskell and colleagues (2012), it is the optimal training intervention for teams. During adaptation and coordination training, team members learn how to alter their coordination strategies and reduce the need for explicit communication during performance.

7. Teams Are Adaptable Social Entities

Teams are capable of adopting new procedures, but it's not something that can be accomplished overnight. Change initiatives that rely on a quick solution or easy fix often fail. In actuality, change requires a long-term approach, systematically developed and implemented in successive stages. Adjusting existing team norms is a challenge and must address not only task-relevant issues but longstanding beliefs and attitudes as well (Beatty & Smith, Chapter 5). Curtis (Chapter 2) asserts that a change initiative should be implemented through a system of "continual process improvement." Clear, achievable goals must be in place, and each goal should represent an organizational plateau to overcome before the team can move forward.

Both management and staff must work together closely to bring about organizational change. Rassouli (Chapter 3) outlines a plan for change management in which the first step is to clearly define the existing problem and its underlying causes through such means as reviewing the organization's history and conducting interviews with staff members. A solution that embodies the vision and organizational goals should be agreed on by all stakeholders. Finally, leadership should focus on measuring the effectiveness of initiatives and be ready to adjust strategies accordingly.

8. Leadership Matters!

Multifaceted leadership functions are outgrowing the capabilities of any one individual and necessitating the use of leadership teams. Members of a leadership team are often responsible for representing a smaller subset of stakeholders while maintaining interdependence for the collective organizational goal (Wageman, Chapter 4). Leadership teams enable a diverse range of perspectives from which to draw and the ability to leverage multiple resources when implementing policies and procedures (Beatty & Smith, Chapter 5). In addition, various members may assume leadership responsibility as the task changes or requires a different set of knowledge, skills, and abilities (Pearce, Manz, Sims, 2009).

A clear vision and purpose are essential when creating leadership teams, especially if the team is comprised of intra-organizational members. Organizational values must be shared among the team, and member interdependencies and mutual goals should be highlighted to encourage collaboration. As stated earlier by Wageman (Chapter 4), a challenging yet attainable team purpose should be in place to drive motivation. Members should be chosen for their ability to analyze complex information, with special attention paid to availability and willingness to contribute as well the functional expertise required to achieve goals. In addition, choosing members who possess empathy and integrity contributes to leadership teams by enabling constructive communication and facilitating decision making.

A variety of leadership approaches can be used to successfully guide a team, but it's essential that leadership style be appropriate for both contextual features and internal team characteristics. A leader must consider factors such as the team's goals, cultural norms, and available resources to create a structure that leverages both leader and team strengths (Clark, Chapter 7). While certain personality characteristics have been associated with effective leadership (such as extraversion), training can also be used to promote effective leadership behaviors. Organizations can provide support through leader development programs and adequate resource allocation (Beer, Chapter 1).

9. Engage Team Members with a Shared Vision, Clear Mission, and Compelling Purpose

Engaged employees display higher levels of job satisfaction, organizational commitment, and organizational citizenship behaviors (Saks, 2006). Creating a positive climate for employees includes establishing a clear mission as well as clear and challenging goals to pursue (Rassouli, Chapter 3). Providing mission and goal clarity also helps when coordinating internal organizational behavior and agreeing on decisions about organizational priorities (Meisinger, Chapter 6). In addition, employees who are given the opportunity to develop new knowledge and skills will display higher levels of job satisfaction and drive higher organizational performance.

An inexpensive and easily executable method of engaging employees is to establish an employee recognition program. Employees can be reinforced for achieving goals and motivated to perform well in the future. Furthermore, over time, social recognition has been shown to be equally as effective as financial rewards (Peterson & Luthans, 2006). Acknowledgements that are personal and demonstrate gratitude and respect achieve the greatest effect. Finally, make sure that policies and procedures are transparent throughout organizational levels. Involve employees in policy decisions that will affect their work or compensation. Giving employees a voice can mitigate negative reactions by producing a climate for justice and reducing feelings of unfairness (Wilkinson & Fay, 2011). Further, participative organizational structures have been linked to such positive organizational outcomes as job satisfaction and organizational commitment.

10. There's Still a Lot to Learn About Teamwork

Valuable contributions from those who study and practice teamwork have undoubtedly advanced the state of the science. However, we are far from knowing everything there is to know about teamwork. New windows of opportunity open every time a development is made. For example, it has been effectively demonstrated that team debriefings work and that they work best when facilitators are trained and the event is structured. However, the authors in this volume have made it clear that many questions still remain unanswered. What tools and techniques can enhance debrief outcomes? Can a team member debrief with one team and carry the benefits on to future teams? (Tannenbaum, Beard, & Cerasoli, Chapter 15).

Researchers have begun to identify the factors that impact performance in distributed teams, as well as strategies and training interventions that help teams overcome the boundaries imposed by spatial separation. However, future research must focus on how teamwork in distributed teams evolves and matures over time. Furthermore, teams of teams, or multi-team systems (MTSs), are often distributed in nature and represent both an emerging organizational trend and an avenue ripe for research. MTSs are being increasingly utilized to address dynamic, multifaceted tasks that exceed the ability of any one team. While some of the team literature may be applicable to these larger systems, the interaction of component teams with the overall system adds another level of complexity to MTS process and performance that requires further investigation.

Yet another underexplored area poised for future research initiatives is that of training sustainability. Researchers and organizations alike devote enormous amounts of time and money to developing effective training programs. However, less attention has been paid to the transfer of learned skills to the work environment and the long-term sustainability of learning gains obtained during training. As previously stated, training is not a one-time event. If organizations wish to realize the full range of benefits from training, they must have organizational policies and procedures in place to support the use of new skills after training takes place. As we seek to maximize team performance potential, it is important to remember that there is still much to learn.

References

Cannella, A.A., Park, J., & Lee, H. (2008). Top management team functional background diversity and firm performance: Examining the roles of team member co-location and environmental uncertainty. *Academy of Management Journal, 51,* 768–784.

Driskell, T., Lazzara, E.H., Salas, E., King, H.B., & Battles, J. (2012). Does team training work? Where is the evidence? In E. Salas & K. Frush (Eds.), *Improving patient safety through teamwork and team training* (pp. 201–217). New York: Oxford.

Entin, E.E., & Serfaty, D. (1999). Adaptive team coordination. *Human Factors, 41,* 312–325.

Kraiger, K., Ford, J.K., & Salas, E. (1993). Application of cognitive, skill-based, and affective theories of learning outcomes to new methods of training evaluation. *Journal of Applied Psychology, 78,* 311–328.

Pearce, C.L., Manz, C.C., & Sims, H.P., Jr. (2009). Where do we go from here? Is shared leadership the key to team success? *Organizational Dynamics, 38*(3), 234–238.

Pelled, L.H., Eisenhardt, K.M., & Xin, K.R. (1999). Exploring the black box: An analysis of work group diversity, conflict, and performance. *Administrative Science Quarterly,* pp. 1–28.

Peterson, S.J., & Luthans, F. (2006). The impact of financial and nonfinancial incentives on business-unit outcomes over time. *Journal of Applied Psychology, 91*(1), 156–165.

Rousseau, V., Aube, C., & Savoie, A. (2006). Teamwork behaviors: A review and an integration of frameworks. *Small Group Research, 37*(5), 540–570.

Saks, A.M. (2006). Antecedents and consequences of employee engagement. *Journal of Managerial Psychology, 21,* 600–619.

Salas, E., DiazGranados, D., Klein, C., Burke, C.S., Stagl, K.C., Goodwin, G.F., & Halpin, S.M. (2008). Does training improve team performance? A meta-analysis. *Human Factors, 50*(6), 903–933.

Salas, E., Tannenbaum, S.I., Kraiger, K., & Smith-Jentsch, K.A. (2012). The science of training and development in organizations: What matters in practice. *Psychological Science in the Public Interest, 13*(2), 74–101.

Tannenbaum, S.I., & Cerasoli, C.P. (2013). Do team and individual debriefs enhance performance? A meta-analysis. *Human Factors: The Journal of Human Factors and Ergonomic Society, 55,* 231–245.

Wilkinson, A., & Fay, C. (2011). New times for employee voice? *Human Resource Management, 50*(1), 65–74.

Name Index

A

Abbott, A. S., 627
Abts, C., 49
AbuAlRub, R. F., 345
Acton, B., 466
Adair, F., 187
Adler, L., 200
Admasachew, L., 341
Aggarwal, R., 611
Aguinis, H., 560, 569, 576
Ahuja, M., 273
Akdere, M., 553
Alge, B. J., 272, 277
Alimo-Metcalfe, B., 347, 350
Allen, D., 219
Allen, J. A., 497
Allen, W. C., 452
Alliger, G. M., 489, 520, 530, 651
Allport, F. H., 446
Allport, G. W., 390
Almeida, P. A., 308
Almeida, S. A., 298, 308, 648, 653
Alonso, A., 239, 301, 302, 407, 413, 563, 633, 653
Alper, S., 574
Alvarez, K., 471
Amalberti, R., 618
Amason, A. C., 585
Ames, C., 505
Amir, Z., 339, 355
Amodeo, A. M., 350, 351
Anantharaman, R. N., 339
Ancona, D., 121, 126, 127, 144, 584, 593
Andersen, P. O., 349
Anderson, J. F., 272, 277
Anderson, N. R., 343, 471, 472, 560, 570
Andreatta, P. B., 357, 611
Andrews, S., 497
Anelay, S., 342
Angell, L., 588
Antino, M., 373, 381, 387, 389, 390, 650, 651
Argyris, C., 30, 39
Armenakis, A. A., 529
Armour, F., 413
Armstrong, C., 348
Armstrong, D. J., 408
Arriaga, A. F., 620
Arrivabene, S., 222, 223–225, 233–234
Arrow, H., 527, 589, 611
Arthur, W. R., 449, 460
Artman, H., 622
Ashforth, B., 271
Atwater, L., 285
AubeC., 649
Augenstein, J. S., 312, 451
Avolio, B. J., 276, 284, 285
Avrahami, M., 71

B

Ba, S., 408
Bader, A. M., 620
Bader, P., 268
Bagian, J. P., 300
Bailey, D. E., 268, 336, 408
Bailey, J., 49
Baker, D. P., 250, 301, 302, 304, 308, 331, 350, 351, 353, 355, 357, 449, 450, 459, 467, 512, 529, 563, 618, 619, 631

Bal, V., 248
Baldwin, T. T., 299, 308, 311, 314, 319, 447, 450, 473, 474
Ballard, D. I., 497
Baltes, B. B., 561
Balzer, W. K., 503
Bandow, D., 458
Bandura, A., 461, 504
Barach, P., 250, 301, 304, 459
Baran, B. E., 497
Barbaccia, J. C., 331, 342
Barczak, G., 408
Barker, J. R., 574
Barksdale, J., 309
Barley, S., 424
Barmeyer, C. I., 502
Barnes-Farrell, J. L., 530
Barrick, M. R., 530, 587
Bartel, C. A., 583, 585, 590, 591, 592, 600
Bass, B. M., 210, 211
Batalden, P. B., 343
Bate, P., 299, 311
Battles, J., 301, 302, 459, 653
Bauer, C. C., 561
Baum, K. D., 460
Bazarova, N. N., 278
Beard, R. L., 449, 488, 657
Beatty, K. C., 154, 160, 655
Beaubien, J. M., 250, 301, 304, 451, 467, 512, 586
Becker, T. E., 92
Bedwell, W. B., 443, 453, 458, 553
Beele, P., 581
Beer, M., 27, 28, 29, 30, 31, 33, 34, 35, 36, 38, 39, 40, 44, 162, 649
Beersma, B., 334, 335
Behson, S. J., 510
Belau, L., 530
Bell, B. S., 473, 522, 527, 532, 610
Bell, S. T., 449, 450, 460, 523, 530, 532
Ben-Hur, S., 185
Ben-Yosef, O., 619
Benbunab-Fich, R., 279, 284
Bendersky, C., 458
Bennett, W. R., 449, 460
Bennis, W., 121, 218
Beranek, P. M., 282
Berdahl, J. L., 611
Berg, D. N., 126, 127, 129, 137, 144
Berger, D. L., 300
Berns, S. D., 300, 341, 351
Beroggi, G.E.G., 122
Berry, W. R., 620
Berwick, D. M., 335
Besharov, M. L., 131
Bettencourt, B., 388
Bezrukova, K., 379, 400
Bienefeld, N., 630, 633
Bienefeld-Seall, N., 611, 629, 631
Billig, C., 378
Birkmeyer, J. D., 620
Birnbach, D. J., 312, 451
Bishop, M., 333
Bizzari, L., 609
Blackburn, R., 282
Blair, V., 458
Blickensderfer, E., 449, 459, 465
Bliese, P. D., 585
Blount, S., 582
Bluedorn, A. C., 587
Blume, B. D., 308, 311, 314, 447, 473
Bobko, P., 504, 507
Bodenheimer, T., 354
Boehm, B. W., 49, 57
Boehm-Davis, D., 49, 451
Bogenstätter, Y., 612
Boh, W. F., 413
Bohmer, R.M.J., 335, 489
Bojke, C., 337
Bolam, F., 343
Bonacum, D., 351
Bond, J., 343
Bonevento, M., 272
Bonito, J., Jr., 272
Bono, J., 284
Boorman, D. J., 620
Boos, M., 611, 612, 626
Bordia, P., 271, 277
Borgatti, S. P., 424
Borilla, C. S., 131, 343, 347

Borman, W. C., 555, 570, 575
Borrill, C., 337, 338, 339, 341, 342, 350, 355
Bos, N., 277, 285
Bostrom, R. P., 268
Botero, I. C., 611
Bowen, J. L., 628
Bowers, C. A., 447, 448, 449, 459, 465, 529, 633
Bowers, J. B., 156
Boyatzis, R. E., 201
Boyd, J. N., 587
Boyett, L., 338
Braithwaite, J., 354
Brandl, J., 269, 272
Brannick, M. T., 447, 467, 471, 559
Braun, C., 633
Brennan, T. A., 620
Brett, J. F., 530
Breuer, M., 609, 612
Brewer, M., 271, 378, 381, 388, 390
Briggs, A. L., 530
Brinkerhoff, R. O., 299
Broad, M. L., 308
Brodbeck, F., 132
Brooks, A. N., 503
Brooks, F., 419
Brousseau, K. R., 592
Brown, A. W., 49
Brown, K. G., 475
Brown, R., 389
Brown, R. J., 271
Buffalo, E. A., 511
Buhl, S. L., 581
Buljac-Samardzic, M., 351, 352
Bundy, M. R., 378
Bunz, U., 284, 285
Burchill, C. N., 300
Burgess, K. A., 472
Burgoon, J., 272, 277
Burke, C. S., 74, 77, 250, 251, 252, 254, 255, 355, 443, 445, 448, 453, 458, 459, 460, 461, 465, 472, 533, 609, 611, 618, 626, 632, 633, 634
Burke, K., 277
Burke, L. A., 299, 308, 319, 473
Burns, C., 341
Burruss, J. A., 121, 126, 130, 133, 139, 189
Burtscher, M. J., 609, 611, 612, 613, 618, 619, 623, 627, 629, 634
Bushe, G. R., 356
Buttigieg, S. C., 337, 338
Buzachero, V. V., 13

C

Cacioppo, J., 381
Cameron, K. S., 162
Campbell, D. J., 410, 415, 429
Campbell, G. E., 441, 474, 556
Campbell, M., 161
Campbell, R. J., 585
Campbell, S. M., 341
Campion, M. A., 353, 355, 523, 529
Cannella, A. A., 650
Cannon-Bowers, J. A., 210, 212, 250, 255, 285, 302, 308, 335, 356, 410, 412, 442, 445, 446, 447, 448, 449, 450, 451, 452, 453, 459, 460, 465, 466, 468, 472, 474, 501, 510, 529, 585, 592, 621
Cannon, M. D., 503
Carleton, A., 74
Carlson, J. R., 270, 281
Carmack, A. L., 300
Carmel, E., 407, 408, 409, 411, 414, 416, 417, 418, 422, 428, 429, 430
Carpenter, M. A., 584
Carroll, J. S., 624, 627
Carter, A. J., 337, 338, 345, 355
Carter, M., 346, 354, 357
Cartilidge, A. M., 343
Cascio, W. F., 284, 285, 560, 569, 576
Cashman, S., 343
Casper, W. J., 475
Castellana, M. J., 3
Cerasoli, C. P., 488, 498, 508, 654, 657
Cervone, D., 504
Challagalla, G. N., 467
Chan, D.W.L., 446, 449, 461, 474
Chandler, M. K., 121, 122

Chang, A., 271, 277
Chen, G., 219, 553
Chermont, K., 339
Chervany, N. L., 283
Chidambaram, L., 277
Chipman, S. F., 449
Chong, C. L., 584
Chrissis, M. B., 61, 68
Christensen, C., 627
Chrobot-Mason, D., 162, 178, 179, 379
Chu, A., 356
Chudoba, K., 272, 407, 420
Chulani, S., 49
Claessens, B.J.C., 582
Clark, B. K., 49, 71
Clark, M. A., 208, 413, 656
Clark, P. R., 352
Clark, T. D., 281
Clay-Williams, R., 354
Clayton, L. D., 552
Clinton, M., 337
Cody, K., 343
Cohen, D. J., 239, 240, 260, 407, 413, 488, 653
Cohen, D. S., 319
Cohen, S. G., 283, 336
Cole, F. S., 343, 344
Cole, P., 408
Collins, J., 198
Colquitt, J. A., 281, 445, 446, 451, 474
Compton, W. D., 194
Connell, J., 268
Connor, D., 215*e*, 220
Conte, J. M., 584, 587
Converse, S. A., 250, 413, 585
Cooke, N. J., 282, 529
Cooley, E., 352
Cooper, C. D., 278
Cooper, D. M., 530
Corbin, J., 213
Cordery, J., 269, 275, 278
Corrigan, J. M., 300
Coutts, R., 231, 232
Coutu, D., 189
Cramton, C. D., 272, 278, 282, 284, 285, 408
Crisp, C. B., 279, 414
Crittenden, M. D., 300
Crolla, R.M.P.H., 619
Cronin, G., 497
Cropanzano, R., 111
Crosby, P., 58
Cross, R., 171, 172–173, 175, 177, 424
Cross, R. L., 171, 177
Crowston, K., 407, 409, 410, 420
Culbertson, B. H., 354
Cummings, J. N., 269, 279, 281, 284, 407, 408, 409, 410, 413, 414, 416, 419, 424, 425, 426, 428, 599
Cummings, L. L., 283
Curtis, B., 48, 49, 50, 51, 52, 55, 56, 57, 61, 68, 72, 649, 651, 655
Cuthbertson, B. H., 336, 354, 609, 610, 618, 620
Cutherbertson, B. H., 618

D

D'Abate, C. P., 506
Daellenbach, U., 271
Dalton, M., 379
Daly, R. C., 341
Dambach, M., 628, 631
Daniels, D., 95
Danjoux Meth, N., 345
Dannenhoffer, J. F., 282
D'Aveni, R. A., 126
Davenport, S., 271
Davidi, I., 489, 502
Davidson, B., 381
Davidson, B. D., 282
Davis, N., 74
Davison, R. M., 279
Dawes, R., 271
Dawson, J. F., 131, 337, 338, 339, 341, 342, 346, 347, 348, 350, 354, 356, 357
Dawson, R., 172, 173, 175
Day, R., 301, 302, 308, 331, 353, 355, 357, 563
Days, R., 619
Dayton, E., 629

De Cremer, D., 389
De Dreu, C., 344, 345, 353, 355, 380, 387, 392, 501
De Gilder, D., 360
de Meuse, K. P., 610
de Vries, E. N., 619, 621
Dearani, J. A., 341
DeChurch, L. A., 221, 340, 381, 490, 501, 503, 504, 591, 595, 612, 633
Deci, E. L., 446
Decker, B., 71
DeDreu, C.K.W., 195, 196
DeJordy, R., 138
Dekker-van Doorn, C. M., 351, 352
Delbecq, L. A., 407, 409, 410
DeLone, W., 408, 414, 422
DeMatteo, J. S., 553
Deming, W. E., 59, 70
den Outer, A. J., 619
DeNisi, A., 504, 511, 553, 557
Denison, D. R., 445
Dennis, A. R., 411, 429, 430
DeRue, D. S., 156, 157
DeSanctis, G., 407
DeShon, R. P., 448, 553
Detert, J. R., 39, 630
Devine, D. J., 523, 530, 552
Diaz, M., 71
DiazGranados, D., 350, 351, 352, 461, 465, 553
Dickinson, T. L., 250
Dickson, C., 222, 228–230, 233
Dickson, M., 375
Dickson, M. W., 561
Digman, J. M., 587
Dino, R. N., 284
Dion, R., 65, 71, 78
Dipboye, R. L., 451
Dismukes, R. K., 505, 509
Dodds, F., 129, 143, 147
Doebbeling, B. N., 349
Doherty, M. E., 503
Donaldson, M. S., 300
Donchin, Y., 619
Donsbach, J. S., 489, 520, 530, 651
Dorsey, D., 556, 570
Dossett, D. L., 94, 95
Doty, M. M., 333
Douglas, C., 193
Dreachslin, J. L., 347
Drewery, G. P., 269
Driskell, J. E., 276, 465, 466
Driskell, T., 441, 649, 653, 654
Drucker, P. J., 13, 407
Dube, L., 274, 275, 276, 277, 281
Dubinsky, Y., 408, 411, 418
Dufresne, R. L., 626, 631, 643
Duggirala, M., 339
Dukes, K. A., 300, 341, 351
Dumville, B. C., 253, 501
Dunbar, N., 272
Dunford, B. B., 552
Dunn, E. J., 300
DuRue, D. S., 155
Dweck, C. S., 219
Dwyer, J., 629

E

Eberhardt, D., 611
Eby, L. T., 553
Eddy, E. R., 506
Edens, P. S., 450, 460
Edmondson, A. C., 39, 127, 147, 185, 195, 196, 334, 335, 339, 346, 458, 489, 503, 609, 610, 629, 630, 631
Edwards, B. D., 449
Egan, T. D., 278
Egido, C., 272
Ehrlich, K., 172, 173, 175
Einav, Y., 619
Eisenhardt, K. M., 650
Eisenstat, R., 29, 30, 35, 38, 39, 40
El Ansari, W., 347, 350
Elam, J. J., 51
ElBardissi, A. W., 341
Ellemers, N., 360
Ellis, A.P.J., 441, 532
Ellis, S., 489, 502, 503
Ellison, L., 228, 229, 230
Elstein, A. S., 627
Ely, K., 475
Ely, R. J., 392

Enayati, J., 129, 143, 147
Endsley, M. R., 618, 619, 621
Ensley, M. D., 219
Entin, E. E., 458, 465, 612, 650
Erez, M., 285, 458
Ernst, C., 162, 178, 179
Ernst, H., 279, 281
Espinosa, J. A., 406, 407, 408, 409, 410, 411, 413, 414, 416, 417, 418, 419, 420, 422, 424, 425, 426, 428, 429, 430, 652
Eubanks, P., 388
Eva, K. W., 626, 628

F

Fahey, T., 276
Fanning, R. M., 497
Faraj, S., 424
Farmer, S., 585
Farr, J. L., 569
Fay, D., 339, 355, 657
Feitosa, J., 441, 649
Felipe Gomez, L., 497
Ferguson, S. L., 351
Fernandez Castelao, E., 611
Field, H. S., 529
Field, R., 346
Finholt, T. A., 283, 408
Fiol, C. M., 282
Fiore, S. M., 51
Firth-Cozens, J., 354
Fischer, J., 272
Flanagan, M. E., 349
Fleishman, E. A., 459
Fletchers, G.C.L., 611
Fletchers, K. P., 194
Flin, R. H., 336, 338, 354, 609, 610, 611, 618, 620, 622
Florey, A. T., 380, 592
Flowe, R. M., 71
Flyvbjerg, B., 581
Fogli, L., 560
Folger, R., 111
Ford, J. K., 299, 308, 311, 314, 319, 447, 450, 471, 473, 474, 475, 654
Fowlkes, J. E., 471
Franklin, N., 627
Franz, T. M., 627
Frederick, E., 504, 507
Freeman, M., 581
Frese, M. D., 449, 472, 589, 591
Friedman, D. M., 300
Fuller, R. M., 411, 430
Furne, A., 340, 342
Furst, S., 282
Futrell, D., 610

G

Gaba, D. M., 497, 618, 620, 621, 633
Gacki-Smith, J., 338
Gajendra, R. S., 281
Galegher, J., 272
Galin, D., 71
Gallagher, C. A., 219
Gandhi, 186
Ganz, M., 126, 131, 134, 135
Gardner, R., 612
Garman, A. N., 299, 308, 311, 317, 318
Garofano, C. M., 471
Gaston, E. H., 208
Gautschi, D., 610, 611
Gavan, J., 380
Gawande, A. A., 620
Gay, G. K., 282
Gerencser, M., 126, 129, 143, 147
Gergle, D., 277
Gersick, C.J.G., 51, 221, 593, 596
Gevers, J.M.P., 581, 582, 585, 586, 587, 590, 591, 592, 596, 650
Giambatista, R. C., 582, 590, 593, 594
Gibbs, J. L., 273, 284
Gibson, C. B., 252, 275, 281, 282, 283, 284, 285, 458, 584, 612
Gil, F., 252, 458, 612
Giles, M., 347
Giles, W. F., 529
Gill, K. M., 343
Gilson, L., 522, 527
Ginnett, R. C., 155, 631
Givens-Skeaton, S., 506
Glasby, J., 347, 350

Glavin, R. J., 611, 622
Glickman, A. S., 59, 67, 555
Glynn, M. A., 138
Goeters, K.-M., 618
Golden, T. D., 284
Goldenson, D., 71, 77
Goldhaber-Fiebert, S., 497, 510
Goldman, M. B., 352
Goldstein, A. P., 461
Goldstein, I. L., 319, 447, 449, 475
Goleman, D., 201
Golhaber-Fiebert, S., 475
Goñi, S., 342
Goodbody, J., 193
Goodwin, G. F., 77, 285, 335, 356, 443, 459, 461, 465
Gopher, D., 619
Gordon, R., 627
Gouma, D. J., 619
Graber, M. L., 627
Graham, S., 351
Grande, B., 628, 629, 631
Grant, A., 338
Gratton, L., 269, 275, 276, 281
Gravelle, H., 337
Green, D., 627
Green, S. G., 194
Greenberg, J., 94, 111
Greenhalgh, T., 299, 311
Greenleaf, R. K., 211
Gregory, M. E., 441, 465, 649, 653
Gregson, B. A., 343
Greitemeyer, T., 612, 627
Grinter, R. E., 407, 408
Grommes, P., 626
Gross, D., 349
Grossman, R., 299, 308, 314, 319, 473, 474
Grote, G., 354, 609, 611, 612, 613, 619, 623, 626, 628, 630, 631, 634
Grumbach, K., 354
Gudanowksi, D. M., 500
Gully, S. M., 210, 212, 585
Gupta, A. K., 581
Gurtner, A., 596, 609
Gustafson, S., 250, 301, 304
Guthrie, J., 462
Guttentag, M., 451
Guzman, M. J., 350, 553
Guzzo, R., 375, 585

H

Haas, C. D., 591, 595
Haas, M. R., 599
Hacker, J., 341
Hacker, W., 584, 589
Hackman, J. R., 27, 31, 37–38, 39, 98, 121, 122, 125, 127, 130, 131, 133, 135, 139, 145, 150, 189, 210, 212, 316, 335, 353, 356, 386, 592, 596, 611
Halfhill, T., 531
Hall, R. J., 585
Halpin, S. M., 461, 465
Halverson, R. R., 585
Hambrick, D. C., 121, 126, 377
Hamliton, K., 588
Handy, C., 285
Hann, M., 341
Hannover, B., 591
Hardy, G., 347, 350
Harrell, M. M., 350, 553
Harris, T. C., 530
Harrison, D. A., 281, 380, 592
Harrison, M. I., 299, 308, 311, 317, 318
Hart, R. K., 276
Harter, D. E., 71
Haskins, C., 6
Haslam, C., 360
Haslam, S. A., 360, 379, 391, 392
Haward, B., 132, 355
Haward, R., 339
Hawryluck, L., 345
Hayes, W., 71, 77
Haynes, M. C., 575, 576
Hays, R. T., 570
Headrick, L. A., 343
Hebl, M. R., 339
Hedlund, J., 531
Heffner, T. S., 285, 335, 356
Hefley, W. E., 72

Heide, J. B., 277
Heidemeier, H., 559
Heilman, M. E., 575, 576
Hein, M. B., 459
Heinemann, G. D., 331
Helferich, J., 172, 173, 175, 308, 311
Helfrich, C. D., 299, 318
Helmreich, R. L., 331, 339, 442
Hemmati, M., 129, 143, 147
Henriksen, K., 629
Henry, K. B., 589
Hepner, D. L., 620
Herbsleb, J. D., 71, 77, 283, 407, 408, 413
Herrera, H., 350, 351
Herscovitch, L., 92
Hertel, G., 281
Heslin, P. A., 575
Heslin, R., 527
Hetlevik, O., 336
Higgs, A. C., 353
Hiltz, S. R., 279, 284
Hinds, P. J., 268, 271, 272, 277, 278, 284, 408
Hinsz, V. B., 240
Hirschfeld, R. R., 529
Hirst, G., 193, 356, 501
Hobman, E. V., 271, 277
Hoegl, M., 279, 281
Hofer, E. C., 283
Hogan, R., 559
Hogg, M. A., 379, 381, 386, 388
Hollenback, J. R., 281, 334, 335, 389, 504, 522, 527, 531
Holm, M.K.S., 581
Holt, R. W., 451
Holton, E. F., III, 473
Holtzman, A., 301, 302
Homan, A. C., 281, 380, 387, 389, 392
Homeyer, C., 338
Hörmann, H.-J., 618
Hornsey, M., 388
Horowitz, E., 50
Houlette, M. A., 388
House, P., 627
Howard, S. K., 618, 620
Howitt, A. M., 122
Howse, W. R., 250, 252, 254, 632
Huang, H., 278, 279, 280, 284
Huang, J. L., 308, 311, 314, 447, 473
Huber, G. P., 57
Hughes, R. L., 160
Humphrey, S. E., 281, 389, 532
Humphrey, W. S., 58, 59, 60, 73, 74
Hung, Y.-T., 284
Hunskår, S., 336
Hunt, P. L., 347
Hunter, J. E., 202
Hunziker, P., 610, 611, 612
Hutchins, H. M., 299, 308, 319, 473

I

Iacono, C., 285
Ilgen, D. R., 281, 389, 523, 527, 531, 532, 584
Incalcaterra, K. A., 586
Insko, C. A., 271
Irmer, B., 271, 277
Iscoe, N., 50, 52, 56
Ives, B., 279, 281, 408

J

Jørgensen, M., 581
Jackson, C. L., 506, 571
Jackson, S. E., 530
Janicik, G. A., 582, 583, 590, 591, 592, 600
Janis, I., 185
Jansen, L., 334
Jaravenpaa, S. L., 279
Jarman, R., 279
Jarvenpaa, S. L., 57, 271, 272, 284, 285, 414
Jawahar, I. M., 508, 559
Jay, G. D., 300, 341, 351
Jehn, K., 379, 381, 382, 400, 458
Jensen, J. M., 611
Jensen, M. K., 349
Jentsch, F., 448, 629, 630, 632, 633
Jetten, J., 360

Jex, S. M., 500
Jobe, K. K., 505, 509
Johnson, L., 530
Johnson, M., 522, 527
Johnson, R. A., 387
Johnston, D., 338
Johnston, J. H., 555
Joiner, B. L., 194
Jones, C., 55
Jones, M., 338
Jones, R., 157, 164
Jonsen, K., 185
Jordan, M. H., 529
Joseph, M., 340, 346, 354
Joshi, A. A., 386, 387, 394, 586
Juarez, A. M., 338
Judd, C., 390
Judge, T. A., 566
Julin, J. A., 530
Jundt, D., 522, 527
Jung, D. I., 530

K

Kaarna, M., 336
Kahai, S. S., 276, 284, 285
Kahn, K., 408
Kaiser, P., 282
Kamdar, D., 630
Kanfer, R., 219, 553
Kaps, S., 612
Kara, I., 619
Karadeen, K., 272
Karam, E. P., 155, 156, 157
Karlgaard, R., 186
Karnik, A., 340, 354
Katz-Navon, T. Y., 458
Katzenbach, J. R., 193
Kavanagh, M. J., 473, 475
Kayworth, T. R., 284
Keeni, G., 71
Keil, C., 556
Keith, N., 449, 472
Kellogg, D., 74
Kelly, C., 126, 129, 143, 147
Kelly, J., 584
Kerr, N. L., 503
Khoo, H. M., 281
Khurana, R., 131
Kiekel, P. A., 529
Kiesler, S., 272, 281, 408
Kim, B. H., 611
Kim, J. W., 279
Kim, P. L., 489
Kim, W. Y., 414
King, E. B., 339
King, H. B., 298, 301, 302, 312, 319, 352, 354, 451, 459, 460, 509, 648, 653
King, N., 408
Kinley, N., 185
Kinney, S. T., 429
Kinni, T., 497
Kirkeby, S., 273
Kirkman, B. L., 219, 269, 275, 278, 281, 282, 283, 285, 335
Kirkpatrick, D., 471
Kirkpatrick, J. D., 319
Kirkpatrick, W. K., 319
Kirton, M. J., 157
Kivimaki, M., 337
Klausen, T. W., 349
Klehe, U. C., 471, 472, 560, 570
Klein, C., 461, 465
Klein, H. J., 272, 277, 504
Klein, K. J., 527, 531, 610, 611
Klimoski, R. J., 413, 459, 585
Kluger, A. N., 504, 553, 557
Knauth, A., 628, 631
Knight, A. P., 610, 611
Knoll, K., 271, 272, 285
Kobayashi, H., 630
Kock, N., 282
Koenig, R. J., 407, 409, 410
Kohn, L. T., 300
Kolbe, M., 354, 609, 611, 612, 613, 618, 619, 623, 624, 626, 627, 628, 629, 631, 634, 650
Konovsky, M., 111
Konradt, U., 281
Korotokin, A. L., 459
Koslowski, S.W.J., 584
Kotter, J., 305, 308, 319

Kozlowski, S.W.J., 210, 212, 448, 473, 506, 522, 527, 531, 553, 610, 611
Krackhardt, D., 424
Kraiger, K., 299, 300, 308, 311, 314, 316, 318, 445, 447, 471, 653, 654
Kraimer, M. L., 424
Kramer, G. P., 503
Krapels, R. H., 193
Krasner, H., 50, 52, 56
Kraut, R. E., 272, 412, 413
Krishnan, M. S., 71
Kriz, W. C., 631
Krokos, K. J., 350, 351, 563, 564
Kruesi-Bailey, V., 49
Kruglanski, A. W., 503
Kruyt, M., 191
Kukenberger, M., 530
Kunitz, S. J., 349
Künzle, B., 354, 609, 611, 612, 613, 619, 623, 628, 634
Kurland, N. B., 278
Kurtzberg, T. R., 285
Kwan, V., 390
Kyriakidou, O., 299, 311

L

Labovitz, G., 309
LaGanke, J. S., 561
Landy, F. J., 569, 587
Lao-Tse, 234
Larman, C., 57
Larson, J. R., 627
Lassiter, D. L., 527
Latane, B., 272
Latham, G. P., 91, 92, 93, 94, 95, 96, 97, 100, 101, 102, 105, 109, 200, 446
Lau, D. C., 373, 375, 377, 381, 385, 387, 389, 390, 414, 650
Lauche, K., 618
Laufer, N., 619
Law, K. S., 574
Lawless, B., 345
Lawlis, P. K., 71
Lawn, M., 619
Lawrence, P. R., 27, 32
Lazzara, E. H., 308, 312, 443, 453, 458, 653
Lea, M. T., 270, 271
Leach, L. P., 600
Leape, L. L., 335
Leblanc, V. R., 346, 354
Lee, C., 504, 507
Lee, E. A., 349
Lee, G., 408, 414, 422
Lee, H., 650
Leggat, S. G., 354, 355
Leggett, E.L.A., 219
Leidner, D. E., 271, 272, 284, 285
Lemay, C., 343
Lemieux-Charles, L., 336
Lencioni, P., 194
Leonard, H. B., 122
Leonard, M., 351
LePine, J. A., 281, 445, 451, 474, 506, 531, 571, 573, 595
Letsky, M. P., 51
Levesque, L. L., 51
Levin, K. Y., 459
Lewicki, R. J., 137
Lewis, P. J., 339
Li, J. T., 126, 377
Liang, T. Y., 194
Liden, R. C., 424
Lientz, B. P., 581
Lim, A., 588
Limpus, A., 340, 354
Lipnack, J., 268, 276
Lippert, A., 349
Lipshitz, R., 506
Lipsitz, S. R., 620
Littlepage, G., 489
Littrell, L. N., 460
Liu, J. H., 272
Locke, E. A., 97, 100, 102, 446, 504, 507
Lohman, M. C., 507
Lombardi, V., 209
Lorsch, J. W., 27, 32
Love, T., 57
Lowton, K., 357
Lu, M., 407

Lukasik, M. A., 530
Lum, H., 51
Lundmark, V., 272
Luthans, F., 657
Lyons, R., 51, 308
Lyubovnikova, J., 331, 346, 354, 357, 649

M

MacCoun, R. J., 503
MacFarlane, F., 299, 311
MacLean, S. L., 338
Madachy, R., 50
Maddux, J. E., 458
Mael, F., 271
Majchrzak, A., 408
Makary, M. A., 351
Malan, J., 191
Malhotra, A., 408
Malone, T., 409, 410
Mann, L., 193
Mann, R. D., 527
Mann, S., 352
Mannix, E., 272
Mannor, M. J., 532
Manser, T., 331, 609, 611, 612, 613, 618, 619, 628, 629, 634
Manz, C. C., 210, 211, 219, 655
Maran, N. J., 611
March, J., 409, 410
Marcus, R. G., 352
Marks, M. A., 75, 138, 210, 212, 221, 250, 251, 255, 391, 458, 459, 504, 559, 571, 590, 595, 611, 619, 633
Markus, H., 445, 446
Marrow, S. E., 156
Marsch, S. U., 609, 610, 611, 612
Marsick, V. J., 502, 507
Martin, A., 248
Martin, J. S., 193
Martin, L., 618
Martin, R., 386
Martins, L. L., 240, 582
Marton, K. I., 331, 342
Massey, A. P., 278, 284
Matheson, K., 277
Mathieu, J. E., 75, 240, 250, 255, 269, 275, 278, 285, 335, 356, 391, 458, 488, 489, 500, 504, 506, 520, 522, 527, 530, 559, 571, 587, 591, 595, 611, 619, 633, 651
Maxwell, R. J., 344
Maynard, M. T., 522, 527
Maznevski, M., 272
McAlearney, A. S., 299, 308, 311, 317, 318
Mcarthur, M., 347
McCauley, C. D., 156
McComb, S. A., 194
McConnell, C. R., 311
McCormick, E. J., 529
McDnough, E. F., 408
McDonnell, L. K., 505, 509
McEvily, B., 277
McGarry, F., 71
McGeorge, P., 611
McGrath, J. E., 250, 527, 582, 584, 592, 611
McGuire, J. B., 164, 166, 167
McGuire, W. L., 336
McHarry, J., 129, 143, 147
McHugh, M., 299, 308, 311, 317, 318
McKee, A., 201
McKee, L., 338
McKinney, M. M., 299, 308, 311, 318
McKnight, D. H., 283
McLeod, P. L., 276
McPherson, S. O., 275, 281, 282, 285, 466
McQuillan, R., 308
Mead, N., 341
Mearns, K., 336, 354, 618, 620
Medsker, G. J., 353
Meertens, R. W., 585
Meisinger, S. R., 182, 649, 656
Meliza, L. L., 490
Melner, S. B., 552
Mendonca, D., 122
Merritt, D., 530
Mesmer-Magnus, J. R., 381, 490, 501, 503, 504, 612
Metiu, A., 272, 273–274, 280, 284

Meyer, J. P., 92
Mickan, S. M., 338, 354, 355
Milanovich, D. M., 441, 471, 474, 592
Milham, L., 445, 448, 451, 452, 474
Miller, A., 340, 346, 354
Miller, S. A., 72
Milliken, F. J., 30, 582, 585
Milliman, P., 57
Mills, H., 56
Mills, P. D., 300
Milner, K. R., 553
Milton, L., 377
Minasian, L., 299, 308, 311, 318
Minehart, R. D., 612, 626, 632
Miner, A. S., 277
Minton, J. W., 137
Mitchell, R., 347
Mitchell, T. R., 94, 95
Mockus, A., 408
Moenaert, R. K., 272, 277, 408
Mohammed, S., 253, 413, 459, 501, 582, 585, 588, 590, 592, 600
Moløkken, K., 581
Molix, L., 388
Molleman, E., 390, 391
Molyneux, J., 347
Monsell, S., 359
Montesino, M. U., 299
Montoya-Weiss, M. M., 278, 284
Moore, C., 164, 165, 169
Moore, D. A., 285
Mooreland, R. L., 589
Morello, D., 269
Morey, J. C., 300, 341, 351
Morgan, B. B., Jr., 59, 67, 537, 555, 557
Morgenson, F. P., 155, 156, 157
Morgeson, F. P., 529, 532
Morisio, M., 76
Morris, M. W., 285
Morrison, E. W., 30, 628, 630
Morrison, J. B., 624, 627
Morrison, J. E., 490
Mortensen, M., 271, 272, 277, 278, 279, 358, 359, 582
Moser, K., 559
Mount, M. K., 530, 587
Mukamel, D., 349
Mukopadhyay, T., 272
Mullaney, J., 74
Mumford, M. D., 459, 529
Murnighan, J., 375, 377, 381, 385, 414
Murphy, C. E., 459
Murrells, T., 337
Murthy, N. N., 467
Murukutla, N., 333
Musselwhite, C., 157, 164

N

Nadkarni, S., 582, 588, 590, 592, 600
Nadler, D. A., 121, 126, 127, 144
Nan, N., 409, 414, 428, 429, 430
Napolitano, F., 126, 129, 143, 147
Neale, M., 272, 381
Neily, J., 300
Nembhard, I. M., 334, 339, 610, 631
Nenadál, J., 575
Nesdale, D., 272
Nestel, D., 611
Neubert, M. J., 530
Neyer, A. K., 269, 272
Ng, P. T., 194
Nichols, D. R., 465, 466
Nicholson, D., 250, 252, 254, 632
Nicolopoulos, D., 227
Nielsen, P. E., 352
Nielsen, T. M., 531
Nijhuis, H., 618
Nijstad, B. A., 612
Noe, R. A., 445, 451, 474, 507
Nohynkova, R., 629
Northcraft, G., 381
Nowak, A., 272
Nunes, D. A., 121, 126, 127, 130, 133, 139, 189

O

Oakes, P., 388
Oakes, P. J., 379

Ochsenbein, G., 590
Ocker, R. J., 278, 279, 280, 284
O'Connor, E. J., 283
O'Connor, K. M., 582, 584
O'Connor, R., 503
Ohlott, P., 379
Okhuysen, G. A., 593
Oldman, G. R., 98
O'Leary, G., 17
O'Leary, K. J., 349, 350, 356
O'Leary, M. B., 269, 278, 279, 358, 359, 428, 582
Oliver, D., 341
Olson, G. M., 277, 285, 408
Olson, J. S., 277, 285, 408
O'Lynn, C. E., 347
Orav, E. J., 620
O'Reilly, C. A., 375
Orlikowski, W. J., 281, 407, 419, 420, 581
Osborn, R., 333
Overman, S., 200
Ovretveit, J., 348

P

Palmisano, S., 190
Panteli, N., 279
Panzer, F. J., 633
Park, D. W., 272, 277
Park, J., 650
Parker, A., 171, 177
Parker, V., 347
Parks, M. R., 272
Patel, P. C., 381, 382, 400, 588
Patrashkova-Volzdoska, R. R., 194
Patterson, M., 272, 342
Paulk, M. C., 61, 68, 71, 77
Payne, S. C., 555
Pearce, B. M., 407
Pearce, C. L., 186, 219, 655
Pearce, J. L., 381
Peeters, M.A.G., 582, 586, 587
Pelled, L. H., 650
Penn, M. L., 68
Peters, K., 157, 159–160
Peters, L. D., 194
Peterson, C., 458
Peterson, R., 195
Peterson, S. J., 657
Pettigrew, T. F., 284
Petty, R., 381
Peugh, J., 333
Peyronnin, K., 530
Philips, J. L., 523, 530, 552
Philips, P. R., 343
Pian-Smith, M.C.M., 612, 630, 632
Piccoli, G., 281, 408
Piccoli, R. F., 506, 571
Pickering, C., 408, 409, 410, 413, 414, 416, 419, 420, 424, 425, 426
Picoli, G., 279
Piquette, D., 346, 354
Pisano, G. P., 335, 489
Pitterman, B., 71
Platow, M. J., 392
Ployhart, R. E., 71, 532
Plsek, P. E., 348
Podlny, J. M., 131
Podraza, M., 632
Polzer, J. T., 278, 377, 414
Poole, M. S., 407, 589
Popper, M., 506
Porter, L. W., 381
Porzio di Camporotondo, N., 213, 217
Postmes, T., 360
Poulton, B. C., 338, 343, 344
Powell, A., 279, 281, 408
Powers, C., 281
Pozner, C. N., 620
Pratt, S. D., 352
Preskill, H., 452
Price, K., 380
Priest, H., 355, 460, 462, 465, 533, 626, 633, 634
Prince, C., 449, 450, 471, 618
Prins, H. A., 619
Pritchard, R. D., 350, 553
Proell, C. A., 284

Pronovost, P. J, 11, 509
Purvanova, R., 284

Q

Quinn, R. E., 162
Quiñones, M. A., 445, 447, 475

R

Radke, P. H., 276
Raemer, D. B., 612, 626, 630, 631, 632
Rafferty, L. A., 441
Rajendran, C., 339
Rall, M., 621, 622, 633
Ramanujam, R., 333
Ramirez, A., 272
Randolph, J., 331, 342
Rao, V. S., 57
Rapp, T., 522, 527, 591
Rassouli, K., 85, 651, 656
Rathgeber, H., 305, 308
Rea, K. P., 581
Reader, T. W., 336, 354, 609, 610, 618, 620
Ready, D. A., 190
Ream, E., 334
Reddington, K., 489
Rees, A., 247, 337, 338, 343, 349
Reeves, S., 346, 354
Reicher, S., 379, 388
Reidy, P., 343
Reifer, D., 50
Rentsch, J. R., 585
Reynard, J., 629
Reynolds, A. M., 441, 474
Reynolds, J., 629, 629
Rhodenizer, L., 447
Rhodes, G. B., 164, 166, 167
Rice, D. J., 282
Rice, R. E., 408
Richards, A., 350
Richardson, J., 336, 354
Richter, A., 337, 340, 356
Rico, R., 252, 373, 381, 387, 389, 390, 391, 458, 612, 650
Riethmüller, M., 611
Riley, D., 222, 225–228, 233
Ringseis, E., 585
Rink, E., 340, 342
Rittman, A. L., 138, 210, 212, 459
Rivard, P., 626, 631, 632
Roach, R. M., 559
Robbins, S. P., 566
Robert, G., 299, 311
Roberto, M. A., 127, 147, 334
Roberts, K. H., 611
Robey, D., 274, 275, 276, 277, 281
Robinson, D. W., 312, 451
Robinson, G., 506
Robinson, S., 337
Robison, J., 346
Robison, W., 489
Rocco, E., 283
Rodger, S. A., 338, 354, 355
Roe, R. A., 584
Rogers, D. G., 497
Rogers, E. M., 299
Rogers, G. C., 28, 31, 33, 34, 44
Rogers, W., 201–202
Roh, H., 386, 387, 394
Ron, N., 506
Rosansky, V., 309
Rosen, B., 219, 269, 275, 278, 281, 282, 283, 285, 335
Rosen, M. A., 252, 254, 282, 354, 443, 451, 452, 459, 460, 465, 475, 509, 632
Rosen, R. M., 187
Rosenbaum, S., 71
Ross, F., 340, 342
Ross, L., 627
Rouiller, J. Z., 447, 475
Rousseau, D. M., 333, 649
Rucolph, J., 632
Ruderman, M. N., 156, 379
Rudolph, J. W., 612, 624, 626, 627, 631, 632
Russ-Eft, D. F., 446, 449, 452, 461, 474
Russell, S., 556
Rutherford, J., 347

Rutte, C. G., 581, 585, 586, 587, 590, 591, 592, 596, 650
Ryan, R. M., 446

S

Sabella, M. J., 251
Sackett, P. R., 560, 564, 570
Saks, A. M., 656
Salas, E., 51, 59, 67, 74, 77, 210, 212, 240, 250, 251, 252, 254, 255, 276, 282, 285, 299, 300, 301, 304, 308, 311, 312, 314, 316, 318, 319, 331, 335, 351, 352, 353, 354, 355, 356, 357, 410, 412, 413, 441, 442, 443, 445, 446, 447, 448, 449, 450, 451, 452, 453, 458, 459, 460, 461, 462, 465, 466, 467, 468, 471, 472, 473, 474, 488, 501, 506, 509, 510, 529, 530, 533, 553, 555, 559, 585, 592, 609, 611, 618, 619, 621, 626, 631, 632, 633, 634, 643, 647, 649, 653, 654
Salisbury, M. L., 298, 300, 301, 302, 341, 351, 451, 459, 648
Salter, C., 510
Sánchez-Manzanares, M., 252, 373, 381, 387, 389, 390, 391, 458, 612, 650
Sappidi, J., 55
Sarker, S., 273, 426, 426
Sato, M., 630
Saul, J. R., 506, 571
Saunders, D. M., 137
Savoie, A., 649
Sawa, R., 630
Sawyer, J. E., 388
Sayles, L. R., 121, 122
Scheinkestel, C., 340, 346, 354
Scherlis, W., 272
Schilpzand, M. D., 240
Schippers, M., 346, 347, 355, 375, 376
Schlack, W. S., 619
Schmidt, A. M., 553
Schmidt, F. L., 202
Schmolck, H., 511
Schnatterly, K., 387
Schoen, C., 333
Scholtes, P., 194
Schon, D., 503
Schopler, J., 271
Schraagen, J. M., 449
Schroeder, K., 276
Schuck, P., 556
Schulz-Hardt, S., 612, 627
Schwalb, J., 74
Schwartz, A., 627
Scott, C. W., 497
Scully, J., 340, 342, 356
Seashore, D. G., 156
Seers, A., 221, 585
Sego, D. J., 447, 475
Sehgal, N. L., 349, 350, 356
Seijts, G. H., 101
Semmer, N. K., 609, 610, 611, 612
Serfaty, D., 458, 465, 612, 650
Seshagiri, G., 74
Sessa, V. I., 530
Sexton, J. B., 331, 339
Shae, G. P., 585
Shalin, V. J., 449
Shapiro, D. A., 132, 337, 338, 343, 347, 349
Shapiro, D. E., 352
Sharit, J., 332
Sheldon, O. J., 284
Shelton, D., 559
Sheppard, L., 281
Sheppard, S. B., 49, 57
Sherif, M., 389
Sherman, M. P., 561
Shervani, T. A., 467
Shewhart, W., 68
Shin, Y., 269, 276
Shipton, H., 348
Shouten, M. E., 334, 335
Shrestha, L., 618
Shuffler, M. L., 443, 453, 458
Shurygailo, S., 284, 285
Sibbald, B., 337
Siebdrat, F., 279, 281
Sierra, M. J., 552, 654

Simmer, G., 222, 230–232, 234
Simon, H. A., 409, 410
Simon, R., 300, 341, 351, 611, 612, 626, 631, 632
Simons, T., 195
Sims, D. E., 74, 211, 250, 255, 448, 458, 460, 465, 472, 609, 618, 632, 633
Sims, H. P., 210, 219, 655
Sitzmann, T., 475
Siviy, J. M., 68
Slater, J. A., 344
Slaughter, S. A., 71, 413
Sligo, J., 71
Slonin, A., 350, 351
Small, S. D., 618, 620
Smink, D. S., 620
Smith, D. K., 194
Smith, D. M., 185, 195, 196
Smith, J. R., 343, 344
Smith-Jentsch, K., 299, 300, 308, 311, 314, 316, 318, 441, 445, 447, 449, 451, 465, 466, 467, 468, 474, 510, 552, 553, 555, 629, 630, 631, 632, 651, 653, 654
Smith, R. B., 154, 161
Smither, J. W., 97, 113
Snipes, J., 316
Sommers, L. S., 331, 342
Song, M., 278, 284
Song, P. H., 299, 308, 311, 317, 318
Soo, C., 269, 275, 278
Sorcher, M., 461
Sorra, J. S., 447, 475
Sosick, J. J., 530
Spahn, D. R., 619, 623, 628, 630, 631
Sparrowe, R. T., 424
Spears, R., 270, 271
Spector, B., 38, 465
Spell, C. S., 400
Sprainer, E., 347
Sproull, L., 424
Spychiger, M., 609, 610, 611, 612
Squire, L. R., 511
Stagl, K. C., 461, 465, 611
Stamps, J., 268, 276
Stanton, N. A., 441
Staples, D. S., 269, 282
Stasser, G., 393, 410, 412, 503, 612, 623
Steece, B., 50
Steele, F., 202, 203
Stein, A., 626
Steiner, I. D., 531, 599
Stevens, M. J., 353, 355, 523, 529
Stevenson, P., 629
Stevenson, W. B., 381
Stewart, D. D., 393
Stewart, G. L., 530
Stewart, J., 591
Stoddard, R. W., 68
Stout, R. J., 471, 529, 592
Strack, M., 612, 626
Straus, S., 277
Strauss, A., 213
Streeter, L. A., 412
Streibel, B. J., 194
Stride, C., 349
Struening, E. L., 451
Studdert, D. M., 620
Sulsky, L. M., 575
Sundstrom, E., 531, 553, 610
Sundt, T. M., 341
Swann, J. W., 377
Swezey, R. W., 445, 449, 451, 472
Szynkarski, A., 55

T

Taekman, J. M., 618, 619, 621
Tajfel, H., 359, 378
Takeshita, T., 630
Talley, A., 388
Tan, A.-H., 284
Tang, M.M.L., 345
Tang, V., 164, 165, 169
Tani, D. W., 22
Tannenbaum, S. I., 240, 250, 255, 299, 300, 308, 311, 314, 316, 318,

442, 445, 447, 449, 451, 465, 466, 468, 473, 475, 488, 489, 497, 498, 501, 506, 508, 509, 510, 520, 530, 621, 651, 653, 654, 657
Tasa, K., 92
Taylor, P. J., 446, 449, 461, 474
Temkin-Greener, H., 349
Terrell, G., 349, 350, 356
Tesluk, P. E., 275, 281, 282, 283, 285, 500, 559
Thaler, R. H., 271
Thapar, A., 341
Thatcher, S.M.B., 381, 382, 400, 588
Thayer, A. L., 443, 453, 458
Thoen, W., 284
Thomas, D. A., 392
Thomas, D. M., 268
Thomas, E. J., 331, 339
Thomas-Hunt, M. C., 284
Thompson, J., 409, 410
Thompson, L. L., 285
Thordahl, J. B., 71
Tilin, F., 300
Timmermann, A., 611
Titus, W., 503, 623
Tjosvold, D., 345, 574
Todd, P., 272
Toomey, L., 301, 302
Toon, P. D., 344
Topakas, A., 341
Towler, A., 451
Tracey, P. J., 473, 475
Trezzini, B., 385
Tripoli, A. M., 592
Tschan, F., 589, 590, 609, 610, 611, 612, 622, 623, 625, 626, 627, 628
Tuckman, B. W., 67, 221
Tuffield, R., 191
Tuggle, C. S., 387
Tullar, W., 282
Tully, M. P., 339
Turner, J. C., 359, 379, 381, 388, 389
Tuzinski, K. A., 564

U
Uggerslev, K. L., 575
Uitdewilligen, S., 609, 623
Upenieks, V. V., 349

V
Valach, L., 590
Valacich, J. S., 411, 430
Valley, K., 272
Valot, C., 618
van Andel, G., 619
Van Buskirk, W., 556
Van de Ven, A. H., 407, 409, 410
Van den Bulte, C., 272, 277, 408
Van der Vegt, G. S., 390, 391
Van Dick, R., 356
Van Eerde, W., 582, 586, 587, 590, 591, 592, 596
van Ginkel, W. P., 393, 586
van Helden, S. H., 619
Van Iddekinge, C. H., 529
Van Kleef, G. A., 281, 387, 389, 392
van Knippenberg, D., 281, 347, 360, 375, 376, 380, 387, 389, 391, 392, 393, 586
Van Lee, R., 126, 129, 143, 147
van Leeuwen, E., 360
van Putten, M.A.S., 619
Van Velsor, E., 156
Van Vugt, M., 389
van Wijk, K. P., 351, 352
van Wijngaarden, J.D.H., 351, 352
Vanderberghe, C., 92
Vanderstoep, S., 592
Vaughan, S. I., 612
Veiga, J. F., 284
Venkatesh, B., 340, 354
Vescio, T., 390
Vesey, J. T., 581
Vessey, W. B., 441, 649
Vickery, C. M., 281
Villado, A. J., 449, 530
Vincent, L. H., 467

Volpe, C. E., 250, 255, 465, 501, 621
Volpe, M., 507, 592
Von Cranach, M., 590
Voss, K., 281

W

Wacker, J., 611, 618, 619, 623, 629
Wageman, R., 121, 125, 126, 127, 130, 131, 133, 134, 135, 139, 145, 189, 210, 212, 316, 353, 655, 656
Walker, A. G., 97, 113
Walker, G. H., 441
Walker, K., 611
Wallace, D. M., 240
Wallace, W., 122
Waller, M. J., 582, 584, 590, 593, 594, 596, 609, 611, 623
Walther, J. B., 269, 270, 272, 277, 278, 284, 285
Walton, E., 27
Walz, D. B., 51
Walzer, T. B., 612, 632
Warkentin, M., 282
Warner, N., 51
Watkins, K. E., 507
Watkins, M. D., 127, 147, 334
Watola, D. J., 611
Watson-Manheim, M. B., 407, 420
Watson, W. E., 530
Wayne, S. J., 424
Wears, R. L., 300, 341, 351
Weaver, S. J., 319, 352, 460, 465
Webb, D. R., 74
Webber, S. S., 255
Weber, C. V., 61, 68, 72
Weber, T., 379
Webster, J., 269, 271, 277, 279, 282, 301, 302
Weeden, K., 386
Wegeman, R., 31
Wegner, D., 413, 423
Weichmann, D., 553
Weick, K., 413, 611
Weilbaecher, A., 531
Weinberg, G., 56
Weiner, B. J., 299, 308, 311, 318
Weingart, L. R., 195, 196, 344, 501, 592
Weisband, S., 285
Weiss, J. A., 592
Weiss, M., 628, 631
Wærn, Y., 622
West, M. A., 131, 331, 336, 337, 338, 339, 340, 341, 342, 343, 344, 345, 346, 347, 348, 350, 354, 355, 356, 357, 503, 596, 649
Wetherell, M., 379, 388
Wheelan, S. A., 300, 589
Wheeler-Smith, S., 630
White, N., 347
Wholey, D. R., 51
Whyte, K., 92
Widmer, P., 346, 355
Wiegmann, D. A., 341
Wiese, C. W., 552, 654
Wiethoff, C., 272, 277
Wilcock, P. M., 343
Wildman, J. L., 553, 561, 566, 571, 575
Wilemon, D. L., 581
Wiles, R., 346
Wilk, S. L., 507
Wilke, H.A.M., 389, 585
Wilkinson, A., 657
Williams, C. R., 504, 508, 559
Williams, K. J., 511
Williams, K. Y., 375
Williams, M. V., 349, 350
Williams Woolley, A., 582
Wilson-Donnelly, K., 355, 533, 633, 634
Wilson, J. M., 51, 268, 271, 273, 277, 281, 284, 407, 653
Wilson, K. A., 308, 312, 451, 459, 462, 626, 633
Wilson, T., 348
Wit, A., 389
Wittenbaum, G. M., 393, 410, 412, 612
Woehr, D. J., 569
Wohlwend, H., 71

Wong, J. M., 620
Wong, W.K.P., 271, 277, 279
Wood, R. E., 415, 429
Woodruff, S., 221
Woolley, A. W., 358, 359
Wright, M. C., 618, 619, 621
Wright, N. S., 269
Wright, Z., 277
Wynn, E., 407

X

Xiao, Y., 610, 611
Xin, K. R., 650
Xyrichis, A., 334, 357

Y

Yakura, E. K., 582, 584
Yates, J., 581
Yeagley, E. L., 388
Yilmaz, T., 553
Yost, P. R., 585
Yourdon, E., 58, 59
Yukl, G., 171, 311

Z

Zaccaro, S. J., 75, 138, 210, 212, 250, 251, 255, 268, 340, 391, 458, 459, 504, 559, 571, 591, 595, 611, 619
Zack, M., 272, 277
Zajac, S., 647
Zajonc, R. B., 445, 446
Zala-Mezö, E., 611, 619, 623
Zanna, M. P., 277
Zanutto, E., 382
Zapf, D., 589
Zazanis, M., 458
Zedeck, S., 560
Zeffane, R., 268
Zeisig, R. L., 466
Zeiss, A. M., 331
Zellmer-Bruhn, M. E., 582, 590, 593, 594
Zheng, J., 272, 285
Ziegert, J. C., 610, 611
Ziewacz, J. E., 620
Zimbardo, P. G., 587
Zimmerman, R. D., 475
Zinner, M. J., 620
Zmud, R. W., 270
Zubrow, D., 71, 77

Subject Index

Page references followed by *fig* indicate an illustrated figure; followed by *t* indicate a table; followed by *e* indicate an exhibit.

A

Action regulation theory: applied to meeting deadlines, 589–597; description of, 589

Action team process phase, 571, 572*t*,573

Adaptability: description of, 252; virtual team, 252–253

Agency for Healthcare Research and Quality (AHRQ), 299, 301, 351

Alcoa virtual teams, 278

Alinghi (America's Cup sailing team), 225–228, 233–234

America's Cup sailing team lessons: build in feedback, acknowledge wins, and plan for the future, 222; coach for peak performance at the right time, 220–222; create a structure that leverages team's strengths, 220; examine leadership styles, beliefs, and fit, 218–220; identify team goals and resources, 217–218

America's Cup sailing team vignettes: Chris Dickson at BMW Oracle, 228–230; Dawn Riley at Areva, 225–228; Grant Simmer at Alinghi, 230–232; Silvio Arrivabene at Mascalzone Latino Capitalia, 223–225

America's Cup sailing teams: America's Cup Management (ACM) charge over, 214, 215*e*; examining team leadership in context of, 212–213; history of the, 214–216*e*; leader challenges for, 213–214

Areva (America's Cup sailing team), 225–228

Army leadership, 8

Assessment instruments. *See* Measurement instruments

Aston Team Facilitation Programme (ATFP) [UK], 351

Asynchronous communication, 411*t*, 423

Atomic Energy Organization of Iran (AEOI), 90

B

Backup behavior, 252

"Bad" team members, 199

BMW Oracle (America's Cup sailing team), 222, 225, 227, 228–230, 233

Boundaries: clarifying executive team, 189; complexity of global, 410*t*, 413–415; complexity of temporal separation, 410*t*, 415–416; five types of, 178; high-impact teams spanning, 178–180. *See also* Faultlines

Boundary spanning: high-impact team practices and strategies for, 179*fig*; strategic change through, 178, 180

Bridge building: high-impact team practices and strategies for, 179*fig*; strategic change through, 178, 180

C

Calendar efficiencies issue, 417–419
Capability maturity model (CMM): adopting to workforce development, 72–73; examining teams in the context of software organizations using, 76–79; five evolutionary stages or maturity level of, 61–70; origins and development of, 60–61; team software process application of, 73–76; validating the, 70–71. *See also* Process maturity framework
Capability maturity model (CMM) levels: level 1: inconsistent, 63*t*, 64; level 2: stabilized, 63*t*, 65–66; level 3: standardized, 62*fig*, 66–67; level 4: optimized, 62*fig*, 68–69; level 5: innovating, 62*fig*, 69–70
Categorization mechanism, 378
Center for Creative Leadership (CCL): on leadership of high-impact teams, 155–157*fig*; on nature of strategic change, 157–162; on participation on face-to-face and virtual teams, 248–249; on team experience in leading strategic change, 162–163; tools to lead strategic change, 163–180; work on developing high-impact teams by, 154–155
CEO succession planning, 199–200. *See also* Executive team leaders
Champions (TeamSTEPPS program), 315–316
Change: leading a major technology development and, 86–116; planning for, 88*t*, 99–103, 313–314. *See also* Organizational change; Strategic change
Change plan: major technological development step of creating, 88*t*, 99–103; TeamSTEPPS program, 313–314
Closed-loop communication: behavioral markers and recommendations for, 617*t*; benefits of, 633; as high-risk team process, 609, 632–633; situations that require, 633–634; ways to train, 634
Co-management health care teams, 16
Coaching, 459
Cockpit Resource Management (CRM), 302
Collaborations: team time management during, 581–601; TeamSTEPPS program establishment of, 317; temporal synchronization during, 584; temporally separated team work during, 406–433; threats to shared temporal cognitions in, 587–589; time zone coordination during, 411*t*, 417–419, 423–428, 431. *See also* Teamwork
Command-and-control health care teams, 14–15
Communication: asynchronous, 411*t*, 423, 431; closed-loop, 609, 617*t*, 632–634; distributed groups and frequent, 272–273, 275–276; holding honest conversations, 38–39, 42–43; meeting deadlines and role of, 590; myth about having to use "richest" medium for, 278; synchronous, 411*t*, 423, 431; team performance barrier of poor coordination and, 30, 35; during team training, 459; virtual team, 255. *See also* Feedback
Competencies: list of leader, 201–202; TeamSTEPPS skills, tools, and, 304*t*. *See also* Knowledge, skills, and abilities (KSAs)

Computer aided software engineering (CASE) tools, 57
Computer supported cooperative work (CSCW) ["groupware"], 57–58
Conflict: attacking silo, 4–5; between subgroups of the same group, 273–274; executive team, 195–197; faultline teams and, 381–382; between individual and collective interests, 144; myth about completely dispersed groups and high, 278–279; team priority, 30, 33–34; during team training, 458
Conflict management: in faultlines teams, 382–386; health care team, 344–345; three practices for executive team, 196
Contingency leadership, 211
Continuous learning (TeamSTEPPS program), 316–317
Cooperation: managing virtual teams to promote, 280*t*; during team training, 458. *See also* Team coordination
Core values: Google, 188–189; TeamSTEPPS, 309–310; Zappos, 188
Corporate culture: attacking silo conflict through shared purpose and, 4–5; SEFUS-Style's BWP (banking with a purpose) and, 5; shared by executive leader and team, 188–189; tips for creating a team training climate as part of, 321*t*–326*t*; variations between norms and, 144–145. *See also* Organizations
Crew resource management (CRM): description of, 22; spaceflight teamwork using strategy of, 22–24
Crisis Resource Management (CRM), 621
Cross-training, 465
Curiosity competency, 202

D

D-Day press statements (Dwight Eisenhower), 9
Deadlines: action regulation theory applied to meeting, 589–597; communication role as central to meeting, 590; ideal cycle of action regulation for making, 590; temporal adaptation for making, 595–597; temporal evaluation for making, 593–595; temporal preparation for making, 591–593
Debriefings. *See* Team debriefings
Decision making: constraints to team composition, 535–538, 544–546; KSAO distributions consideration for team composition, 525, 526, 528*t*–529, 530, 533–534, 535, 548, 554; for team composition, 523–527; on what should be measured for team performance, 554–558
Demographic team boundaries, 178
Distributed work groups: description and special issues of, 268–269; how nature of teamwork is changing to include, 652–653; implementation of, 279; mechanisms that affect social information in, 271–276; myth about highest conflict in, 278–279; myths and misconceptions about, 276–285; performance in temporally separated, 406–433; social information acquired and used by, 269–270. *See also* Virtual teams
Diversity management. *See* Team diversity management
Dyad team work: description of, 424; findings on temporally separated, 424–426
Dynamic model of team time management: illustrated diagram of, 598*fig*; introduction to, 597–599; practical implications of, 599–601

Dynamics Outcome Management (DOM), 301

E

Emirates Team New Zealand (TNZ), 224, 225, 230, 232
Emotional intelligence competency, 201
Empathy: description of, 140; look for team members with, 140–141
Esfahan Nuclear Technology Center (ENTC or Center) [Iran]: definition of the problem and conceptual solution, 91–94; development and communication of policies and strategies, 94–99; examining the two-year joint efforts of, 89–90; goals and change plan developed at, 101–103; governance development at, 106–108; implementation and measurement of success at, 111–113; keeping staff motivated at, 113–116; origins and background of, 90–91; staffing, training, and professional development at, 108–111; stakeholder involvement and management at, 103–106; vision statement of, 99–100
Evaluation: instruments for performance measurement and, 349–350, 562–568; making deadlines by conducting temporal, 593–595; team training, 471–473. *See also* Team performance measurement (TPM)
Executive team leaders: defining team boundaries, 189; developing shared culture with team, 188–189; developing trust among team members, 193–195; five suggestions for, 204; know themselves first quality of, 185–188; recognizing their need for executive team, 184–185. *See also* CEO succession planning
Executive team members: the bad, 199; developing trust among, 193–195; the good, 199–202; nature of conflict by, 195–197; proper rewards and recognition provided to, 197; the ugly, 198–199
Executive teams: care and feeding of, 184; clear operational responsibilities of the, 193; conflict resolution practices for, 196; defining the role of the, 189–193; developing shared culture with leader, 188–189; five suggestions for leading, 204; leader work done through, 184–185; leaders must clarify boundaries of, 189; location and day-to-day contacts of, 202–203; recognizing unique attributes of, 182–184
Expert leader-dominated health care teams, 15
Expertise: getting buy-in for training from those with, 449; health care team leaders with, 15; transactive memory of sources of, 423–424. *See also* Subject-matter experts (SMEs)
Explicit reasoning process: behavioral markers and recommendations for, 615*t*; benefits of, 626–627; as high-risk team process, 609, 625–626; situations that require, 627–628; ways to teach, 628

F

Face-to-face teams: comparing challenging behaviors for virtual and, 243*t*; comparing successful behaviors for virtual and, 242*t*; myths about virtual work as requiring meetings by, 276–278

Faultline strength: description and level of, 382; team constellation with varying degrees of diversity and, 384*t*–385*t*
Faultline teams: information elaboration in, 380–381; interventions for, 391–400; management of faultlines in, 382–386; psychology and triggers of faultlines forming, 378–380; team conflict in, 381–382; theory of faultlines to understand, 376–378
Faultlines: description of, 375; global boundary complexity context of, 414–415; palliative management of activated, 394; preventing activation of, 394; preventing occurrence of, 394; psychology and triggers of, 378–380; when leaders should intervene, 393–394, 400. *See also* Boundaries
Faultlines-performance framework: illustrated diagram of, 383*fig*; management of fraultlines teams using the, 382–386; relational level managerial strategies, 391–394, 398*t*–399*t*; structural level managerial strategies for, 386–391, 395*t*–397*t*
Favoritism principle, 378
Feedback: America's Cup sailing team lesson on building in, 222; post-performance feedback exercises, 467; team debriefings form of, 467–468, 488–514; team level training, 467. *See also* Communication
Financial institutions: as balance-sheet driven, 3–4; importance of teamwork in, 3–5
The Five Dysfunctions of a Team (Lencioni), 194
Floyd D. Spence National Defense Authorization Act (NDAA), 301
Follow-the-sun tactic, 411*t*, 418–419
Follower team members, 18
The Four Obsessions of an Extraordinary Executive (Lencioni), 198
Functional intelligence competency, 201

G

Gender differences in hospital staff, 347
Global boundary complexity, 410*t*, 413–415
Global competence, 202
Goals: action regulation theory on achieving deadline, 589–597; America's Cup sailing team lesson on identifying team, 217–218; established team training prior to training, 446–447; health care team performance improvement with explicit, 354*e*; major technological development step of creating, 88*t*, 99–103
"Good" team members, 199–202
Google core values, 188–189
Group identity: authentic team membership aspect of, 357–358; description of, 271; multiple team membership and, 358–360; subgroup, 273–274; virtual teams and, 271
"Groupware" (computer supported cooperative work) [CSCW], 57–58
Guided team self-correction training, 465–466

H

Health care organizations: complexity and specialized roles in, 12–13, 331–332; five based teams in, 14; implications for future of team trainings in, 319–320; training outcomes for, 341–342
Health care team performance: CMHTs (community mental health teams) questionnaire on, 349–350; conflict management to improve, 344–345; diversity management to improve, 346–347;

Health Care Team Vitality Instrument (HTVI) to assess nursing, 349; leadership role in, 348–349; participation to improve, 343–344; practical recommendations for promoting effective, 354*e*–356*e*; ProMES (Productivity Measurement and Enhancement System) to assess, 350; recommendations for improving, 350–353; reflexivity to improve, 345–346, 355*e*; team objectives to improve, 342–343

Health care team training: eight principles for designing, 352*e*; implications for future of, 319–320; I/O psychology used in, 332–333, 353; TeamSTEPPS performance improvement, 298–299, 301–320, 351, 462; VHA (Veterans Health Administration), 11–12

Health care team types: co-management, 16; command-and-control, 14–15; expert leader-dominated, 15; multi-disciplinary, 15–16; team of equals, 14

Health Care Team Vitality Instrument (HTVI), 349

Health care teams: authority differentiation characteristic of, 335; context and characteristics of, 333–335; five basic types of, 14; future challenges for research on, 353–360; importance of effective teamwork by, 11; individual level outcomes, 336–338; Input-Process-Output (IPO) framework of, 336; multiple team membership of members of, 358–360; National Health Service (NHS) hospital (England), 337–338; "needle stick injuries" of, 338; organizational level outcomes of, 341–342; providing authentic membership on, 357–358; the science of, 336; skill differentiation characteristic of, 334; team level outcomes of, 338–341; temporal stability characteristic of, 334–335; types of, 14–16; WHO Surgical Safety Checklist for OR, 631; widespread threat of violence against, 337–338. *See also* High-risk team processes; Hospitals

Hewlett-Packard, 129

High-impact team leadership: boundary spanning and bridge building by, 178–180; the collective as, 164–170; interconnected influence agent (influencer) and contextual cartographer in, 171–177; risk and vulnerability as invitation to develop, 169–170; role/identity shift to develop, 166–167; storytelling as invitation to join, 170*e*; Team Leadership Responsibility Tool for, 168*e*

High-impact teams: collective as leader approach by, 164–170*e*; comparing traditional and, 158*fig*; leadership functions during strategic change, 157*fig*; leadership of, 155–156; network mapping by, 172–177; team levers, traditional view, and network view of, 175*t*; team network analysis of, 176*e*; team social network of, 177; tools to lead strategic change, 163–180

High-risk team processes: closed-loop communication, 609, 617*t*, 632–634; explicit reasoning, 609, 615*t*, 625–628; maintaining situation awareness (SA), 609, 614*t*, 618–622; organized along two-dimensional taxonomy, 613*fig*; speaking up, 609, 616*t*, 628–632; talking to the room, 609, 615*t*, 622–625. *See also* Health care teams

High-risk teams: five processes of, 609, 611–634; specifics and examples of, 610–611

Honest conversations: for rapid change through SFP facilitated, 42–43; team performance benefits of, 38–39
Horizontal team boundaries, 178
Hospitals: complex human organization of health care teams and, 12–13, 331–332; VHA (Veterans Health Administration), 11–12. *See also* Health care teams

I

IBM's Enterprise Leadership Team, 190
Ideal cycle of action regulation, 590
I'm Working While They're Sleeping (Carmel & Espinosa), 417
Implicit cooperation, 410*t*, 412–413, 420
Information elaboration. *See* Social information
InfoSys, 417
Input-Process-Output (IPO) team structure, 336
Institute of Medicine (IOM), 300
Integrated Team Effectiveness Model (ITEM), 336
Integrity: description of, 141; how team members manifest, 141–142
Intellect competency, 201–202
Intergroup accentuation principle, 378
International Atomic Energy Agency (IAEA), 95, 96
International Space Station (ISS) teamwork, 23–24
Interpersonal team process, 571, 572*t*, 573
Iran: Atomic Energy Organization of Iran (AEOI), 90; ENTC's team leadership during major technological development, 89–116
Iraq-Iran war, 98

K

"Know thyself," 185–188
Knowledge, skills, and abilities (KSAs): health care team performance improvement by training for, 355*e*; the optimal team composition of, 522–523; refresher training to maintain, 476; selected team members with, 353; shared mental model (SMM) of, 253–254, 465; as team composition consideration, 525, 526, 528*t*–529, 530, 533–534, 535, 544, 548; team diversity as adding to, 374. *See also* Competencies
Kone Americas, 164–165

L

Lack of engagement, 257*t*–258
Laissez faire leaders, 30, 34–35
Leader competencies: curiosity, 202; emotional intelligence, 201; functional intelligence or proven track record, 201; global competence, 202; intellect, 201–202; political savvy, 202
Leadership style: America's Cup sailing team lessons on, 218–220; laissez faire, 30, 34–35; top-down, 30, 34–35
Leadership teams: cross-organizational, 121–122; description and functions of, 122–124; increasing use of, 121; Team 1 case study on, 124–125; Team 2 case study on, 125–126; tripwires and conditions for great, 123*t*, 126–151. *See also* Team leadership
Leadership teams conditions: compelling directions and purpose, 123*t*, 132–136; convene the right people, 123*t*, 140–143; create an enabling structure for the team, 123, 146*fig*–149; listed, 123*t*

Leadership teams tripwires: listed, 122, 123*t*; meetings are a waste of time, 123*t*, 143–146; unclear purposes, 123*t*, 126–132; the wrong people are convening, 123*t*, 136–140

Loser team members, 18–19, 21

M

Major technological development. *See* Technological development

Mascalzone Latino Capitalia (America's Cup sailing team), 223–225, 233

Measuring performance. *See* Team performance measurement (TPM)

Mechanistic coordination, 409, 410*t*, 412, 413, 420

Medical errors: description and rates of, 339; health care training outcomes for, 339

Medical Team Management, 301

MedTeams, 301

Meetings. *See* Team meetings

MIR Space Station teamwork, 23

Mission: engaging team members with clear, 656–657; TeamSTEPPS, 309–310

Motivation: extrinsic or external training, 446–447; intrinsic or internal training, 446; major technological development step of facilitating staff, 89*t*, 113–116

Multi-disciplinary health care teams, 15–16

Multi-team systems (MTSs), 657–658

Mutual performance monitoring: description of, 251; virtual team, 251–252

Mutual trust: among executive team members, 193–195; managing virtual teams to promote, 280*t*; by virtual team members, 255–256

Myers-Briggs Type Indicator (MBTI), 194

N

Narratives, 134–135

NASA: CRM (crew resource management) strategy used at, 23–24; teamwork issue at, 23

National Health Service (NHS) hospitals [England]: Aston Team Facilitation Programme (ATFP) used in, 351; gender segregation in health care teams, 347; individual level outcomes of team training at, 337–338; "needle stick injuries" at, 338; organizational outcomes of team training at, 341–342; violence against health care staff at, 337–338

National Outdoor Leadership School, 23–24

NAVAIR: "team process integration" method developed at, 75; training software development teams in team software process, 74–75

"Needle stick injuries," 338

Network mapping: comparing traditional and network views of teams, 175*fig*; creating a high-impact team for business development, 174*fig*; high-performing and low-performing information flow, 173*fig*; strategic change role of, 172, 176

Nigerian Society of Engineers, 129

9/11 terrorist attacks, 623

Non-governmental organizations (NGOs) teams, 121–122

Norms: establishing and revisiting, 148–149; variations and conflict between, 144–145

Northeast Air Defense Sector of the United States (NEADS), 623

O

Optimal team composition. *See* Team composition

Organic coordination, 410*t*, 412, 420

Organizational change: developing high-impact teams to lead strategic, 154–180; Hewlett-Packard's SRSD division transformation and, 44–45; SFP (strategic fitness process) used to facilitated rapid, 42–43. *See also* Change

Organizations: advice on effective use of team debriefings by, 512–513; conditions that drive team performance, 651–652; core values of, 188–189, 309–310; enhancing the practice of teamwork in, 647–658; health care, 13–14, 298–327, 331–360; importance of teamwork for, 648–649; narratives of, 134–135; software, 58–79; succession planning for sustaining, 199–200; team norms in, 144–145, 148–149; tips for creating a team training climate in, 321*t*–326*t*. *See also* Corporate culture

P

Paradox of team leadership dilemma, 210

Partnerships (TeamSTEPPS program), 317

Patient Safety Program (DoD-AHRQ), 301–302

Performance. *See* Team performance

Personnel model with teamwork considerations model, 528*t*, 529–530

Plan execution: description of, 254; virtual team, 254–255

Political savvy competency, 202

Power-law distribution of talent, 7–8

Practice: guided, 470*t*; team training principle of, 461–462

Problem identification: definition of problem, 91, 254; leading technical team step of, 87*t*, 91–94; by virtual team, 254

Process maturity framework: applied to software development teams, 59–60, 77–78; origins and development of the, 58–59. *See also* Capability maturity model (CMM)

Productivity of software teams, 56–58

Professional development, 89*t*, 108–111. *See also* Team training

Purpose: authorize an individual to articulate, 135–136; creating a compelling and clear, 132–136; engaging team members with clear, 656–657; obstacles to clarifying, 128–132; unclear team, 123*t*, 126–128*fig*

Purpose obstacles: conceptual challenge of specifying purpose, 130–131; differences in interests as, 129–130; teams are poor at articulating common purposes, 131–132

Q

Quality: challenges of quantifying measurements of, 55; early methods used by software teams to improve, 56–58

R

Raytheon, 71

Reflexivity: description for improving health care team performance, 345–346; health care team performance improvement by taking time for, 355*e*

Relationships: faultlines-performance framework strategies for, 391–394, 398*t*–399*t*; frequent communication for building, 272–273, 275–276; time and familiarity for developing, 271–275

Relative contribution model, 528*t*, 531–534

Resources: America's Cup sailing team lesson on identifying team, 217–218; Cockpit Resource Management (CRM), 302; crew resource management (CRM),

22–24; inadequate leadership development of, 30, 32
Rewards/recognition: America's Cup sailing team lesson on, 222; to executive team members, 197

S

Santa Rosa Systems Division (SRDS) [Hewlett-Packard]: description and functions of, 28; overcoming silent barriers through SFP (strategic fitness process) at, 38–45; performance challenges facing, 28–29; silent barriers to team performance of, 29–38; structural and procedural changes made at, 44–45
Scheduling flexibility: description of issue, 258; as virtual team challenge, 257*t*, 258–259
SEFCU credit union: BWP (banking with a purpose) model adopted at, 5; description of, 4; their approach dealing with silo conflict at, 4–5
Senior teams: management of executive, 182–204; team performance barrier of ineffective, 30, 32–33
Servant leadership, 211
Shared mental models (SMM): description of, 253; team training use of, 465; virtual team, 253–254
Silent killer syndrome: illustrated diagram showing interrelatedness of, 36–37*fig*; overcoming silent barriers of, 38–46; six barriers of the, 29–38
Silo conflict, 4–5
Situation awareness (SA): behavioral markers and recommendations for, 614*t*; benefits of, 619–620; as high-risk team process, 609; maintaining, 618–619; situations that require, 620–621; ways to train, 621–622
Skylab: CRM (crew resource management) teamwork on, 22–23; description and operation of, 22–23
Social competition principle, 378
Social information: acquisition and use of, 270; description of, 269–270; in faultlines team, 380–381; frequent communication for sharing, 272–273, 275–276; managing team-distributed information awareness of, 392–393; mechanisms affecting distributed groups, 271–276; transactive memory of sources of, 423–424
Social information mechanisms: allow for time and familiarity, 271–272, 274–275; group identity, 271, 273–274
Society for Human Resource Management (SHRM): on challenges to virtual team success, 244*t*; comparing virtual and traditional, 242*fig*–243*t*
SoftCo virtual team failure, 239–240, 249
Software development team performance: CMM (capability maturity model) to improve, 60–79; early methods to improve productivity and quality, 56–58; impact of individual differences on, 49–51; measuring, 53, 55; model of factors affecting, 54*fig*; process maturity framework used to improve, 58–60, 77–78; software industry factors driving, 48
Software development teams: CMM (capability maturity model) application to, 60–79; dissecting characteristics and interactions of, 51–53; Humphrey's personal software process applied to, 73–74; percentage of agreement during meetings, 51, 52*fig*. *See also* Technological development

Software Engineering Institute, 75
Software organizations: CMM (capability maturity model) to improve team performance at, 60–79; process maturity framework to improve team performance at, 58–60, 77–78; team performance in the context of, 76–79
Solutions (conceptual), 87*t*, 91–94
Space Shuttle teamwork, 23
Speaking up process: behavioral markers and recommendations for, 616*t*; benefits of, 629–630; as high-risk team process, 609, 628–629; situations that require, 630; ways to train, 630–632
Staffing: major technological development step of developing, 89*t*, 108–111; major technological development step of motivating, 89*t*, 113–116
Stakeholder team boundaries, 178
Stakeholders: major technological change involvement of, 88*t*, 106–108; team network analysis, 176*e*; team social network of, 177
Storytelling, 170*e*
Strategic change: leadership functions during, 157*fig*; nature of, 157, 159–162; systematic and contextual understanding of challenges of, 161*fig*–162; three levels and dimensions of, 160; tools for high-impact teams to lead, 163–180. *See also* Change
Strategic change tools: boundary-spanning strategies, 178–180; network mapping, 172–177; role/identity shift, 166–167; storytelling as invitation, 170*e*; Team Leadership Responsibility Tool, 168*e*
Strategic fitness process (SFP): description of the, 29; development of the, 39; for enabling honest conversation for rapid change, 42–43; iterating between advocacy and inquiry, 40*fig*; overcoming silent barriers to team performance using, 38–46; steps in effective use of the, 41*fig*–42
Subgroup differentiation: categorization mechanism behind, 378; management of faultlines and, 382–386; relational level managerial strategies to manage, 391–400; structural level managerial strategies to manage, 386–391; team faultlines and, 375, 376–382
Subgroups: conflict between two different, 273–274; description of, 273
Subject-matter experts (SMEs): commenting on team staffing decisions, 523–527; team needs analysis by, 449. *See also* Expertise
Succession planning, 199–200
Super leadership, 211
Synchronous communication, 411*t*, 423
Systems thinking, 142

T

Talent power-law distribution, 7–8
Talking to the room process: behavioral markers and recommendations for, 615*t*; benefits of, 623–624; as high-risk team process, 609, 622; situations that require, 624–625; ways to train, 625
Team composition: additional considerations for research and

application of, 546–548; constraints to decision making about, 535–538, 544–546; examining how to create the optimal, 520–522; important to effective teamwork, 522–523; KSAO distributions as consideration for, 525, 526, 528*t*–529, 530, 533–534, 535, 548, 554; models of, 527–534; recommended approach for practitioners, 538, 539*t*–543*t*; types of decisions made for, 523–527. *See also* Team members

Team composition models: personnel model with teamwork considerations, 528*t*, 529–530; relative contribution model, 528*t*, 531–534; research on different, 527–528; synthesis of the, 532; team profile model, 528*t*, 530–531; traditional personnel–position fit model, 528*t*–529

Team coordination: break down barriers to intra- and inter-team, 649–650; challenges related to temporally separated team work, 406–409; dyad-level findings on, 424–426; implicit, 410*t*, 412–413, 420; mechanistic type of, 409, 410*t*, 412, 413, 420; organic type of, 410*t*, 412, 420; studies on global, 408; tactics for time zone, 417; team-level findings on, 426–428; during team training, 458–459. *See also* Cooperation

Team debriefing types: alternative types and application to different team, 492*fig*; alternative types and applications to the same team, 491*fig*; six different, 493*t*–496

Team debriefings: advice for organizations on using, 512–513; description and purpose of, 489–490; desired improvements/outcomes from, 499*t*–502; efficacy of, 498–499; future trends for use of, 513–515; lessons learned on promoting effective, 508–513; participates in, 496–498; pitfalls and obstacles to successful, 505–508; proposed framework on how they work, 502–505*fig*; team training and follow-up, 467–468; tips for leaders on using, 513; when to conduct, 490–498

Team diversity: dimensions and mixed results of, 376–377; managing diverse beliefs, 391–392; team constellation with varying degrees of faultline strength and, 384*t*–385*t*; team faultlines basis for subgroup differentiation, 375, 376–382

Team diversity management: additional considerations for, 400–401; faultlines approach to, 382–391; health care team, 346–347; importance for team success, 375–376; relational level managerial strategies for, 391–400; Team A case study on, 373–375, 377

Team faultlines: information elaboration in, 380–381; leadership interventions for, 382–400; psychology and possible triggers of, 37–380; relational level managerial strategies for, 391–394, 398*t*–399*t*; structural level managerial strategies for, 386–391, 395*t*–397*t*; subgroup differentiation and, 375; understanding theoretical basis of, 376–378

Team leader development: challenges of, 17–18; individual plan of action of, 19–20; teamwork aspect of, 20–21

Team leaders: assessing importance to teams, 9–10; assigned credit or blame to, 6–7; defining characteristics and roles of, 210–212; team performance barrier of top-down or laissez faire, 30, 34–35; tips for effective use of team debriefings, 513; two reasons why they matter, 7–8

Team leadership: Army context of, 8; defining, 210–212; of ENTC during major technological development, 89–116; as essential virtual team process, 251–252; examined in the context of America's Cup sailing teams, 212–234; of executive teams, 182–204; health care team performance improvement by establishing, 354*e*; improving virtual team, 283–285; intervention for team faultlines by, 382–400; paradox of team leadership dilemma of, 210; team performance barrier of inadequate development of, 30, 32; TeamSTEPPS program engagement of, 310–312; teamwork theme on importance of, 655–656; ten steps for leading technological development, 86–90; traditional/historical and new definition of, 158*fig*. *See also* Leadership; Leadership teams

Team Leadership Responsibility Tool, 168*e*

Team leadership types: contingency, 211; servant, 211; super, 211; transformational, 211; universal, 211

Team meetings: establishing ground rules for, 145–146; myths about virtual work as requiring face-to-face, 276–278; that are a waste of time, 123*t*, 143–146; variations in institutional cultures and norms during, 144–145

Team member types: the bad, 199; derailers, 138–140; followers, 18; the good, 199–202; losers, 18–19, 21; the ugly, 198–199; winners, 18, 19, 21

Team members: achieving optimal composition for success, 520–548; convening the right people to be, 140–143; convening the wrong people to be, 123*t*, 136–140; with empathy and integrity, 140–142; engaging with shared vision, clear mission, and compelling purpose, 656–657; health care team performance improvement with stability in, 356*e*; identifying categories of individual, 18–19; KSAs (knowledge, skills, and abilities) of, 353; multiple team membership of, 358–360; mutual performance monitoring by, 251–252; providing authentic membership to, 357–358; shared temporal cognition of, 584–589; systems thinking by, 142. *See also* Team composition

Team needs analysis, 449–451

Team network analysis, 176*e*

Team performance: coach for peak performance at the right time, 220–222; five conditions required for effective, 37–38; five team processes to improve high-risk, 609–635; health care, 342–353; major themes about teamwork and, 648–658; organizational conditions driving, 651–652; overcoming silent barriers to, 38–46; research on creating high levels of, 27; silent barriers to, 29–38; team time management importance to, 581–601; team training objective of improved, 442–443; in temporally separated team work, 406–433; temporally separated team work and, 406–433; time zone coordination to enhance, 411*t*, 417–419, 423–428, 431; transition, action, and interpersonal process phases of, 571–573

Team performance barriers: discussion of problems related to each silent killer, 31–38; inadequate leadership development resources, 30, 32; ineffective senior team, 30, 32–33; interrelationships of the, 36–37*fig*; poor coordination and communication, 30–32; poor vertical communication down, 30, 35; top-down or laissez fair leader, 30, 34–35; unclear strategy and conflicting priorities, 30, 33–34

Team performance measurement (TPM): during both action and transition phases, 571–573; decisions on what should be measured, 554–558; major technological development step of, 89*t*, 111–113; on-the-job or during simulation-based exercises, 569–571; potential of using, 552; rater training for conducting, 568–569; rating formats for, 562–568; rating sources for, 558–562; reasons for, 553–554; software development team, 53, 55; TeamSTEPPS program assessed by, 317–319; of training program, 451–453. *See also* Evaluation

Team performance measuring instruments: BARS rating scales, 566, 568; checklists for raters, 563*e*–564; CMHTs (community mental health teams) questionnaire for, 349–350; frequency scales, 564, 565*e*; Health Care Team Vitality Instrument (HTVI) for, 349; latency/deviation-based formats, 564, 566; Likert-type rating scales, 566, 568; ProMES (Productivity Measurement and Enhancement System), 350; rating sources, 558–562; subjective rating scales, 566, 567*e*

Team processes: to improve high-risk team effectiveness, 609–635; measured after enough time to affect performance outcomes, 573; transition, action, and interpersonal phases of, 571–573

Team profile model, 528*t*, 530–531

Team roles: defining executive, 189–193; defining team leader, 210–212; health care team performance improvement by providing clear, 354*e*; identity shift to develop in high-impact team, 166–167; of leaders in health care teams, 348–349

Team social network, 177

Team structure: crafting interdependent activities for, 147–148; create one that leverages team's strengths, 220; creating enabling, 146*fig*–149; establishing team norms as part of, 148–149; faultlines-performance framework strategies for, 386–391, 395*t*–397*t*; Input-Process-Output (IPO) of health care teams, 336

Team time management: action regulation toward meeting deadlines, 589–597; dynamic model of, 597–601; increasing importance of effective, 581–583; role of shared temporal cognitions, 584–587; temporal synchronization in collaborative action, 584; threats to shared temporal cognitions, 587–589; time zone coordination, 411*t*, 417–419, 423–428, 431. *See also* Temporally separated team work

Team training: checklist for evaluating, 447*t*–478*t*; cross-training, 465; eight principles for designing, 352*e*; guided team self-correction training, 465–466; intrinsic and extrinsic motivation of, 446–447; pros and cons of delivery methods of, 463*t*–464*t*; providing virtual team, 282–283; scientific grounding and systemic approach to, 653–654; team coordination training, 465; TeamSTEPPS for health care performance improvement, 298–299, 301–320, 351, 462; teamwork improvement goal of, 442–443; tips for creating a successful organizational climate for, 321*t*–326*t*; VHA (Veteran s Health Administration), 11–12; virtual team challenge of absence of, 257*t*, 258. *See also* Professional development

Team training checklists: after team training, 477*t*–478*t*; pre-training, 454*t*–457*t*; during training, 469*t*–470*t*

Team training principles: appropriate team-based content, 453, 458–460; conduct a team needs analysis, 449–451; create conditions for teamwork, 447–449; design a measurement plan, 451–453; evaluate the team training, 471–473; incorporate the appropriate instructional strategy, 460–462, 465–466; prepare the climate for learning, 445–447; promote transfer of team training, 473–475; support team development activities, 466–468; sustain the conditions to foster teamwork, 475–476; temporal display of the, 444*fig*

Teams: as adaptable social entities, 654–655; assessing importance of team leaders to, 9–10; boundary spanning/bridge building by, 178–180; comparing most challenging behaviors for virtual and traditional, 243*t*; comparing most successful behaviors for virtual and traditional, 242*t*; composition variables influencing management of, 650–651; five types of boundaries within, 178; honest conversations within, 38–39, 42–43; strategic change through high-impact, 154–180; traditional/historical and new definition of, 158*fig*; virtual, 239–263

Teams of teams, 652–653, 657–658

TeamSTEPPS Masters, 305

TeamSTEPPS program: champions of, 315–316; competencies, skills, and related tools for, 304*t*; continuous learning aspect of, 316–317; curriculum core content and instructional framework of, 302, 303*fig*; description of, 298–299, 462; field-testing and subject-matter expert input, 305, 307; implications for the future of health care team training, 319–320; lessons learned about drivers of success, 307–308; scientific evolution of the, 301–302; three-phased organizational change approach, 303, 305, 306*fig*; training course delivery of, 302–303

TeamSTEPPS program success factors: applied after training delivery, 314–319; before training delivery, 309–314

Teamwork: appreciating importance in financial institutions, 3–5; CRM (crew resource management) strategy for, 22–24; enhancing the practice of, 647–658; as essential in health care, 11; health care team performance improvement by inter-team, 356*e*; major technological development, 86–116; performance in temporally separated, 406–433; pre-training strategies for creating conditions for, 447–449; sustain conditions to foster effective, 475–476; team leader development role of, 20–21; team training objective of improved, 442–443. *See also* Collaborations

Teamwork themes: break down barriers to intra- and inter-team coordination, 649–650; composition variables influence the management of teams, 650–651; engage team members with shared vision, clear mission, and purpose, 656–657; leadership matters, 655–656; organizational conditions drive team performance, 651–652; team training works but must be scientifically grounded, 653–654; teams are adaptable social entities, 654–655; teamwork does matter, 648–649; technology is changing nature of teams, 652–653; that there is still a lot of learn about teamwork, 657–658

Techno-literacy, 257*t*

Technological development: changing nature of teams due to, 652–653; Iran's ENTC team leadership during major, 89–116; ten steps for leading a team to a major, 86–90, 91–108. *See also* Software development teams

Technological development team leadership: step 1: review the background, 87*t*, 90–91; step 2: define the problem, 87*t*, 91–94; step 3: develop a conceptual solution, 91–94; step 4: developing change strategies, 88*t*, 94–99; step 5: crafting vision, goals, and change plans, 88*t*, 99–103; step 6: stakeholder involvement and management, 88*t*, 103–106; step 7: establish governance, 88*t*, 106–108; step 8: staffing, training, and professional development, 89*t*, 108–111; step 9: measure and monitor success, 89*t*, 111–113; step 10: keep staff motivated, 89*t*, 113–116

Temporal adaptation: advice for practitioners on, 597; for making deadlines, 595–596

Temporal cognitions: collaboration role of shared, 584–587; team composition issues related to, 589; threats to shared, 587–589

Temporal evaluation: advice for practitioners on, 594–595; for making deadlines, 593–594

Temporal planning: advice for practitioners on, 592–593; for making deadlines, 591–592

Temporal separation complexity, 410*t*, 415–416

Temporal synchronization, 584

Temporally separated team work: asynchronous communication of, 411*t*, 423, 431; conveyance and convergence of, 411*t*; dyad-level findings on, 424–426; global boundary complexity issue of, 410*t*, 413–415; issues to consider for, 406–409; role of interaction synchronicity in, 411*t*, 428–431; synchronous communication of, 411*t*, 423, 431; team coordination role in, 408–413, 420–422; team level findings on, 426–428; temporal distance and calendar efficiencies issue of, 417–419; temporal vs. spatial distance issue of, 419–424. *See also* Team time management; Time zone coordination

Time and familiarity: distributed group context of, 271–272; forming relationships among distributed group members with, 274–275
Time shifting tactic, 411*t*, 431
Time zone coordination: asynchronous and synchronous, 411*t*, 423, 431; dyad-level findings on, 424–426; follow-the-sun tactic for, 411*t*, 418–419; InfoSys study on, 417; team-level findings on, 426–428; time shifting tactic for, 411*t*, 431. *See also* Temporally separated team work
To Err is Human: Building a Safer Health System (IOM), 300
Top-down leaders, 30, 34–35
Traditional personnel–position fit model, 528*t*–529
Transactive memory, 423–424
Transfer appropriate processing (TAP), 448–449
Transformational leadership, 211
Transition team process phase, 571, 572*t*, 573
TRICARE Management Activity, 301
Trust: developing among executive team members, 193–195; managing virtual teams to promote, 280*t*; virtual team need for, 255–256

U

"Ugly" team members, 198–199
UNESCO, 129
United Kingdom: Aston Team Facilitation Programme (ATFP), 351; National Health Service (NHS) hospital teams, 337–338, 341–342, 347, 351
Universal leadership, 211
U.S. Department of Defense (DoD), 299, 301–302
U.S. Military Health System (MHS), 299

V

Vertical team boundaries, 178
Veterans Health Administration (VHA) team training program, 11–12
Virtual team members: mutual trust between, 255–256, 280*t*; providing training and support to, 282–283; selecting, 281–282
Virtual team success: behaviors that challenge, 243*t*, 244*t*; best behaviors for, 242*t*; factors and questions leading to, 245*t*–247*t*; how to strive for, 244, 248–249
Virtual teams: car metaphor used for, 241; challenges to success of, 244*t*; comparing most successful behaviors for traditional and, 242*t*; continuing and future issues for, 261–262; definition and purposes of, 240–241; designing, 279–281; how nature of teamwork is changing to include, 652–653; improving leadership and facilitation, 283–285; managed to promote trust and cooperation, 280*t*; mechanisms that affect social information in, 271–276; myths and misconceptions about, 276–285; performance of temporally separated, 406–433; reasons why they fail, 241; review of processes of, 249–256; social information acquired and used by, 269–270; SoftCo's failed experience with, 239–240, 249. *See also* Distributed work groups
Virtual teams processes: adaptability, 252–253; backup behavior, 252; communication, 255; mutual performance monitoring, 251–252;

mutual trust, 255–256; overcoming challenges by using, 259–261; plan execution, 254–255; problem identification, 254; shared mental models, 253–254; team leadership, 251
Virtual teamwork challenges: common process, 257*t*–259; comparing traditional team and, 243*t*; logistical, 256; processes to overcome challenges, 259–261; SHRM poll on common, 244*t*
Virtual teamwork process challenges: absence of training and preparation, 257*t*, 258; lack of engagement, 257*t*–258; scheduling flexibility, 257*t*, 258–259; techno-literacy, 257*t*
Vision: engaging team members with shared, 656–657; major technological development step of creating, 88*t*, 99–103; shared mental models (SMM), 253–254, 465; TeamSTEPPS, 309–310

W

WHO Surgical Safety Checklist, 631
Winner team members, 18, 19, 21
Workforce development (CMM model), 72–73
World Bank, 129

Z

Zappos core values, 188

Printed and bound by CPI Group (UK) Ltd, Croydon, CR0 4YY

23/04/2025

14660926-0001